ESSENTIALS OF MANAGEMENT SCIENCE/ OPERATIONS RESEARCH

The Wiley/Hamilton Series in Management and Administration
Elwood S. Buffa, Advisory Editor   University of California, Los Angeles

PRINCIPLES OF MANAGEMENT: A Modern Approach   Fourth Edition
    Henry H. Albers
OPERATIONS MANAGEMENT: Problems and Models   Third Edition
    Elwood S. Buffa
PROBABILITY FOR MANAGEMENT DECISIONS   William R. King
MODERN PRODUCTION MANAGEMENT: Managing the Operations Function
    Fifth Edition   Elwood S. Buffa
CASES IN OPERATIONS MANAGEMENT: A Systems Approach
    James L. McKenney and Richard S. Rosenbloom
ORGANIZATIONS: Structure and Behavior, Volume I   Second Edition
    Joseph A. Litterer
ORGANIZATIONS: Systems, Control and Adaptation, Volume II   Joseph A. Litterer
MANAGEMENT AND ORGANIZATIONAL BEHAVIOR: A Multidimensional
    Approach   Billy J. Hodge and Herbert J. Johnson
MATHEMATICAL PROGRAMMING   Claude McMillan
DECISION MAKING THROUGH OPERATIONS RESEARCH,   Second Edition
    Robert J. Thierauf and Robert C. Klekamp
QUALITY CONTROL FOR MANAGERS & ENGINEERS   Elwood G. Kilpatrick
PRODUCTION SYSTEMS: Planning, Analysis and Control   Second Edition
    James L. Riggs
SIMULATION MODELING: A Guide to Using Simscript   Forrest P. Wyman
BASIC STATISTICS FOR BUSINESS AND ECONOMICS,   Second Edition
    Paul G. Hoel and Raymond J. Jessen
COMPUTER SIMULATION OF HUMAN BEHAVIOR   John M. Dutton and
    William H. Starbuck
INTRODUCTION TO GAMING: Management Decision Simulations
    John G. H. Carlson and Michael J. Misshauk
PRINCIPLES OF MANAGEMENT AND ORGANIZATIONAL BEHAVIOR
    Burt K. Scanlan
COMMUNICATION IN MODERN ORGANIZATIONS   George T. and
    Patricia B. Vardaman
THE ANALYSIS OF ORGANIZATIONS,   Second Edition   Joseph A. Litterer
COMPLEX MANAGERIAL DECISIONS INVOLVING MULTIPLE OBJECTIVES
    Allan Easton
MANAGEMENT SYSTEMS,   Second Edition   Peter P. Schoderbek
ADMINISTRATIVE POLICY: Text and Cases in the Policy Sciences
    Richard M. Hodgetts and Max S. Wortman, Jr.
THE ECONOMICS OF INTERNATIONAL BUSINESS   R. Hal Mason, Robert R. Miller
    and Dale R. Weigel
BASIC PRODUCTION MANAGEMENT,   Second Edition   Elwood S. Buffa
FUNDAMENTALS OF MANAGEMENT COORDINATION:
    Supervisor, Middlemanagers and Executives   Thomas A. Petit
QUANTITATIVE BUSINESS ANALYSIS   David E. Smith

OPERATIONS MANAGEMENT: The Management of Productive Systems
    Elwood S. Buffa
PERSONNEL ADMINISTRATION AND HUMAN RESOURCES MANAGEMENT
    Andrew F. Sikula
MANAGEMENT SCIENCE/OPERATIONS RESEARCH: Model Formulation and
    Solution Methods   Elwood S. Buffa and James S. Dyer
MANAGEMENT PRINCIPLES AND PRACTICES   Robert J. Thierauf, Robert Klekamp
    and Daniel Geeding
ESSENTIALS OF MANAGEMENT SCIENCE/OPERATIONS RESEARCH
    Elwood S. Buffa and James S. Dyer
AN INTRODUCTION TO MANAGEMENT   Joseph A. Litterer
FORECASTING: METHODS AND APPLICATIONS   Spyros Makridakis and
    Steven Wheelwright
POLICY FORMULATION AND STRATEGY MANAGEMENT   Robert Schellenberger
    and Glenn Boseman
DECISION SYSTEMS FOR INVENTORY MANAGEMENT AND PRODUCTION
    Rein Peterson and Edward A. Silver

ESSENTIALS OF MANAGEMENT SCIENCE/ OPERATIONS RESEARCH

Elwood S. Buffa
University of California, Los Angeles

James S. Dyer
University of California, Los Angeles

John Wiley & Sons
Santa Barbara □ New York □ Chichester □ Brisbane □ Toronto
A Wiley/Hamilton Publication

Copyright © 1978 by John Wiley & Sons, Inc.

All rights reserved. Published simultaneously in Canada

No part of this book may be reproduced by any means, nor transmitted, nor translated into a machine language without the written permission of the Publisher.

Library of Congress Cataloging in Publication Data

Buffa, Elwood Spencer, 1923-
　Essentials of management science.

　(The Wiley/Hamilton series in management and administration)
　"A basic version of . . . [the authors'] book, Management Science/Operations Research: model formulation and solution methods."
　"A Wiley/Hamilton publication."
　Includes bibliographical references.
　1. Operations research. 2. Management. I. Dyer, James S., joint author. II. Title.
T57.6.B82　　　　　　658.4'034　　　　　　77-23799
ISBN 0-471-02003-6

Printed in the United States of America

10　9　8　7　6　5　4　3　2　1

This book was copyedited by Carolyn Geiger and set in 10 point Souvenir by Allservice Phototypesetting. Text and cover were designed by Christy Butterfield, illustrations were prepared by Graphics Two, and printing and binding were done by Halliday Lithograph Corporation. Jean Varven supervised production.

ABOUT THE AUTHORS

Elwood S. Buffa is Professor of Management Science and Operations Management at the Graduate School of Management of the University of California, Los Angeles. He received his B.S. and M.B.A. degrees from the University of Wisconsin, and his Ph.D. from the University of California, Los Angeles. He worked as an Operations Analyst at the Eastman Kodak Company before entering the teaching profession, and has engaged in consulting activities in a wide variety of settings during the past twenty years. He has served as Assistant Dean and Associate Dean at the Graduate School of Management, and has held visiting appointments at IPSOA in Turin, Italy and at the Harvard Business School. Professor Buffa has published many research papers and books in Management Science and Operations Management. Currently he serves on the Board of Directors of On-Line Decisions Incorporated.

James S. Dyer is Associate Professor of Management Science at the Graduate School of Management, University of California, Los Angeles. He received his B.A. degree in physics and his Ph.D. degree in business administration from the University of Texas at Austin. At UCLA, he teaches courses in the areas of systems analysis and operations research. These courses emphasize materials on mathematical programming and utility theory.

Dr. Dyer has consulted for such organizations as the RAND Corporation, the Jet Propulsion Laboratory, the Western Interstate Commission on Higher Education (WICHE), Standard Oil Company (Indiana), and the County of Los Angeles. His articles have appeared in various professional journals, including *Decision Sciences, Management Science,* and *Operations Research.* He is an Associate Editor of *Management Science* and a participant in the ORSA/TIMS Visiting Lecturers Program in Operations Research and the Management Sciences.

CONTENTS

PREFACE   xi

Part I. INTRODUCTION   1

1. An Introduction to Management Science   3

Part II. EVALUATIVE MODELS   17

2. Probability and Expected Value   24
3. Decision Trees   52
4. Evaluative Models Based on Utility Functions   78

Part III. PREDICTIVE MODELS   103

5. Forecasting the Environment   110
6. Building Mathematical Models to Predict System Performance   140
7. Predicting the Effects of Risk—Markov Chains   172
8. Predicting the Effects of Risk—Waiting Line Theory   196
9. Predicting the Effects of Risk—Monte Carlo Simulation   220

Part IV. OPTIMIZING MODELS   247

10. Elementary Optimizing Models for Inventory Management   254
11. Linear Optimization Models   284
12. Applications of Linear Optimization Models   326
13. The Simplex Method   368
14. Network Models: Transportation and Transshipment   404
15. Network Scheduling Models: PERT and CPM   446

Part V. SYNTHESIS   469

16. What Should the Manager Know?   472

Part VI. APPENDIXES   489

A. Review of Some Mathematical Concepts   491
B. Review of Some Concepts of Statistics   503
C. Tables   517

PREFACE

The Essentials of Management Science/Operations Research is a basic version of our book *Management Science/Operations Research: Model Formulation and Solution Methods*. The "essentials" version has been rewritten for a basic coverage of the field in beginning courses. It is specifically designed for students who do not intend to specialize in MS/OR, who will never be involved in the details of formulating sophisticated mathematical models and obtaining solutions through the use of special-purpose algorithms. At one extreme, this kind of student may be a user of the results of large-scale MS/OR studies. Operating in this role, he must have the following skills:

1. The ability to recognize situations in which MS/OR might be used effectively.
2. The ability to communicate with a technical specialist both ways; that is, he must be able to
   a. explain the nature of his problem to a specialist in a meaningful way, and
   b. understand the product of the specialist sufficiently well to verify the appropriateness and potential usefulness of the result.
3. The ability to understand the results of MS/OR studies so that he obtains full value from the information available to him from such studies.

At the other extreme, we have the student who plans to work in a small business. The size of the operations would make it unlikely that a formal MS/OR analysis would ever be performed. For this student, we can provide a way of thinking and organizing information that should aid his intuitive decisions. The general concept of model building as an integral part of problem solving is stressed throughout the book. We are convinced that the process of problem definition associated with MS/OR (bound the problem, identify the decision variables, the objective function, and the constraints) can provide a useful conceptual framework for any manager if it is presented properly. We devote considerable attention to this point.

Somewhere between these two extremes is the individual who occasionally encounters relatively small straightforward problems amenable to analysis using MS/OR techniques. Examples are simple inventory problems, project scheduling problems, and even simple resource allocation problems. We would expect the user of this book to be able to formulate models appropriate for analyzing these problems, utilize canned computer programs (perhaps in time-share) to obtain solutions, and evaluate results.

The recognition of the needs of the users of this book is important, since these needs should determine both the content and the level of presentation of materials. For example, these needs seem to stress the importance of model building and formulation skills among all users of the book. At the same time, there is little justification for devoting much space to technical details of algorithms or computer codes. The only apparent justification for introducing such materials would be to remove some of the mystery from the solution strategies and to provide a basis for understanding the limitations of the various approaches.

Thus, we emphasize model building and formulation, and interpretation and use of the results from an analysis. In order to implement these objectives, transfer to reality is emphasized with examples of the use of quantitative methodology in real organizations. Relatively less emphasis is placed on algorithms. When they are presented, an effort is made to provide an intuitively appealing description of the solution process. The mathematical treatment has been kept very light, and no mention is made of theorems or mathematical derivations without a significant pedagogical justification.

These same considerations have also been the basis for omitting some topics found in many other introductory textbooks in MS/OR. For example, we can find little justification for requiring a future manager to learn about duality theory in linear programming, even though the MS/OR specialist would rightfully consider this to be an extremely important topic. On the other hand, the related concepts of sensitivity analysis based on information provided by standard computer programs do have important managerial implications, so this material is covered. Similarly, the details of the relatively complex algorithms for solving nonlinear programming problems are not covered, although they would also provide important tools for the specialist. Another topic, game theory, was omitted because of our inability to find a significant number of real-world applications of the methodology. We have restricted our coverage to the MS/OR models and methods that have proven useful in practice.

Other topics have been omitted because of our assumptions regarding the background of the reader. We do presume that he has been exposed to the fundamentals of probability and statistics, although a brief summary of some basic concepts of statistics are included in Appendix B as a convenient reference and review. We do not cover the fundamentals of statistical decision making. The only other required mathematical background is an understanding of basic algebra. Again, a review of the rudiments of basic mathematics is provided in Appendix A.

Topics that are included in the more extensive coverage in *Management Science/Operations Research* but omitted or briefly summarized here in the "essentials" version are methods for dealing with multiple criteria, dynamic structural models (systems dynamics, etc.), finite waiting line models, probabilistic inventory models, integer programming models and solution methods, and dynamic programming. Readers who seek exposure to these topics should consider the alternate text. The materials remaining in this book provide what we consider to be an exposure to the fundamental *essentials* of MS/OR.

Another unique feature of this book is an attempt to provide numerous examples from the public and not-for-profit sectors of the economy. There are several arguments for including these types of examples. The student can be impressed with the generality of both the techniques and mathematical models by avoiding a series of "maximize profit" or "minimize costs" objective functions. In addition, more and more students entering schools of business administration or management plan to work in the public and not-for-profit sectors. Finally, it is conceivable that the book might be appropriate for use in similar introductory courses that are now evolving in schools of education, public administration, and public health.

The organization of a book as well as its content should depend on the needs of its users. When a specialist learns about the models and methods of MS/OR, he must be concerned with the basic mathematical structure that is involved. Therefore, it seems natural to organize the materials according to mathematical structure, with an obvious dichotomy being deterministic versus stochastic models and methods. Many introductory textbooks intended for managers rather than specialists seem to maintain this same organization of the materials, and simply "water down" the mathematics. Other textbooks seem to organize the presentation on the basis of the relative importance of the topics, and generally begin with linear programming.

In our opinion, neither of those approaches is appropriate for the presentation of these materials to the nonspecialist. The manager is not really concerned with the mathematical structure of the models and methods, but rather with how and when they should be used. Similarly, managers need some assistance in relating what may seem like a confusing list of models and solution techniques, and an organization of materials based on relative importance cannot offer this assistance. We have attempted to organize the materials in a manner that will assist the manager in relating the various models and methods by defining a relationship among evaluative, predictive, and optimizing models.

The book draws heavily on the literature of Management Science and Operations Research and where specific materials have been used, they are cited. We have benefited greatly from reviews and comments by well-known professors such as William A. Manning, Portland State University; Kenneth Schneider, St. Cloud State University; William Wright, Stephan F. Austin University; Linus Schrage, University of Chicago; Steven C. Wheelwright, Harvard University; Robert Winkler, Indiana University; Edwin Shapiro, University of San Francisco; Norman R. Baker, University of Cincinnati; David Goodman, Southern Methodist University and Ross E. Lanser, San Jose State University.

Elwood S. Buffa
James S. Dyer

INTRODUCTION

AN INTRODUCTION TO MANAGEMENT SCIENCE

Whether he is in a private, not-for-profit, or public organization, the most important and the distinguishing function of a manager is problem solving. The field of management science is dedicated to aiding the manager in his problem-solving efforts. This is accomplished through the use of mathematical models to analyze the problems. We shall provide some perspective for understanding the importance of mathematical model building by first considering the problem-solving process.

Much has been written about problem solving and various authors have provided their own descriptions of the problem-solving process. These descriptions tend to be influenced by the experiences and concerns of the individual authors, but they do exhibit a significant degree of commonality.

Problem Solving Defined Just what is problem solving? Certainly it is an activity in which you are successful, or you would not be in a position to read this book. You have solved the basic problems of survival and of education in the modern world, but perhaps you have never explicitly considered what problem solving is all about. Jackson [1974] defines problem solving very simply as "the business of *purposefully* inventing and choosing among ways to get you where you want to go." Perhaps the simplest description of the problem-solving process was provided by John Dewey [1910]:

1. define the problem
2. identify the alternatives
3. select the best alternative

This description seems straightforward enough. The key, of course, is to go through this process in such a manner that the "best" alternative is actually identified and selected. In a similar spirit, Jackson [1974] suggests that the most crucial tasks of a problem solver are identifying "things that might be done," determining "ways to anticipate results," and developing "ways to evaluate results." While other authors have elaborated on certain aspects of the problem-solving process and provided suggestions regarding how these tasks might be accomplished, these basic statements are common to most descriptions of the problem-solving process.

The Problem-Solving Process At this point, it may be helpful to provide some additional detail regarding the problem-solving process. One extended view of this process is provided in Figure 1-1. First, the existence of a problem must be recognized. That is, someone must observe reality and note that his perception is not consistent with his conception of how things ought to be. This recognition may occur because of changes in reality (we elect to ignore the

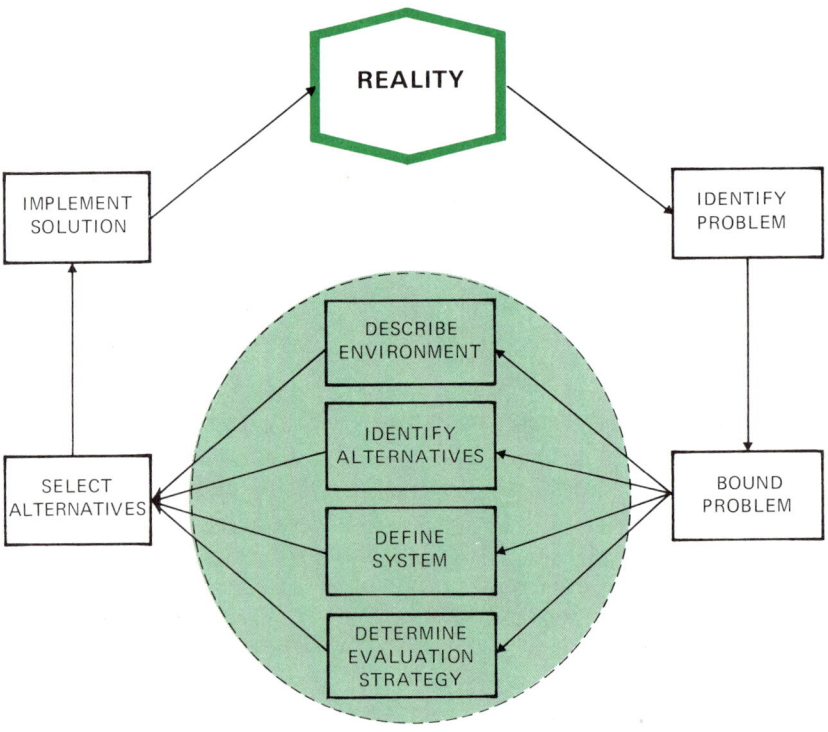

Figure 1-1. **The problem-solving process**

philosophical issues related to the notion of *reality*), because of changes in the individual's perception, or because of changes in his notion of what ought to be. This perceived problem may be actually occurring, or the observer may be forecasting a potential problem that will occur unless some action is taken. He may also be recognizing an opportunity for improvement.

The reason for this recognition of a problem or of an opportunity for improvement need not concern us here, although we do suggest that the management problem solver take an active role in identifying problems before they become so serious as to create a crisis. Rather, we are more concerned with what he should do once a problem or opportunity has been identified.

A problem solver's first task is bounding the problem. In essence, he must think about what to think about. The event that created his awareness of a problem may be only a symptom of the actual problem. For example, the event that caused his concern may have been an unusually large number of items out-of-stock in inventory. If he decides to "solve" the problem by focusing his attention on inventory policies, he may overlook the "real problem," which may lie in the production scheduling operations.

As a second example, a problem solver may consider the de facto racial segregation of public schools to be undesirable. While busing or redistricting may provide some racial balance in the schools, the real problem may lie in the housing patterns of individuals and in the concept of the neighborhood school. The long-term solution of this difficult problem may require a strategy focused on issues quite different from the transportation of students.

Certainly the task of bounding a problem is not a trivial one. It may be the most important step in the problem-solving process, since asking the right questions may be the most significant determinant of a successful solution. One way of getting started is the use of an exploratory scenario as suggested by Jackson [1974]. The problem solver begins by letting his mind "run loose" and talking about or writing down ideas concerning possible alternatives, their potential effects, obstacles that might be encountered, etc. In essence, this process is simply an active way of "mulling things over," and clearly requires insight and judgment on the part of the problem solver.

After the problem has been recognized and bounded, the problem solver can begin the other required tasks. He must devise alternative means of dealing with the problem. He must have an understanding, or definition, of the system he is dealing with and its environment so that he can predict the effects of implementing his alternate solutions. Finally, he must determine the criteria by which he will evaluate these different effects.

In some instances, the search for alternate solutions may require a great deal of creativity. New ways of dealing with problems may be sought. In other cases, it may be relatively easy to identify the alternatives because constraints eliminate many courses of action.

The system definition is an attempt to specify how the implementation of an alternative will actually affect the system. That is, if you take a particular action, your system definition should provide the means of predicting the results. In some cases, this system definition may remain implicit and never be verbalized by the problem solver. He may indicate that he cannot describe how a particular system behaves, and yet he comfortably predicts the effects of different alternatives based on his intuition. Unless his intuition is equivalent to a wild guess, he must at least have some gross hypothesis about how things work in the system of concern.

The behavior of the system may also be influenced by some aspects of its environment that cannot be controlled by the problem solver. For example, the profitability of a manufacturer will be influenced by the demand for the product. In order to predict the effects of implementing alternate production plans, the manufacturer must be able to describe the environment in sufficient detail to obtain forecasts of future demand.

Finally, the problem solver must determine a strategy for evaluating the effects of the alternatives. In some cases this strategy will be obvious. If the only effect of the selection of an alternative is on the profits of an organization, his evaluation strategy may be to rank one alternative higher than another if it generates more profit. In other cases involving uncertain or risky effects from the alternatives, or involving multiple effects that must be considered, the determination of the evaluation strategy may not be so straightforward. For example, how would you evaluate alternative plans for deploying ambulances, even if the results from the different alternatives could be forecasted with complete certainty? How would you trade off the cost of the alternative versus the number of lives saved? What is it worth to save another human life? Is your answer different if you know that the person whose life you save will be a rich man or a poor man? A young man or an old woman? A member of your family or a stranger? You? These are difficult questions that have no simple answers acceptable to everyone.

After forecasting the effects of implementing each alternative and determining his evaluation strategy, the problem solver should be in a position to select an alternative. This alternative becomes the solution to the problem he has identified. One final step remains: he must implement this solution in the real world.

By now it should be clear why organizations are not being run by the models of management science. Time and again we saw the need for human judgment during our discussion of the problem-solving process. It seems unlikely that machines will ever be created that are sufficiently sensitive to detect all the problems of an organization. Mechanical sensors might very well detect changes in the real world or even improve our perception of it. However, the concept of the way the world ought to be is purely artificial and dependent on human judgment. Once a problem has been identified, judgment is required in thinking about what to think about. Obviously, creating alternatives, defining the system, and determining an evaluation strategy all require judgmental inputs. Finally, after an alternative has been selected, only a trivial technological change can be implemented in an organization without involving the manager in the role of change agent.

Where then do the models of management science fit into the problem-solving process? The use of these models generally falls into the area within the dashed circle in Figure 1-1. That is, management science models can be used to help forecast what the environment will be like, identify alternatives, provide a system definition that predicts outcomes, and implement an evaluation strategy. The intent of these models is to aid the problem solver in performing these vital tasks in the problem-solving process. Seldom, if ever, can it be said that these models actually solve his problem.

MANAGEMENT SCIENCE MODELS

Models and Problem Solving As we have seen, the management problem solver has an interest in being able to predict "how things work." One important role of the model is to increase an individual's understanding of how things work. This potential for increased understanding should motivate a manager to learn more about model building as an aid to problem solving.

Broadly defined, a model is a device for aiding rational thinking. More specifically, the models we are interested in provide a simplified representation of a complex system or phenomenon. To be helpful in problem solving, a model must include the essential, relevant features of the system being studied.

In order to deal with the complexity of the world, all individuals use models to aid their understanding of the surrounding environment. For example, we have models of certain shapes within our heads that help us to recognize important traffic signs, such as stop signs, from among the multitude of other shapes we perceive in our environment. A model is an economizing device that reduces the infinite number of possibilities to a much smaller, finite number of categories. It ignores much information potentially available to the problem solver and uses categories to collect together many other bits of information that may be considered similar for the process of problem solving. While all stop signs differ at some level of detail, they may all be placed in the same category when determining a driver's behavior.

If a model simplifies a problem solver's view of a problem by leaving out much information and by creating categories, what features must it retain in order to be useful? Ideally, a model used for problem solving will include the important features, or elements, of the system under study, as well as the interrelationships among these elements that determine causes and effects. If such a model exists, the problem solver may actually manipulate the elements of the system within the model and observe their effects. Either by trial and error or by using more sophisticated approaches, he will determine how to adjust these elements so that the resulting impact on the system is consistent with his objectives.

Thus, the managerial problem solver can use such a model, if it exists, to perform experiments and test hypotheses much as a natural scientist uses his laboratory. Because of this similarity, the area of management concerned with model building is often referred to as management science.

FIGURE 1-2. **Aircraft shape in a wind tunnel**

Examples of Models Let us now consider three examples of models that have been used in problem solving. Figure 1-2 shows a model of an aircraft in a wind tunnel. The problem that is being studied is the determination of the appropriate external shape of the aircraft. This model captures the central features of shape very well. However, it does not include important elements of the aircraft, such as the internal workings, that are largely irrelevant to this problem.

Figure 1-3 illustrates a dummy under observation during a staged automobile accident. This model captures the essential features of the behavior of a human body involved in an accident, but detailed physical appearance, skin coloring, and internal workings are omitted because they are irrelevant to the problem being studied.

A third example of a model is provided by the diagram of the problem-solving process shown in Figure 1-1, as you may have recognized. The problem-solving process is exceedingly complex and may vary from individual to individual according to his own unique style. Nevertheless, in Figure 1-1, we have attempted to capture the essential elements of this process in order to solve the problem of organizing our discussion. In doing so we have omitted certain details. For example, the steps in the process are all interdependent. The task of defining the system may affect the range of alternatives that are considered, and vice versa. Similarly, there may be interactions between the evaluation strategies and the alternatives that are considered. Thus, this model would be more realistic if arrows were drawn in both directions between all pairs of blocks. However, such arrows would make the drawing extremely messy and would perhaps defeat our purpose of presenting a simplified view of a complex

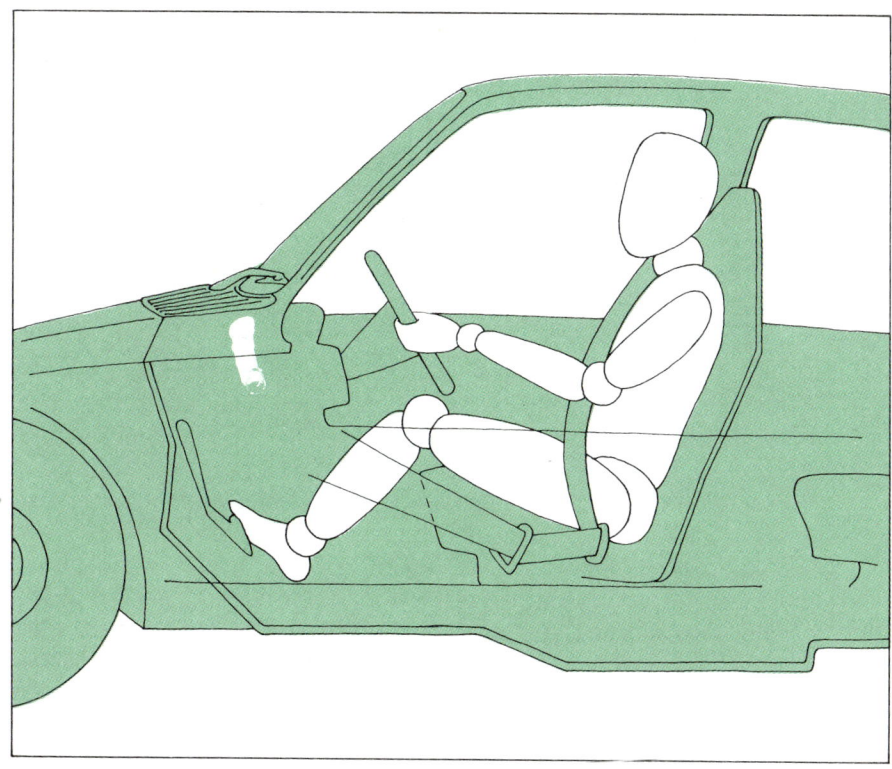

FIGURE 1-3. **Automobile testing dummy**

process. In addition, it is important to note that this is not the only model of the problem-solving process that could be drawn. (Try to construct your own.) Nevertheless, this model will have been useful if it aided your understanding of the important aspects of the process.

This same feature of nonuniqueness is common to almost any model of a complex process. Other models, perhaps very different ones, may also be useful in enhancing a problem solver's understanding of a complex process. The danger of model building is that the problem solver will come to regard the model as the problem and forget that it is only one way (generally very limited) of looking at the problem.

Mathematical Models We have been describing models in general. While any form of a model may be useful to the problem solver, and thus should be encouraged, the field of management science is generally concerned with mathematical models. Why, you may ask, is this so? You may feel that the world is complex enough without hiding it behind a screen of mathematical symbols and notation. However, those who have mastered the language of mathematics (even to a very limited extent) find that they can benefit significantly from the use of mathematical models. A mathematical model forces the model builder to make explicit his assumptions about the important elements of the problem and the cause-effect relationships that exist within the system of interest. Using the logical rules of mathematical analysis, he can check these assumptions and relationships to ensure their internal consistency. The logic of mathematics also provides a means of exploring the consequences of these assumptions. Further, the results of these analyses can be independently verified by others.

THE MODERN MANAGER AND MANAGEMENT SCIENCE

We have argued that problem solving is the most important function of a manager, that model building is an aid to problem solving, and that the mathematical models of management science are an important special class of models. Hopefully, you are persuaded that you should learn something about the field of management science. We do not feel that you should be subjected to a detailed discussion of mathematical techniques and theories. However, you should learn enough about the field so that you will be in a position to use effectively the models and techniques that are available in real-world situations.

We shall presume that the typical reader of this book does not intend to specialize in management science and become a professional in this field. Thus, it seems unlikely that he will ever be involved in the details of formulating sophisticated mathematical models and obtaining solutions through the use of special-purpose computer programs. At one extreme, he may be the user of the results of large-scale management science studies. Operating in this role, he should have the following skills:

1. The ability to recognize situations in which management science might be used effectively.
2. The ability to conduct two-way communication with a technical specialist; that is, he must be able to
    a. explain the nature of his problem to a specialist in a meaningful way and
    b. understand the specialist's product sufficiently well to verify its appropriateness and potential usefulness.
3. The ability to understand the results of management science studies so that he can obtain full value from the information available to him.

At the other extreme, he may find himself working in a small business. The size of the operations would make it unlikely that a formal management science analysis would ever be performed. Nevertheless, the models of management science provide a way of thinking and of organizing information that should aid his intuitive decision making. One of the most powerful aids in problem solving is the use of analogies. A justification for the case method in management education is the expectation that the graduate, when faced with a real-world problem, will be able to say, "Aha, this problem is similar to the problem faced by the company in the XYZ case. With only a few modifications, the analysis and solution for that case may apply here." Similarly, by gaining an exposure to the models of management science, the manager may be able to recognize a problem as being similar to those analyzed using a particular management science technique. This recognition should be helpful to him in identifying the data he needs and in exploring possible alternative solutions.

Somewhere between these two extremes, the manager may be in an organizational position in which he occasionally encounters relatively small, straightforward problems amenable to analysis by management science techniques. He should be able to formulate models appropriate for analyzing these problems, utilize standard computer programs written by others to obtain solutions, and interpret the results.

In each of these contexts, the manager should have the ability to recognize problems amenable to analysis using management science models and should have some model formulation skills. Therefore, we will present numerous examples of models throughout this text and attempt to illuminate the process of thought that developed these formulations. In order to avoid extraneous details, the initial presentations of these example formulations will be in the context of "toy" problems that we have created to illustrate certain points. We then will discuss examples of real-world implementations of management science models and techniques and attempt to examine their significance critically. At the same time, we will emphasize the interpretation of the results obtained from these models and attempt to point out where managerial discretion and judgment must be used to provide a meaningful interpretation in the real world.

We shall avoid devoting a great deal of time to the technical details of the mathematical analyses associated with the different management science models. Nevertheless, the manager should have some idea how these analyses are performed. This knowledge is important to his understanding of both the power and the potential limitations of these techniques. Further, such understanding will help remove the mystique often associated with the "black box" known as the computer, and should increase his self-confidence in challenging and analyzing the results that pour from it. In order to obtain this understanding, it will be necessary for you to work through some small examples by hand. Please keep in mind while you are pushing the pencil that these exercises are not suggested because they are "good for you" per se, or because we expect that you will actually be performing similar analyses by hand in your position as a manager. Rather, you should concentrate on understanding what each technique is doing in a substantive sense. What kinds of results are being generated, and how do these results follow from your formulations of the problem? Although we will attempt to help you in gaining this insight, it will require careful reflection on your part.

THE PLAN OF THE BOOK

We have seen that management science is primarily concerned with those aspects of problem solving related to identifying alternatives, understanding

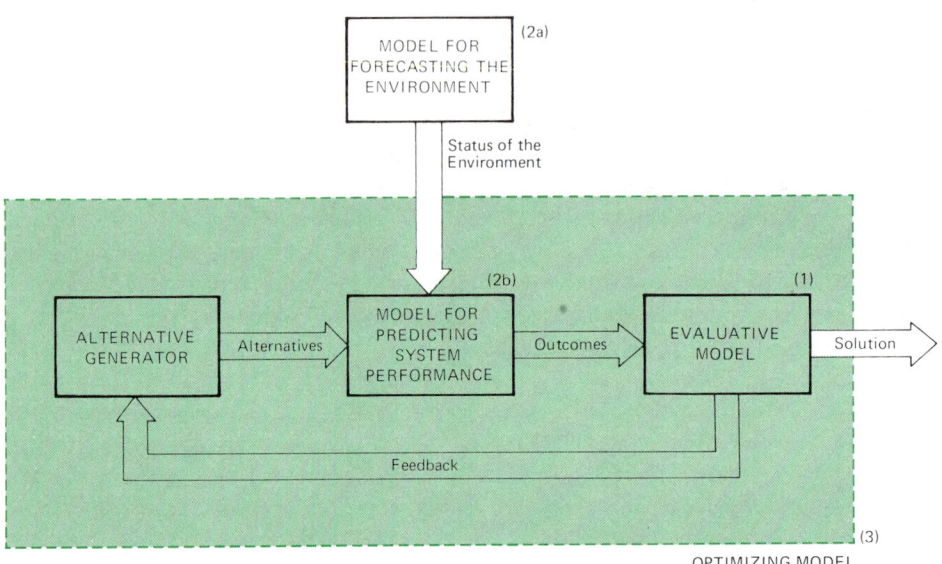

FIGURE 1-4. **Models of management science**

"how things work," and evaluating the predicted effects of implementing alternatives. Each different mathematical model of management science may focus on one or more of these aspects. Therefore, it is helpful to categorize these models according to their primary functions.

Figure 1-4 provides more detail regarding the items within the circle in Figure 1-1. One important category of managment science models is represented by the *evaluative model* [(1) in Figure 1-4]. While a natural scientist would be satisfied with a predictive model that describes "how things are," a manager also needs an evaluative model to determine "how things ought to be." Such models may be implicit in simple cases involving decisions that produce only a single, certain effect on the system. However, in cases involving risk so that different effects may occur with different probabilities, a manager may require an explicit evaluative model in order to select the alternative most consistent with his view of the way things ought to be.

In Part II of this book, we shall assume that we know how things work. That is, given an alternative, we can predict the result of choosing it, subject, perhaps, to factors in the environment beyond our control. For example, our alternatives might be 1) to take an umbrella to work or 2) not to take an umbrella to work. We can easily predict the result of selecting either alternative if we know whether or not it will rain. Unfortunately, we cannot control whether or not it will rain. How do we go about making decisions in cases like this? As we shall see, we can construct an evaluative model to help us analyze this problem. These evaluative models are based on a field of management science known as decision theory. An understanding of decision theory can be a very practical aid to a manager, even when the required mathematical calculations are made on the back of an envelope rather than on a computer.

The model for forecasting the environment and the model for predicting system performance [2(a) and 2(b) respectively in Figure 1-4] represent two important categories of models concerned with understanding "how things work" and with predicting the effects of alternative decisions. Part III will be concerned with these *predictive models*. First, we shall see how models may be used to predict, or forecast, the status of the environment. For example, our decision regarding whether or not to take an umbrella to work might be greatly simplified if we could forecast the weather more accurately. Similarly, a decision regarding what price to charge for a new product might be much simpler if we could accurately forecast demand. Again, we could easily determine the appropriate staffing for a hospital emergency room if we knew how many patients to expect.

Next, we shall make more precise the notion of a *system* and a *system definition,* and see how a mathematical model may be used to provide this system definition, thus becoming a predictive model of system performance. We shall illustrate how the familiar break-even model may be viewed as a predictive model, then provide several real-world examples of the actual use of predictive models in the form of large-scale corporate planning models in private, public, and not-for-profit organizations. Finally, we shall study predictive models that explicitly include risk and uncertainty. These models are generally required when we are unable to control the effects of the environment on our system of interest or to forecast them with certainty. Even the most experienced weatherman often offers rainfall predictions in terms of probability statements rather than simply stating that it will or will not rain. Many of the predictive models incorporating risk are based on the fields of queuing (waiting line) theory and Monte Carlo simulation.

There is a third category of models (3) indicated by the dashed line in Figure 1-4, which combines predictive and evaluative models with a feedback mechanism to an alternative generator. These models actually allow the rules of mathematical analysis (usually implemented on a computer) to generate and search through the set of all alternate solutions and to select the one with the best predicted outcome according to an evaluative model. These models are termed *optimizing* (or prescriptive) models, since the result of their use is actually a proposed solution to the problem that is optimal (or "best") in terms of the evaluative model.

In Part IV, we shall see how evaluative and predictive models can be combined in certain special cases to create an optimizing model. These models include the important class of mathematical programming models. It will be important for you to understand the characteristics of problems that can be analyzed using these methods, the manner in which these models are formulated, and the way the associated mathematical analysis produces a solution.

You should study Figure 1-4 carefully to ensure that you understand this classification of models. This figure will be repeated at the beginning of each subsequent chapter with one or more aspects highlighted in order to emphasize how the particular topic under discussion fits into this overall framework. By referring to this figure, you should avoid becoming so absorbed in technical details that you lose sight of the basic purpose of the management science model or solution technique. As a manager, this conceptual understanding may be of much more potential value than any mathematical details.

Appendixes A and B present the rudiments of mathematics and statistics that are necessary to understand the materials included in this text. These appendixes provide a convenient review and reference. Readers who seek a "refresher" in these topics should study them carefully before proceeding. Others may prefer to consult some basic programmed texts such as those offered by Martin [1969a, 1969b] and Mason [1970, 1971]. Before doing so, look over the material in the appendixes to identify which topics should be covered.

Check Your Understanding

1. Consider each of the following hypothetical situations:
   a. Suppose you are an urban planner who has been involved in the study of a large-scale, sociotechnical system, such as a rapid transit system. What would you consider to be the most important phase of the problem-solving process (refer to Figure 1-1)?
   b. Suppose you are an architect who must design a new building. Again referring to Figure 1-1, what do you consider to be the most important phase of the design process?
2. Are there fundamental differences in the problem-solving processes followed by an urban planner and an architect, or are there only different emphases on phases of the process? Discuss.
3. Select a problem of personal interest to you, such as the choice of a career, the purchase of a new car, or the travel plans for your vacation. Create an exploratory scenario by listing possible alternatives, potential effects of alternatives, obstacles that might be encountered, etc. Intermix these items while letting your mind "run loose." Did you gain any additional insights into the problem?
4. Although you will be able to sharpen the definition of the following terms as you proceed through the book, on the basis of the discussion in this chapter, define:
   a. predictive model
   b. evaluative model
   c. optimizing model

   What are the relationships among them?

5. Are the models of the aircraft in Figure 1-2 and of the dummy in Figure 1-3 examples of evaluative, predictive, or optimizing models? Explain.
6. List three examples of problems you may be required to solve in following your own career plans. For each example, discuss how a model might be a potential aid. What do you need to know about the models of management science?

References

1. Dewey, J., *How We Think*. D. C. Heath, 1910.
2. Jackson, J. R., "Coping with Complexity," mimeographed, Graduate School of Management, University of California, Los Angeles, 1974.
3. Martin, E. W., *Mathematics for Decision Making: A Programmed Basic Text*, Vols. 1 and 2, Richard D. Irwin, Inc., Homewood, Ill., 1969a.
4. ———, *Programmed Learning Aid for Basic Algebra*, Learning Systems Company, Homewood, Ill., 1969b.
5. Mason, R. D., *Programmed Learning Aid for Business and Economic Statistics*, Learning Systems Company, Homewood, Ill., 1970.
6. ———, *Programmed Learning Aid for College Mathematics*, Learning Systems Company, Homewood, Ill., 1971.

PART II

EVALUATIVE MODELS

INTRODUCTION TO EVALUATIVE MODELS

In Part II we shall assume that we know how things work, subject perhaps to factors in the environment beyond our control. However, even for situations in which the environment is not known with certainty, we shall assume that we can list each of the possible states of the environment and provide probability estimates of their occurrence. To illustrate this point, consider again the decision of whether or not to take an umbrella to work. If we take the umbrella to work and it actually rains, having the umbrella is a desirable outcome. On the other hand, if we take the umbrella and it does not rain, we have unnecessarily burdened ourselves. We may not know with complete certainty whether or not it will rain. However, in Part II we shall assume that we can estimate the probability of rain. Given this information, we can use the concepts of decision theory to develop an *evaluative model* that aids in making decisions.

Thus, in Part II we shall be concerned primarily with the evaluative models of management science as shown in Figure II-1. Later, we shall turn our attention to the issue of how we obtain these predictions regarding the state of the environment (for example, rain or no rain) and how we predict the outcome of choosing an alternative given a particular state of the environment.

The purpose of an evaluative model is to reflect the subjective judgments of the decision maker regarding the desirability of an outcome resulting from a decision. The choice of the appropriate evaluative model will depend on the circumstances under which the decision is actually being made. One of the important considerations is whether the outcome is known with certainty or only in terms of probability statements. For example, suppose we have $100 to invest. If we place it in a federally insured savings account paying 7 percent

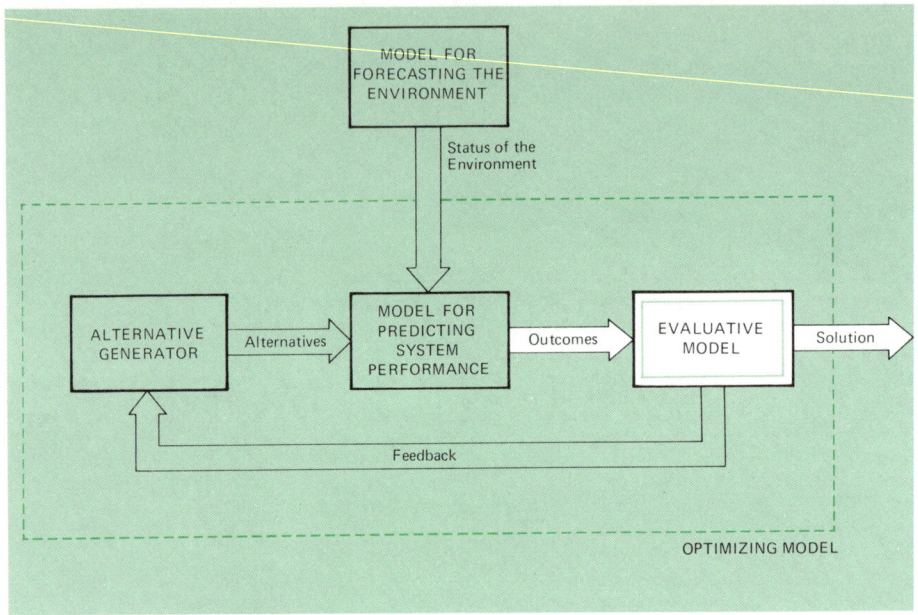

FIGURE II-1 **The evaluative model in relation to the environment forecasting model, the alternative generator, and the predictive system model**

interest, we will receive $107 in return at the end of one year. We know this result with certainty. Naturally, we are ignoring such events as a political revolution, a world war, or other such catastrophes that might prevent the bank from meeting its obligations. (In most real-world situations, we also ignore these surprise events that could happen, but that are sufficiently unlikely.) For practical purposes, we can say that the outcome of the decision to place $100 in a federally insured savings account is known with certainty.

The second important consideration in defining the appropriate evaluative model is the number of different criteria that are relevant for evaluating the desirability of an action. For example, if we are trying to invest $100, the only important criterion may be the amount of money we receive in return. Thus, we would say that there is only a single criterion to be considered. In other cases, there may be multiple goals involved, and therefore multiple criteria must be considered. In purchasing an automobile, we consider not only cost but also such criteria as appearance and performance.

The simplest decisions from the viewpoint of the evaluative model involve only a single criterion, and the outcome associated with each alternative is known with complete certainty. An appropriate evaluative model in such cases can easily be identified. However, even with a single criterion, the introduction of risk creates the need for an explicit evaluative model to aid in the decision making. The introduction of risk recognizes that there are several possible outcomes, each of which may occur with a known probability.

Properties of an Evaluative Model

Since the purpose of an evaluative model is merely to reflect subjective judgments, it would be natural to question the model's practical usefulness. After all, the decision maker should simply be able to look at the different outcomes and state which one he prefers. However, in truly complicated situations involving risk and multiple criteria, this may be a difficult task. The development of an evaluative model can proceed on a step-by-step basis, so that the decision maker is not overwhelmed with the complexity of the total problem. In addition, for certain problems having very specific characteristics, the explicit identification of an evaluative model may allow the use of the powerful optimizing models of management science, which identify the best, or optimal, solution to a problem on the basis of this evaluative model.

Suppose we have only two alternatives for consideration, A_1 and A_2. We have assumed that we can predict the outcome of choosing each alternative and have labeled these O_1 and O_2, respectively. Now, suppose we construct an evaluative model to aid us in choosing between these alternatives. What properties should such a model have? First, it would seem reasonable to require this model to be a function of information regarding the outcomes O_1 and O_2 alone. That is, the choice of the alternative should not be influenced by extraneous information unrelated to the effects of selecting either alternative. While this point may appear to be trivial, in complex situations it will be a difficult task to identify correctly all of the potential impacts from adopting an alternative.

Therefore, let us define our evaluative model U as a function of the outcomes O_1 and O_2. Since U is a function, $U(O_1)$ and $U(O_2)$ are simply numbers. For example, we may obtain $U(O_1) = 0.6$ and $U(O_2) = 0.4$. (It may be helpful at this point to review the notion of a function presented in Appendix A.)

Now let us consider a second desirable property of an evaluative model. Suppose the decision maker prefers O_1 to O_2. Then this preference should be indicated by requiring $U(O_1)$ to be a larger number than $U(O_2)$. If the decision maker is actually indifferent between O_1 and O_2, we should have $U(O_1) = U(O_2)$ to indicate this feeling. Clearly, if O_1 is preferred to O_2, then alternative A_1 is the correct decision, and vice versa. In our previous example, if $U(O_1) = 0.6$ and $U(O_2) = 0.4$, then we should choose alternative A_1 over A_2.

These are the two essential properties of an evaluative model: first, that it be a function solely of information regarding the outcomes of the decision, and second that $U(O_1)$ is greater than $U(O_2)$ if and only if O_1 is preferred to O_2. We shall now turn our attention to the problem of constructing such models in practical situations. The choice of U depends on the preferences of the decision maker. We shall investigate what kind of information the decision maker must provide in order to allow the construction of U.

An Example: A Single Criterion Under Certainty

The simplest case from the standpoint of evaluative models involves a single criterion under conditions of certainty. To illustrate this case, let us return to our bank example. Suppose we have $100 to invest. For simplicity, assume that there are only two alternate investments available to us. The first, A_1, is a bank deposit paying 7 percent per year, and the second alternative, A_2, is another bank deposit paying 5 percent per year. Both accounts are fully insured and alike in every respect except for the interest rate.

Certainly this example seems trivial. No doubt you have already noted that the outcome O_1 from the first alternative A_1 is $107, while O_2 is only $105. Thus, we have identified the alternatives A_1 and A_2 and predicted their associated outcomes with certainty. According to our diagram of the models of management science, we still need an evaluative model in order to make the decision. However in this case, the correct decision A_1 seems obvious. Why is this so?

The reason is deceptively simple. There is a single criterion, money. Further, at least in our culture, most persons would agree that more money is preferred to less. That is, most persons would prefer having $107 to having $105. Therefore, we have actually used an evaluative model in making our decision, but since we agree that more money is preferred to less, and since there is no risk involved to complicate matters, the choice of the evaluative model is not a critical issue.

An obvious evaluative model can be constructed by defining $U(O_i) = O_i$ for $i = 1$ or 2. That is, we simply define the evaluative function as the identity function, so that this function assigns the number 107 to the outcome $107, and the number 105 to the outcome $105. Notice that this definition satisfies both desirable properties of an evaluative model. It is a function of the outcome, and $U(O_1) > U(O_2)$ if and only if O_1 is preferred to O_2. Further, this accurately reflects the feelings of *most* persons in our culture. When we are dealing with a single criterion such as money, we can often let $U(O_i)$ equal O_i. Therefore, we can speak of maximizing profit (or minimizing cost) without making explicit our evaluative model. Nevertheless, the choice of such a model is implied.

The function $U(O_i) = O_i$ is not the only function that satisfies these properties. For example, $V(O_i) = 2O_i$ would be acceptable. Since $V(\$107) = (2)(107) = 214$ and $V(\$105) = 210$, and 214 is greater than 210, this function also indicates bank deposit A_1 should be chosen. Try to think of other functions that preserve the same ordering of these two outcomes as the simple identity function $U(O_i) = O_i$.

It is clear that we have a wide choice of evaluative models that will lead to the same decision. We could easily agree on the correct decision for our problem, A_1, without much concern regarding the appropriate form of U. As we shall see, this will not always be the case when risk is introduced.

One should not conclude, however, that decision making under certainty is always simple. In many problems of interest to managers, the models required to generate the alternatives may be very complex, involving possibly thousands of alternatives. Given the explicit identification of an evaluative model as a basis for ranking alternatives, it may be possible to use certain optimizing models of management science, such as linear programming, as aids in these more complex situations.

An Overview of Part II

In order to be useful, the evaluative model must reflect the manager's concept of what ought to be. This latter concept requires a subjective judgment on the part of the manager. Thus, the evaluative model can only be considered right or wrong on the basis of how well it reflects these subjective judgments. In this sense, the evaluative model is also subjective. Some individuals make the mistake of interpreting this to mean that the evaluative model is arbitrary, since it is not objective. However, there is a significant difference between a subjective model and an arbitrary model. An evaluative model is a good one if it reflects the subjective judgments of the manager. It cannot be arbitrary, since if it were it might not reflect these judgments properly. This point is important, and we shall return to it as we proceed through this section.

In Chapter 2, we shall see how decision making with a single criterion becomes more complicated when risk is involved. In order to provide a background for this discussion, we shall review some basic probability concepts and then discuss the use of *expected value* as an evaluative model. In Chapter 3, we introduce decision trees as a technique for simplifying the complex relationships and the calculations associated with risky choices. Finally, in Chapter 4 we study how to deal with situations in which the expected value of the outcomes is not an appropriate evaluative model. These situations often occur because the stakes are very high in a decision involving risk. In such situations, the concepts of utility theory may be used to determine the appropriate evaluative model.

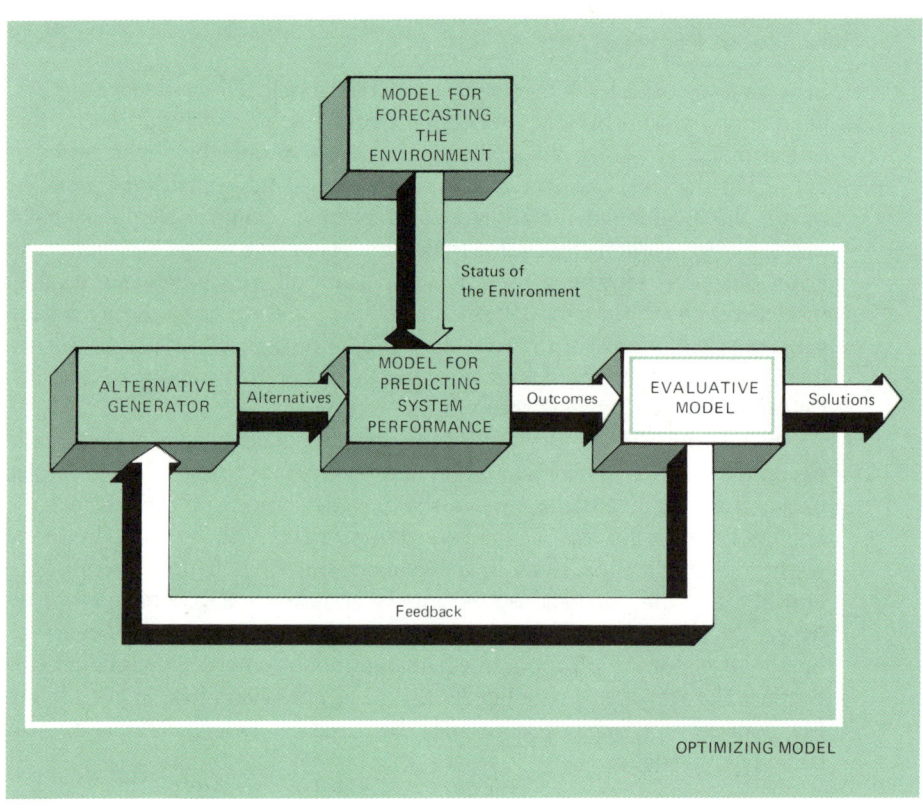

2

PROBABILITY AND EXPECTED VALUE

Most managerial decisions involve some risk. For example, the decision regarding how many items to stock in a retail store must consider risk in the form of different probabilities for different levels of demand. The decision to drill a wildcat oil well involves risk in the form of the probability that an underground pool of oil actually exists on the site. The decision to build a new hospital involves risk in the form of different probabilities for different levels of demand for service. The decision to market a new product involves risk in the form of different probabilities for different costs of the production process and the raw materials, different probabilities for the price level that will be appropriate for the product, and different probabilities for the demand for the product at each price level.

Thus, it is essential that the manager be comfortable with the basic concepts of probability theory and that he understand the alternate evaluative models that may be applied to decisions involving risk. In this chapter, we first review the basic concepts of probability theory, then we consider the use of *expected value* as an evaluative model for decisions involving a single criterion under risk.

REVIEW OF SOME PROBABILITY CONCEPTS

Loosely speaking, a probability is a measure of how likely something is to occur. This something that either does or does not occur is called an *event*. For example, an event might be a coin landing on heads after it is flipped or it might be a second oil embargo by the major oil producing nations before 1985. In either case, a probability number can be assigned to each event to express the likelihood of its occurrence. These probability numbers range from 0.0, which means that an event cannot occur, to 1.0, which means that it definitely will occur.

In the case of the flip of an ordinary coin, most of us would agree that the probability number that should be assigned to the event *heads* is 0.5. One interpretation of this number is that 0.5, or one-half, is the proportion of the times that the coin will land on heads if it is flipped many times. But what about the probability number that should be assigned to the oil embargo? Will we all agree on this number? Can we observe the world many times from the present to 1985 and note in what proportion of these alternative futures an oil embargo actually occurs? No, of course not.

Subjective Versus Objective Probabilities

The concept of probability is often introduced in terms of the notion of a *relative frequency of occurrence*. In our coin flipping example, the more times we flip the coin, the closer we would expect the *relative frequency* of heads to approach 0.5, the probability of the coin landing on heads on a single toss. The definition of the probability of an event as the relative frequency of the occurrence of that event in a long series of trials is *objective,* since it relates to a phenomenon we can observe in the real world.

Suppose you are shown a coin and asked to state the probability that it will land on heads if it is tossed. You might assume that it is a fair coin (one with an equal probability of landing heads or tails) and state that this probability is 0.5. In doing so, you would say that this is an objective probability. Now suppose you are shown a thumb tack and asked to state the probability that it will land point up if it is tossed. More than likely you have never conducted a long series of experiments of tossing thumb tacks and observing the relative frequency of a *point up*. Moreover, you may not have any information regarding such experiments by others, and you probably do not have the information and skills necessary to develop a predictive model based on the laws of physics. Nevertheless, you are forced to respond. After some reflection, suppose you say, "Well, I feel that the thumb tack is more likely to fall point up than point down. In fact, based on my understanding of how physical bodies behave when they hit the ground, I would say it is about twice as likely to land point up. Therefore, given the toss of a thumb tack, I would estimate the probability of a *point up* at about 0.67."

Since this estimate is not based on any historical experience or rigorous analysis, we would call 0.67 a *subjective probability.* In decisions faced by managers, subjective probabilities generally play a much more important role than objective probabilities. Organizations and their environments are in a constant state of flux, making the development of actual data on the relative frequency of important events a difficult task. In some cases, predictive models can be used to provide objective probability estimates. However, in most cases, the assignment of a probability to an event will be based on some individual's personal experience and understanding of the event, and it will thus be *subjective*. Further, it is only natural that two persons might make different probability assignments to the same event, since their experiences and understandings of the event may differ. Thus, the probability assigned to the occurrence of a second oil embargo before 1985 would be a *subjective probability*.

The decision maker is the person who has the responsibility for the decision to be made. It follows that the decision should be based on *his* preferences and expectations regarding future events. But he may choose to designate other persons as his experts when it comes to estimating the probability of occurrence of a particular event, since the expert may have a better information base.

In a practical application, experts will be drawn from different fields. Estimates of market variables, such as sales volume, are likely to come from the marketing department; production variables, such as manufacturing costs, will be provided by accountants and industrial engineers. Some variables may even require experts from outside the organization.

We may be able to simply ask these experts to "think hard," and give us these probability assessments. However, if an individual experiences difficulty in expressing his feelings about the likelihood of an event in the form of a probability number, then some techniques that simplify the process of assessing subjective probabilities can be used. These techniques are reviewed by Spetzler and Stael von Holstein [1975]. In the following discussion, we will assume that the relevant probabilities have been determined objectively or that they are subjective estimates from the appropriate experts.

Mutually Exclusive Events

Events are called *mutually exclusive* if one and only one of them can occur. For example, on the flip of a coin, either "heads" or "tails" will be the event that occurs, but not both. Similarly, the events "a second oil embargo occurs before 1985" and "a second oil embargo *does not* occur before 1985" are mutually exclusive. On the other hand, the events "a second oil embargo occurs before 1985" and "a second oil embargo occurs before 1990" are *not* mutually exclusive, since both events occur if the oil producing nations declare a second embargo between the present and 1984.

If A and B are mutually exclusive events, then the probability that A or B occurs, written $P(A \text{ or } B)$, is equal to the probability of A, written $P(A)$, plus the probability of B, written $P(B)$. That is,

$$P(A \text{ or } B) = P(A) + P(B). \tag{1}$$

For example, if H represents the event of a coin landing on heads, and T the event of its landing on tails, then

$$P(H \text{ or } T) = P(H) + P(T)$$
$$= 0.5 + 0.5 = 1.0.$$

Since either heads or tails must occur, the probability of heads or tails must equal 1.0, the result we obtained. When exactly one event from a list of events must occur, we say the list of events is *collectively exhaustive*. That is, the list contains all of the future events that could possibly happen that relate to a given phenomenon. If a list of events is collectively exhaustive and the events are mutually exclusive, then the sum of the probabilities assigned to the events must equal to 1.0. This summing of probabilities provides a means of checking the logical consistency of subjective probability estimates.

Example The Pacific Oil Company (POCO) is engaged in a study that requires an estimate of the price of a barrel of crude oil in five years. Suppose the manager identifies the purchasing agent of the company as the appropriate expert for questions involving crude oil prices and asks him to estimate the probability that the price will be lower than $10, between $10 and $12, and more than $12, assuming that there is *no oil embargo* during the period.

Suppose the purchasing agent responds with the following estimates:

Price Range	Probability
less than $10	0.125
$10–$12	0.375
more than $12	0.500
	1.000

Notice that these events are mutually exclusive and collectively exhaustive, since exactly one of them must occur. Therefore, the sum of the probabilities must equal 1.0. If the initial set of probability estimates had not summed to 1.00, but it was "close" (say within ± 0.05), the manager might have normalized them by simply dividing each estimate by the initial sum. Otherwise, he would have to interact further with the purchasing agent.

Independent Events

Two or more events are independent (or statistically independent) if the occurrence of one has no effect on the probability of the occurrence of the others. If the events A and B are independent, then the probability of both A and B occurring, written P(AB), is equal to the product of their individual probabilities. That is,

$$P(AB) = P(A) \cdot P(B), \tag{2}$$

where P(AB) is called the *joint* probability of A and B.

Example Suppose we flip a fair coin twice, so that the probability of heads on each flip equals the probability of tails, which equals 0.5. Let H_1 denote the event of heads on the first toss of the coin, and let H_2 denote heads on the second toss. Similarly, T_1 and T_2 denote tails on the first and second tosses of the coin, respectively.

Now, the occurrence of heads (or tails) on the first flip of the coin has no effect on the probability of heads or of tails on the second flip, and *vice versa*. Therefore H_1H_2, H_1T_2, T_1H_2, and T_1T_2 are pairs of independent events. We can compute the joint probability of heads on both tosses of the coin from

$$P(H_1H_2) = P(H_1) \cdot P(H_2)$$
$$= (0.5)(0.5) = 0.25.$$

Thus, the probability of two heads in a row is 0.25.

Dependent Events

Two events are dependent (or statistically dependent) if the occurrence of one *does affect* the probability of the occurrence of the other. Suppose we know that event A has occurred, and we wish to compute the probability that B will now occur. If B is dependent on A, we write $P(B|A)$ to indicate the probability of B, given that A has occurred. The probability $P(B|A)$ is called a *conditional* probability since it depends, or is conditional on, the event A.

The conditional probability $P(B|A)$ can be computed from the expression

$$P(B|A) = \frac{P(AB)}{P(A)}, \qquad (3)$$

as long as $P(A) \neq 0$. Thus, the conditional probability of B, given that A has occurred, is equal to the joint probability of A and B divided by the probability of A.

Notice that the probability of A in equation (3) is *not* a conditional probability. In order to distinguish $P(A)$ from a conditional probability, we call it an unconditional or marginal probability. The reason for the term *marginal* will become clear momentarily.

We can rearrange equation (3) by multiplying both sides by $P(A)$, and obtain

$$P(AB) = P(B|A) \cdot P(A). \qquad (4)$$

This equation provides a means of calculating the joint probability of A and B from the product of the conditional probability of B and the unconditional probability of A. Notice that a second expression for $P(AB)$ can be obtained from

$$P(AB) = P(A|B) \cdot P(B),$$

since the designation of the events A and B is *arbitrary*.

The relationship between independent and dependent events can be seen if the expression for the joint probability of independent events in (2) is substituted for $P(AB)$ in equation (3). We obtain

$$P(B|A) = \frac{P(A) \cdot P(B)}{P(A)} = P(B).$$

If B is independent of A, then the conditional probability of B, given that A has occurred, is not affected and can be written simply as $P(B)$, the unconditional probability of B.

A Simple Example   Let us consider a simple example in order to clarify the relationships among conditional, unconditional, and joint probabilities. Suppose we have two boxes; box 1 contains three balls (two red and one white), and box 2 contains four balls (two red and two white). We first select one of the two boxes at random, so that each has a probability of 0.5 of being chosen. Then we choose one ball from the box we have selected, again so that each ball in the box has an equal probability of being selected.

Figure 2-1 shows a tree diagram of the sequential process indicating all of the possible outcomes. Taking the upper branch, the probability of selecting box 1, $P(1)$, is 1/2. Given that box 1 has been selected, the conditional probability of drawing a red ball is $P(R|1) = 2/3$, since there are two red balls in the box of three. Similarly, the probability of drawing a white ball, given that box 1 was selected, is $P(W|1) = 1/3$. Now, the joint probability of drawing box 1 and a red ball is

$$P(R1) = P(R|1) \cdot P(1)$$
$$= (2/3)(1/2) = 1/3,$$

and of drawing box 1 and a white ball is

$$P(W1) = P(W|1) \cdot P(1)$$
$$= (1/3)(1/2) = 1/6.$$

The other main branch probabilities are calculated in a similar way. Notice that the joint probabilities at the right-hand side of the tree enumerate all of the possible outcomes. Thus, the events are mutually independent and collectively exhaustive, so the probabilities must sum to 1.0.

Let us now assemble the joint probability data from Figure 2-1 in the form of Table 2-1. The *unconditional* probabilities associated with selecting box 1 or box 2 are the sums of the two joint probabilities of $P(R1)$ and $P(W1)$ for box 1 and $P(R2)$ and $P(W2)$ for box 2, and are 1/2 each, shown as the marginal probabilities in the right-hand column. Similarly, the unconditional probabilities associated with selecting red or white balls are the sums of the two joint probabilities in the bottom row. These probabilities are called *marginal* simply because they occur in the margins of the table as shown. Their significance is that they are the probabilities of the ending events without stated conditions; that is, they are unconditional.

A POCO Example   The manager of the Pacific Oil Company (POCO) asked the purchasing agent for the probability that the price of crude oil in five years

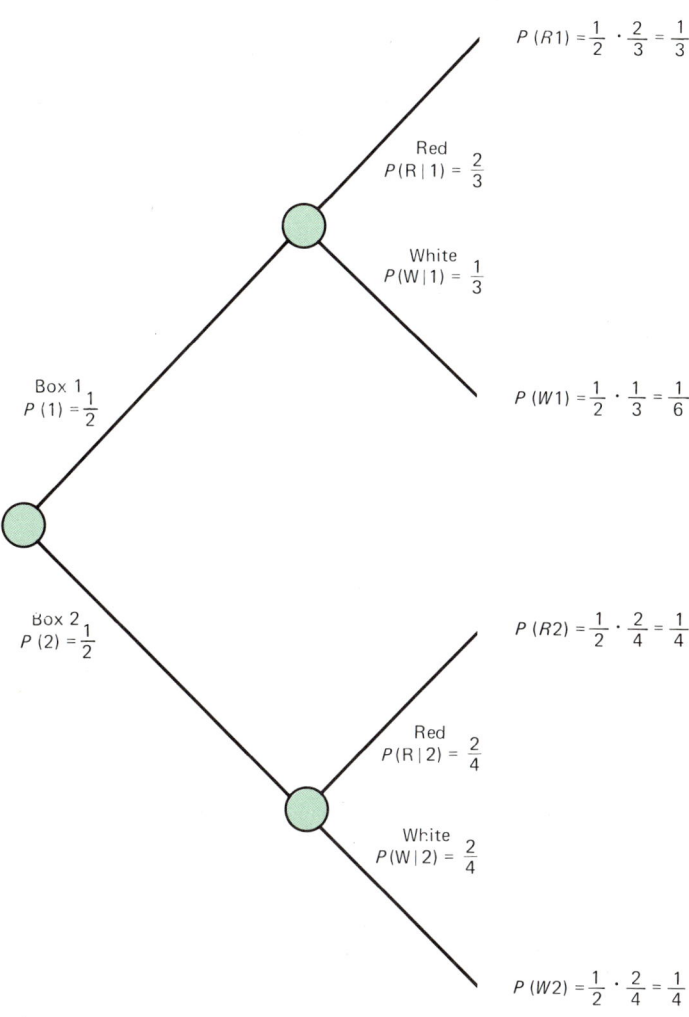

Figure 2-1. **Tree diagram of the box-ball drawing process**

would fall in one of three ranges, *given* that there is no oil embargo during the period. For simplicity, the price range of less than $10 per barrel will be termed *lower,* between $10 and $12 will be termed *current,* and more than $12, *higher.*

Now, suppose the manager really needs the probabilities that prices will be in each of these ranges *and* that there will be no embargo. That is, he wants the joint probabilities of lower prices and no embargo, current prices and no

CHAPTER 2 PROBABILITY AND EXPECTED VALUE

TABLE 2-1. **Joint and Marginal Probabilities for the Box-Ball Drawing Process**

Second Draw: Which Ball? / First Draw: Which Box?	Joint Probabilities		Marginal (Unconditional) Probabilities of Outcomes on First Draw
	Red Ball	White Ball	
Box 1	$P(R1) = \frac{1}{3}$	$P(W1) = \frac{1}{6}$	$\frac{1}{3} + \frac{1}{6} = \frac{1}{2}$
Box 2	$P(R2) = \frac{1}{4}$	$P(W2) = \frac{1}{4}$	$\frac{1}{4} + \frac{1}{4} = \frac{1}{2}$
Marginal (Unconditional) Probabilities of Outcomes on Second Draw	$\frac{1}{3} + \frac{1}{4} = \frac{7}{12}$	$\frac{1}{6} + \frac{1}{4} = \frac{5}{12}$	1.00

embargo, and higher prices and no embargo. Why did he not ask for these probabilities directly? Perhaps because his purchasing agent might feel that he has no knowledge about the prospects of another embargo. Therefore, he has very little confidence in his ability to estimate the joint probability of a price level *and* the embargo. However, he does feel confident about his estimates of the probability of the different price ranges, *given* the assumption of no embargo.

Now the manager can consult a different expert, perhaps someone outside the company, to obtain an estimate of the probability of an embargo during the next five years. Suppose he obtains an estimate of 0.2 as the probability of an embargo, so P(no embargo) $= 1.0 - 0.2 = 0.8$ since *embargo* and *no embargo* are mutually exclusive events. He can then use the formula for a joint probability when the events are dependent to modify his probability estimates for his prices as follows:

P(lower prices and no embargo) = P(lower prices|no embargo) · P(no embargo)
= (0.125)(0.8) = 0.1;
P(current prices and no embargo) = P(current prices|no embargo) · P(no embargo)
= (0.375)(0.8) = 0.3;
P(higher prices and no embargo) = P(higher prices|no embargo) · P(no embargo)
= (0.5)(0.8) = 0.4.

Notice that the sum of these joint probabilities is $0.1 + 0.3 + 0.4 = 0.8$, less than 1.0. Thus, these events are not collectively exhaustive. The missing event is *embargo,* and $P(embargo) = 0.2$ which, when added to the sum of the joint probabilities, does make it equal to 1.0.

TABLE 2-2. **Calculation of Probabilities for POCO**

Price Range	Conditional Probability of Price Range Given No Embargo		Marginal Probability of No Embargo		Joint Probability of Price Range and No Embargo
Lower	0.125	×	0.8	=	0.1
Current	0.375	×	0.8	=	0.3
Higher	0.5	×	0.8	=	0.4
	1.0				0.8

The results of this analysis are summarized in Table 2-2. Notice that the sum of the conditional probabilities is 1.0. That is because the price ranges are mutually exclusive, and, *given* that an embargo does not occur, one of these three events must occur (an embargo is treated as a distinct event involving a combination of higher prices and higher demand). The probability of no embargo, 0.8, is called a marginal probability because it is not affected by another event.

Revision of Probabilities

In many managerial problems we may start with some probabilities of occurrence, but be able to revise (improve) them as we obtain new information. For example, suppose we have a process that has been shown to produce products that are 95 percent good when it has been set up properly. On the other hand, when it is improperly set up, only 20 percent of the products are acceptable. Previous data also indicate that 90 percent of the process settings have been correct in the past. Suppose we set up the process and the first output is *good.* What is the probability that the process has been properly set up?

We can compute the probability that the setup is correct, given the new information, through the use of the expression

$$P(A_i|B) = \frac{P(A_iB)}{P(B)} \quad \quad \quad (5)$$

Notice that (5) is simply a restatement of expression (3) for computing conditional probabilities. However, when it is used in this form to revise probabilities, it is known as *Bayes theorem.*

Suppose we define the event A_1 as *a correct setup*, the event A_2 as *an incorrect setup*, and the event B as *a good product*. From previous data, we know that $P(A_1) = 0.9$ *prior* to observing the first output of the process. This is called the *prior probability* of the event A_1. Similarly, the prior probability of a bad setup, $P(A_2)$, is 0.1.

We know the conditional probability of a good product given a correct setup, $P(B|A_1)$, is 0.95, while the conditional probability of a good product given a bad setup, $P(B|A_2)$ is 0.20. From expression (4) for joint probabilities, we can compute

$$P(A_1 B) = P(B|A_1) \cdot P(A_1)$$
$$= (0.95)(0.9) = 0.855,$$

the *joint probability* of A_1 and B. Similarly, we obtain the *joint probability* of A_2 and B from

$$P(A_2 B) = P(B|A_2) \cdot P(A_2)$$
$$= (0.2)(0.1) = 0.02.$$

The *unconditional* or *marginal* probability of a good product, event B, is obtained from the sum of these two joint probabilities, so that

$$P(B) = P(A_1 B) + P(A_2 B)$$
$$= 0.855 + 0.02 = 0.875.$$

We can now compute the probability that the process has a correct setup given the *additional information* that the first output of the process is good. Using Bayes theorem (5), we obtain

$$P(A_1|B) = \frac{P(A_1 B)}{P(B)}$$
$$= \frac{0.855}{0.875} = 0.977,$$

which is the *revised prior* or *posterior probability* of A_1. Additional information regarding the output of the process could be used in an iterative fashion to continue to revise the probability of A_1.

A SINGLE CRITERION UNDER RISK

We can now use these probability concepts to investigate the problem of making a decision on the basis of a single criterion under conditions of risk. One of several different outcomes will result from a decision, and the probability of each outcome can be specified. The simplest examples of decisions involving a single criterion and some risk regarding the outcome are provided by several gambles. Suppose you are offered the possibility of playing one of two games. In either game, you will flip a fair coin. In the first game (A_1) you win $10 if the coin lands on heads, but lose $2 if it lands on tails. In the second game (A_2), you win $2 if heads occurs, but lose $1 if the coin falls on tails.

What are the outcomes O_1 and O_2 for the two games? In this case, the outcomes depend on an external event, heads or tails on the coin flip, as well as on our decision. Thus, we may call the payoffs for the gambles conditional outcomes; that is, they are conditional on the result of the coin flip. We also know the probability of receiving each conditional outcome, given the choice of either alternative. This information may be summarized in tabular form as shown in Table 2-3.

Study Table 2-3 carefully; this approach to summarizing the information for a decision involving risk can be very helpful. Notice that there is a row in the table corresponding to each alternative decision and a column corresponding to each future event or future state of the world. The *conditional outcomes* in the table represent the result of choosing an alternative, given each of these future states.

Expected Value

Now let us consider an evaluative model that might be appropriate for decision making in situations such as this one. A widely used evaluative model calculates the *expected value* of each outcome. The *expected value* of an outcome is simply the sum of the possible conditional values that can result for the outcome weighted by their respective probabilities of occurrence. For example, the expected value of the first gamble A_1 is

$$(0.5)(\$10.00) + (0.5)(-\$2.00) = \$5.00 - \$1.00 = \$4.00.$$

Similarly, for A_2 we have

$$(0.5)(\$2.00) + (0.5)(-\$1.00) = \$1.00 - \$0.50 = \$0.50.$$

The expected value of an outcome has an intuitively appealing interpretation. If we were to accept the first gamble A_1 many times, we would expect to win $10 half of the time, and to lose $2 the other half of the time. The net result would be equivalent to winning the expected value of the gamble, $4, on each coin flip; thus, $4 is what we expect to gain per flip if the coin is flipped many times. However, it is important to emphasize that this expected value is not one of the actual outcomes of the coin flip, which will be either "win $10" or "lose $2."

TABLE 2-3. **Representation of Alternatives Involving Risk**

	Events	
Alternatives	Heads ($p_1 = 0.5$)	Tails ($p_2 = 0.5$)
Game 1 (A_1)	$10	-$2
Game 2 (A_2)	$ 2	-$1

Because of this interpretation, the expected value of an outcome has desirable properties for use as an evaluative model by managers. During the course of his career, a manager may be faced with many decisions involving risky outcomes. If he selects only those alternatives with positive expected values, there is a high probability that his decisions will result in a positive increment to his company's profits. That does not mean that every decision will result in a desirable outcome, but rather that the odds are in favor of the manager who abides by this evaluative model.

Expected Value and Dependent Events Even when the relationships among the events are more complicated, with some being dependent on others, the expected value can still be calculated. As an example with dependent events, let us introduce a third alternative, A_3, for a comparison against our original two. Suppose this gamble has the following rules: if the fair coin lands on heads, you flip it again. On the second flip if it lands on heads, you win $20, but if it lands on tails, you lose $5. If the fair coin lands on tails on the first flip, you flip a second coin which is *unfair*. This coin is weighted and has only a 0.4 chance of landing on heads and a 0.6 chance of landing on tails. Nevertheless, if it falls on heads, you will win $5; but if it lands on tails, you lose $10. Which alternative do you prefer using the expected value evaluative model?

Alternative A_3 has four conditional outcomes: you either win $20, win $5, lose $5, or lose $10. However, the probability of receiving each of these outcomes is not immediately clear, so we must do some additional calculations.

In order to deal with the dependence of one outcome on several events, we need to be able to compute both conditional and joint probabilities. At this point, it will be helpful to introduce some new notation; let H_1 denote the event of heads on the first toss of the coin, and let H_2 denote heads on the second toss. Similarly, T_1 and T_2 denote tails on the first and second tosses of the coin respectively.

Since the first coin is fair, the probability of heads on the first toss, written $P(H_1)$, equals 0.5. In addition, the probability of heads on the second toss, *given* that heads appeared on the first toss, written $P(H_2|H_1) = 0.5$, is a *conditional probability*. That is, the probability of the event H_2 is dependent on the occurrence of the event H_1. However, if T_1 occurs, then $P(H_2|T_1) = 0.4$, since we would be using the unfair coin for the second toss. We say that $P(H_1)$ and $P(T_1)$ are *unconditional* (or *marginal*) *probabilities*, since they are not dependent on any other event.

Thus, we have $P(H_1) = P(T_1) = P(H_2|H_1) = P(T_2|H_1) = 0.5$, $P(H_2|T_1) = 0.4$, and $P(T_2|T_1) = 0.6$. However, what we really need to know is the probability of receiving each outcome. The outcome of a $20 win will occur if we obtain both H_1 and H_2. We may write $P(H_1H_2)$ as the *joint* probability that *both* H_1 and H_2 occur.

Using expression (4) for joint probabilities, we obtain the following results:

$$P(H_1 H_2) = P(H_2|H_1) \cdot P(H_1) = (0.5)(0.5) = 0.25$$
$$P(H_1 T_2) = P(T_2|H_1) \cdot P(H_1) = (0.5)(0.5) = 0.25$$
$$P(T_1 H_2) = P(H_2|T_1) \cdot P(T_1) = (0.4)(0.5) = 0.20$$
$$P(T_1 T_2) = P(T_2|T_1) \cdot P(T_1) = (0.6)(0.5) = \underline{0.30}$$
$$1.00$$

Now we can use these probabilities to compute the expected value of this third alternative A_3, which involves the second coin flip. We have the following data:

Events	$H_1 H_2$	$H_1 T_2$	$T_1 H_2$	$T_1 T_2$
Probabilities	0.25	0.25	0.2	0.3
Outcomes	$20	−$5	$5	−$10

which give the expected value

$$(0.25)(\$20.00) + (0.25)(-\$5.00) + (0.2)(\$5.00) + (0.3)(-\$10.00) = \$1.75.$$

Thus, on the basis of the expected value evaluative model, A_3 is preferred to gamble A_2, which had an expected value of $0.50, but not to A_1 with an expected value of $4.00.

Example The Pacific Oil Company (POCO) is concerned with determining the appropriate strategy for developing its oil shale leases in Colorado and Canada. Oil shales are actually mined, much like coal, but liquid petroleum products can be extracted from the oil shales through a heating process. Given the current state of the art, it is not economical to obtain oil in this manner even with the recent increases in the price of crude oil. However, as the world's reserves of crude are depleted, it is likely that this price will eventually rise even further. In addition, improvements in techniques for extracting the petroleum from oil shales would reduce the costs of obtaining this resource. Thus, it appears that oil shales may eventually be an economical source of petroleum.

POCO has identified three basic strategies for developing their oil shale leases over the near term (the next 10 to 15 years). The choice of a near-term strategy will have little effect on long-run profits after this 10- to 15-year time horizon. The *first strategy* would concentrate exclusively on research work related to oil shale processing. Such a strategy would place POCO in a position to exploit these resources eventually, but they would be unable to respond significantly to any opportunities for actually selling petroleum products from oil shales over the near term. These opportunities might occur because of higher crude prices or as a result of an oil embargo from the major oil-producing nations. An embargo would ensure higher crude prices coupled with a high demand for domestically produced oil.

The *second strategy* would be to combine a research program with some actual development of production capabilities. At the current world prices of crude, the output from this process would not quite break even, but the loss would not be great. However, the company would be in a position to actually profit from increases in crude oil prices or from the excess demand for domestic oil created by an embargo.

The *third strategy* would be a crash program aimed at developing the capability to produce petroleum products from oil shales in quantity as quickly as possible. Such a venture would lose money at the current crude oil prices and only break even at higher prices. However, POCO would be in a position to make considerable profits if another embargo occurred.

If crude oil prices were to fall in the near term due to significant new discoveries of additional reserves, all three of these strategies would result in losses. However, such an event is considered unlikely by POCO.

How can POCO go about making a decision in this case? First, the manager may recognize that he can gain some insights into this problem by viewing it as a decision involving a single criterion (money) under risk. There are three alternatives, and each has a different conditional outcome, depending on the future price of oil or the occurrence of an oil embargo. Thus, the manager may construct a table to display the relevant alternatives and the events that affect the outcomes from selecting each alternative. Such a display is shown in Table 2-4.

The construction of this table is an important exercise, since the manager now has identified the primary alternatives for consideration as well as the events that will determine the outcomes from these alternatives. It will generally be advantageous for the manager to discuss his assumptions with others at this point using this table as the basis for this discussion. In such a discussion, additional alternatives or other important events might be identified. For the sake of simplicity, we have used the events of lower prices, current prices, higher prices, and embargo. In an actual study, a manager might consider many more events. For example, he might consider all possible crude oil prices from $5 to $20 per barrel in increments of $1. This would lead to sixteen possible events regarding prices plus the additional event of an embargo. Even the latter could be stated in more detail by specifying embargos of various lengths of time.

TABLE 2-4 **Identification of Alternatives and Events**

Alternatives	Events			
	Lower Prices	Current Prices	Higher Prices	Embargo
Research only				
Combined research and development				
Crash				

The next task would be to predict the conditional outcome associated with each alternative and event. Such a task will be simplified if the manager has access to explicit predictive models such as those we shall describe in Part III of this book. Finally, he must provide an estimate of the probability of the occurrence of each event. For our example, we suppose that the manager has performed these tasks and now has the information available in Table 2–5.

TABLE 2–5. **Identification of Conditional Outcomes and Probabilities**

Alternatives	Events			
	Lower Prices ($p = 0.1$)	Current Prices ($p = 0.3$)	Higher Prices ($p = 0.4$)	Embargo ($p = 0.2$)
Research only	−50	0	50	55
Combined research and development	−150	−50	100	150
Crash	−500	−200	0	500

Note. Conditional outcomes given in millions of dollars.

Finally, the manager must identify some evaluative model in order to choose an alternative. In many practical situations, once the analysis has come this far, the solution will be obvious. However, in other cases the use of an explicit evaluative model may be helpful in making the final decision. The manager of POCO may apply the expected value evaluative model to these data and obtain the following results:

research only: $(0.1)(-50) + (0.3)(0) + (0.4)(50) + (0.2)(55) = 26$

research and development: $(0.1)(-150) + (0.3)(-50) + (0.4)(100) + (0.2)(150) = 40$

crash development:
$(0.1)(-500) + (0.3)(-200) + (0.4)(0) + (0.2)(500) = -10$

Thus, on the basis of the expected value model, the choice of a combined research and development strategy would be preferable.

However, it would be naive to think that a manager facing a decision with such important consequences would stop his analysis at this point. For example, the conditional outcomes and the probabilities of the events are only estimates and may contain some errors. Thus, the manager would want to test the sensitivity of his decision to small changes in these estimates. For example, if the probability of current prices had been 0.5, and of higher prices 0.2, then alternative 1 (research only) would have been preferred. (Check this yourself.)

In addition, the manager may question the value of being able to resolve the risk in his decision. Suppose he could invest some additional time and effort and determine which future event will occur with certainty. How much should he be willing to spend for this information? The answer to this question will be our next topic.

The Value of Information

To examine the value of information, let us return to our coin flipping example. Suppose someone tells you he is clairvoyant; that is, he can predict the future, including the result of flipping a coin. How much should you offer to pay him for his services? In other words, what is the value of resolving the risk in the gambling situation?

To compute this value, we need to identify the best alternative, given that each possible event has occurred (see Table 2-3). For example, if we know that the coin will land on heads, we would choose alternative A_1 and win $10. However, if we know it will land on tails, we would choose alternative A_2 to minimize our losses. Thus, we would have the following strategies and outcomes:

Event	Strategy	Outcome
Heads	A_1	+ $10
Tails	A_2	− 1

Now, suppose the clairvoyant tells us whether the coin will land on heads or tails just prior to its being flipped. Since the coin is fair, the probability that it will fall on heads is 0.5, and the probability that it will fall on tails is 0.5. Therefore, the probability that the clairvoyant will predict heads prior to a flip is also 0.5, as is the probability that he will predict tails. He *cannot* control the future by changing the probability of each event, but his prediction is always correct.

If he predicts heads, we will choose A_1 and win $10, and if he predicts tails we will choose A_2 (assuming we must play) so that we only lose $1. Thus, given the predictions of the clairvoyant just prior to each flip of the coin, we have a 0.5 chance of winning $10 and a 0.5 chance of losing $1.

We can compute the *expected value* of playing the game with perfect information. It is simply the probability of being told each event will occur multiplied by the outcome we would receive if we knew that event were going to occur. In this case, it would be

(0.5) ($10.00) + (0.5) (−$1.00) = $4.50.

However, the expected value of choosing alternative A_1 *without* perfect information was $4. Thus, the expected value of playing the game with the clairvoyant (with perfect information) is $4.50, while the expected value of playing the game without the clairvoyant, but choosing alternative A_1, is $4. So the value of having a clairvoyant (perfect information) in this case is only

$4.50 − $4.00 = 0.50. The value of perfect information is obtained by determining the expected value of the decision made with perfect information, and subtracting the expected value of the best alternative without this information. This amount is an important upper limit or bound on what we should be willing to pay for the information.

A POCO Example Given the data in Table 2-5, the choice of the appropriate oil shale strategy for POCO would be trivial *if* the occurrence of future events were known with certainty. For example, if prices drift lower, POCO would be well advised to delay work in oil shales entirely, but if prices stay constant a research-only strategy would just break even. For higher prices, a combined research and development program would provide the greatest returns, while the crash program would be most desirable, given the occurrence of an oil embargo in the near future. Clearly, it would be worth something to POCO to obtain a certain forecast of the future, but how much?

The computation of this value of information is straightforward. First, we note what the outcome would be for each event if we knew it were going to occur. For example, if we knew that current prices were going to continue over the near term, we would choose a research-only strategy with a break-even outcome. For simplicity, let us assume that even if prices in the near term were to fall, we would still continue the research strategy at a cost of $50 million in anticipation of long-run payoffs. Thus, we would have the following decisions summarized from Table 2-5:

Event	Probability	Strategy	Outcome
lower prices	0.1	research only	− 50
current prices	0.3	research only	0
higher prices	0.4	research and development	100
embargo	0.2	crash development	500

Our current expectations are that there is a 0.1 chance of lower prices, a 0.3 chance of current prices continuing, a 0.4 chance of higher prices, and a 0.2 chance of an embargo in the near term. If we resolve this uncertainty and obtain perfect information, we will determine which event will actually occur. However, the probability of finding that each event will occur is simply the same as our current expectation. For example, the probability that we will find that prices will be lower when we resolve the risk in this problem is simply 0.1. Similarly, the probability that perfect information will reveal that prices will move higher is 0.4. Thus, we calculate

$$(0.1)(-50) + (0.3)(0) + (0.4)(100) + (0.2)(500) = 135$$

as the expected return from a decision, *given* that we do obtain perfect information.

What is this information worth? To find the value of the perfect information, we subtract the expected value of the best decision under risk, which was $45 million for the research and development strategy. Thus the value of perfect information would be $135 - $45 = $90 million. Clearly, this is a substantial sum.

Again, the practicing manager would recognize that he will be unable to obtain perfect information regarding the future in most realistic situations. Nevertheless, this analysis does suggest that additional marketing research to obtain better estimates would be a worthwhile investment. In addition, this result provides an upper bound on such expenditures.

WHAT SHOULD THE MANAGER KNOW?

Up to this point, we have been involved in some of the technical details associated with basic probability concepts and with calculating expected values. In order to ensure that we have an overall grasp of the practical significance of this material, it will be worth our time to step back and ask the question, "What does the manager really need to know?"

With regard to decision making with a single criterion under certainty, the situation is really straightforward. As long as all persons agree that more (or less) of the criterion is always better, the simple decision rule of finding the alternative that maximizes (or minimizes) this criterion obviously holds. Thus, the real task is in predicting the outcomes associated with each alternative.

However, when risk is involved in the problem, the situation becomes more complicated. First of all, the manager must understand the basic concepts of probability theory. The majority of the significant decisions made by a manager do involve risk in some form. Probability theory provides a language for describing and analyzing these problems.

The introduction of risk means that there is no longer a single outcome associated with each alternative. Rather, the outcome consists of several conditional outcomes, each with an associated probability of occurrence. In order to rank alternatives, some means of transforming these conditional outcomes and probabilities into a single number may be helpful. One evaluative model that performs this task is the expected value model, which weights each conditional outcome by its associated probability of occurrence.

Interpretation of Results

The interpretation of the expected value has an intuitive appeal. Basically, this value represents what the manager would receive, *on the average,* if the decision were made many times. But we continually emphasize that the expected value does not represent the actual profit or loss that the company will obtain based on its decision. Rather, one of the conditional outcomes will actually occur (if all the predictions are accurate). This point is important and should not be overlooked by a manager. An alternative with a high expected value may have some small probability of leading to a disastrous result, and *such a result could actually occur.* If it does, it does not mean that the original decision was bad, but merely that an unfortunate conditional outcome occurred. All that the manager can hope for in situations involving risk is to keep the odds in his favor. However, if the manager is really averse to making a decision involving even a small probability of an undesirable outcome, he can compensate with another evaluative model, as we shall see in Chapter 4.

As a second point, the results from the calculation of expected values should always be subjected to an analysis of their sensitivity to the predictions of the conditional outcomes and the probabilities of the events. One approach is to deliberately bias the outcomes and probabilities against the best alternative from the initial analysis, then recompute the expected values. If this alternative remains the most desirable even when this deliberate bias is introduced, the manager's confidence that he has identified the best alternative should be improved. However, if the rankings of the alternatives are changed drastically by this second analysis, he may be well advised to spend more time and effort in obtaining better predictions. The value of perfect information can be used as a guide in these efforts.

Problem Characteristics

A key characteristic of problems that should be analyzed by using the expected value evaluative model is that the decisions are made repetitively. An example of such a problem would be the determination of the appropriate daily inventory level when probabilities can be assigned to various levels of demand. On any given day, the company might incur a relatively high cost from leaving too much or too little in inventory. But over a longer time horizon, the actual inventory costs will approximate their expected value. Routine capital budgeting decisions that do not require a high proportion of the company's resources are also a natural area for the use of expected values as a guide to decision making.

Limitations

One of the limitations of using expected values is that real-world problems are much more complex than the examples we have used to illustrate the basic concepts. The number of alternatives and of possible future events can be extremely large, making it especially difficult to summarize the information in tabular form as shown in Tables 2–3 through 2–5. When some events are dependent on others, the calculation of probabilities can also become a confusing task. However, many of the difficulties of implementing the expected value calculations can be overcome or simplified through the use of decision trees. This important decision aid is discussed next in Chapter 3.

Check Your Understanding

(Exercises 1 through 3 are based on concepts presented in the Introduction to Evaluative Models.)

1. When a decision is made on the basis of a single criterion under certainty, why is it often very easy to identify an acceptable evaluative model?
2. Give an example of a decision involving a single criterion under certainty for which it is *not* appropriate to simply maximize or minimize the criterion.
3. Suppose we have five alternatives under consideration that result in the following monetary returns with certainty:

Alternative	Outcome
A_1	$ 20
A_2	$100
A_3	$ 20
A_4	$ 50
A_5	$ 70

    a. Using the obvious evaluative model of maximizing returns $[U(O_i) = O_i]$, rank these alternatives.
    b. Rank these same alternatives using the following evaluative models:
       1) $U(O_i) = (2)(O_i) - 300$
       2) $U(O_i) = 3(O_i^2)$
       3) $U(O_i) = O_i - (0.1)(O_i^2)$
       4) $U(O_i) = \$1000/O_i$
    c. Which of these evaluative models give the same rankings of the alternatives as $U(O_i) = O_i$?
    d. Would your answer to (c) change if a sixth alternative A_6 with a certain outcome of $-\$20$ (a loss) were introduced?
4. For each of the following probabilities, state whether it is objective or subjective. If it is objective, identify the data or basis for its determination. If it is subjective, identify the "expert" who should assess it.
    a. The probability of rain tomorrow.
    b. The probability of drawing an ace from a well shuffled deck of playing cards.
    c. The probability that the demand for a company's product will increase by at least 5 percent next year.
    d. The probability that the demand for a company's product will increase by at least 5 percent next year given that it has increased by at least 5 percent in each of the past 10 years.
    e. The probability that a light bulb will "burn out" after 100 hours of use.

5. Which of the following sets of events are mutually exclusive? Which are independent? Dependent? Collectively exhaustive?
    a. 1) an oil embargo before 1985; 2) an oil embargo before 1990; 3) an oil embargo before 2000.
    b. 1) an oil embargo before 1985; 2) an oil embargo between 1985 and 1990; 3) an oil embargo after 1990.
    c. 1) price rise of less than $0.05; 2) price rise of between $0.05 and $0.10; 3) price rise of between $0.10 and $0.20.
    d. 1) price rise of less than $0.05; 2) rain tomorrow; 3) obtaining heads on the flip of a fair coin.
    e. 1) price rise for product A of less than $0.05; 2) price rise for product A of $0.05 or more; 3) an increase in the demand for product A of 10 percent or more.
6. Suppose we have two boxes, and box 1 contains six balls (two red, three white, and one blue), and box 2 contains three balls (one red, one white and one blue). We first select one of the two boxes at random, so that each has a probability of 0.5 of being chosen. Then we choose one ball from the box we have selected, again so that each ball in the box has an equal probability of being selected.
    a. Draw a tree diagram similar to Figure 2–1 and show the conditional and joint probabilities of drawing each color ball after choosing each box.
    b. Construct a table similar to Table 2–1 showing the marginal probabilities of obtaining a red, white, or blue ball.
7. Recall the process that produces 95 percent good products when set up properly, but only 20 percent acceptable products when improperly set up. In the past, some 90 percent of the setups have been correct.
    a. Suppose we set up the process and the first output is *bad*. What is the probability that the process has been properly set up?
    b. Suppose we set up the process and the first *two* units of output are good. What is the probability that the process has been properly set up?
        1) Compute this probability by revising the probability of 0.977 that the process is set up properly that was obtained after the first unit was found to be good.
        2) Compute this probability directly by defining A_1 and A_2 as before, and the event B as *two good products*.
8. Explain why the expected value evaluative model may be appropriate for repetitive decisions, but perhaps not appropriate for very significant decisions that are made rarely. Give an example of each type of decision.
9. Explain the difference between a good decision and a good outcome. Should managers be evaluated on the basis of their decisions or on the basis of the outcomes that result from their decisions? Discuss.
10. What is meant by the term *perfect information*?
11. What are the limitations of a tabular presentation of alternatives and events?
12. Which of the three oil shale development strategies would be preferred for POCO if the probabilities in Table 2–5 were revised as follows:

	Lower Prices	Current Prices	Higher Prices	Embargo
a.	0.1	0.4	0.3	0.2
b.	0.0	0.3	0.4	0.3
c.	0.0	0.2	0.5	0.3

Use the expected value evaluative model and the data in Table 2-5 to determine your answers. What are the implications of this analysis? How does it relate to the value of perfect information for POCO?

Problems

13. A hospital ward has kept a record of the number of new patients admitted each day over a long period of time. The results are summarized below:

Number of Patients Admitted	Number of Days
0	15
1	27
2	53
3	45
4	18
5 or more	5

  a. What is your best estimate of the probability that exactly two patients will be admitted on a given day? What concept of probability did you use in making this judgment?
  b. What is your best estimate of the probability that three or more patients will be admitted? What property of the events justifies your method for calculating this number?
  c. Can you foresee any problem in predicting admissions based on these data? For example, would you expect any differences in the number of admissions on Monday or on Sunday?

14. Suppose that 30 percent of the units produced by a machine are defective. What is the probability of:
  a. producing two good units in a row?
  b. producing a good and then a bad unit in that order?
  c. producing at least one bad unit in a lot of three?

15. How did you define the "events" and what assumption did you make about them in answering exercise 14?

16. Raw materials have arrived from supplier 1 and supplier 2. From past records, we know that 20 percent of the units provided by supplier 1 are defective, and 40 percent of those provided by supplier 2 are defective.

a. Suppose we pick two units from the shipment of supplier 1. What is the probability of:
   1) two defective units being selected?
   2) at least one good unit being selected?
b. Suppose we pick one unit from the shipment of supplier 1 and test it. If it is good, we take a second unit from supplier 1's shipment, but if it is defective we take the second unit from supplier 2. What is the probability of:
   1) two defective units being selected?
   2) at least one good unit being selected?
   3) one good unit being selected from the shipment by supplier 2?
c. Suppose we pick one of the two shipments at random, so that we have a 0.5 chance of selecting the shipment from either supplier. Next, we choose a unit from this shipment and test it.
   1) Draw a tree diagram of the process similar to Figure 2–1.
   2) Assemble the probability information in a table similar to Table 2–1.
   3) What is the probability that a defective unit was chosen?
   4) If a defective unit was chosen, what is the probability that the unit was from supplier 2?

17. A company is considering the introduction of a new product. It is estimated that there is a 0.9 probability that the product will be successful if there is no competition within two years. However, there is only a 0.3 probability that it will be successful if competition does appear in the first two years. An independent estimate of the probability of competition within two years is 0.3. What is the probability that the product will be successful?

18. An analysis of the credit card data of the Pacific Oil Company is focused on persons who avoided being classified as bad risks during the first year they held the card. Of these persons, 95 percent continue to be good customers, but 5 percent are classified as bad risks at some later point because of unpaid balances. The analysis reveals that 80 percent of the persons who continue to be good customers did not let their credit balance accumulate beyond $100 during the first year, but 70 percent of those who became bad risks did let their balances exceed $100 the first year. Suppose a new credit card customer lets his balance exceed $100 during the first year. What is the probability that he will become a bad risk?

19. The Pacific Oil Company has an interest in some offshore lands. They estimate the probability of finding oil on this land to be 0.3. Additional seismographic tests could be used to revise this probability. If there is oil on the land, there is a 0.95 probability that the test will be positive, but a .05 probability that it will be negative. If there is no oil, there is still a 0.1 probability of a positive test. If a positive test is obtained, what is the probability that the well will be a "dry hole" (no oil)?

20. P. R. Noid, the noted consumer advocate, has led the fight to require automobile manufacturers to install heavy-duty bumpers on new cars. The new bumpers cost an additional $200 per car, and these costs are passed along to the purchaser of the automobile. The bumpers were "justified" because *if* the

automobile is in a minor collision, the savings on repairs that result from the bumpers is $500. However, if the collision is a major one, the repair charges are *increased* by $100 because these heavy-duty bumpers cost more to fix than the older ones. Suppose you expect to purchase a car and keep it for five years. You estimate that there is a 0.7 probability that you will not have an accident over that period. If you do have an accident, you estimate that there is a 0.5 chance that it will be a minor collision, and a 0.4 chance that it will be a major one. There is also a probability of 0.1 that you will have two minor accidents. The probabilities of more than two minor accidents or more than one major accident are so small that they can be set equal to 0.0.

   a. Compute the expected savings from the bumper and compare it to the cost to the purchaser of $200.

   b. Recall that an automobile insurance company does not pay the $200 extra for the bumper, and will pay for repairs only if an accident occurs. What is the expected savings of your insurance company as a result of the bumper?

   c. Is the expected value evaluative model appropriate for the purchaser of an automobile? For the insurance company? Discuss.

21. POCO owns a lease that will allow it to explore for oil on the Aleutian Islands just west of Alaska. They have been offered $80 million for this lease by the Essex Oil Company. The three possible results of the exploration are shown below, along with their associated probabilities and monetary returns. The latter are based on the most recent estimates by the POCO engineers.

Result	Probability	Monetary Outcome (millions of $)
Dry well	0.4	−$100
Discovery of oil reserves of moderate size	0.4	$200
Discovery of oil reserves of major proportions	0.2	$300

   a. Compute the expected value of the decision to explore the islands. Should POCO sell the lease to Essex?

   b. Do you think that the expected value evaluative model is appropriate for a decision such as this one? Would you use the results of this analysis if you were a manager of POCO? Discuss.

22. Consider the question of whether to take an umbrella to work. The best results would be not to take an umbrella on a pretty day. Suppose you consider this to be the nominal case and assign it a value of $0. You might carry an umbrella on a pretty day, which would be an unnecessary bother. Suppose you decide that you would pay $2 to avoid this encumbrance. If it rains and you have an umbrella, you will stay dry. However, you would pay $4 to avoid the hassle of

using the umbrella on a rainy day. If it rains, and you do not have an umbrella, you get soaking wet. You would pay $10 to avoid this inconvenience.
   a. Set up a table like Table 2–3 which shows the alternative decisions, the possible events, and the outcomes. Give both a verbal description of the outcomes and the associated payments you would be willing to make to avoid them.
   b. Using the expected value evaluative model with the payments, determine the best decision when the forecasts of the probability of rain are the following:
      1) 0.0
      2) 0.25
      3) 0.5
      4) 0.75
      5) 1.0
   c. What is the value of perfect information regarding rain, given each of the above forecasts?

23. A small grocery store must decide how many loaves of bread to stock each day. The store must pay $0.50 per loaf, and each loaf sells for $1 when it is fresh (deliveries are made each morning). However, if it is not sold on the day it is delivered, it must be sold for $0.25 per loaf as day-old bread. The demand for the bread varies between six and eight loaves per day. The probabilities for the different levels of demand are as follows:

Level of Demand	Probability
6	0.25
7	0.60
8	0.15

   a. Compute the profit if six loaves are stocked and all six are sold when fresh.
   b. Compute the profit if eight loaves are stocked and only six are sold on the day they are delivered.
   c. Construct a table similar to Table 2–3 for which the alternatives are "stock 6," "stock 7," and "stock 8," and the events are demands of 6, 7, and 8 loaves respectively. Compute the conditional outcomes [see (a) and (b) above] and place them in the table.
   d. What is the best decision according to the expected value evaluative model? Discuss whether or not this evaluative model is appropriate for this decision.
   e. What is the value of perfect information regarding the demand for bread?

References

1. Bierman, H., C. P. Bonini, and W. H. Hausman, *Quantitative Analysis for Business Decisions,* fifth edition, Richard D. Irwin, Inc., Homewood, Ill., 1977.

2. Hodges, J. L., and E. L. Lehmann, *Basic Concepts of Probability and Statistics,* Holden-Day, San Francisco, 1964.
3. Jones, J. M., *Statistical Decision Making,* Richard D. Irwin, Inc., Homewood, Ill., 1977.
4. Levin, R. I., and C. A. Kirkpatrick, *Quantitative Approaches to Management,* third edition, McGraw-Hill, New York, 1975.
5. Mason, R. D., *Programmed Learning Aid for Business and Economic Statistics,* Learning Systems Company, Homewood, Ill., 1970.
6. Schlaifer, R., *Probability and Statistics for Business Decisions,* McGraw-Hill, New York, 1959.
7. Spetzler, C. S., and C. S. Stael von Holstein, "Probability Encoding in Decision Analysis," *Management Science,* Vol. 22, No. 3, November 1975.

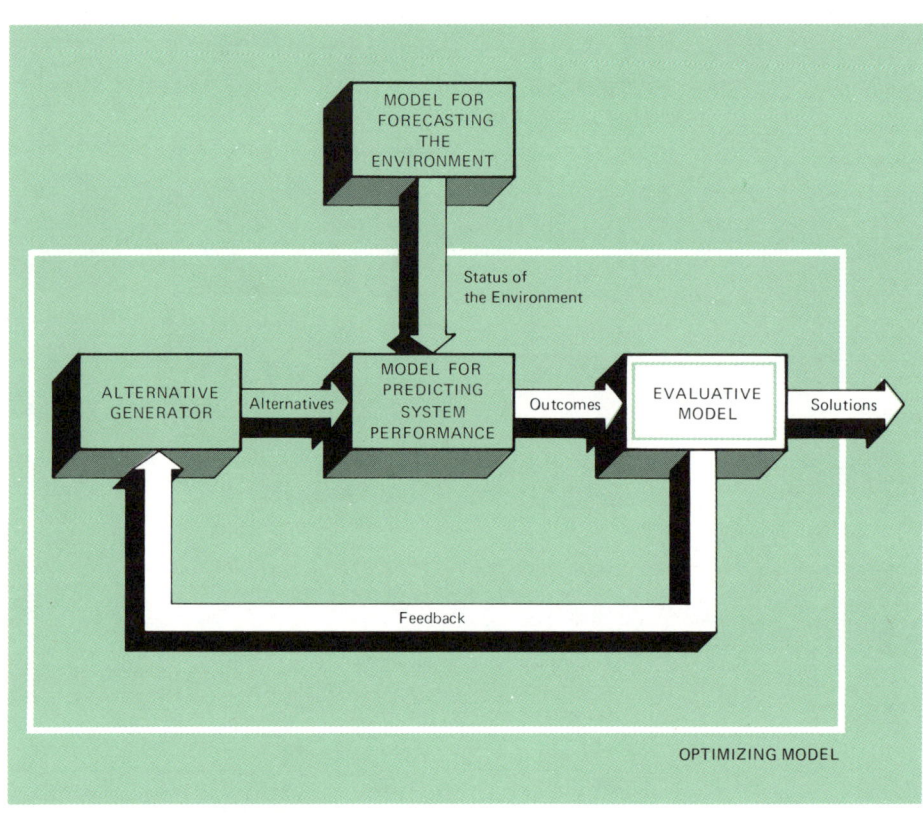

3

DECISION TREES

We can use the concept of expected value as an evaluative model for decisions involving a single criterion and risk. This approach can be applied even in rather complex situations, but we must be very careful to keep track of the relationships among events and to perform our probability calculations correctly. What we really need is a tool to aid us in structuring or visualizing these complex relationships more easily and a means of simplifying the probability calculations. The decision tree is just such a tool. It is one of the most practical and useful quantitative managerial aids. Decision trees are now routinely used in the analysis of major capital budgeting decisions, major marketing strategies, and competitive bidding policies.

The idea of the decision tree is delightfully simple. Instead of compressing all of the information regarding a complex decision into a table such as those we have used previously, one draws a schematic representation of the problem that displays the information in a more easily understood fashion. In addition, the complex probability computations can be simplified through the use of this tree. This idea is an extension of the simple probability tree shown in Chapter 2 Figure 2–1.

A Simple Example

To begin this discussion, let us refer again to the problem of selecting from the three games that were introduced in Chapter 2. In each of the games, you flip a fair coin. In the first game (A_1) you win $10 if the coin lands on heads, but lose $2 if it lands on tails. In the second game (A_2), you win $2 if heads occurs, but lose $1 if the coin falls on tails. In the third game (A_3), you flip the fair coin again if it lands on heads. On the second flip, you win $20 if it lands on heads, but if it lands on tails, you lose $5. If the fair coin lands on tails on the first flip, you flip an unfair coin with a 0.4 probability of landing on heads and a 0.6 probability of landing on tails. If this unfair coin lands on heads, you win $5; if it lands on tails, you lose $10.

Growing the Tree How can we schematically represent the problem of choosing from among the three alternatives? Very simply by showing each alternative as one of three possible branches on a tree, as illustrated in Figure 3-1.

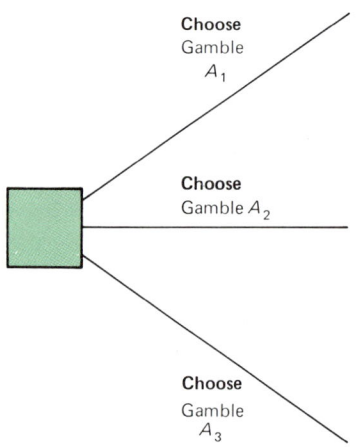

FIGURE 3-1. **The beginnings of a decision tree**

The next step is to show the events that could occur in a similar fashion, as branch points on the tree with each branch representing the occurrence of a particular event. In the case of alternative A_3, the second toss of each coin can be represented with additional branches in the tree. Finally, the outcomes can be written on the branches where they are realized. A careful study of Figure 3-2 should clarify these concepts.

In the decision tree in Figure 3-2, we have indicated a decision point by a box, and a chance point where events are realized by a circle. There is no hard and fast rule requiring that the tree be drawn in this way. However, in more complex trees it may be helpful to distinguish decision points from chance points in some manner such as this. Further, we have shown the decisions, then the events, and finally the outcomes, in that order. In some practical situations, we will make an initial decision, and then have the opportunity to wait until some events have actually occurred before making another decision. This situation can also be represented in the decision tree format as we shall see in a later example.

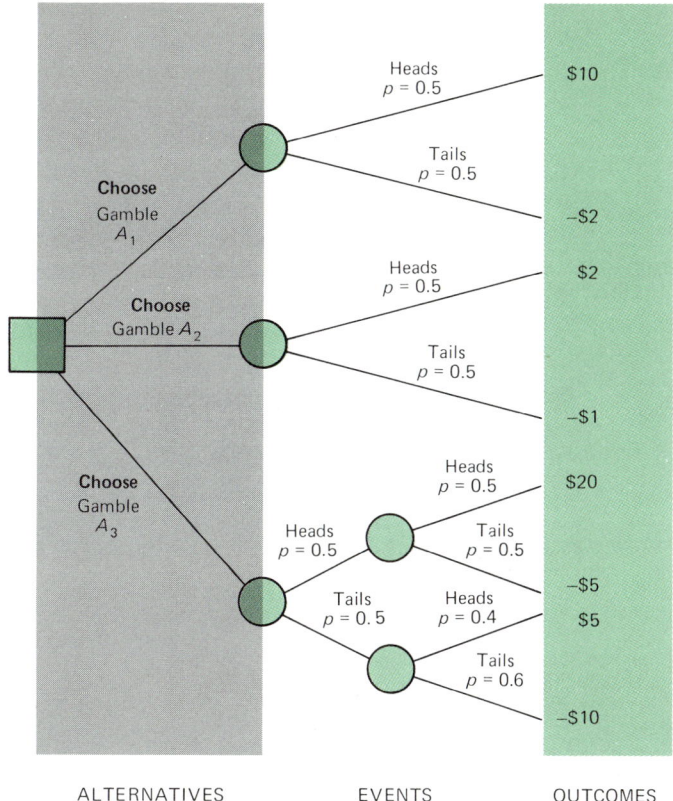

FIGURE 3-2. **A decision tree for the gamble selection problem**

One important advantage of the decision tree is that a manager can quickly visualize the alternatives, the possible future events, and their outcomes. The logic and the assumptions that are the basis for a decision are laid out for easy scrutiny. Such trees can be useful in promoting a healthy discussion regarding the alternatives, the possible events, their probabilities, and the outcomes. In practical situations, a decision tree may be modified many times before general agreement can be reached that it accurately portrays the real problem. However, each revision of the tree will represent some additional learning about the nature of the problem.

Rolling Back These advantages mean that merely drawing a decision tree can have a significant benefit for the manager. In addition, the calculation of the expected values associated with the alternative decisions can be simplified by studying each branch point, beginning at the tips of the branches. For example, let us begin by considering the one branch point for alternative A_1. We compute the expected value of this branch point by multiplying the probability on each

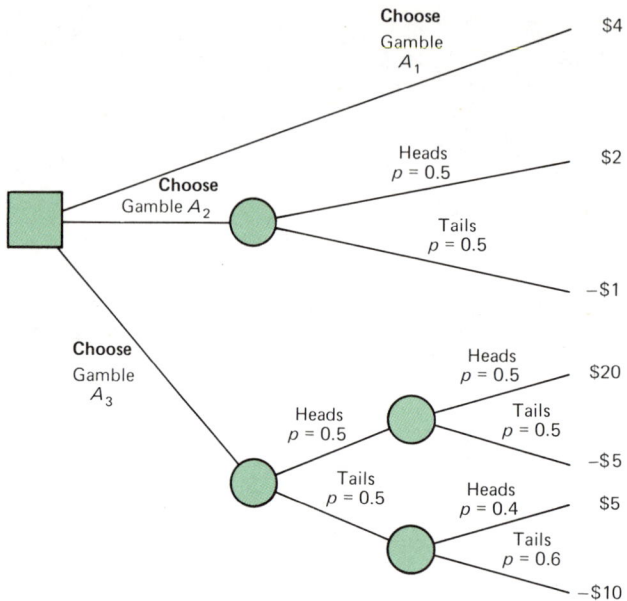

FIGURE 3-3. **Simplifying the branch for alternative A_1**

branch by the outcome associated with the branch, and summing these results. For the branch point of A_1 we obtain $(0.5)\,(\$10) = \$5$ on the first branch, and $(0.5)\,(-\$2) = -\$1$ on the second branch. Summing these, we get $\$4$, and we replace the branch point on the tree by its expected value, as shown in Figure 3-3.

Since there was only one branch point for alternative A_1, the result is that the expected value of the branch point is also equal to the expected value of alternative A_1. A similar analysis would determine an expected value of $\$0.50$ for alternative A_2.

Now consider alternative A_3, which includes a series of branches. Again, let us begin at the far right and compute the expected value of each chance branch. The first branch of alternative A_3 corresponds to the toss of the fair coin on the second trial and has an expected value of $(0.5)\,(\$20) + (0.5)\,(-\$5) = \$7.50$. The other branch corresponds to the toss of the unfair coin and has an expected value of $(0.4)\,(\$5) + (0.6)\,(-\$10) = -\$4$. Now, and this is important, we replace each of these two branches by their respective expected values. We now have the tree shown in Figure 3-4.

We now have only one chance branch point in the tree for alternative A_3, corresponding to the toss of the first coin. The two chance branch points corresponding to the toss of the second coin have been replaced by their respective expected values. Finally, we compute the expected value of this

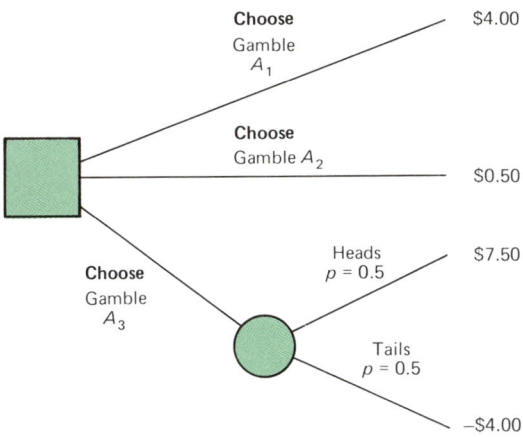

FIGURE 3-4. **Further simplifications**

remaining chance branch point in exactly the same manner as before, and obtain (0.5) ($7.50) + (0.5) (−$4.00) = $1.75, the expected value of alternative A_3. Notice that this number was computed *without* using the concepts of joint or conditional probabilities. It is important to realize, however, that the probabilities on the second branch of the tree actually are *conditional* probabilities (conditional on the first [leftmost] chance outcome). Thus, the use of the decision tree also simplifies the probability calculations that are required to obtain expected values.

This process of starting at the right and successively replacing each branch by its associated expected value is referred to as "rolling back" the tree. Even when the tree gets very large and many different calculations are involved, they always remain simple in the sense that only expected values are calculated for each branch point. As a final result, the tree of Figure 3-2 has been reduced to Figure 3-5, and the desirability of alternative A_1, based on the expected value evaluative model, is apparent.

The Value of Perfect Information   The value of perfect information can be computed directly from the decision tree. Further, this concept can be illustrated on the decision tree. Suppose our clairvoyant friend says that he can predict the outcome of the flip of the fair coin. We would still have to leave the result of flipping the second coin in alternative A_3 to chance.

Let us construct a decision tree to represent the problem, given the assistance of our friend. He can predict the outcome of flipping the fair coin before it occurs. Therefore, we will *know* whether heads or tails will occur before we must choose A_1, A_2, or A_3. However, since the first coin flip is fair, there is still a 0.5 chance that he will tell us it will be heads and a 0.5 chance he will tell us tails. The first branch in our revised decision tree must, therefore, be a chance

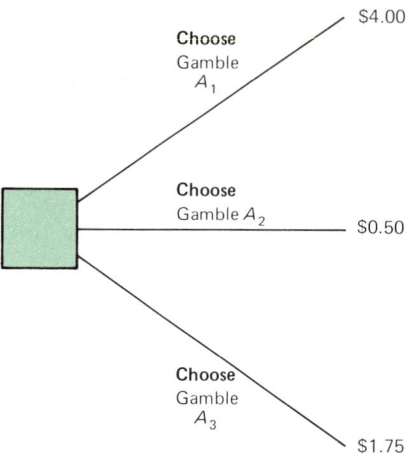

FIGURE 3-5. **The results of the analysis; expected values for three alternatives**

branch which represents the 0.5 probability that our friend predicts heads and the 0.5 probability he predicts tails.

The concept of perfect information does not mean that the chance branch point regarding the flip of the fair coin can be removed from the tree. Rather, it means that the result of the event will be known *prior* to our decision, so the chance branch point appears *before* the decision branch points, as shown in Figure 3-6, rather than after the decision branch points, as shown in Figure 3-2. In order to understand this important concept, carefully compare Figure 3-2 and 3-6.

If our clairvoyant friend predicts heads, we have the option of choosing alternative A_1 with outcome "win $10," A_2 with outcome "win $2," or A_3 with an expected value of $(0.5)(\$20) + (0.5)(-\$5) = \$7.50$. Using our expected value model, we would choose A_1. Similarly, if our clairvoyant says tails on the first flip, we would choose A_2 with a loss of $1. Thus, we would have a 0.5 chance of winning $10 and a 0.5 chance of losing $1 prior to the flip of the coin when the clairvoyant is on our side. The expected value of our decision using this perfect information regarding the first flip of the coin is $(0.5)(\$10) + (0.5)(-\$1) = \$4.50$. Comparing this value with the expected value of $4 without this information, we find that again our friend's advice is worth only $0.50.

What would be the value of his advice if he could successfully predict the results of *both* coin flips (if we choose A_3) before we select an alternative? We shall leave this question for an exercise.

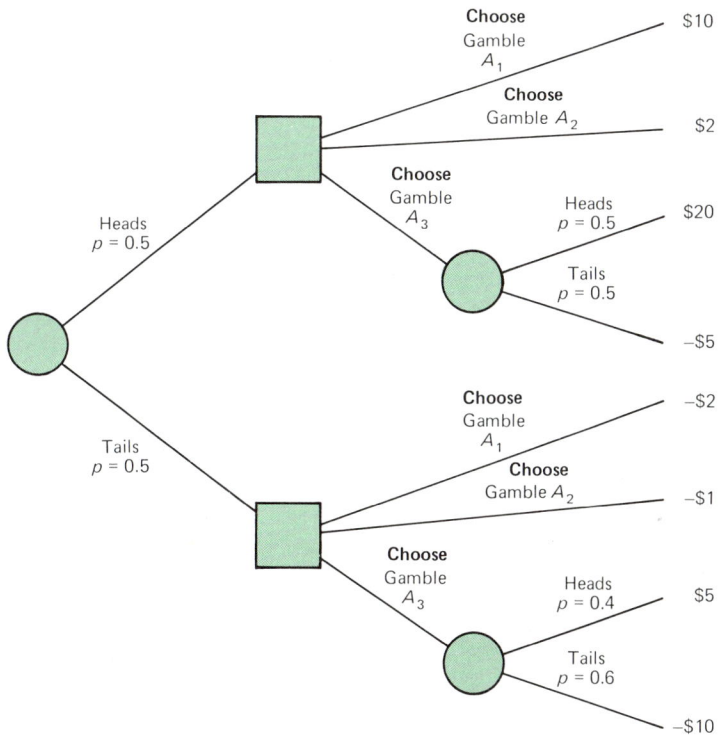

FIGURE 3-6. **A decision tree for calculating the value of perfect information regarding the flip of the first coin**

A POCO Example

Suppose we complicate the problem of the Pacific Oil Company (POCO) described in Chapter 2 by recognizing the possibility of a breakthrough in oil shale processing technology resulting from the research efforts carried out either under the research-only strategy or under the combined research and development strategy. This breakthrough would significantly reduce the costs of extracting petroleum products from oil shales. POCO estimates the probability of such a breakthrough from following the research-only strategy at 0.4 and from following the combined research and development strategy at 0.3. Under the alternative of a crash development of production capabilities, the current state-of-the-art technology would be used.

If such a breakthrough occurred, POCO would have the option of changing strategies. If they had initially selected a research-only posture and a breakthrough occurred, they would begin either a combined research and development effort immediately or shift into the crash development program. If they were already in a combined research and development operating mode and the breakthrough occurred, they could continue in this mode or begin crash development. The conditional outcomes would depend on both the strategy selected after the breakthrough and the strategy the company selected initially. For example, the costs of shifting from a combined research and development strategy to a crash development program would be less than shifting from a research-only strategy to a crash development program. In addition, the news of the breakthrough in oil shale technology would reduce the probability of higher oil prices or an embargo, because the oil shales would provide additional supplies of petroleum products. The conditional outcomes for the different strategies and the probabilities of each event, *given* the occurrence of a breakthrough, are shown in Table 3–1.

It would be difficult to organize all of this information regarding POCO's options in tabular form. However, the decision tree can be used to advantage here.

TABLE 3–1. **Conditional Outcomes and Probabilities, Given the Occurrence of a Breakthrough**

Alternatives	Events			
	Lower Prices ($p = 0.1$)	Current Prices ($p = 0.5$)	Higher Prices ($p = 0.3$)	Embargo ($p = 0.1$)
Change to research and development from research only	−100	0	100	120
Change to crash from research only	−150	−50	200	300
Continue research and development	−50	50	150	200
Change to crash from research and development	−125	100	300	500

Note: Conditional outcomes given in millions of dollars.

Growing the Tree The first branch in a decision tree used to analyze this problem would be the choice of an initial strategy—research only, a combined research and development activity, or a crash development program. At the end of the research-only and the combined research and development branches there would be a chance branch point representing the possibility of a breakthrough in technology. If a breakthrough occurs, another decision point

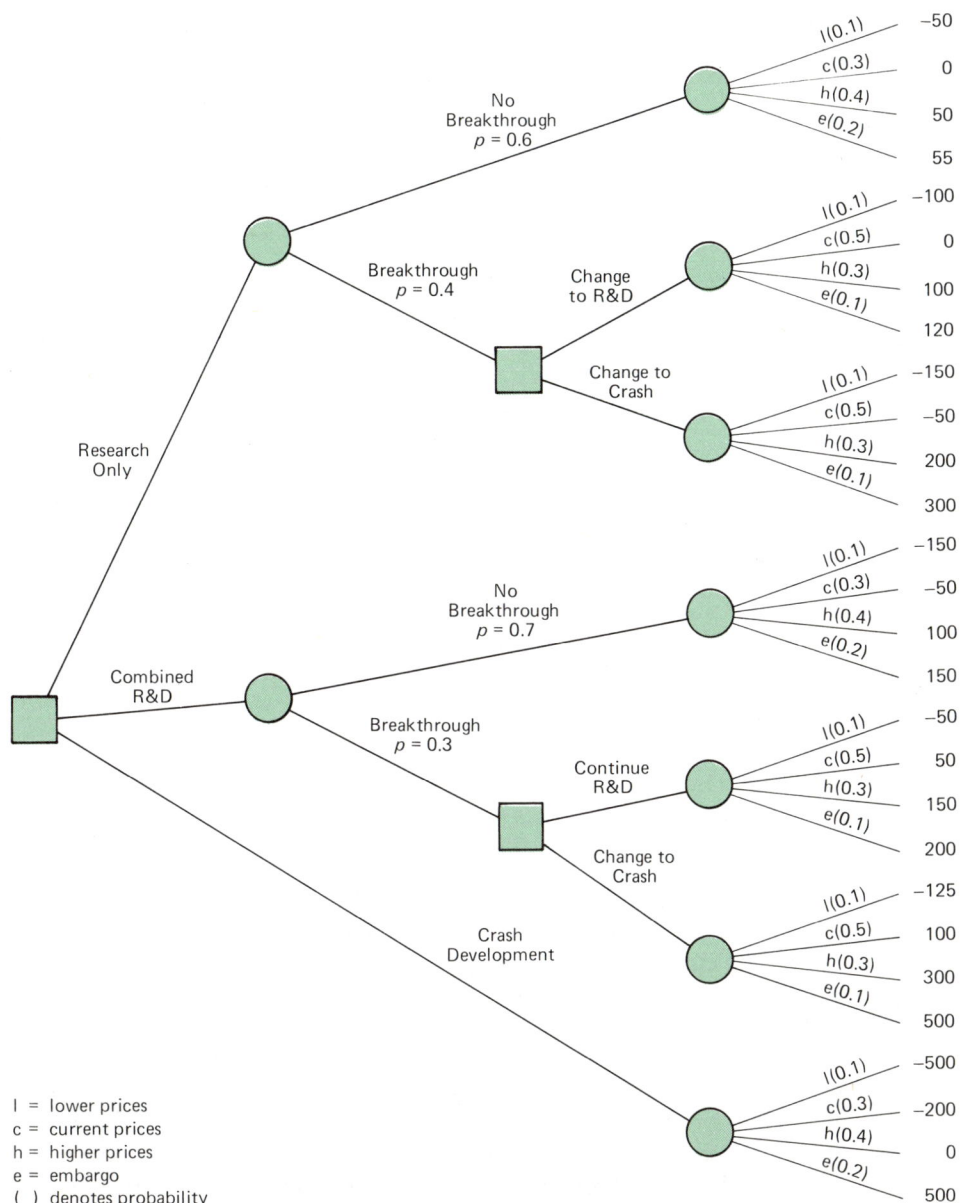

FIGURE 3-7. **Initial decision tree for POCO**

would follow allowing POCO to modify its initial strategy. The decision tree for this problem is shown in Figure 3-7. Notice that there are 28 different paths through the tree, and each leads to a distinct outcome. Also notice that there are several decision branch points in the tree, as well as the chance branch points.

CHAPTER 3 DECISION TREES

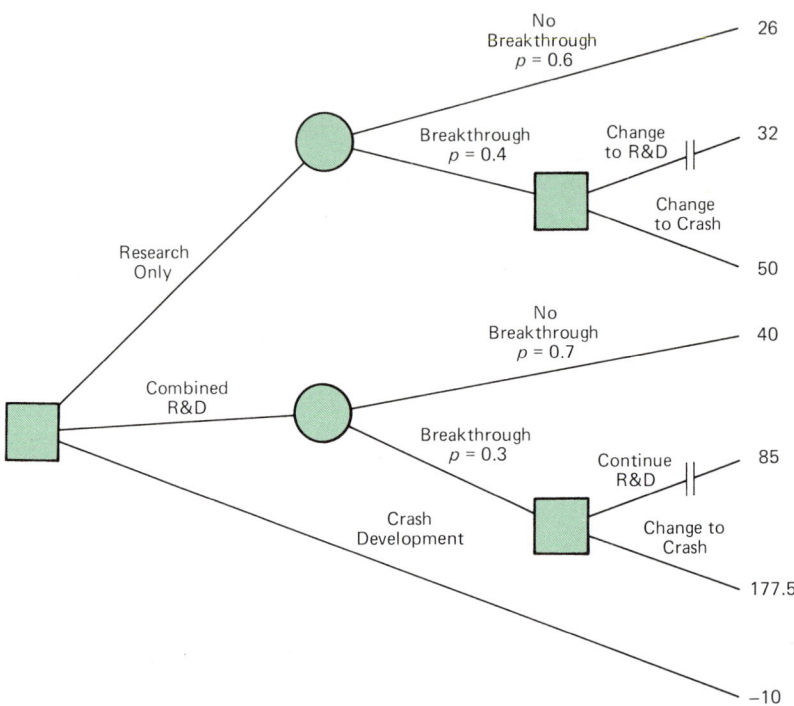

FIGURE 3-8. **Rolling back the tree**

Rolling Back Now let us analyze this situation by rolling back the tree. First we replace the chance branch points at the far end of the tree by their respective expected values and obtain the tree shown in Figure 3-8. Notice that the results at the end of the no-breakthrough branches are the same expected values that we computed in Chapter 2 for each strategy. At the end of the breakthrough branches, we have the decision branches with an expected value for each strategy. On the basis of the expected value model, the best strategy in each case would be to begin a crash development program if a breakthrough occurs.

Branches broken by vertical parallel lines (see Figure 3-8) would be ignored if this decision point were reached. Thus, we can represent the decision point by the expected value of the best decision at that point, and continue to roll back the tree. That is, we would replace the decision point following the breakthrough from the research-only strategy by 50, the expected value of the crash development strategy at that point. Similarly, the decision point following a breakthrough resulting from an initial combined research and development effort would be replaced by the expected value of the crash development effort, 177.5.

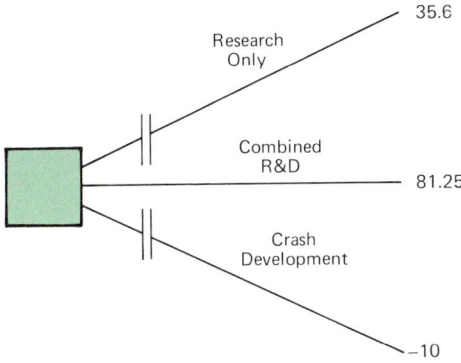

FIGURE 3-9. **The results of the analysis for POCO**

Thus, the expected value of the initial research strategy and of the initial combined research and development strategy would be computed as

research only: (0.6) (26) + (0.4) (50) = 35.6
combined research
and development: (0.7) (40) + (0.3) (177.5) = 81.25.

Even allowing for the possibility of a breakthrough, the combined research and development strategy still remains the best alternative according to the expected value evaluative model. The tree reflecting these final calculations is shown in Figure 3-9.

At this point, there are several important observations to be made:

1. POCO does not expect to make $81.25 million from following an initial research and development strategy. They will actually receive one of eight different outcomes, which range from losing $150 million to making $500 million. *The expected value evaluative model provides a means of ranking alternatives under risky choice situations, but it does not give the actual result that will occur.*
2. Even though the problem was becoming complex because of the different strategies and events, the decision tree provided a useful means of organizing the relationships and the data.
3. The probability calculations at each step were straightforward and consisted of simple expected values.

As can be seen, even when the problem becomes rather "messy" in terms of several alternate strategies, some of which may depend on future events, and when many different future events are possible, the decision tree can provide a practical, useful means of analyzing a problem.

The Value of Perfect Information What if POCO could spend additional research funds immediately and determine whether or not a breakthrough in the

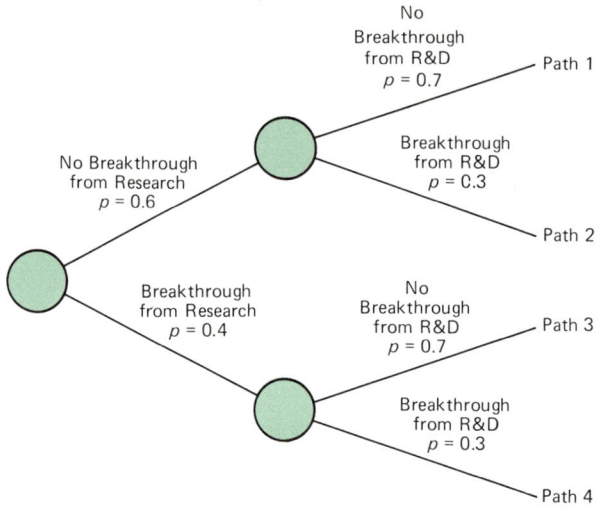

FIGURE 3-10. **Partial tree**

processing technology could be made? How much would this information be worth? In order to answer this question, we must revise the decision tree using an approach like the one employed in determining the value of perfect information from our clairvoyant friend regarding the toss of the coin. If we could resolve the uncertainty of the breakthrough, we would decide on an initial strategy after having this knowledge. When we obtain perfect information, the probability of discovering that a breakthrough will occur from an initial research-only strategy is 0.4, while there is a 0.6 chance we will be told that no breakthrough will occur from this strategy. Therefore, the first branch point in our revised tree (Figure 3-10) represents the resolution of the uncertainty regarding whether or not a breakthrough will occur, given that we follow a research-only strategy.

Next, we need chance branches to represent the resolution of the uncertainty regarding the probability of a breakthrough, given that we follow initially a combined research and development strategy. There is a 0.3 probability that such a breakthrough will occur and a 0.7 probability that it will not. The chance node representing this event should be placed at the tips of both branches from the chance node representing the research-only strategy, as ilusrated in Figure 3-10.

There are four paths through the partial decision tree in Figure 3-10. Path 1 corresponds to discovering from our source of perfect information that no breakthrough would occur from a research-only strategy, *and* no breakthrough would occur from a combined research and development effort. Path 2 corresponds to discovering that no breakthrough would occur from a research-only strategy, but that a breakthrough *would occur* if we choose a combined research and development strategy initially. Similar interpretations hold for paths 3 and 4, with path 4 indicating that a breakthrough would occur given either of these initial strategies.

Notice that the partial tree in Figure 3-10 could have begun with a single chance point representing the resolution of the uncertainty regarding the combined research and development strategy. Then two chance points corresponding to the research-only strategy would have been placed at the tips of these branches. Verify that the same four paths can be identified in such a partial tree.

At the end points of the four resulting paths through the partial tree, the uncertainty regarding the possibility of a breakthrough has been resolved, and the decisions that can be made in each case are shown in Figure 3-11. Notice that the final chance branch points, labeled A through G, occur two or more times in the tree. For example, the chance branch point A appears following the research-only decision after the two decision points at the top of the tree. By labeling these redundant chance branch points as shown, we simplify the presentation of the tree.

On the uppermost path in Figure 3-11, corresponding to no breakthrough from a research-only strategy and no breakthrough from a combined research and development strategy, the decisions are simply to choose the research-only strategy, the combined research and development strategy, or a crash program initially, without hope of a breakthrough. The outcomes are still conditional on the price of oil or the possibility of an embargo, as before. The expected value of each decision would be the same as the expected value that we computed using the tabular display of information in the previous discussion of the POCO problem (see Table 2-5).

However, the lower path in the tree corresponds to knowing that a breakthrough will occur if we initially choose the research-only strategy *and* also if we choose the combined research and development strategy. Therefore, our alternatives are as follows:

1. to begin the research-only strategy, then change to either a combined research and development strategy or to a crash development strategy when a breakthrough occurs
2. to begin with and continue the combined research and development strategy when a breakthrough occurs
3. to begin with a research and development effort and switch to a crash development program when the breakthrough occurs
4. to start the crash development program using the state-of-the-art technology immediately

The expected value of resolving these uncertainties is computed by rolling back this tree as before, and the result is $84.05 million. This result compares with the expected value of $81.25 million for choosing the combined research and development strategy without resolving the uncertainty regarding the breakthrough. Therefore, POCO should be willing to spend *up to* $84.05 − $81.25 = $2.8 million immediately to determine if a breakthrough

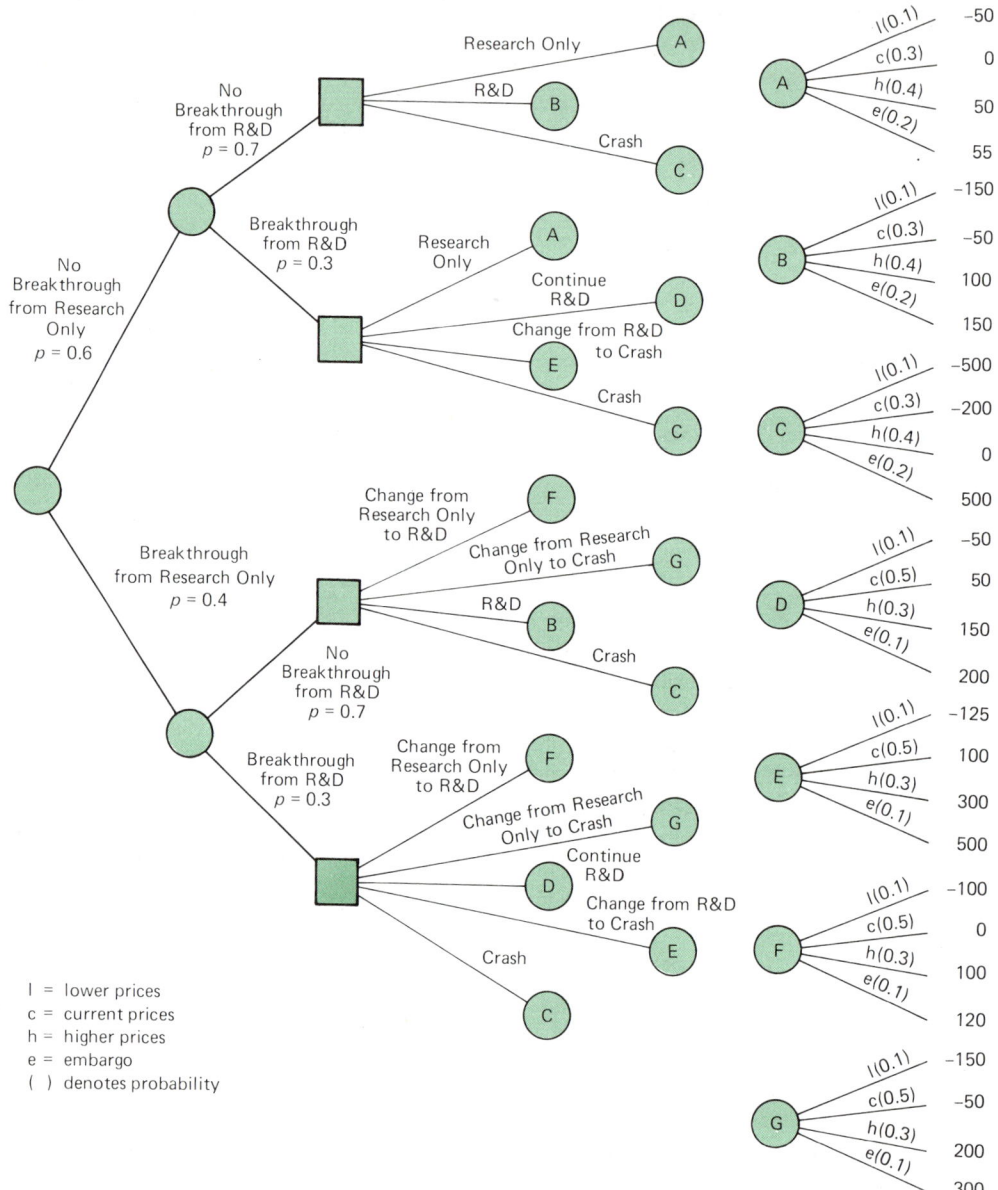

FIGURE 3-11. **The decision tree for computing the value of perfect information regarding a breakthrough for POCO**

will actually occur given an initial research-only or a combined research and development strategy.

WHAT SHOULD THE MANAGER KNOW?

As problems under risk become more complicated, it becomes difficult to organize the information and to maintain an understanding of the logical relationships among the possible decision alternatives and the chance events. One important aid in dealing with these problems is the decision tree.

The central issues related to the use of quantitative aids such as the decision tree are the following:
1. What are the characteristics of problems that should be analyzed with decision trees?
2. How should the decision tree be formulated?
3. What are the information requirements of the procedure?
4. How are the computations performed?
5. How should the results of the analysis be interpreted?

And, finally,

6. What are the advantages of using decision trees?
7. What are the possible problems and pitfalls that must be overcome in practice?

Let us briefly consider each of these issues in turn.

Problem Characteristics

Decision trees are especially helpful in analyzing nonrepetitive decisions that involve risk and substantial costs or potential rewards. In problems of this type, simply identifying the alternative strategies and the possible events that may influence the outcomes, and gaining some appreciation of the probabilities of the occurrence of these events may be the most important part of the analysis. Certainly these are steps that successful managers must perform in any case, even if they have never heard of decision trees. However, the manager who has a knowledge of this technology has a means of organizing his thoughts and improving his understanding of a complex problem.

Several examples of the actual use of decision trees have been reported. Notable examples are the following:

> Pillsbury switched from a box to a bag for one of its grocery products—and even scrapped plans to undertake an extensive market test—when the analysis indicated high expected profitability from this strategy. The switch was successful.
>
> General Electric decided to raise prices, rather than increase manufacturing capacity, for a mature industrial product. As part of the strategy, research and development expenditures were increased twenty-fold, and the decision resulted in a highly profitable sales of some $20 million a year.
>
> Ford Tractor chose to introduce a new model into a regional market suffering from competitive inroads, rather than reduce prices. The strategy worked. [Raiffa, 1974]

Notice that these applications tend to be in the area of determining a marketing strategy for products. This fact is not surprising, since such situations often involve nonrepetitive decisions, risk, and the potential for significant costs or profits.

Other areas that offer potential applications are decisions to expand production or service capacities, the determination of competitive bidding strategies, and the analysis of major government policies such as the decision to seed hurricanes (for an example see Howard, Matheson, and North[1972]). Thus, the manager should be sensitive to problems with these characteristics in order to take advantage of this useful decision-making aid.

Formulation

The issue of who should actually formulate the decision tree is an important one. In extremely complicated problems involving perhaps millions of dollars, the manager may wish to call on his analytic staff or on outside consultants for assistance. However, the *manager* should be involved in the formulation of the decision tree in order to ensure that he understands the assumptions made by the analysts and to ensure that the analysts actually understand the real problem. It is important that the manager have confidence in the analysis, which is unlikely to happen without his personal involvement.

One approach would be for the manager to actually sketch out the first decision tree in gross terms. The major alternatives and events would be shown, perhaps with rough estimates of probabilities, in order to obtain some idea of the important aspects of the problem. Using only a crude analysis of this sort, that would be carried out "on the back of an envelope" in only an hour or so, the manager might be able to eliminate some alternatives as being undesirable, thus reducing the complexity of the problem. The rough tree consisting of the remaining alternatives could then be presented to the professional analysts as a takeoff point for a more detailed analysis.

Information Requirements

The information requirements for a decision tree are basically the same as those for the manager who does not use the decision tree. That is, he must obtain the following:
1. the alternative decisions and their relationships to possible future events
2. the outcomes of selecting each alternative, given the occurrence of each future event
3. the probabilities of the occurrence of each event

In a complex, real-world problem, the decision tree could grow to enormous proportions and require many bits of information. However, a preliminary analysis can be used to eliminate some alternatives from a detailed consideration and to determine the sensitivity of the results to various future events, so that the number of chance branches can be held down. This process requires judgment on the part of the analyst, and it is another reason for encouraging the active participation of the manager in the initial formulation and analysis of the problem. The eventual information requirements can be significantly reduced by this process. In the following chapters we will be concerned with how the estimates of the outcomes and probabilities can actually be obtained.

Computations

Since the computation of expected values is a straightforward task, there is no reason why managers cannot perform their own analyses of decision trees that are of reasonable size. It would be especially desirable to do so in the initial phase of the analysis of a large, complex problem, or perhaps might be sufficient in the case of a problem where the potential losses or rewards do not justify a more elaborate analysis. Thus, the decision tree is one practical analytical aid for which the modern manager should actually be able to perform the required simple computations.

However, in larger, complex problems, the information regarding the decision tree can be input into specially programmed computer routines. Use of a computer would be especially helpful in checking the sensitivity of the solution to various estimates, since the results from changes in the information can be obtained instantly. In addition, the calculations necessary to compute the value of perfect information could also be accomplished quite easily.

Interpretation of Results

We continually emphasize that the expected value does not represent the actual profit or loss that the company will obtain as a result of its decision. Rather, one of the conditional outcomes will actually occur (if all the predictions are accurate).

The expected value evaluative model is appropriate for repetitive decisions or for decisions in which the stakes are not high. For the nonrepetitive problems involving substantial costs or potential rewards, the expected value calculations may provide a means of discarding obviously inferior alternatives at an early stage in the analysis. However, it may be necessary to resort to an alternative evaluative model, expected utility, in order to make the final decision. As we shall see in Chapter 4, the decision tree format can also be used to simplify calculations with this alternative evaluative model.

Advantages of Decision Trees

The crucial question for the practicing manager is whether the use of a decision-making aid is really worth the effort. Will the actual decision be improved over the decision he would make based on his intuition? This question is difficult to answer, since the manager seldom has the opportunity to make the same decision both with and without a decision-making aid.

Certainly, we can point to numerous advantages of using decision trees. They force the manager to organize his thoughts and to specify his alternatives and the important events that will affect the outcomes of these alternatives. Further, the decision tree can be scrutinized by others and used as the basis for a discussion regarding the alternatives and the assumptions that have been made by the manager. This discussion can be carried on by a manager and his advisers or by a committee. Without being overly dramatic, we can say that the decision tree structure provides a useful *language* for discussing complex problems among those who understand the technology. Even when the actual computation of expected values is not carried out, the construction of the decision tree with outcomes described in qualitative terms can be an extremely useful exercise.

Disadvantages of Decision Trees

The only objection to the use of decision trees is that problems in the real world are so complex that the tree expands beyond the limits of human comprehension. There are so many uncertain events and so many alternatives that the decision tree quickly becomes a "bushy mess." However, at this point the involvement of the manager in the preliminary analysis of the problem is required to quickly eliminate some alternatives and to aid in identifying the uncertain events that will have a major impact on the decision. There are no hard and fast rules for this pruning of the decision tree; it requires the judgment and, yes, perhaps the intuition of the manager. The final result of this combination of analysis and intuition would seem to provide the basis for improved decisions that the responsible manager is seeking.

Check Your Understanding

1. What are the advantages of a decision tree presentation of alternatives and events?
2. What is the role of the manager in a decision tree analysis of a substantive, real-world problem?
3. Consider the three gambles A_1, A_2, and A_3 illustrated in Figure 3–2.
    a. Suppose your clairvoyant friend will predict the outcome of flipping the second coin in A_3, but not the first coin in A_1, A_2, and A_3. He charges $0.50 for this service. Should you pay him?
    b. Now suppose he offers to predict the outcome of flipping the first coin in A_1, A_2, and A_3, *and* the outcome of the second coin in A_3 (if you select A_3) for only $1. Should you accept this offer?
4. Refer to Figure 3–7, and POCO's strategy decision. What if POCO could spend additional funds immediately and determine if a breakthrough in the processing technology could be made *from the initial research-only strategy*? The probability of a breakthrough from the initial strategy of a combined research and development effort would remain at 0.3. How much would this information be worth? Draw a decision tree appropriate for analyzing this question and perform the necessary roll-back calculations.

Problems

5. The objective of the U.S. Hurricane Modification Program is to determine whether any hurricane threatening the U.S. coast should be seeded with silver iodide crystals in an attempt to mitigate its destructive effects. In order to analyze this question, probability estimates were obtained concerning the likely impacts of seeding a hurricane on the maximum sustained surface wind speed. A predictive model was then developed to estimate the property damage that results from hurricanes with various wind speeds. As a result of the analysis, the following estimates were obtained for seeding and not seeding a hurricane.

Probability (Hurricane seeded)	Probability (Hurricane not seeded)	Change in Maximum Sustained Wind (%)	Property Damage Loss (millions of $)
0.038	0.054	+32	335.8
0.143	0.206	+16	191.1
0.392	0.480	0	100.0
0.255	0.206	−16	46.7
0.172	0.054	−34	16.3

The cost of seeding a hurricane is relatively cheap, only $0.25 million.
   a. Compute the expected monetary values of the decisions to seed a hurricane and not to seed a hurricane.
   b. Draw a decision tree to summarize the decisions and the outcomes. Compute the expected monetary values of the decisions by rolling back this simple tree.
   c. As stated by Howard, Matheson, and North [1972], "The results of extensive sensitivity analysis may be summarized as follows: The expected loss in terms of property damage appears to be about 20 percent less if the hurricane is seeded. Varying the assumptions of the analysis causes this reduction to vary between 10 and 30 percent but does not change the preferred alternative."

   Place yourself in the position of a government administrator responsible for making the hurricane seeding decision. Why might you recommend against seeding, despite the results of this analysis? In other words, what considerations may have been left out of the analysis? Discuss.

6. Assume that you are president of a company that manufactures electrical relays. The position in which you find yourself requires some interrelated decisions involving a labor dispute and bids on two government contracts.

   The union has set a strike deadline of midnight tonight if you do not accept their demand for a 10 percent wage increase. You are certain that the union will carry out its threat and the resulting strike will cost you about $300,000. If you give in to the demand, the total cost per relay unit will increase to $4.05, compared to the present cost of $3.80 per unit. On the other hand, you feel certain that the union will be defeated if it strikes, and therefore your present costs will remain fixed for the coming year. You must decide whether to give the employees the wage increase and suffer the higher cost of production or to hold to the present wage scale and suffer the resulting strike loss.

The labor dispute is complicated by the fact that the government is letting a large contract for 10 million relay units within the next month and *you will not be in a position to bid on this contract if your employees go on strike.* However, even if you give in to the union demands and avert a strike, you still are not assured of getting the contract unless you can underbid your competitors. Possible bids and resulting probabilities of winning the contract are estimated as follows:

Bid (price per unit)	Probability of Getting Contract
$4.15	0.3
$4.12	0.5
$4.10	0.6
$4.07	0.8

Fortunately a second major government contract is anticipated in the latter part of the year if you do not receive the lucrative contract mentioned previously. (Because of production limitations it will not be possible for you to assume both contracts should you receive the first contract.) To be in a position to bid on the second contract, it is necessary at this time for you to secure adequate financial backing to guarantee the government that you can provide certain expensive testing equipment.

The larger the test facilities you can provide, the more likely it is that you will be awarded the contract. The anticipated net profit for this second project is $3 million if your unit cost is $4.05 and $4 million if your unit cost is $3.80. These figures do not include the large investment in special test equipment that must be written off over the life of the contract. This investment is actually made only if you are awarded the contract. The investment costs and the probabilities of winning the second contract are shown below:

Investment	Probability of Getting Contract
$2,000,000	0.2
$2,400,000	0.4
$2,600,000	0.5
$2,900,000	0.6

a. Draw a decision tree for analyzing this problem.
b. On the basis of the expected value evaluative model, should you accept the union's demand for a 10 percent wage increase?

c. If your answer to (b) above was to grant the pay increase and avert the strike, what should you bid on the first contract?
d. How much should you invest in test facilities if you bid on the second contract?

7. Mid-Valley Manufacturers has the opportunity to bid on a government contract for 100,000 high pressure valves to be used in the hydraulic systems of aircraft. They estimate that these valves could be manufactured by their existing equipment at a cost of $12.50 per unit. However, one of their engineers has suggested a new process for manufacturing the valves.

The unit cost estimates for the new process are only $7.50 if all goes exceptionally well. If there are minor complications, the cost estimate is $9.50 per unit; but if major complications arise, the costs would be prohibitive, so they would have to return to the old process. The engineers estimate the probability of minor complications at 0.5, the probability of major complications at 0.2, and the probability of no complications at 0.3. The investment required for the new process is $100,000, which would not be recoverable even if the process is a failure.

The company must make its bid on the contract before the new process can be tested. The various bids under consideration and the estimated probability of obtaining the contract associated with each bid are shown below:

Bid	Probability of Receiving Contract
$17	0.2
14	0.6
12	0.9

a. Construct a decision tree to analyze this problem using the expected value evaluative model. What should Mid-Valley bid? Which process should they use if they get the contract? Does the choice of the process depend on the bid price?
b. What would be the value to Mid-Valley of resolving the risk regarding the new process?
c. For an investment of $20,000, the company can conduct a pilot test on the new process. Unfortunately, the results of the pilot test would not be conclusive. However, if the results are positive, the engineers would revise their probability estimates to 0.6 for no complications, 0.3 for minor complications, and only 0.1 for major complications. If the results of the test are negative, the probabilities would remain as before. The probability is 0.5 that the results will be positive. If they receive the contract, should Mid-Valley conduct this pilot test? Does your answer depend on the bid price? Why or why not?

8. A chemical company must decide whether to build a small plant or a large one to manufacture a new product with an expected market life of 10 years.* If the company decides to build a small plant now, then finds demand high during the initial period, it can choose to expand its plant after two years.

Marketing estimates indicate a probability of 0.6 of a large market in the long run, and a 0.4 probability of a long-term low demand, developing intially as follows:

Demand Pattern	Probability
Initially high demand, sustained high	0.60
Initially high demand (yrs. 1–2), long-term low (yrs. 3–10)	0.10
Initially low demand, long-term low	0.30
Initially low demand, long-term high	0.0

Estimates of annual income are made under the assumptions of each alternative demand pattern:

1) A large plant with high volume would yield $1,000,000 annually in cash flow.
2) A large plant with low volume would yield only $100,000 because of high fixed costs and inefficiencies.
3) A small plant with low demand would be economical and would yield annual cash income of $400,000.
4) A small plant, during an initial period of high demand, would yield $450,000 per year, but this yield would drop to $300,000 yearly in the long run because of competition. (The market would be larger than under alternative 3, but would be divided up among more competitors.)
5) If the small plant were expanded to meet sustained high demand, it would yield $700,000 cash flow annually (less efficient than a large plant built initially).
6) If the small plant were expanded but high demand were not sustained, estimated annual cash flow would be $50,000.

It is estimated further that a large plant would cost $3 million to put into operation, a small plant would cost $1.3 million, and the expansion of the small plant would cost an additional $2.2 million.

a. Draw a decision tree to structure the problem.
b. What should the initial decision of the company be on the basis of the expected value evaluative model?

---

*From J. F. Magee, "Decision Trees for Decision Making," *Harvard Business Review*, July–August 1964.

c. Repeat the above analysis using a discount factor of 0.10 to adjust for the time value of money. Assume that the first year cash flow is not discounted, the second year cash flow is discounted one year, etc.
d. If you were the manager of this company, what additional information would you wish to obtain before making your decision? Discuss.

9. A large manufacturer of heavy capital equipment operates on a multinational basis.* The firm's treasurer was concerned about a large, recently completed sale of equipment to a French firm. The balance on the terms of this sale was 25 million francs (about $5 million at the current exchange rate), which was receivable in a little less than 30 days. Recent events in France had shaken people's confidence in the franc. The current exchange rate for the franc was 0.2011 U.S. dollars, just above the lower rate of $0.2010 guaranteed by the French government. In addition, the franc could be bought or sold "forward" 30 days at only $0.2000, which reflected the possibility that it would be devalued.

If a devaluation did occur, the firm would lose a great deal of money. For example, a 20 percent devaluation would result in a loss of about $1 million.

The treasurer has two basic alternatives. He can hedge against devaluation by selling forward the 25 million francs for a sure return of $5 million. If he does *not* hedge, he estimates that there is only one chance in twenty that a new government will be formed within 30 days. If the old government remains in power, he is certain that the franc will *not* be devalued, and the return will be $5,025,000. However, if a new government is formed, he estimates that there is a 0.5 chance of an immediate devaluation.

Given a devaluation, the treasurer estimates that the possible range is from 5 to 20 percent, so he assigns returns of $4,750,000; $4,500,000; $4,250,000; and $4,000,000 equal probabilities of 0.25.

a. Construct a decision tree and analyze this problem. What is the better decision on the basis of the expected value evaluative model?
b. The argument has been made that a large company should *never* hedge against exchange devaluations because the market for currency futures is "perfect." Thus, it represents the expectations of persons involved in the market who obviously know more than a corporate treasurer (see Wheelwright [1975]). Would you support this argument or prefer the use of the decision tree? Discuss.

*From S. C. Wheelwright, "Applying Decision Theory to Improve Corporate Management of Currency-Exchange Risks," *California Management Review,* Summer 1975.

References

1. Brown, R. V., "Do Managers Find Decision Theory Useful?" *Harvard Business Review*, Vol. 48, 1970.
2. Howard, R. A., "Social Decision Analysis," *Proceedings of the IEEE*, Vol. 63, No. 3, March 1975.
3. Howard, R. A. (ed.), "Special Issue on Decision Analysis," *IEEE Transactions on Systems Science and Cybernetics*, Vol. SSC-4, No. 3, September 1968.
4. Howard, R. A., J. E. Matheson, and D. W. North, "The Decision to Seed Hurricanes," *Science*, Vol. 176, June 17, 1972.
5. Jones, J. M., *Statistical Decision Making*, Richard D. Irwin, Inc., Homewood, Ill., 1977.
6. Magee, J. F., "Decision Trees for Decision Making," *Harvard Business Review*, July–August 1964.
7. ———, "How to Use Decision Trees in Capital Investment," *Harvard Business Review*, September–October 1964.
8. Raiffa, H., *Decision Analysis*, Addison-Wesley, Reading, Mass., 1968.
9. ———, *Analysis for Decision Making* (an audiographic, self-instructional course), Encyclopedia Britannica Educational Corporation, Chicago, 1974.
10. Schlaifer, R., *Analysis of Decisions Under Uncertainty*, McGraw-Hill, New York, 1969.
11. Wheelwright, S. C., "Applying Decision Theory to Improve Corporate Management of Currency-Exchange Risks," *California Management Review*, Vol. 17, No. 4, Summer 1975.

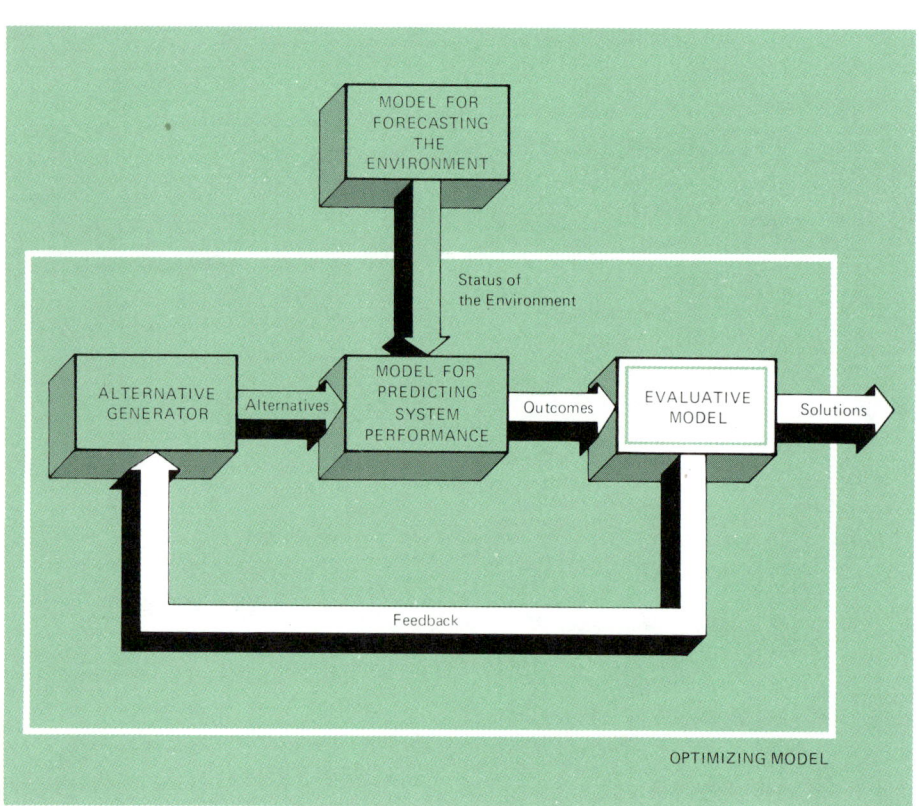

4

EVALUATIVE MODELS BASED ON UTILITY FUNCTIONS

We have seen that the expected value evaluative model can be a useful guide to decisions involving risks, especially when the decisions are to be made over and over again, as in many low- to middle-level company decisions. The expected value represents the average return a manager expects to receive, given that the same (or similar) decision is made many times. Thus, a manager who makes many capital budgeting decisions under conditions of risk might be well advised to adopt the expected value evaluative model as a useful aid.

However, suppose you face a decision involving risks, and you make the decision only once. For example, suppose you are offered the following choice, and you have only one opportunity to accept it. You may receive $25 with certainty, or you may accept the results of a gamble in which a fair coin will be tossed. If the coin falls on heads, you will win $150; but if the coin lands on tails, you will lose $50. Which do you prefer? Think hard about this. Many people, including perhaps yourself, would prefer taking the $25 even though the expected value of the gamble is $50, *twice as much* $[(0.5)($150) + (0.5)(-$50) = $50]$. Does this mean they are irrational? No, they are simply expressing their feelings, and they would prefer to accept the $25 rather than run the risk of losing $50 even though there is an equal chance of winning $150.

If the people who prefer the certain value of $25 are not irrational, then something must be wrong with the expected value evaluative model. This conclusion would also be incorrect. Expected value is a useful evaluative model only so long as it adequately reflects the preferences of the decision maker. In situations involving similar choices that are repeated many times or that have relatively low stakes, the decision maker may feel that his preferences are consistent with the simple expected value of the outcomes. However, in decisions made only once involving relatively high stakes, he may wish to avoid the possibility of an unfortunate outcome, even though the odds are actually in his favor. If so, we would say he is risk averse.

Most persons are risk averse in their decision making, at least in some decision situations, although the degree of risk aversion varies greatly and is a personal matter. A few individuals, including some oil wildcatters, actually prefer to accept high risk situations. For example, they might prefer accepting the gamble we have posed to accepting say $60 with certainty, because there is a good chance they can win $150. However, numerous experiments have shown that such individuals are in the minority.

A second complicating factor in many significant, real-world problems is the existence of several criteria of approximately equal importance. The strategy of using an evaluative model with a single criterion may not be particularly helpful in these instances. For example, the effects of an alternative on the share of the market, prestige, and labor relations might be considered roughly as important as the effect on profit or loss in some business decisions. In the context of educational decision making, the number of students actually enrolled at the undergraduate, Master's, and Ph.D. levels might be important criteria for some decisions [Geoffrion, Dyer, and Feinberg, 1972]. Similarly, the design of a rapid transit system must be evaluated on such criteria as noise pollution, air pollution, appearance, safety, and the number of persons utilizing the system, as well as the costs [Pardee et al., 1969].

The really important decisions that a manager makes generally represent unique opportunities and involve high stakes, and often there are multiple criteria. Since the expected value evaluative model may not be appropriate for such decisions, the manager should be aware of alternative evaluative models. As we shall see, these alternative models have the disadvantage of requiring the decision maker to explicitly reveal information about his preferences. Therefore, the information requirements are much more demanding than those of the simple expected value evaluative models. Nevertheless, these evaluative models do help the decision maker in dealing with perhaps the most important class of problems that he must solve—one-time, high-stake problems.

UTILITY FUNCTIONS FOR A SINGLE CRITERION

The expected value of several conditional outcomes does not consider what each conditional outcome is actually worth to the decision maker. Thus, we need some means of transforming conditional outcomes to measures of worth or utility. Let us think about how this transformation might be made.

Consider again the three games introduced in Chapter 2 and displayed in the decision tree in Figure 3-2 of Chapter 3. The conditional outcomes are expressed in dollars. How can we transform them into measures of utility? The best and worst conditional outcomes are "win $20" and "lose $10," respectively. To get started, we might assign the conditional outcome "win $20" a utility of 1.00, and the conditional outcome "lose $10" a utility of 0.0. Then we would assign each of the other conditional outcomes some utility between 1.00 and 0.0, depending on how it compares with "win $20" and "lose $10." Thus, the utility number we assign to "win $10" will be larger than the one we assign to "win $2," since we would prefer the former to the latter.

We might assign these numbers on the basis of our personal reactions regarding what seems right. For example, you might think that winning $14 would make you almost as happy as winning $20, so you would assign the conditional outcome "win $14" a utility of perhaps 0.9. Similarly, you might think that you would be really happy if you won $20, but really sad if you lost $10. If you broke even, that would be about halfway between these two extremes *in terms of your feelings*, so you would give "win/lose $0" a utility of 0.5. You might continue assigning utility values and search you own mind until you felt comfortable with the responses. However, such a process is *ad hoc*, and you may feel uncomfortable with it no matter how long or how hard you think about the problem.

Constructing the Utility Function

What we really want to do is generate values for these outcomes that can be used in risky situations. Therefore, we should introduce risk into a procedure for obtaining these values. Consider a simple gamble where you win $20 if a fair coin lands on heads but lose $10 if it lands on tails. The coin will be flipped only once, and you either win or pay off immediately. As an alternative, you can take a fixed sum rather than play the game. Suppose you are offered the choice of taking the expected value of the game or having the coin flipped. The expected value of this game is (0.5) ($20) + (0.5) (−$10) = $5. Which would you prefer? Think seriously about this.

To continue the example, suppose you responded after considerable thought that you would take $5. Instead of being paid, you are asked a similar question, except this time the payoff is only $2 for sure, or the result of the coin flip. Again, suppose you prefer the certain payoff of $2 because you really do not like the 0.5 chance of losing $10. The next question, then, is would you *pay* $1 rather than have the coin flipped? Suppose you respond that you would accept the result from the gamble rather than pay to avoid it. After a few more questions of this sort, suppose you finally agree that if you are offered *any* certain winning, you would accept this certain payoff, but you would not *pay* to avoid the coin flip. Thus, at $0 for certain, you are indifferent about having the coin flipped. That is to say, you would just as soon walk away without winning or losing anything, or you would accept the result of the coin flip. You just do not care at that point.

Thus, you are indifferent between receiving $0 for sure and the gamble shown in Figure 4–1. We would like to use this information to assign a utility number to the outcome of winning or losing $0 (breaking even), relative to the utility number 1.0 assigned earlier to winning $20, and of 0.0 assigned to losing $10. These utility numbers are also shown in parentheses in Figure 4–1.

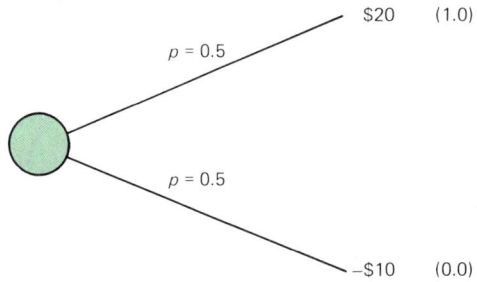

FIGURE 4–1. **The gamble**

In our previous analysis, we have used the expected value of the conditional outcomes of a chance point to replace the chance point in a decision tree. This time, let us compute the expected value of the *utility numbers* associated with the conditional outcomes of the chance point, obtaining $(0.5)(1.0) + (0.5)(0.0) = 0.5$. Much as before, we can let 0.5 be the utility number that we assign to this chance point. Since we were indifferent between breaking even ($0) and this risky situation, we will assign $0 a utility value of 0.5 also. This procedure is summarized in Table 4–1.

We can continue this procedure by creating 50-50 gambles between $0 and win $20, and between lose $10 and $0. For example, suppose you are asked to indicate the least amount you would take for certain, rather than have a fair coin flipped with a $20 payoff on heads and a break-even payoff on tails. If you think hard about this question, you might say to yourself:

> Well, I would certainly rather have $15, and also I would prefer $10. However, I would rather flip the coin than accept only $5 for sure, so it's somewhere between $5 and $10. Let's see, I would prefer flipping the coin if I were offered only $6, $7, or even $8. However, if I could get $9 for sure . . . well, I think I would take it. So, the least I would take is somewhere between $8 and $9, probably closer to $8, say $8.25.

Thus, we assign $8.25 a utility number equal to the expected value of the utility numbers of the new gamble, which is $(0.5)(1.0) + (0.5)(0.5) = 0.75$.

Now suppose we ask a similar question regarding a coin flip between losing $10 and breaking even. This time you say you would pay up to $5.85 to avoid

TABLE 4-1. **Summary of the Estimation of $u(\$0) = 0.5$**

Question	Response	Implication
Do you prefer $5 for sure or the coin toss in Figure 4-1?	$5	utility of $5 is greater than 0.5
Do you prefer $2 for sure or the coin toss in Figure 4-1?	$2	utility of $2 is greater than 0.5
Do you prefer to pay $1 or to have the coin toss in Figure 4-1?	coin toss	utility of −$1 is less than 0.5
Do you prefer to neither gain nor lose any money for sure ($0), or to have the coin toss in Figure 4-1?	indifferent	utility of $0 is equal to 0.5

facing this coin toss. Notice that you are willing to *pay more* than the expected monetary value of the coin flip in order to avoid the possibility of losing $10. The expected value of the utility number for this gamble is 0.25, which we assign to "lose $5.85."

What we are obtaining are values for some function that assigns utility numbers to conditional outcomes. We call such a function a utility function and denote it as $u(O_i)$. For example, we have $u(+\$20) = 1.0$, $u(-\$10) = 0.0$, $u(\$0) = 0.5$, $u(\$8.25) = 0.75$, and $u(-\$5.85) = 0.25$. We could continue this process to obtain more utility numbers by creating hypothetical gambles between $20 and $8.25, between $8.25 and $0, between $0 and −$5.85, and between −$5.85 and −$10.

As an alternative, we could ask the same type of question in another way. Suppose you are offered the choice of either $5 for sure or a gamble with payoffs of "win $20" or "lose $10." If the probability of winning $20 is 0.5 (and of losing $10 is $1.0 - 0.5 = 0.5$), you say you would prefer taking the $5. Now suppose there is a 0.9 chance of winning $20, but only a 0.1 chance of losing $10. Then, you might prefer the gamble. What we are looking for is the *probability* of winning the $20 that would make you indifferent between the $5 for certain and the gamble. To help you find this probability, questions such as those above might be asked explicitly. Alternatively, you might find it easier to ask such questions of yourself.

After much thought, suppose you say that if the odds favor the outcome of "win $20" by at least 2 to 1, then you would take the gamble. Thus, the probability of winning $20 must be about 0.67 for you to be indifferent between the $5 for sure and the gamble, so we have $u(\$5) = 0.67$.

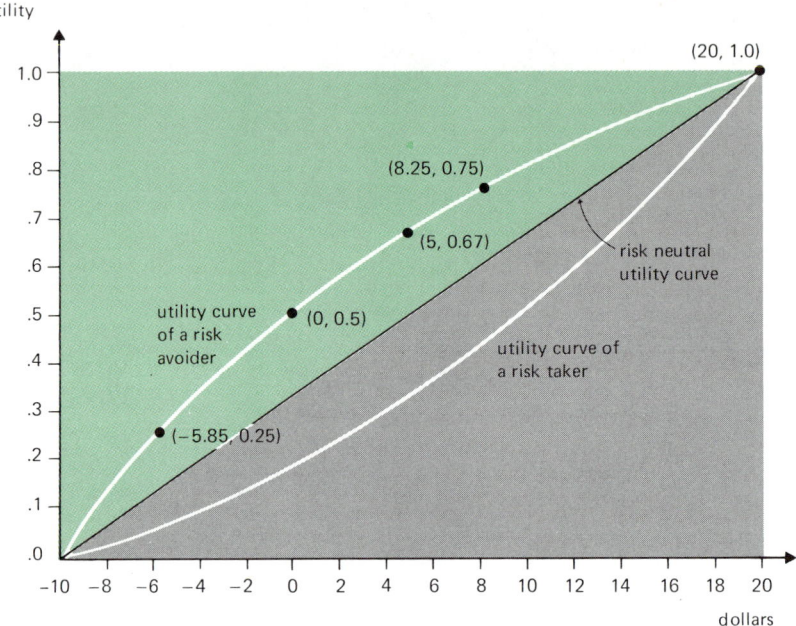

FIGURE 4-2. **A utility function**

We can now plot these utility function values as shown in Figure 4-2, and sketch a smooth curve (the upper white line) that goes through these points. Notice that the curve is bowed slightly. This bow is a characteristic of utility functions that reflect risk averse preferences. Relatively more bow in the curve reflects relatively more risk aversion. A person who is risk neutral would make choices based directly on the expected values of the conditional outcomes of a gamble, and his utility function would be a straight line (also shown in Figure 4-2 for comparison). The utility curve of a risk taker, a person who prefers high risk situations, would have an inverted bow as illustrated by the lower white line in Figure 4-2. It is also possible that a person might be a risk taker for certain values of money and a risk avoider for others, so he would have an S-shaped utility curve.

These two ways of asking questions in order to estimate a utility function are the most commonly used ones and have a sound theoretical basis. Other approaches have been suggested; these are reviewed by Fishburn [1967]. (For a more detailed discussion, see Keeney and Raiffa [1976, Chapter 4].)

The Utility Function As an Evaluative Model

The purpose of constructing a utility function for a decision maker is to use it in an evaluative model. In the decision tree, we replaced a chance point with conditional outcomes by the expected value of the conditional outcomes. Thus we implicitly assumed that the decision maker was indifferent between the chance point and the expected value of the conditional outcomes. As we have discussed, this assumption is only appropriate if the decision maker is risk neutral, but many persons are risk averse.

The assignment of the utility numbers was based on the following procedure. Consider a chance point or a gamble where the utility numbers of the conditional outcomes are known. Find a certain outcome such that the decision maker is indifferent between receiving that outcome and the chance point. Then assign that certain outcome a utility number equal to the expected value of the *utility numbers* associated with the conditional outcomes. The certain outcome may not be the expected value of the conditional outcomes, but by our rules for constructing the utility function, the utility number associated with the certain outcome will be the expected value of the utility numbers of the conditional outcomes.

This result suggests that rather than using the expected value of the conditional outcomes to evaluate alternatives, we can use the expected value of the utility numbers associated with these outcomes. This evaluative model is identical to the simple expected value model except for the introduction of the utility function u, which is unique to a particular decision maker. The practical disadvantage of the model is that it requires more information, since we must interact with the decision maker to obtain an estimate of u. Further, the result will be different for different decision makers, so there is no single answer.

Some persons would object to the use of this model on the grounds that it is not objective, as is the simple expected value model, because it incorporates subjective judgments. However, as we have stressed, the proper criterion for choosing an evaluative model is how well it captures the true preferences of the decision maker. Since the expected utility model explicitly incorporates these preferences, it is superior on this criterion. Notice that if the decision maker is actually risk neutral and is willing to act on the basis of the expected values of conditional outcomes, this attitude will also be reflected as a special case of the utility function, which is the straight line shown in Figure 4–2.

In problems involving a single criterion under certainty, the decision maker sometimes has a specific goal in mind for the criterion. For example, an individual purchasing an automobile might consider 300 horsepower to be superior to any smaller value because of performance considerations *and* superior to any larger value because of safety considerations. In such a case, it is not true that either more or less of the criterion is always preferred. The same techniques can be used to construct a utility function for use as an evaluative model in these instances.

An Example With Gambles Consider again the problem originally presented in Chapter 2 of choosing among three alternative gambles. The decision tree for analyzing the problem is shown again in Figure 4–3. However, this time, the utility function values associated with the outcomes are shown in parenthe-

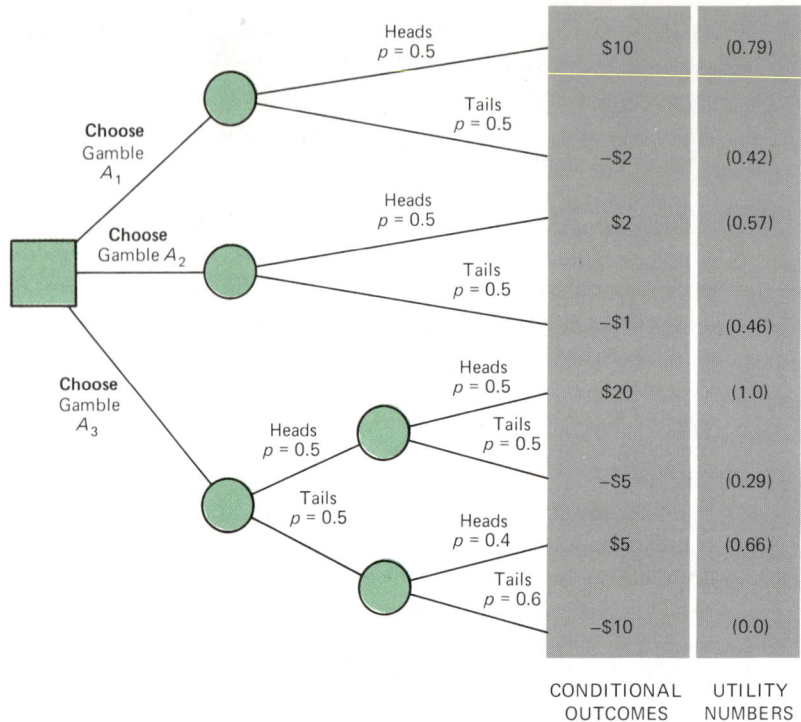

FIGURE 4-3. **Utility numbers for the gamble selection decision tree**

ses to the right of the outcomes. These values were obtained from the utility function we constructed earlier, as illustrated in Figure 4-4. Now let us roll back this decision tree by taking expected values at the chance points. However, rather than taking the expected values of the conditional outcomes, we take the expected values of the utility numbers associated with those outcomes. Performing these calculations, we have the results shown in Figure 4-5, with A_1 receiving an expected utility number of 0.605, A_2 of 0.515, and A_3 of 0.455. According to the expected utility evaluative model, the decision maker for whom we constructed this utility function should prefer A_1 to A_2 or A_3, and A_2 to A_3.

This result is the same for A_1, which was also preferred according to the expected value of the conditional outcomes model. However, using the expected value of the conditional outcomes, A_3 with a value of $1.75 was preferred to A_2 with a value of $0.50. By the expected utility model, A_2 is preferred to A_3. Looking at the decision tree (Figure 4-3), we see that very little risk is involved in A_2. Although you can win only $2, you can lose only $1, at worst. However, A_3 includes the possibilities of losing either $5 or $10. These negative outcomes are penalized heavily by the utility function, so the safer alternative, A_2, is now preferred to A_3.

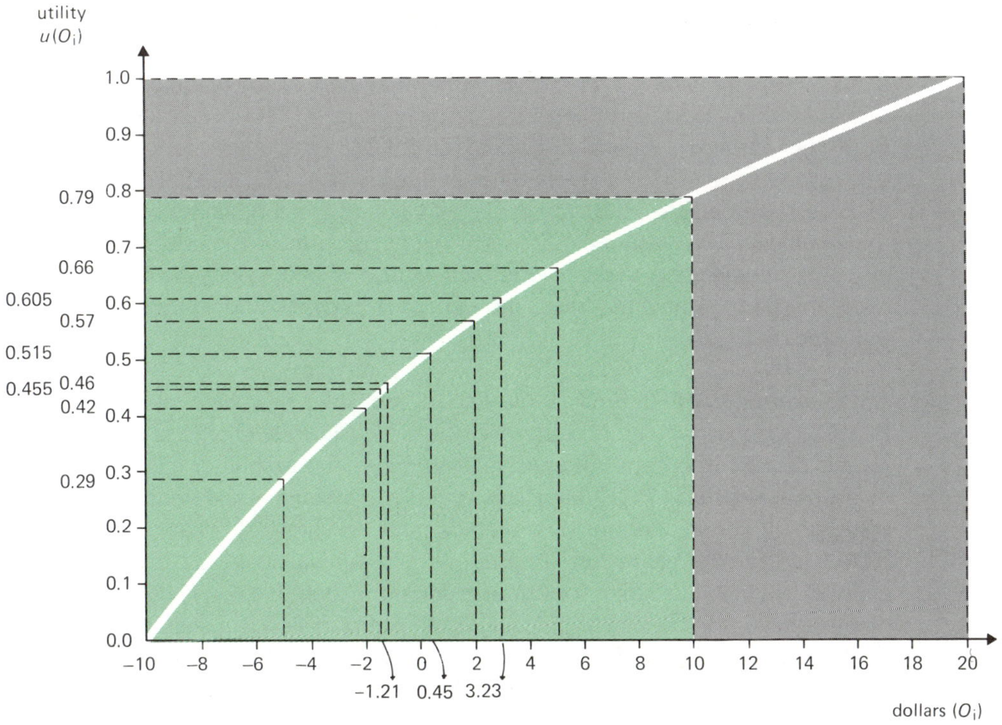

FIGURE 4-4. **Estimating the utility numbers for the gamble selection problem**

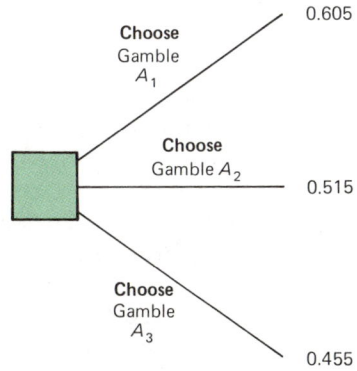

FIGURE 4-5. **The results of the analysis with utility numbers**

CHAPTER 4 EVALUATIVE MODELS BASED ON UTILITY FUNCTIONS

We can also transform these utility numbers associated with the alternatives back into dollars. These results represent the least amount the decision maker would accept for certain in each case, rather than choose the gamble. For A_1, the monetary value corresponding to a utility number of 0.605 can also be read from the curve in Figure 4-4, and is $3.23. Similarly, the dollar value corresponding to 0.515 or A_2 is $0.45, and for A_3 it is $-$1.21. Notice that each of these numbers is less than the expected value of the conditional outcomes for the gambles, as we would expect since the decision maker is risk averse. Note also that this decision maker would actually be willing to *pay* up to $1.21 to avoid the third gamble, A_3, even though the expected value of the conditional outcomes is $1.75.

An Example With POCO Now let us reconsider the shale oil problem of POCO. Suppose we can find the decision maker in POCO who is responsible for this decision (perhaps not an easy task). He may say that for relatively small investment decisions, POCO is willing to make decisions based on the expected value of the conditional outcomes. Since many such decisions are made, they expect to actually realize total returns roughly equivalent to the total of these expected values. However, for a major decision, such as the oil shale development strategy, the possibility of losing up to $500 million is a serious outcome. Therefore, he agrees to answer several questions involving 50-50 gambles, and we eventually construct the utility curve for him displayed in Figure 4-6.

You may question why we should use this decision maker's utility function. What we really want is a utility function for POCO, if such a thing exists. Perhaps so, however, we may assume that the decision maker is not reflecting his *personal* risk aversion in his responses. Rather he is reflecting his view of how POCO should respond in risky situations. If so, his responses may provide the basis for the best approximation to a utility function for POCO that we can hope to obtain. After all, POCO does not actually make decisions, this person makes the decisions. For an example of an attempt to determine such a utility function for a real company, see the account by Spetzler [1968].

Now, let us substitute the corresponding utility function values for the conditional outcomes in the decision tree for POCO, as shown in Figure 4-7. Rolling back the tree, we obtain expected utility function values of 0.722 for the initial research-only strategy, 0.752 for the research and development strategy, and 0.633 for the crash development strategy. These results and the expected utility function values at the other chance branch points and decision points are shown in Figure 4-7. Notice that the relative ranking of these three strategies is the same when the utility function values are used as when the expected values of the conditional outcomes were computed. The certain returns corresponding to these utility values, which can be obtained from Figure 4-6, are $29.34 million for the initial research-only strategy, $69.48 million for the initial research and development strategy, and a loss of $78.27 million for the crash development strategy. Again, each of these certain equivalents is less than the corresponding expected value of the associated conditional outcomes.

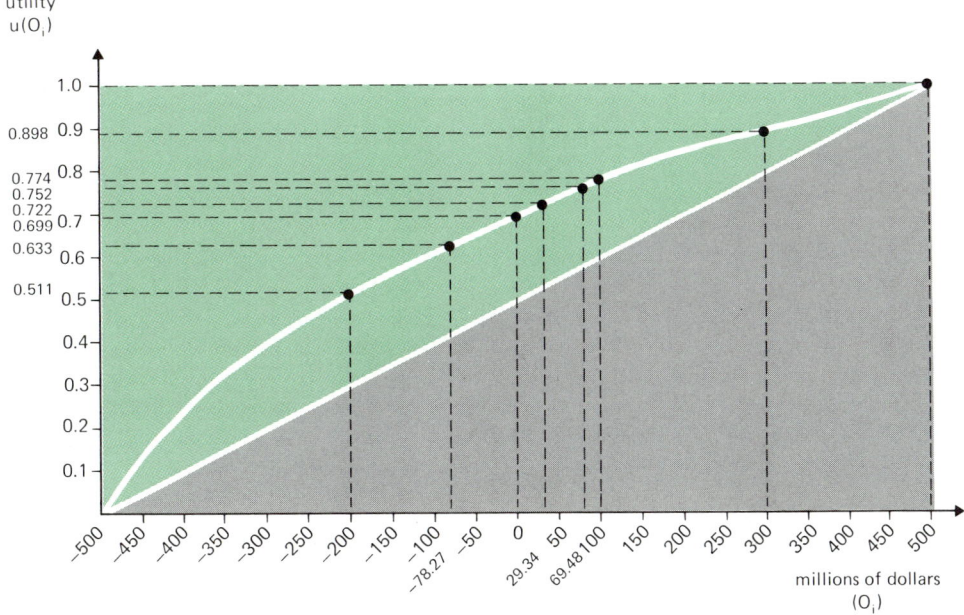

FIGURE 4-6. **A utility function for POCO**

UTILITY FUNCTIONS FOR MULTIPLE CRITERIA

Evaluative models may be used as an aid to decision making when there are multiple criteria. In Chapters 2 and 3, we assumed that there was only one outcome, or criterion, relevant for evaluating the alternatives. A more realistic interpretation would be that there was only one criterion of overriding importance, such as profit or loss. Other considerations (which could be thought of as secondary criteria) could be brought into play to choose among alternatives that were "close" on the primary criterion. Thus, the approaches we have described could be used to identify a smaller subset of alternatives that are roughly equivalent based on a criterion of overriding importance such as profit (loss), but they are inappropriate for explicitly dealing with multiple criteria.

Multiple criteria of approximately equal importance generally arise because the problem is complex. Major decisions involving a significant allocation of resources often exhibit this complexity. First we shall consider the initial issue in the case of a complex problem: the identification of the criteria. Next, an evaluative model for problems involving multiple criteria will be briefly described.

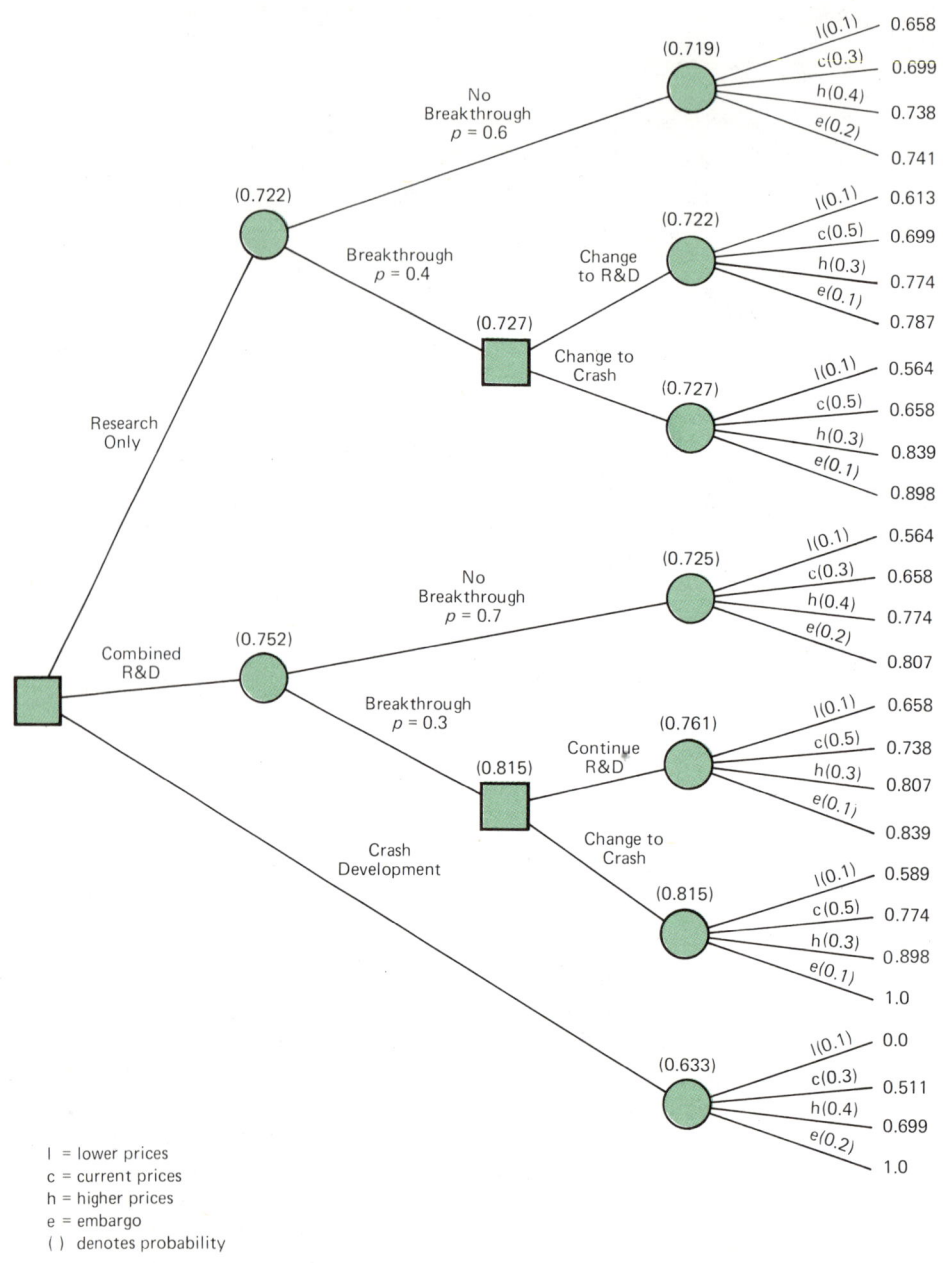

FIGURE 4-7. **The decision tree for POCO with utility numbers**

Identifying the Criteria

An important issue that should be considered early in the problem-solving effort is the actual identification of the criteria that are relevant for comparing alternatives. These criteria (attributes, objectives, outcomes, or goals) are simply the outcomes that are affected by the choice of an alternative and that affect the decision maker's preference for the alternative. The task of recognizing the aspects of the system that will be affected by the choice of an alternative may be the most difficult and the most important task in the analysis. The development of an evaluative and a predictive model may have to be accomplished simultaneously or iteratively, since the criteria may change as the decision maker learns more about the problem.

As an example, consider the imposition of a 55-mile-per-hour speed limit during the oil embargo in 1974. The stated objective of this law was to conserve fuel by forcing automobiles to travel slower. It also had the effect of communicating the seriousness of a situation to the general public. In addition, deaths and injuries from traffic accidents fell drastically during this period. On the negative side, this law also touched off a nationwide strike by truckers and curtailed the demand at businesses depending on motorists and tourists. It is not clear that Congress or the president were aware of all of these outcomes prior to the passage of the legislation.

Thus, the criteria may include outcomes, such as the probability of a strike by truckers, not directly related to the primary purpose of the alternative, conserving gasoline in this case. Nevertheless, these criteria must be included in the evaluative model if they affect the preference of the decision maker.

An Additive Evaluative Model for Multiple Criteria

The most complex and important managerial decisions generally involve both multiple criteria and risk. Because of the importance of these decisions, the modern manager should know that evaluative models for dealing with them do exist. For example, suppose we are trying to decide which automobile to purchase, and we have narrowed our choice to two alternatives, a Starburst (A_1) or a Palomino (A_2). The Starburst and the Palomino are approximately the same in size and weight, so we have decided to base our decision on only two criteria, cost measured in dollars and performance measured in horsepower. We assume that the outcome of either alternative decision is certain, so if we purchase the Starburst (A_1), we obtain the outcome $O_1 = (\$3500, 140 \text{ hp})$ and if we purchase the Palomino (A_2), we obtain $O_2 = (\$3600, 170 \text{ hp})$. Now, which automobile should we choose?

The Additive Model   Suppose we have only two criteria, and let (O^1, O^2) represent an outcome where O^1 and O^2 are the values of the two criteria. For example, O^1 might be the cost and O^2 might be a measure of performance, like horsepower. We would like to obtain a utility function $U(O^1, O^2)$ of the multiple outcomes. However, it would be difficult to interact with a decision maker to approximate such a function without some simplifying assumptions.

The simplest assumption is that $U(O^1,O^2)$ is additive. This means that it can be written

$$U(O^1,O^2) = w_1 u_1(O^1) + w_2 u_2(O^2),$$

where u_1 and u_2 are single criterion utility functions scaled from zero to one, and w_1 and w_2 are scaling constants or weights. The practical implication is that we can apply the methods for estimating a single criterion utility function to obtain u_1, and then to obtain u_2. We then adjust for the relative importance of the two criteria by assessing w_1 and w_2.

For example, suppose we interact with a decision maker using the methods for estimating a single criterion utility function over cost, and obtain u_1 shown in Figure 4–8. Next, we assess a single criterion utility function over horsepower, and obtain u_2 in Figure 4–9. Finally, suppose the decision maker estimates that a change in horsepower from 100 to 200 is about twice as important as a change in cost from $3375 to $3750; these changes are the ranges over which the utility functions are defined. Therefore, the weight w_2 for u_2 should be twice as large as the weight w_1.

We have estimated the additive utility function

$$U(O^1,O^2) = 1.0\ u_1(O^1) + 2.0\ u_2(O^2),$$

where u_1 and u_2 are shown in Figures 4–8 and 4–9, respectively. We now wish to evaluate the Starburst and the Palomino. The outcome for the Starburst is ($3500, 140 hp). From Figure 4–8, we estimate $u_1(\$3500) = 0.7$ approximately, and from Figure 4–9, $u_2(140\text{ hp}) = 0.67$. Therefore we have the total utility function value

$$U(\$3500, 140\text{ hp}) = (1.0)(0.7) + (2.0)(0.67) = 2.04$$

for the Starburst.

In a similar manner, we obtain

$$U(\$3600, 170\text{ hp}) = (1.0)(0.42) + (2.0)(0.87) = 2.16$$

for the Palomino. Since the result is larger for the Palomino, it should be preferred by the decision maker. It should also be noted that these same concepts can be applied in situations involving risk.

Unfortunately, it is not always true that the evaluative model over multiple criteria for a particular decision maker can be written in this additive form. That is, it may not be possible to determine the functions u_1 and u_2, and the weights w_1 and w_2 so that the additive model accurately reflects the preferences of the decision maker. In such cases, alternate evaluative models can be used.

Additional details regarding evaluative models for multiple criteria are presented by Keeney and Raiffa [1976]. For real-world applications, these evaluative models are sufficiently complex to require the assistance of an analyst. However, the manager should recognize that such evaluative models do

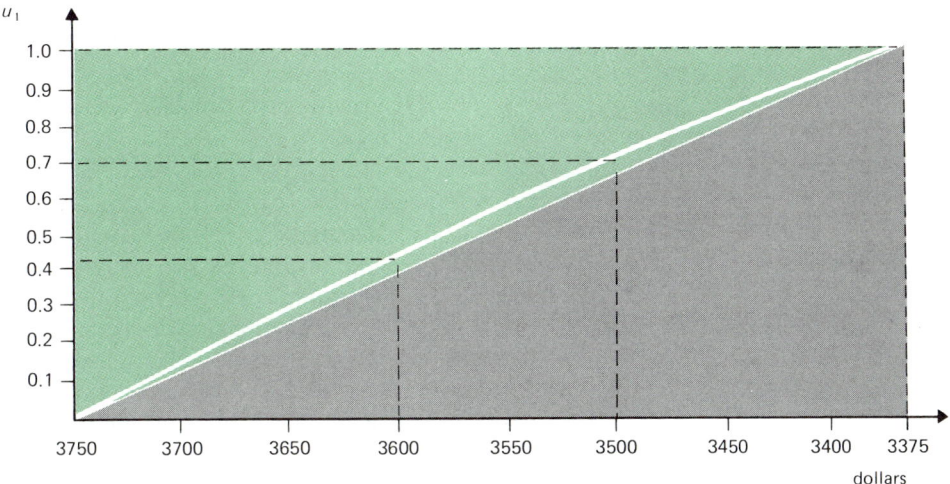

FIGURE 4–8. **The utility function u_1 for total cost**

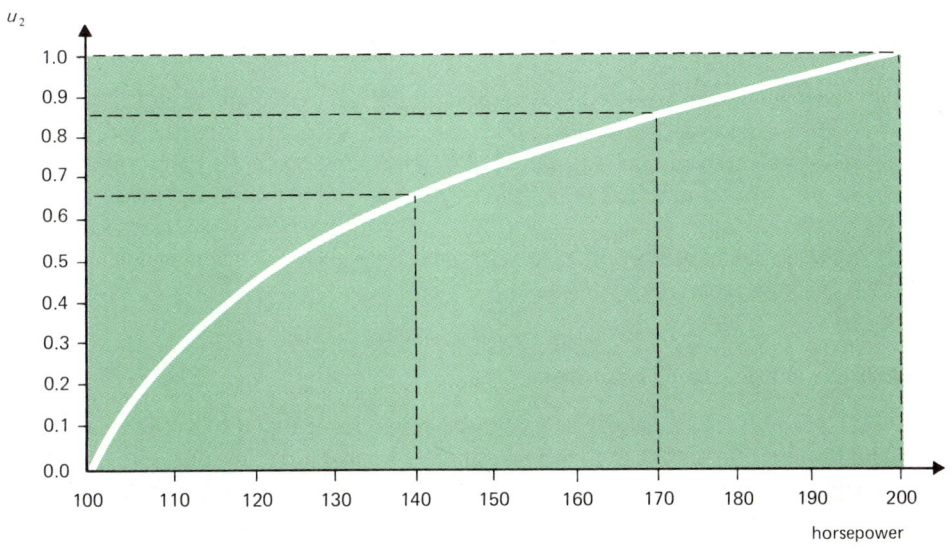

FIGURE 4–9. **The utility function u_2 for horsepower**

exist, and that they can be constructed as a straightforward extension of the approach for a single criterion utility function.

WHAT SHOULD THE MANAGER KNOW?

The manager should recognize that the expected value of conditional outcomes is not the only available evaluative model for use in decisionmaking when risk or multiple criteria are involved. The simple expected value model does not take into consideration the decisionmaker's feelings regarding risk, and it does not deal at all with the problem of reconciling multiple criteria.

A utility function that reflects a decision maker's risk aversion can be constructed. In problems involving a single criterion and risk, the utility function values can be substituted for the corresponding conditional outcome values. The expected values of the utility numbers, which can be organized in tabular form or in a decision tree, can be computed and used to rank the alternatives. Most persons are risk averse, so the outcome value associated with the expected utility function value of an alternative is generally smaller than the expected value of the conditional outcomes.

When multiple criteria are involved, an additive evaluative model can be used in some situations. Then a single criterion utility function can be assessed on each of the criteria, and weights can be determined to compensate for the relative importance of the different criteria. Although the assistance of an analyst may be required to implement these more complex evaluative models, the manager should be aware of their existence.

Problem Characteristics

Utility functions involving single and multiple criteria are useful in analyzing nonrepetitive decisions involving risk and substantial costs and potential rewards. The nonrepetitive nature of the decision is especially important with the single criterion utility function, since otherwise simple expected value would be an appropriate evaluative model. In addition, the potential rewards and costs must be substantial in order to justify the time and effort required to obtain the subjective estimates.

Obtaining Subjective Estimates

The modern manager may find himself in the position of the decisionmaker from whom information is required to estimate a utility function for single or multiple criteria. It seems unlikely that he will ever be interviewing others and trying to obtain subjective estimates from them. Why, then, did we present the methodology for eliciting this information in some detail?

If the manager is questioned by an analyst, he should recognize what the analyst is doing and cooperate with him. Perhaps more important, the manager may be drawing a decision tree and performing the necessary calculations himself. If so, he may find it helpful to carry on a structured dialogue *with himself* to elicit the necessary information; that is, he may pose these questions involving gambles to himself in order to crystallize his own thinking. Therefore, it is important that he be aware of the basic approaches for eliciting judgmental response.

Information Requirements

The information requirements for utility functions for single or multiple criteria are relatively severe. Therefore, the manager may wish to ignore all but one criterion and perform a preliminary analysis with simple expected values. In many practical problems, the best alternative will be obvious from such an analysis. Recall that the decision for POCO was not changed by the introduction of utility function values. However, if two or more alternatives are "close" on the basis of an expected value model, an analysis using utility functions might then be performed.

No quantitative aid should be applied blindly. Why use a procedure requiring the gathering of expensive information when a simpler approach will work just as well? The manager should always trade off the benefit of using a quantitative aid against the cost of the required information.

Interpretation of Results

The expected utility function values may be used to rank the alternatives. When there is only a single criterion, the outcome value corresponding to the expected utility value for an alternative can be estimated from the utility function. This estimate is the least amount that the decision maker should actually be willing to accept for certain rather than choose the alternative. Again, we must emphasize that this certain value of the alternative will not actually occur; rather any one of the conditional outcomes of the alternative will be the result of the decision.

A sensitivity analysis should be performed to ensure that small errors in estimating the utility functions and/or in eliciting the subjective probabilities will not affect the decision. It would be inappropriate to blindly follow the rankings resulting from these models, especially if several outcomes are relatively "close" according to the models.

These approaches do not relieve the manager of the task of making a decision. They simply provide a systematic way of analyzing the alternatives. Often a manager may wish to revise his utility functions and weights as he learns more about the problem. Such revisions are especially likely to occur in the public sector where inputs from citizens and public reactions to initial proposals may provide a basis for these revisions.

Check Your Understanding

1. In the following situations, would the expected value of the outcomes or expected utility be a more appropriate evaluative model? Explain your reasoning.

a. the determination of daily inventory policies
   b. the expansion of capacity by building a large plant
   c. the selection of a new product to market when approximately 20 new products are introduced by the firm each year
   d. the selection of a new product to market when a commitment of a high proportion of the firm's capital will be required
   e. the purchase of personal life insurance
   f. the decision to seed hurricanes
2. Distinguish between an outcome and the *worth* of the outcome to the decision maker.
3. Distinguish between a person who is risk averse and a risk taker. What professions might appeal to a risk taker?
4. Estimate the utility function values for each of the outcomes in the gamble selection decision tree of Figure 4-3 from the utility curve of a *risk taker* shown in Figure 4-2.
   a. Which gamble would the risk taker prefer?
   b. What is the least amount he would accept for certain in each case rather than choose a gamble?
5. Obtain the cooperation of a friend, a roommate, or your spouse. Using questions involving gambles, find at least five points on his or her utility function over the range of monetary values from $-\$10$ (lose \$10) to $+\$20$ (win \$20).
   a. Is the individual risk averse, risk neutral, or a risk taker?
   b. Plot these five points and draw in the corresponding utility curve. Using these results, analyze the gamble selection decision tree in Figure 4-3. Which gamble should he or she prefer?
   c. Describe the three alternative gambles to your friend. Ask him to choose one. Did this choice agree with your prediction in (b)?
6. By posing questions involving gambles to yourself, develop and plot your own utility curve over the range from $-\$10$ to $+\$20$.
   a. Are you risk averse, risk neutral, or a risk taker?
   b. Using your own personal utility function values, analyze the gamble selection decision tree in Figure 4-3. Which gamble should you prefer according to this analysis?
   c. Study the three alternative gambles carefully. Does your "gut reaction" agree with the analysis in (b)?
7. List two or more criteria that might be considered of approximately equal importance for each of the following decision situations.
   a. the selection of a jet fighter from several alternative prototypes
   b. the design of an emergency medical system for a city
   c. the choice of a dam site on a river
   d. the creation of a new national park
   e. the purchase of a new computer system
   f. the selection of a particular product for further develoment and marketing

g. the determination of the terms of a bargaining settlement in negotiating a labor contract

8. Suppose the decision maker wishes to apply the additive utility function with u_1 and u_2 shown in Figures 4-8 and 4-9 respectively, and with $w_1 = 1.0$ and $w_2 = 2.0$, to a new alternative, the Champion. The Champion is described as follows:

Champion (A_3)	
Cost	$3400
Horsepower	120 hp

Estimating the appropriate values of u_1 and u_2 from Figures 4-8 and 4-9 respectively, calculate the utility function value associated with the Champion from the additive utility function. Should it be preferred to the Palomino?

Problems

9. Suppose an individual is interested in purchasing an automobile and is concerned with the acceleration and performance of the automobile as determined by its horsepower. Without even considering other criteria such as cost and mileage, he may feel that 300 horsepower is the ideal figure. Suggest two different evaluative models that could be used to select an automobile for this individual based on the single, certain criterion of horsepower. Graph each one as a function of horsepower over the interval from 0 horsepower to 600 horsepower.

10. Consider the problem of POCO in determining whether to drill in the Aleutian Islands as described in exercise 21 of Chapter 2.
    a. Find the utility function values of POCO for $80 million, −$100 million, $200 million, and $300 million from Figure 4-6.
    b. Repeat the analysis of exercise 21 in Chapter 2 substituting the utility function values for the monetary outcomes. Does the decision change?
    c. If you were a manager of POCO, would you feel more comfortable with the analysis based on expected monetary value or the one based on expected utility? Explain.

11. Consider the problem of a government decision maker who must decide if a particular hurricane is to be seeded. He finds the analysis of the hurricane seeding issue as described in exercise 5 of Chapter 3 most interesting, but it omits an important consideration. Once a hurricane has been seeded, it is no longer an "act of God," but it becomes an "act of man." As a result, once a hurricane has been seeded, the government will be blamed for damages, even if they are smaller than they would have been otherwise. Hurricanes are unpredictable. If the surface wind speed should actually *increase* after the hurricane is seeded, or if its direction of travel should shift into a heavily populated area, the public outcry would be tremendous.

Thus, the value of the outcome to the decision maker depends both on the property damage *and* on whether the hurricane was seeded. The best outcome would be the least damage, estimated at $16.3 million in exercise 5 of Chapter 3, and no seeding. The worst outcome would be the highest property damage of $335.8 million after the hurricane was seeded. Suppose he assigns the best outcome a utility function value of 1.0, the worst outcome a utility function value of 0.0, and uses the approach involving gambles to assign utility function values to the remaining outcomes. The results and the probability estimates are shown below:

Property Damage Loss (millions of $)	Hurricane Seeded		Hurricane Not Seeded	
	Probability	Utility	Probability	Utility
$335.8	0.038	0.0	0.054	0.30
191.1	0.143	0.61	0.206	0.68
100.0	0.392	0.82	0.480	0.89
46.7	0.255	0.89	0.206	0.98
16.3	0.172	0.90	0.054	1.0

Notice that the decision maker is indifferent between a property damage loss of $46.7 million from a seeded hurricane and a loss of $100 million from an unseeded hurricane because of the difference in government responsibility in each case.

The utility function value assigned to the cost of seeding, only $0.25 million, is negligible and can be ignored.

a. Compute the expected utility associated with each of the two decisions. Which one should be preferred?
b. Does the preferred decision differ from the one that would be obtained using the expected monetary value model? Is this surprising?
c. As a practical matter, would you, in the role of the government decision maker, like for these utility function values to be publicized? How would you defend the use of this procedure before a congressional committee?

12. Consider the problem of whether to take an umbrella to work as described in exercise 22 of Chapter 2.
    a. Use the plot of the utility function in Figure 4–4 to assign utility numbers to the outcomes of $0, −$2, −$4, and −$10.
    b. Using the expected utility evaluative model, determine the best decision when the forecasts of the probability of rain are the following:
        1) 0.00
        2) 0.25
        3) 0.50
        4) 0.75
        5) 1.00
       How do these decisions compare with those that result from using the expected value evaluative model?

c. What are the certain returns (payments in this case) corresponding to the decisions for each of the five forecast probabilities?
13. Consider the problem of managing currency-exchange risks as described in exercise 9 of Chapter 3. Suppose we ask the treasurer a series of questions involving gambles, and estimate the utility function for the firm shown in Figure 4–10.
   a. Estimate the utility function values associated with the relevant outcomes and perform the decision tree analysis using the expected utility evaluative model. Do the results change?
   b. It has been argued that we should *not* obtain the utility function from the treasurer. Since he will be blamed if an unfortunate outcome occurs, he will be too risk averse. Thus, his views are not in the best interests of the firm. Do you agree? If so, suggest a remedy for this problem.

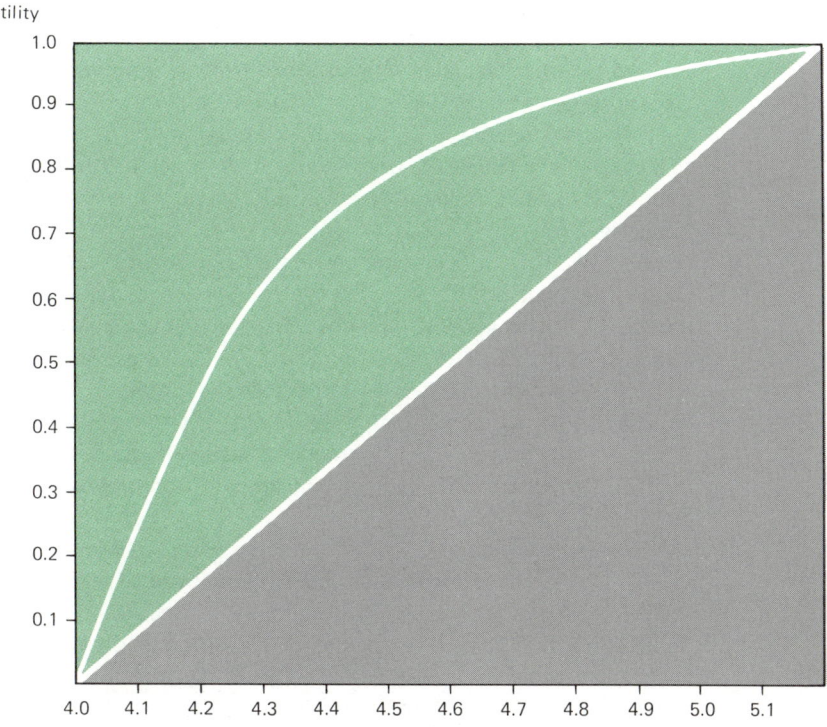

FIGURE 4–10. **A preference curve for the treasurer**

Adapted from S. C. Wheelwright, "Applying Decision Theory to Improve Corporate Management of Currency-Exchange Rates," California Management Review, Vol. 17, No. 4, Summer 1975.

References

1. Brown, R. V., "Do Managers find Decision Theory Useful?" *Harvard Business Review,* Vol. 48, 1970.
2. Fishburn, P. C., "Methods of Estimating Additive Utilities," *Management Science,* Vol. 13, No. 7, March 1967.
3. ———, "Utility Theory," *Management Science,* Vol. 14, No. 5, January 1968.
4. Geoffrion, A., J. Dyer, and A. Feinberg, "An Interactive Approach for Multi-Criterion Optimization with an Application to the Operation of an Academic Department," *Management Science,* Vol. 19, No. 4, 1972.
5. Grayson, C. J., "Decisions Under Uncertainty: Drilling Decisions by Oil and Gas Operators," Division of Research, Harvard Business School, Boston, Mass., 1960.
6. Hammond, J. C., "Better Decisions with Preference Theory," *Harvard Business Review,* November–December 1967.
7. Howard, R. A., "Decision Analysis in Systems Engineering," in *Systems Concepts,* edited by R. Miles, John Wiley & Sons, New York, 1973.
8. Jackson, J., "Coping with Complexity," mimeographed notes, Graduate School of Management, University of California, Los Angeles, 1974.
9. Keeney, R., and H. Raiffa, *Decisions with Multiple Objectives,* John Wiley & Sons, New York, 1976.
10. North, D. W., "A Tutorial Introduction to Decision Theory," *IEEE Transactions on Systems Science and Cybernetics,* Vol. SSC-4, No. 3, September 1968.
11. Pardee, F., T. Kirkwood, K. Kraemer, K. MacCrimmon, J. Miller, C. Phillips, J. Ranftl, K. Smith, and D. Whitcomb, "Measurement and Evaluation of Transportation System Effectiveness," RM-5869-DOT, The Rand Corporation, Santa Monica, California, September 1969.
12. Raiffa, H., *Analysis for Decision Making* (an audiographic, self-instructional course), Encyclopedia Britannica Educational Corporation, Chicago, Illinois, 1974.
13. ———, *Decision Analysis,* Addison-Wesley, Reading, Mass., 1968.
14. ———, "Preferences for Multiattribute Alternatives," RM-5868-DOT/RC, The Rand Corporation, Santa Monica, California, April 1969.
15. Spetzler, C. S., "The Development of a Corporate Risk Policy for Capital Investment Decisions," *IEEE Transactions on Systems Science and Cybernetics,* Vol. SSC-4, No. 3, September 1968.
16. Wheelwright, S. C., "Applying Decision Theory to Improve Corporate Management of Currency-Exchange Risks," *California Management Review,* Vol. 17, No. 4, Summer 1975.

PART III

PREDICTIVE MODELS

INTRODUCTION TO PREDICTIVE MODELS

In Part II, we assumed that we knew how our basic financial, productive, marketing, and behavioral systems would respond to forecasts of the environment and to alternatives that we might pose. Recall our basic diagram relating these models, which we reproduce here as Figure III–1. Our emphasis in Part II was to develop methodologies for deciding what the best strategies would be if we knew the outcomes from predictive models. Now, however, we shall focus our attention on the predictive models themselves.

Forecasting the Environment

In the context of predictive models, the means we use to forecast the behavior of the environment is also a predictive model with a special character. Forecasting models focus attention on the prediction of the exogenous (outside) factors that are normally not within our control, but that have a tremendously important influence on what happens. The most obvious of these outside factors in managerial systems is demand for the product or service with which we deal. Demand is a fundamental driving force for all of our systems in both private and public enterprises, as well as product and service systems. These exogenous factors drive the basic systems for which we wish to establish predictive models and have an extremely important influence on the behavior of these systems.

It is important that we think in broad terms about the kinds of systems, for there is an unfortunate currency for the idea that demand functions are related only to business enterprises, when in fact every organization is driven by some

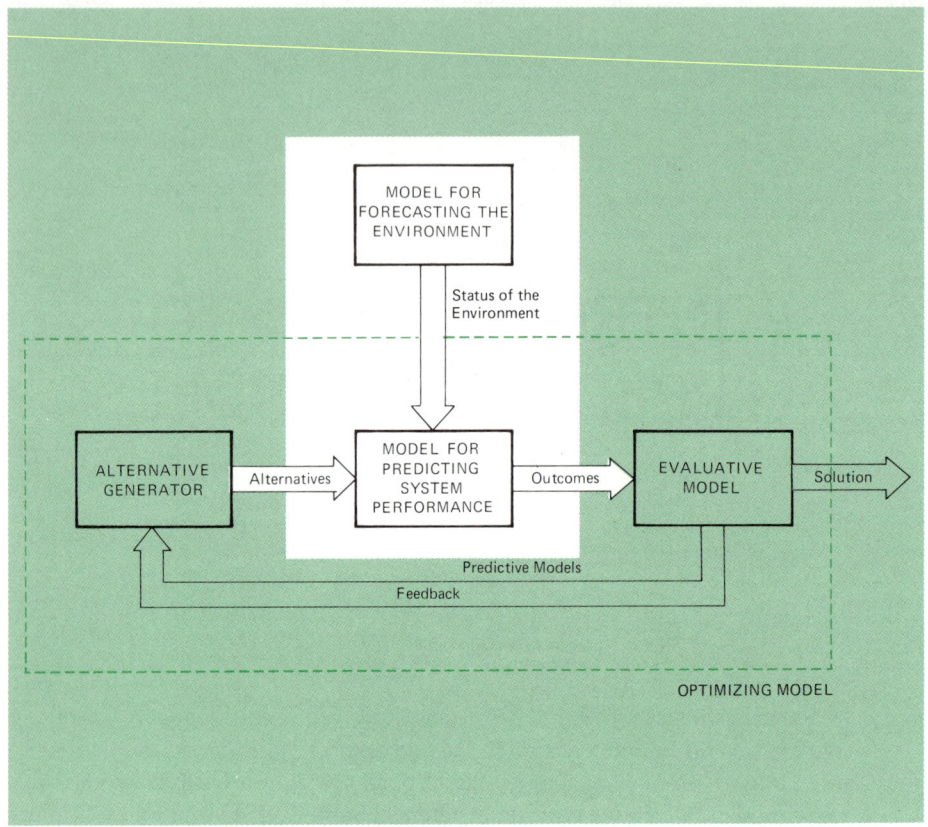

FIGURE III-1. **Predictive models in relation to alternatives and evaluation of outcomes**

kind of demand function. Knowing more than naive information about the demand function may suggest some of the most important strategies for managerial systems. For example, the delivery of mail to the post office peaks between 4:00 and 8:00 P.M. when 40 to 60 percent of the daily mail is delivered because of the day-end mailing practices of business. Given this fact, what are the best allocations of work force during the day and night shifts? With such a variable load pattern, how effective are proposals for mechanization likely to be?

Furthermore we all know that there is a very important seasonal pattern in mail volume. How do we forecast the mail volume pattern and also, the corollary question, what are the best strategies for allocating productive resources for a given forecast? Taking an even longer term viewpoint, what are the factors in our society that control the need for postal service in the future? How do we forecast the longer term needs for facilities and for systems appropriate to possibly much larger loads in the future?

The questions are similar for all kinds of systems. There are short-range, medium-range, and long-range variations in the demand for products and services of all kinds. In order to predict system performance we must forecast demand as an input.

Predicting System Performance

We can view our problem of predicting system performance (including the performance of the preceding forecasting models) in the context of any productive process as indicated in Figure III-2. In Figure III-2 we have input, process or transformation, and output in the general format of systems theory. Figure III-2 simply says that given an input to a process, that input will be transformed in some way to produce an output.

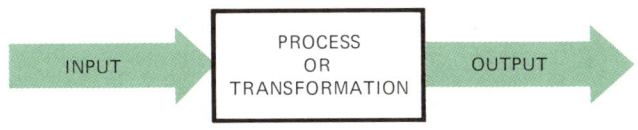

FIGURE III-2. **Input-transformation-output module as a basis for predictive models.**

First, let us take a physical process such as steel making with an electric furnace. As shown in Figure III-3 (a), the inputs are basically iron ore, coke, limestone, and labor, and the output is steel. Between input and output there was a transformation process that we have simply called an electric furnace. We could replace "electric furnace" with a transformation function in order to compute output for given inputs. Suppose we are interested in output *quantity*. The transformation function would then be a simple mathematical statement of the tons of steel output for given quantities of the inputs. The mathematical transformation is a predictive model for output, given stated inputs. Now suppose you are a metallurgist. Your interest is in the transformation for certain qualities of steel alloys. In this case, the metallurgist's transformation function is in terms of the recipe and timing necessary to obtain the output of a specific alloy, rather than the quantity of output. His predictive model has a different purpose and is expressed in different units, but it is still a model that indicates how a system works.

Now let us expand our thinking to include a more highly aggregated system. The system is now an economic enterprise with inputs of consumer demand,

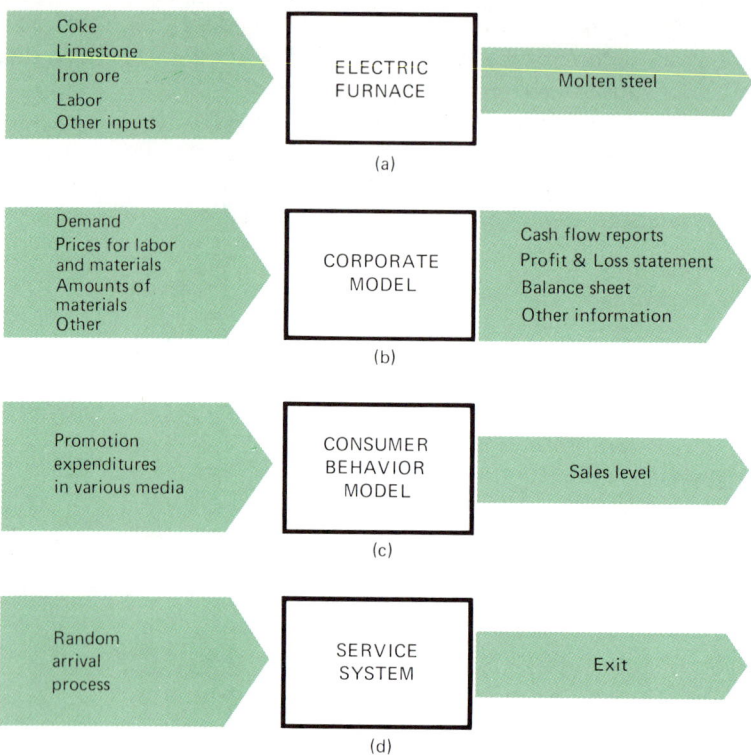

FIGURE III-3. **Input-transformation-output modules. In each case a predictive model can be substituted for the actual process or transformation to predict the outputs or outcomes**

labor, materials, and other costs, and the outputs are predictions of cash flow, profit and loss, balance sheet, and other information of interest. The transformation of input to output is accomplished by the enterprise itself, but we will substitute a model for the enterprise, which gives the equivalent transformations. We show the corporate model as a predictive model in Figure III-3 (b). Such corporate models are now in common use in industry and some service and government operations as mechanisms for predicting performance, given stated inputs. Managers can use such models to test the effects of possible changes in demand, prices, wages, market structures, new equipment, and so on.

Obviously now, we can see that predictive models can be of any type. In Figure III-3 (c), we show a model of consumer behavior, which might be developed to indicate the effect on sales of expenditures for promotion in various media. In Figure III-3 (d), we show a service system model in which people arrive at the service window of a bank or post office, probably randomly. Since the time for service is itself variable, depending on many factors, there may be some interacting effects on the size of the waiting line and waiting time that will result.

The predictive models that we will discuss in Part III are designed as the mechanisms for predicting the outcomes of alternative courses of action. These courses of action may be generated in some systematic way that attempts to exhaust a range of possibilities, or they may be hypotheses for what a manager thinks could be good strategies. In any case, the outcomes of the predictive model must still be evaluated according to the general methods of Part II.

Plan for Part III

We will begin in Chapter 5 with a survey of the models that can be used to forecast, or predict, the future status of the environment. These models play an important role as an input to other predictive models. Chapter 6 then discusses the general concepts of mathematical model building as applied to models for predicting system performance. Many of these concepts are illustrated by the corporate simulation models that are also described in the chapter.

Chapters 7 through 9 deal with *dynamic* predictive models, which analyze the behavior of a system over time. These models also include relationships among the important elements that can only be described in terms of probabilistic statements. The Markov chain models of Chapter 7 describe how elements of a system move from one state, or condition, to another over time. In an important application of Markov chains, changes in the brand loyalty of consumers of a particular product are predicted over time. Chapters 8 and 9 deal with systems characterized by the formation of waiting lines.

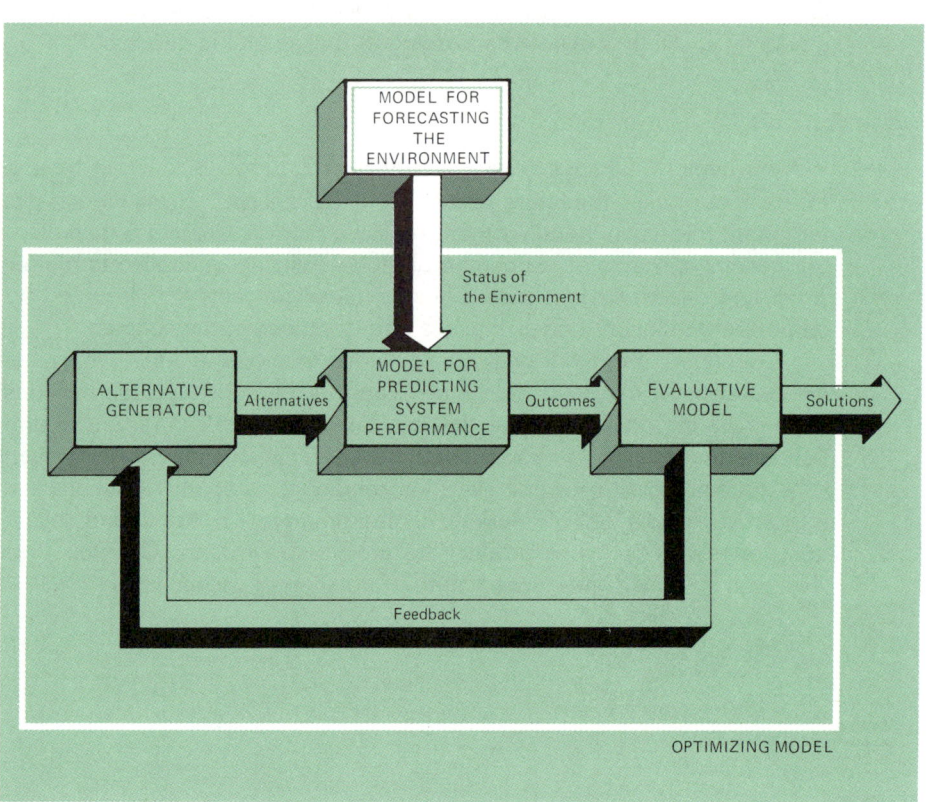

5

FORECASTING THE ENVIRONMENT

As we pointed out in the Part III Introduction, forecasting models are predictive models that drive other predictive models. They fit into the input-transformation-output format. Normally historical data are the input that is transformed by a forecasting model to produce forecasts as the output. The models range from rather simple ones that process historical data through some averaging procedure, to sophisticated models that involve a rigorous framework of theory for the causes of changes in demand. Forecasting models can also be identified in terms of other dimensions such as qualitative versus quantitative, and in terms of the appropriate range or horizon for the forecast.

Uses of Forecasts

While we have already stated that forecasts are generally inputs to models that predict system performance, it may be of value to indicate the range of possible systems. We will not attempt to be exhaustive; rather we will relate uses to the dimension of range or horizon of the forecast.

Shortest Range Suppose we are concerned with the scheduling of personnel (and possibly facilities) in service-oriented situations. We wish to provide the necessary short-term capacity in order to give good service. Capacity may be measured in practical terms such as the number of windows open for service in a post office or a bank, the number of nurses on duty in a hospital, the number of fire units ready to answer emergency calls, the number of ambulance units available to answer calls, or the number of police patrol units cruising. There is clear evidence in all of the kinds of systems just mentioned that the service load varies significantly over the day and that patterns are significant and sometimes stable, but sometimes depend on the day of the week and/or the season of the year. Since wide variation in load may exist from hour to hour and day to day, one of the opportunities available to managers of such systems is to forecast the shortest term demand and to key personnel schedules to the forecasts.

Short Range Forecasts in the range of one week to one month are common as inputs to guide current operations for the control of inventories and to set personnel and facility schedules. In industrial systems, managers need to make plans for production and employment levels for the upcoming period (commonly a month), and for the corollary plans to build or drain seasonal inventories. Such plans have an immediacy because there is often a minimum lead time to change plans and produce at a different level.

In service-oriented systems the one-week to one-month plans can be even more crucial because we cannot store the output of such systems, and therefore managers do not enjoy the flexibility provided by inventories. In such systems, if the capacity is not available when demanded, we may experience lost sales and grumbling over poor service, or possible disastrous effects in emergency situations requiring fire, police, or health services.

Medium Range In the medium term, managers need to be able to anticipate the impact of seasonal variations in demand. A manufacturer can reduce costs substantially by the adroit combination of overtime, seasonal inventories, back ordering policies, and part-time workers, together with seasonal hiring and layoff.

In nonmanufacturing and service systems, forecasts in the medium term can provide managers with the bases for planning employment levels. These plans can perhaps take advantage of natural turnover during seasonal lulls and use overtime, part-time, and new hires to meet peak seasonal demands.

Long Range In the longer term, managers need to make plans for new products and services, and for changes in product and service mix, locations, and facilities, as well as for financing to provide the needed future capacity. While looking far into the future is difficult and often unreliable, it must be done. Such forecasts, real or implied, must be made. Though the techniques are somewhat closer to "crystal ball gazing" than the more quantitative models we shall discuss, they are at a minimum conscious, systematic ways of scanning the future.

Forecasting Models and Uses The preceding survey of the managerial uses of forecasts indicates a rather wide range and implies that substantially different models may be involved. While we did not identify these uses as predictive models, this is exactly what they are. The manager is always using some rationale for the kinds of plans discussed. Our entire thrust will be to analyze and organize the rationale into as rigorous a model as is possible.

Figure 5-1 summarizes the uses in relation to the time spans, indicating the general kinds of forecasting methodologies that have been found useful and appropriate. In general, special studies to determine hourly and/or daily load distributions are appropriate for the shortest range, with continued sampling to be sure that the system is stable. Moving averages, exponential smoothing, and adaptive smoothing are appropriate in the short range and the causal methods for the short and medium range.

For the longer range, we are forced to use somewhat more qualitative methods such as the Delphi method, market surveys, and historical analogy and life-cycle analysis. *Technological forecasting* is a term used in connection with the longest term predictions, and the Delphi technique is the methodology often used as a vehicle. The objective of the Delphi technique is to probe into the future in the hope of anticipating new products and processes in the rapidly changing environment of today's culture and economy. Market surveys and the analysis of consumer behavior involve the use of questionnaires, consumer panels, and tests of new products and services in various kinds of surveys. Historical analogy and life-cycle analysis scan the performance of an ancestor of the product or service under consideration, applying an analysis of the S-curve. The S-curve traces demand for an ancestor product in the initial phases of development, accelerating in the middle-growth period, and culminating in market saturation. Comparisons are made, providing guidelines for future products.

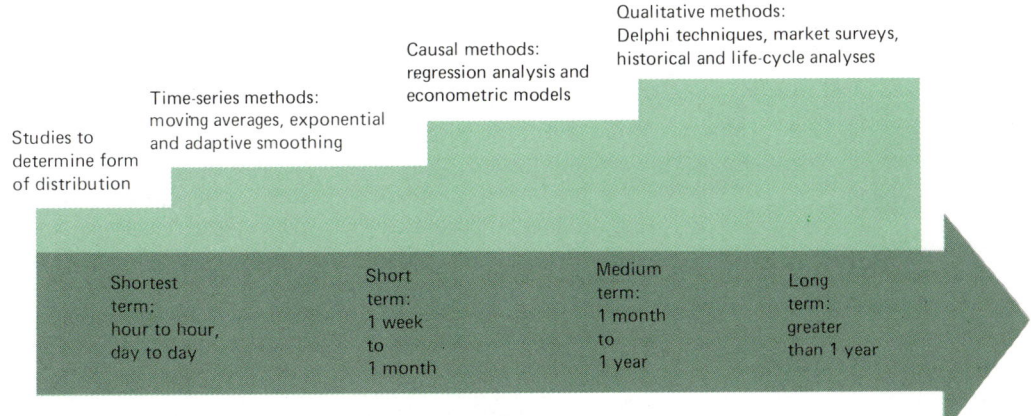

FIGURE 5-1. **General applicability of forecasting methods to the intended range or horizon of the forecast**

Comparative Costs The various forecasting methodologies are not all equally expensive to install and maintain. In general, the shorter range time-series analyses such as moving averages and exponential forecasting models are relatively inexpensive to install and maintain. They are appropriate for item inventories, for example, and can be computerized to handle a large number of different items efficiently. On the other hand, the causal methods require a great deal of statistical analysis to establish relationships, and these special studies can easily cost in the range of $5,000 to $10,000. The increased costs must be justified by the value of higher quality forecasts. In general, the shorter range time-series methods are most useful for lower valued items, while the causal methods may justify their costs when applied to higher valued items. The longer range qualitative methods are relatively expensive, costing in the range of $1,000 to $5,000 per item forecast [Chambers, Mullick, and Smith, 1971].

Components of Demand

We can break down the components of demand changes into a few situations and use them to characterize the combinations of components we may encounter. The components are average demand, random variation around the average, trends in the average, seasonal variations, and cyclic variations. Longer term cyclic variations dealing with the concept of the business cycle are beyond our scope.

We shall use a five-year record of demand for three hypothetical products or services as a basis for discussion. These three demand patterns typify the components of demand for a large number of actual products and services.

1. Figure 5-2 shows the record for product A, an item whose demand is affected by a large number of factors. The result is that there seems to be no dominant pattern other than considerable variation around the average of 102.33 units per month (standard deviation, 23.99 units). The maximum demand during the five-year period was 158 units in October of 1974, and the minimum was 42 units in January of 1975.
2. Figure 5-3 shows the five-year record for product B, and is typical of an item that is enjoying modest but steady growth throughout its five-year record. The average demand for the entire five years is 548 units and the average for 1977 was 654 units, but given the month-to-month variation, neither of these averages seems of much value for projecting into 1978.
3. Figure 5-4 shows product C. At first glance, product C may seem to be characterized by the random variation similar to product A; however, if one examines the timing of the peaks and valleys there appears to be seasonal variation with a summer peak, followed immediately by a seasonal low in the early fall. The average demand for the five years is 104 units; however, the seasonal cycle is the most intriguing component of demand for product C.

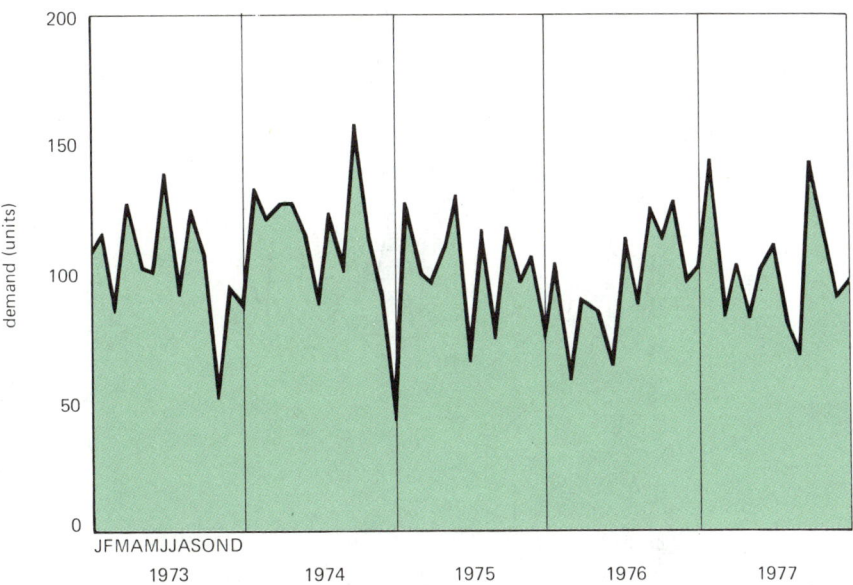

FIGURE 5-2. **Monthly demand for product A**

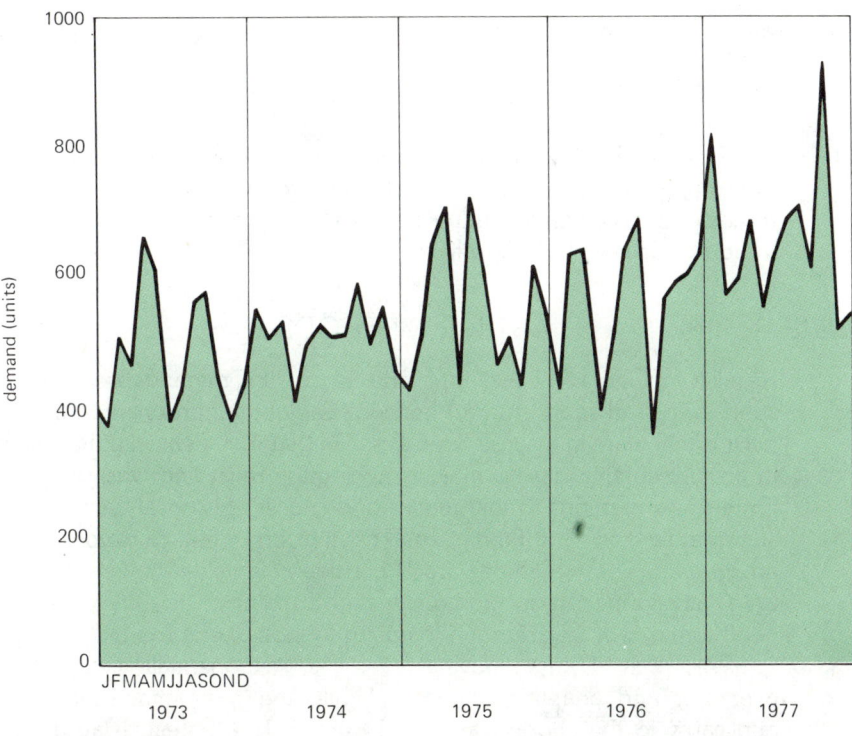

FIGURE 5-3. **Monthly demand for product B**

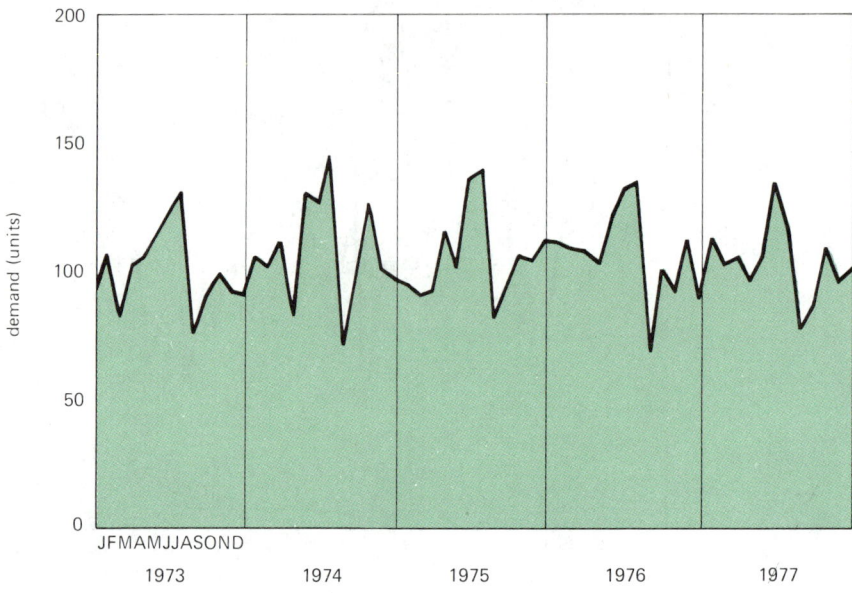

FIGURE 5-4. **Monthly demand for product C**

Through the time-series forecasting methods, we shall look more closely at the components of demand illustrated by products A, B, and C. In general, all three exhibit a certain amount of random variation, but products B and C exhibit trend and seasonality respectively.

TIME-SERIES FORECASTING METHODS

Recall from Figure 5-1 that time-series forecasting methods are applicable to the short-term (and shortest term) horizon. They are appropriate to the short term because they are in a sense "mindless" in that they deal with the historical data in an indiscriminant way, making no inquiry regarding why variations occur. Time-series methods simply record and process historical data in a consistent statistical fashion. The fundamental driving forces that cause demand changes are ignored. These methods are of considerable value, however, because they are relatively inexpensive to construct and maintain. In addition, they provide good forecasts if we are not attempting to look ahead too far.

We shall discuss moving averages, exponentially weighted moving averages, and adaptive methods. While the basic time-series models are applicable to the shortest term in Figure 5-1, we shall delay discussing the special problems of the shortest term until the end of this section.

Moving Averages

When we look at the actual demand for product A in Figure 5-2, we note wide variation from a possibly large number of chance causes. If in fact the variation from the mean is random, we wish to discount the effects of these causes. The common way of smoothing the effects of random variations in demand is to estimate average demand by some kind of moving average. Table 5-1 gives some sample demand data from Figure 5-2 (product A) for the first few months.

A moving average is simply the average of the n values centered on the month in question. For example, from Table 5-1, the first three months of actual demand are 106, 116, and 85, and the three-month average is $(106 + 116 + 85)/3 = 102.33$. Thus, an estimate of February demand that discounts random variations is 102.33. In moving to the March estimate, we drop the January figure of 106 and add the April figure of 127, and the new moving average centered on March is then $(116 + 85 + 127)/3 = 109.33$. In general, moving averages are centered on the month for which the average is quoted. For example, a five-month moving average for March would be the sum of the five demand figures from January through May divided by 5 or $(106 + 116 + 85 + 127 + 102)/5 = 107.20$.

Both Figure 5-2 and Table 5-1 show that actual demand is quite variable. The three-month moving average, however, is much more stable because the demand for any one month receives only one-third weight. Extreme values are discounted, and if they are simply random variations in demand, we are not strongly influenced by them if we gauge demand by the three-month moving average.

Greater smoothing effect is obtained by averaging over a longer period, as is shown by the five-month moving average in Table 5-1. Extreme values are discounted even more since each period's demand carries only a one-fifth weight in the moving average. Figure 5-5 shows the three- and five-month moving averages plotted in comparison with actual demand for product A. Note

TABLE 5-1 **Actual Demand for Product A and Three- and Five-Month Moving Averages**

Date (1973)	Actual Demand	Three-Month Moving Average	Five-Month Moving Average
Jan.	106	---	---
Feb.	116	102.33	---
Mar.	85	109.33	107.20
Apr.	127	104.67	105.80
May	102	109.33	110.40
June	99	113.33	111.40
July	139	109.33	111.00
Aug.	90	118.00	---
Sept.	125	---	---

the smoothing effects and the way in which the moving average lines reveal the most current average demand.

The five-month moving average discounts random variation more effectively; note that in the peaks and valleys of the two moving averages, the five-month line responds less to the extreme values. On the other hand, the three-month moving average gives more weight to the most recent data, and if demand were changing fundamentally it would track these changes more rapidly. In forecasting with moving averages, one extrapolates the last average into the future to obtain the forecast. Methodology is also available that can take account of trend and seasonal factors.

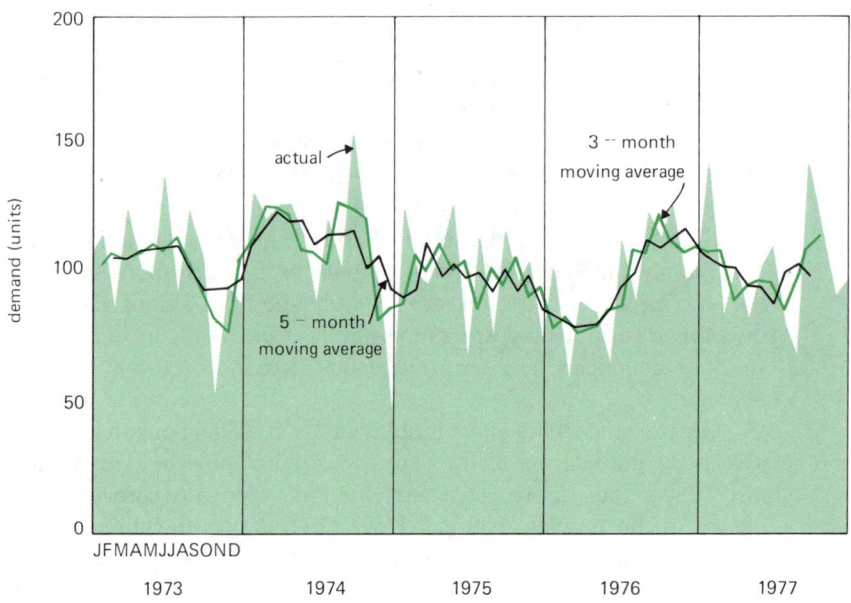

FIGURE 5-5. **Actual demand and three- and five-month moving averages for product A**

Exponentially Weighted Moving Averages

When demand is actually changing rather than reflecting only random variations, we have a keen interest in emphasizing the most current data in a moving average. One effective and convenient method for accomplishing differential weighting and smoothing is the use of exponentially weighted moving averages. The simplest exponential smoothing model estimates average smoothed demand for the current period $\bar{F}_t$ by adding or subtracting a fraction α of the difference between actual current demand D_t and the last smoothed average

$\bar{F}_{t-1}$. The new smoothed average $\bar{F}_t$ is then

new smoothed average = old smoothed average
+ α (new demand − old smoothed average),

or stated symbolically.

$$\bar{F}_t = \bar{F}_{t-1} + \alpha(D_t - \bar{F}_{t-1}). \qquad (1)$$

The smoothing constant α is between 0 and 1 with commonly used values of 0.01 to 0.30. Equation (1) can be rearranged in a more convenient and possibly more understandable form as follows:

new smoothed average = α (new demand)
+ (1 − α) (old smoothed average),

or stated symbolically,

$$\bar{F}_t = \alpha D_t + (1 - \alpha)\bar{F}_{t-1}. \qquad (2)$$

If $\alpha = 0.10$, then equation (2) says that the smoothed average in the current period $\bar{F}_t$ will be determined by adding 10 percent of the new actual demand information D_t and 90 percent of the last smoothed average $\bar{F}_{t-1}$. For example, if $\alpha = 0.10$, $D_t = 106$, and $\bar{F}_{t-1} = 100$, then the new smoothed average is

$$\bar{F}_t = 0.1 \times 106 + 0.9 \times 100 = 10.6 + 90 = 100.6$$

Since the new demand figure D_t includes possible random variations, we are discounting 90 percent of those variations. Obviously then, small values of α will have a stronger smoothing effect than large values. Conversely, large values of α will react more quickly to real changes (as well as random variations) in actual demand. As an example, if $\alpha = 0.4$ and the previous data remain the same, the new smoothed average would be

$$\bar{F}_t = 0.4 \times 106 + 0.6 \times 100 = 42.4 + 60 = 102.4.$$

Note that the components of current actual demand and the old average are now weighted quite differently, giving considerably more weight to current actual demand. The choice of α is normally guided by judgment, though studies could produce economically best or near best values.

Equation (2) actually gives weight to all past actual demand data, though this is not obvious. This weighting occurs through the chain of periodic calculations to produce smoothed averages for each period. In equation (2), for example, the term $\bar{F}_{t-1}$ was computed from

$$\bar{F}_{t-1} = \alpha D_{t-1} + (1 - \alpha)\bar{F}_{t-2},$$

which includes the previous actual demand D_{t-1}. The $\bar{F}_{t-2}$ term was calculated in a similar way, which included D_{t-2}, and so on back to the beginning of the series. Therefore, the smoothed averages are based on a sequential process representing all previous actual demands.

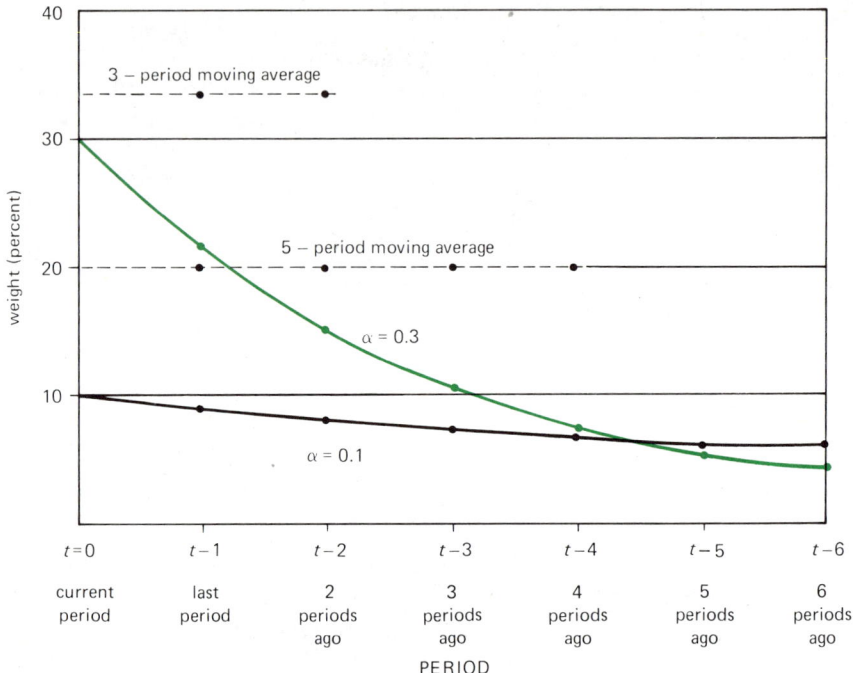

FIGURE 5-6. **Comparative weightings given past data by three- and five-period moving averages and by exponentially weighted moving averages with $\alpha = 0.1$ and 0.3**

Figure 5-6 shows comparative weightings given data by three- and five-period moving averages and by exponentially weighted moving averages with $\alpha = 0.1$ and 0.3. Note the effectiveness of the exponentially weighted averages in placing heavier weight on the most recent data.

Another factor implicit in Figure 5-6 is that exponentially weighted data give a weight to all prior data, though the effect of the old data will be small. Simple moving averages give weight only to the periods included in the average.

It is important to place the time periods for $\bar{F}_t$, D_t, and $\bar{F}_{t-1}$ in perspective and to recognize that the so-called new smoothed average $\bar{F}_t$ is not an extrapolation beyond known demand data. Rather, it is the most current smoothed average. It is not a forecast but a statement of current demand.

Extrapolation and Forecast Since no trend or seasonality is expected in the model of equation (2), direct extrapolation from $\bar{F}_t$ to infer a forecast is justified. Therefore, the forecast for upcoming period D^*_{t+1} is taken directly as the computed value of $\bar{F}_t$. (Starred symbols [D^*] represent extrapolated or forecast values.) Table 5-2 shows the computations and forecasts for the first few months of the data for product A, when $\alpha = 0.10$.

TABLE 5-2 Sample Computations for $\bar{F}_t$ and the Forecast D^*_{t+1} for the Simple Exponential Smoothing Model ($\alpha = 0.1$)

Date (1973)	Actuals†	Smoothed Average ($\bar{F}_t$)	Forecast (D^*_{t+1})
Initial	---	100	---
Jan.	106	100.600	---
Feb.	116	102.140	100.600
Mar.	85	100.426	102.140
Apr.	127	103.083	100.426
May	102	102.975	103.083
June	99	102.578	102.975
July	---	---	102.578

†Data from Table 5-1.

Frequently, a forecast is needed for more than one period in advance. Using equation (2) as a model, one simply extrapolates further into the future. For example, in January $\bar{F}_t = 100.6$ and the forecast for February is also $D^*_{t+1} = 100.6$ from Table 5-2. If we were to forecast for July based only on the information available in January, $D^*_{t+6} = 100.6$, the same forecast as for February. We must point out, however, that the accuracy of such forecasts declines rapidly as the forecasting range increases.

Trend and Seasonal Adjustments

If there were a trend present in the data, equation (2) would respond to it, but with a lag. But, the apparent trend each period is simply the difference between the last two smoothed averages $\bar{F}_t - \bar{F}_{t-1}$. This difference represents another series that can be smoothed by exponentially weighted averages, just as with average demand. The expected demand for the current period including the trend adjustment is then the smoothed average $\bar{F}_t$ computed in equation (2) plus a fraction of the new average trend adjustment. A forecast is obtained by extrapolating the estimate of current demand by adding the most recent trend adjustment.

Figure 5-7 shows a graph of exponentially smoothed forecasts with and without trend adjustment for the product B data. Note that the two forecasts are similar in form; however, since the actual data have considerable trend in them, the forecast without trend adjustment lags behind and is lower than the forecast with trend adjustment. If the actual data were to stabilize, exhibiting no trend, the two forecasts would tend to converge. (See Brown [1959]; Buffa and Taubert [1972] for computed examples).

The basis for including a seasonal adjustment to an exponentially smoothed forecast model is to develop a *base series* that represents the seasonal cycle. The base series is usually constructed from last year's experience in some way. If the seasonal pattern is strong and relatively invariant, then the base series could simply be the period-by-period demand for last year, or an idealized cycle. If the peaks and valleys shift forward or backward slightly from year to year, then an averaging process may be used. For example, a three-month moving average could be used, centered on the month for which the average is being determined as in Table 5-1. The general methods used are similar to the trend model, though there is more complexity because of the seasonal component.

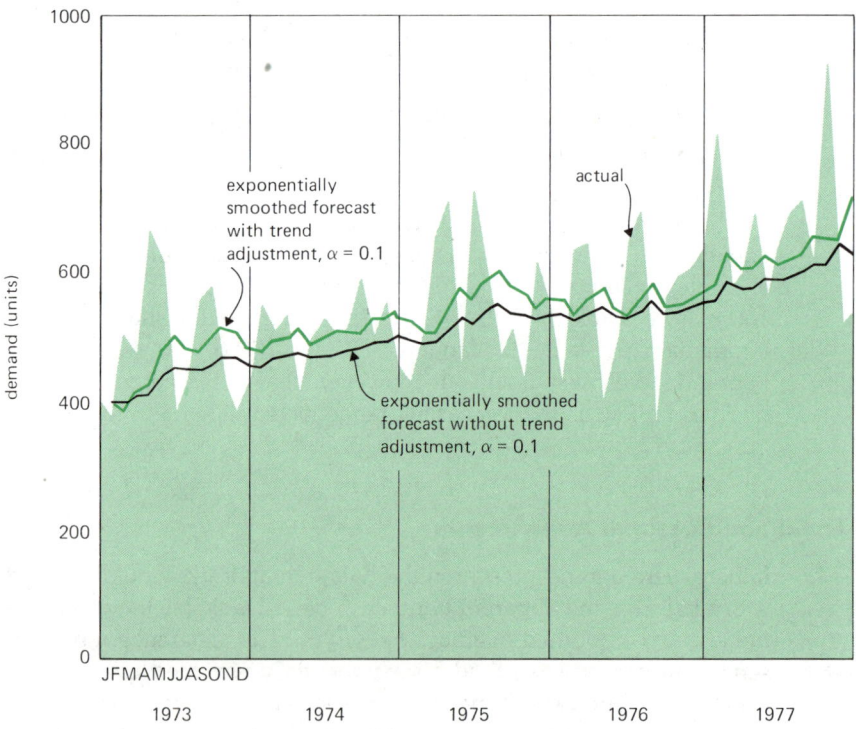

FIGURE 5-7. **Forecasts for product B using exponential smoothing models with and without trend adjustments**

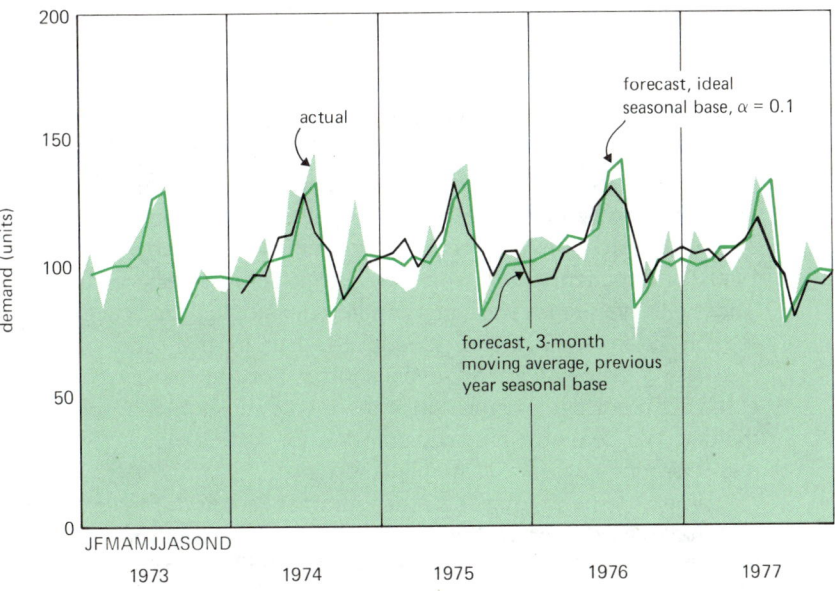

FIGURE 5-8. **Forecasts for product C using exponential smoothing models with trend and seasonal adjustments**

Figure 5-8 shows an exponentially smoothed forecast with trend and seasonal adjustments for product C. Two different base series were used in computing the forecasts in Figure 5-8. One used the ideal seasonal series from which the data were generated originally, and the other used the previous year's three-month moving average.

A common practical measure of the forecast accuracy is the Mean Absolute Deviation (MAD). MAD is simply the sum of the absolute deviations between actual demand and forecasts, divided by the number of observations. The MAD measure for the forecast using the ideal base series was 8.69 and for the three-month moving average base series it was 12.25.

Modifications for the Shortest Term

In general, the time-series methods discussed also apply to the shortest term. The forecasting horizon can be as short as desired; however, the limitation is that we must have an information system that can react and provide a useful forecast within the shortest time frame defined. In most instances, the time and cost to gather the data for current actual demand, D_t, will place a lower limit on the forecasting period. If there is a need to have demand forecasts for an even shorter time period than can be justified for the basic forecasting system, then

CHAPTER 5 FORECASTING THE ENVIRONMENT

special studies can be made of the distribution of weekly demand by days of the week, or daily demand by hours of the day. The assumption is then made that for each forecast, the proportionate distribution applies in the shorter time frame. Periodic monitoring of the distribution to ensure that the system remains stable is then required.

Service systems are the typical situations in which the shortest term of the forecasts may be monthly, weekly, or daily, but distributions of that forecast on an even shorter term are needed. For example, in a study of a University Health Service Outpatient Clinic, there was considerable daily variation of demand. These daily variations were important in developing predictive models involving the physician staffing and scheduling. But in this kind of service system, forecasting demand for an even shorter horizon was important in order to construct predictive models, since there was substantial hourly variation within the day. We deal with predictive models for service type systems in Chapters 8 and 9 on queuing and waiting line systems.

When demand data can be summarized and forecasts made entirely automatically, the forecasting period can be extremely short. That was the case in a system installed in the business office of Bell, Canada [Church, 1973]. The office manager had to schedule enough service representatives to take calls throughout the day in order to give good service to calling customers. The office also was responsible for other activities such as arranging for telephone installations, investigating annoyance calls, and collecting accounts. The basic problem was to develop a predictive model for allocation and scheduling of effort between the two kinds of activities in such a way that good customer service was given and the other work was also accomplished.

In order to forecast the call load, an exponential smoothing system was developed that forecasted daily load, treating daily variations through the week as the equivalent of seasonal variations. The base series was taken from the previous week and the general technique of exponential smoothing with trend and seasonal adjustments discussed previously was used. The forecast was then made for the following day, projecting call load for each half hour.

CAUSAL FORECASTING METHODS

When we have enough historical data and experience, it may be possible to relate forecasts to the factors in the environment that *cause* the trends, seasonals, and fluctuations. Thus, if we can *measure* the causal factors and have determined their *relationships* to the product or service of interest, we may be able to compute forecasts of considerable accuracy.

The factors that enter causal models are of every conceivable type: gross national product, disposable income, new marriages, housing starts, inventories, cost-of-living indexes, as well as predictions of dynamic factors and disturbances such as strikes, actions of competitors, sales promotion campaigns, and so on. The causal forecasting model expresses mathematical relationships between the causal factors and the demand for the item being forecast, and is indeed a most sophisticated forecasting tool. As indicated in Figure 5-1, there are two general types of causal models, regression and econometric, and the costs range from medium to high for installation and operation.

Regression Analysis

Forecasting based on regression methods establishes a forecasting function called a regression equation. The regression equation expresses the series to be forecast, such as dollar sales or quantities sold, in terms of other series that presumably control or cause the sales to increase or decrease. The rationale can be general or specific. For example, in furniture sales we might postulate that sales are in general related to disposable personal income — if disposable income is up, sales will increase, and if people have less money to spend, sales will be down. Establishing the empirical relationship is accomplished through the regression equation. To take more specific factors, we might postulate that furniture sales are controlled to some extent by the number of new marriages and/or the number of new housing starts. These are both specific indicators of possible demand for furniture. For a review of simple regression and correlation, see Appendix B.

Table 5-3 gives data on these three independent variables — housing starts, disposable income, and new marriages — and on sales of a hypothetical furniture company, the Cherryoak Company. We can build a relationship between the observed variables and company sales, where the volume of sales is dependent on or caused by the observed variables. Therefore sales is termed the dependent variable and the observed variables are called the independent variables. The correlation coefficients between sales (S) and each of the independent variables are:

1. disposable personal income (I)   0.805
2. housing starts (H)   0.435
3. new marriages (M)   0.416

Since disposable income (I) correlates most strongly with company sales, let us start with it as an example. Using regression analysis, we can determine the straight line that best fits the data expressing the relationship between sales (S) and disposable income (I). From statistics, we know that the regression equation represents a straight line that minimizes the square of the deviations from it and sets the sum of the simple deviations to zero. The regression equation for the data of company sales (S) versus disposable income (I) is

$$S = 72.5 + 0.23I, \qquad (3)$$

where the constant, 72.5, is the y-axis intercept and the slope of the straight line is 0.23. Note that the form of the equation is in the standard format of the equation of a straight line, $y = a + bx$, where y is the dependent variable, x the independent variable, a the y intercept, and b the slope. In regression analysis, a and b are termed the regression coefficients and are estimates of the parameters that specify the equation.

TABLE 5-3. **Data Used in Performing Regression Analysis to Forecast 1971 Sales of Cherryoak Company**

Year	Housing Starts (H) (thousands)	Disposable Personal Income (I) ($ billions)	New Marriages (M) (thousands)	Company Sales (S) ($ millions)	Time (T)
1947	744	158.9	2,291	92.920	1
1948	942	169.5	1,991	122.440	2
1949	1,033	188.3	1,811	125.570	3
1950	1,138	187.2	1,580	110.460	4
1951	1,549	205.8	1,667	139.400	5
1952	1,211	224.9	1,595	154.020	6
1953	1,251	235.0	1,539	157.590	7
1954	1,225	247.9	1,546	152.230	8
1955	1,354	254.4	1,490	139.130	9
1956	1,475	274.4	1,531	156.330	10
1957	1,240	292.9	1,585	140.470	11
1958	1,157	308.5	1,518	128.240	12
1959	1,341	318.8	1,451	117.450	13
1960	1,531	337.7	1,494	132.640	14
1961	1,274	350.0	1,527	126.160	15
1962	1,327	364.4	1,547	116.990	16
1963	1,469	385.3	1,580	123.900	17
1964	1,615	404.6	1,654	141.320	18
1965	1,538	436.6	1,719	156.710	19
1966	1,488	469.1	1,789	171.930	20
1967	1,173	505.3	1,844	184.790	21
1968	1,299	546.3	1,913	202.700	22
1969	1,524	590.0	2,059	237.340	23
1970	1,479	629.6	2,132	254.930	24

Note: Company sales and disposable per capita income have been adjusted for the effect of inflation and appear in constant 1959 dollars.
Source: G. G. C. Parker and E. L. Segura, "How to Get a Better Forecast," *Harvard Business Review*, March–April, 1971; used by permission. Data from Statistical Abstract of the United States (Washington, Bureau of the Census).

The regression line is plotted in Figure 5-9, showing some specific points for selected years. These points illustrate the kinds of forecast errors that would have resulted if one had used this equation to forecast Cherryoak furniture sales. To use the regression equation to forecast sales, one simply inserts the value of I and computes sales S. For example, if $I = 700$, then the forecaster could compute the value of S as $S = 72.5 + 0.23 \times 700 = \$233.5$ (million).

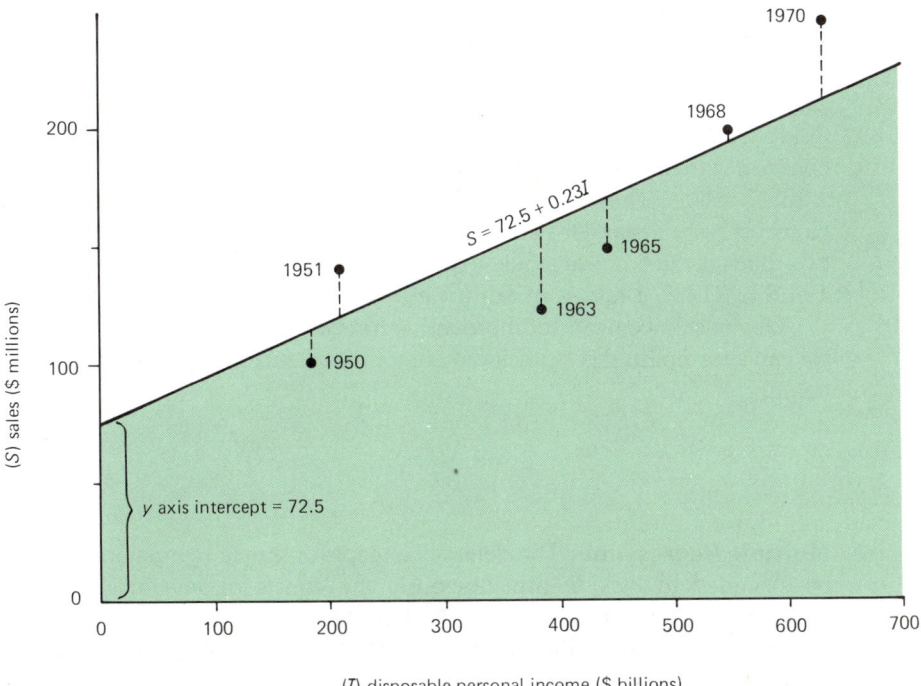

FIGURE 5-9. **Simple regression line for sales dependent on disposable income (data from Table 5-3)**

Reliability of Forecast There are a number of statistical tests that can be performed to help determine how reliable the regression equation is as a forecasting device. Data resulting from these statistical tests are commonly generated automatically in standard regression analysis computer programs. Our interest is particularly in the coefficient of determination and the standard error of estimate. In addition, there are important statistical tests concerning the significance of the regression coefficients, but these tests are beyond our scope.

The coefficient of determination is simply r^2, the correlation coefficient squared. For our example, $r^2 = (0.805)^2 = 0.65$. The coefficient of determination states the proportion of the variation in the dependent variable of the regression equation that is associated with the independent variable. For our equation then, 65 percent of the variation in sales is controlled by variation in I, and 35 percent is unexplained. Thus, we can expect large forecast errors if we use equation (3). Apparently, other variables account for a substantial fraction of the changes in S that actually occur.

The standard error of estimate indicates the expected range of variation from the regression line of any forecast made. For example, the standard error of estimate for our data and equation (3) is 38.7. Since we assume a normal distribution of sales for each value of I, this means that we can expect with some confidence that two-thirds of the time our estimate of S will be in the range of $\pm\$38.7$ million. Therefore, if $I = 700$, then $S = 233.5$ as computed previously. However, with a standard error of estimate of 38.7, we are actually stating that two-thirds of the time we would expect the actual value of S to be in the range of 194.8 to 272.2, a rather broad range.

Obviously, we need to improve the forecasting ability of equation (3), and we can accomplish this by including other causal factors in the regression equation.

Multiple Regression The general concepts of simple regression analysis can be extended to include simultaneously the effects of several causal factors through multiple regression analysis. For the data of Table 5-3, Parker and Segura [1971] have developed a multiple regression equation based on disposable income, time trend, gross sales lagged one year, and new housing starts lagged one year. The resulting forecasting accuracy was indicated by an $r^2 = 0.95$ and a standard error of estimate of 9.7.

A considerable historical record is necessary for regression analysis to have validity. As rules of thumb, a five-year record is needed for one independent variable, eight years for two independent variables, and a longer history for three or more independent variables [Parker and Segura, 1971]. These data requirements are often severe limitations to application.

In addition, there are important assumptions made in regression analysis that should be met. The nature and importance of these assumptions is covered in greater detail in Benton [1972], Huang [1970], and Wheelwright and Makridakis [1977]. Obviously, considerable knowledge of statistical methods is required for the appropriate application of regression analysis.

Beyond possibly ignoring one or more of the important assumptions, one of the great dangers in misapplying regression analysis is in assuming that a good fit to historical data guarantees that the regression equation will be a good forecasting device. The regression equation itself should be an expression of a good causal theory relating the factors in the regression model. In addition, we also need an understanding of the potential importance of factors that are not included in the model.

One of the differences then between time-series forecasting models and causal methods is that time series accept increases or decreases in demand in an unbiased way, not questioning the reasons for the increase or decrease. On the other hand, causal methods demand an explanation within the rationale of the forecasting system for demand changes that occur.

Econometric Forecasting Methods

In simplest terms, econometric forecasting methods are an extension of regression equations. If, for example, in the multiple regression equation we attempted to include the effect of price and advertising, then we see the possibility of an interdependence, where our own sales can have an effect on these factors as well as vice versa.

For example, assume that sales is a function of GNP, price, and advertising. In regression terms, we would assume that all three independent variables are exogenous to the system and thus are not influenced by the level of sales itself or by one another. This is a fair assumption as far as GNP is concerned. If, however, we consider price and advertising, the same assumption may not be valid. For example, if the per unit cost is of some quadratic form, a different level of sales will result in a different level of cost. Furthermore, advertising expenditures will certainly influence the price of the product, since production and selling costs influence the per unit price. The price, in turn, is influenced by the magnitude of sales, which can also influence the level of advertising. As can be seen, all four of the variables in our equation are interdependent.

When this interdependence is at all strong, regression analysis cannot be used. If we want to be accurate, we must express this sales relationship by developing a system of four simultaneous equations that can deal with the interdependence directly.

Thus, in econometric form we have

```
sales            = f (GNP, price, advertising),
cost             = f (production and inventory levels),
selling expenses = f (advertising, and other selling expenses),
price            = f (cost + selling expenses);
```

that is, instead of one relationship, we now have four. As in regression analysis, we must 1) determine the functional form of each of the equations, 2) estimate in a simultaneous manner the values of their parameters, and 3) test for the statistical significance of the results and the validity of the assumptions [Wheelwright and Makridakis, 1977].

Thus far, econometric models have been used largely in connection with relatively mature products where a considerable historical record is available and in industry and broad economic forecasts. For example, the Corning Glass Works developed econometric models to forecast TV tube sales [Chambers, Mullick, and Smith, 1971]. These models were used to forecast sales six months to two years in the future to help spot turning points far enough in advance to assist in making decisions for production and employment planning.

Industry econometric models have been developed to forecast activity in the forest products industry. Also, the economic forecasting models developed at the Wharton School are econometric models.

SELECTION OF AN APPROPRIATE FORECASTING MODEL

Autocorrelation is an important concept in determining the nature of the raw demand data and the kind of forecasting model that might be appropriate. Autocorrelation measures the degree to which demands in different time periods are correlated. For example, a strong trend in demand data would result in a high correlation between demands in different time periods. Also, a strong seasonal pattern would produce intercorrelation between demands in periods 1, 13, 25; 2, 14, 26; 3, 15, 27, and so on. Analyses of autocorrelation coefficients are therefore used to determine the best type of forecasting model to use.

Box and Jenkins [1970] have developed a highly sophisticated forecasting methodology in which a general class of forecasting methods is postulated for a particular situation. In stage 1, a specific model is tentatively identified as the forecasting method best suited to that situation. The forecasting models may range from moving averages through exponential and adaptive methods to regression analysis. In stage 2 the postulated model is fit to the available historical data and a check is run to determine whether or not the postulated model is adequate. Various statistical tests are involved, including the presence or absence of autocorrelation. If the postulated model is rejected, stage 2 is used to identify an alternative model, which is then tested. The process is repeated until a model that can be used to make forecasts for future time periods has been identified. Thus, the approach involves a philosophy that makes model selection dependent on a statistical analysis of data, so that the most appropriate specific model is selected. (See Nelson [1973] or Mabert [1975] for accessible discussions of the Box-Jenkins methods.)

An Interactive Forecasting System   Makridakis, Hodgsdon, and Wheelwright [1974] have developed a generalized interactive forecasting system within the framework of the Box-Jenkins philosophy. A flow chart for the system is shown in Figure 5-10; the system is divided into two main segments: SIBYL and RUNNER. After data input, SIBYL allows the user to perform preliminary analyses in order to identify two or three forecasting models as the most likely candidates. The interactive system makes inquiries about the data and the characteristics of the situation, including the following:

1. the time horizon for decision making—immediate term, short term, medium term, and long term
2. the pattern of data—seasonal, horizontal, trend, cyclical, or random
3. the type of model desired—time series, causal, statistical, or nonstatistical
4. the value of the forecast, and thus the costs that can be allocated to obtaining it
5. the accuracy that is required and justified
6. the complexity that can be tolerated
7. the availability of historical data

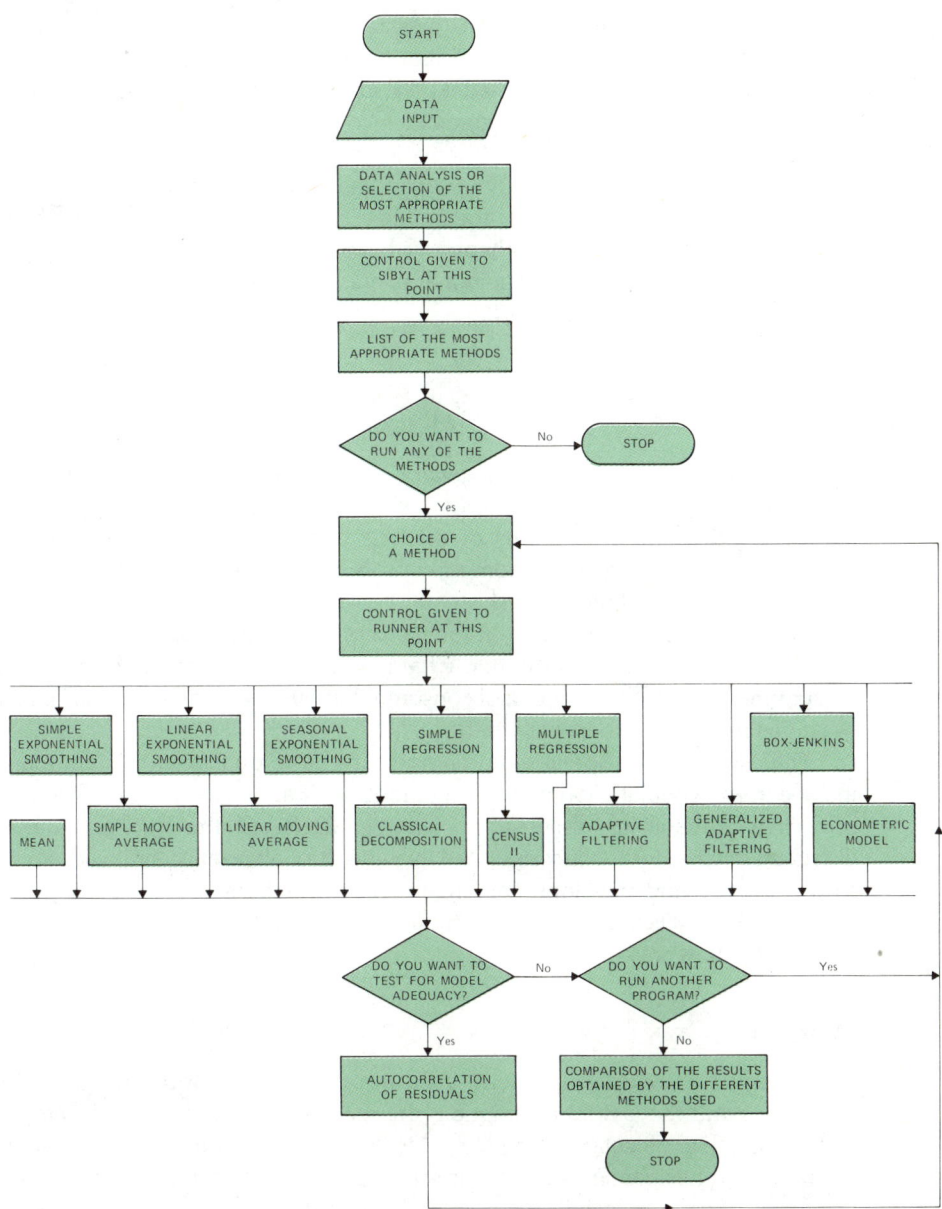

FIGURE 5-10. **Flow chart of an interactive forecasting system**

From S. Makridakis, A. Hodgsdon, and S. C. Wheelwright, "An Interactive Forecasting System"; used by permission; © 1974, The American Statistician. November 1974. Vol. 28, No. 4, pp. 153-158.

CHAPTER 5 FORECASTING THE ENVIRONMENT

Autocorrelations for various time lags are computed and may be graphed. Through a series of queries, the program obtains information on the factors needed to select a forecasting model and supplies the user with a list of three or four that appear to be logical candidates, together with comparative statistics on those methods.

The user can then select any of the candidate methods and have that model used in the RUNNER portion of the system. The models listed in Figure 5-10 include those discussed in this chapter with some variations. Through a system of queries, the user can run additional candidate models with the same data and obtain comparison results.

LONG-TERM FORECASTING METHODS

Some of the most important managerial decisions are made in terms of longer term broader horizons and involve the commitment of resources to future products and services, locations of markets and facilities, and investment in physical facilities. Forecasts become the most crucial element in these kinds of predictive models. Unlike the short- and medium-term forecasting methods discussed previously, there is no historical record of a statistical nature on which to base long-term forecasts. Rather, what people think, samplings of how they react to market tests, knowledge of consumer behavior, and analogy with similar situations may be the best we can do.

Thus, longer term forecasting methods are more qualitative in nature and may be used in conjunction with the methods of Chapters 2 and 3 involving the subjective probabilities discussed in Chapter 2. Recall the POCO example discussed in Chapter 3 concerning the evaluation of alternative strategies for oil shale research and development. Implicit in that example were forecasts of longer term results for alternative strategies tempered by probabilities of the occurrence of events.

Delphi Method

Technological forecasting is a term used in connection with the longest term predictions and the Delphi technique is the methodology often used [Gerstenfeld, 1971]. The objective of the Delphi technique is to probe into the future in the hope of anticipating new products and processes in the rapidly changing environment of today's culture and economy. In the shortest range covered by this technique, it can also be used to estimate market sizes and timing.

The technique draws on a panel of experts in a way that eliminates the possible dominance of the most prestigious, the most verbal, the most persuasive, and so on. The attempt is to gain the benefit of expert opinion in the form of a consensus rather than a compromise. The result is pooled judgment showing the range of expert opinion and the reasons for differences of opinion. The Delphi technique was first developed by the RAND Corporation as a means of eliminating the undesirable effects of group interaction that may occur in conferences and panels where the individuals are in direct communication.

The panel of experts can be constructed in various ways and often includes individuals both inside and outside the organization. It may be true that each panel member is an expert in some aspect of the problem, but no one may be an expert on the entire problem. In general, the procedure involves the following:

1. Each expert in the group makes independent forecasts in the form of brief statements.
2. A coordinator edits and clarifies these statements.
3. The coordinator provides a series of written questions to the experts that combine the responses of the other experts.

One of the most extensive probes into the technological future was reported by TRW, Inc. [North and Pyke, 1969]. The project involved the coordination of 15 different panels corresponding to 15 categories of technologies and systems that were felt to have an effect on the company's future. Anonymity of panel members was maintained to stimulate unconventional thinking. The Delphi method was then used to question and requestion the experts. The result was a composite rating of each event on the basis of its desirability, its feasibility, the probability that the event would occur, and probability estimates of the timing of occurrence.

The extensive results of the project were then formed into logic networks. One such network shown by North and Pyke [1969] shows the milestone events that had to precede the technical achievement of holographic color movies. Holography is an optical projection technique that gives the viewer the illusion of the third dimension. The network also showed events that were likely to occur as "fallout" from the basic developments.

Market Surveys

Market surveys and the analysis of consumer behavior have become quite sophisticated and the resulting data become an extremely valuable input to forecasting market demand. In general, the methods involve the use of questionnaires, consumer panels, and tests of new products and services in various kinds of surveys. The entire field is a specialty in itself and beyond the scope of our discussion.

There is considerable literature dealing with the estimation of new product performance based on consumer panels [Ahl, 1970], analytical approaches [Bass, 1969; Claycamp and Liddy, 1969], and simulation and other techniques [Bass, King, and Pessemier, 1968]. Proposed products and services may be compared with the products and known plans of competitors, and new market segments may be exploited with variations of product designs and quality levels. In such instances, comparisons can be made with data on existing products. These kinds of data are often the best available to refine the designs of products and facilities for new ventures.

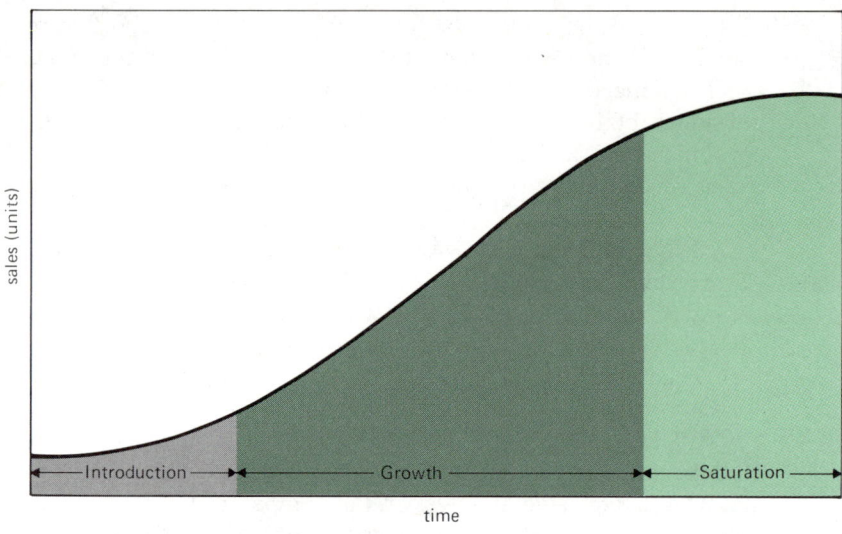

FIGURE 5-11. **Typical *S*-curve of the introduction, growth, and market saturation in the life cycle of a product or service**

TABLE 5-4. **Summary of Forecasting Methods**

Methods	Applications	Data Needs	Relative Cost	Development Time
Moving averages, and exponentially weighted moving averages	Short-range forecasts for operations, inventory control, scheduling, pricing, timing of special promotions	Minimum of a one-year history, two years if seasonals are present	Low	Very short
Regression analysis	Short- and medium-range forecasts for existing products and services; marketing strategies, production and facility planning	Several years history; rules of thumb: five years history for one variable, eight for two variables	Medium	Medium
Econometric models	Same as for regression analysis	Same as for regression analysis	High	Medium
Delphi, market surveys, historical analogy, and life-cycle analysis	Long-range predictions, new products and product development, market strategies, pricing, and facility planning	Variable for different methods; several years history for analogy and life cycle	Medium to high	Medium

134   PART II PREDICTIVE MODELS

Historical Analogy and Life-Cycle Analysis

Market research studies can sometimes be supplemented by reference to the performance of an ancestor of the product or service under consideration, applying an analysis of the S-curve. A typical S-curve is shown in Figure 5-11 where demand in the initial phases of market development accelerates to the middle growth period, culminating in market saturation. Of course, following saturation there may be an actual decline.

For example, the assumption was made that color TV would follow the general sales pattern experienced with black and white TV, but that it would take twice as long to reach a steady state [Chambers, Mullick, and Smith, 1971]. Such comparisons provide guidelines during the initial planning phases and may be supplemented by other kinds of analyses and studies as initial actual demand becomes known.

WHAT SHOULD THE MANAGER KNOW?

The manager's interest in forecasting is significant because forecasts are invariably an input to decisions, and, as we have noted, forecasts drive the predictive models we shall discuss thoughout Part III.

The manager's use of forecasts and the required forecasting methodology can be related to the S-curve shown in Figure 5-11. During the product development phase, which actually preceeds the introductory phase shown in Figure 5-11, the manager is concerned with decisions about the amount of development effort, product designs and their suitability for the market, and strategies for penetrating the proposed markets. He needs long-term forecasting methodologies in order to scan the future, and the only techniques available to him are the Delphi method, historical analysis of comparable products or services, and the various forms of market surveys. The decisions are risky and the manager will be interested in assessing these risks and employing the concepts discussed in Part II.

During the introduction phase of a new product or service, the nature of managerial decisions shifts somewhat because delivery systems must now be developed. Therefore, the decisions focus on marketing strategies, pricing, optimum facility size and location, and distribution systems. Again, however, the manager must rely mainly on nonquantitative forecasting methods involving consumer surveys and market tests, historical analogy and life-cycle analysis, and early warning tracking systems regarding the market. The decisions still involve considerable risk.

During the growth phase of the S-curve, the decisions become more operational and the manager is concerned with facilities expansion coupled with marketing strategy, and with mobilizing production and inventory planning decisions. The causal methods of forecasting can also provide excellent input regarding marketing and pricing decisions.

We have summarized the nature of applications, data needs, costs, and development time for the various forecasting methods in Table 5–4. In general, development time and cost are correlated with forecasting range. It is important for the manager to understand the limitations imposed by data needs for each of the methods. Usually, even the short-term methods require considerable historical data for statistical significance. For example, the moving average methods require a minimum of a one-year history and at least two years if seasonals are present. The causal methods require at least five years of historical data and considerably more if we are attempting to correlate demand with two or more variables. Obviously, the data requirements dictate that causal methods will be most useful in the saturation or steady state phase of the product life cycle.

Check Your Understanding

1. Thinking in terms of the horizon or range of forecast needed, state the requirement for each of the following as shortest, short-, medium-, or long-range:
    a. the decision concerning the size of a new manufacturing plant
    b. the market forecast for TV sales as a basis for 1) allocating promotion funds to alternative media, and 2) scheduling production
    c. the forecast as a basis for controlling component parts inventories for a lawn mower manufacturer
    d. the forecast of call load as a basis for shift scheduling of telephone operators
    e. the decision to make internally or purchase component parts
    f. the forecasts of demand for service at a four-window post office
2. Following is a list of products and services. Based on general knowledge, what components of demand do you think are likely to be found if statistical analyses of data on actual demand were made:
    a. swim suits
    b. automobiles
    c. hula hoops
    d. X-ray service
    e. hospital inpatient census
    f. gross national product (annual)
3. If $\alpha = 0.2$, the last smoothed average is 102, and the current demand is 105, compute the current smoothed average, assuming no trend in the model. How much weight is given the current demand? Based on this model, what forecast would be made for the next period?
4. When the forecasting need is for the very short term, perhaps demand for service on an hourly or half-hourly basis, more aggregate forecasts are often made on a daily or even weekly basis. The aggregate forecast is then

distributed on the shorter term basis following known distributions resulting from special studies. Why not simply make the forecasts on an hourly or half-hourly basis, updating for each short time period?

5. If disposable income was $I = \$590$ billion in 1969, compute the sales forecast for the Cherryoak Company using equation (3). Actual sales in 1969 were $237.34 million. Is the forecast within the standard error of estimate? What is the significance of whether or not the forecast is within the standard error?

6. Explain the significance of the coefficient of determination and the standard error of estimate in judging the overall effectiveness of a regression equation as a forecasting device.

7. Examine Figure 5–9, the regression line for forecasting sales based on disposable income. Explain why it is not simply an extrapolation of existing trends.

8. What are the assumptions and limitations of regression analysis for forecasting?

9. If our regression equation included terms of GNP, new marriages, price, time trend and advertising expenditures, and we found a significant correlation between price and advertising, why would this relationship not actually improve our forecasting equation?

Problems

10. Table 5–5 gives monthly data on the sales of a product for two years.
    a. Compute a three- and a 5-month moving average for the data.
    b. Compute an exponentially weighted moving average using equation (2) for $\alpha = 0.1$ and 0.3.

TABLE 5–5. **Monthly Sales for a Product**

	Jan.	Feb.	Mar.	Apr.	May	June	July	Aug.	Sept.	Oct.	Nov.	Dec.
1976	47	42	16	47	38	34	45	50	47	54	40	43
1977	22	44	42	29	46	45	56	50	39	44	24	46

11. Based on the computations for exercise 10, compute the forecasts that would be made for the months of 1976 using equation (2) for $\alpha = 0.1$ only, and compute the monthly forecast errors. Compute the mean absolute deviation of errors and compare them.

12. Based on the forecasts computed in exercise 11 for the months of 1976, what forecasts for the months of 1977 do you think might be justified, assuming of course that the actuals for 1977 in Table 5–5 did not exist? How many months in advance do you feel justified in forecasting, using equation (2)?

13. The Cherryoak Company discussed in the text was jolted by the economic downturn in 1974, as were many companies. The president of the company reacted badly to the fact that the forecast did not predict the downturn until sales had disintegrated substantially. "Last year I didn't need the forecast. This year I needed it and it was off. What good is it?" Table 5-6 provides data for the years 1971, 1972, 1973, and midyear and year-end estimates for the annual rates for 1974. The multiple regression model developed by Parker and Segura [1971] for the company is

$$S_t = -33.51 + 0.373 S_{t-1} + 0.033 H_{t-1} + 0.672 I - 11.03 T,$$

where S = sales in millions of dollars, H = new housing starts during the year, I = disposable personal income during the year, and T = time trend (T = 1, 2, 3, ..., n). The coefficient of determination is 0.95, and the standard error of estimate is 9.7.

Based on the regression model, what forecasts would have been made based on midyear and year-end estimates of the indicators? How bad is the forecast? Should the president drop the forecasting model?

TABLE 5-6. **Data for Cherryoak Company**

Year	Housing Starts	Disposable Income	Actual Sales
1971	1522	679.4	295.79
1972	1621	705.3	305.24
1973	1320	725.8	320.62
1974 (midyear)*	1024	726.5	291.32
1974 (year-end)	857	701.1	272.21

*Midyear values are annual rates.

References

1. Ahl, D. H., "New Product Forecasting Using Consumer Panels," *Journal of Marketing,* Vol. 7, No. 2, May 1970, pp. 159–67.
2. Bass, F. M., "A New Product Growth Model for Consumer Durables," *Management Science,* Vol. 16, No. 5, January 1969.
3. Bass, F. M., C. W. King, and E. A. Pessemier, *Applications of the Sciences in Marketing Management,* John Wiley & Sons, 1968.
4. Benton, W. K., *Forecasting for Management,* Addison-Wesley, Reading, Mass., 1972.

5. Box, G. E. P., and G. M. Jenkins, *Time Series Analysis, Forecasting,* and *Control,* Holden-Day, San Francisco, 1970.
6. Brown, R. G., *Statistical Forecasting for Inventory Control,* McGraw-Hill, New York, 1959.
7. Buffa, E. S., and W. H. Taubert, *Production-Inventory Systems: Planning and Control,* revised edition, Richard D. Irwin, Inc., Homewood, Ill., 1972.
8. Chambers, J. C., S. K. Mullick, and D. D. Smith, "How to Choose the Right Forecasting Technique," *Harvard Business Review,* July–August 1971.
9. Church, J. G., "SURESTAF: A Computerized Staff Scheduling System for Telephone Business Offices," *Management Science,* Vol. 20, No. 4, December, Part II, 1973, pp. 708-20.
10. Claycamp, H. J., and L. E. Liddy, "Prediction of New Product Performance: An Analytical Approach," *Journal of Marketing Research,* Vol. 6, No. 4, November 1969, pp. 414-21.
11. Gerstenfeld, A., "Technological Forecasting," *Journal of Business,* Vol. 44, No. 1, January 1971, pp. 10-18.
12. Huang, D. S., *Regression and Econometric Methods,* John Wiley & Sons, New York, 1970.
13. Mabert, V. A., "The Box-Jenkins Forecasting Technique," Paper No. 529, Institute for Research in the Behavioral, Economic, and Management Sciences. Purdue University, September 1975.
14. Makridakis, S., A. Hodgsdon, and S. C. Wheelwright, "An Interactive Forecasting System," *The American Statistician,* Vol. 28, No. 4, November 1974, pp. 153-58.
15. Nelson, C. R., *Applied Time Series Analysis for Managerial Forecasting,* Holden-Day, San Francisco, 1973.
16. North, H. Q., and D. L. Pyke, "Probes of the Technological Future," *Harvard Business Review,* May–June, 1969.
17. Parker, G. G. C., and E. L. Segura, "How to Get a Better Forecast," *Harvard Business Review,* March–April, 1971, pp. 99-109.
18. Trigg, D. W., and A. G. Leach, "Exponential Smoothing with an Adaptive Response Rate," *Operational Research Quarterly,* Vol. 18, No. 1, March 1967, pp. 53-59.
19. Wheelwright, S. C., and S. Makridakis, *Forecasting Methods for Management,* John Wiley & Sons, New York, 1973.
20. Whybark, D. C., "A Comparison of Adaptive Forecasting Techniques," *The Logistics and Transportation Review,* Vol. 8, No. 3, 1972, pp. 13-26.

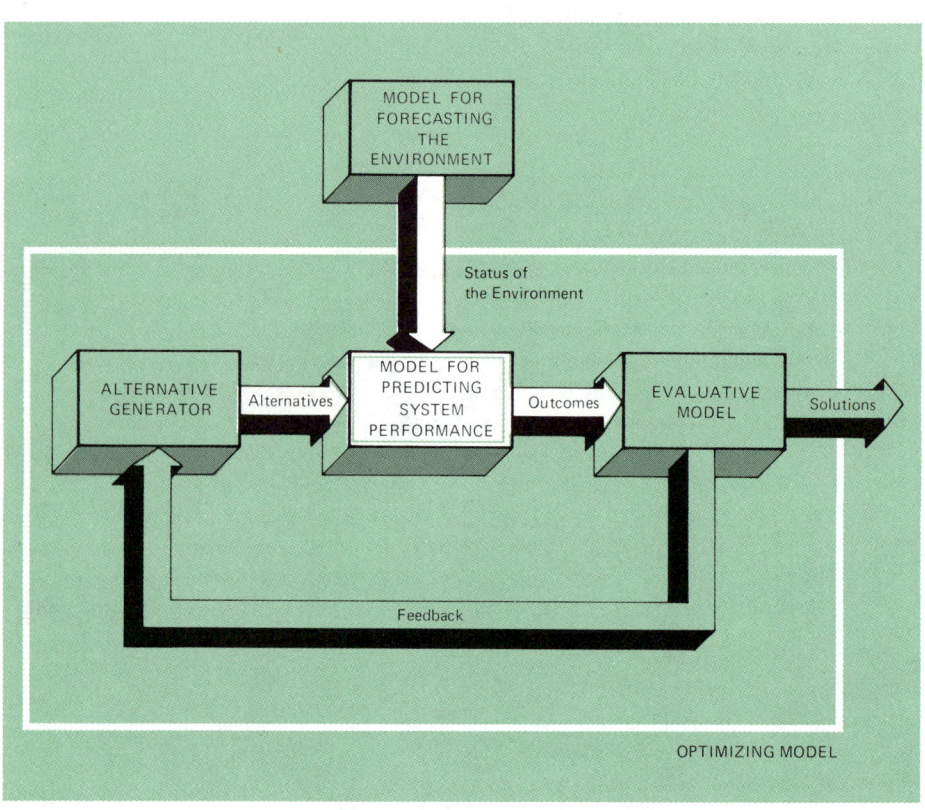

6

BUILDING MATHEMATICAL MODELS TO PREDICT SYSTEM PERFORMANCE

Models for predicting system performance are probably the most familiar type of mathematical model. These models are designed to predict the outcomes of alternative courses of action. The alternatives may be generated in some systematic manner that attempts to exhaust the feasible alternatives, or they may be hypotheses for what a manager thinks could be a good strategy. The alternatives may be viewed as inputs being transformed by the predictive model into a set of outcomes. This transformation of alternatives into outcomes may be influenced by the nature of the environment.

The Components of a Model for Predicting System Performance

Variables We often speak of the *variables* within a mathematical model. These are the elements of the model that can take on different values. An *alternative* is expressed as a particular set of values for these variables. For example, suppose we model a physical process such as steel making with an electric furnace as discussed in the Introduction to Part III. The variables in this model would be the quantities of ore, coke, limestone, and labor that are used. An alternative would consist of specific values for these variables. That is, we would identify an alternative by specifying the exact quantities of ore, coke, limestone, and labor to be used. These variables are often called *decision variables* or *controllable* variables, since their values can be determined by the decision maker.

Parameters The *parameters* of a model are the known entities not directly controllable by the decision maker. Some parameters may be determined by the nature of the environment. For a specific set of assumptions regarding the environment, these parameters are constants. However, they may vary as the environment changes. These parameters are often called *uncontrollable variables* to indicate that they do vary with the environment but are not controlled by the decision maker. The values of some of these uncontrollable variables are determined from forecasting models as discussed in Chapter 5.

Other parameters are known and are not affected by the environment. They may be determined by physical laws and always maintain constant values in the model no matter how the environment may change.

The corporate model discussed in the Introduction to Part III included costs of labor and materials as essential elements. These parameters would be considered uncontrollable variables, since the company cannot directly manipulate their values. For a given set of assumptions regarding the environment, these values will be determined within the model.

In the steel making example, the number of pounds of steel produced from quantities of iron ore and scrap is determined by physical laws. It does not change at the discretion of the decision maker, and it is not influenced by the environment. Thus, parameters reflecting these physical laws would be included in the model.

Logical Relationships The logical relationships in a mathematical model are explicit statements regarding how the system actually functions. They are cause-effect relationships among the variables and parameters of the model. For example, we might write

$$I_t = I_{t-1} + P_t - D_t$$

to indicate that the inventory of a product at the end of time period t (I_t) equals the inventory at the end of period $t - 1$ (I_{t-1}) plus the production of the product in period t (P_t) minus the demand for the product in period t (D_t). This is a mathematical statement of a simple accounting relationship.

Other logical relationships place upper and lower limits on the values of variables or on mathematical expressions involving several variables. For example, we might write

$$P_{t-1} + P_t \geq 100$$

to indicate that the production in time period $t - 1$ plus the production in time period t must be greater than or equal to 100. The production levels are variables in this expression, while the number 100 is a particular value for the two-period production level parameter. Other logical relationships may involve probabilistic statements.

In some mathematical models, most notably the optimizing models to be discussed in Part IV, these logical relationships are called *constraints*.

The Purpose of a Model for Predicting System Performance

Commonly, the manager will play the role of alternative generator for a model for predicting system performance. In this role, he will specify values of the decision variables in the model. In addition, the manager will specify some scenario regarding the nature of the environment in which the system will be operating. The specification of this scenario must be sufficiently detailed to provide information to any forecasting models used to determine the parameters of the model for predicting system performance. In some cases, the manager may subjectively assign values to these parameters based on his implicit forecasting model for the environment.

Given this information, the model should predict the outputs of the system that would be created if the same alternative were actually chosen under identical environmental conditions in the real world. These outcomes would then be evaluated by the manager, perhaps using one of the evaluative models discussed in Part II.

Notice that the manager has the option of analyzing many different alternatives under the same environmental assumptions or of analyzing the same alternative under many environmental assumptions. If the logical relationships are computerized, the process of making these analyses can be greatly simplified.

CREATING A MODEL FOR PREDICTING SYSTEM PERFORMANCE

Creating a useful mathematical model for predicting system performance is not a trivial task in a complex, real-world environment. Nevertheless, the investment of time and effort, especially by the manager who will eventually use the model, can lead to significant benefits. We shall now consider how such a model might be constructed. In order to provide a concrete reference for this discussion, we shall illustrate the concepts by developing a simple model for break-even analysis. It is important to emphasize that our interest here is on the model building procedure rather than on the break-even analysis per se.

Initial Formulation

Getting Started Suppose a manager recognizes that he has a problem and believes that a model for predicting system performance might be useful to him. His first task is to *bound* the problem by identifying as specifically as possible those questions he would like to have answered by the model.

For example, suppose the manager of a small manufacturing firm that produces one item is having difficulty determining a proper pricing strategy and in forecasting profits or losses. He might feel that a predictive model could be useful to him in dealing with this task. He could bound his problem by identifying the following set of initial questions he would like to have assistance in answering:

1. For a given set of costs, production, and price figures, what will my profit or loss be?
2. What will be the effect on profits (or losses) if I change my price, given that costs and demand remain constant?
3. How will my profit or loss be affected if demand changes?
4. What if my variable costs of production increase? How will my profit or loss be affected?

Notice that such a list of questions should be provided by the manager who will actually be *using* the system. It should not be generated by a professional analyst on the basis of what he thinks the manager should want. The responsibility for such a list falls on the manager, and his developing the list is most important in ensuring that a mathematical model created for the manager will actually be used by him. Thus, he needs to have the proper expectations regarding the types of questions on which he can legitimately expect help from a mathematical model.

Identifying the Important Elements The model builder must now abstract from the real world those essential elements of the system relevant to answering the questions posed by the manager. As illustrated in Figure 6-1, this process is one of *simplification* of the complexity of the real world.

The circles in Figure 6-1 indicate elements in the real world to be represented by variables and parameters in the model. The lines between the

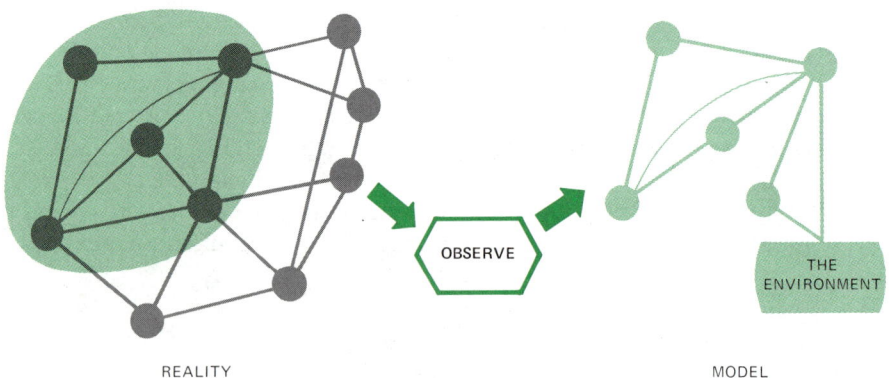

FIGURE 6-1. **Modeling as a simplification of the real world**

circles suggest that the connected elements are interdependent in some fashion, and this interdependence should be specified using logical relationships. Finally, the shaded area places bounds on the problem in the real world. It is the task of the model builder to observe this reality and to abstract a simplified model.

In our example, it is clear that the questions posed by the manager can be answered by considering the internal workings of one company, and then only its financial aspects. The linkage of this company to its environment will be through the demand for the product produced by the company. From studying the questions, it seems that the profit (or loss) is the most important element. Further, we know that the profit (or loss) of a company is determined by the relationship between revenues and costs.

Determine Logical Relationships Next, the model builder must hypothesize the logical relationships among these elements to create the model. In some cases, these relationships may be based on empirical data, while in other cases we can only appeal to the criterion of "reasonableness." In our example, we know that

profit (loss) = revenues − costs,

which is a mathematical statement of the logical relationship among these elements.

This simple mathematical relation serves as our initial formulation of a model for predicting system performance. What have we learned from this model? It is clear from an analysis of this model that

1. if revenues increase, so do profits, or
2. if costs decrease, profits increase.

Further, this interpretation of the results seems reasonable in the real world. Although these statements may seem trivial and self-evident, the basic concepts employed in the more elaborate model building efforts in the real world are essentially the same.

Adding Additional Detail We have begun with a simple model as our initial formulation. However, we do not have sufficient detail in this model to answer some of the questions posed by the manager. For example, we do not have logical relationships in the model that determine the effects of price, demand, and variable costs on revenues and total costs. Therefore, we must add additional detail to the model.

First let us consider the revenues in the model. Revenues are generated by selling items at a particular price. Therefore, the sales price and the number of items sold must be important elements in our model. The specific relationship among revenues, price, and items sold is

revenues = (price)(items sold).

Let us use some simple mathematical notation to condense this model, defining

p as the price per unit of our product and x as the number of units produced and sold. Now, we have the expression

revenues = px

to summarize this relationship. This expression is a logical relationship written in algebraic form.

The costs are a bit more complicated. First we have the costs of being in business, the fixed costs. These include rent or lease payments, license fees, and other costs that must be met even if we do not produce a single item. Next, there are the costs of doing business, the variable costs. These costs include expenditures for labor and raw materials and are influenced by the number of units we produce. Mathematically, the logical relationship dealing with costs is written

total costs = fixed costs + (variable costs per unit) (number of units sold).

This logical relationship adds the fixed costs to the variable costs, which are determined by the product of the variable costs per unit produced times the number of units produced and sold. Now, let us simplify this expression by defining f as the fixed costs and c as the variable costs per unit sold. Then, the total costs equal $f + cx$.

We can now replace the elements of revenues and costs in our original model and obtain a new model with additional detail:

profit (loss) = $px - (f + cx)$

Now, do we have sufficient detail in the model shown in Figure 6-2? Perhaps so. The manager may substitute values for the elements of this model and determine his profit or loss. Simultaneously, he may answer the other questions that he posed in his list.

Bootstrapping We shall use the term *bootstrapping* to refer to a strategy of model formulation based on beginning with a simple model and adding detail. We have illustrated this strategy with the simple break-even model, and it is a most important strategy in real-world applications.

Specialists in management science and operations research are often tempted to study a problem, then go off in isolation to develop an elaborate mathematical model for use by the manager. Unfortunately the manager may not understand this model and may either use it blindly or reject it entirely. The specialist may feel that the manager is too ignorant and unsophisticated to appreciate his model, while the manager may feel that the specialist lives in a dream world of unrealistic assumptions and irrelevant mathematics.

Such difficulty can be avoided if the manager works with the specialist to develop first a simple model that provides a crude but understandable analysis. After the manager has built up confidence in this model, additional detail and sophistication can be added, perhaps only a bit at a time. This process requires an investment of time on the part of the manager and sincere interest on the part

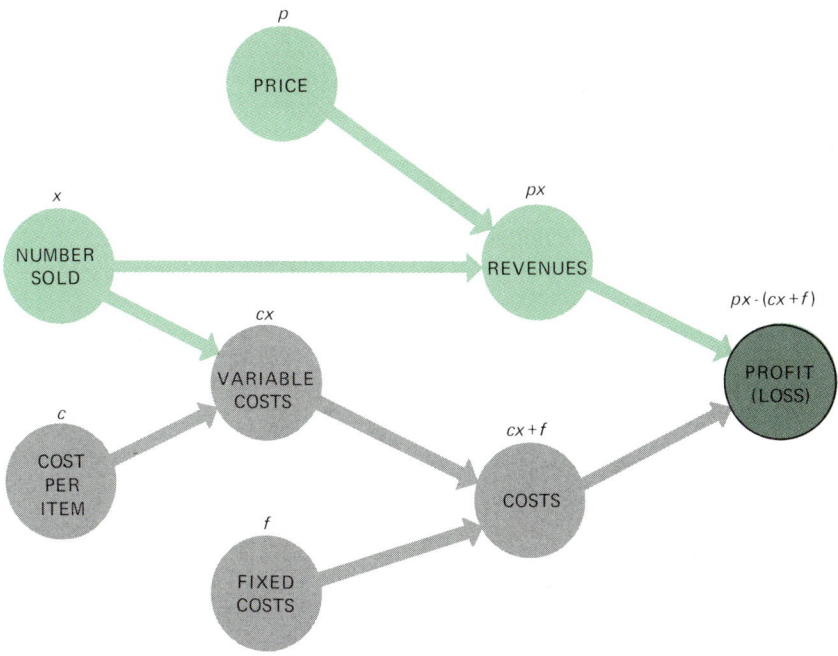

FIGURE 6-2. **The simple break-even model**

of the specialist in solving the manager's real problem, rather than in playing with sophisticated models. However, a bootstrapping approach to model building seems to be one of the most important factors in determining the successful implementation of a mathematical model (for examples see Morris [1967], Little [1970], and Urban [1974]). This approach also simplifies the difficult task of validating the model.

The Appropriate Level of Detail The creation of a mathematical model is still very much an art rather than a science. Although there are a number of generally accepted rules of thumb, there is no simple list of steps that will lead automatically to a successful model. The objective of modeling is to obtain the benefits of a mathematical model at a relatively low cost. Naturally, the benefits from a model will increase, other things being equal, as the level of detail in the model increases to provide an improved representation of reality. Unfortunately, the costs of modeling also increase, since more detail requires more information and a heavier computation burden. The art of modeling requires trading off the benefits of an increased level of detail against their associated increases in the costs of information and computation.

Validation of the Model

The next task is to validate the model. The objectives of this task are to ensure that the model accurately predicts the outcomes of alternatives and to simultaneously increase the manager's confidence in the model.

There are two potential dangers in not adequately validating a mathematical model. The first is that the manager will be so impressed by the elegance and sophistication of the mathematical model and its computer printouts that he will never question whether the basic assumptions on which it depends are actually sound. As Churchman [1973] points out, a mathematical model may be precisely wrong. He suggests that we often mistakenly believe that he who thinks elaborately thinks well.

At the other extreme, the manager may not have sufficient confidence in the mathematical model to actually rely on it. Most individuals prefer a simple, crude analysis they can understand to a sophisticated analysis they cannot comprehend.

Reasonableness Criterion The validation should consider the internal logic of the model as determined by the logical relationships. All of the assumptions on which these relationships were based should be specified and made known to the manager. The logic of the model should reflect the manager's view of the real world and not the analyst's view. For example, analysts often assume that the variables in the model are related by linear rather than nonlinear relationships. While this assumption is valid in many real-world situations, in others it may seriously distort the model.

A second issue is the validity of the data used in the model. Forecasting models may be required to provide values for some of the parameters. These data sources should also be scrutinized.

Finally, the model must be run several times to ensure that the logical relationships and the mathematical analysis were correctly programmed in the computer. Geoffrion [1976] refers to these as probationary exercises. He suggests that the model be restricted by fixing many of the decision variables and logical relationships so that the appropriate answer will be obvious, or at least can be calculated by an experienced staff analyst. Then the results of the model can be compared against those obtained by hand. The source of any discrepancies should then be identified, whether it be errors in the basic assumptions, the logical relationships, the input data, or a bug in the computer program.

Predictive Criterion A second approach is to match the model against past history. The actual data used in prior time periods in the real-world system that the model is to represent can be put into the model, and the outcomes can be compared. Again, it should be possible to justify any discrepancies that occur.

Thus, validation requires that we manipulate the model and compare the results with what has happened (or what we would expect to happen) in the real

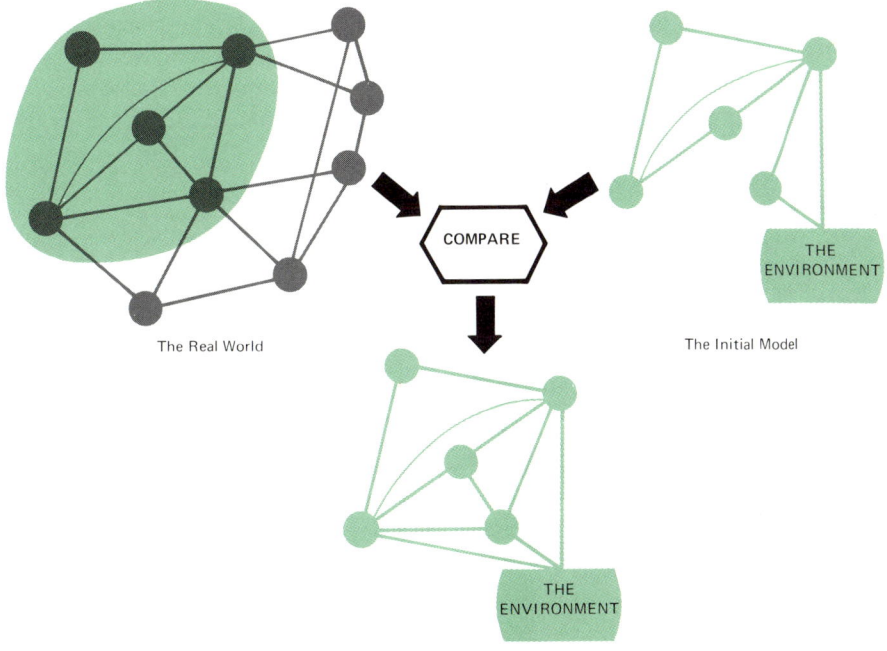

FIGURE 6-3. **Revision of a model**

world. This process may cause us to revise the model until we are satisfied with the results.

Figure 6-3 illustrates that the initial model formulation is compared against the real world. In this example, additional logical relationships are identified in the revised model in order to represent reality more closely.

The break-even analysis model should be validated by questioning whether the basic assumptions are appropriate. For example, we have assumed that costs consist of a variable component, and a fixed component that remains constant no matter what the level of production actually is. In a real-world situation, a more elaborate cost model would probably be required (for examples see Reisman and Buffa [1962]).

Analysis

A model for predicting system performance is analyzed by exploring the structure and behavior of the model as a consequence of the initial assumptions and the logical relationships. This analysis is "objective" in the sense that it can be verified or repudiated on the basis of logical arguments alone.

Let us consider an example of analysis based on the break-even model. The manager may ask, "What if my fixed costs are $2000 per week, my price is $30 per unit, my variable costs are $15 per unit, and I sell 300 units per week? What will my profit or loss be?" We can use the break-even model to calculate the profit or loss using the logic of mathematical analysis. Substituting for the decision variables and parameters we have

$f = 2000, \quad c = 15,$
$p = 30, \quad x = 300.$

Using the logical relationship, we obtain

profit (loss) $= (30)(300) - (15)(300) - 2000$
$= 9000 - 4500 - 2000 = 2500.$

Thus the profit in this situation would be $2500 per week.

The creation of a mathematical model requires a significant investment of time and money. However, once this capital investment has been made, the actual use of the model is generally very cheap. Therefore, it should be used often, even at the whim of the manager.

In addition to the probationary exercises to validate a model, Geoffrion [1976] suggests a series of computer runs. These include the following:

1. *Base case runs.* The model should be run with several future scenarios for the organization.
2. *Sensitivity analysis.* Additional runs should be made to test the sensitivity of the model to any questionable assumptions made in the model. The objective is to learn if these assumptions have significantly affected the results from the model. Other runs can be made to test the sensitivity of the results to the values of key parameters.
3. *"What if" questions.* Managers may wish to explore basic questions of interest to them such as, "What if a new competitor enters the market?" or "What if we suffer a strike that lasts for n weeks? or "What if fuel shortages reduce our effective trucking capacity by 10 percent?"

Interpretation

Once the model has been analyzed and the results have been obtained, the manager must *interpret* their meaning back in the real world. In the few cases where the model captures the problem perfectly, interpretation may be a straightforward task. More commonly, the model is not a perfect fit, so the results of the analysis may require careful scrutiny, since the best solution for the model may not be the best solution for the real-world problem.

Formulation is a process of simplification or extraction from the real world. During interpretation, the manager must reconsider the results from the mathematical analysis in the context of the complexities omitted or ignored during formulation because of intangibility or technical difficulties. The results may need to be modified to allow for other considerations. Returning to the

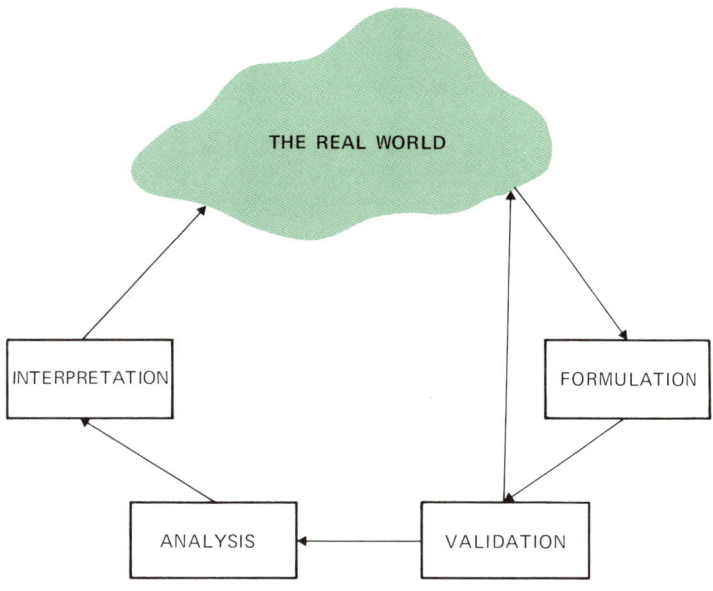

FIGURE 6–4. **The steps of mathematical modeling**

break-even model, the manager finds from the analysis that a weekly profit of $2500 could be realized if he sells 300 units per week at a price of $30. He must decide whether he can actually sell 300 units per week at this price, since the model provides the profit calculation only for successful sale of these units. Could he sell more than 300 units at this price, or could he sell 300 units at an even higher price? These issues must be confronted before the results of the analysis are implemented in the real world.

The basic steps of model building are illustrated in Figure 6–4. Model formulation and interpretation of the results of analysis require skill and insight on the part of a manager. Once the relatively straightforward tools of mathematical analysis are understood and available to a manager, formulation and interpretation become the intellectually challenging activities.

COMPUTER-BASED CORPORATE SIMULATION MODELS

Computer-based corporate simulation models are a particular kind of predictive model. These models have been well received by practicing managers, partly because the model itself makes no pretense for making managerial decisions. Rather, these models represent the financial or other flows of an enterprise and can therefore be queried with *what if* questions by managers. Since the models simulate the enterprise, a range of hypotheses concerning prices, volume, various costs, etc. can be tested to form a sound planning base. The models provide answers to questions asked, but the manager retains his traditional role as decision maker.

Computer-based corporate models have commonly been developed in computer interactive mode to facilitate a "manager active" situation in which results from one query may stimulate new questions. We have then an extremely powerful combination of decision maker and predictive model in a loop. Very complex computations reflecting assumptions about volume, price, costs, or the effects of a labor dispute, can be handled in a short turn-around time as low as a few minutes, including data input, computing, and output.

Basically, the mathematical relationships are as simple as the accounting flows discussed earlier in the chapter in connection with the break-even analysis example of model building. We summarized those relationships in Figure 6–2, which showed eight elements that enter break-even models. Previously, we used the simple break-even model as a vehicle for developing the concepts of model building. We shall now build on those ideas to develop a more sophisticated model. It will be more sophisticated because it will more closely represent the complexities of an enterprise and because we shall assume the power of a computing system. However, the relationships are no more sophisticated than those used to construct the simple break-even model.

PLYWOOD MANUFACTURING AS AN EXAMPLE

The physical flow of material for a plywood manufacturing operation is shown in Figure 6–5 where we see that the material inputs are company-owned logs together with purchased logs (if required). These materials are processed through the veneer manufacturing phase that involves cutting a thin sheet of veneer from the surface of the log (peeling) and drying it to a specified moisture content. By-products of the peel-dry process are green lumber cores and chips, which are sold at transfer prices to other divisions of the enterprise. Plywood is then glued and pressed with veneer produced in the previous operation or (if required) purchased veneer.

While this description of the process is simplified, it serves as an adequate basis for our discussion. The capacity of the glue-press operation in relation to the available company-produced veneer determines the amount of purchased veneer required. Similarly, the capacity of the peel-dry operation in relation to desired veneer output determines the amount of purchased logs required.

Model Formulation

Let us begin with simple relationship diagrams that describe the profit or loss of the plywood company.

Revenue The three outputs that produce revenue are chips, lumber cores, and, of course, plywood, as shown in Figure 6–6 (a). For plywood, revenue is simply the quantity produced and sold multiplied by the price as indicated in

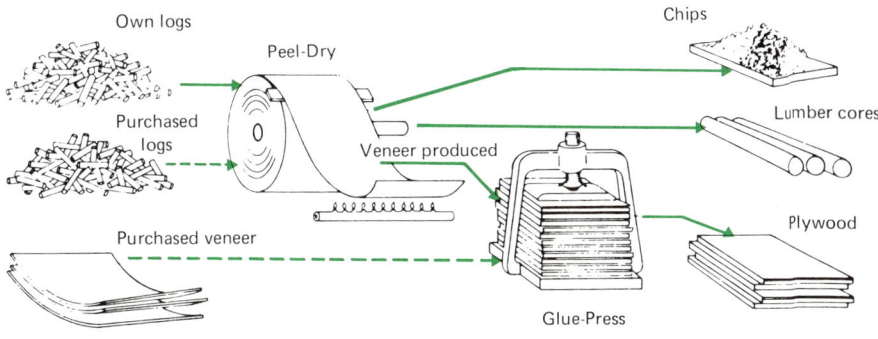

FIGURE 6-5. **Overall flow of plywood operations**
From J. B. Boulden and E. S. Buffa, "Corporate Models: On-Line Real-Time Systems," Harvard Business Review, *July–August 1970, used by permission.*

Figure 6-6 (b). The price is an estimate or an actual market price; however, the quantity is the lesser of two figures—the plant capacity or the desired production level determined by forecasts coupled with a planning process—as indicated by Figure 6-6 (c). Now, if we enter into our model the specific numbers for plywood price, desired quantity, and capacity, we can obtain the total revenue generated by plywood sales through the simple mathematical relationship,

plywood revenue = price × minimum of (desired quantity, capacity).

A similar analysis could be used to determine revenue from chips and lumber cores; we could then specify a model to estimate total revenues as the sum of the three components of revenue.

Costs Now let us consider the cost model. In an actual application we may wish to include very detailed cost breakdowns of the marketing costs, variable production costs, fixed costs, and miscellaneous costs shown as components in Figure 6-7 (a). Each of these separate components of the total cost must be analyzed to develop the appropriate relationships. For example, the marketing costs might be generated from subcomponents of discounts and allowances, sales commissions, and freight charges, as shown in Figure 6-7 (b).

Each of these costs might be estimated as a percentage of the total plywood sales revenues, for example. Therefore, our model would use the plywood sales revenue generated and apply specific percentages to determine marketing costs. Similar analyses would be required to develop models representing the behavior of the other costs.

FIGURE 6-6. **Plywood company revenue model formulation: (a) revenue components, (b) factors entering plywood revenue, and (c) factors determining quantity of plywood**

We see now that the process of *formulating* a profit (loss) model is quite straightforward. The logic consists primarily of simple arithmetic operations, though the number of calculations will be large as we try to represent a real

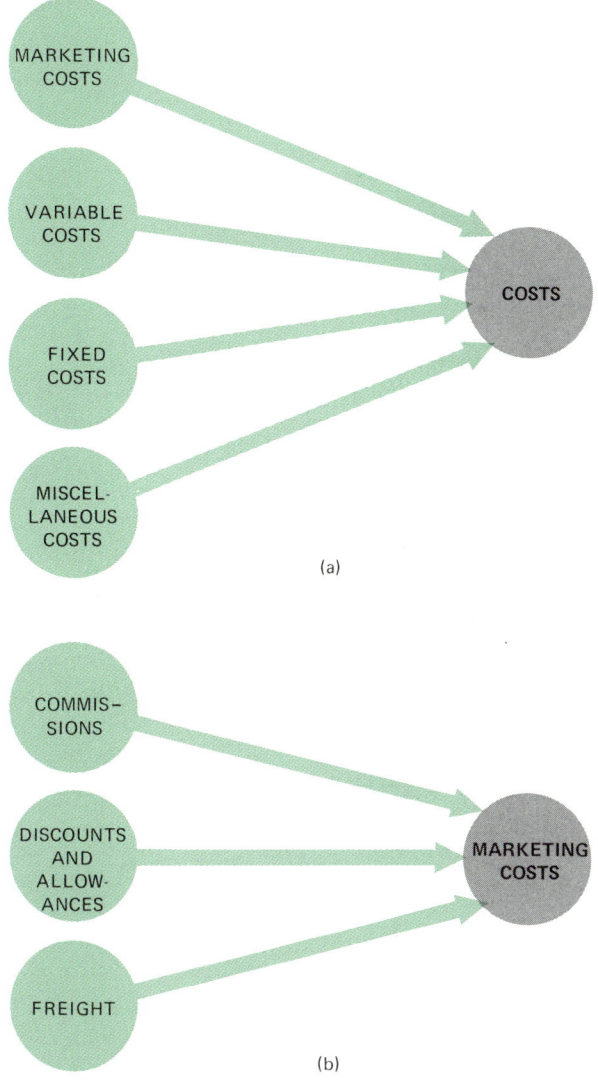

FIGURE 6-7. **Plywood company cost model formulation: (a) cost components and (b) marketing cost components**

organization, since there will be various sizes, types, and grades of plywood. Because of the complexity, we program such models on a computer in order to retain the logic for repetitive use and to achieve rapid turnaround time for computing the effects of alternatives that reflect price and cost changes. To use such a profit (loss) model we must specify the inputs or values of the elements of

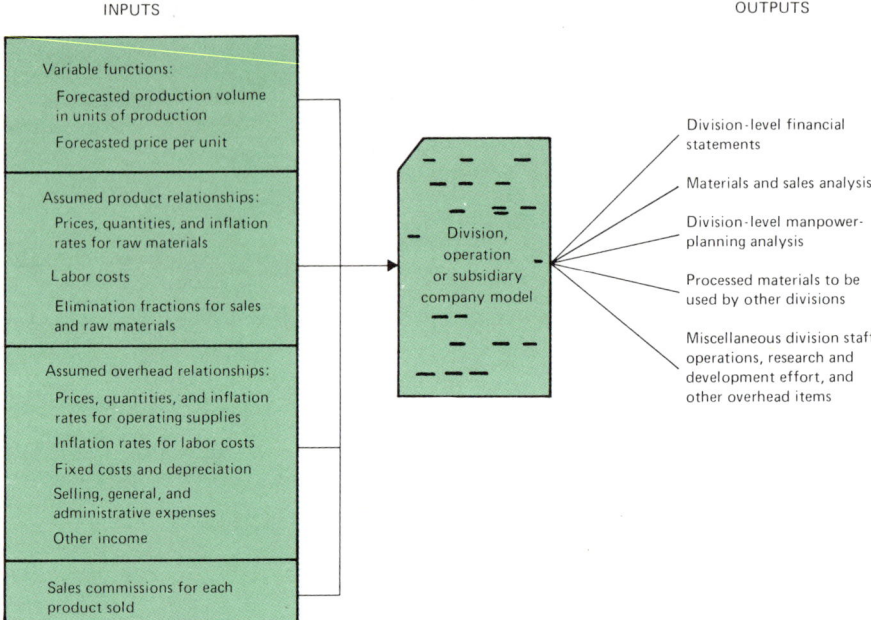

FIGURE 6-8. **Input-output relationships for a division**

From J. B. Boulden and E. S. Buffa, "Corporate Models: On-Line Real-Time Systems"; used by permission.

the model. These values include the *parameters* that define specific conditions as we discussed previously, and the *decision variables* that may be changed at the discretion of the manager.

Use of Computer Version of the Plywood Model

Let us now assume the power of the computer and see how the plywood model can be of managerial use. We also assume now that the plywood operation is really only a division of a larger concern. The inputs and outputs of the plywood model are shown in Figure 6-8. We have added the product and overhead relationships to the forecasts of production volume and prices.

Depending on our needs, we can structure outputs in various ways, such as profit and loss statements, materials and sales analyses, manpower planning schedules, etc. The computer will not provide the necessary inputs for the model or the logical relationships—that is our function. The computer's function is to carry out the computations defined by the logic we provide.

```
YEAR 76

        LINE ITEMS          YRT
        SALES PLY        138550.0
        SALES CHIPS        7051.5
        SALES LUMBER       4545.0
        SALES ELIM
        TOTAL SALES      150146.5
        D&A PLYWOOD        2771.0
        COM PLY            8313.0
        FREIGHT PLY        1122.0
        TOT COM           12206.0
        NET SALES        137940.5
        RAW MATERIAL      25570.0
        VENEER PURCH      32356.5
        OP SUPPLIES       14101.2
        LABOR             33860.4
        COST ELIMIN
        COST OF SALE     105888.1
        GROSS PROFIT      32052.4
        FIXED COSTS        5000.0
        SELLING EXP        3000.0
        G&A EXPENSE        3000.0
        OTHER EXPENSE       500.0
        TOT IND EXP       11500.0
        NET PROFIT        20552.4
        GP/NS                 .23
        TIE/NS                .08
        NP/NS                 .15
```

FIGURE 6-9. **Computation of profit and loss statement from predictive model. Output could have been called for by quarters or months and could have included actual experience plus projections based on forecasts, depending on input.**

From J. B. Boulden and E. S. Buffa, "Corporate Models: On-Line Real-Time Systems"; used by permission.

Using a system of precoded commands we can call for model output in various forms. For example, in Figure 6-9 we have called for the profit and loss statement based on a set of parameters. Note that the model provides summary ratios such as gross and net profit to sales. Also, the output could have been called for by quarters or in some other format.

The problem-solving value of such a model lies in our ability to ask meaningful questions that may involve changing the values of the decision variables. Each set of values for the decision variables represents a different alternative. In addition, we may wish to determine the outcomes associated with each alternative, given several future scenarios. These scenarios are described

```
DESIRED YEARLY PROFIT = 0/
    TUT SALES      PROFIT     FRAC 1
    150146.50      20552.36   1.0000
     53870.76           .00    .3588
```

FIGURE 6-10. **Computation of break-even sales and fraction from predictive model**

From J. B. Boulden and E. S. Buffa, "Corporate Models: On-Line Real-Time Systems"; used by permission.

```
P-L MODE =
PARAMETER SENSITIVITY
P#/MIN/MAX/INCREMENT/ = 24/5/6/.25/

    YEAR 76                   P/L

P24 = 5.000

    LINE ITEMS                YRT
    NET PROFIT                20552.4

P24 = 5.250

    LINE ITEMS                YRT
    NET PROFIT                18859.3

P24 = 5.500

    LINE ITEMS                YRT
    NET PROFIT                17166.3

P24 = 5.750

    LINE ITEMS                YRT
    NET PROFIT                15473.3

P24 = 6.000

    LINE ITEMS                YRT
    NET PROFIT                13781.0
```

FIGURE 6-11. **Sensitivity of net profit to the parameter $P24$, labor cost per hour for the plywood case**

From J. B. Boulden and E. S. Buffa, "Corporate Models: On-Line Real-Time Systems"; used by permission.

by modifying the parameter values. For example, we can ask for a profit and loss report for a given profit objective and specific assumptions regarding the state of the environment. Also, using that concept we can perform a break-even analysis by specifying a profit objective of zero in response to the system's query as shown in Figure 6–10. The system responds by computing the sales and percentage of current forecasted sales necessary for break-even operation.

Now suppose we wish to assess the impact on profits of a labor cost increase. By reference to a parameter list, we know that labor cost is coded as P24. We call for "parameter sensitivity," and the system responds by asking which parameter we wish to test as well as the minimum-maximum limits of the test and the increments of variation. We respond by typing 24 for parameter 24, a minimum of $5, a maximum of $6, in increments of 0.25; that is, 24/5/6/.25, as shown in Figure 6–11. The system then computes net profit for each value of the labor cost parameter automatically generating outcomes, given four different scenarios (see Figure 6–11). Such a computation might be of great importance during a labor negotiation.

Larger Systems of Models Now, assuming that the plywood operation is a division of a much larger corporation, a straightforward extension of the concepts we have discussed can result in the consolidation of the outputs of the plywood division model with other divisions into a "group" consolidation model as shown in Figure 6–12. This process would require the specification of similar additional relationships.

Finally, the results of several group models can be consolidated at the corporate level, also shown in Figure 6–12. Top executives are likely to be most interested in the group and corporate consolidation models. Yet, by using the kind of structure illustrated by the plywood model as a basic building block, together with the successive layers of aggregation we have indicated, management can ask for effects of proposed changes in prices, costs, equipment, financing, and so on, at any level within the organization. Also, management can quickly estimate the net effects on the total enterprise.

MANAGERIAL USE OF COMPUTER-BASED PREDICTIVE MODELS

Predictive models of enterprise operations of the type we have just discussed are in general use. Large-scale applications have been made at Van den Bergh & Jergens, a subsidiary of Unilever, [Buffa, 1972] and for a division of Imperial Chemical Industries [Stephenson, 1970] in England. Reports have been published of the use of corporate planning models at Xerox Corporation [Seaberg and Seaberg, 1973], in financial institutions [Hamilton and Moses, 1973, 1974], and for aggregate production planning [Lee and McLaughlin, 1974]. Here we shall discuss an application at the Inland Steel Company.

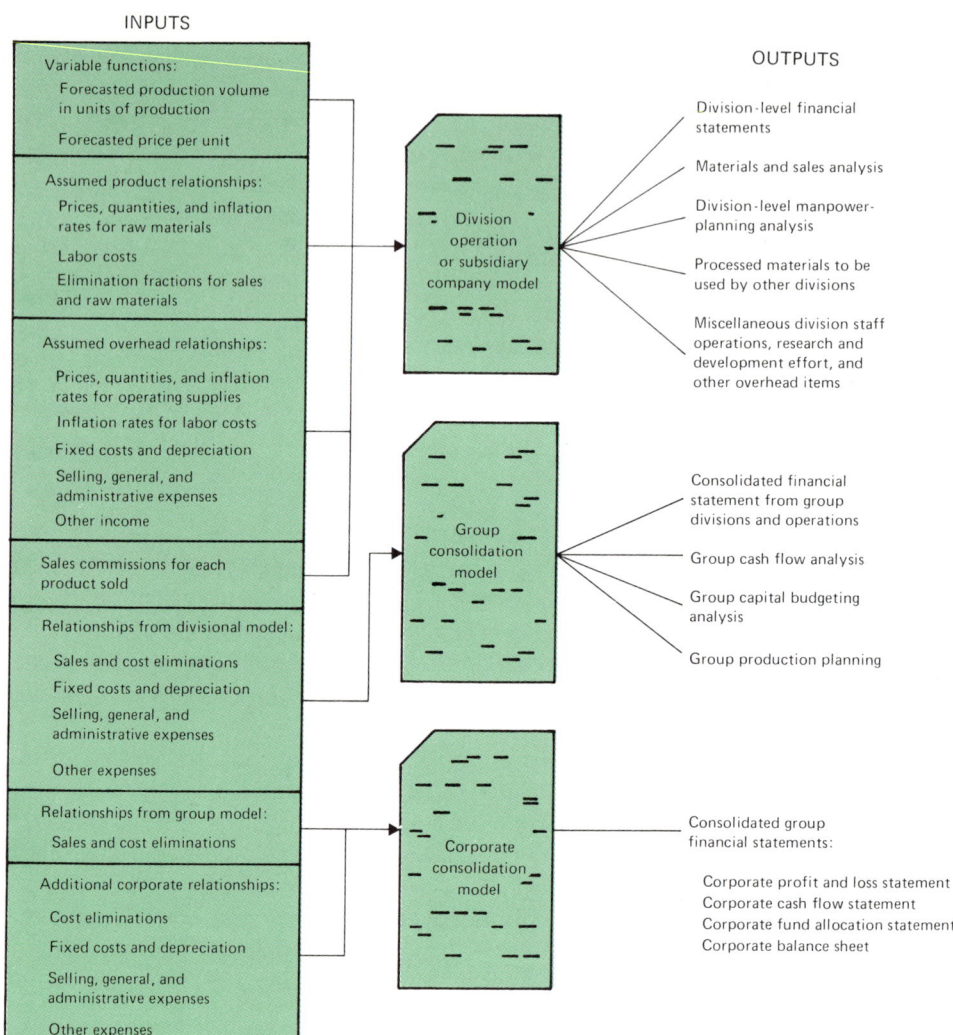

FIGURE 6-12. **Input-output relationships for division or subsidiaries, group consolidation, and corporate consolidation**

From J. B. Boulden and E. S. Buffa, "Corporate Models: On-Line Real-Time Systems"; used by permission.

Inland Steel Company

Inland Steel's use of predictive models focuses on the production process [Boulden and Buffa, 1970]. The models that have been developed and their relationships are shown in Figure 6-13. Using the models, corporate planners can quickly simulate the effects of a wide variety of planning assumptions. Each model deals with a basic process in the sequence from raw materials to finished products. The models simulate the various costs incurred in converting ores to molten iron, converting molten iron to steel ingots, processing ingots, and finishing the steel to various end products.

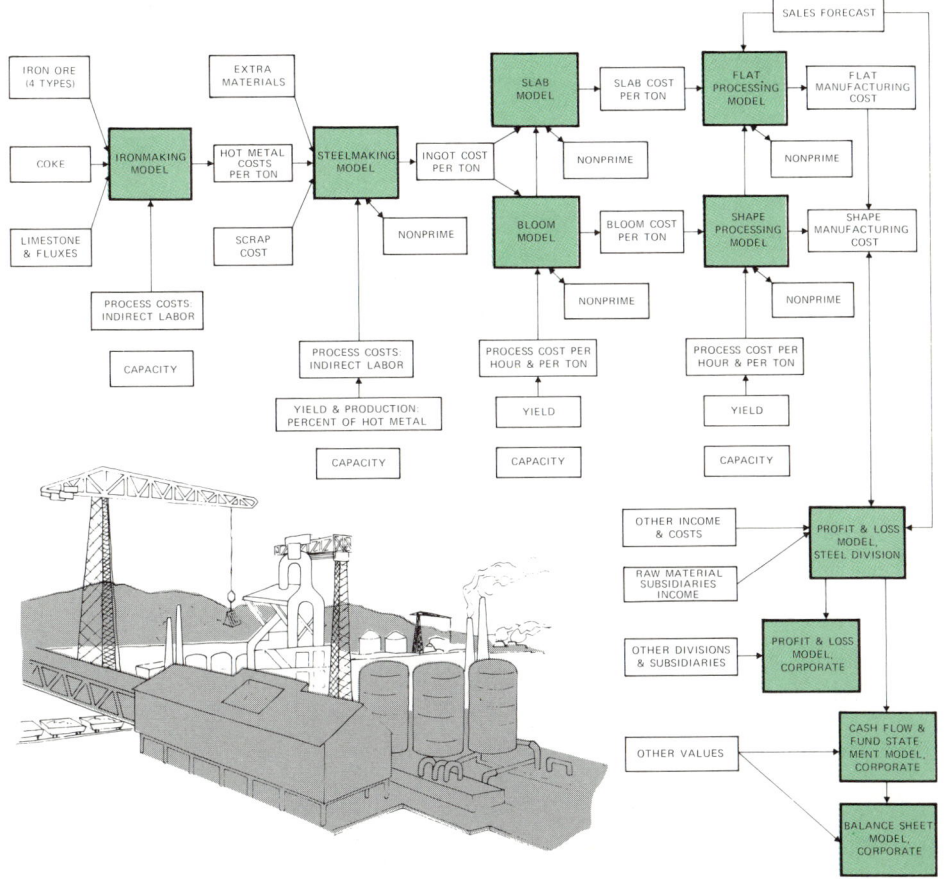

FIGURE 6-13. **Relationships in Inland Steel model, courtesy *Inland Steel* and *Planmetrics, Inc.***

From J. B. Boulden and E. S. Buffa, "Corporate Models: On-Line Real-Time Systems"; used by permission.

The types of questions asked by Inland Steel management using the models are typified by the following: How much raw material is required to meet production forecasts? What are the cost effects of various hot metal to scrap ratios and the resulting yield under various assumptions of raw material costs? What are the capacity requirements for proposed levels of operation?

The first actual test of the models was in the preparation for the 1971 profit plan and the related five-year profit and cash projection. For the first time, alternative strategies and assumptions were used during the planning process and during the executive review of the total corporate plan.

In approaching the profit-planning cycle for 1971, the company management was faced with unusual uncertainties. This situation led to the use of the models to simulate operations, given four significantly different scenarios. All four were based on a basic premise that a strike in the automotive industry was a near certainty during the fourth quarter of 1970, and that if this should occur there would be a significant impact on fourth-quarter shipments for the company. However, the sales forecast for 1971 indicated a very strong sales demand for the first seven months of that planning period, ending with the August 1 deadline date for negotiations with the Steel Workers Union, and a possible steel strike.

The *first scenario* of this basic premise was that the sales forecast for 1971 would follow a normal seasonal distribution of shipments, much like what would happen in any normal year, with no impact from the actions of customers through hedge buying of steel inventories in anticipation of a possible steel strike. This assumption gave a base condition for planning.

The *second scenario* was that the historic pattern of prestrike hedge buying would occur in the first seven months of 1971, as it had in all similar periods in the postwar period, and that there would be no steel strike, since agreement would be reached late on July 31. In this condition, sales demand would decline sharply in August, September, and October, with some recovery in the later months of the fourth quarter of 1971.

The *third scenario* involved the previous basic premise, but assumed a 30-day strike in the steel industry, with resumption of production and shipments after 30 days.

The *fourth scenario* assumed a 90-day steel strike, with the same prestrike hedge-buying sales pattern occurring, as stated in the basic premise.

The financial model was used to simulate operations, given these four basic scenarios, all with the premise that there would be an auto strike in the fourth quarter of 1970. Management determined a formal profit plan for 1971 consistent with scenario two, which included a prestrike build up of inventories, but no strike occurring in the steel industry. However, the other options were maintained in the profit-planning manual as alternative strategies in the event conditions should change as they approached the August 1 strike deadline.

In September 1970, top management made a major decision to build semifinished and finished inventories to the largest level in the company's history to capitalize on the strong demand forecast for the first half of 1971. The reason for this decision was that if the forecast were correct and inventories were not accumulated, the mills would not be able to produce steel fast enough to meet the customer delivery requirements, and there would be a loss of sales revenue. This plan was followed. The excess inventory was liquidated on schedule by June 1, 1971, and the company achieved an all-time record industry market share of 6.8 percent versus a normal rate of 4.8 to 5.2 percent.

In late June 1971, it became apparent that the sales demand would not hold up through July 31 as anticipated, and that the odds for a strike on August 1 were growing. Because the preliminary sales forecast from market research for 1972 indicated a very strong market, the company also evaluated similar inventory buildup strategies for both the poststrike period, should a steel strike occur, and for production over the last five months of 1971, should there be no strike.

In early July 1971, the management requested the five-year cash projection for the years 1972 through 1976 and an accelerated updating of the annual cash forecast for 1971. Management recognized that rigorous planning of capital expenditures and long-term financing was required to meet the heavy capital needs for normal expansion and replacement, pollution control equipment, long-term bond issues scheduled for retirement, and very large requirements and opportunities for investment in new projects.

The Inland Steel Company continues to develop the use of predictive models for production scheduling, developing raw materials and mines, and planning subsidiary operations.

WHAT SHOULD THE MANAGER KNOW?

Formulation

The manager must play an active role in the creation and use of mathematical models. This task cannot be successfully accomplished by a technical staff or outside consultant working in isolation. The manager must be involved. He must bear the principal responsibility for recognizing problems that can be analyzed successfully by mathematical models. He must create the list of questions to be answered by the model as an aid in bounding the formulation. He must express his understanding of the system in a manner that can be captured by logical relationships. He must participate in the probationary exercises with the model in order to gain confidence in its validity. Finally, he must use the model in a creative way to attack and solve the problem of interest.

Models only reflect what has been structured; they cannot create a new structure. The model should serve to reduce the routine, pencil-pushing work of the manager, leaving him even more time for creative thought and innovation. The model can also assist by quickly computing the results of some of his innovative ideas and by helping him to develop his intuition regarding a particular problem area.

However, the most dramatic and creative new solutions will "break the model" in the sense that they cannot be represented with the existing structure of the model, even though a conscious effort has been made to provide sufficient flexibility to allow the manager to try a wide range of alternatives. These creative solutions are ideas that were not considered during model building because they were not a simple extension of the existing system or operations, but represent a significant innovation. Perhaps the highest compliment that could be paid to a model would be that it contributed to its own obsolescence by providing the insights to the manager that allowed him to leap beyond it. Certainly, the manager should be alert for such opportunities.

Although he may often seek the aid of specialists trained in modeling and the technology of management science, the manager must play the role of catalyst in guiding the model building effort. He knows the problem and his needs better than anyone else, and it is his responsibility to ensure that this information is clearly communicated to the specialist. Managerial participation may require a significant commitment of time, but without it the model building activity may be merely an academic exercise.

The important point to remember is that the manager will still be left with the responsibility of making the decision, and this responsibility cannot be delegated to the model. The model can aid the manager by sharpening his intuition and by predicting for him the outcomes from choosing alternative solutions. However, in the final analysis, the decision will be made by the manager. The degree to which this decision is improved as a result of the use of a mathematical model will generally be determined by the involvement of the manager in its creation.

Computer-based predictive models take a position in a manager's organizational environment similar to that of his staff. The manager calls on various members of his staff to perform special studies for him. In essence, the staff is providing him with answers to *what if* questions. Managers have always asked these kinds of questions in order to improve their own planning and decision making. By manual methods, however, the staff had to labor for many man-months to provide answers. Computer-based predictive models perform the same basic functions except that because they are constructed to represent certain phases of operations, the models can provide answers to the questions very quickly.

What the manager needs to know about predictive models is in general what he must know about his staff. He must have faith in his staff's competence to evaluate properly the alternatives he raises. Thus, for predictive models, the manager needs to be close enough to the original design of the models to be sure that they will have the capabilities he wants. He needs to know the kinds of questions he is likely to raise and be sure that the models will have the flexibility required to deal with them.

Also, the manager must be interested in the model validation phase; he must be convinced that the models truly predict system performance in order for him to have the required faith. Given faith in the models, he is limited only by his imagination and the capability limits of the models.

Validation

The manager should insist on initial runs of these kinds of predictive models using historical data input to test their validity. The nature of the straightforward relationships within such models should produce a high level of conformance between model and known result. If the model builder approximates some functions by using averages, the manager should determine the sensitivity of the model to changes in the averages, and whether or not an approximation is justified. For example, if product mix is fairly stable in sales, an average price could be used at higher levels of aggregation.

Formulating Scenarios

The manager's greatest interest will be in formulating alternate hypotheses or scenarios for what would happen if certain events were to occur. The specific questions may become quite detailed and quite dependent on the nature of the enterprise. However, the manager can take advantage of the sensitivity analysis capability of computer-based predictive models to determine which variables are really important in his operations and which ones may be of only minor significance. A good manager will already have a feel for which variables are important, but by using the model he can quantify the effects.

In general, in profit-oriented organizations the manager will be interested in what happens if prices, material costs, and labor costs change. In the Van den Bergh & Jurgens Ltd. (a subsidiary of Unilever) use of computer-based predictive models, a list of seventeen typical *what if* questions are reported [Buffa, 1972], including the testing of prices and costs, marketing plans for specific products and their effects, response to competitors' price actions, alternate forecasts, and the effect on resources and profits of the acquisition of a competitor.

In a banking application, management focused on the effects of changes in discount rate, reserve requirements, banking regulations, levels of earning assets, and changes in the deposit base.

Interpretation of Results

The entire focus of computer-based predictive models seems to be on quantitative factors. On the surface it appears that such models would be useful only for problems in which we accept a quantifiable criterion such as cost or profit. In fact, however, a modern manager is likely to use them as a part of a more complex decision process in which he considers the quantitative effects produced by the models as well as other factors that are not quantifiable. He then makes the trade-offs required in his decision process.

The predictive models actually facilitate this trade-off process because the manager can ask for and obtain quickly and efficiently the quantitative effects of a scenario, which allows him to "price" the nonquantifiable advantages or disadvantages. In the case of Inland Steel's use of its computer-based models, management was undoubtedly using a complex set of criteria in deciding on its strategy. These criteria included the risk of inventory building in the face of market uncertainties, the impact on labor relations and the community, the reaction of stockholders, and so on. The models provided information regarding costs and profits for alternatives, and this information could then be used in the judgmental trade-off process.

In essence then, the models provide input to the evaluative models discussed in Chapters 2, 3, and 4 where formal models, perhaps involving utility theory, provide mechanisms for trade-offs. For example, subjective estimates of the probabilities of the occurrence of each of the scenarios could be made and this information could be used in a decision tree.

Check Your Understanding

1. Consider each of the following problems:
    a. the development of a long-range plan for a large integrated forest products company
    b. the development of a production plan for a large steel manufacturing company
    c. the development of a plan for locating and dispatching ambulances

    For each problem, assume that a predictive model is to be developed to aid in its resolution and that you are the manager with the primary responsibility for the plan.

    1) Bound the problem by listing the questions you would expect a predictive model to answer.
    2) Identify the important elements in each problem. Indicate whether each element is a decision variable or a parameter.
    3) Determine the important logical relationships among these elements using a diagram such as the one illustrated in Figure 6–2.
2. Explain the differences between a controllable variable, an uncontrollable variable, and a parameter determined by physical laws. Describe a problem in which you identify examples of each.
3. What is meant by the term *bootstrapping,* and why is it so important?

4. For each of the problems in exercise 1, provide the following:
   a. At least two examples of future scenarios that you would expect to be used in base case runs of the predictive model. Be specific.
   b. At least two questionable assumptions or key parameters on which you would perform a sensitivity analysis.
5. For the break-even model developed in this chapter, develop the following:
   a. Base case analyses with forecasted sales of 200 and 400 units per week.
   b. Base case analyses with variable costs of $14 and $20 per unit.
   c. A sensitivity analysis of the assumption of linearity in the variable costs by supposing that the first 100 units produced per week have a variable cost of $25 per unit, the next 100 cost $15 per unit, and the remaining units cost $10 per unit. Is there a serious discrepancy with the linear model when the sales are 300 per week? 400 per week? 200 per week?
   d. A *what if* analysis of a new production system that would lower unit costs to $10 but would increase fixed costs to $3000. For what levels of weekly sales would the old production system be superior, and for what levels would the new system be superior?
6. Explain why model formulation and interpretation are the intellectually challenging activities in mathematical modeling for a manager.
7. A small fiberboard company is in the process of constructing a budget model and wishes to construct the model in the general format of computer-based corporate simulation. It is decided that the model will be set up for the first and second half plus the year summary. The fixed costs are simple, $1 million per six months. The company produces only one product, and sales forecasts in units by six-month periods are: 200,000 and 300,000, or 500,000 for the year. The price is $2 per unit and variable cost is $1.50 per unit.

   The output of the model will have six lines, as defined in Figure 6-14 under the heading *Output Description*.
   a. Define the relationships required for each line of output in column (3). Output line 1 is simply listed as *volume* in column (3). Other lines of output might be the sum or product of items such as price, costs, etc.
   b. Following the relationships defined in column (3), define equivalent algebraic relationships in column (4), with the definitions of variables used in column (5). As symbols, use V for vectors of numbers, P for parameters, and D for previously computed values in a line of output. For example, $D4$ would represent the result of the computation in line 4 and could be used in subsequent computations. As an example, we have shown $V1$ for output line 1 under column (4), and defined it as the vector of volume per six months.
   c. List the input data required to "drive" the budget model in column (6). For example, we have shown the volume vector previously given by six-month periods. Note that some lines will have no data input.
8. When Figure 6-14 is completed, the budget model is complete. If the variable costs increase by $0.10 per unit, what will be the impact on annual profits?

(1) Output Line	(2) Output Description	(3) Relationship	(4) Model Logic	(5) Definitions	(6) Input Data
1	Volume (units)	Volume	V1	V1 = Volume per quarter (units)	200,000/300,000
2	Sales ($)				
3	Variable cost				
4	Gross Margin				
5	Fixed cost				
6	Profits				

FIGURE 6-14. **Work sheet for budget model**

What parameters, vectors, or other input data need to be changed to run the model with the new assumption?
9. Referring to the budget model, determine the sensitivity of profit in each of the two periods, and annually, to changes in variable cost. Compute the profit for variable costs of $1.50, $1.60, and $1.70 per unit. How would this computation be accomplished in the computer model?
10. Assuming that variable costs increase by $0.10 as in exercise 8, how many units must be sold during the first six months to break even for the first six months?
11. Why is it of value to maintain a modular concept in building large-scale computer-based corporate models?
12. In a structural sense, how can a multitude of divisions, groups, and subsidiary companies be related in large-scale corporate models?

Problems

13. The president of a large bank (assets of more than $2 billion) is considering the development of a computerized financial planning system to facilitate rapid analysis and comparison of short and longer term policies and performance.

    The present system requires largely manual computation of only a few alternatives that management feels are the most likely and promising. It is time consuming both in terms of man-hours and overall time to evaluate an alternative. In addition, the manual system does not consider all important interrelationships of financial flows and therefore does not reflect the full financial impact of alternatives. Specifically, the manual system is not able to evaluate rapidly and accurately the full impact of changes in the discount rate, reserve requirements, earning assets, and the deposit base.

In structuring the system of planning models, the bank decided on six functional modules plus a composite planning model to predict overall performance. The six functional models centered on commercial loans and installment loans in the fund-using category, deposits in the fund-providing category, plus modules for noninterest income and expenses. The structure of basic inputs and outputs of the six functional models and the composite model is shown in Figure 6–15, along with the key bank variables.

List as many *what if* questions as you can, that the bank president should be able to pose and expect to be answered by the model. The detailed design of the models must take account of these kinds of questions.

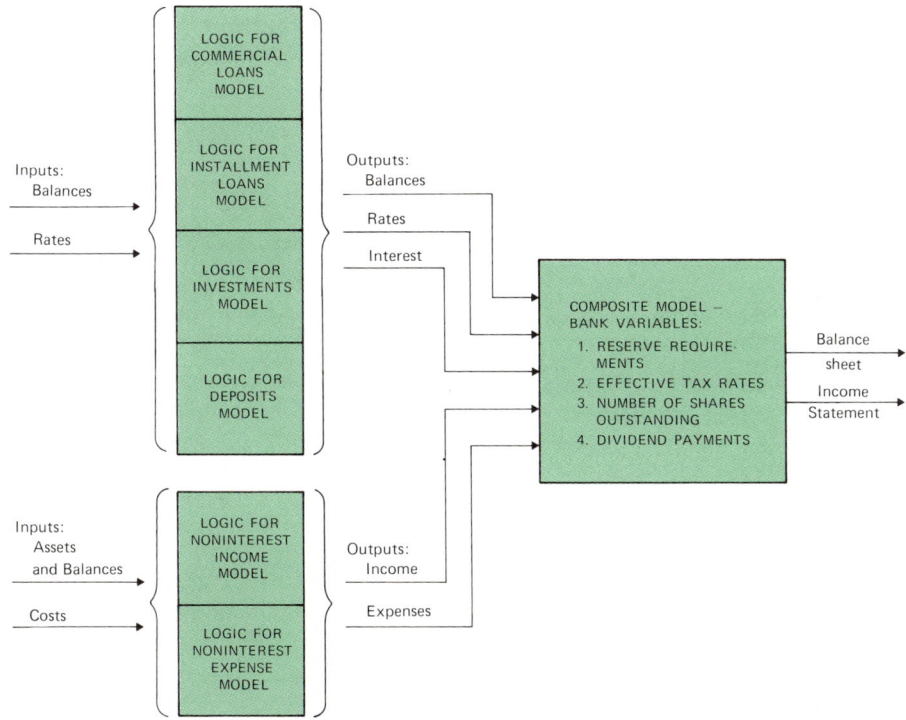

FIGURE 6–15. **Inputs and outputs for six functional models and a composite model for a bank**

14. Tax planning is an important reality for many individuals and most profit enterprises. Design the structure of a tax planning model by developing a block

diagram of the basic modules, indicating the inputs, transformations (what functions performed), and outputs for each module. The blocks in the diagram need not be thought of as separate models.

Begin by listing the key factors, or *what if* questions that might be important in determining the short-and long-term impact on taxes. Who would use such a tax model? Can it reflect tax laws as well as tax rulings? How can it be made flexible enough to allow for changes in tax laws and rulings?

15. The NEWSprint Company is a large supplier of paper to the newspaper industry. It operates through a system of four paper mills located in the United States and has an international division that operates two Canadian plants. Paper is supplied to the United States and international markets from both the domestic and Canadian plants; however, organizationally the international division is separate.

    NEWSprint is considering the development of computer-based corporate planning models. Discussions with management indicate that primary problems revolve around shifting patterns and changes in demand forecasts, demand at individual mills, distribution costs, and inventory levels. In addition, capital expenditures for the company as a whole are an important aspect of planning and affect mill output and productivity. Propose a structure of models and their linkage to meet company needs.

References

1. Ackoff, R. L. *A Concept of Corporate Planning,* Wiley-Interscience, New York, 1970.
2. Barkdoll, G., "Models—New Management Decision Aid," *Industrial Engineering,* December 1970, pp. 32–40.
3. Boulden, J. B., *Computer Based Planning Systems,* McGraw-Hill, New York, 1975.
4. ———, and E. S. Buffa, "Corporate Models: On-Line, Real-Time Systems," *Harvard Business Review,* July–August 1970.
5. ———, and E. R. McLean, "An Executive's Guide to Computer-Based Planning," *California Management Review,* Vol. 17, No. 1, Fall 1974, pp. 58–67.
6. Buffa, E. S., *Operations Management: Problems and Models,* third edition, John Wiley & Sons, New York, 1972, Chapter 21.
7. Churchman, C. W., "Reliability of Models in the Social Sciences," *Interfaces,* Vol. 4, No. 1, November 1973.
8. Dietz, R. V., and R. V. Scavullo, "Industrial Progress: A System to Develop Utility Systems Planning," *Public Utilities Fortnightly,* May 9, 1974.
9. Elmaghraby, S. E., "The Role of Modeling in IE Design," *The Journal of Industrial Engineering,* Vol. 19, No. 6, June 1968.
10. Geoffrion, A., "Progress in Computer Assisted Distribution System Planning," Working Paper No. 219a, Western Management Science Institute, University of California, Los Angeles, revised June 1975.

11. ——, "Better Distribution Planning with Computer Models," *Harvard Business Review,* Vol. 54, No. 4, July–August 1976.
12. Gershefski, G. W., "Building a Corporate Financial Model," *Harvard Business Review,* January–February 1969, pp. 72–82.
13. ——, "Corporate Models—The State of the Art," *Management Science,* Vol. 16, No. 6, February 1970.
14. Hamilton, W. F., and M. A. Moses, "An Optimization Model for Corporate Financial Planning," *Operations Research,* Vol. 21, No. 3, May–June 1973, pp. 677–92.
15. ——, "A Computer-Based Corporate Planning System," *Management Science,* Vol. 21, No. 2, October 1974, pp. 148–159.
16. Lee, W. B., and C. P. McLaughlin, "Corporate Simulation Models for Aggregate Materials Managment," *Production & Inventory Management,* 1st Quarter, 1974, pp. 56–67.
17. Little, J. D. C., "Models and Managers: The Concept of a Decision Calculus," *Management Science,* Vol. 16, No. 8, April 1970.
18. Morris, W. T., "On the Art of Modeling," *Management Science,* Vol. 13, No. 12, August 1967.
19. Naylor, T. H., and H. Schauland, "A Survey of Users of Corporate Planning Models," *Management Science,* Vol. 22, No. 9, May 1976, 927–37.
20. Ogden, J., "'What Happens If': A Planning System for Utilities," *Public Utilities Fortnightly,* March 1972.
21. Reisman, A., and E. S. Buffa, "A General Model for Investment Policy," *Management Science,* Vol. 8, No. 3, April 1962.
22. Rivett, P., *Principles of Model Building,* John Wiley & Sons, New York, 1972.
23. Rosenthal, B., and R. C. Murphy, "Instant Manpower Replanning Is Here," *State Government Administration,* February 1975.
24. Ruhl, G. J., "Conservation: What is It Worth? A Quantitative Approach Using a Rate and Revenue Model," *Public Utilities Fortnightly,* December 19, 1974, pp. 33–37.
25. Schrieber, A. N., editor, *Corporate Simulation Models,* Graduate School of Business Administration, University of Washington, 1970.
26. Seaberg, R. A., and C. Seaberg, "Computer Based Decision Systems in Xerox Corporate Planning," *Management Science,* Vol. 20, No. 4, December, Part II, 1973, pp. 575–84.
27. Stephenson, G. G., "A Hierarchy of Models for Planning in a Division of I.C.I.," *Operational Research Quarterly,* Vol. 20, 1970, pp. 221–45.
28. Strauch, R. E., "'Squishy' Problems and Quantitative Methods," The Rand Corporation, Santa Monica, California, P-5303, October 1974.
29. Urban, G. L., "Building Models for Decision Makers," *Interfaces,* Vol. 4, No. 3, May 1974.
30. Wheelwright, S. C., and S. G. Makridakis, *Computer-Aided Modeling for Managers,* Addison-Wesley, Reading, Mass., 1972.
31. Zeleny, M., "Managers Without Management Science," *Interfaces,* Vol. 5, No. 4, August 1975.

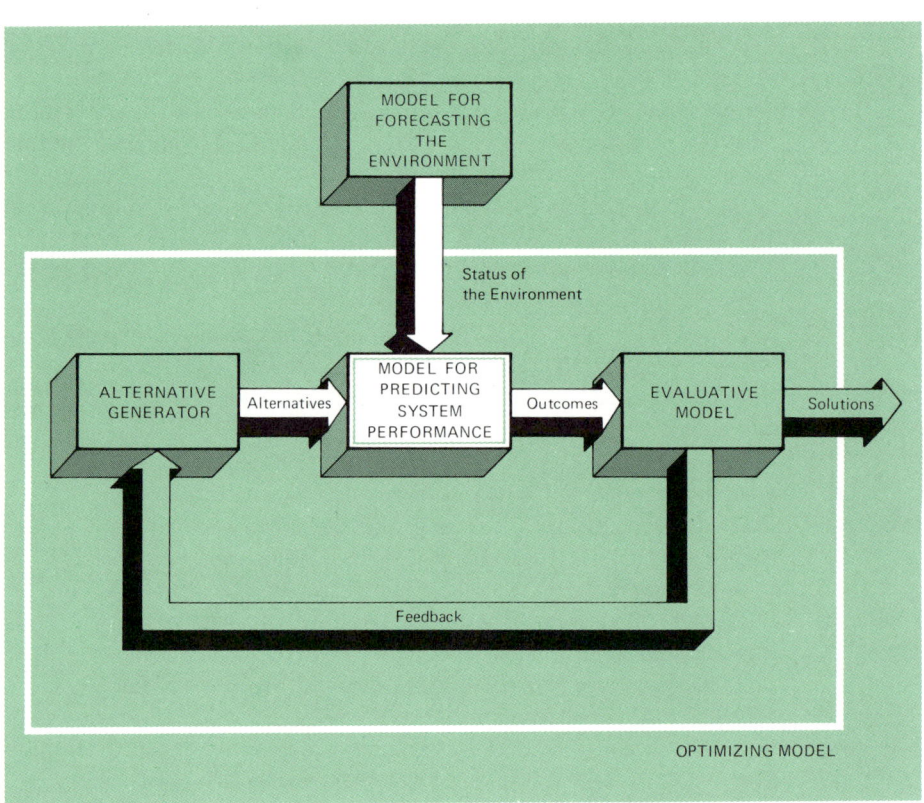

7

PREDICTING THE EFFECTS OF RISK— MARKOV CHAINS

Suppose a person enrolls as a freshman in a four-year college. What is the probability that he will be enrolled as a sophomore the next year? What is the probability that he will actually graduate after four years? Suppose a person chooses brand X from three competitive products X, Y, and Z. What is the probability that he will purchase brand Y next time? Suppose a person is in a mental hospital in January. What is the probability that he will be in an outside home in May? Suppose a person has a job as a department head in a major corporation. What is the probability that he will be promoted to a corporate vice-president in five years?

In many real-world problems, it is convenient to classify individuals or items into distinct categories or *states*. We can then analyze the transitions of these individuals or items from one state to another over time. For example, if we are analyzing college enrollments, we may use the classifications of freshman, sophomore, junior, senior, graduated, and dropout as our states. We can then investigate the probability that a freshman will become a sophomore after one year, or a senior after three years. If we are concerned with analyzing alternative marketing strategies, we may use the classification of a purchaser of brand X, a purchaser of brand Y, or a purchaser of brand Z as our states. What would be the appropriate states to use in the analysis of a mental hospital or of job advancement in a major corporation?

Generally, we speak in terms of the probability that a person or an item will move from one state to another during time period n. Suppose the probability that a person moves from state i to state j during time period n depends only on the previous state i, and is independent of the time period n. Then the process can be analyzed using Markov chains. This approach will be illustrated through the use of several examples.

FORECASTING COLLEGE ENROLLMENTS

Accurate forecasts of college enrollments are extremely important for many decisions that relate to the management of higher education. The decision to expand the facilities at various campuses or to add a new campus may depend on enrollment forecasts. Questions that may be important include the following:
1. If 100 new students enroll as freshmen each year in a four-year college, what will the total increase in the enrollment be after four years?
2. If 100 new students enroll as freshmen each year, how many will actually graduate?

These questions can be answered by using the concepts of Markov chains.

Estimation of Transition Probabilities

The analysis of enrollments begins with the classification of students into mutually exclusive categories or states. The appropriate classification will depend on the particular problem that is being analyzed. For example, the states used to analyze enrollments in a major university might be lower division undergraduate, upper division undergraduate, master's level, and doctoral studies. For simplicity, we shall assume that we are analyzing enrollments in a four-year college with no graduate programs. The major student flows are illustrated in Figure 7-1.

Suppose we confine our interest to the states of dropout (Do), freshman (Fr), sophomore (So), junior (Jr), senior (Sr), and graduated (Gr). According to Figure 7-1, a freshman in one academic year either becomes a sophomore the next academic year or drops out. For simplicity in this example, we are ignoring the relatively small proportion of individuals who may drop out of college for a year or more and then return, and the individuals who make less than "normal" progress and do not move from one state to another after each academic year. However, these complicating factors could be incorporated into a similar, more detailed analysis.

Now we need the probability that a freshman will become a sophomore, and the probability that he will become a dropout. Actual data on the progress of students in the public four-year colleges of Texas from 1960 through 1967 are shown in Table 7-1. The number of sophomores as a percentage of freshmen is relatively constant with a mean value of 54.0 and a range of from 51.3 to 55.4. Thus, it would seem reasonable to use 0.54 as an estimate of the probability that

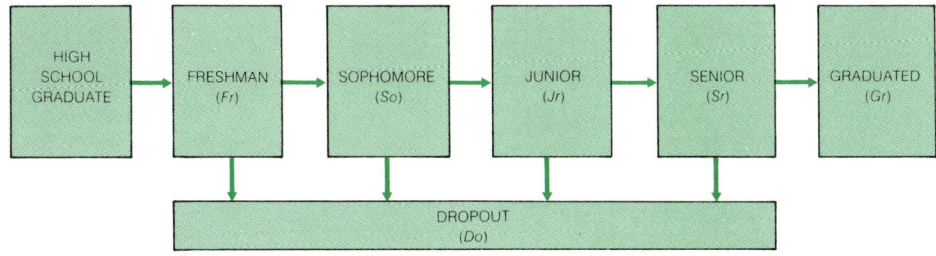

FIGURE 7-1. **Major student flows in a four-year college**

a freshman will become a sophomore, and to assume that this probability does not depend on the particular academic year, since the figures show no notable trend or other systematic variation. It follows that $1.0 - 0.54 = 0.46$ is the probability that a freshman will drop out after one academic year, since this is the only other state possible according to the student flow diagram of Figure 7-1.

Stated symbolically, we have the conditional probability that a freshman during academic year $n - 1$ will become a sophomore the next academic year n, $P(So_n|Fr_{n-1}) = 0.54$. Similarly, $P(Do_n|Fr_{n-1}) = 0.46$, and $P(Jr_n|So_{n-1}) = 0.87$ and $P(Do_n|So_{n-1}) = 0.13$ from Table 7-1.

TABLE 7-1. **Progress of Entering Freshman Classes in the Public Four-Year Colleges of Texas**

Fall Class Entered	No. of Freshmen	No. of Sophomores 1 Year Later	No. of Sophomores as Percentage of Freshmen	No. of Juniors 2 Years Later	No. of Juniors as Percentage of Sophomores	No. of Seniors 3 Years Later	No. of Seniors as Percentage of Juniors
1960	18,451	9,913	53.7	8,468	85.4	8,260	97.5
1961	20,687	11,473	55.4	9,235	80.5	9,350	101.2
1962	22,253	11,414	51.3	10,226	89.6	10,335	101.1
1963	23,611	12,695	53.8	11,446	90.2	11,373	99.4
1964	26,474	14,283	53.9	12,351	86.5	12,526	101.4
1965	30,484	16,652	54.6	14,685	88.2	---	---
1966	32,933	18,103	55.0	---	---	---	---
1967	33,411	---	---	---	---	---	---
Total	174,893	94,533	54.0	66,411	86.9	51,844	100.2

Source: Coordinating Board, Texas College and University System, unpublished reports of enrollment, Fall 1960–Fall 1967.

Notice that the number of seniors as a percentage of the number of juniors has a mean value of 100.2, indicating perhaps that there are individuals who remain classified as seniors for two or more academic years. For simplicity, we assume that $P(Sr_n|Jr_{n-1}) = 1.0$ and $P(Do_n|Jr_{n-1}) = 0.0$ are reasonable estimates. We also assume that every individual who becomes a senior will actually graduate, so $P(Gr_n|Sr_{n-1}) = 1.0$ and $P(Do_n|Sr_{n-1}) = 0.0$.

These conditional probabilities can be conveniently summarized in tabular form as illustrated in Table 7–2. Each entry in Table 7–2 is the probability of moving from the state indicated by the corresponding row to the state indicated by the corresponding column. For example, the 0.87 entry indicates that the probability that a sophomore will become a junior after one academic year is 0.87.

Since the entries in Table 7–2 represent the probabilities of transition from one state to another, they are called *transition probabilities*. The table or matrix of probabilities is called the *transition matrix* for the problem.

TABLE 7–2. **Probabilities of Transition from One State to Another**

From	To: Do	Fr	So	Jr	Sr	Gr
Do	1.0	0.0	0.0	0.0	0.0	0.0
Fr	0.46	0.0	0.54	0.0	0.0	0.0
So	0.13	0.0	0.0	0.87	0.0	0.0
Jr	0.0	0.0	0.0	0.0	1.0	0.0
Sr	0.0	0.0	0.0	0.0	0.0	1.0
Gr	0.0	0.0	0.0	0.0	0.0	1.0

Use of Transition Probabilities

The transition probabilities in the transition matrix can be used to answer the questions posed initially regarding the impact of 100 new students enrolling as freshmen. Since $P(So_n|Fr_{n-1}) = 0.54$, there would be $(100)(0.54) = 54$ additional sophomores the following year, and since $P(Jr_n|So_{n-1}) = 0.87$, there would be $(54)(0.87) \cong 47$ new juniors two years hence.* Finally, since $P(Sr_n|Jr_{n-1}) = 1.0$, there would be 47 incremental seniors. The total increase in enrollment in the college after four years from an increase of 100 new students as freshmen each year would be 248, as calculated in Table 7–3. The number of additional persons who graduate each year would also be estimated as 47, since $P(Gr_n|Sr_{n-1}) = 1.0$.

---

*The symbol $\cong$ is read "is approximately equal to."

TABLE 7-3. **Total Increase in Enrollment After Four Years From an Additional 100 Freshmen Each Year**

Increase in:	
Freshmen	100
Sophomores	54
Juniors	47
Seniors	47
Total	248

This example has illustrated how transition probabilities can be obtained and used to analyze a problem of enrollment forecasting. Additional insights can be obtained when the transition matrix is actually used in the analysis. This process will be illustrated through a second example.

BRAND SWITCHING

An important application of transition matrices is in the analysis of *brand switching* among consumers. For example, suppose there are three major automobile manufacturers who dominate the automobile market. During the previous month, manufacturer X sold a total of 120,000 automobiles, manufacturer Y sold 203,000, and manufacturer Z sold 377,000. However, the sales totals do not tell the full story regarding customer preferences.

Customers do not always purchase a new automobile from the same producer that manufactured their previous automobile. This phenomenon, called *brand switching,* has important implications for marketing analysis and for planning advertising strategies. In order to analyze this phenomenon, data are needed on the manufacturer of the car previously owned by each of these purchasers.

Table 7-4 shows how these data might be displayed. From Table 7-4, we see that the market share of manufacturer Z has declined from $400/700 = 0.571$ to $377/700 = 0.539$, with most of the gain going to manufacturer X. Of the 120,000 new automobiles purchased from manufacturer X, 85,000 customers previously owned an automobile manufactured by X, 20,000 owned an automobile manufactured by Y, and 15,000 owned an automobile manufactured by Z. Of the 100,000 previous owners of automobiles manufactured by X, 8,000 purchased a new automobile from manufacturer Y, while only 7,000 purchased from Z. These data show not only the total sales and the market shares, but also indicate the relationship among the manufacturers in terms of customer brand loyalty and brand switching.

TABLE 7-4. **Automobile Brand Switching**

Previously Owned Automobile Made by:	Purchased New Automobile Made by:			Total	Previous Market Share
	X	Y	Z		
X	85	8	7	100	0.143
Y	20	160	20	200	0.286
Z	15	35	350	400	0.571
Total	120	203	377	700	
New Market Share	0.171	0.290	0.539		

Note: Data given in thousands.

On the basis of these data, questions such as the following might be asked and analyzed:

1. Should the advertising campaign of manufacturer Z be directed toward attracting previous purchasers of automobiles manufactured by X or Y, or should it concentrate on retaining a larger proportion of the previous purchasers of automobiles manufactured by Z?
2. The purchaser of a new automobile keeps the car an average of three years. If this trend in brand switching continues, what will the market shares of the three companies be in three years? In six years?
3. If this trend in brand switching continues, will the market shares continue to fluctuate, or will an equilibrium eventually be reached?

These questions can be analyzed by developing and using transition probabilities and the transition matrix.

The Matrix of Transition Probabilities

Given the data in Table 7-4, it is a simple matter to compute the transition probabilities. The probability that a previous owner of an automobile manufactured by X will purchase a new automobile from Y is $8/100 = 0.08$, and from Z is $7/100 = 0.07$. The probability that X will retain a customer is $85/100 = 0.85$. Thus we simply divide each entry in Table 7-4 by the corresponding row total, as follows:

	X	Y	Z
X	$85/100 = 0.8500$	$8/100 = 0.0800$	$7/100 = 0.0700$
Y	$20/200 = 0.1000$	$160/200 = 0.8000$	$20/200 = 0.1000$
Z	$15/400 = 0.0375$	$35/400 = 0.0875$	$350/400 = 0.8750$

These calculations determine the transition matrix shown in Table 7-5.

Notice that the sum of the entries in each row in the transition matrix is 1.0. This is an important characteristic of a transition matrix. The columns of the transition matrix yield the following information:

(1) X retains 85 percent of its customers, gains 10 percent of Y's customers, and gains 3.75 percent of Z's customers.
(2) Y gains 8 percent of X's customers, retains 80 percent of its customers, and gains 8.75 percent of Z's customers.
(3) Z gains 7 percent of X's customers, gains 10 percent of Y's customers, and retains 87.5 percent of its customers.

We shall now consider how this matrix can be used to analyze marketing strategies.

TABLE 7-5. **Transition Matrix for Brand Switching**

From	To: (1) X	(2) Y	(3) Z
X	0.8500	0.0800	0.0700
Y	0.1000	0.8000	0.1000
Z	0.0375	0.0875	0.8750

An Example of a Markov Chain The matrix of transition probabilities can be used to study the dynamic behavior of consumer purchasing patterns if the following assumptions can be justified:

1. The probability that a customer will switch to another manufacturer or purchase again from the same manufacturer depends only on the brand of the automobile he now owns. The brands of the automobiles he has owned previously are irrelevant.
2. The probability that a customer will switch to another manufacturer or purchase again from the same manufacturer is independent of how many previous purchases he has made.

For example, suppose customer Jones owned an automobile manufactured by Z and then purchased an automobile from X, while customer Smith owned an automobile manufactured by X and purchased a new one from X. According to assumption 1, the probabilities that Jones and Smith will purchase their next cars from X, or switch to Y or Z, must be identical.

If these assumptions are reasonable, and in many real-world marketing analyses they are, then the series of purchases by consumers constitute a *Markov chain* of the first order. Under such conditions, the matrix of transition probabilities can be used to provide further insights into consumer purchasing patterns.

Prediction of Market Shares in Future Periods

The current market share for each of the manufacturers is 0.171 for manufacturer X, 0.290 for manufacturer Y, and 0.539 for manufacturer Z. These numbers appear in Table 7–4 and were obtained by dividing the number of automobiles sold by each manufacturer by the total number of automobiles sold by all three manufacturers.

The average length of time that a new automobile purchaser keeps his automobile is three years. If the brand switching behavior of the customers continues in the same manner as described in the transition matrix of Table 7–5, what will the market shares be in three years, when the customers purchase new automobiles again? We can write the current market shares as the column of numbers shown below:

	Market Share
X	0.171
Y	0.290
Z	0.539

where the numbers represent the proportion of the total new automobile sales attributable to each manufacturer.

By using the following procedure we can estimate the market share of manufacturer X in three years. From column (1) of Table 7–5, we know that X retains 85 percent of its customers, or 85 percent of its market share. Thus, we expect X to retain $(0.171)(0.85) = 0.145$ of its current market share. X also gains 10 percent of the customers of Y, or 10 percent of Y's market share. Therefore, X would gain $(0.290)(0.10) = 0.029$ of the market from Y. Likewise, X would gain 3.75 percent of the market of Z, or $(0.539)(0.0375) = 0.020$. Adding the proportion of the market share retained, 0.145, the proportion of the market gained from Y, 0.029, and the proportion of the market gained from Z, 0.020, gives

$$0.145 + 0.029 + 0.020 = 0.194$$

as the estimate of the market share of X in three years. This estimate represents a net gain of $0.194 - 0.171 = 0.023$, or 2.3 percent of the market.

Notice that these calculations are equivalent to simply multiplying the numbers in the market share column shown previously by the corresponding numbers in column (1) of the transition matrix (Table 7–5) and summing the results. That is, we have

Market Share Column		Column (1) of Transition Matrix		
0.171	×	0.8500	=	0.145
0.290	×	0.1000	=	0.029
0.539	×	0.0375	=	0.020
				0.194

To obtain the estimated market share for Y in three years, we can multiply the market share by the corresponding numbers in column (2) of the transition matrix as follows:

Market Share Column		Column (2) of Transition Matrix		
0.171	×	0.0800	=	0.014
0.290	×	0.8000	=	0.232
0.539	×	0.0875	=	0.047
				0.293

The net increase is 0.293 percent for the market share of Y. Verify that the estimate of the market share for Z in three years is 0.513.

Thus the estimated market share column in three years is

	Market Share
X	0.194
Y	0.293
Z	0.513

Now, to estimate the market shares of X, Y, and Z six years hence, when the typical customer will again purchase an automobile, we can multiply the new values in the column of market shares times the corresponding numbers in the columns of the transition matrix in Table 7–5. Thus the estimated market share of X in six years would be found as follows:

Market Share Column		Column (1) of Transition Matrix		
0.194	×	0.8500	=	0.165
0.293	×	0.1000	=	0.029
0.513	×	0.0375	=	0.019
				0.213

Again the market share of X has increased. If the estimated total sales six years hence is 900,000, then the estimated sales for manufacturer X would be $(0.213)(900,000) = 191,700$.

By continuing this process, we can find the estimated market shares for each manufacturer for any multiple of three years into the future. To find the estimated market shares nine years hence, simply take the estimated market shares in six years found as indicated above, and multiply them times the columns in the transition matrix. Using these estimates and the transition matrix, we can find the estimated market shares twelve years hence, etc. Naturally, this analysis assumes that the brand switching behavior of the customers as indicated in Table 7–5 remains constant (assumption 2).

In our analysis, the market shares of X and Y increased, while that of Z fell. If the brand switching behavior of the customers remains constant, will this shift of customers from Z to X and Y continue indefinitely, or will an equilibrium point be reached at which there are no more changes in the market shares?

Equilibrium

Suppose we assume that at some future time, an equilibrium point will be reached so that the market shares of X, Y, and Z do not change. At that point, the same proportion of customers would switch *to* each brand as switch *from* each brand over each purchase cycle of three years.

Let us assume that these equilibrium market shares are x for manufacturer X, y for manufacturer Y, and z for manufacturer Z. Thus the column of market shares at equilibrium is

	Equilibrium Market Share
X	x
Y	y
Z	z

To estimate the market shares of each manufacturer in another three years, we would simply multiply the numbers in this column times the corresponding numbers in the transition matrix columns (Table 7–5), and sum the results. However, we know the results will remain unchanged at the equilibrium point, so the sum for X will be the market share for X, which is simply x.

That is, to calculate the market share for X in three years *after* equilibrium has been reached, we would simply perform the following calculations:

Equilibrium Market Share Column		Column (1) of Transition Matrix		
x	×	0.8500	=	$0.8500x$
y	×	0.1000	=	$0.1000y$
z	×	0.0375	=	$0.0375z$
		Equilibrium market share for X	=	x

But we know that the sum will simply be x, since the market share of X remains unchanged when equilibrium has been reached. We can rewrite this summation in the form of an equation,

$$0.8500x + 0.1000y + 0.0375z = x,$$

which simplifies to

$$0.1500x - 0.1000y - 0.0375z = 0. \qquad (1)$$

Performing similar calculations for the market share of Y gives

$$0.0800x + 0.8000y + 0.0875z = y,$$

which simplifies to

$$0.0800x - 0.2000y + 0.0875z = 0. \qquad (2)$$

Similarly, for Z we obtain

$$0.0700x + 0.1000y - 0.1250z = 0. \qquad (3)$$

Since the market shares are proportions, we also know that

$$x + y + z = 1. \qquad (4)$$

Thus, we have four equations and three unknowns. We may use equation (4) and any two of equations (1) through (3) and solve for the values of x, y, and z, using one of the methods reviewed in Appendix A. Substituting these values back into the fourth equation provides a check on our computations.

Suppose we choose equations (2), (3), and (4), and solve them by the method of substitution. We can eliminate y from (2) and (3) by multiplying (3) by 2 and adding it to (2) as follows:

$$
\begin{array}{ll}
0.1400x + 0.2000y - 0.2500z = 0 & \text{[(3) multiplied by 2]} \\
\underline{0.0800x - 0.2000y + 0.0875z = 0} & (2) \\
0.2200x \qquad\quad - 0.1625z = 0. & \qquad (5)
\end{array}
$$

We can eliminate y from (3) and (4) by multiplying (3) by -10 and adding it to (4) as follows:

$$
\begin{array}{ll}
-0.70x - 1.00y + 1.25z = 0 & \text{[(3) multiplied by } -10] \\
\underline{x + y + z = 1} & (4) \\
0.30x + 2.25z = 1. & \qquad (6)
\end{array}
$$

Finally, we can eliminate x from (5) and (6) by multiplying (5) by -0.3, multiplying (6) by 0.22, and adding the resulting equations:

$$
\begin{array}{ll}
-0.066x + 0.04875z = 0 & \text{[(5) multiplied by } -0.3] \\
\underline{0.066x + 0.49500z = 0.22} & \text{[(6) multiplied by 0.22]} \\
0.54375z = 0.22. &
\end{array}
$$

Therefore, $z = 0.22/0.54375 = 0.4046$. Substituting this value back into (6), we have

$$0.30x + (2.25)(0.4046) = 1,$$

which simplifies to

$$0.30x = 0.0897,$$

so that $x = 0.0897/0.30 = 0.2990$. Finally, we substitute these values of x and z into (4) to obtain

$$y = 1.0 - 0.2990 - 0.4046$$

or $y = 0.2964$.

We can check these results by substituting them into equation (1), which gives

$$(0.1500)(0.2990) - (0.1000)(0.2964) - (0.0375)(0.4046) = 0.0,$$

as we expected. Note that these calculations are straightforward, but admittedly somewhat tedious, even for a problem with only three states. In real-world applications, there will generally be more than three states, but these calculations can be done efficiently on a computer in only a few seconds.

These results tell us that at equilibrium the market shares of manufacturers X, Y, and Z will be 0.30, 0.30, and 0.40, respectively (rounding to two decimal places). This result assumes that the brand switching behavior of the consumers continues according to the pattern in Table 7–5. Thus we would expect X's market share to continue to grow from its current value of 0.17, but to stabilize at 0.30. The market share of Y will remain virtually unchanged, since its current value is 0.29. Manufacturer Z will continue to lose customers from its current share of 0.539, but will fall only to 0.40, and will still be the dominant manufacturer in the industry.

Use of the Markov Chain Analysis

The Markov chain analysis can be used to analyze the effects of various marketing strategies. Recall that the equilibrium market shares of 0.30, 0.30, and 0.40 were derived on the basis of the assumption that the brand switching behavior of the consumers as described in Table 7–5 remains unchanged. What if manufacturer X undertakes an aggressive marketing strategy designed to encourage more of the customers who previously purchased automobiles from manufacturer Z to switch to automobiles manufactured by X? Recall advertisements that you have seen in which one manufacturer focuses its marketing campaign on one competitor while ignoring others.

Suppose the market analysts feel that such a campaign would increase the percentage of Z's customers who switch to automobiles manufactured by X from 3.75 to 7.5, so that the transition matrix for the automobile industry would become the one illustrated in Table 7–6. Verify that the new long-run (equilibrium) market shares of the three manufacturers based on this change would become 0.366 for X, 0.295 for Y, and 0.339 for Z. Thus, *a successful marketing campaign would make X the dominant force in the industry and relegate Z to second place.*

TABLE 7-6. **New Transition Matrix for Brand Switching**

		To:		
		X	Y	Z
From	X	0.8500	0.0800	0.0700
	Y	0.1000	0.8000	0.1000
	Z	0.0750	0.0875	0.8375

AN ANALYSIS OF A GERIATRIC WARD

Meredith [1973] presents an example of an analysis of a real-world problem using Markov chains. At the California Napa State Hospital, a resocialization program was instituted in 1964 to deinstitutionalize geriatric (elderly) patients so that they could be placed in boarding homes or their equivalent outside the hospital. The analysis was performed to determine the costs and the benefits of the program.

For the purposes of the analysis, it was convenient to classify current or former patients into the following states:
1. in the Geriatric Resocialization Program (GRP)
2. in one of the hospital wards
3. in a home but placed from GRP
4. in a home but placed directly from a ward
5. deceased

It seemed reasonable to assume that the movement of a patient from one state to another could be described by a Markov chain. This assumption implies that the probability of movement to the next state depends only on the patient's current state and not on the time period. The only concern was that for long-term projections, the probability of a patient's death would actually increase; however, since the probability of death is quite small, this effect was not considered significant, so the Markov chain assumption was made.

The probabilities of movement among the five states for a period of one month are given in Table 7-7. The cost of keeping a patient in each state for one month is shown in the right-hand column of Table 7-7. These probabilities were determined from actual hospital records in the same manner illustrated in the enrollment forecasting and in the brand switching examples.

Notice in Table 7-7 that the probability of moving to another state from *deceased* is 0.0, and the probability of remaining deceased is 1.0, as we would expect. What if we calculate the long-run, equilibrium probability of patients in each state? Once a patient reaches the state *deceased*, he can never leave it. In general terms, this is called an *absorbing state* in a transition matrix. In the enrollment forecasting example with the transition matrix shown in Table 7-2, the states *dropout* and *graduated* are absorbing states also. If an absorbing state exists in a transition matrix, all of the persons or items will eventually move into the absorbing state (unless the transition matrix has other unusual characteristics which need not concern us here).

For the transition matrix in Table 7-7, the long-run proportion of patients in each state is obviously 0.0 in GRP, ward, home (from GRP), and home (from ward), and 1.0 in deceased. In other words, in the long run, all of the patients are deceased. This analysis provides little useful information, so another type of long-run analysis is required when the transition matrix has absorbing states.

Using techniques slightly more involved than those presented here, Meredith computed the mean number of months a patient starting in each of the five nonabsorbing states would stay in each of these states before entering the absorbing state *deceased*. He multiplied these results times the costs of being in each of these states for one month, and obtained the results shown in Table 7-8. For example, these figures indicate that a patient starting in the GRP can be expected to be in the program for a total of 26 months, in a ward for 38 months, in a home after placement from the GRP for 95 months, and in a home after direct placement from a ward for 4 months before dying.

The total cost to the state of treating this patient will be $64,950. Notice that a patient starting in a ward expects to spend much more time in the hospital ward and much less time in a home, since all patients are not selected for the GRP. Also notice that the expected total cost of treating a patient in the GRP is about $13,000 less than for one in the ward.

What if there were no GRP? A transition matrix similar to Table 7-7 was developed with only three states—ward, home (from ward), and deceased. The expected stay times for the average patient in each of the two states—ward and home (from ward)—before dying are shown in Table 7-9, along with the associated costs. The costs are significantly higher, about 30 percent. In addition, the average patient currently in the ward can now be expected to spend approximately 13 of his remaining 14 years in the ward (152 months in the ward and 15 months in a home after direct placement from a ward).

On the basis of this analysis Meredith was able to estimate that the GRP had resulted in a net savings to the state of some $15 million after only 5.5 years of operation. This amount corresponds to a savings of approximately $3 million per year.

WHAT SHOULD THE MANAGER KNOW?

Markov chains can be the basis for a predictive model for forecasting the future state of a person, a company, or an item. This predictive model is used when risk is involved in the form of probabilities of transition from one state to another.

TABLE 7-7. **One-Month Transition Probabilities and Costs**

	To:					
From	GRP	Ward	Home (from GRP)	Home (from Ward)	Deceased	Cost per Month ($)
GRP	0.854	0.028	0.112	0.000	0.006	682
Ward	0.013	0.978	0.000	0.003	0.006	655
Home (from GRP)	0.025	0.000	0.969	0.000	0.006	226
Home (from Ward)	0.000	0.025	0.000	0.969	0.006	226
Deceased	0.000	0.000	0.000	0.000	1.000	0

Source: J. Meredith, "A Markovian Analysis of a Geriatric Ward," *Management Science*, June 1972; used by permission.

TABLE 7-8. **Expected Stay Times (months) and Costs**

Initial State	GRP	Ward	Home (from GRP)	Home (from Ward)	Cost ($)
GRP	26	38	95	4	64,950
Ward	17	77	63	7	77,800
Home (from GRP)	21	31	109	3	59,900
Home (from Ward)	14	62	51	38	70,250

Source: J. Meredith, "A Markovian Analysis of a Geriatric Ward," *Management Science*, June 1972; used by permission.

TABLE 7-9. **Expected Stay Times (months) and Costs Without GRP**

Initial State	Ward	Home (from Ward)	Cost ($)
Ward	152	15	102,900
Home (from Ward)	123	44	90,400

Source: J. Meredith, "A Markovian Analysis of a Geriatric Ward," *Management Science*, June 1972; used by permission.

The approach is limited to problems with very special characteristics, but it does provide useful information to managers in those cases where it can be applied.

Problem Characteristics

It must be possible to classify the items involved in the problem into unique states. For example, students were classified by academic level or by dropout or graduated status; the customers were classified according to the brands of automobiles they purchased; and patients were classified according to whether they were in a program, a home, a hospital ward, or deceased.

Next, it must be possible to determine the probability that a person or an item in each state will be in any other state in the next time period. This probability must

1. depend only on the current state, and
2. be independent of the particular time period.

These probabilities form a transition matrix.

Examples of real-world problems that often have these characteristics include enrollment forecasting, brand switching analysis, and health care system analysis. Trinkl [1974] presents an analysis of programs for the mentally retarded in Hawaii that is very similar to the analysis of Meredith [1973] in California. Pegels and Jelmert [1970] report the use of Markov chains to evaluate blood-inventory policies.

Several models for the evaluation of human resources and manpower planning also include Markov chains. For example, Flamholtz [1974] has used Markov chains to calculate the probabilities that individuals within an organization will occupy each of several jobs in the future. Charnes, Cooper, and Niehaus [1972] report that similar transition matrices have been developed for manpower planning in the U.S. Navy.

Formulation and Data

The transition matrices are not particularly difficult to formulate. The manager should be involved in the identification of the relevant states. An attempt should be made to keep the number of states to a minimum. For example, in a brand switching analysis, it may be possible to ignore a large number of minor competitors or to group them into the single state *other*.

The required data are the transition probabilities. In cases such as the enrollment forecasting, mental retardation studies, and manpower planning studies, there may be sufficient historical data to determine proportions that can be converted into probabilities. However, the data must be carefully scrutinized. Adjustments may be required to compensate for recent trends or unusual patterns in the past that are not likely to repeat themselves. For example, data on college enrollments just before or just after a war should not be the basis for forecasts during peacetime. Similarly, brand switching data could be distorted by a strike in one of the companies during a particular year. The manager should be alert for such problems.

As a note of interest, the Market Research Corporation of America (MRCA) has established a sample of families who report their purchases of certain branded items to MRCA. These reports can be used as the basis for transition matrices in a brand switching analysis. Similar services are provided by other organizations.

When actual data are unavailable or of questionable validity for future projections, subjective probabilities can be used. Again, the manager should play an active role in the assessment of these subjective probabilities.

Computations

The computations are straightforward, but quickly become tedious. It is simple to develop or obtain computer programs that can rapidly perform the onerous arithmetic and present the results to the manager for interpretation.

Interpretation

There are three important results that can be obtained from the use of the transition matrices. First, forecasts of the proportion of individuals or items in each state can be attained for future time periods. These forecasts are obtained by multiplying a column of proportions (market shares in the brand switching example) times each column in the transition matrix, and summing the results. This information can be extremely useful for short-term forecasting of enrollments or sales.

Second, the long-run or equilibrium proportions can be developed for some transition matrices. The equilibrium state was illustrated for the brand switching problem. In the long run, these results indicate that the proportion of customers in each state will reach equilibrium values and remain unchanged. The sensitivity of these equilibrium values to changes in the probabilities in the transition matrices can be used as the basis for choosing among alternative marketing strategies.

Third, in some transition matrices, it is impossible to leave a state once it has been reached. Such a state is called an absorbing state. When absorbing states occur, the equilibrium analysis must take another form. The most relevant information is usually the expected number of time periods spent in each of the other states by an individual (or an item) before being absorbed. An example of this form of analysis was used in the study of the Geriatric Resocialization Program by Meredith [1973]. Although the mathematical details are straightforward, they are so tedious that they would be performed on a computer for any real-world application and have been omitted here. However, the manager should be aware of the use of this analysis. As illustrated, if the costs of being in each state are known, the results can be used in a cost analysis.

Check Your Understanding

1. List the appropriate *states* to use in the analysis of the following:
   a. consumer credit policies
   b. a blood-inventory system
   c. the long-run ratio of tenured to nontenured professors in a university
2. Identify the two absorbing states in Table 7-2. Is it reasonable to assume that each of these are absorbing states? Why or why not?
3. Suppose that forecasts indicate that 34,000 students will enter the four-year colleges of Texas next year, 36,000 in two years, and 40,000 in three years. There are 30,000 enrolled in the current freshman class.
   a. Using the transition probabilities in Table 7-2, compute the expected total enrollment in the four-year colleges in three years.
   b. Suppose the average variable cost per student in the four-year colleges of Texas is estimated to be $800 for a freshman, $900 for a sophomore, $1100 for a junior, and $1400 for a senior. What should the variable portion of the state budget for higher education in the four-year colleges be in three years time?
4. Suppose that the *proportions* of students in each of the states in the four-year colleges of Texas are as follows:

State	Proportion
Do	0.00
Fr	0.40
So	0.25
Jr	0.20
Sr	0.15
Gr	0.00

   a. Using the data in Table 7-2, what will the proportions in each state be next year if just enough freshmen are admitted to maintain the *same* total enrollment?
   b. If the total current enrollment is 100,000 students, how many freshmen should be admitted next year to allow the total enrollment to increase to 105,000?
5. Discuss the assumptions that must be justified in order to use a Markov chain analysis in the enrollment forecasting problem, the brand switching problem, and the analysis of the geriatric ward.
   a. Are the assumptions met in each case?
   b. If not, would you expect the potential error to be so large that the results would be in question?
6. Determine the following, using the transition matrix for brand switching (Table 7-5):
   a. the market share of Z in three years

b. the estimated sales for manufacturers Y and Z in six years if the estimated total sales is 900,000 automobiles
c. the equilibrium market shares for X, Y, and Z using equations (1), (3), and (4).

7. Verify that the long-run (equilibrium) market shares of the three manufacturers based on Table 7-6 are 0.366 for X, 0.295 for Y, and 0.339 for Z.

8. Suppose there are 100 geriatric patients in the Napa State Hospital in January. There are 20 in GRP, 60 in one of the hospital wards, 15 in a home but placed from GRP, and 5 in a home but placed directly from a ward. Using the information in Table 7-7, determine the following:
   a. the cost of caring for the patients in January
   b. the expected number of patients in each state in February
   c. the expected number of patients in each state in March
   d. the expected cost of caring for the patients in March

Problems

9. Suppose that new razor blades were introduced on the market by three companies at the same time. When they were introduced, each company had an equal share of the market, but during the first year the following changes took place:
   1) Company A retained 90 percent of its customers, lost 3 percent to B and 7 percent to C.
   2) Company B retained 70 percent of its customers, lost 10 percent to A, and 20 percent to C.
   3) Company C retained 80 percent of its customers, lost 10 percent to A, and 10 percent to B.

   Assume that no changes in the buying habits of the consumers occur.
   a. What are the market shares of the three companies at the end of the first year? The second year?
   b. What are the long-run (equilibrium) market shares of the three companies?

10. The University of Lufkin employs nontenured and tenured professors to teach its classes. By obtaining a promotion, a nontenured professor may receive tenure (security of employment). Currently there are 100 nontenured and 50 tenured professors. On the basis of past records, 20 percent of the nontenured professors are promoted each year, and another 20 percent leave the university because of resignation or retirement. Similarly, 10 percent of the tenured professors leave the university each year. For every two faculty members who leave the university, one nontenured faculty member and one tenured faculty member are hired to replace them.

TABLE 7-10. **Transition Probabilities and Mean Salaries for Faculty Members at the University of Lufkin**

From	To: Nontenured	Tenured	Outside	Mean Salary
Nontenured	0.60	0.20	0.20	$14,000
Tenured	0.00	0.90	0.10	$20,000
Outside	0.50	0.50	0.00	---

This situation may be summarized in the transition matrix shown in Table 7-10, where the state *outside* serves to indicate both resignations and new hires. (If the number of resignations did not equal the number of new hires, separate states would be required.) The mean salaries of tenured and nontenured faculty members are also shown. Assume that the number of faculty members initially classified as *outside* is 25.

a. Compute the current total annual cost of salaries at the University of Lufkin and the estimated total annual cost of salaries next year.

b. What are the long-run (equilibrium) proportions of nontenured and tenured faculty members? What total annual salary cost would be associated with these proportions, assuming that the total number of faculty members remains at 150?

c. Suppose a new policy is adopted so that every faculty member who leaves the university must be replaced by a nontenured faculty member (i.e., no one can be hired with tenure). What are the resulting long-run (equilibirum) proportions of tenured and nontenured faculty members? What total annual cost would be associated with these proportions assuming that the total number of faculty members remains at 150?

11. Suppose we assume that approximately the same number of patients enter the geriatric program of the Napa State Hospital each month as the number who leave the system (die). Thus, we could ignore the absorbing state *deceased* in Table 7-7. By combining the states of *home* (*from ward*), we obtain the simplified data in Table 7-11.

a. In January, there are 20 persons in GRP, 70 persons in a ward, and 10 persons in a home. What is the cost of caring for these patients?

b. How many patients are expected to be in each state in February? In March? What are the expected costs in each month?

c. What are the long-run (equilibrium) proportions of patients in each state? What would be the cost of caring for 100 patients after equilibrium has been reached?

TABLE 7-11. **One-Month Transition Probabilities and Costs for the Simplified GRP Analysis**

From	To: GRP	To: Ward	To: Home	Cost per Month ($)
GRP	0.859	0.028	0.113	682
Ward	0.013	0.984	0.003	655
Home	0.012	0.012	0.976	226

TABLE 7-12. **Modified Transition Probabilities and Costs Without GRP**

From	To: Ward	To: Home	Cost per Month ($)
Ward	0.997	0.003	655
Home	0.024	0.976	226

TABLE 7-13. **Transition Probability Matrix and Costs for Credit Card Receivables**

Days Past Due at Month t	Days Past Due at Month $t+1$: 0–29	30–59	60+	Costs ($)
0–29	0.94	0.06	0.00	1
30–59	0.70	0.10	0.20	2
60+	0.65	0.10	0.25	4

TABLE 7-14. **Modified Transition Matrix for Credit Card Receivables**

Days Past Due at Month t	Days Past Due at Month $t+1$: 0–29	30–59	60+	Costs ($)
0–29	0.94	0.06	0.00	1
30–59	0.85	0.10	0.05	2
60+	0.60	0.10	0.30	4

12. To compare the long-run costs of treating patients without GRP, we assume "that only those patients who would have been placed directly from the ward will now be placed at all, since the patients who actually *were* selected for GRP had been in the hospital for over five years already without being placed and no reason exists to assume things would change suddenly."[Meredith, 1973] The resulting transition matrix is shown in Table 7-12.
    a. What are the long-run (equilibrium) proportions of patients in each state?
    b. What would be the cost of caring for 100 patients after equilibrium has been reached?
    c. Does this analysis provide sufficient justification for the GRP program? What weaknesses do you see in the analysis? What other considerations might influence a decision?
13. Finally, suppose a program is being contemplated that would double the number of placements from GRP. Then the probability of going from GRP to home in Table 7-11 would increase to 0.226, and the probability of staying in GRP would fall to 0.746.
    a. What are the long-run (equilibrium) proportions of patients in each state?
    b. What would be the cost of caring for 100 patients after equilibrium has been reached?
    c. What other noncost issues might be influential in a final decision regarding this new program? If you were the decision maker, what other information would you want?
14. A major travel and entertainment credit card company analyzed its credit history file to determine the transition probability matrix shown in Table 7-13. For example, 6.4 percent of all current accounts (0 to 29 days past due) age to 30 to 59 days past due. The costs are based on estimates of the rate of return that the firm could obtain on investments if the money were not tied up in accounts receivable.
    a. What are the long-run (equilibrium) proportions of accounts in each state?
    b. Suppose the company estimates that sending a letter to all account holders in the 30 to 59 days past due state would result in the modified transition matrix of Table 7-14. What would be the effect on the long-run (equilibrium) proportion of accounts in each state? Suppose that the incremental cost of sending 100 letters is $25. Would this strategy be justified on an economic basis?

---

*Adapted from L. H. Liebman, "A Markov Decision Model for Selecting Optimal Credit Control Policies," *Management Science,* Vol. 18, No. 10, June 1972.

References

1. Charnes, A., W. Cooper, and R. Niehaus, *Studies in Manpower Planning,* U.S. Navy Office of Civilian Manpower Management, Washington, D.C., 1972.
2. Dyer, J., "Cost-Effectiveness Analysis for a Public System of Higher Education," Ph.D. dissertation, The College of Business Administration, The University of Texas at Austin, May 1969.
3. Flamholtz, E., *Human Resource Accounting,* Dickenson Publishing Co., Encino, California, 1974.
4. Kemeny, J., and J. Snell, *Finite Markov Chains,* Van Nostrand, Princeton, New Jersey, 1960.
5. Liebman, L. H., "A Markov Decision Model for Selecting Optimal Credit Control Policies," *Management Science,* Vol. 18, No. 10, June 1972.
6. Meredith, J., "A Markovian Analysis of a Geriatric Ward," *Management Science,* Vol. 19, No. 6, February 1973.
7. Pegels, C., and A. Jelmert, "An Evaluation of Blood-Inventory Policies: A Markov Chain Application," *Operations Research,* Vol. 18, 1970, pp. 1087–98.
8. Trinkl, F., "A Stochastic Analysis of Programs for the Mentally Retarded," *Operations Research,* Vol. 22, No. 6, November–December 1974.

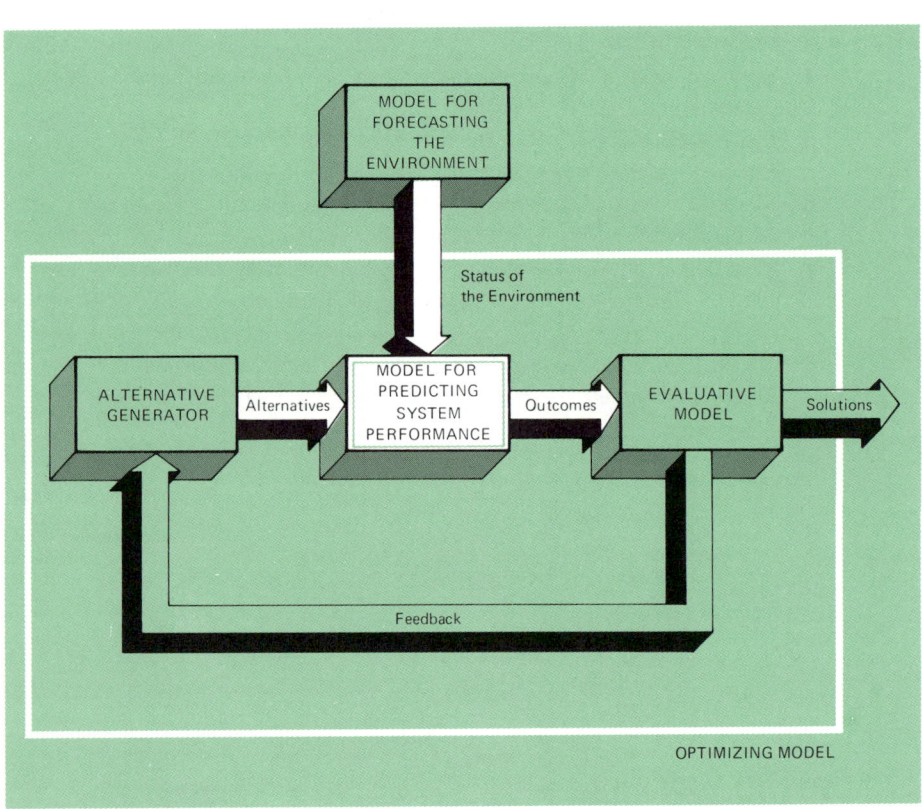

8

PREDICTING THE EFFECTS OF RISK— WAITING LINE MODELS

Many systems and subsystems that occur throughout organized society can be conceptualized by the input-transformation-output module presented in Figure III–2 of the Introduction to Part III. The service facility module has the input-transformation-output structure we have used as a basis for all of the predictive models discussed in Part III, but the input and the transformation have special characteristics.

The input is composed of *arrivals,* and arrival times are controlled by some stochastic or probabilistic process. Similarly, the time required to process the input follows a probability distribution. The output of such a system will depend on the interplay between the random arrivals and the variable service times. Predicting the output depends on this complex interplay, and queuing or waiting line theory is the basis for these predictions.

We normally have or can obtain information about the probability distributions that control the arrivals and the service times, so we are dealing with decision problems involving risks.

In this chapter, we shall develop the concepts and methods of queuing theory and the mathematical solutions to relatively simple queuing problems. However, when the mathematical analysis becomes too complex, we must resort to simulation. That approach to formulating and using queuing models will be discussed in the next chapter.

TABLE 8–1. **Waiting Line Model Elements for Some Commonly Known Situations**

Situation	Unit Arriving	Service or Processing Facility	Service or Process Being Performed
Ships entering a port	Ships	Docks	Unloading and loading
Maintenance and repair of machines	Machine breaks down	Repair crew	Repair machine
Assembly line, not mechanically paced	Parts to be assembled	Individual assembly operations or entire line	Assembly
Doctor's office	Patients	Doctor, his staff, and facilities	Medical care
Purchase of groceries at a supermarket	Customers with loaded grocery carts	Checkout counter	Tabulation of bill, receipt of payment, and bagging of groceries
Auto traffic at an intersection or bridge	Automobiles	Intersection or bridge with control points such as traffic lights or toll booths	Passage through intersection or bridge
Inventory of items in a warehouse	Order or withdrawal	Warehouse	Inventory maintenance
Machine shop	Job order	Work center	Processing

WAITING LINE MODELS OF SERVICE SYSTEMS

Queuing or waiting line concepts provide insight into many problems in productive systems. The original work in waiting line theory was done by A. K. Erlang, a Danish telephone engineer. Erlang started his work in 1905 in an attempt to determine the effect of fluctuating demand (arrivals) on the utilization of automatic dial equipment. Since the end of World War II, Erlang's work has been extended and applied to a variety of situations that are now recognized as being described by the general waiting line model.

In all instances, the input-transformation-output module is in operation, with the time between the arrival of individual inputs at the service facility commonly being random. Also, the time for service or processing is a random variable. Table 8–1 shows the waiting line model elements for a number of commonly known situations.

Structure of Waiting Line Models

There are four basic waiting line structures that describe the general conditions at the service facility. The simplest structure, shown in Figure 8–1 (a), is our basic

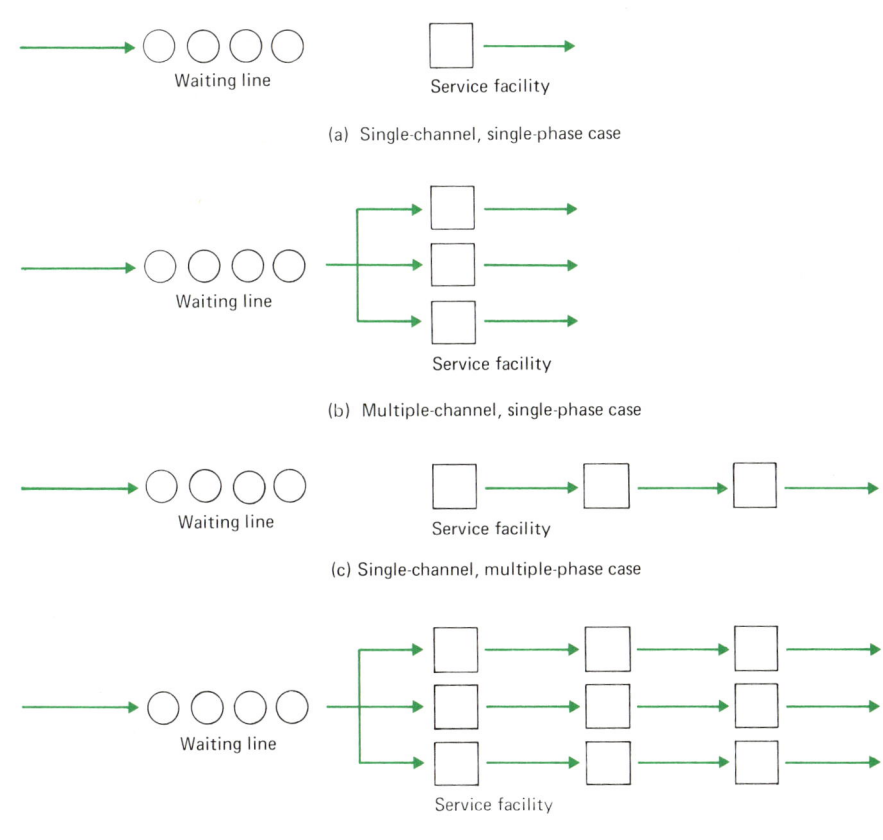

FIGURE 8–1. **Four basic structures of waiting line situations**

module. It is called the single-channel, single-phase case. There are many examples of the simple module: the cashier at a restaurant, any single-window operation in a post office or bank, a one-man barber shop. If the number of processing stations is increased but still draws on a single waiting line, we have the multiple-channel, single-phase case shown in Figure 8–1 (b). A simple assembly line or a cafeteria line has, in effect, a number of service facilities in tandem and is called the single-channel, multiple-phase case shown in Figure 8–1 (c). Finally, the multiple-channel, multiple-phase case can be illustrated by two or more parallel assembly lines as shown in Figure 8–1 (d). Combinations of any or all of the basic four structures could also exist in networks of queues in very complex systems.

The analytical methods for waiting lines divide into two main categories for any of the basic structures in Figure 8–1, depending on the size of the source population of the inputs. When the source population is very large, and in theory at least the length of the waiting line could grow without fixed limits, the applicable models are termed *infinite*. On the other hand, when the arriving unit comes from a source having a fixed upper limit, the applicable models are termed *finite*. For example, if we are dealing with the maintenance of a bank of 20 machines and a machine breakdown represents an arrival, the maximum waiting line is 20 machines waiting for service, and a finite model is needed. If, on the other hand, we operated an auto repair shop, the source population of breakdowns is very large and an infinite model would be appropriate. We shall restrict our discussion to infinite waiting line models, since the mathematical formulas for the finite models are relatively more complex, but the important managerial implications are the same for both models.

There are other variations in waiting line structures that are important in certain applications. The "queue discipline" implied in Figure 8–1 is first-come first-served. Obviously there are many other possibilities involving priority systems. For example, in a medical clinic, emergencies and patients with appointments are taken ahead of walk-in patients. In machine shop scheduling systems there has been a great deal of experimentation with alternate priority systems. Because of mathematical complexity, simulation has been the common mode of analysis for systems involving queue disciplines other than first-come first-served.

Finally, the nature of the probability distribution of arrivals and service is an important structural characteristic of waiting line models. The distribution of arrivals gives the probability of the arrival of any number of units during a specified time period, while the distribution of service times gives the probability that service will require any given time. Some mathematical analysis is available for very simple distributions or when the time between arrivals or the service time is constant. If distributions are relatively complex, or are taken from actual records, simulation is likely to be the necessary mode of analysis.

INFINITE WAITING LINE MODELS

We shall not cover all possibilities of infinite models, but will restrict our discussion to situations involving the first-come first-served queue discipline and the Poisson distribution of arrivals. We will deal initially with the single-channel, single-phase case [Figure 8–1 (a)], but later we shall also discuss the multiple-channel case [Figure 8–1 (b)].

Poisson Arrivals

The Poisson distribution function has been shown to represent arrival rates in a large number of real-world situations. It is a discrete function dealing with whole units of arrivals, so that fractions of men, products, or machines do not have meaning, nor do negative values.

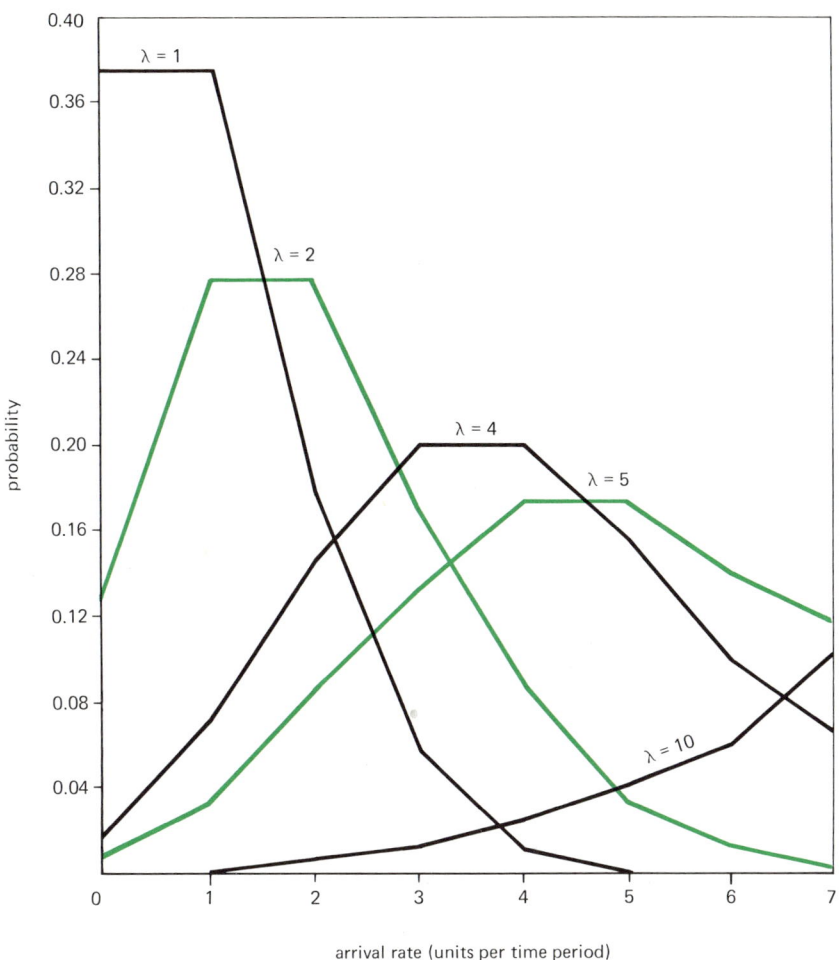

FIGURE 8-2. **Poisson distributions for several mean arrival rates**

The Poisson distributions for mean arrival rates of $\lambda = 1$, $\lambda = 2$, $\lambda = 4$, $\lambda = 5$, and $\lambda = 10$ are shown in Figure 8-2. For example, if the mean number of units that arrive during a given time period (e.g., an hour) is $\lambda = 4$, then from Figure 8-2, the probability that exactly five units will arrive is 0.16. The Poisson distribution is typically skewed to the right. The distribution is simple in that the standard deviation is expressed solely in terms of the mean, $\sigma_\lambda = \sqrt{\lambda}$.

Evidence that the Poisson distribution in fact represents arrival rates in many applications is indeed great. Many empirical studies have validated the Poisson arrival rate in general industrial operations, traffic flow, and various service operations.

Arrival distributions are sometimes given in terms of the time between arrivals, or interarrival times. Such distributions often follow the negative exponential distribution. However, if the *number* of arrivals in a given interval is Poisson distributed, then necessarily the times *between* arrivals are independent and exponentially distributed, and vice versa.

Although we cannot say that all distributions of arrivals per unit time are adequately described by the Poisson distribution, we can say that it is usually worth checking to see if it is true, for then a fairly simple analysis may be possible. It is logical that arrivals may follow the Poisson distribution when many factors affect arrival time, since the Poisson distribution corresponds to completely random arrivals. That means that each arrival is independent of other arrivals as well as of any condition of the waiting line. The practical question, of course, is whether or not the Poisson distribution is a reasonable approximation to reality.

Poisson Arrivals—Service Time Distribution Not Specified

Since Poisson arrivals are common, a useful model is one that depends on Poisson arrivals but accepts any service time distribution. We assume also that the mean service rate is greater than the mean arrival rate, otherwise the system would be unstable and the waiting line would become infinitely large. The queue discipline is first-come first-served, and arrivals wait for service; that is, they neither fail to join the line nor leave it because it is too long. Under these conditions the expected length of the waiting line is

$$L_q = \frac{(\lambda\sigma)^2 + (\lambda/\mu)^2}{2(1 - \lambda/\mu)} \qquad (1)$$

where

L_q is the expected length of the waiting line,
λ is the mean arrival rate from a Poisson distribution,
μ is the mean service rate,
σ is the standard deviation of the distribution of service times.

Because the ratio λ/μ is itself a useful concept, since it represents the average utilization of the service facility, we define $\rho = \lambda/\mu$. For example, if the mean arrival rate is $\lambda = 3$ units per hour, but the mean service rate is $\mu = 4$ units per hour, then the service facility will be busy only $\rho = \lambda/\mu = 3/4$ of the time.

Since ρ represents the fraction of time that the service facility is in use, by analogy it also represents the expected number of individuals or units being served at any instant in time. For example, if $\rho = 0.4$ the service facility is in use 40 percent of the time. Also, $(1 - \rho)$ is the fraction of service facility idle time, or the fraction of time when no one is being served. Since ρ is the expected number being served, the expected total number in the waiting line plus the expected number being served is the expected total number in the system, L,

$$L = L_q + \rho. \tag{2}$$

Similar simple logic leads to the expected waiting time in line W_q, and time in the system including service W. The reciprocal of the mean arrival rate is the mean time between arrivals $(1/\lambda)$. The multiplication of the mean time between arrivals and the expected length of the waiting line gives the waiting time.

$$W_q = L_q/\lambda \tag{3}$$

Similarly, the total time a unit spends in the system is obtained by multiplying the mean time between arrivals and the expected total number in the system,

$$W = L/\lambda. \tag{4}$$

Equations (1), (2), (3), and (4) are useful relationships. The general procedure would be to compute L_q from (1), and compute the values of L, W_q, and W as needed, given the value of L_q. Note that equations (1) through (4) deal only with steady state or long-run equilibrium conditions.

An Example Trucks arrive at the truck dock of a wholesale grocer at the rate of 8 per hour and the distribution of arrivals is Poisson. The loading and/or unloading time averages 5 minutes, but the estimate s of the standard deviation of service time is 6 minutes. Truckers are complaining that they must spend more time waiting than unloading and the following calculations verify their claim:

$\lambda = 8/\text{hour}$; $\mu = 60/5 = 12/\text{hour}$; $s = 6/60 = 1/10$ hours

$$L_q = \frac{(8/10)^2 + (8/12)^2}{2(1 - 8/12)} = 1.63 \text{ trucks in line}$$

$L = 1.63 + 8/12 = 2.30$ trucks in the system
$W_q = 1.63/8 = 0.204$ hours, or 12.24 minutes in line waiting for service
$W = 2.30/8 = 0.288$ hours, or 17.28 minutes in the system

The calculations yield another verification of logic in that the average truck waits 12.24 minutes in line plus 5 minutes for service, or 17.28 minutes in the system. Thus, another logical relationship is $W = W_q + 1/\mu$.

Let us pause for a moment to reflect on the model. Which are the decision variables and which are the uncontrollable parameters? The service-related variables can be altered by the manager if he is willing to invest capital in new capacity or if he can devise new procedures that can reduce the variability of service time. On the other hand, the arrival rate of trucks is presumably not under managerial control, and thus is a parameter.

The grocer knows that he could probably solve the problem by expanding the truck dock so that two trucks could be handled simultaneously. This solution, however, would require a large capital expenditure and disruption of operations during construction. Instead, he notes the very large standard deviation of service time, and on investigation he finds that some orders involve uncommon items that are not stored in a systematic manner. Locating these items takes a great deal of search time.

The grocer revamps the storage system so that all items can be easily located. As a result, the standard deviation is reduced to 3 minutes. Assuming that mean service time is not affected, we have an indication of the sensitivity of the system to changes in the variability of service time. The new values are $L_q = 0.91$, $L = 1.57$, $W_q = 6.8$ minutes, and $W = 11.8$ minutes. Waiting time has been almost cut in half. The truckers are happier, and the grocer has improved his system without a large capital expenditure.

SERVICE TIME DISTRIBUTIONS

While there is considerable evidence that arrival processes tend to follow the Poisson distribution as has been indicated, service time distributions seem to be much more varied in their nature. It is for this reason that the previous model involving Poisson arrivals and an unspecified service time distribution is so valuable. With equation (1), one can compute the queuing statistics, knowing only the mean service rate and the standard deviation of service time.

The negative exponential distribution has been one of the prominent models for service time, and there is evidence that in some instances the assumption is valid. However, Nelson's study [1959] of distributions of arrivals and service times in a Los Angeles jobbing machine shop did *not* indicate that the exponential model fit the actual service time distributions adequately for all of the machine centers.

Figure 8-3 shows the service time distributions at a university outpatient clinic. The distributions for *walk-in* and *appointment* patients are definitely not exponential, while the *second-service* distribution is reasonably close to being represented by a negative exponential distribution. Second-service patients are those who have been seen by a physician, have been routed for tests or some other medical procedure, and are returning to complete the consultation with a physician.

Other evidence indicates that in some cases the negative exponential distribution fits. Figure 8-4, for example, shows that the service time at a tool crib was nearly exponentially distributed. The distribution of local telephone calls not made from a pay station has also been shown to be exponential.

Model for Poisson Input and Negative Exponential Service Times

Since the negative exponential distribution is completely described by its mean value, the standard deviation being equal to the mean, we can describe this model as a special case of equation (1). The mean of a negative exponential distribution is the reciprocal of the mean service rate, that is, $1/\mu$. Equation (5) can easily be derived from equation (1) (verify this derivation yourself):

$$L_q = \frac{\lambda^2}{\mu(\mu - \lambda)}. \tag{5}$$

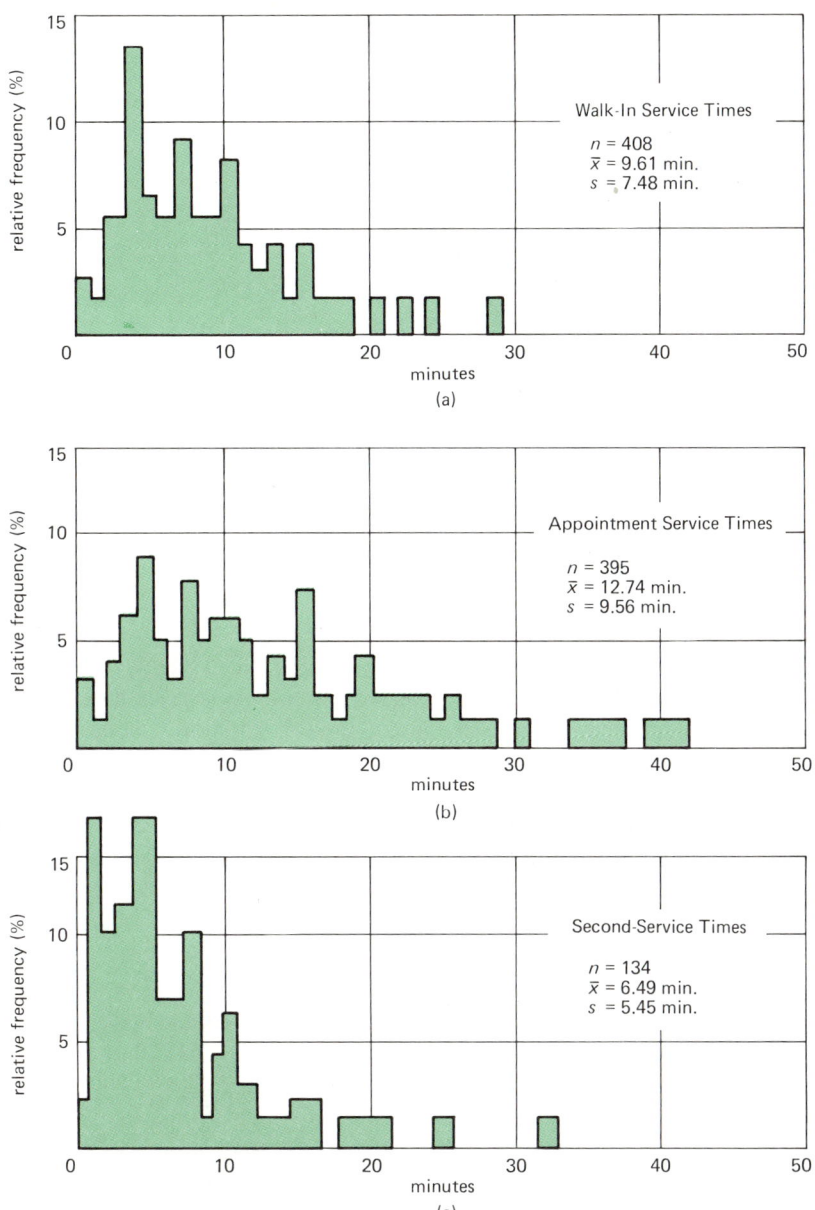

FIGURE 8-3. **Histograms of service time for (a) walk-in, (b) appointment, and (c) second-service patients**

From E. J. Rising, R. Baron, and B. Averill, "A Systems Analysis of a University-Health-Service Outpatient Clinic," Operations Research, Vol. 21, No. 5, Sept.-Oct. 1973, pp. 1030-1047, used by permission.

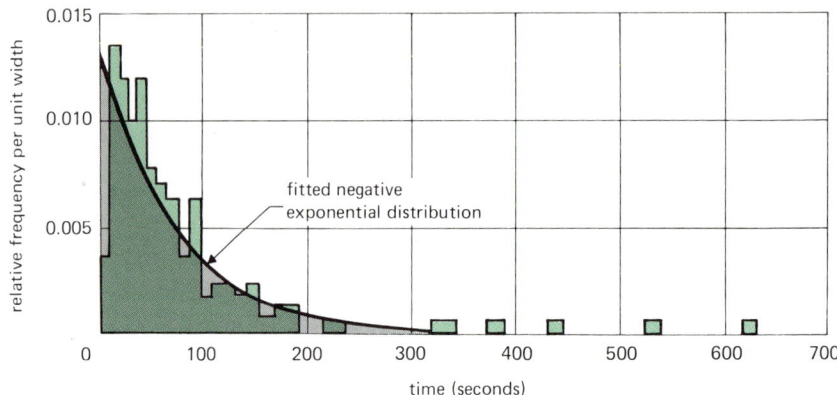

FIGURE 8-4. **Service time at a tool crib**
From G. Brigham, "On a Congestion Problem in an Aircraft Factory," Operations Research, Vol. 3, No. 4, 1955, pp. 412-28; used by permission

The other relationships between L_q, L, W_q, and W, expressed by equations (2), (3), and (4), hold for the negative exponential service time distributions as well as for the case where no service time distribution is specified. For the sake of simplicity, many individuals prefer to use equation (1), using the appropriate value of σ to reflect the special case.

We can now check to see the effect of exponential service times on queuing statistics for the truck dock problem. If we assume that the service time in that situation was represented by a negative exponential distribution, then $\sigma = 1/\mu = 1/12$, and the value of L_q from equation (1) is 1.33. The other queue statistics are $L = 2$, $W_q = 10$ minutes, and $W = 15$ minutes. The values are intermediate between the previous two calculations for the grocer's problem, since the value of σ is between the two previous values.

Model for Poisson Input and Constant Service Times

While constant service times are not common in actual practice, they may be reasonable in cases where a machine processes arriving items by a fixed time cycle. Also, constant service times represent a boundary or lower limit on the value of σ in equation (1). As such, constant service time is also a special case of equation (1). The resulting equation for constant service times is

$$L_q = \frac{\lambda^2}{2\,\mu(\mu - \lambda)}. \tag{6}$$

You should derive equation (6) from equation (1) by substituting $\sigma = 0$ in equation (1).

Again, for comparison, and to gain insight into what happens in waiting lines, let us see what the result would have been if the grocer could have made service time constant at 5 minutes, that is, reduced the standard deviation to zero. Substituting in equation (1), we have $L_q = 0.67$, $L = 1.33$, $W_q = 5$ minutes, and $W = 10$ minutes. Again, the other relationships between L_q, L, W_q, and W expressed by equations (2), (3), and (4) hold for the constant service time distribution as well as for the case where no service time distribution is specified.

We can consider equation (1) as a fairly general model with service time distributions described by the negative exponential, or constant service times as special cases.

Relationship of Queue Length to Utilization

Recall that the ratio of $\lambda/\mu = \rho$ represents the service facility utilization. If $\lambda = \mu$, then $\rho = 1$, and theoretically the service facility is used 100 percent of the time. But let us see what happens to the length of the queue as ρ varies from zero to one. Figure 8–5 summarizes the result for Poisson input and exponential service times. As ρ approaches unity, the number waiting in line increases rapidly and approaches infinity. We can see that this must be true by examining equations (1), (5), and (6) for L_q. In all cases, the denominator goes to zero as ρ approaches unity and the value of L_q becomes infinitely large.

We see now that one of the requirements of any practical system is that $\mu > \lambda$; otherwise we cannot have a stable system. If units are arriving faster on the average than they can be processed, the waiting line and waiting time will increase continuously and no steady state can be achieved. This simple fact also indicates that there is a value to be placed on idle time in the service facility. We must trade off the value of rapid service against service facility costs, which may include substantial service facility idle time.

Multiple-Channel, Single-Phase Case

In the multiple-channel case we assume the conditions of Poisson arrivals, exponential service times, and first-come first-served queue discipline. The effective service rate $M\mu$ must be greater than the arrival rate λ, where M is the number of channels. The facility utilization factor now becomes $\rho = \lambda/M\mu$, and we define $r = \lambda/\mu$. First, it is necessary to calculate L_q, the mean number in the waiting line. The formula for L_q becomes relatively complex in the multiple-channel, single-phase case, so we have computed L_q for various values of M (the number of service channels) and $r = \lambda/\mu$ in Table C–2 of Appendix C.

Given the value of L_q, then L, W_q, and W are easily computed from the following equations:
mean number in system, including those being serviced,

$$L = L_q + r, \tag{7}$$

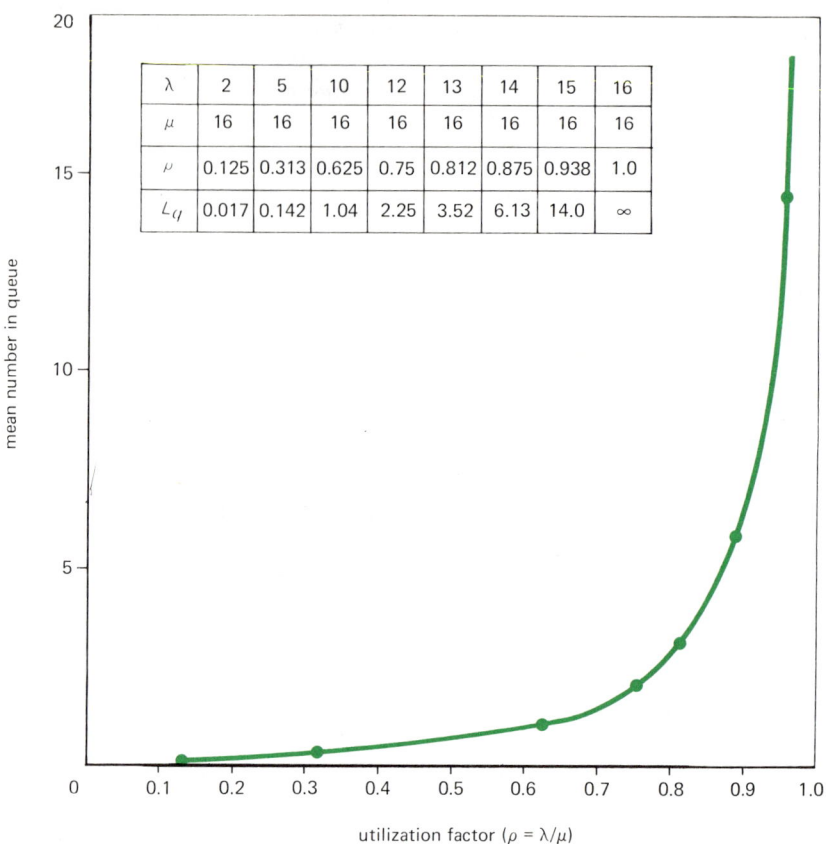

FIGURE 8-5. **Relationship of queue length to the utilization factor ρ**

mean waiting time

$$W_q = \frac{L_q}{\lambda}, \tag{8}$$

and mean time in system, including service,

$$W = W_q + \frac{1}{\mu} = \frac{L}{\lambda}. \tag{9}$$

As an example, assume that the wholesale grocer decides to expand facilities and add a second truck dock. What is the effect on average truck waiting time? Recall the basic data: $\lambda = 8$ per hour, $\mu = 12$ per hour, but now $M = 2$. From Table C-2 of Appendix C, for $M = 2$ and $r = \lambda/\mu = 8/12 =$

0.67, we find, by interpolating, that $L_q = 0.085$ trucks in line. Then $W_q = L_q/\lambda = 0.085/8 = 0.0106$ hours or 0.64 minutes. Compare these results with the single channel solution for exponential service time of $W_q = 10$ minutes. Obviously, adding the second dock eliminates the truck waiting problem. Note that overall utilization of the facilities declines from $\rho = \lambda/\mu = 0.67$ to $\rho = \lambda/M\mu = 0.34$.

The Effect of Pooling Facilities

To compare the effects of increasing or decreasing the number of channels, we can refer to Table C-2 in Appendix C for different numbers of channels for a given value of r. If for example, we were faced with a situation where $r = 0.9$ for the single channel case, then L_q is approximately 8 from Table C-2 of Appendix C. Adding a second channel reduces the average line length to $L_q = 0.23$. Adding a third channel reduces it to $L_q = 0.03$. The effects on L_q are surprisingly large; that is, we can obtain disproportionate gains in waiting time by increasing the number of channels. We can see intuitively that this might be true from Figure 8-5, since queue length (and waiting time) begins to increase very rapidly at about $\rho = 0.8$. A rather small increase in the capacity of the system (decrease in ρ) at these high loads can produce a large decrease in waiting line length and waiting time.

We can examine pooling effects by comparing the doubling of capacity within the same service facility with doubling capacity through parallel service facilities. Assume that $r = 0.8$ for the base case with a single channel ($M = 1$), as indicated in Table 8-2. From Table C-2 of Appendix C and the interrelationships, the mean number in the system is $L = 4$ and the mean time in the system is $W = 0.5$ hours, or 30 minutes.

If we double capacity by increasing the service rate within the same channel, the mean number in the system falls to only $L = 0.67$, and the mean time in the system falls to $W = 5$ minutes, 16.7 percent of the former values (see Table 8-2).

If we double capacity by adding a second parallel channel, service improves, but not as dramatically. The mean number in the system falls to only $L = 0.95$ and the mean time to $W = 7.15$ minutes, 23.8 percent of the base values.

Looking at just the two alternatives of providing the same capacity with one large facility versus two equivalent smaller facilities (the two right-hand columns of Table 8-2), it is clear that the single larger facility gives better service. While with the single large facility there is a larger queue ($L_q = 0.27$ versus 0.15) and waiting time is proportionately greater, this condition is compensated for by faster service, and the mean number in the system as well as the *total* time in the system are smaller for the system that pools resources.

An Example A large manufacturing concern with a 100-acre plant had a well-established medical facility, which was located at the plant offices at the eastern edge of the property. The plant had grown over the years from east to

TABLE 8-2. **Effects of Doubling Capacity Within the Same Service Facility Versus Parallel Service Centers**

	Base Case ($M = 1$, $r = 0.8$)	Capacity Doubled	
		Within Single Channel ($M = 1$, $r = 0.4$)	By Adding Second Channel ($M = 2$, $r = 0.8$)
L_q†	3.2000	0.2666	0.1533
$L = L_q + r$	4.0000	0.6666	0.9533
$W = L/8$	0.5000 hr. or 30.0 min.	0.0833 hr. or 4.99 min.	0.1191 hr. or 7.15 min.

†Values from Table C-2 of Appendix C.

west and currently travel time to the medical facility was so great that management was considering dividing the facility. The second unit was to be established near the center of the west end of the plant. A study had been made of weighted travel times for the present single facility and for the proposed two-facility system. The result indicated that average travel time for the present large medical facility was 15 minutes. The volume averaged 1000 visits per week, or 250 man-hours for travel time. The two-facility plan would reduce the average travel time to 8 minutes, or 133 man-hours per week.

The question now was, what would happen to waiting time in the waiting rooms? For the one large facility, $\lambda = 25$ per hour, and the average service rate is $\mu = 3$ per hour ($r = 25/3 = 8.33$). There were 10 physicians who handled the load. Interpolating in Table C-2 of Appendix C, $L_q = 2.45$, and $W_q = 2.45 \times 60/25 = 5.88$ minutes per person or 98 man-hours per week. Therefore, travel plus waiting time was $250 + 98 = 348$ man-hours per week.

The plan was to divide the medical staff for the two facilities, and it was assumed that the load would divide equally, so comparable data for the divided facilities are $\lambda = 12.5$ per hour per facility, $\mu = 3$ per hour, $M = 5$, and $r = 4.2$. From Table C-2 of Appendix C, $L_q = 3.3269$ and $W_q = 16$ minutes per person or 267 man-hours per week. The travel plus waiting time for the dual facility plan was therefore $133 + 267 = 400$ man-hours per week, compared to 348 for the single large facility. Other alternatives could of course be computed, probably involving an increased medical staff.

The waiting time for the single large facility was 5.88 minutes per person compared to 16.0 minutes per person for the two-facility plan. Obviously one large facility can give better service than the two smaller facilities. If we visualize the two decentralized facilities functioning side by side, we can see intuitively why waiting time increases. If facility one were busy and had patients waiting while at the same time facility two happened to be idle, someone from the facility one waiting room could be serviced immediately by facility two, thereby reducing average waiting time. In this situation the two facilities are drawing from one waiting line. When they are physically decentralized, the facilities must draw on two independent waiting lines and the idle capacity of one cannot be used by the waiting patients of the other.

COSTS AND CAPACITY IN WAITING LINE MODELS

While many decisions concerning service systems may turn on physical factors of line length, waiting time, and the service facility utilization, very often system designs will depend on comparative costs for alternatives. The costs involved are commonly the costs of providing the service *versus* the waiting time costs. In some instances the waiting time costs are objective, as when the enterprise is employing both the servers and those waiting. The company medical facility just discussed is such a case. The company absorbed all of the travel time and waiting time costs, as well as the cost of providing the service. In such an instance, a direct cost-minimizing approach can be taken balancing the waiting costs, or the time-in-system costs, against the costs of providing the service.

When the arriving units are customers, clients, or patients, the cost of making them wait is less obvious. If they are customers, excessive waiting may cause irritation and loss of goodwill and eventually sales. Placing a value on goodwill, however, is not a straightforward exercise. In public service operations and other monopoly situations, the valuation of waiting cost may be even more tenuous because the individual cannot make alternate choices. In these situations where objective costs cannot be balanced, it may be necessary to set a standard for waiting time; for example, to adjust capacity to keep average waiting time at or below three minutes at supermarket checkout counters. The following examples involve costs and waiting time standards.

Example One   Let us refer to the data for the company internal medical facility. Recall that there were 10 physicians, whom we will assume are paid $3000 per month, or about $6928 per week for the 10 physicians. Let us also assume that the average hourly wage of employees coming to the medical facility is $5. Computations for the single central facility yield a travel time cost of $250 \times 5 = \$1250$ per week, and a waiting time cost of $98 \times 5 = \$490$ per week. The total weekly cost is then $8668, including physicians' salaries. First, with the central facility only, how many physicians will minimize affected costs? Using Table C–2 of Appendix C, we can easily determine average waiting time for 9, 10, and 11 physicians, and the resulting weekly costs. The results are shown in Table 8–3. So, the present policy of having 10 physicians is a little less costly than having either 9 or 11.

Now, let us consider the dual facility concept, where travel cost is also affected. The travel, waiting, and physicians' cost for the central facility was $\$5(250 + 98) + \$6928 = \$8668$ per week. The comparable figures for the dual

TABLE 8-3. **Utilization, Waiting Time, and Costs for Different Levels of Medical Service**

	Number of Physicians		
	9	10	11
Utilization ($\rho = \lambda/M\mu$)	0.93	0.83	0.76
Mean waiting time (min.)	23.40	5.88	2.26
Weekly waiting time (hr.)	390	98	38
Cost of waiting time/week	$1950	$ 490	$ 190
Physicians' cost/week	6235	6928	7620
Total affected cost	$8185	$7418	$7810

facilities were $5(133 + 267) + $6928 = $8928. Would increased capacity in either or both of the dual facilities improve affected costs? The answer is no. The weekly travel and waiting costs and service costs for 5 physicians in each facility, 5 in one and 6 in the other, and 6 in each are respectively $8928, $9109, and $9292.

Now, of course, an important observation concerning the company medical facility is that the unit cost of providing the service is very large and tends to dominate, compared to unit waiting time costs. The physician is paid $3000 per month while the average employee waiting is paid only about $866 per month. If the unit costs change relative to each other, the best solution may be different.

Example Two The manager of a large bank has the problem of providing teller service for customer demand, which varies somewhat during the business day from 10:00 A.M. to 4:00 P.M. He has a total capacity of six windows and can assign unneeded tellers to other useful work. He also wishes to give excellent service, however, which he defines in terms of customer waiting time as $W_q \leq 1$ minute. In order to give the best service for any situation, he has arranged the layout so that customers form one waiting line from which the customer at the head of the line goes to the first available teller.

The arrival pattern is as follows:

	Customers per Minute (λ)
10:00 A.M.–11:30 A.M.	1.8
11:30 A.M.– 1:30 P.M.	4.8
1:30 P.M.– 3:00 P.M.	3.8
3:00 P.M.– 4:00 P.M.	4.6

and each mean rate follows the Poisson distribution. The mean value of arrivals varies, but is always from a Poisson distribution. The mean service time is one minute and the distribution of service times is negative exponential. The service rate is $\mu = 1/1 = 1$ per minute.

The bank manager can make plans to adjust teller capacity to daily demand patterns very easily, maintaining the waiting time standard. The basic data comes from Table C–2 of Appendix C and is tabulated here in Table 8–4. We see there that to maintain the one-minute standard for W_q, the number of windows open must be:

	No. of Windows Open
10:00 A.M.–11:30 A.M.	3
11:30 A.M.– 1:30 P.M.	6
1:30 P.M.– 3:00 P.M.	5
3:00 P.M.– 4:00 P.M.	6

TABLE 8–4. **Waiting Time for Different Numbers of Teller Windows Open at Different Times of Day**

No. of Windows Open (M)	Length of Waiting Line (L_q)	Waiting Time in Minutes (W_q)
10:00–11:30 A M		$r = \lambda/\mu = 1.8$
2	7.67	4.26
3	0.53	0.29
11:30 A M–1:30 P M		$r = \lambda/\mu = 4.8$
5	21.64	4.51
6	2.07	0.43
1:30–3:00 P M		$r = \lambda/\mu = 3.8$
4	16.94	4.46
5	1.52	0.40
3:00–4:00 P M		$r = \lambda/\mu = 4.6$
5	9.29	2.02
6	1.49	0.32

WHAT SHOULD THE MANAGER KNOW?

The waiting line models we have discussed have particular value in providing us with insight into what happens in service systems. These models show why waiting lines form and why waiting is probably necessary or at least costly to eliminate.

Problem Characteristics

Whenever we have the typical module in which something or someone arrives for some kind of service or processing by an unpredictable pattern, we have a problem that has the potential of being analyzed by a waiting line model. As we noted in Figure 8-1, there are four basic structures, and in some situations these structures may be assembled into networks of queues. The problem itself may appear as a capacity problem, or one of giving rapid enough service.

Formulation

The formulation of waiting line models involves identifying arrival and service time distributions and validating the assumptions about the basic model and the form of the distributions. Validating the assumption of random arrivals (Poisson distribution) is important if any of the basic models discussed are to be used.

Validating the form of the service time distribution is of lesser importance in the simple situation where equation (1) applies as long as we have a good estimate of the standard deviation of the service time distribution. In order to use the multiple channel models discussed, we must be reasonably sure that the assumptions for both arrival and service time distributions are valid.

Interpretation

Managers can gain considerable insight into many problems of operations through the interpretations that flow from waiting line analyses. For example, with variable arrival rates and service times, it becomes immediately obvious that good facility utilization and good service are at odds. Indeed, there is a positive value to idle time for the service facility if we hope to provide rapid response in medical services, fire protection, police protection, machine maintenance, and a variety of other services.

Waiting line analyses can indicate the effects of increased capacity, pooling of facilities, and variability in service time distributions. We noted that variation in the service time can have a very important effect on line length, waiting time, and total time in the system. In the Poisson input, exponential holding time case, half of the congestion is in the service time variation, as a comparison of equations (5) and (6) shows. The other half of the congestion is due to the variable arrival process. Thus, managers who understand the source of the congestion can possibly make important improvements in service by *not* assuming that the arrival process is a given and outside of their control. It may be possible to schedule arrivals or resort to other techniques to reduce variation in the arrival process. Indeed, a manager would wish to do everything possible to smooth demand, as has been commonly practiced in manufacturing systems.

With a knowledge of waiting line models, a manager knows that adding parallel channels causes more than a proportional effect. Line length and waiting time drop dramatically with the addition of capacity through parallel channels. Also, the effect of pooling facilities becomes clear through waiting line analyses. If we wish to give good service, we can do it better with one large facility than with a number of smaller facilities offering equivalent capacity. Furthermore, the pooling effect is not one of economy of scale in the traditional sense, but results from the unique interplay between arrivals and service that allows the use of what would be idle time in decentralized smaller facilities.

Check Your Understanding

1. Discuss the nature of service systems. What characteristics of these systems make them candidates for study as waiting line systems?
2. Classify the following in terms of the four basic waiting line structures:
   a. assembly line
   b. large bank—six tellers (one waiting line for each)
   c. cashier at a restaurant
   d. one-chair barbershop
   e. cafeteria line
   f. general hospital
   g. post office—four windows drawing from one waiting line
3. Define the following terms:
   a. arrival process
   b. queue discipline
   c. infinite waiting line model
   d. finite waiting line model
   e. single-phase model
   f. multiple-phase model
   g. single-channel model
   h. multiple-channel model
4. Identify the unit being processed, the server or service facility, and the waiting line structure for each of the following:
   a. car wash
   b. fire station
   c. toll bridge
   d. shipping dock

e. appliance repair shop
  f. TV repair
  g. supermarket
  h. large department store
5. Given a Poisson distribution of arrivals with mean of $\lambda = 5$ per hour, what is the probability of an arrival of $x = 4$ within an hour? What is the probability of the occurrence of 15 minutes between arrivals? See Figure 8-2.
6. A machine in a processing line is designed to perform its function automatically in a constant time of one minute. Items to be processed are fed from the operation upstream, which is manual. The arrival rate to the machine is Poisson distributed and averages 50 units per hour. In spite of the fact that the machine is faster than the preceding manual operation, the foreman is perturbed by the fact that there is an in-process inventory piled up in front of the machine and at the same time, the machine utilization is only 83 percent.

    Explain how the system functions. What is the average in-process inventory in front of the machine? Verify the machine utilization figure. How can the foreman improve the machine utilization?
7. A taxi cab company has four cabs that operate out of a given taxi stand. Customer arrival rates and service rates are described by the Poisson distribution. The average arrival rate is 12 per hour and the average service time is 17.5 minutes. The service time follows a negative exponential distribution.
  a. Calculate the utilization factor.
  b. From Table C-2 of Appendix C, determine the mean number of customers waiting.
  c. Determine the mean number of customers in the system.
  d. Calculate the mean waiting time.
  e. Calculate the mean time in the system.
  f. What would be the utilization factor if the number of taxi cabs were increased from four to five?
  g. What would be the effect of the increase in the number of cabs from four to five on the mean number in the waiting line?
  h. What would be the effect of reducing the number of taxi cabs from four to three on the mean number in the waiting line?
8. Explain the benefits that accrue from pooling facilities.

Problems

9. Present day universities have become complex systems of scholars where a value must be placed on communication, both within systems that are now multicampus giants and between systems throughout the nation. It is not surprising then that WATS (wide area telephone service) should be considered

to allow faculty members and administrators to make unlimited toll-free long-distance calls.

Data were gathered for one such system, that yielded the following information:

1) The frequency of calls was estimated to be 10.4 per hour, based on present use of long-distance service plus an estimate of increased use if WATS were available (Poisson distribution).
2) The length of calls was estimated to be 15 minutes (exponential distribution).
3) The current long-distance telephone bill average was $10,000 per month.
4) After much haggling, average faculty-administrator time was valued at $10 per hour.
5) A WATS line costs $2000 per month.

Assume an average of 173 hours per month. The central issue finally resolved into the number of WATS lines that would be justified.

a. Formulate the problem as a decision to determine the number of WATS lines to install. What cost components are involved and how do the costs vary with the number of lines installed?
b. Determine the number of WATS lines to install. What criteria have you used?

10. A supermarket chain has 30 stores in a large metropolitan area and supplies its stores from a central warehouse. The general routine is to supply each store every day on the basis of the store order list. Store managers compile these lists daily and transmit them to the warehouse.

At the warehouse, store orders are taken in sequence as they arrive and "order picker" crews assemble the order in designated staging areas using a hand truck system for smaller items and dispatching fork truck operators to fill skid load items. When a store order is complete, it awaits transportation.

A fleet of five large closed trucks transports the orders. Trucks are loaded at the truck dock, which can accommodate three trucks simultaneously. A special crew of loaders is used to load trucks from the staging areas. While the trucks are being loaded, the driver obtains the documents that indicate the list of items shipped and the store destination.

After loading, the trucks are driven to the store destination, and the contents are unloaded at the store truck dock by store personnel. The driver then returns the truck to the warehouse. At the end of the day, the truck is returned to the maintenance area at the warehouse where it is washed, refueled, and serviced for general maintenance and repair.

Formulate the system as a sequence of waiting line problems by first developing a flow chart that identifies the arrival, service, and exit processes. Identify each waiting line situation in terms of its structure and the type of waiting line model that might apply. In order to analyze the system as a waiting line system, what information is needed?

References

1. Buffa, E. S., *Operations Management: Problems and Models,* third edition, John Wiley & Sons, New York, 1972, Chapters 14 and 15.
2. Cox, D. R., and W. L. Smith, *Queues,* John Wiley & Sons, New York, 1961.
3. Morse, P. M., *Operations Research for Public Systems,* MIT Press, Cambridge, Mass., 1967.
4. ———, *Queues, Inventories and Maintenance,* John Wiley & Sons, New York, 1958.
5. Nelson, R. T., "An Empirical Study of Arrival, Service Time, and Waiting Time Distributions of a Job Shop Production Process," Research Report No. 60, *Management Sciences Research Project,* University of California, Los Angeles, 1959.
6. Saaty, T. L., *Elements of Queuing Theory,* McGraw-Hill, New York, 1961.
7. Thierauf, R. J. and R. C. Klekamp, *Decision Making Through Operations Research,* second edition, John Wiley & Sons, New York, 1975.
8. Wagner, H. M., *Principles of Operations Research,* second edition, Prentice-Hall, Englewood Cliffs, N.J., 1975.

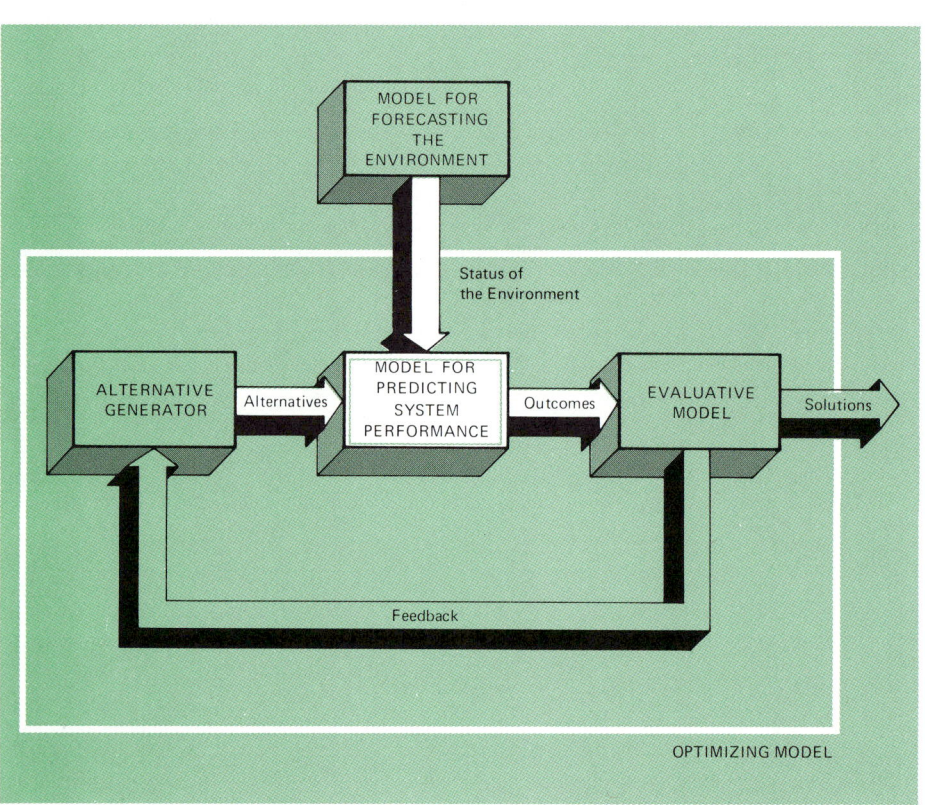

9

PREDICTING THE EFFECTS OF RISK—MONTE CARLO SIMULATION

The complexity of many managerial systems, as well as the need to include empirical data, often makes the prediction of performance by analytical models either impossible or impractical. In such situations, simulation is the common methodology for predicting performance.

Simulation is a general term that means *imitation*. In fact, the rigorous technique of simulation that has developed in operations research and management science does imitate the essential characteristics of processes, usually with the aid of a computer. Most of the simulation models with which we deal in management science represent a problem by imitating what would happen in the real system, then keeping track of what happens in the model. By driving the model with a large sample of input data and recording results, we can build a representative record of what would probably happen if the policy, design, or system were actually installed. Simulation models are in a real sense management's laboratory.

Kinds of Simulation Models

Simulation models may be discrete or continuous, deterministic or stochastic. In continuous systems, the parameters that describe the system can take on any values within the ranges specified. Wind tunnel simulation of flight is an example of a continuous simulation system. Discrete systems take on only particular values within the possible ranges of parameters. These systems are characterized by the events that occur, and we keep track of the events, their timing, and other parameters that may describe them. In managerial systems we commonly deal with discrete simulation systems.

As noted, a system may also be deterministic or stochastic, depending on the nature of input, process, and output at various stages of the system. The output of a deterministic system, or the process within a system, is known exactly when the input is specified—there is no unaccounted for variation. In other words, the transformation function of the predictive model provides a completely determined output. The simple relationship in physics between force, mass, and acceleration is an example, $F = ma$. Given the mass m and the input state of the acceleration a, the force F is assumed to be determined exactly. The model admits no other variables. Deterministic simulation models are often used in management science, and the corporate planning models discussed in Chapter 6 were simulations involving only deterministic values.

Stochastic systems, however, respond to a given input with a range of possible outputs, following some distribution of values. For example, if in an emergency medical system there is a call for service, the time to perform the service is not a fixed time. Service time will depend on many things that in themselves are not predictable, such as distance to the scene, traffic density, time of day, and availability of the ambulance. In addition, there may be random variation in service time that has no logical explanation.

Probably most processes in managerial systems are in fact stochastic; however, we often use deterministic relationships and average relationships when they reasonably represent what happens. They are simpler to handle and require less execution time in complex simulation models. On the other hand, many processes are only described adequately by probability distributions, such as those reflecting variable demand for services and products, and the queuing or waiting line models of Chapter 8. Special simulation techniques called Monte Carlo, or simulated sampling, are used to introduce statistical variations in simulation models.

Simulation models in managerial systems, then, are usually of the discrete type and are often a combination of deterministic and stochastic processes, especially in models representing a complex system. In this chapter we will concentrate on stochastic simulation models.

THE SIMULATION PROCESS

Conceptually, the simulation process is a simple one, once we have a carefully specified model. While many other variables may be involved in discrete event simulations, they are usually related in some way to the passage of time. There are in general two ways of organizing the simulation process: around the occurrence of discrete events and around updating events for discrete time periods.

In the *discrete event* approach, the entire process follows the sequence of events or steps in the process, keeping track of what happens. The emergency medical system simulation described later in the chapter uses the discrete event process.

If we were to attempt to simulate the *discrete time updating* approach, we would select a smallest time unit for the study and examine the state of the system in all of its aspects at the end of each time interval, recording and updating the status of each element. The time interval might be 0.01 minute, 1 minute, 5 minutes, or 1 hour, as appropriate. When the total planned simulation time is equaled or exceeded, the process is stopped and the results printed out.

In both the discrete event and the discrete time updating approaches, repetitions might be programmed to provide sample sizes large enough to average out stochastic effects. In either the discrete event or discrete time updating simulation systems we could be dealing with stochastic processes or combinations of both deterministic and stochastic processes. Since dealing with stochastic processes as well as empirical data is so important in simulation, we now turn our attention to this subject.

MONTE CARLO—SIMULATED SAMPLING

Simulated sampling, generally known as Monte Carlo, makes it possible to introduce into a system data that have the statistical properties of some empirical distribution. If the model involves the flow of orders according to the actual demand distribution experienced, we can simulate the "arrival" of an order by Monte Carlo sampling from the actual distribution, so that the timing and flow of activities in the simulated system parallels the actual experience. If we are studying the breakdown of a certain machine (perhaps an office copying machine) caused by bearing failure, we can simulate typical breakdown times through simulated sampling from the distribution of bearing lives.

An Example

Suppose we are dealing with an emergency medical system, and we wish to estimate the level of service that can be maintained by one ambulance. We have available, or must obtain, data concerning the frequency of calls for service and the service time. As we noted earlier, if these distributions followed certain mathematical functions, we could compute directly the results that we will determine here by simulation methods, using the formula for the waiting line models from Chapter 8. However, the data summarized by Figures 9-1 and 9-2 are empirical data, and we shall assume that they are not adequately described by any known mathematical model that we can solve. Our procedure follows the steps described in the following paragraphs.

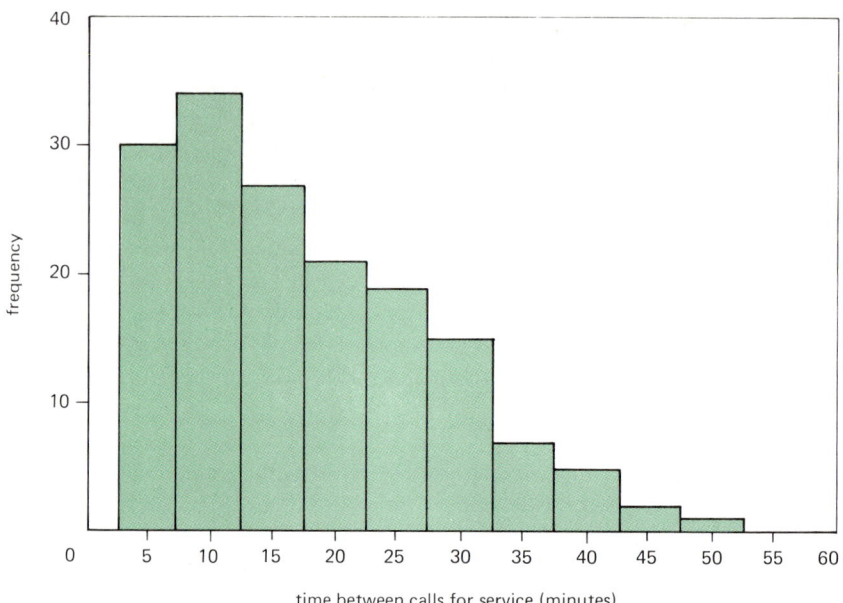

FIGURE 9-1. **Frequency distribution of the time between calls for 161 emergencies ($n = 161$, $\bar{x} = 17.5$ minutes)**

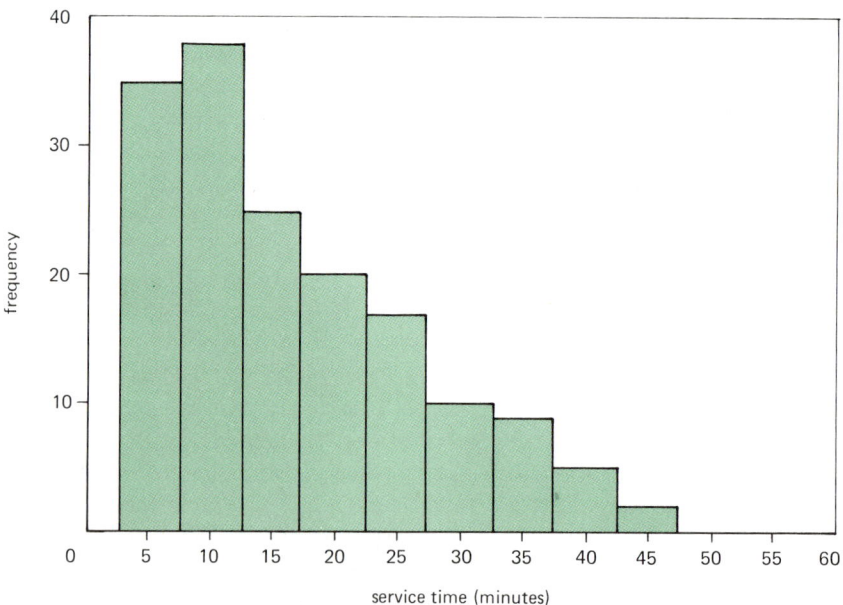

FIGURE 9-2. **Frequency distribution for the service time of 161 emergency calls ($n = 161$, $\bar{x} = 16.5$ minutes)**

Step 1. *Determine the distributions of the time between calls for service and service time.* If they were not available directly, we would have to make a study to determine these distributions, or use records of calls for service and service time, if available, from which the distributions might be constructed. Figures 9-1 and 9-2 show the distributions of the time between calls for service and the service times for 161 emergencies. These distributions will be the basis for our simulation.

Step 2. *Convert the frequency distributions to cumulative probability distributions* (see Figures 9-3 and 9-4). This conversion is made by summing the frequencies that are less than or equal to each call or service time and plotting them. The cumulative frequencies are then coverted to probabilities.

As an example, let us take Figure 9-1 and convert it to the cumulative distribution of Figure 9-3. Beginning at the lowest value for the time between calls, 5 minutes, there are 30 occurrences. For the call time 5 minutes, 30 is plotted on the cumulative chart. For the call time 10 minutes, there were 34 occurrences, but there were 64 occurrences of 10 minutes or less, so the value 64 is plotted for 10 minutes. For the call time 15 minutes, there were 27 occurrences recorded, but there were 91 occurrences of calls for 15 minute intervals or less.

Figure 9-3 was constructed from Figure 9-1 by proceeding in this way. When the cumulative frequency distribution is completed, a cumulative probability scale is constructed on the right of Figure 9-3 by assigning the number 1.0 to the maximum value, 161, and dividing the resulting scale into 10 equal parts. This process results in a cumulative empirical probability distribution. From Figure 9-3 we can say that 100 percent of the call time values were 50 minutes or less; 99 percent were 45 minutes or less, and so on. Figure 9-4 was constructed from Figure 9-2 in a comparable way.

Step 3. *Sample at random from the cumulative distributions to determine specific times between calls for service and service times; use these data in simulating the emergency medical operation.* This sampling is conducted by selecting numbers between 001 and 100 at random (representing probabilities). The random numbers could be selected by any random process, such as drawing numbered chips from a box. The easiest way is to use a table of random numbers such as those included in Table C-3 of Appendix C. (For example, select a starting point in the table at random and take two-digit numbers in sequence in that column.)

The random numbers were used to enter the cumulative distributions to obtain time values in proportion to their occurrence in the distributions. An example is shown in Figure 9-3 where the random number 30 is shown to select a call time of 10 minutes.

By using random numbers to obtain call time values in this fashion from Figure 9-3, we will obtain call time values in proportion to the probability of occurrence indicated by the original frequency distribution. As a matter of fact, at this point we can construct a table of random numbers that selects certain call and service times. For example, reading from Figure 9-3, the random numbers

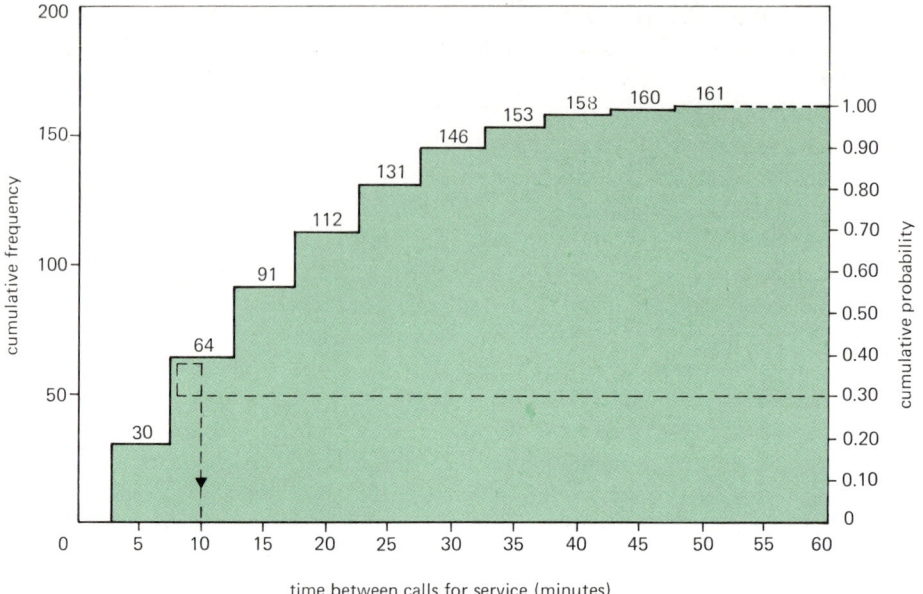

FIGURE 9-3. **Cumulative distribution of the time between calls for service**

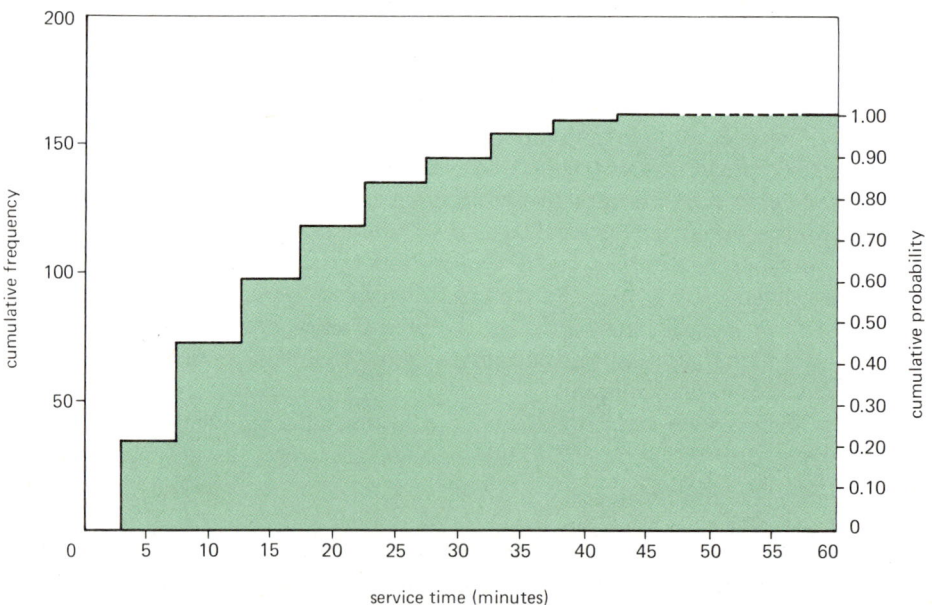

FIGURE 9-4. **Cumulative distribution of service times**

226 PART III PREDICTIVE MODELS

TABLE 9-1. **Random Numbers Used to Select Calls for Service and Service Times**

Time Between Calls for Service			Service Times		
These Random Numbers	Select ⟶	These Call Times (min)	These Random Numbers	Select ⟶	These Service Times (min)
1–19		5	1–20		5
20–40		10	21–44		10
41–57		15	45–60		15
58–70		20	61–72		20
71–81		25	73–83		25
82–91		30	84–89		30
92–95		35	90–94		35
96–98		40	95–99		40
99		45	100		45
100		50			

Note: These data are in proportion to the occurrence probabilities of the original distribution.

1 through 19 give us a call time of 5 minutes, etc. That is to say, 19 percent of the time we would obtain a call time of 5 minutes, $40 - 19 = 21$ percent of the time we would obtain a call time of 10 minutes, and so on. Table 9-1 shows the random number equivalents for Figures 9-3 and 9-4.

Sampling from either the cumulative distributions of Figures 9-3 and 9-4 or from Table 9-1 will now give call times and service times in proportion to the original distributions, just as if actual calls and services were happening. Table 9-2 gives a sample of 20 times between calls for service and service times, determined in this way.

Step 4. *Simulate the actual operation of calls and services.* The structure of what we wish to do in simulating the emergency medical operation is shown by the flow chart of Figure 9-5. This operation involves selecting a call time, then determining whether or not the ambulance is available. If the ambulance is not available, the patient must wait until it is, and we can compute the wait time easily. If the ambulance is available, the question is, did the ambulance have to wait? If it did, we compute the ambulance idle time. If the ambulance did not have to wait, we select a service time and proceed according to the flow chart, repeating the overall process as many times as desired, providing a mechanism for stopping the procedure when the desired number of cycles has been completed.

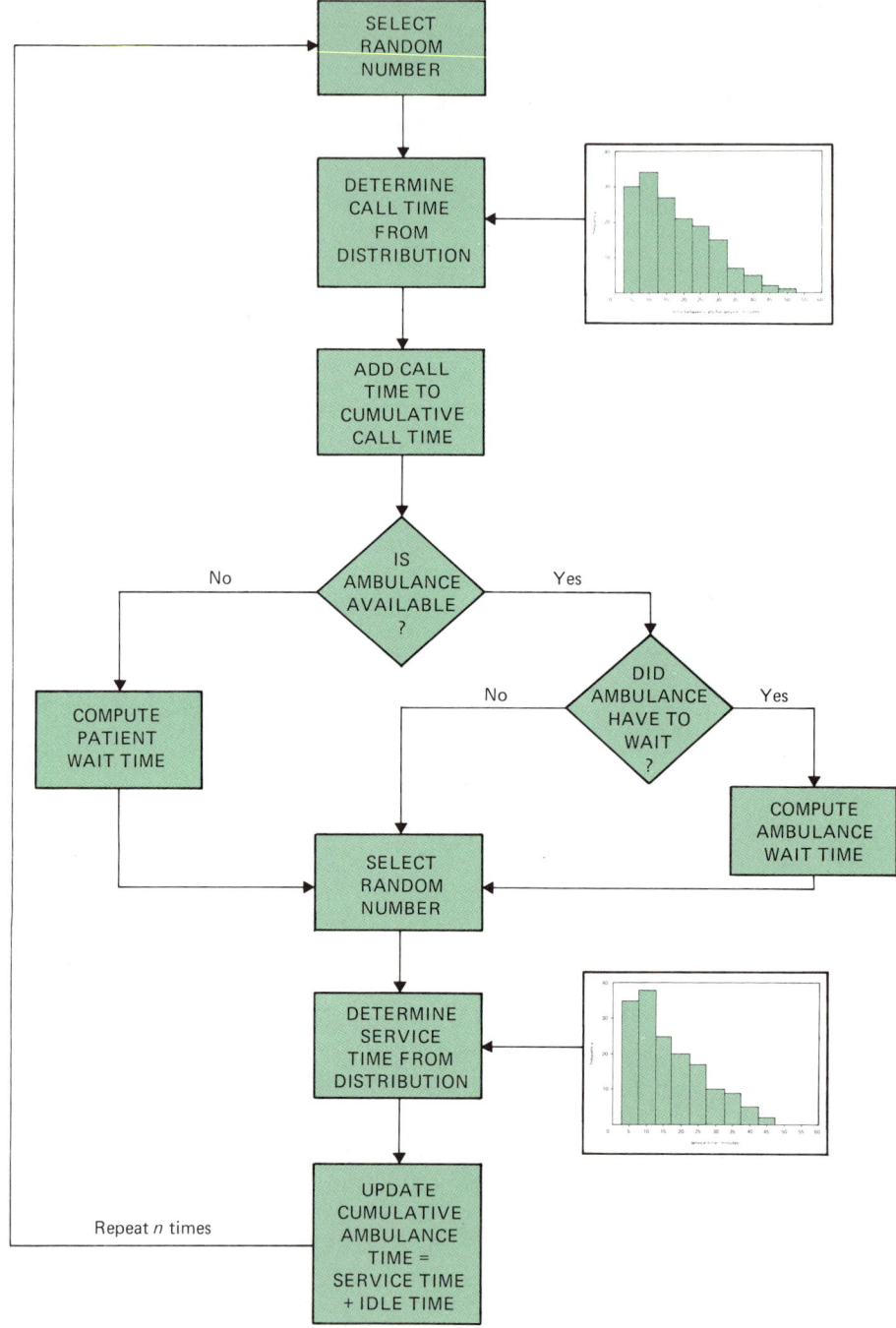

FIGURE 9-5. **Flow chart showing structure of ambulance simulation**

TABLE 9-2. **Simulated Sample of 20 Times Between Calls for Service and Service Times**

Times Between Calls for Service		Service Times	
Random Number	Call Time* (min)	Random Number	Service Time† (min)
27	10	71	20
89	30	43	10
27	10	16	5
51	15	64	20
96	40	75	25
54	15	28	10
13	5	54	15
53	15	11	5
14	5	12	5
87	30	86	30
54	15	92	35
63	20	06	5
00	50	49	15
13	5	03	5
28	10	63	20
15	5	41	10
83	30	09	5
29	10	72	20
49	15	14	5
01	5	83	25

*Data from Figure 9-3.
†Data from Figure 9-4.

The simulation of the emergency medical operation for 20 calls for service is shown in Table 9-3. Here we have used the call times and service times selected by random numbers in Table 9-2. We assume that time begins when the first call occurs, and we accumulate call time from that point. The service time required for the first call was 20 minutes, and since this occurrence is the first in our record, neither the patient nor the ambulance had to wait. The second call occurred at 30 minutes, but the ambulance was available at the end of 20 minutes, so it waited 10 minutes for the next call to occur. Note that we are using the *discrete event* simulation process.

We proceed in this fashion, making computations according to the requirements of the simulation model to obtain the record of Table 9-3. At the bottom of Table 9-3 we show that for the sample of 20 emergencies, total patient waiting time was 145 minutes, and total ambulance idle time was 70 minutes. Of course, to obtain a realistic picture we would have to use a much larger sample.

TABLE 9-3. **Simulated Ambulance Calls and Service**

Time of Call for Service	Time Service Begins	Time Service Ends	Patient Waiting Time	Ambulance Idle Time
0	0	20	0	0
30	30	40	0	10
40	40	45	0	0
55	55	75	0	10
95	95	120	0	20
110	120	130	10	0
115	130	145	15	0
130	145	150	15	0
135	150	155	15	0
165	165	195	0	10
180	195	230	15	0
200	230	235	30	0
250	250	265	0	15
255	265	270	10	0
265	270	290	5	0
270	290	300	20	0
300	300	305	0	0
310	310	330	0	5
325	330	335	5	0
330	335	360	5	0
			145	70

Interpretation of Results

Interpreting the results of the emergency medical system simulation is rather hazardous in view of the small sample; however, it would appear that the system is too heavily loaded for one ambulance to give really excellent service, since patient waiting time was required for 55 percent of the calls because the ambulance was servicing another call.

The manager of such an emergency medical system would undoubtedly ask about the effect of doubling capacity by adding a second ambulance. We can predict the general effect from our knowledge of queuing systems—the patient waiting time will drop dramatically. In fact, using the same sample of call and service times from Table 9–2, but simulating for a system of two ambulances, a 5-minute patient waiting time is required in only one instance. The price paid for the improved service is the cost of a second ambulance and the added operating costs. The ambulance idle time increases from only about 20 percent to almost 60 percent for the small sample.

COMPUTER SIMULATION

If a computer were programmed to simulate the emergency medical system, we would place the two cumulative distributions in the memory unit of the computer. Through the random number generator program, the computer would generate a random number and thereby select a call time. By comparing cumulative call time with cumulative ambulance time, the computer program could determine whether or not the ambulance was available, and if it was available, whether or not it had to wait. The computations of patient waiting time, or ambulance idle time, would be routinely made and the program would direct the selection of another random number, thereby determining a service time. The necessary computations could then be made, with the resulting values being held in memory. The cycle would then repeat as many times as desired, so that a large run (i.e., a large number of service calls) could be made easily and with no more effort than a small run. With the aid of a computer, a simulation model can become very realistic, reflecting all sorts of contingency situations that may be representative of the real problem.

The ambulance system example is a demonstration of a manual Monte Carlo simulation. Its value is in the close contact with the problem and the sequence of simulated sampling and resulting calculations. Often, however, the performance evaluation of systems through simulation is complex and large scale so that manual methods are entirely impractical. In addition, even for simple systems such as the emergency medical system example, the need for large samples to describe adequately the performance of stochastic elements of a system eliminates manual methods from consideration. Digital computer simulation is therefore almost synonymous with the term *simulation* so far as management science is concerned.

Validation of Simulation Models

Validation of all kinds of models is an important phase in their useful application. Given the model, how closely does it represent reality? Validation of complex simulation models has some extraordinary problems because their complexity raises some issues of validation that may be more important with simulation than with other kinds of models. Complexity puts a greater burden on verifying internal logic, including program debugging. Thus in a first phase we must determine whether or not the simulation program actually represents what was intended in the program design by checking assumptions and reviewing the program with people familiar with the problem.

The second and crucial phase of validation requires us to determine in some satisfactory way whether the program represents the reality it was intended to simulate. If the simulation is meant to forecast the performance of a new system design, we are somewhat in the dark because there is no existing real system for comparative validation checks. In such situations, the nature of results can be reviewed by experts. Also, parts of a complex system may represent existing subsystems where direct validity checks can be made. Finally, statistical tests can be used to test hypotheses regarding general logic and validity.

Even though the final objective may be the design of a new system, we may develop simulation models to predict performance of an entire class of systems, a special case of which is an existing system. For example, in analyzing traffic

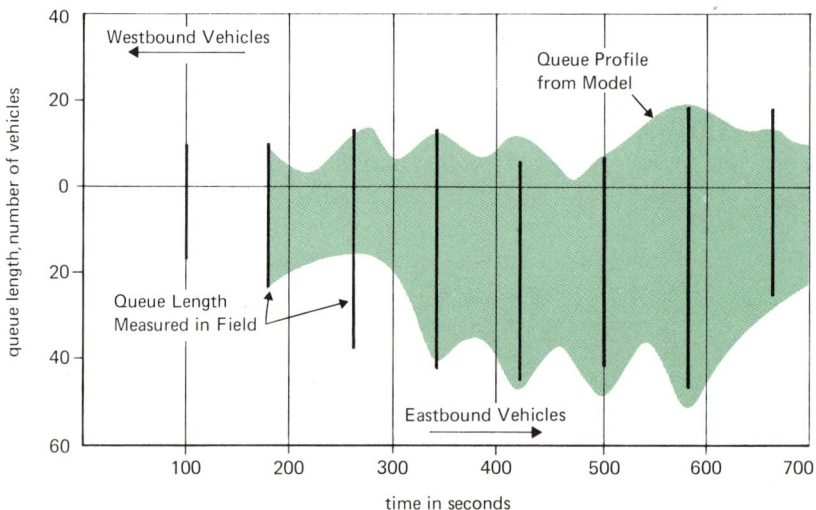

FIGURE 9-6. **Queue length field data versus model**

From J. Reitman, Computer Simulation Applications, *John Wiley & Sons, New York, 1971. Figure 12.13, p. 321; used by permission.*

flow, a simulator might be designed to take account of all of the main variables such as traffic density, traffic light settings, number of lanes, rules for left and right turns, special left turn lanes, etc. The simulator can be validated by predicting performance with the model for specified conditions, and comparing these results with actual field data.

Figure 9-6 represents just such a comparison in a traffic study. An intersection was selected within a network of five signalized intersections, and queue length predicted by the model (curved lines) was compared with measured queue length (vertical lines). The queue lengths are measured at 80-second intervals during the peak 15-minute period of the day. Eastbound traffic was 300 cars per 15 minutes over two through lanes and one left turn lane, and westbound traffic was 220 cars per 15 minutes. Average eastbound speed was measured as 7.3 mph compared to 6.3 mph predicted by the model, and westbound speed was measured as 10.2 mph versus 9.0 mph for the model. The comparison was judged to be satisfactory validation for the model.

Validation studies may result in model changes that could be as drastic as reformulating the problem. Thus, the comments on validation in Chapter 6 are especially significant for large-scale simulation models.

SIMULATION OF AN EMERGENCY MEDICAL SYSTEM

Earlier in this chapter, we developed the general Monte Carlo methodology around arrival and service distributions for an emergency medical system. Now, however, we wish to place these inputs in context with an actual simulation study of the emergency medical system of the City of Los Angeles. The managerial objectives of the study were focused on the appropriate capacity and deployment of emergency medical facilities, and the results were an important input to the deployment decision.

The prediction of the performance of an emergency medical system is an ideal example of the need for a "systems" view because in such a system, performance cannot be inferred by examining the components separately. The demand for service, nature and location of medical need, ambulance availability, traffic problems, the location of hospitals, and so on, are all interacting parameters that define the system and have a bearing on the decision variables. The decision variables themselves are complex, involving deployment strategy, response time, system cost, and other factors.

The simulation methodology is an ideal vehicle for studying complex systems such as an emergency medical system, because it would not be feasible to perform the experiments on the real system in a controlled way. Since factors of known risk in the form of probability distributions enter the process, we can perform a large number of replications of the experiments to determine the expected values of measures of performance, and thus be able to make decisions based on the expected long-run conditions. In addition, with simulation we can assess the response of the system to peak loads. Indeed, in all kinds of emergency service systems such as police and fire protection, as well as medical systems, how the system performs when its capacity is stressed may be of the greatest importance.

The Computer Simulation Model

Fitzsimmons [1970, 1973] programmed the emergency medical system, driving the simulation process with an incident generator (call for service) that provided the forecasts of load.

The Incident Generator Based on studies of past actual loads for each hour of the day, the hourly pattern shown in Figure 9-7 was developed. Therefore, a specific mean hourly rate could be determined from Figure 9-7 in proportion to load experience through the day. Furthermore, previous statistical studies had shown that the Poisson distribution was a good description of call rates for the mean values of Figure 9-7. For each hourly mean call rate, the generator could determine a specific call rate based on Monte Carlo methods. Recall that the shape of the Poisson distribution varies with the mean; three sample distributions at different load levels are shown in Figure 9-7. Note that at low loads the Poisson distribution has a fairly sharp peak with a relatively high probability of arrival rates near the mean. At high loads, however, the variability is rather great and there is a reasonably high probability of call rates substantially lower and higher than the mean rate. Finally, an exact time for an incident was determined by sampling over the hour from a uniform distribution.

The Simulator The main program of the simulator begins with an incident at a specific time, and the incident is processed according to the general logic of the flow chart shown in Figure 9-8. Travel time is computed as the sum of x and y distances converted to travel time, to correspond to the usual urban layout plan. Additional Monte Carlo sampling is required to compute the time required at the scene, the type of incident, and the delay at the hospital. Thus, the simulation contains both deterministic and stochastic elements.

While each vehicle has a home base, the simulator is designed to accommodate a mobile system (which can be dispatched en route), since vehicles can be reassigned in transit. The simulator includes capability for both ambulances and helicopters.

Model Validation The model was validated both in terms of equivalent analytical models for simple cases and for a portion of the existing Los Angeles Ambulance System.

Fitzsimmons [1970] constructed single and multiple ambulance waiting line models. The assumptions were first-come first-served queue discipline, Poisson input and exponential service time, and an infinite queuing system. On-scene care was assumed constant at seven minutes, all patients were transported to hospitals, and hospital transfer time was constant at three minutes in the

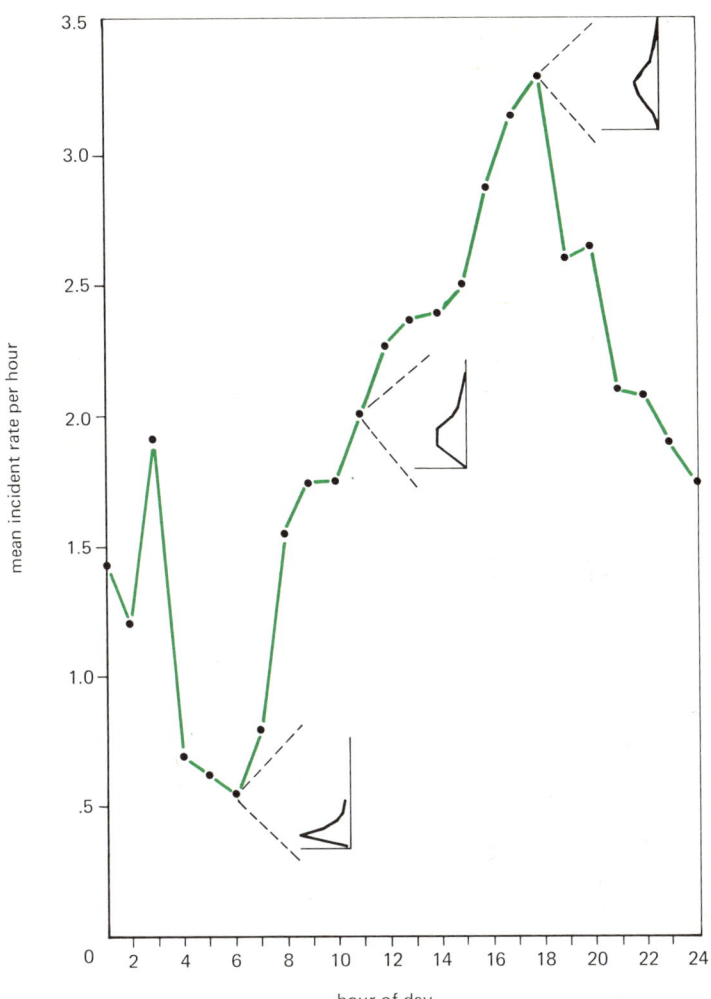

FIGURE 9-7. **Mean call for service rate (incident rate) for the Los Angeles emergency medical system. Three sample miniature Poisson distributions are shown for widely differing mean incident rates**

From J. A. Fitzsimmons, "Emergency Medical Systems: A Simulation Study and Computerized Method for Deployment of Ambulances." Unpublished Ph.D. Dissertation, UCLA, 1970; used by permission.

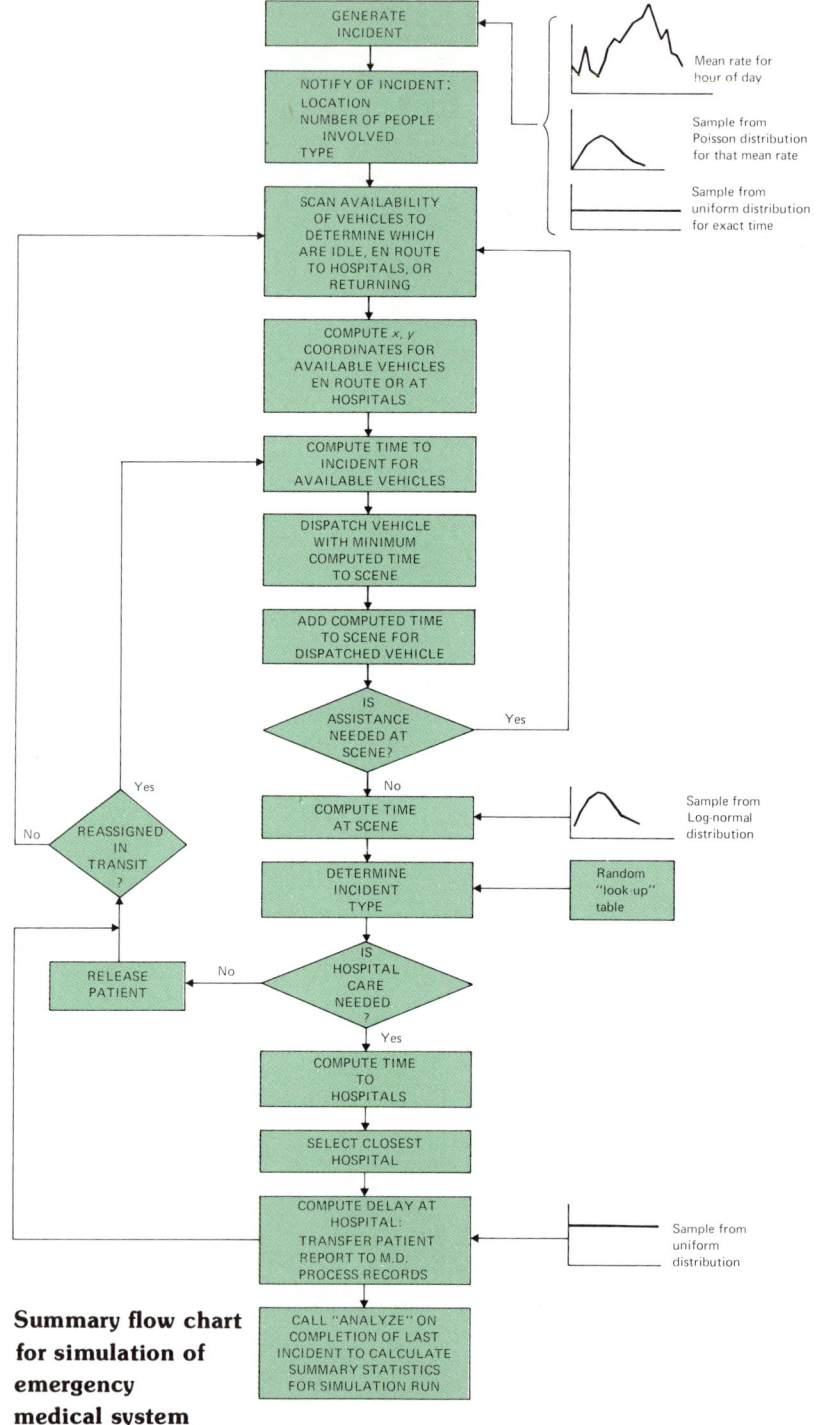

FIGURE 9-8. **Summary flow chart for simulation of emergency medical system**

validation studies. Simulation runs included 10,800 and 3,240 calls for the single and multiple ambulance cases respectively. Test of significance of various queue statistics were made comparing analytical and simulation results, and all results indicated high conformance between the simulation and analytical models.

In validating the computer simulation model against the real-world Los Angeles Ambulance System, Fitzsimmons tested its ability to predict the behavior of the San Fernando Valley portion of the Los Angeles system. Actual data for 1967 were used in developing the model and historical verification was performed by comparing records for 1967 with simulated results for the same period. A number of statistical tests were performed. Again, statistical tests confirmed that the simulation system duplicated reality adequately. Figure 9-9 shows a comparison between distributions of actual and simulated response times.

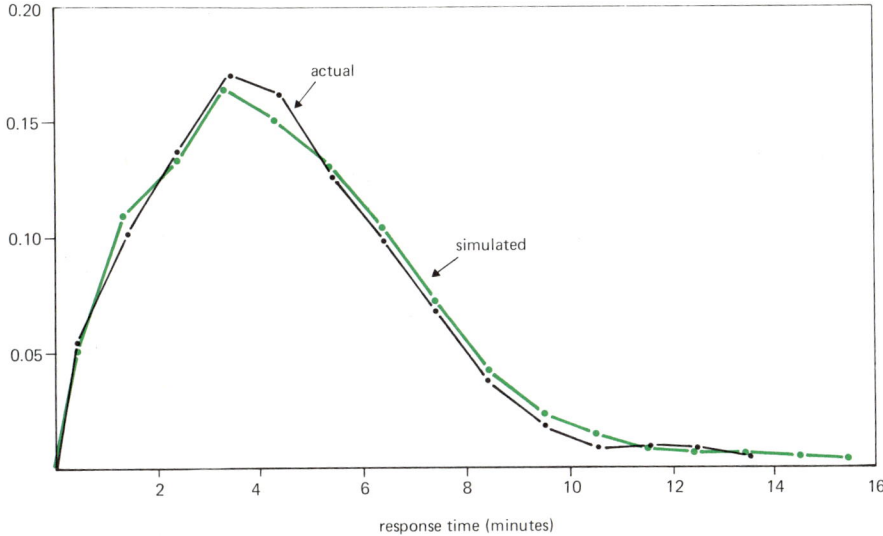

FIGURE 9-9. **Distribution of response times for the San Fernando Valley Ambulance System**

From J. A. Fitzsimmons, "Emergency Medical Systems: A Simulation Study and Computerized Method for Deployment of Ambulances." Unpublished Ph.D. Dissertation, UCLA, 1970; used by permission.

Use of the Emergency Medical Simulation Model

Given the validated simulation model, we have an effective vehicle for the managerial evaluation of practical alternatives in the form of sensitivity analysis and the evaluation of alternative control policies. The alternatives were evaluated mainly in terms of response time.

Number and Location of Ambulances Fitzsimmons evaluated the effect on response time of having one to ten ambulances in the system for single and dispersed home stations. The single home stations were at a hospital. In general, the response time for a single station leveled off at about three ambulances in the system; however, response time for dispersed deployment continued to decline. Waiting time for the single station fell to near zero with three ambulances in the system.

A series of 20 experimental runs evaluated hypotheses concerning location deployment patterns, and dispersed deployment dominated the single station alternative for all system performance criteria. Furthermore, optimal locations improved mean travel time to the scene by about 12 percent, compared to existing locations. Finally, it was found that optimal deployment was a function of incident or call rate.

Number and Location of Hospitals A series of runs was made in which the number of hospitals was varied from one to four, using a single ambulance located centrally. Mean time to the hospital was reduced considerably with the addition of hospitals to the system, but response time and waiting time were only slightly reduced, and ambulance utilization declined about 2 percent. Mean travel time to the scene actually increased slightly. Locating hospitals optimally reduced mean waiting time only slightly, because of reduced ambulance utilization.

Control Policies Alternate dispatch policies were evaluated for no radio communication, radio dispatch without mobile transmitters on board ambulances, and two-way radio communication. These alternate policies were evaluated under loads varying from call rates of 15 to 45 per day. Simulated response time was reduced by 7 to 8 percent with radio dispatch; however, the two-way radio dispatch system was very little better than the basic system. Nevertheless, the two-way system was recommended, since it effected some improvement.

Even when ambulance stations were physically dispersed, simulation experiments showed a definite advantage of pooling ambulances into one central dispatch command, as would be predicted from waiting line theory.

Alternate ambulance deployment policies were also evaluated, indicating an advantage for an adaptive system that allows repositioning of vehicles as load builds up, rather than having each vehicle return to its home base at the end of an incident. Fitzsimmons [1973] developed a computer program named Computerized Ambulance Location Logic (CALL) to determine optimum ambulance deployment. Based on evaluations for particular ambulance locations, a computer search routine directs changes in the ambulance locations to progressively decrease the system's mean response time.

WHAT SHOULD THE MANAGER KNOW?

Problem Characteristics

Computer simulation is a powerful tool, and simulated sampling is an extremely important component that makes it possible to assess the risk factors entering complex problems. The manager should have an understanding of the kinds of problems for which simulation might be useful. These problems are in general those that must reflect the complexities of systems—problems in which there are probabalistic interactions between components of the system. The emergency medical simulation is such a problem. The effectiveness of the emergency medical system depends on the demand for service, the number of vehicles available and their locations, the number and locations of hospitals, population and traffic densities and patterns, and the control and deployment policies used. Most organizations have some problems that require a systems approach in order to represent the problem adequately, and simulation has been used effectively in industrial planning and control systems, hospital admissions systems, urban transportation systems, weapons systems, and others.

Model Formulation

In deciding whether or not to place faith in the results of a simulation model, a manager needs to be involved in the initial phases of model formulation to be sure that the model will have the capability to examine the kinds of questions in which he is interested. The manager's sense of the problems may be particularly important when risk factors need to be accounted for. While managers cannot be expected to know simulation languages and to program simulation problems, they need to be able to communicate effectively with the technical people who will implement the detailed formulation of the model. Thus, a manager should be able to make a flow chart of a problem, to indicate at least the major progressions involved and the decision points that he feels will be useful. In this process, the manager may also be defining basic data needs.

Problems for which simulation is particularly useful tend to be ones involving the evaluation of alternative policies and procedures. As such, they are commonly one-time studies. Thus, while a manager need not know programming languages in detail, he may nevertheless find it worthwhile to know the general characteristics of languages. For example, simulation languages are efficient in terms of programming effort, but not necessarily efficient in terms of computer run time. Languages such as FORTRAN and PL/1 have the opposite characteristics. For a large-scale simulation program, it may be worthwhile to obtain capability in specialized simulation languages.

Interpretation of Results

The validation process should be of great interest to managers in interpreting results. The manager should not use the results of a simulation model if the validation is not satisfactory. With satisfactory validation, however, the sensitivity analysis should be of significant help to managers. These studies can provide insight into how the real system functions and which variables are important and which are relatively unimportant, even though they may be under managerial control.

Check Your Understanding

1. What are the essential differences between discrete event and discrete time updating simulations? Illustrate by indicating how the simulation of the activities of a single ambulance might be handled in each of the two simulation modes.
2. Outline the procedure for simulated sampling (Monte Carlo). What is the purpose of each step?
3. How does Monte Carlo sampling ensure that data enter the simulation in proportion to their occurrence in the original distribution? Can you envision a situation where the data entering the simulation might not be representative of the original distribution?
4. The manager of a small post office is concerned that his growing township is overloading the one-window service being offered. He decides to obtain sample data concerning 100 individuals who arrive for service. The data obtained are summarized in Table 9-4.
   a. Convert the distributions to cumulative probability distributions.
   b. Using a simulated sample of 20, estimate the average customer waiting time and the average percentage of idle time of the postal clerk.
5. The manager of a bank is attempting to determine how many tellers he needs during his peak load period. He wishes to offer service so that the average waiting time of a customer does not exceed two minutes. How many tellers does he need if the arrival and service distributions are as shown in Table 9-5? Customers form a single waiting line and are serviced by the next available teller. Simulate for alternative numbers of tellers with a sample of 20 arrivals in each instance.
6. You have carried through two simple simulations in connection with exercises 4 and 5. How could you validate the results?
7. The discussion of the simulation of an emergency medical system is a report of how an extensive simulation was carried through, validated, and used. Place yourself in the position of the policy and decision maker responsible for the operation of the Los Angeles Emergency Medical System. Assume that a presentation has just been made to you similar to the report of the study given in the text. What questions would you ask the researcher? How would you

TABLE 9-4. **Arrival and Service Time Data for a One-Window Post Office**

Time Between Arrivals (min)	Frequency	Service Time (min)	Frequency
0.5	2	0.5	12
1.0	6	1.0	21
1.5	10	1.5	36
2.0	25	2.0	19
2.5	20	2.5	7
3.0	14	3.0	5
3.5	10		100
4.0	7		
4.5	4		
5.0	2		
	100		

TABLE 9-5. **Arrival and Service Time Data for a Bank**

Time Between Arrivals (min)	Frequency	Service Time (min)	Frequency
0.0	10	0.0	0
1.0	35	1.0	5
2.0	25	2.0	20
3.0	15	3.0	40
4.0	10	4.0	35
5.0	5		100
	100		

satisfy yourself concerning the value of the study? What criteria would you use in making such decisions as the number of ambulances to use, the number of hospitals to establish for the system, and the type of radio communication to use?

Problems

8. A manufacturing company has a large machine containing three identical electronic components that are the major cause of downtime. The current practice is to replace the components as they fail. However, a proposal has been made to replace all three components whenever any one of them fails in order to reduce the frequency with which the machine must be shut down.

    In the current situation, the machine must be shut down for one hour to replace one component or for two and one-fourth hours to replace all three.
    a. What are the data requirements to analyze and compare the alternatives using simulation?
    b. Formulate the problem in terms of a simulation system using the discrete event method. Prepare a flow chart of the simulation system similar to Figure 9-8 in the text.

9. Suppose we are dealing with the maintenance of a bank of 30 machines, and we wish to estimate the level of service that can be maintained by one mechanic. In order to make judgments about the effectiveness of the system, we need to have the simulation system generate data concerning the time that machines are down while waiting for service and being repaired. We also wish to know how well the mechanic is utilized in the system.
    a. What are the data requirements necessary to construct a simulation of the system?
    b. Formulate the problem in terms of a simulation system using the discrete event method. Prepare a flow chart of the simulation system similar to Figure 9-8 in the text.

10. A bank of 20 automatic machines is being maintained by a crew of six mechanics. Production forecasts indicate the need for two more machines to meet capacity needs. The question of whether or not the size of the repair crew should be enlarged has been raised.

    There are two basic kinds of repair situations: the *run* call and the *downtime* call. A run call is one in which the mechanic can service the machine while it is still operating. On the average, 67 percent of the calls for service are of the run type. A downtime call for service normally comes from a more serious problem resulting in machine breakdown. In such situations, the mechanic completes the repair and the machine is put back in service. However, the mechanic spends additional time with the machine after it has started again to make final adjustments and ensure that it is ready for service. This period is the mechanic's *run-in time*.
    a. What are the data requirements to develop a simulation of the repair system in order to analyze and compare the system for different numbers of machines in service and different numbers of mechanics?
    b. Formulate the problem in terms of a simulation system using the discrete event method. Prepare a flow chart of the simulation system similar to Figure 9-8 in the text.

11. There are numerous full reports of simulations of complex systems, including those on the list that follows:
    a. Simulation of a district office of the United States Social Security System [Maisel and Gnugnuoli, 1972, pp. 343–94].
    b. Simulation in business [Meier, Newell, and Pazer, 1969, Chapter 2].
    c. Simulation in economic analysis [Meier, Newell, and Pazer, 1969, Chapter 4].
    d. Prediction of passenger railroad system performance [Reitman, 1971, Chapter 8].
    e. Performance of a computer system [Reitman, 1971, Chapter 11].
    f. Auto traffic flow through a series of intersections [Reitman, 1971, Chapter 12].

    Read one of the simulation studies from the preceding list. Prepare a report giving a brief summary and reviewing data requirements, methodology, and interpretation of results. If the report were presented to you as decision maker, what questions would you raise? What criteria other than those specifically included in the simulation do you think are pertinent in judging and deciding on the issues raised by the simulation study?

12. A professional football coach has six running backs on his squad. He wants to evaluate how injuries might affect his stock of backs. A minor injury causes a player to be removed from the game and miss only the next game. A major injury puts the player out of action for the rest of the season. The probability of a major injury in a game is 0.05. There is at most one major injury per game. The probability distribution of minor injuries per game is:

Number of Injuries	Probability
0	0.2
1	0.5
2	0.22
3	0.05
4	0.025
5	0.005

    Injuries seem to happen in a completely random manner, with no discernible pattern over the season. A season is ten games.

    Using random numbers given in Table C–3 of Appendix C, simulate the fluctuations in the coach's stock of running backs over the season. Assume that he hires no additional running backs during the season.

References

1. Emshoff, J. R., and R. L. Sisson, *Design and Use of Computer Simulation Models,* Macmillan, New York, 1970.

2. Evans, G. W., G. F. Wallace, and G. L. Sutherland, *Simulation Using Digital Computers,* Prentice-Hall, Englewood Cliffs, N.J., 1967.
3. Fitzsimmons, J. A., "Emergency Medical Systems: A Simulation Study and Computerized Method for the Deployment of Ambulances," unpublished Ph.D. Dissertation, University of California, Los Angeles, 1970.
4. ———, "A Methodology for Emergency Ambulance Deployment," *Management Science,* Vol. 19, No. 6, February 1973, pp. 627–36.
5. IBM Corporation, *GPSS V Users' Manual,* Form No. SH20-0851-0, 1970.
6. Kiviat, P. J., R. Villanueva, and H. M. Markowitz, *The Simscript II Programming Language,* Prentice-Hall, Englewood Cliffs, N.J., 1969.
7. Maisel, H., and G. Gnugnuoli, *Simulation of Discrete Stochastic Systems,* Science Research Associates, Chicago, 1972.
8. Meier, R. W., T. Newell, and H. L. Pazer, *Simulation in Business and Economics,* Prentice-Hall, Englewood Cliffs, N.J., 1969.
9. Naylor, T. H., J. L. Balintfy, D. S. Burdick, and K. Chu, *Computer Simulation Techniques,* John Wiley & Sons, New York, 1966.
10. Reitman, J., *Computer Simulation Applications,* John Wiley & Sons, New York, 1971.
11. Schriber, T. J., *Simulation Using GPSS,* John Wiley & Sons, New York, 1974.
12. Wyman, F. P., *Simulation Modeling: A Guide to Using SIMSCRIPT,* John Wiley & Sons, New York, 1970.

PART IV

OPTIMIZING MODELS

INTRODUCTION TO OPTIMIZING MODELS

The use of optimizing models is the most exciting and potentially valuable method of management science. That is true because, given a criterion, these models combine the elements of alternative generator, predictive, and evaluative models in such a way that the *best possible* solution can be determined. Best possible means that, given the criterion, there exists no superior combination of the decision variables for the model. These are the powerful optimizing methods of management science such as mathematical programming, network optimization, inventory models, and others.

Implicit in the preceding euphoric statement about best possible solutions are the assumptions that the submodel that predicts system performance is a valid representation of how the system works and that the evaluative model reflects the preferences of the decision maker. As we shall see these are important assumptions, and it may be difficult to always meet them when we are combining the functions of alternative generator, system performance prediction, evaluation, and optimization in one grand system.

Let us begin by recalling the scheme of models in management science from Chapter 1, shown again in Figure IV–1. Parts II and III of this book have dealt with the processes of the models shown in Figure IV–1. Part II focused on evaluative models. We assumed that we knew how the system worked and models that depended on utility theory, decision trees, and expected values were developed to evaluate outcomes. In Part III we removed the assumption that we knew how the system performed and developed models and methodologies for predicting system performance under conditions of certainty and risk. In both Parts II and III we assumed that the decision maker played the role of alternative generator.

Optimizing models combine the alternative generator, predictive model, and the evaluative model, as indicated by the highlighted area in Figure IV-1. The output of the combined system is a combination of values for the decision variables that produces the best solution; we call this the optimum solution. In the optimizing models we shall study, the different elements of Figure IV-1 will not have a separate and distinct identity, yet their functions will be performed.

Let us see in general how the coupling can be made. In Figure IV-2 we have developed a flow chart that contains all of the elements of Figure IV-1. In addition, below the evaluative model we have inserted a test for optimality in which we determine whether or not the solution just produced can be improved. If it can be improved, we need some mechanism to determine the direction of change and the amount of change we should make in the decision variables for the next iteration. This information is sent back to the alternative generator to produce a new alternative. System performance is predicted and evaluated, and the cycle is repeated until the test for optimality indicates that no further improvement is possible. We have diagramed the process as an iterative one; however, some of the solution techniques combine these steps and go directly to the optimum solution, while others actually do iterate in the manner we have described.

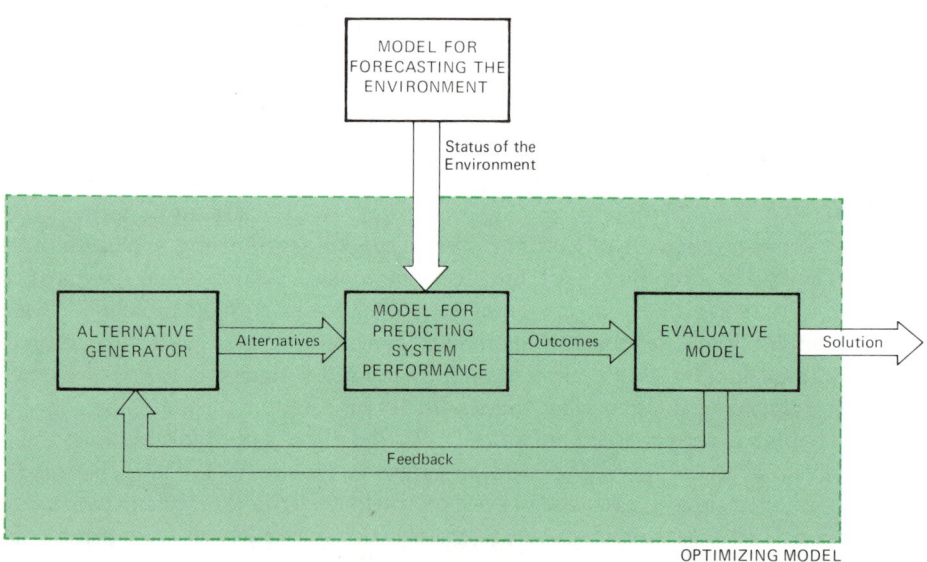

FIGURE IV-1. **Elements of an optimizing model**

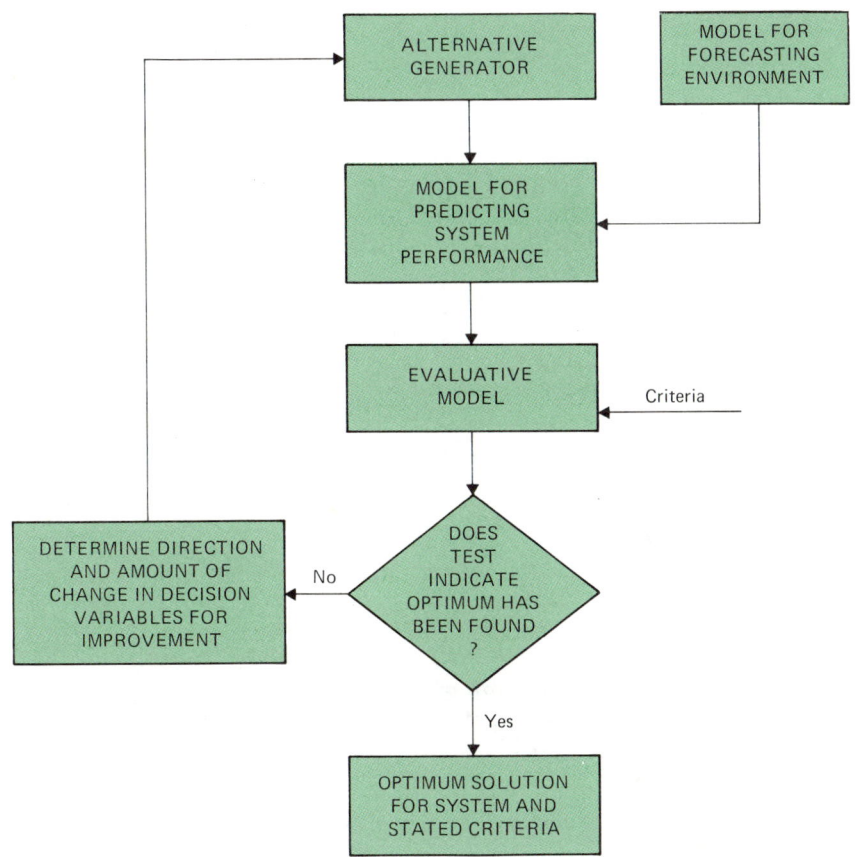

FIGURE IV-2. **Flow chart showing test for optimality and coupling to alternative generator**

CONCEPT OF A TEST FOR OPTIMALITY

The simplest case of a test for optimality is one in which we have a single decision criterion such as cost or profit, and the value of the criterion varies as a function of a single decision variable. Suppose, for example, that we wished to determine the least cost inventory to hold as a buffer to absorb variations in demand. The larger the buffer inventory, the greater the inventory holding cost, but the lower the cost of lost sales and back ordering. Since one component of cost is increasing and the other decreasing as buffer inventory increases, the composite cost function plotted in relation to buffer inventory size would be similar to Figure IV-3; that is, cost decreases to a minimum and then increases again as inventory holding costs become the dominant cost factor.

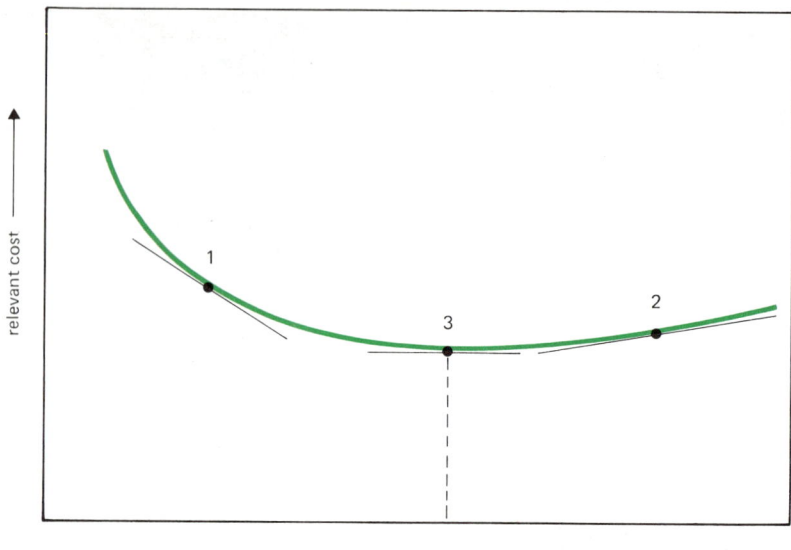

FIGURE IV-3. **Typical curve of relevant cost versus the size of buffer stock indicating optimum at a point where the slope of the curve is zero**

We can see by inspection that the optimum inventory size is at point 3 in Figure IV-3, the minimum point of the cost curve. Mathematically, the test for the minimum point is in terms of the slope of the curve. The minimum will be where the slope of the curve is zero. In this kind of situation the iterative process is not necessary since we can test for the minimum (or maximum) much more directly using appropriate mathematical techniques as we shall see in Chapter 10.

PLAN FOR PART IV

All of the models discussed in Part IV will be of the optimizing type. They combine the separate elements or functions in our framework of alternative generator, predictive model, and evaluative model in an optimizing system. This system automatically determines the best possible solution for the model. We shall begin with elementary optimizing models used in inventory management in Chapter 10. We shall then discuss linear optimization models and linear programming methods in Chapters 11, 12, and 13. Finally, we shall consider network models in Chapters 14 and 15. The network models of Chapter 14 can be used to design and analyze alternative product distribution systems, and the network models of Chapter 15 are used to plan and schedule major projects.

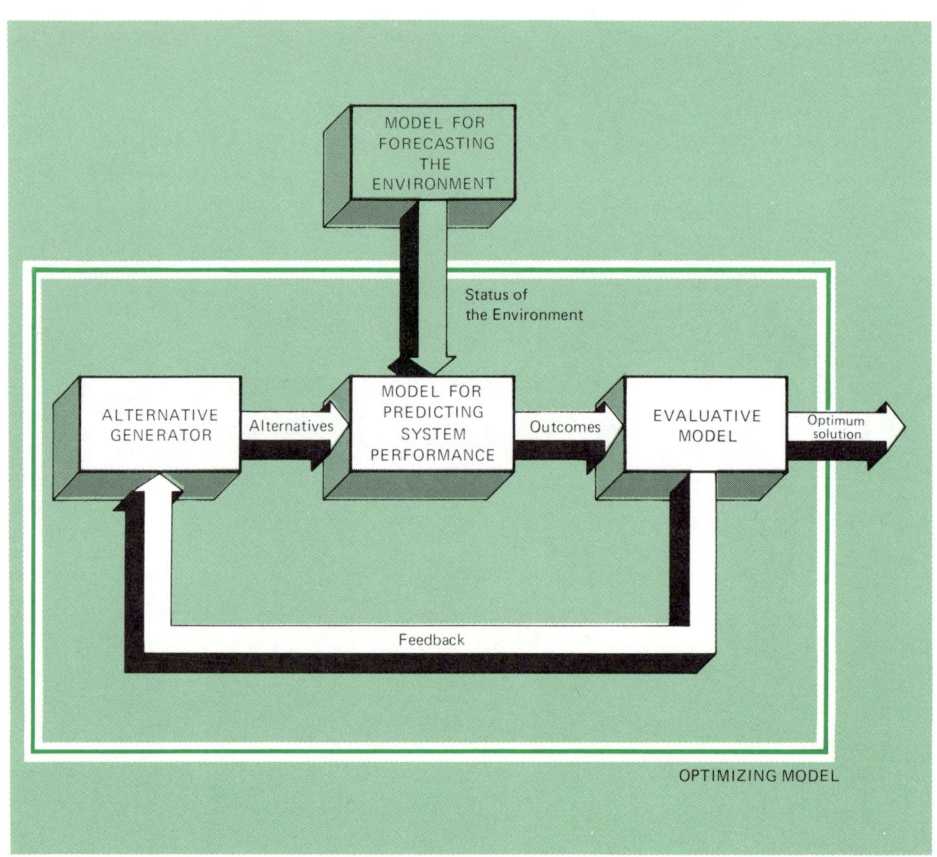

ELEMENTARY OPTIMIZING MODELS FOR INVENTORY MANAGEMENT

It is perhaps fitting that we should use an inventory problem as a vehicle to introduce optimizing models. The first optimizing model used by managers was an inventory model developed by F. W. Harris in 1915. Harris derived a formula for the Economic Order Quantity (EOQ), the optimum quantity of materials or items to purchase at one time.

Since World War II a great deal of research has been focused on inventory problems. We shall begin with a general discussion of inventories and their functions in managerial systems, and the relevant costs associated with inventories. We shall then formulate the alternative generator and the predictive and evaluative submodels, and show how these elements can be combined in a system that functions as an optimizing model to guide inventory reordering decisions and policy. Given the conceptual framework, we will then develop extensions that take account of some complicating factors, such as stock shortages, quantity discounts, and risk.

Functions of Inventories

Inventories are necessary in many managerial systems in order to provide "off the shelf" service for stock items in retailing and wholesaling operations, and

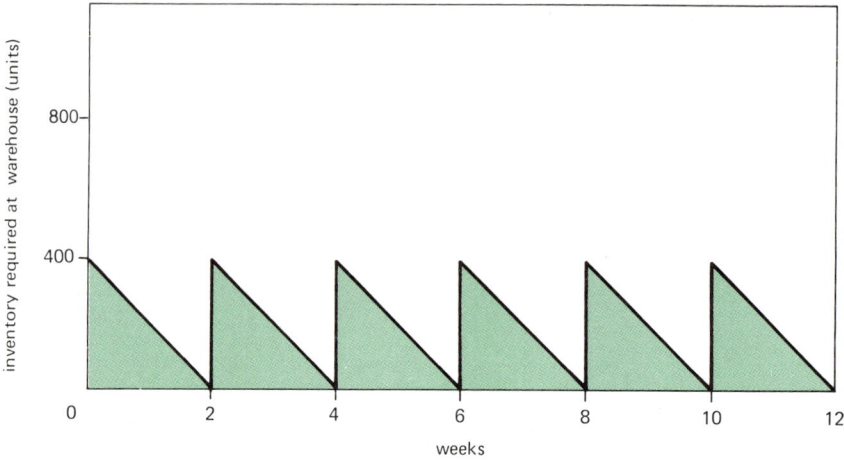

FIGURE 10-1. **Idealized graph of inventories required at the warehouse to cover trucking time from the factory. The average transit inventory component of pipeline inventory is the product of truck time and demand rate, or $2 \times 200 = 400$ units. Average inventory for the transit function is $400/2 = 200$ units**

these needs are reflected back into the manufacturing and raw material supply functions as well. In systems that produce a service rather than a physical product, the proper functioning of that service is usually partially dependent on supply items—paper and forms in governmental and other offices, medical supplies in hospitals, repair parts in a maintenance operation, and so on.

Throughout the supply-manufacturing-distribution system, inventories are the "shock absorbers" that absorb the normal variations in demand and in supply lead time at each stock point. As such, they perform a *decoupling* function, which makes it possible to carry on activities relatively independently and efficiently. Without inventories, such systems could not function effectively, and when inventories fall to dangerously low levels, we need virtually perfect coordination and scheduling to compensate. Unfortunately this perfection is not normally attainable. When such enterprises are forced into a hand-to-mouth supply situation by strikes or other choking of supply lines, the smoothly functioning machine breaks down. The vital nature of inventories is seen by examining the kinds of inventories in a supply system.

Pipeline Inventories To illustrate the function of pipeline inventories, assume a production-distribution system with one product for which there is an

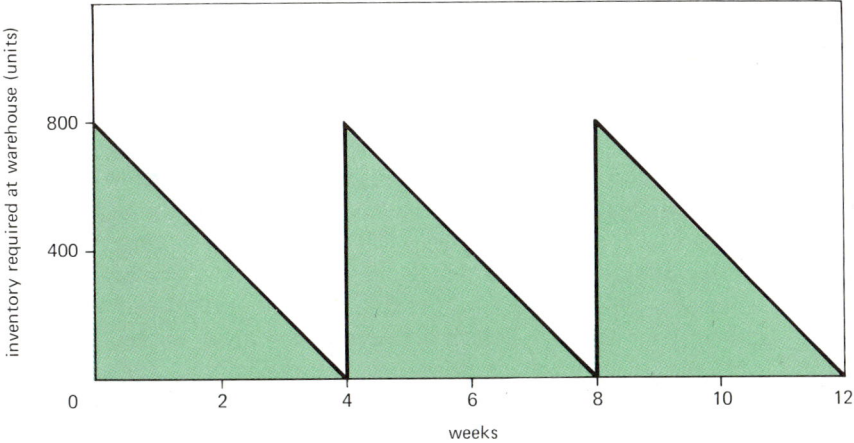

FIGURE 10-2. **Inventories required at the warehouse when orders are placed for a truckload of 800 units. Average inventory for this component is 800/2 = 400 units. Transit inventories are unchanged.**

average demand of 200 units per week at the warehouse. Let us assume that normal warehousing procedures are to prepare a procurement order to the factory when the warehouse inventory falls to a critical level called the *reorder point*. It takes one week to prepare the order, get it approved, and have it received by the factory. Once the order is received at the factory, it takes two weeks for loading, trucking, and unloading at the warehouse.

The warehouse must carry enough stock on hand to meet demand during the transit time. Figure 10-1 shows an idealized graph of the inventories required at the warehouse just to cover trucking time from the factory. The average transit inventory is the product of the truck time and the demand rate, or $2 \times 200 = 400$ units. At all times, then, 400 units are in motion from the factory to the warehouse, or in an equivalent sense, the factory must maintain an inventory that takes account of this fact. The order time delay of one week has the same effect as a transit time, since the warehouse must also carry inventories to cover this delay. In general then, every lag in the system generates the need for inventory to fill the pipeline. These are the in-process inventories in production systems; however, the concept is completely general.

Lot Size or "Cycle" Inventories To examine lot size inventories, let us continue with our simple example. Since the truck is to make the trip from the factory to the warehouse, how many items should be moved at one time? Most of the trucking costs are fixed regardless of lot size, so hand-to-mouth supply would be prohibitively expensive. Let us assume that orders are placed for a truck load of 800 units, equivalent to a four-week supply. Figure 10-2 shows an idealized graph of inventories required at the warehouse when orders are placed for a truckload. Warehouse inventories must therefore be increased to take account of the fact that materials are trucked 800 at a time to gain transportation cost advantages.

Buffer Inventories At times, inventories must provide a buffer against variations. Figure 10-2 assumes that demand rate, truck time, and order time are all constant. We know, however, that these factors are not ordinarily constant, so we must have some way to protect against unpredictable variations in demand and in supply time. Figure 10-3 shows the contrast in inventory levels at the warehouse that might occur if the maximum demand* of 300 units per week occurred during the supply time of three weeks. In order to ensure that we do not run out of stock, a buffer inventory of 300 units is required [the difference in the maximum and average demand rates during the three-week supply time, $(300 - 200)\,3 = 300$ units].

Seasonal Inventories Many products have a fairly predictable but seasonal pattern through the year. Where this is true, management has the choice of changing production rates over the year to absorb the fluctuation in demand or of absorbing some or all of the fluctuation in demand with inventories. If we attempt to follow the demand curve through the seasonal variations by changing production rates, the capital investment for the system must provide for the peak capacity, and we must absorb costs for overtime, hiring, training, and separating labor.

The discussion to this point has indicated the vital nature of inventories and the advantages gained by recognizing their functions. The question, however, is not one-sided. Inventories cost money and a knowledge of the behavior of inventory-related costs will be important to building inventory models and to the formulation of managerial objectives and an evaluative model.

Costs and Management Objectives

The following types of cost items are often relevant to inventory models: costs that depend on the number of orders, price or production costs, handling and storage costs, shortage costs, and capital costs.

Costs Depending on the Number of Orders In deciding on purchase order quantities, there are certain clerical costs of preparing orders. These costs

---

*The maximum demand is a point on the demand distribution curve that would not be exceeded more than a preset percentage of time. It is established in relation to a desire not to run out of stock.

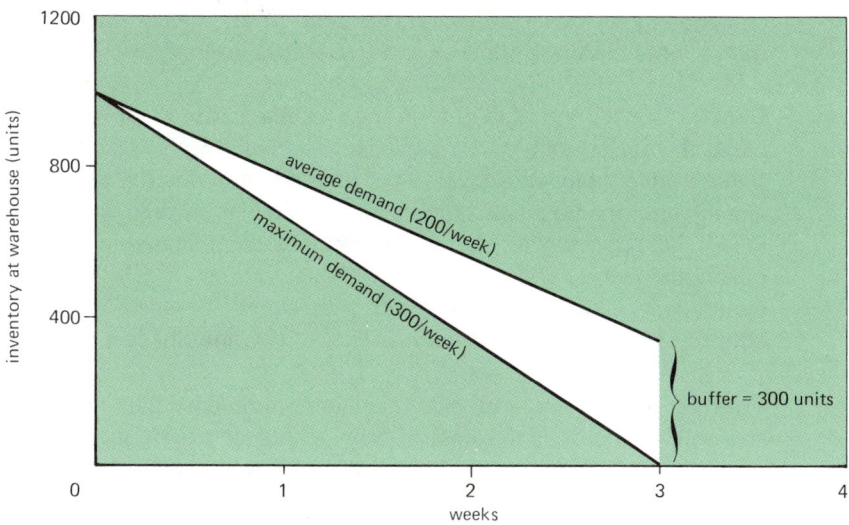

FIGURE 10–3. **Buffer inventory required to avoid shortages. Difference between idealized average and maximum demand rates over the supply lead time represents a minimum or buffer stock required to protect against the occurrence of shortages resulting from random fluctuations in demand.**

are the same regardless of the quantity ordered. They are important in the models with which we shall deal; however, our interest is in the true incremental cost of order preparation (or its equivalent). The average ordering cost derived by dividing the total cost of the purchasing operation by the average number of orders processed is not appropriate, since a large segment of the total costs are fixed. Our interest is in the variable cost component.

The parallel cost in production systems is the cost to prepare production orders, set up machines, and control the flow of orders through the plant.

Price or Production Costs When quantity discounts must be taken into account, unit price becomes relevant in determining purchase order quantities. Comparably, production cost is relevant to determining the size of production lots.

Costs of Handling and Storing Inventory There are certain costs associated with the level of inventories, represented by the costs of handling material in and out of inventory and the storage costs. The storage costs are made up of components such as insurance, taxes, rent, obsolescence, spoilage, and capital costs. These costs are commonly in proportion to inventory levels.

Capital Costs As alluded to in the preceding paragraph, part of the storage cost is the opportunity cost of capital invested in inventory. The cost figure itself is the product of inventory value per unit, the time that the unit is in inventory, and the appropriate interest rate. In general, the appropriate interest rate should reflect the opportunities for the investment of comparable funds within the organization, and it should not be lower than the cost of borrowed money. Since the funds are tied up in inventories, they cannot be used for the purchase of other profit-producing investments, and an opportunity cost must be imputed.

Cost of Shortages An extremely important cost that never appears on accounting records is the cost of running out of stock. Such costs appear in several ways. In profit-making concerns, sales may actually be lost as a result of stockouts. Or, there may be additional costs for back ordering. In production systems, a part shortage may cause idle labor on a production line or subsequent incremental labor cost to perform operations out of sequence, usually at higher than normal cost. Alternately there may be costs of avoiding shortages. In nonprofit organizations, similar costs may be involved other than the cost of lost sales.

Management Objectives The overall objective of management is to design policies and decision rules that view inventories in a "systems" context so that the broadly construed set of costs discussed are generally minimized. In addition, however, the existence of a cost of shortages raises a question concerning the appropriate service level. (Service level may be defined as the percentage of orders that can be filled from stock.) When shortage costs can be accurately estimated, the most economical service level can be determined by balancing buffer inventory costs against shortage costs. More commonly, however, shortage costs cannot be accurately determined, and the manager must reflect his subjective trade-off for service versus buffer inventory cost in establishing service level policies.

FORMULATION OF A PURCHASE ORDER QUANTITY MODEL

Let us organize our knowledge about the functions of inventories and about inventory-related costs, with the objective of determining managerial policies concerning the number of units of an item to order at one time. We establish the following notation:

C = total incremental cost
C_0 = total incremental cost of an optimal solution
Q = order quantity

Q_0 = Economic Order Quantity (EOQ)
R = annual requirements in units
c_H = inventory holding costs per unit per year
c_P = preparation costs per order
c_S = shortage costs per unit per year
P = reorder point
L = supply lead time
B = buffer inventory level

The decision variable under managerial control is the order quantity Q, and we assume that we have a forecasting model to provide an estimate of the annual requirements R. Our initial objective is to develop a model to determine the order quantity Q_0 that minimizes the relevant incremental costs.

Alternative Generator

In our discussion of predictive models, we generally assumed that the manager determined a specific alternative as input to the predictive model. When an optimizing model is used, rather than identifying a specific alternative, the manager defines the *set of all feasible alternatives*. That is, he must describe the characteristics of alternatives that will be acceptable solutions to his problem. In our inventory management problem the set of feasible alternatives consists of all of the possible order sizes, $Q = 1, 2, 3, \ldots, n$, where n may be an upper bound reflecting warehouse capacity or some other constraint. The optimizing model must search through this entire set of alternatives to identify Q_0.

Model for Predicting System Performance

With the set of feasible alternatives defined, we must develop a model that relates system inputs to system outputs. For the purchase order quantity system, given a specific order quantity Q, the outcome of interest to the decision maker is the total incremental cost C with which it is associated. We must determine a logical relationship between the order quantity and these incremental costs.

Figure 10-4 describes the idealized functioning of the inventory system. When the inventory level of our item falls to the reorder point P, an order for Q units is placed. The reorder point P is set so that inventory is reduced to zero by normal usage at rate R precisely when the order for Q units is received. The inventory is then increased immediately by Q units and the cycle repeats as shown in Figure 10-4. The average inventory is simply $Q/2$.

The total incremental costs C for this simple system are the costs of holding inventory and the costs associated with the procurement of an order of size Q. (We are assuming no price discounts and no shortages, since deterministic usage rate and precise timing of order receipt are a part of the model.) Therefore, the logical relationship for the costs is

C = inventory holding costs + preparation costs.

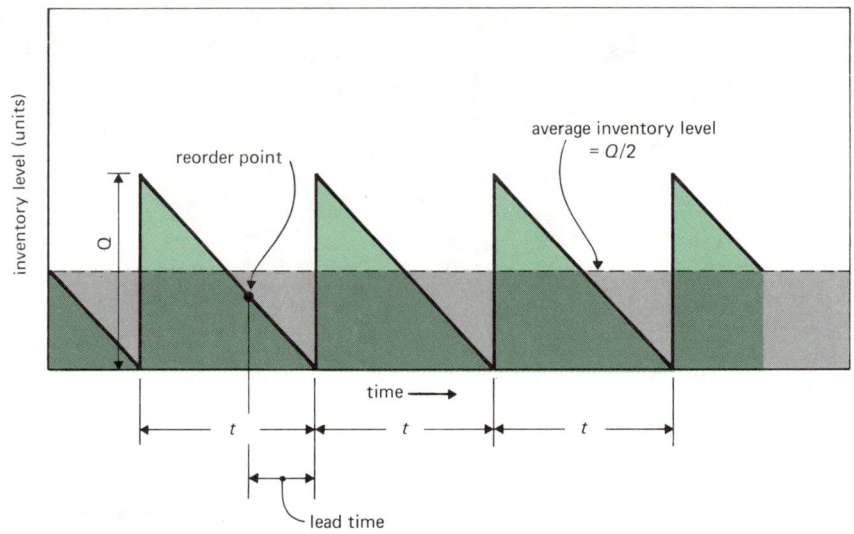

FIGURE 10-4. **Graphic model of inventory levels when the number purchased at one time is Q units. The time between the receipt of orders is t.**

We can see from Figure 10-4 that if Q is increased, the average inventory level $Q/2$ will increase proportionately. If the inventory holding cost per unit per year is c_H, the annual incremental costs associated with holding inventories are

$c_H(Q/2)$.

If the cost to hold a unit of inventory was $c_H = \$0.10$, we could express the inventory holding cost function as $0.10Q/2 = 0.05Q$, a simple linear function. The inventory holding cost function is plotted in Figure 10-5 as curve (a).

Similarly, the annual preparation costs depend on the number of times orders are placed per year and the cost to place an order. The number of orders required for an annual requirement of R will vary with the lot size Q of each order; that is, the number of orders equals R/Q. If it costs c_P to place an order, the annual preparation costs are

$c_P(R/Q)$.

If, for example, $R = 1600$ units per year, and $c_P = \$5$, we could express the annual preparation costs as $(5 \times 1600/Q) = 8000/Q$. This preparation cost function is plotted for different values of Q in Figure 10-5, curve (b).

The total incremental costs C are represented by the sum of the two cost components

$C = c_H(Q/2) + c_P(R/Q).$ \hfill (1)

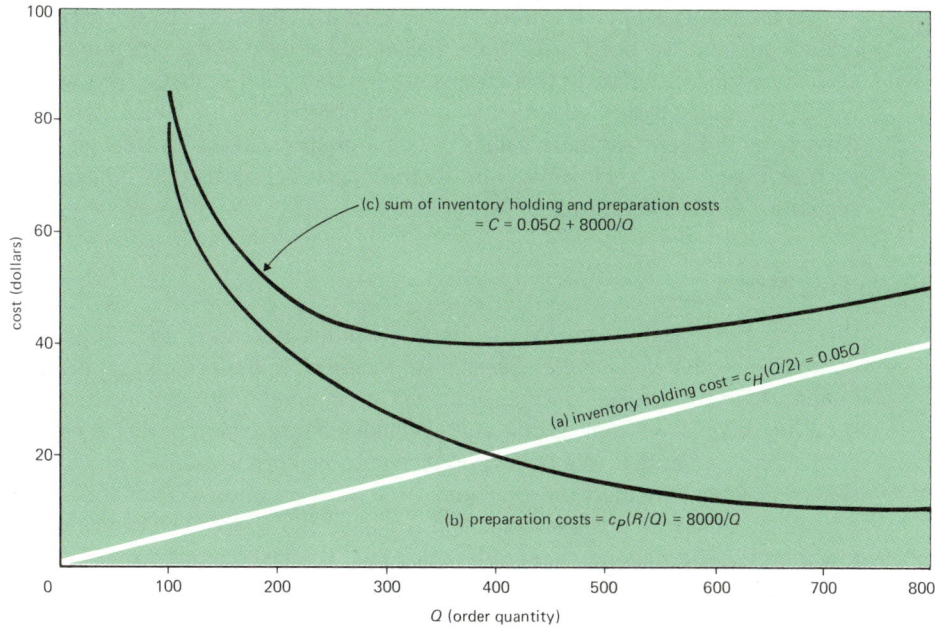

FIGURE 10-5. **Graphic representation of evaluative model.** $R = 1600$ **units per year,** $c_P = \$5.00$, $c_H = \$0.10$.

Equation (1) is our predictive model. For the specific values of the parameters given, equation (1) becomes

$$C = 0.05Q + 8000/Q. \qquad (2)$$

Curve (c) in Figure 10-5 shows this total cost function plotted for different values of Q. Note that curve (c) declines to a minimum as order size increases and then increases again as inventory holding costs become dominant. We can now use equation (2) to evaluate different order quantity policies.

Evaluative Model

Given the predictive model, we must now evaluate the outcomes it produces. The simple inventory problem we have described involves a single criterion, total incremental costs, and complete certainty. That is, we have assumed that there is no uncertainty regarding demand, inventory holding costs, preparation costs, the supply lead time, or other elements of the problem. These assumptions may or may not be appropriate in a specific real-world application. Later, we shall see how additional detail can be added to this simple model, so that more realistic models may be obtained by bootstrapping.

As we discussed in the Introduction to Part II, in the case of a single criterion under certainty, we need only agree that more (or less) of the criterion is desirable. Since the criterion in this case is total incremental costs C, obviously we would like to minimize C. That could be accomplished by trial and error calculations using different alternate values of Q in equation (2), or by creating graphs such as Figure 10-5. However, an optimizing model exists that simplifies this search for Q_0, the economic order quantity.

Optimizing Model

We now have all but one of the basic elements necessary to construct the optimizing model. We have an alternative generator in that we can set the order quantity Q to some initial low value and with each iteration we can increase Q by small increments (as small as one unit). We have a forecasting model to estimate annual requirements R. We have a predictive model of the manner in which the system functions in the form of equation (1), or equation (2) for the specific parameter values of our example, and we have the simple evaluative model, minimize C. The missing element is, of course, the test for optimality.

By inspecting Figure 10-5, we can see that the form of the total incremental cost curve is such that the minimum cost occurs when the slope of the curve is zero. We have placed all of the elements of the optimizing model in the flow chart shown in Figure 10-6.

To use the iterative procedure we would start with a value of Q and evaluate it by equation (1) and determine the direction of the slope in order to get the next value of Q. In fact we will not actually use this iterative procedure, we will simply use a visual examination of the total cost curve of Figure 10-5 as our test. Let us start with $Q_1 = 100$ units and use increments of 100 units for sample calculations. using equation (2) for the specific parameters of our example,

$C = 0.05Q + 8000/Q$
$= 0.05 \times 100 + 8000/100 = \$85$.

Table 10-1 summarizes the successive calculations for $Q_2 = 200$, $Q_3 = 300$, $Q_4 = 400$, and $Q_5 = 500$ units, indicating the visual check for the direction of slope. In this instance we have actually gone past the zero slope point in calculating for Q_5 to indicate that the slope changes from negative to positive and that the value of C increases beyond the minimum at $Q_0 = 400$ units.

The power of the optimizing model is not in the iterative procedure we have just used to demonstrate conceptually what happens as we converge on the optimum solution, but in using mathematical methods to derive a *general solution* for the entire class of order quantity problems. Using appropriate mathematical methods we can determine the general form of the slope of equation (1):

$$\text{slope} = c_H/2 - c_P(R/Q^2). \tag{3}$$

The value of equation (3) is, in fact, the slope of the line tangent to the total

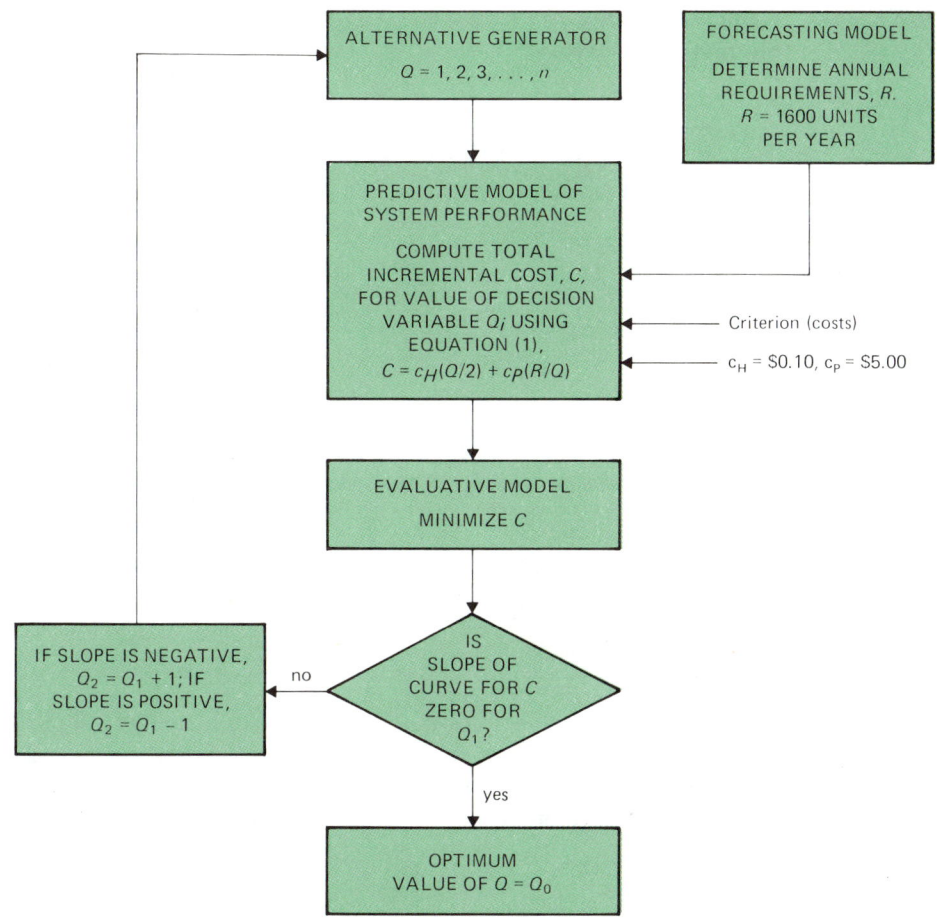

FIGURE 10-6. **Flow chart for an optimizing inventory model that combines a forecasting model, an alternative generator, a predictive model, an evaluative model, a test for optimality, and a mechanism to direct changes in Q based on the test for optimality.**

incremental cost curve. We wish to know the value of Q when this slope is zero. Therefore, we set equation (3) equal to zero and solve for Q_0:

$$0 = c_H/2 - c_P R/Q_0^2$$
$$Q_0^2 = 2 c_P R/c_H$$

and

TABLE 10-1. **Computation of Costs C for Five Successive Values of Q_i**

Order Quantity (Q_i)	Inventory Holding Costs ($0.05\,Q_i$)	Preparation Costs ($8000/Q_i$)	Total Incremental Costs* (C)	Visual Check of Slope of C for Value of Q_i
100	5.0	80.0	85.0	—
200	10.0	40.0	50.0	—
300	15.0	26.7	41.7	—
$400 = Q_0$	20.0	20.0	40.0	0
500	25.0	16.0	41.0	+

Note: $R = 1600$ units per year, $c_H = \$0.10$, and $c_P = \$5$.
*The sum of the second and third columns of the table.

$$Q_0 = \sqrt{2\,c_P R / c_H}. \tag{4}$$

Equation (4) is a general solution for the optimum order quantity Q_0 and may be used for any values of requirements R and the cost parameters c_P and c_H. The cost of an optimal solution may be derived by substituting the value of Q_0 defined by (4) in equation (1),

$$C_0 = c_H Q_0 / 2 + c_P R / Q_0.$$

This reduces to

$$C_0 = \sqrt{2\,c_P c_H R}. \tag{5}$$

Now that we have equations (4) and (5), we may substitute the values for R, c_P, and c_H used in our example to obtain

$$Q_0 = \sqrt{2 \times 5 \times 1600 / 0.10} = \sqrt{160{,}000} = 400 \text{ units},$$

and

$$C_0 = \sqrt{2 \times 5 \times 0.10 \times 1600} = \sqrt{1600} = \$40.$$

The basic EOQ model involves quite restricted assumptions. For example, no shortages or back orders are allowed (the timing of the receipt of orders is assumed to be perfect), there are no price discounts, and all aspects of the model are deterministic (demand is assumed to be known and constant, as is supply lead time). Given the basic model, we can successively relax some of these assumptions and approach reality. In Chapter 6 we called this process of beginning with a simple model and adding detail *bootstrapping*.

Inventory Model That Allows Shortages

If the assumption that shortages and back orders are zero is relaxed, we have the graphical structure of Figure 10-7. The problem is now to determine the minimum cost order quantity when shortages are allowed at a cost of c_S. The inventory level rises to only I_{max} on the receipt of Q because the difference $(Q - I_{max})$ is assumed to meet back orders instantaneously.

When shortage costs are accounted for, the basic EOQ model becomes slightly more general and the optimizing model represented by equation (4) becomes a special case. The rationale for the derivation parallels the basic model, but it is somewhat more complex mathematically. Derivations may be found in Buffa and Taubert [1972], and the resulting formulas are

$$Q_0 = \sqrt{2c_P R/c_H} \cdot \sqrt{(c_H + c_S)/c_S}, \qquad (6)$$

$$C_0 = \sqrt{2c_P c_H R} \cdot \sqrt{c_S/(c_H + c_S)}, \qquad (7)$$

$$I_{max_0} = \sqrt{2c_P R/c_H} \cdot \sqrt{c_S/(c_H + c_S)}. \qquad (8)$$

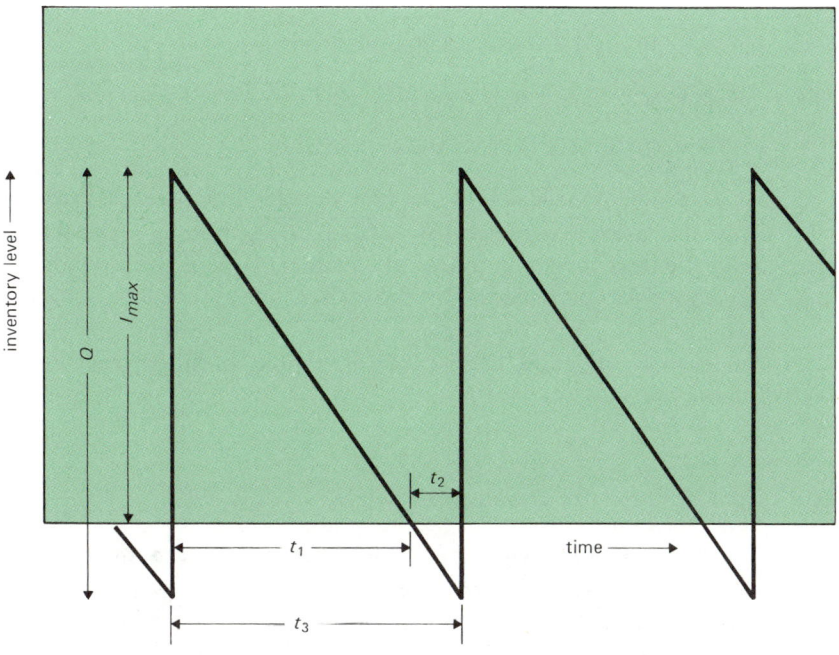

FIGURE 10-7. **Idealized structure of inventory levels with back orders of $Q - I_{max}$ allowed; t_1 = time during which there are inventory balances on hand; t_2 = time during which there is an inventory shortage; t_3 = cycle time.**

Note that when comparing equations (6) and (7) with the comparable equations (4) and (5), Q_0 is increased by the factor $\sqrt{(c_H + c_S)/c_S}$, and C_0 is decreased by the factor $\sqrt{c_S/(c_H + c_S)}$. The influence of shortages, then, is dependent on the relative size of c_H and c_S. If c_H is large relative to c_S, the effect of shortages on Q_0 and C_0 is considerable; that is, Q_0 will be increased and C_0 decreased compared to equations (4) and (5). If, on the other hand, c_H is small relative to c_S, minor changes in Q_0 and C_0 will result.

The net effect of shortage costs on Q_0 and C_0 may at first seem to be strange. Recognize, however, that when the model permits shortages, average holding costs are reduced because of smaller average inventory balances. This reduction will result in a larger Q_0. For the shortage case, C_0 is smaller than when shortages are not included because both holding costs and annual preparation costs are somewhat lower. If we consider shortages in the previous example where $R = 1600$ per year, $c_P = \$5$ per order, $c_H = \$0.10$ per unit per year, and in addition, $c_S = \$0.50$ per unit per year, we have the following results:

$$Q_0 = \sqrt{(2 \times 5 \times 1600)/0.10} \cdot \sqrt{(0.10 + 0.50)/0.50}$$
$$= 400 \ \sqrt{1.2} = 400 \times 1.095 = 438 \text{ units,}$$
$$C_0 = \sqrt{2 \times 5 \times 0.10 \times 1600} \cdot \sqrt{0.50/(0.10 + 0.50)}$$
$$= 40 \ \sqrt{0.833} = 40 \times 0.913 = \$36.51.$$

The limiting values of c_S provide valuable insight. As c_S becomes infinitely large the factor in equation (6), $\sqrt{(c_H + c_S)/c_S}$, becomes 1 in the limit and we have the basic inventory model of equation (4). This corresponds to a policy of no shortages permitted. On the other hand, if c_S is set at zero, then $\sqrt{(c_H + c_S)/c_S}$ and Q_0 become infinity. This corresponds to a policy of infinite back ordering, hand-to-mouth supply, or supply only on the basis of special order.

The Effect of Quantity Discounts

The basic EOQ model assumes a fixed price; therefore, the total cost equation (1) does not include the price of the item, since it is not a relevant cost in the basic model. Let us now consider a model that includes the value of the item as a factor in order to take account of quantity discounts. The total incremental cost associated with such a system is then:

$$\begin{aligned}C =\ & \text{(annual cost of placing orders)} \\ & + \text{(annual purchase cost of } R \text{ items)} \\ & + \text{(annual holding cost for inventory)} \\ =\ & c_P(R/Q) + kR + kF_H(Q/2),\end{aligned} \quad (9)$$

where k = cost or price per unit, and F_H = fraction of inventory value representing inventory holding cost on an annual basis ($kF_H = c_H$). For example, if $k = \$1$ and $F_H = 0.25$, then $c_H = \$0.25$ per unit per year.

Following the rationale developed previously, we seek the value of Q, Q_0, that minimizes this total incremental cost equation. This leads to

$$Q_0 = \sqrt{2c_P R / kF_H}, \qquad (10)$$

$$C_0 = \sqrt{2c_P k F_H R} + kR. \qquad (11)$$

The derivations of equations (10) and (11) parallel the derivations for the previous EOQ formulas.

We may now use equations (10) and (11) in the analysis of inventory systems that involve a price break. For comparison let us assume the previous example data of $R = 1600$ units per year, $c_P = \$5$ per order, and $F_H = 10$ percent per year. Recall that Q_0 was 400 units without quantity discounts. Now let us assume in addition that the purchase prices are quoted as $1 per unit in quantities below 800 and $0.98 per unit in quantities above 800. If we buy in lots of 800, we save $32 per year on the purchase price plus $10 on order costs, since only two orders need to be placed per year to satisfy annual needs. This saving of $42 per year must be greater than the additional inventory costs that would be incurred if the price discount is to be attractive.

Referring to Figure 10-8, we see that there are two ranges of lot sizes where in fact two different total cost curves are effective. For the price $k_1 = \$1$, order sizes in the range of 0 to 799 are effective. For the discounted price of $k_2 = \$0.98$, order sizes greater than or equal to the price break order size of $b = 800$ are effective.

The logic of our analysis is first to note that the total incremental cost curve C_2 will fall below the curve C_1. This configuration is shown in Figure 10-8. The logical thing to do, then, is to calculate Q_{2_0} to see if it falls within the range where the price $k_2 = \$0.98$ applies. Performing this calculation using equation (10), we find that $Q_{2_0} = 404$ units, which is less than the break point $b = 800$ units (below the effective range for C_2). Since 404 units corresponds to the minimum point on the C_2 curve, we know that the lowest possible cost of C_2 within the range where the price k_2 applies is at the order size $b = 800$ units.

If it had happened that Q_{2_0} was in the range for price k_2, this would have determined immediately that the EOQ for the system was the value calculated as Q_{2_0}. Since this is not the case, however, we must continue our analysis to see if the minimum point on the curve C_1 is below C_2 (which we now know is at the order size $b = 800$ units). We may calculate the cost associated with Q_{1_0} (C_{1_0}) easily from equation (11), and its value is $1640. Also, we may calculate the costs associated with the lot size $b = 800$ units (C_b) using equation (9), and we find this to be $1617. The decision is now clear; $Q_0 = b = 800$ units, since the total incremental costs at order size b are less than C_{1_0}.

The results can be seen easily from the graph of Figure 10-8; however, constructing the curves for each case would be laborious compared to the simple

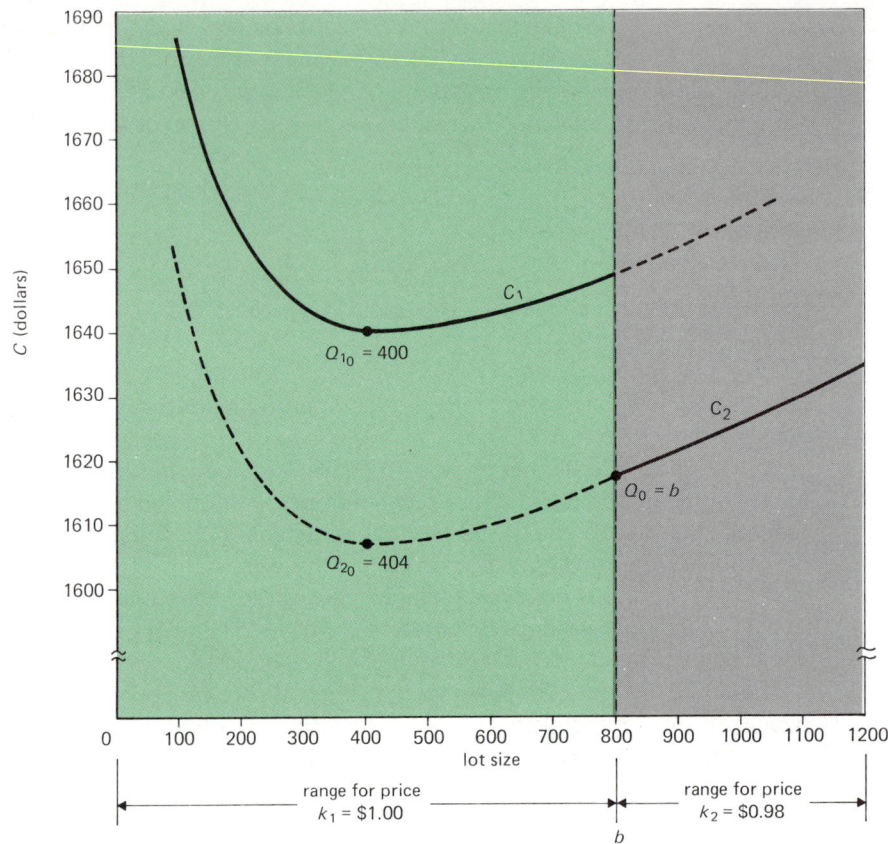

FIGURE 10-8. **Total incremental cost curves for inventory model with one price break at $b = 800$ units. $R = 1600$ units per year; $c_P = \$5$; $F_H = 10$ percent of inventory value**

computations required to come to a decision. Figure 10-9 shows a decision flow chart for the inventory model with one price break, indicating the flow of computations and resulting decisions. In some instances, the final result is obtained with one calculation, as when Q_{2_0} falls in the order size range where the price k_2 is valid. Where this is not the case, simple calculations for comparitive total incremental cost yield a final result.

The flow chart in Figure 10-9 is a series of steps that must be followed in order to solve our optimizing inventory model. In general, the steps required to solve an optimizing model are called an *algorithm*. Often an algorithm can be programmed and implemented on a computer. Although the algorithm required

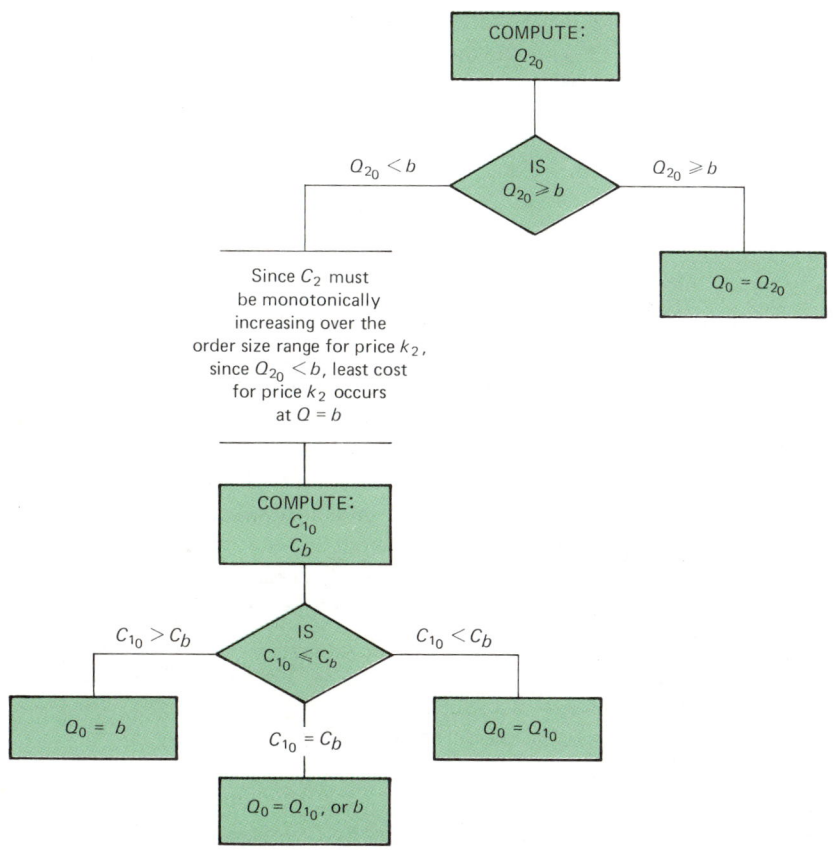

FIGURE 10-9. **Decision flow chart for inventory model with one price break at the lot size b. Price k_1 applies in the order size range $0 < Q < b$, price k_2 applies in the order size range $Q \geq b$.**

to solve this simple inventory model consists of only a few steps, more complex optimizing models will require much more complex algorithms to determine a solution.

Using the same general rationale, we can develop decision processes for inventory models with two or more price breaks. Also, models can be constructed for quantity discount situations that also take account of other factors such as shortage costs.

We have used the purchase order quantity problem as a mechanism for introducing optimizing models. While simple, the conceptual framework for the EOQ involves all of the basic elements of optimizing models in which alternative generator, predictive model, and evaluative model are combined in an optimizing system. Of course, there is a great deal more to know about inventory models for managerial use. Some of the most important concepts in this category are those related to the assessment of risks that result from variability of both demand and supply lead time.

ASSESSING RISKS IN INVENTORY MODELS

In the basic EOQ model and in the simple extensions that we developed, we assumed that both demand and supply lead time were constant; that is, we assumed a deterministic model. Yet, variability of demand and supply lead time are elements of reality that can be of great importance because they impose risks, and the risks are commonly two-sided.

We can cushion the effects of demand and supply lead time variation, absorbing risks by carrying larger inventories, called buffer or safety stocks. The larger we make these buffer stocks, the greater the risk associated with the funds tied up in inventories, the possibility of obsolescence, and so on. But large buffer stocks minimize the risk of running out of stock. On the other hand, the inventory risk can be minimized by reducing buffer inventories, but the risks associated with poor inventory service increase, including the costs of back ordering, lost sales, disruptions of production, and so on. Our objective then will be to find a rational model for balancing these risks.

Service Levels and Buffer Stocks with Constant Lead Time

In order to examine service levels and buffer stocks, let us begin by dealing with the effects of demand variability, assuming that supply lead time is known and constant. Figure 10–10 shows the general structure of inventory balance with a reordering system similar to the one we developed previously in Figure 10–4. When inventory falls to a preset reorder point P, an order for the quantity Q is placed. The reorder point P is set to take account of the supply lead time L, so that if we experience normal usage rates during L, inventory would be reduced to minimum levels when the order for Q units is received.

Note, however, that demand may not be at a constant rate. Inventories may decline to the reorder point P earlier or later than expected. But, what is more important, if demand during lead time is greater than expected values, inventory levels may decline below the minimum or planned buffer stock level. In the limiting situation, if we experienced maximum demand during lead time as shown in Figure 10–10, inventory levels would decline to zero by the time the order for Q units was received. The size of the needed buffer stock is then the difference between the expected or average demand $\bar{D}$ and D_{max}, the maximum demand during the supply lead time, or $B = D_{max} - \bar{D}$. The issue then must focus on how we define D_{max}.

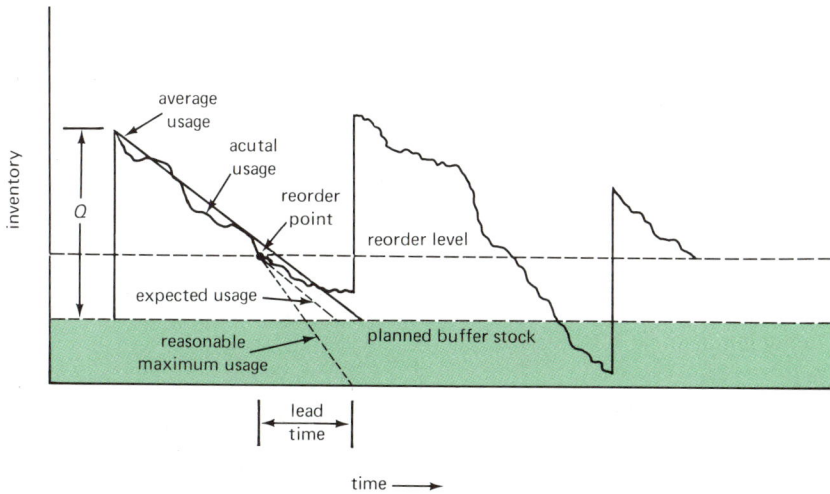

FIGURE 10-10. **Structure of inventory balance for a fixed order quantity system, with safety stocks to absorb fluctuations in demand and in supply time. The buffer stock level is set so that a reasonable figure for maximum usage would draw down the inventory to zero during the lead time. Q is a fixed quantity ordered each cycle.**

Defining Maximum Demand Maximum demand, D_{max}, is not a fixed number that we can simply abstract from a distribution of demand, but depends on an analysis of the risks. Let us take as an example the record for the distribution of demand for an item shown in Figure 10-11. Figure 10-11 represents just the random variations, and if there were other effects such as trend and seasonals, they have been removed by standard statistical techniques. We note that for the sample of $N = 113$, average biweekly demand was $\bar{D} = 1,214$ units and the standard deviation was $s = 313.6$ units. The maximum *recorded* demand in the sample was 2000 units, which occurred twice in the distribution.

Let us convert Figure 10-11 to the form shown in Figure 10-12, so we can conveniently estimate the probability of various demand rates. Figure 10-12 was constructed from Figure 10-11 by plotting the number of periods in which demand exceeded a given level. We then established a percentage scale to estimate the probability of various levels of demand. Since the average

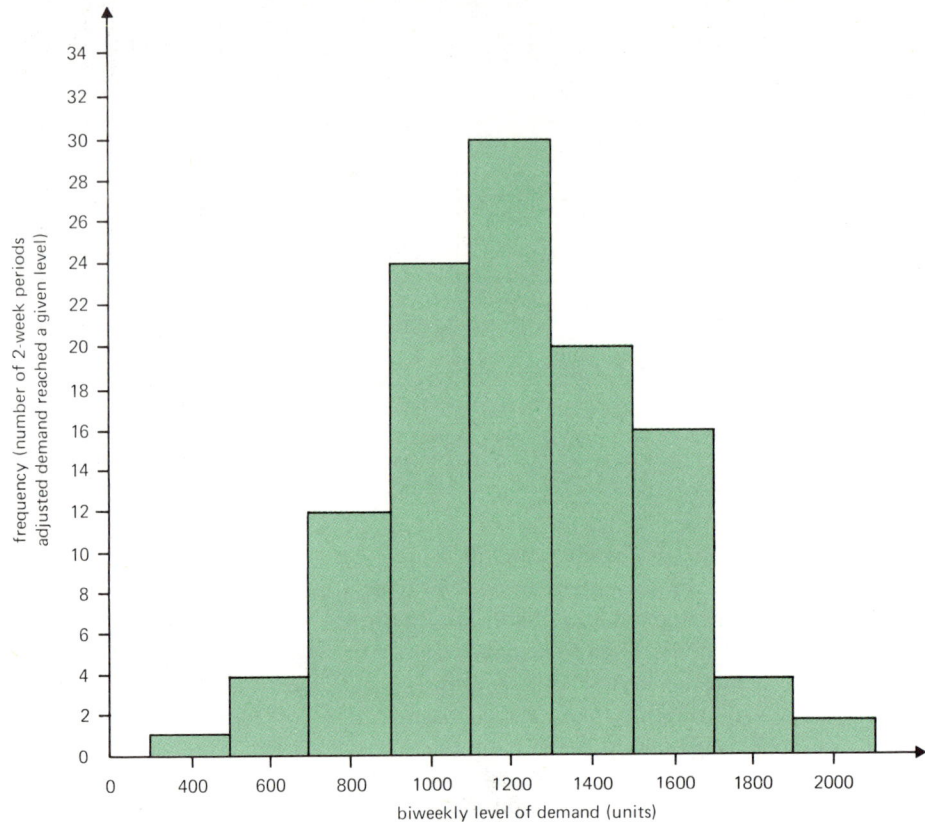

FIGURE 10-11. **Distribution representing expected random variation in weekly sales, exclusive of seasonal and trend variations.** $\overline{D} = 1214$ units per two weeks, $s = 313.6$ units, $N = 113$

two-week usage rate is 1214 units, if we assume a normal lead time of $L = 2$ weeks, we could be 90 percent sure of not running out of stock by having 1520 units on hand when the replenishment order is placed (see Figure 10-12 for the demand rate for 10 percent). The buffer stock required for this 90 percent service level is then $B = 1520 - 1214 = 306$ units. Similarly, if we wish to be 95 percent sure of not running out of stock, then $B = 1640 - 1214 = 426$ units. For a 98 percent service level (2 percent risk of stockout) the buffer stock level must be increased to 786 units.

From the shape of the demand curve, it is clear that required buffer stock goes up rapidly as we increase service level, and therefore the cost of providing this assurance goes up. These effects are shown by the calculations in Table

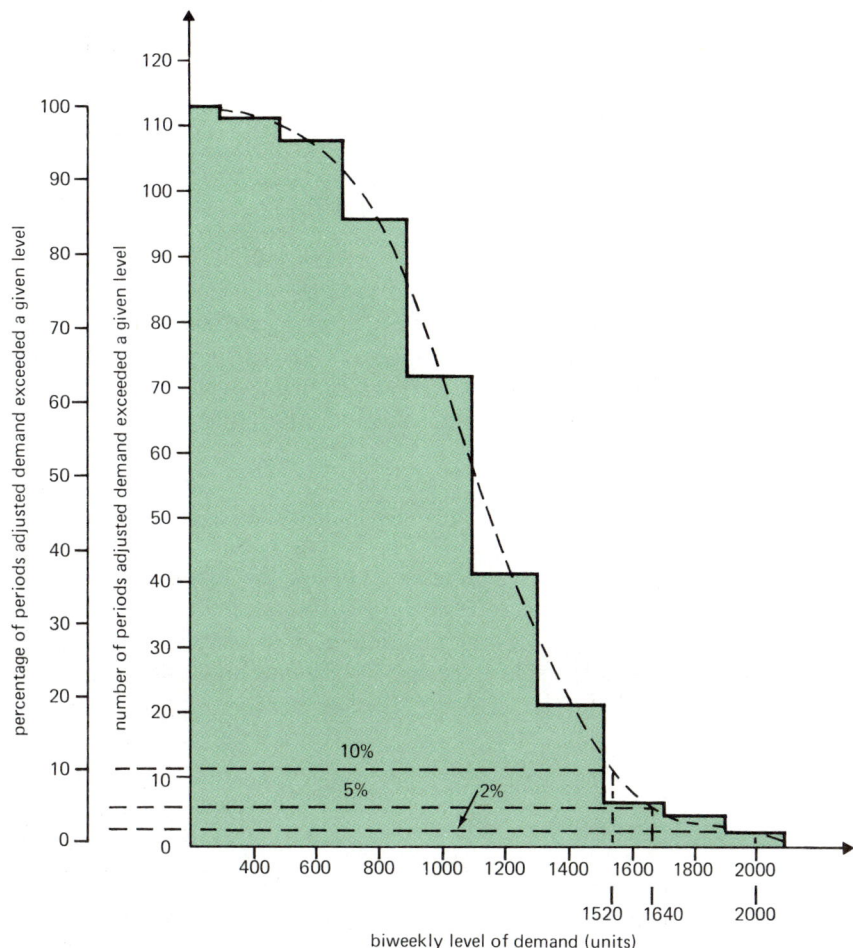

FIGURE 10-12. **Distribution of percentage of periods that demand exceeded a given level, developed from Figure 10-11.** $\bar{D} = 1214$ **units per two weeks,** $s = 313.6$ **units,** $N = 113$

10-2 where we have assumed the demand curve of Figure 10-12, assigning a value of $50 to the item and inventory holding costs of 20 percent of inventory value. The average inventory required to cover expected maximum usage rates during the two-week lead time is calculated for the three service levels shown. To offer service at the 95 percent level instead of the 90 percent level requires an incremental $1200 per year, but to move to the 98 percent level of service from the 95 percent level requires an additional $3600 in inventory cost.

Management could define any of the three levels of demand as D_{max} by setting a service level policy. Given the service level policy, the buffer stock required to implement that policy is simply $B = D_{max} - \bar{D}$.

Practical Methods for Determining Buffer Stocks

The general methodology for setting buffer stocks that we have discussed here is too cumbersome for practical use in systems where large numbers of items may be involved. Computations are simplified considerably if we can justify the assumption that the demand distribution follows some particular mathematical function, such as the normal, Poisson, or negative exponential distributions.

First let us recall the general statement for buffer stocks.

$$B = D_{max} - \bar{D}. \tag{12}$$

Note, however, that $D_{max} = \bar{D} + n\sigma_D$, where σ_D is the standard deviation for the demand distribution during lead time; that is, the defined reasonable maximum demand is the average demand $\bar{D}$ plus some number n of standard deviation units σ_D that is associated with the probability of occurrence of that demand (n is now defined as the safety factor). Substituting this statement of D_{max} in our general definition of B, equation (12), we have

$$B = D_{max} - \bar{D} = (\bar{D} + n\sigma_D) - \bar{D},$$

or

$$B = n\sigma_D. \tag{13}$$

This simple statement allows us to determine buffer stocks that meet risk requirements when we know the mathematical form of the demand distribution. The procedure is as follows:

1. Determine whether the normal, Poisson, or negative exponential distribution approximately describes demand during lead time for the case under consideration. This determination is critically important, involving well-known statistical methodology.
2. Set a service level based on managerial policy, a subjective assessment of the balance of incremental inventory and stockout costs, or an assessment of the manager's trade-off between service level and inventory cost when stockout costs are not known.
3. Using the service level, define D_{max} during lead time in terms of the appropriate distribution.
4. Compute the required buffer stock from equation (13) where n is termed the safety factor and σ_D is the standard deviation for the demand distribution during lead time.

TABLE 10-2. **Cost of Providing Three Levels of Service (from Figure 10-12)**

	Service Level (percent)		
	90	95	98
Expected maximum usage for 2-week replenishment time	1520	1640	2000
Buffer stock required ($B = D_{max} - 1214$)	306	426	786
Value of buffer stock ($50\,B$)	$15,300	$21,300	$39,300
Inventory holding cost at 20 percent	$3060	$4260	$7860

Note: The item is valued at $50 each and inventory holding costs are 20 percent.

WHAT SHOULD THE MANAGER KNOW?

Depending on the nature of the enterprise, inventories can be of extreme importance. It is not uncommon for inventories to account for 15 to 40 percent of assets. Especially in high volume operations, a changing demand pattern can have an important effect on inventories. Recall the fantastic inventory buildup in the automobile industry during the latter part of 1974, when a decrease in demand resulted in an enormous inventory buildup which in turn caused a virtual shutdown of production.

Interpretation of the Results of Inventory Models

In order to manage inventories effectively, managers need to know how they behave in relation to demand changes. The several components of system inventories behave differently in relation to average demand. First, the pipeline inventories vary directly with system volume. If the system is geared up for a higher volume, pipeline inventories must increase in direct proportion. Conversely, if volume declines, the pipeline inventory necessary to sustain the system declines, and management must take action to ensure that inventories are reduced to reflect the change.

Note, however, that required cycle and buffer stocks may be a source of economy of scale in operations. If demand increases, the average cycle stock need increase only as the square root of demand [see equation (4)]. Thus, if demand doubles, cycle stock need increase by a factor of only $\sqrt{2} = 1.4$. There is a definite economy in larger scale operations. There may also be a similar economy of scale in relation to the size of buffer stocks needed to absorb the fluctuations in demand and supply time.

Another dimension in the interpretation of the results of inventory models has to do with the sensitivity of relevant costs to changes in order size from optimal levels. Note in equation (5) that relevant costs are proportional to the square root of demand and the other relevant factors. Thus, near the optimum, costs do not change markedly as we deviate from optimality. We note this effect in Figure 10-5; that is, the total incremental cost curve is "shallow" near the optimum. This fact of relative insensitivity of costs provides managers with flexibility. They can take account of factors not included in the model that may call for deviations from optimal order sizes, realizing that costs will not be affected greatly unless the deviation is quite large. It is important to be operating in the optimal range, but strict adherence to the results of order size models is of little importance.

Information Requirements

Good inventory control systems are dependent on good forecasting and up-to-date inventory records. When this kind of information is available, inventory reordering decisions can be programmed in computing systems and become virtually automatic. In addition, however, the cost parameters need to be maintained up to date and the system parameters such as reorder points need to be examined periodically to ensure that the system remains appropriate to current conditions.

The Manager's Role and Optimizing Models

The manager's role in the predictive models discussed in Part III was basically his traditional role. Those models in no way challenged the manager's traditional decision-making function. Optimizing models by their nature, however, suggest what the decision should be. This suggestive power is perhaps the great optimizing model trap. If the solution is optimum, what is left for the manager to decide? It is at this point that the need for managerial involvement in model formulation becomes crucial. If the manager understands what factors enter the model and the assumptions made, he can determine how to use the results intelligently. He should understand that the solution is optimal for the *model*. It is also optimal for the real-world counterpart of the model only insofar as the predictive component of the model duplicates actual system performance and the evaluative component reflects the criteria that bear on the decisions. If the evaluative component of the model cannot deal with all of the criteria, then the manager must do so by making trade-offs between model results and other criteria.

Check Your Understanding

1. Explain the decoupling function of inventories.
2. An auto manufacturer produces at the rate of 2000 cars per day, seven days per week. The autos are driven off the assembly line to a temporary storage lot where they await shipment for an average of two days. They are then loaded on trains or trucks and are moved to distribution points. The transit time averages five days. The cars remain in storage at distributors for an average of three days and are then shipped to dealers by truck, requiring an average of two days. They are unloaded at the dealers' lots and remain there until sold for an average of two days.
   a. Compute the transit inventory.
   b. Compute the finished goods pipeline inventory.
   c. What is the investment tied up in finished goods inventory if the average value of a car is $2500?
3. Define the following terms:
   a. cycle inventory
   b. buffer inventory
   c. seasonal inventory
4. List and define the cost components that are relevant to the control of inventories. Relate the costs to managerial objectives.
5. Define the following terms:
   a. order quantity
   b. Economic Order Quantity (EOQ)
   c. inventory holding costs
   d. preparation costs
   e. shortage costs
   f. reorder point
   g. lead time
6. If the cost of holding inventory is $c_H = \$0.25$ per unit per year, the cost of order writing is $c_P = \$10$ per order, and the annual requirements are $R = 10,000$ units,
   a. What is the alternative generator?
   b. What is the predictive model?
   c. What is the evaluative model?
   d. What is the test for optimality?
   e. What is the optimizing model?
   f. What is the EOQ?
7. What are the assumptions involved in equation (4)? Which assumptions are relaxed in the shortage model? In the model that allows price discounts?
8. If c_H is $100 \times c_S$, what is the effect on EOQ compared to the basic model of equation (4)? What is the effect on incremental costs compared to the basic model of equation (5)? Explain why this effect should be true in terms of the relative values placed on inventories and shortages.

9. In the text example concerning price discount models, the computed EOQ for the discounted price of k_2 = $0.98 per unit was 404 units. The cost of a lot size of 404 units by equation (11) would be $1608, yet we chose the lot size of 800 units at a cost of $1617 as being more economical. Explain why.
10. If demand changes, perhaps an increase or decline of 50 percent, how do the following components of inventory change?
    a. buffer inventory
    b. cycle inventory
    c. transit inventory
    d. pipeline inventory
    e. decoupling inventory
11. If the EOQ for an item is 500 units, but there is a price advantage in ordering 550 units, how concerned should the manager be about deviating from the computed EOQ?
12. Define the following terms:
    a. service level
    b. maximum demand
    c. safety factor
13. If average demand were $\bar{D}$ = 52 units during the supply lead time and management had designed a system in which the buffer stock was set at B = 23 units, what is management's definition of maximum demand for this situation?
14. Using the demand distribution described by Figures 10–11 and 10–12 as an example, if the service level is set at 85 percent, estimate D_{max} and B.
15. Suppose on statistical analysis of the demand for an item we isolate trend, seasonal, and random components of demand variation. Can we construct a meaningful buffer inventory for the item? How?
16. Rationalize why the cost of providing service goes up rapidly as the service level increases.

Problems

17. The pharmacy of a large hospital has established inventory-related costs to aid them in ordering and maintaining inventory levels of drugs for hospital use.

    In establishing inventory holding costs, there was some controversy over the appropriate interest charge. The hospital was nonprofit, so an internal rate of return would be zero. Interest on borrowed money was 10 percent. The cost of storage, insurance, obsolescence, and pilferage, averaged 15 percent of inventory value. The cost of storing some items such as narcotics, however, was 20 percent because of special precautions taken against theft. The cost of storing ordinary prescriptions was 15 percent, and of nonprescription items only 10 percent.

The cost to place an order seemed to vary considerably because some items, for example narcotics, required special procedures to conform to control laws. At the other end of the spectrum were nonprescription items for which ordering was as simple as ordering any other common supply item. When aggregated, however, the average cost of preparing an order was $10, but the range seemed to be from $5 to $25.

Another problem in controlling inventories was the wide range of item value. The value of aspirin was as low as $2 per thousand, but some exotic drugs could have a value as high as $1000 per ounce.

Formulate an ordering policy for the pharmacy manager that takes account of his rather different supply items.

18. Suppose we are using an EOQ ordering policy on the high valued items in exercise 17, and ordering costs have been established as c_P = $25 per order, and inventory holding costs as c_H = $100 per unit per year. Average annual requirements are R = 1000 per year and, therefore, Q_0 = 22.36.
    a. There is controversy over the appropriate ordering cost. Some think it too high and some too low. What difference in Q_0 results if c_P is $20? $30? What are the percentage differences? What are the incremental cost differences and their percentage differences?
    b. The inventory holding cost is also contested. What difference in Q_0 and C_0 results if c_H is $80? $120?

19. Suppose that the pharmacy manager in exercise 17 has decided to adopt an EOQ policy that recognizes three general categories of items. One of the problems was the lead time of supply from vendors. Each vendor was fairly reliable in meeting his stated supply time; however, there were variations between vendors. Therefore, the manager had set order points for each item that depended on the vendor, the average usage rate, and a safety stock.

    Having installed the system, the manager now wishes to maintain it and adhere to the policy. Which parameters should he monitor most closely? Why?

20. A manufacturing company produces a line of small one-cylinder engines used in lawn mowers, portable compressors, portable pumps, etc. The parts for the engines are produced in lots and stored as manufactured parts for later use in assembly as needed. The costs of preparing manufacturing orders and controlling them through the shop are estimated as $50 per manufacturing order. The cost of holding in-process inventory is estimated as 25 percent of inventory value.

    The cylinder block for one of the engines has a usage rate of 25,000 per year and the value of the completed block including all labor, materials, and overhead is $10 per unit.

    How many manufacturing runs should be scheduled per year if incremental costs are to be minimized?

21. The Jensen Manufacturing Company has organized its inventory system into three main categories depending on urgency and the ordinary amount of follow-up required. It therefore wishes to simplify its use of equation (4) for use

by ordering clerks. For class 1, 2, and 3 items ordering costs are respectively $5, $15, and $40.
   a. Derive formulas for the three classes of items.
   b. Further examination shows that inventory carrying cost is virtually constant at 18 percent of cost value for all items. Derive further simplified formulas for the three classes of items.

22. The Jensen Manufacturing Company converted its entire ordering procedure to the EOQ basis described by exercise 21. On examining one of the class 3 items (c_P = $40), however, they noted very high annual freight costs under the new policy. Freight costs have been $200 per order under the EOQ policy and would cost only $400 for a carload lot of 500 units. R = 5000 units per year, and the average value of the item is $222.22. Should Jensen order in carload lots?

23. The pharmacy discussed in exercise 17 has some items for which a price discount is available. One such item is offered at $10 per unit in lots below 1000 and $9 per unit in lots above 1000. Annual requirements are 5000, c_P = $25, and F_H = 35 percent of inventory value. Q_0 for the $10 price is 267 units and for the $9 price is 282 units. Is the price discount attractive?

References

1. Brown, R. G., *Decision Rules for Inventory Management,* Holt, Rinehart & Winston, New York, 1967.
2. Buchan, J., and E. Koenigsberg, *Scientific Inventory Management,* Prentice-Hall, Englewood Cliffs, N.J., 1963.
3. Buffa, E. S., and W. H. Taubert, *Production-Inventory Systems: Planning and Control,* revised edition, Richard D. Irwin, Inc., Homewood, Ill., 1972.
4. Magee, J. F., and D. M. Boodman, *Production Planning and Inventory Control,* second edition, McGraw-Hill, New York, 1967.
5. Starr, N. K., and D. W. Miller, *Inventory Control: Theory and Practice,* Prentice-Hall, Englewood Cliffs, N.J., 1962.

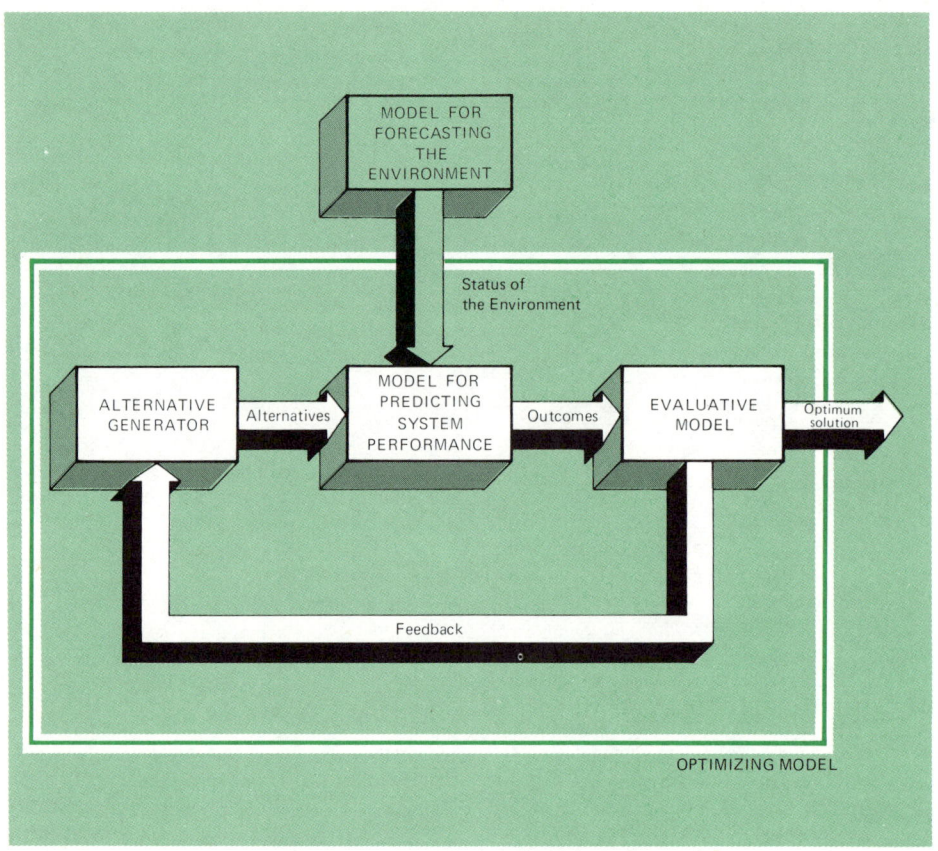

11

LINEAR OPTIMIZATION MODELS

The optimizing models of the greatest significance to managers have been linear optimization models and their associated powerful solution technique known as linear programming. Linear optimization models have been applied in a wide variety of industries and nonprofit activities such as steel, oil refining, utilities, education, meat packing, health care, refuse collection, and many others.

The kinds of applications have included all sorts of resource allocation problems such as long-range financial planning, aggregate capacity planning, portfolio planning and selection, plant location, production planning and scheduling, political districting, corporate financial planning, warehousing and distribution, air pollution control, water pollution control, promotion and advertising decisions, and so on. Obviously, linear optimization models are not simply theoretical concepts applicable to toy problems. They are powerful, useful managerial models.

In this chapter and in Chapter 12, we emphasize formulating linear optimization models and interpreting results. In fact, we assume a computer solution technique exists so that if we learn how to formulate linear optimizing problems, we can use a "black box" to provide solutions. Then we can take the manager's viewpoint and see how the results can be interpreted in the most useful way. In Chapter 13, The Simplex Method, we look inside the black box to see how the solution technique works.

THE NATURE OF LINEAR OPTIMIZATION MODELS

As with all optimizing models, linear optimization models combine the alternative generator, predictive model, and evaluative model with a test for optimality. The combination of these elements functions as a system to produce the best possible solution for the stated conditions and criteria. Just how these elements are combined in linear optimization models can be understood better at a later point. While we will maintain the general conceptual framework of the optimizing system, our first task will be to examine the special characteristics of linear models and their formulations.

Linear optimization models, then, are characterized by linear mathematical expressions. In addition, they are usually deterministic in nature; that is, they do not take account of risk and uncertainty. The parameters of the model are assumed to be known with certainty. Finally, as we shall see, linear optimization models are used most often when we are attempting to allocate some limited or scarce resources in order to make decisions that use the resources in question in such a way that a stated criterion is optimized (either minimized or maximized).

The Meaning of Linearity

In linear models, we *must* use only linear mathematical expressions. Recall our use of simple break-even analysis in Chapter 6. Figure 11-1 shows the elements of the profit (loss) function that we developed there. The relationships in the profit (loss) model are linear because the decision variable, x (number sold), does not appear to any power other than 1. There are no squared or higher powers of variables and there are no cross product terms where more than one variable is involved. Another way to say the same thing is to note that linear variables graph as straight lines.

In Figure 11-2 we show equations of both linear and nonlinear mathematical expressions, together with their graphs. In Figure 11-2, (a) and (b) are graphs of linear expressions and appear as straight lines, but (c) and (d) are graphs of nonlinear expressions, since (c) contains an x^2 term and (d) the cross product of $x_1 x_2$.

Figure 11-2 also illustrates the mathematical form of constraints. In Figure 11-2 (b) in the shaded portion, we see the expression $x_1 - 2x_2 \geq 4$, which states that $(x_1 - 2x_2)$ must be greater than or equal to ($\geq$) 4. When it is equal to 4, we have the straight line. Otherwise, the inequality expression constrains all combinations of x_1 and x_2 to be in the shaded portion of the graph. Conversely, all combinations of x_1 and x_2 that fall above the straight line are not admissible, since they do not satisfy the constraint $x_1 - 2x_2 \geq 4$.

Figure 11-2 (d) shows a nonlinear constraint expression in the shaded portion of the graph. That expression constrains combinations of x_1 and x_2 to be above the curve (in the shaded portion), since the expression states that

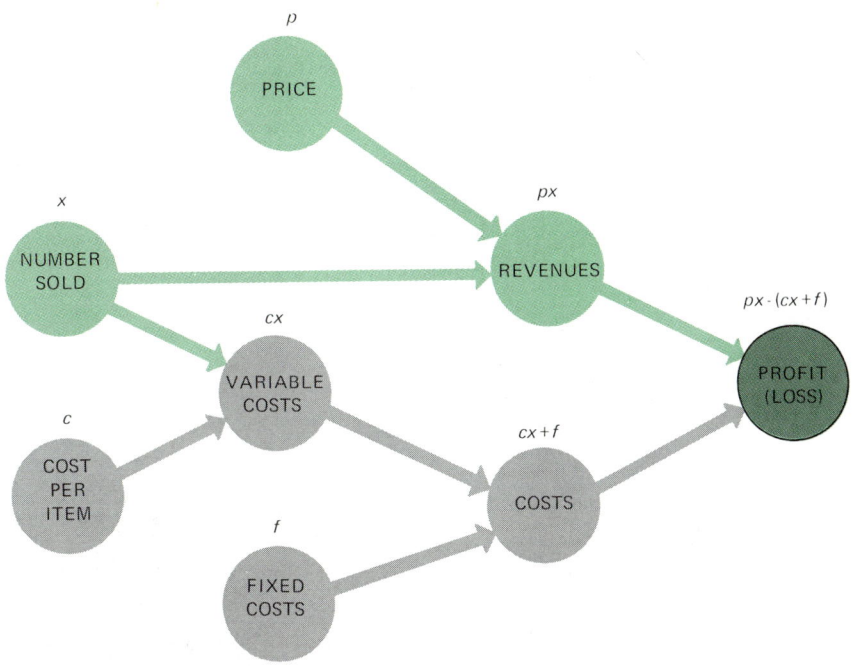

FIGURE 11-1. **Elements entering the formulation of a profit (loss) function**

$(x_1 - 2x_1x_2)$ must be less than or equal to ($\leq$) 4. Again, when the statement on the left-hand side of the expression is equal to 4, all points fall on the curve.

Mathematical statements of constraints may be less than or equal to ($\leq$), equal to ($=$), and greater than or equal to ($\geq$). *Linear* constraints, illustrated by the expression in the shaded portion of Figure 11-2 (b), will be very important in linear optimization models.

Elements of the Model-Building Process

In order to develop a linear optimization model, we use the following process:
1. Define the decision variables.
2. Define the objective function, Z, a linear equation involving the decision variables that identifies our objective in the problem-solving effort. This equation predicts the effects on the objective of choosing different values for the decision variables.
3. Define the constraints—linear expressions involving the decision variables that specify the restrictions on the decisions that can be made. *Alternatives can be generated* by selecting values for the decision variables that satisfy these constraints.

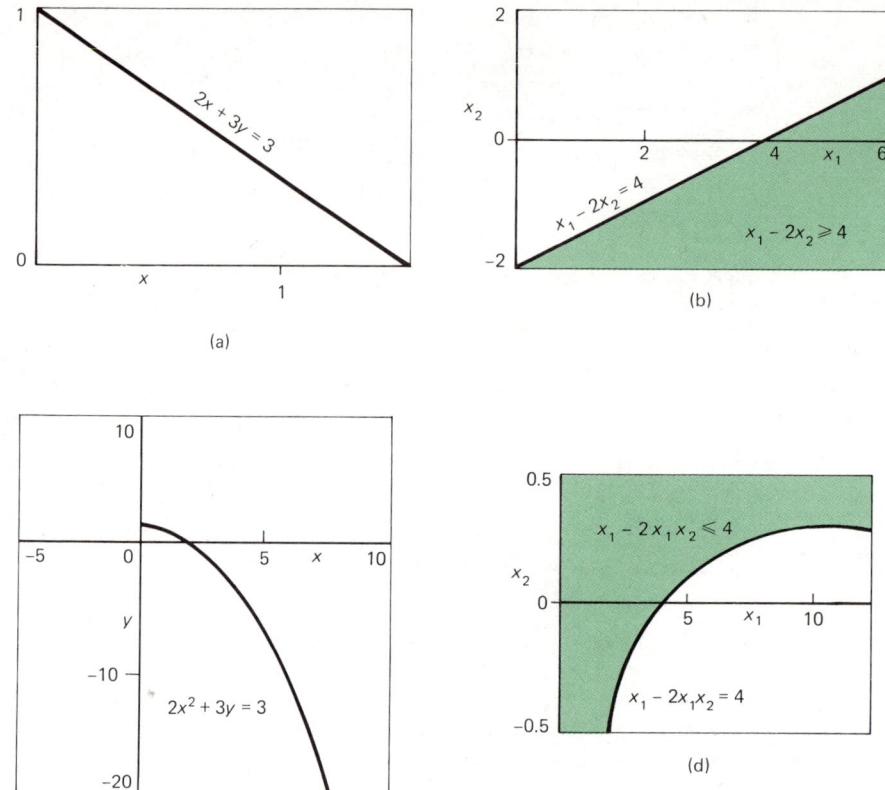

FIGURE 11-2. Examples of linear and nonlinear expressions; (a) and (b) are linear, and (c) and (d) are nonlinear, since (c) has an x^2 term, and (d) contains the cross product term $x_1 x_2$. The shaded portions of both (b) and (d) contain inequality expressions describing constraints; that is, values of x_1 and x_2 falling within the shaded areas are admissible but points beyond the curve are not.

Let us illustrate the process using a simple break-even analysis model, including the structure and definitions that we developed previously and that are shown in Figure 11-1.

Define the Decision Variables In the break-even analysis model we are interested in how profits vary as a function of the number of units sold. Since we are interested in determining a value for x, the number of units produced and sold, it is the decision variable in the model.

Define the Objective Function In the break-even analysis model, the manager wishes to make his profit as large as possible. Therefore the mathematical expression for predicting the effect of the choice of a production level on profits is from Figure 11–1:

profit (loss) = $px - cx - f$.

Now, since the manager wishes to maximize profits our objective function is

maximize $Z = px - cx - f$,

using the evaluative model "maximize profits."

The first two steps in the development of a linear break-even analysis model have been very simple. The decision variable is x, the number of units produced and sold, and the objective function is to maximize the simple mathematical statement of profit. Suppose we stop our model-building effort at this point and examine the break-even chart shown in Figure 11–3. If we attempt to implement the stated objective function to find a value of the decision variable x that maximizes profits, it is obvious that we should make x very large and produce as many units as we possibly can. We see immediately, however, that we do not yet have enough information. We know that we wish to make x large, but how large can we make it? We do not know, because we have not yet defined the constraints on our decision variable x.

Define the Constraints Obviously we cannot ignore possible limitations on the size of x. We may have capacity limitations that restrict the number of units that can be produced within a given time period. If the monthly capacity of the production facility is C units—for example, 300 units per month—then we have a constraint on the decision variable x as follows:

$x \leq C$.

Of course, we can substitute the appropriate specific capacity limitation for C.

In addition, we may not be able to sell all units produced at capacity. Perhaps the forecast for monthly demand is D units, for example 200. We have, then, an additional constraint on the decision variable,

$x \leq D$.

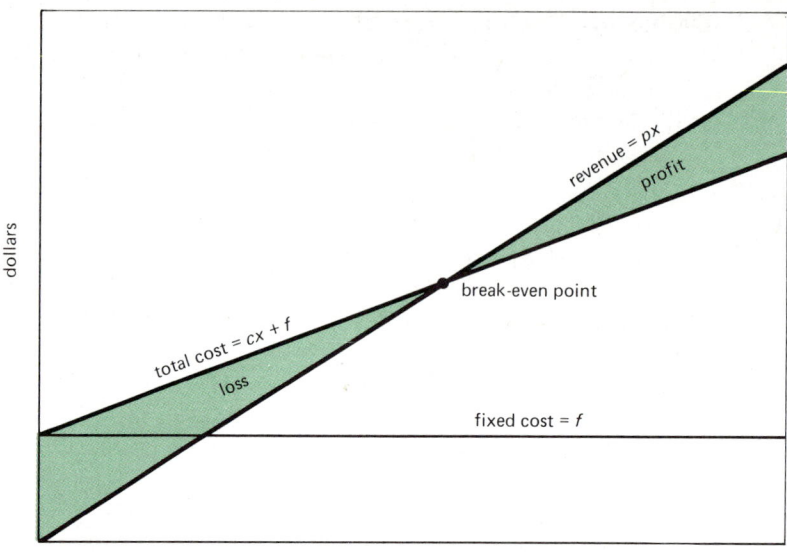

FIGURE 11-3. **Revenue and the relationship of costs with the number of units produced for a simple break-even chart**

To this point, the constraints define how large x can be. The linear model formulation process requires that we be very specific and also indicate how small x can be. Obviously, it cannot be negative, therefore,

$x \geq 0$.

Thus, we can generate alternatives for our analysis by selecting any value for x that satisfies these constraints.

In summary, the linear optimization model for our break-even analysis problem is developed as follows:
1. Define the decision variables: x = the number of units produced and sold.
2. Define the objective function: maximize $Z = px - cx - f$.
3. Define the constraints: $x \leq C$, $x \leq D$, $x \geq 0$.

Figure 11-4 shows the graphic relationships in the form of the well-known break-even chart to which we have added the constraints, the range of feasible solutions within the constraints, and the maximum possible profit for the model.

For the simple break-even model, it would not have been necessary for us to go through the process in order to identify the optimum solution. The solution

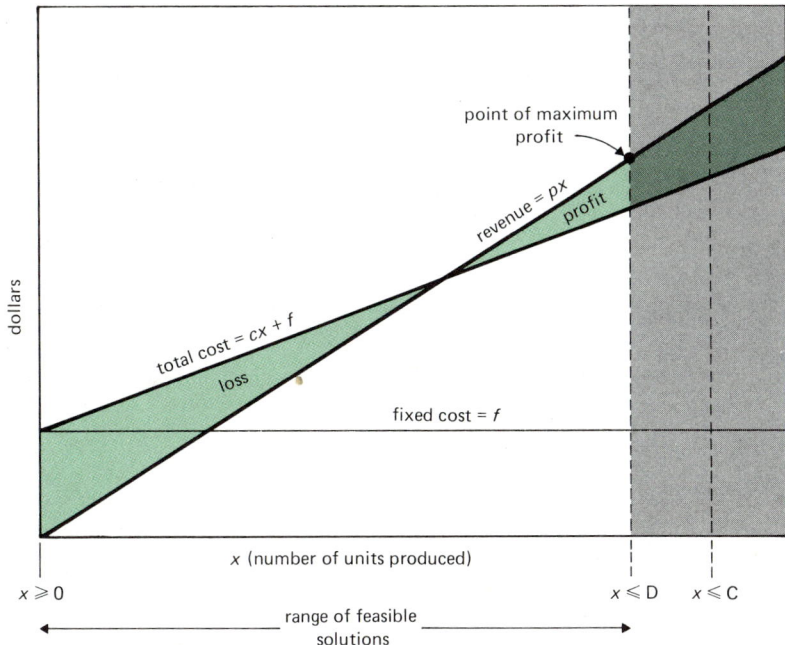

FIGURE 11-4. **Relationship of revenues, costs, constraints, and range of feasible solutions for a simple break-even analysis**

is obvious. What is important, however, is that the more complex linear optimization models with which we shall deal are a straightforward extension of the process we have developed to this point.

Simplifications

While we can deal with the objective function for profit (loss) = $px - cx - f$ in break-even analysis, it can be simplified for linear models. First, let us factor out the decision variable x so that the profit function becomes

$$px - cx - f = x(p - c) - f.$$

Now let us define the term $(p - c)$ as the contribution to profit and overhead, r, per unit sold. The objective function is then simplified to

$$\text{maximize } Z = rx - f.$$

Now let us examine the importance of the fixed cost element f in our decision problem. Note that f is not a function of the decision variable x.

CHAPTER 11 LINEAR OPTIMIZATION MODELS

Therefore, our objective of making x as large as possible within the constraints is not affected by f. Thus, for decision-making purposes, we can eliminate the fixed costs, since they are irrelevant to the decision. This is an important notion in model building for managerial decision making, and we have applied it previously, for example, in the inventory models of the previous chapter where we considered only the costs affected by the decision. The result of this step is that the objective function is further simplified to

maximize $Z = rx$,

that is, maximize the product of contribution per unit times the number of units produced and sold.

Our final linear optimization model written in the special form for linear programming is now

maximize $Z = rx$,
subject to
$\quad x \leq C$,
$\quad x \leq D$,
$\quad x \geq 0$.

A Specific Example

Let us now provide specific numbers for the variables and constraints. Suppose that the price per unit is $3.50, and the variable cost per unit is $2. Then r, the contribution to profit and overhead, is $p - c = 3.50 - 2.00 = \$1.50$. In addition, suppose that production capacity is 300 units per month and the market forecast of demand indicates that we could sell as many as 200 units per month. The specific linear optimization model is then

maximize $Z = 1.5x$,
subject to
$\quad x \leq 300$,
$\quad x \leq 200$,
$\quad x \geq 0$.

The simplified linear optimization model is shown graphically in Figure 11–5 where the objective function $Z = 1.5x$ is a straight line beginning at the origin. The constraints on capacity and demand are shown, but only the demand constraint is effective, since it is more restrictive. The feasible range of solutions is between $x = 0$ and $x = 200$ units, and we have slack (unused) plant capacity of 100 units per month.

While it is true that the break-even analysis example is so simple that the answer is entirely obvious, it displays most of the elements of linear optimization model formulation and also introduces the important concept of a range of feasible solutions and the concept of slack in a resource.

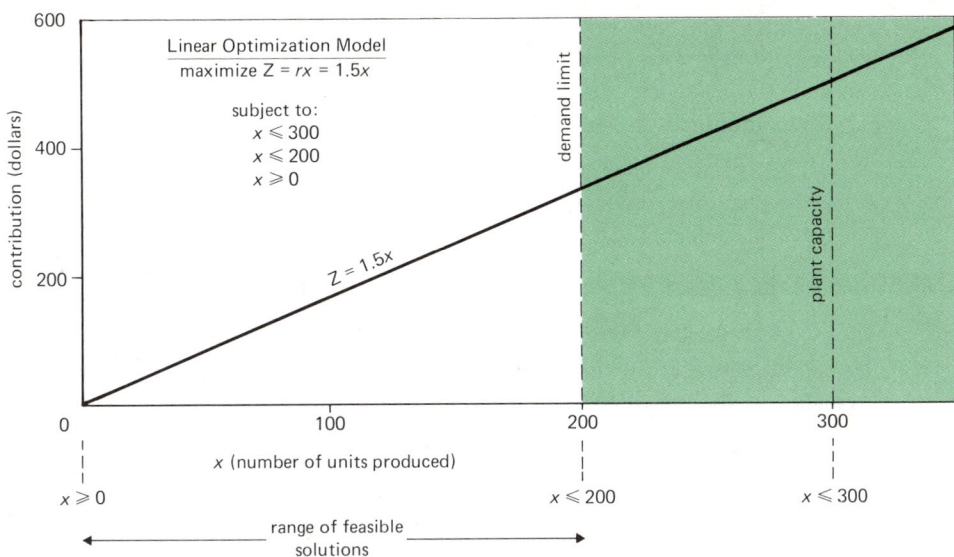

FIGURE 11-5. **Graphic representation of a linear optimization model when $p = \$3.50$, $c = \$2.00$, and contribution per unit produced is $r = p - c = \$1.50$. Plant capacity is 300 units per month, and demand is forecast for a limit of 200 units per month.**

FORMULATION OF A TWO-PRODUCT MODEL

Let us now consider a slightly more complex situation. A chemical manufacturer produces two products, which we shall call chemical x and chemical y. Each product is manufactured by a two-step process that involves blending and mixing in machine A and packaging on machine B. The two products complement each other, since the same production facilities can be used for both products, thus achieving better utilization of these facilities.

Definition of Decision Variables

Since these facilities are shared, and costs and profits from each product are different, there is the question of how to utilize the available machine time in the most profitable way. Chemical x is seemingly more profitable, but the manager once tried producing the maximum amount of chemical x within market limitations, using the balance of his capacity to produce chemical y. He found, however, that such an allocation of machine time resulted in poor profit performance. He feels now that some appropriate balance between the two products is best and he wishes to determine the production rates for each product per two-week period.

Thus, the decision variables are

x, the number of units of chemical x to be produced,
y, the number of units of chemical y to be produced.

Definition of the Objective Function

The physical plant and basic organization exists and represents the fixed costs of the organization. From the previous example, we know that these costs are irrelevant to the production scheduling decision, and they are ignored. The manager, however, has obtained price and variable cost information and has computed the contribution to profit and overhead per unit of each product sold as shown in Table 11-1. He wishes to maximize profit, and the contribution rates have a linear relationship to his objective. Therefore, the objective function that he wishes to maximize is the sum of the total contribution from chemical x, $(60x)$, plus the total contribution from chemical y, $(50y)$, or

maximize $Z = 60x + 50y$.

TABLE 11-1. **Sales Prices, Variable Costs, and Contributions per Unit for Chemicals x and y**

	Sales Price (p)	Variable Costs (c)	Contribution to Profit and Overhead $(r = p - c)$
Chemical x	$350	$290	$60
Chemical y	450	400	50

Definition of Constraints

The processing times for the two products on the mixing machine (A) and the packaging machine (B) are as follows:

Product	Machine A (hours)	Machine B (hours)
x	2	3
y	4	2

For the upcoming two-week period, machine A has available 80 hours and machine B has available 60 hours of processing time.

Machine A Constraint Since we are limited by the 80 hours available on machine A, the total time spent in the manufacture of chemical x and chemical y cannot exceed the total time available. For machine A, since chemical x requires 2 hours per unit and y requires 4 hours per unit, the total time spent on the two products must be less than or equal to 80 hours, that is,

$2x + 4y \leq 80$.

Machine B Constraint Similarly, the available hours on the packaging machine are limited to 60, and since chemical x requires 3 hours per unit and y requires 2 hours per unit the total hours for the two products must be less than or equal to 60 hours, or

$3x + 2y \leq 60$.

Marketing Constraints Forecasts of the markets indicate that we can expect to sell a maximum of 16 units of chemical x and 18 units of chemical y. Therefore,

$x \leq 16$,
$y \leq 18$.

Minimum Production Constraints The minimum production for each product is zero, therefore,

$x \geq 0$,
$y \geq 0$.

These constraints are shown graphically in Figure 11–6. Note that we have now bounded the possible solution by eliminating all of the production schedules in the shaded areas of Figure 11–6. The solution to our problem lies somewhere within the solution space *abcdef*, since any production schedule with a combination of amounts of x and y that falls outside the solution space is not feasible. This is important information for it limits our search for alternatives.

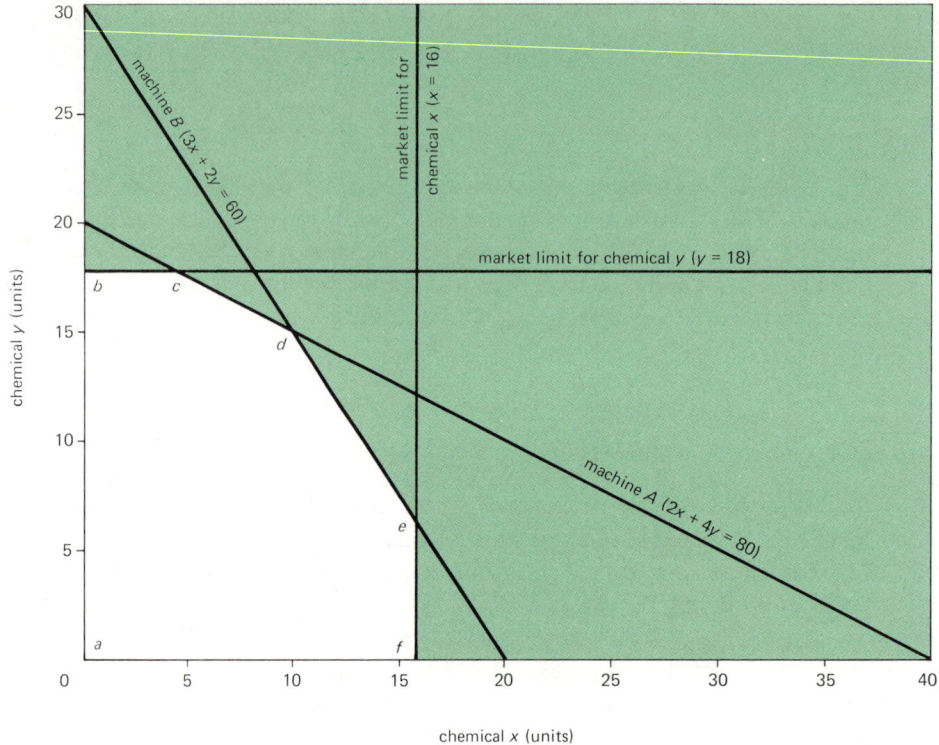

FIGURE 11-6. **Graphic representation of the limitations imposed by machine capacity, marketing, and minimum production constraints. The area enclosed by *abcdef* includes all feasible solutions to the model.**

The Linear Optimization Model

We can now summarize a statement of the linear optimization model for the two-product chemical company in the standard linear programming format, as follows:

maximize $Z = 60x + 50y$,
subject to

$2x + 4y \leq 80$ (machine A),
$3x + 2y \leq 60$ (machine B),
$x \leq 16$ (demand for chemical x),
$y \leq 18$ (demand for chemical y),
$x \geq 0$ (minimum production for chemical x),
$y \geq 0$ (minimum production for chemical y).

Solution and Interpretation of the Two Product Model

As we mentioned earlier, we will assume that we have a mechanism for solving linear optimization models when they are formulated in the preceding standard format. Indeed, linear programming computing codes are commonly available both in interactive mode (available from a time-share terminal) and in batch mode for large-scale linear programming problem solutions. In order to use either of these computing programs for the solution of linear optimization models, the problem must be presented to the "black box" in the precise form required. This input format is usually more user oriented in interactive time-share systems, and we shall use one of these programs to illustrate solutions to problems in this chapter [see Buckley et al., 1974].

Now, let us return to the chemical production problem for which we just formulated the linear optimization model in standard form. Figure 11-7 shows a portion of the computer output for the problem. Let us follow through the input steps as well as the solution output.

Computer Input In Figure 11-7 (a) we see the input steps following the "sign on" and "call up" of the linear programming subroutine. At this point, the user types *LPENTER,* and the terminal prints *ENTER THE NAME OF THIS PROJECT.* The user responds by typing *CHEMICAL PRODUCTION.*

The terminal then asks whether this problem will have an objective of maximizing or minimizing the objective function by typing *MAXIMIZE OR MINIMIZE.* Since our problem is to maximize contribution, the user responds by typing *MAXIMIZE.*

The terminal then asks for the statement of the objective function by typing *OBJECTIVE FUNCTION.* The user simply responds by typing in the objective function, $Z = 60$ *CHEMX* $+ 50$ *CHEMY.* In so doing, the user has named the variables and these names will be used for the balance of the problem. He could have used a purely symbolic notation, but variable names that convey meaning within the context of the problem are common.

Given the objective function, the terminal then requests the constraint equations and tells us how to indicate that all of the constraint equations have been entered, that is, *(STRIKE JUST A CARRIAGE RETURN TO STOP INPUT).* The user responds by typing each constraint on a separate line, using the variable names previously defined. We need not enter the last two constraints of $x \geq 0$ and $y \geq 0$, since the computer program assumes that none of the variables can take on negative values. Therefore, when the constraints have been entered, the user strikes the carriage return key as directed and the program is executed, computing the solution.

We have discussed the computer input in detail only to show how simple it is to use such programs. Many computer programs for linear programming are available; the instructions for each individual program will be unique to that

```
             LPENTER
ENTER THE NAME OF THIS PROJECT CHEMICAL PRODUCTION
MAXIMIZE OR MINIMIZE:  MAXIMIZE
OBJECTIVE FUNCTION:  Z=60CHEMX+50CHEMY
ENTER CONSTRAINT EQUATIONS, (STRIKE JUST A CARRIAGE RETURN TO STOP INPUT)
[001]  2CHEMX+4CHEMY≤80
[002]  3CHEMX+2CHEMY≤60
[003]  CHEMX≤16
[004]  CHEMY≤18
```

(A)

```
        LPRUN
                     CHEMICAL PRODUCTION

    THE OPTIMAL VALUE OF THE OBJECTIVE FUNCTION IS:   1350.000

                   THE VARIABLES IN THE SOLUTION ARE

    VARIABLE   CHEMX   AT LEVEL    1.0000E1
               CHEMY                1.5000E1
               SLK3                 6.0000E0
               SLK4                 3.0000E0
```

(B)

FIGURE 11-7. **The chemical production problem: (a) computer input and (b) computer solution**

program and the documentation indicates exactly how to provide input. The form of the computer output may also vary from program to program, but will be similar in content.

Computer Output Figure 11-7 (b) shows the solution output. First, the terminal prints the optimum value of the objective function, $1350. In other words, it states that $Z = 1350$ in the objective function for an optimal solution.

Next, the terminal prints the values of the variables in the optimum solution. Note that scientific notation is used; that is, the value of each variable is followed by E and some number. This notation means that the number preceding the E is to be multiplied by that number of 10s. For example, $E1$ means multiply by 10, $E2$ by 100, etc. $E0$ indicates that the multiplier is 1, or simply that the value of the variable needs no modification.

Now let us consider only the first two variables listed in the solution, *CHEMX* and *CHEMY*. The solution states that their optimal values are 10 and 15 respectively. Note that this is point *d* in Figure 11-6, the point where the capacity constraint lines for machines *A* and *B* intersect. This is an important observation that we shall use in Chapter 13 in understanding how the linear programming algorithm actually works.

Using the solution values of CHEMX and CHEMY, let us insert them in the objective function and compute Z,

$Z = 60 \times 10 + 50 \times 15 = 1350.$

This result checks with the optimal value of Z given by the computer solution.

Checking one further bit of logic, if the solution to our problem is at the intersection of the two capacity constraint equations, then we should be able to solve the equations for the two lines simultaneously to determine the values of CHEMX and CHEMY that are common to the equations. First, let us use the equation for machine A and solve for x,

$2x + 4y = 80.$

Therefore,

$x = 80/2 - 4y/2 = 40 - 2y.$

We then substitute this value of x in the constraint equation for machine B.

$3(40 - 2y) + 2y = 60,$
$120 - 6y + 2y = 60,$
$4y = 60,$
$y = 15$

This value of y checks with our computer solution. Now, substitute $y = 15$ in the machine A constraint equation to determine the value of x,

$2x + 4(15) = 80,$
$x = (80 - 60)/2 = 10.$

Thus, we have verified that the solution to our problem is at point d of Figure 11-6 where the two constraint equations intersect. Another interpretation of this fact is that machines A and B, our two productive resources, are completely utilized in this solution—there is no residual slack capacity. This fact is important because any of the other feasible solutions in the polygon $abcdef$ of Figure 11-6 would have involved some slack capacity in one or both of the two machines. If there had been slack capacity for either of the machines in the optimum solution, that fact would have been indicated in the computer output for the optimum solution. In some more complex problems, there might be slack capacity of a productive resource in an optimum solution.

Now, note that the computer output gave us the value of variables that we did not ask for explicitly, SLK3 and SLK4. These are the slack values related to constraints [3] and [4], the market constraints. Constraint [3], CHEMX $\leq$ 16, was the market limit for that product. The solution simply points out to us that if we produce according to the optimum solution where CHEMX = 10, there will be unsatisfied demand (slack) of 6, and this fits in with the market constraint, since $CHEMX + SLK3 = 10 + 6 = 16$. Similarly, the value of $SLK4 = 3$ agrees with the market constraint, $CHEMY \leq 18$, since $CHEMY + SLK4 = 15 + 3 = 18$.

These interpretations of the optimum solution to the chemical production problem are rather simple. The important point is that equivalent interpretations of more complex problems are a straightforward extension of these ideas. The solution will state the combination of variables that optimizes the objective function. Some but not all of the constraints will be the controlling ones, and there will be slack in some of the resources; that is, they will not all be fully utilized. In our example, the slack was in the demands for the two products. Note, however, that if the demand for $CHEMY$ dropped to only 14, that is $y = 14$, it would have become one of the controlling ("tight") constraints as may be seen from Figure 11–6, and there would have been some slack capacity in machine A.

```
DO YOU WISH SENSITIVITY ANALYSIS? YES

                          SHADOW          LB          CURRENT         UB
CONSTRAINT      1        3.7500E0      5.6000E1      8.0000E1      8.8000E1
                2        1.7500E1      4.8000E1      6.0000E1      7.2000E1
                3        0.0000E0      1.0000E1      1.6000E1      7.2370E75
                4        0.0000E0      1.5000E1      1.8000E1      7.2370E75


PRICE        CHEMX                     2.5000E1      6.0000E1      7.5000E1
             CHEMY                     4.0000E1      5.0000E1      1.2000E2

-<END>-
```

FIGURE 11–8. **Sensitivity analysis for the chemical production problem**

SENSITIVITY ANALYSIS AND INTERPRETATION OF RESULTS

If we wanted only the solution to the problem—the optimal combination of variables, the value of slack variables, and the optimum value of the objective function—we could stop at this point by answering NO to the next question typed out by the terminal, DO YOU WISH SENSITIVITY ANALYSIS? There is available to the decison maker, however, additional valuable information, and he can obtain it by simply answering the question, YES, as we have done in Figure 11–8 for the chemical production problem.

While the optimum solution states what to do now, given the objective function and the constraints, the sensitivity analysis raises questions about opportunities and perhaps about what could or should be done to improve the solution to the managerial problem.

Figure 11–8 presents the sensitivity analysis in tabular form, first for each constraint and then for the prices (contributions) for each product. For each constraint there is listed a *SHADOW* (shadow price), the *LB* (lower bound of the right-hand size of the constraint), *CURRENT* (current value of the right-hand size), and *UB* (upper bound of the right-hand side). At first this appears complex, but let us define what these terms mean in our chemical production example.

Shadow Prices The shadow prices indicate the value of an additional unit in the right-hand side of the constraint. For example, recall the meaning of the first constraint for machine A (2 *CHEMX* + 4 *CHEMY* ≤ 80). It states that the total available capacity for machine A is 80 hours. What would be the marginal value (in the objective function) of one additional unit of capacity? The answer is given in Figure 11–8 as $3.75. If the capacity of machine A were 81 hours, the extra hour would add $3.75 to the total contribution. Conversely, if only 79 hours were available, this amount would be subtracted from total contribution.

Now observe that the shadow price for machine B capacity is $17.50. The marginal value of capacity for machine B is 17.50/3.75 = 4.7 times that for machine A. The shadow prices tell the manager that the opportunity provided by increasing machine B capacity is relatively large and allow him to appraise expansion proposals for both machines.

The shadow prices for constraints [3] and [4] (demands) are zero because these constraints do not limit us in the current situation. If demand for *CHEMY* dropped to 14, then it would become one of the controlling constraints, as we noted previously. The optimum solution would change, but in addition, the shadow price for constraint [4] would become some positive value, indicating a marginal value to increasing demand for *CHEMY,* perhaps providing the manager with information to appraise programs to stimulate demand.

Lower, Current, and Upper Bounds We just stated the meaning of the shadow prices, that is, the value of marginal units of resources. But, for what ranges are these marginal rates valid? Can we increase capacity for machine B to two or three times its present capacity and expect to obtain an additional $17.50 per unit in the objective function? No, there are limits, and the bounds tell us exactly what they are. Taking the capacity of machine B as an example, it is currently 60 hours as shown in Figure 11–8 under the *CURRENT* column, but we see that the shadow price is valid in the range of 48 to 72 hours.

If we could increase the capacity of machine B to 72 hours, we would obtain an additional 17.5 × 12 = $210 in total contribution. We would be able to increase contribution by 210 × 100/1350 = 15.6 percent. On the down side, if we had a breakdown of machine B, for example, and available hours fell to the lower bound of 48, we would lose $210 in total contribution. The interpretation for the bounds on the capacity of machine A is similar.

Now let us examine the significance of the bounds on the demand for the two products. Take constraint [4], the demand for *CHEMY,* for example. Its lower bound is 15. A shadow price of zero applies if demand falls to 15, that is, the constraint is ineffective in that range. But, as we have already noted, if demand falls below 15 the constraint becomes one of those controlling the solution.

Now, the upper bound for constraint [4] is listed as 7.2370E75. This is the code for infinity in this particular linear programming computer program. There is no upper bound in effect.

Price Sensitivity The contribution rates in the objective function are termed generally *prices*. Recall that the contribution of a unit of *CHEMX* was $60 and of *CHEMY* $50, and these are shown as the *CURRENT* values in Figure 11-8. But, what if prices change? Would the changes affect the solution? The lower and upper bounds for prices shown in Figure 11-8 indicate the range of prices (contribution rates) for which the optimum solution is valid. For example, the contribution rate for *CHEMX* could be anywhere in the range of $25 to $75 and the optimum amount of *CHEMX* and *CHEMY* would still be as indicated in the present solution: produce 10 units of *CHEMX* and 15 units of *CHEMY*. Of course, the total contribution would change because of the change in the contribution rate, but the optimal *decision* would remain the same.

There is a practical significance to the price sensitivity. For example, the manager might estimate contribution for *CHEMX* at $60, but these kinds of figures are seldom absolutely precise. Suppose that the contribution is somewhere in the $55 to $65 range. In this case, the same solution applies. The result is that the use of *rough* estimates for the contribution rate is adequate, and we should not spend additional time and money to refine the estimate. Thus, the bounds help indicate how we should allocate time and money to refine cost information—if the bounds are tight it may be worthwhile to be precise, but if they are loose we would gain nothing by attempting to improve the estimates.

Summary

Let us take a moment to summarize at this point. Given a linear optimization model stated in the format we have specified, we can use a computer program to provide the optimum combination of the decision variables, the optimum value of the objective function, and the values of slack capacity or other resources in the system. In interpreting the solution, however, we can also obtain the value of a marginal unit of each resource (shadow prices) and the range over which the shadow price is valid. In addition, we can obtain the range of prices (contribution rates in our example) in the objective function for which the solution is valid.

Understanding the significance of the optimum solution and the sensitivity analysis in the context of the real problem has great value. The decision maker is in a position to appraise various proposals for changing the optimum solution. He should not look on the optimum solution as necessarily the final decision, but as a basis for asking *what if* questions. The sensitivity analysis provides him with information regarding many possible *what if* questions, and may also suggest variations of the model that may require additional computer runs.

A MODEL INVOLVING RATIO CONSTRAINTS

This example introduces the important concept of the use of *ratios* or *proportions* in the formulation of constraints, providing a bridge to the formulation of many real-world problems.

Suppose a production process is used to manufacture two products. The daily demand for the first product is 50 units, while the demand for the second is 100 units. These products can be processed either manually or by a mechanized system during a two-shift day. However, the capacity of the mechanized system is restricted to less than or equal to 40 units of product 1 per shift, or less than or equal to 75 units of product 2 per shift. Similarly, the manual system is restricted to less than or equal to 30 units of product 1 per shift, or 50 units of product 2 per shift. Suppose that, according to our accounting records, the costs of producing the products vary depending on the system used (mechanized or manual), the type of product, and the shift, as shown in Table 11–2. The obvious question to be answered is how many units should be processed on which system during each shift, assuming that we must meet the demand.

TABLE 11–2. **Production Costs per Unit for Products 1 and 2 on Manual and Mechanized Systems During Shifts 1 and 2**

	Manual	Mechanized
Product 1		
Shift 1	10	8
Shift 2	15	11
Product 2		
Shift 1	5	4
Shift 2	6	6

Definition of Decision Variables

In order to define the decision variables, it is convenient to introduce some notation that may appear complex at first, but that actually simplifies the formulation of the model. We will let M_{ij} be the number of units of product i (1 or 2) processed during shift j (1 or 2) on the manual system and let MCH_{ij} be the number of units of product i processed during shift j on the mechanized system. Thus, if we determine that $M_{11} = 20$ and $MCH_{21} = 60$, this would indicate that

20 units of product 1 are to be processed by the manual system during shift 1, and 60 units of product 2 are to be processed on the mechanized system during shift 1. Since there are two products that can be processed on either of two systems during either of two shifts, there are a total of $2 \times 2 \times 2 = 8$ decision variables.

Definition of the Objective Function

Now we wish to let the computer determine the values of M_{ij} and MCH_{ij} that minimize the cost of meeting our daily production demand. That is, we wish to let the computer minimize the expression

$$Z = 10M_{11} + 8MCH_{11} + 15M_{12} + 11MCH_{12}$$
$$+ 5M_{21} + 4MCH_{21} + 6M_{22} + 6MCH_{22},$$

where the cost coefficients are taken directly from Table 11-2. For example, the cost of processing a unit of product 2 using the manual system during shift 1 is $5, so $5M_{21}$ appears as the fifth term in this objective function.

Definition of Constraints

The constraints result from the demand requirements and the capacity restrictions. In order to meet the demand for product 1, we must have

$$M_{11} + MCH_{11} + M_{12} + MCH_{12} = 50,$$

which says that the total number of units of product 1 produced using manual labor and the mechanized system during both shifts must equal 50. Similarly, for product 2,

$$M_{21} + MCH_{21} + M_{22} + MCH_{22} = 100.$$

Finally, we have capacity restrictions on both the manual and the mechanized systems during each shift. Consider the problem on the manual system during the first shift. Clearly M_{11} must be less than or equal to 30, and M_{21} must be less than or equal to 50. The temptation is to jump to the conclusion that these capacity constraints are very simple; for example, for the manual system during the first shift, we would write

$$M_{11} \leq 30,$$
$$M_{21} \leq 50,$$

and so on for the other shift and for the mechanized system.

The problem with this approach becomes apparent when we note that on shift 1 we seem to be allowing the simultaneous use of the manual system in two different ways. For example, if we use the full capacity for product 1 ($M_{11} = 30$), then M_{21} must be zero. We cannot use the same capacity more than once, and that is the key to the proper construction of the capacity constraints.

During shift 1, the total available capacity of the manual system can be used up to 100 percent. Therefore, the sum of the *fractions* or *proportions* of this capacity used by each product must be less than or equal to *one*. The fraction of the capacity used for product 1 is the number of units of product 1 processed on the manual system during shift 1, M_{11}, divided by the capacity for product 1, or $M_{11}/30$; for product 2, $M_{21}/50$. Thus, if $M_{11} = 10$, then we are using one-third of the available capacity on the manual system during shift 1 to process product 1. The capacity constraint for the manual system during shift 1 is then

$$M_{11}/30 + M_{21}/50 \leq 1.$$

Now, let us simplify this constraint by multiplying through by 150, the common denominator, and we obtain

$$5M_{11} + 3M_{21} \leq 150.$$

Following exactly the same process, we develop a similar constraint for the capacity of the manual system during the second shift. Test your understanding of this important point by writing down the capacity constraints for the mechanized system, using the same reasoning.

Figure 11-9 shows the computer input and solution for the problem. The complete problem formulation is shown as the computer input in (a). According to the computer solution shown in (b), $MCH_{11} = 13.33$, $MCH_{12} = 36.67$, $M_{21} = 50$, and $MCH_{21} = 50$. The optimal values of the decision variables not listed in the computer solution are 0.0. This result indicates that we should produce 13.33 units of product 1 during the first shift and 36.67 during the second shift, all on the mechanized system. Further, we produce 50 units of product 2 on the manual system and 50 on the mechanized system, all during the first shift. Check to see that this result satisfies our constraints. The minimum total cost of this solution is 960. Finally the slack variables $SLK4$ and $SLK6$, corresponding to constraints [4] and [6] respectively, indicate that there is unused capacity on both the manual and mechanized systems during shift 2.

ANALYSIS OF A PRODUCT PLANNING DECISION

Let us now use linear optimization models to analyze some expansion problems of a company that manufactures two products, A and B. The schedule proposed by the production manager calls for a product mix of 615 units of A, and 2600 units of B. One of the current issues is whether or not the mix is most profitable. Also, since a third product may be added to the line, a decision must be made about the possible enlargement of the four manufacturing departments.

Table 11-3 shows the man-hour requirements for each product and the departmental capacities. Also, the contribution rates are $50 per unit for product A, $35 for B, and the objective is to maximize combined contribution.

Model Formulation

First, let us formulate a linear optimization model designed to indicate the best product mix for maximum contribution.

```
LPENTER
ENTER THE NAME OF THIS PROJECT:TWO PRODUCTS-RATIO CONSTRAINTS
MAXIMIZE OR MINIMIZE: MIN
OBJECTIVE FUNCTION: Z=10M11+8MCH11+15M12+11MCH12+5M21+4MCH21+6M22+6MCH22
ENTER CONSTRAINT EQUATIONS, (STRIKE JUST A CARRIAGE RETURN TO STOP INPUT)
 (1) M11+MCH11+M12+MCH12=50
 (2) M21+MCH21+M22+MCH22=100
 (3) 5M11+3M21≤150
 (4) 5M12+3M22≤150
 (5) 7.5MCH11+4MCH21≤300
 (6) 7.5MCH12+4MCH22≤300
 (7)
                                    (A)
      LPRUN
                      TWO PRODUCTS-RATIO CONSTRAINTS

THE OPTIMAL VALUE OF THE OBJECTIVE FUNCTION IS:      960.000

                 THE VARIABLES IN THE SOLUTION ARE

VARIABLE   MCH11    AT LEVEL        1.3333E1
           MCH12                    3.6667E1
           M21                      5.0000E1
           MCH21                    5.0000E1
           SLK4                     1.5000E2
           SLK6                     2.5000E1
                                    (B)
```

FIGURE 11-9. **Model with ratio constraints: (a) computer input and (b) computer solution**

Definition of Decision Variables Since the objective is to determine the optimal product mix, the decision variables are the amounts of each product to produce per month. Therefore, we let A and B be the number of units per month of products A and B respectively.

Definition of the Objective Function We wish to

maximize $Z = 50A + 35B$.

The coefficients of A and B are the contribution rates.

Definition of Constraints The constraints are the expressions limiting the use of departmental man-hours to the monthly capacities indicated in Table 11-3. Since Table 11-3 indicates man-hours per unit for each product, the total man-hour requirement in each department is the sum of the amounts used by each product. Department one, for example, is used only by product A, so the total is simply 3 times the number of units of product A, or $3A$, since product A requires 3 hours per unit in department one. This amount cannot be larger than the capacity of department one, so the constraint is

$3A \leq 6000$.

Department two is used only by product B and its constraint expression is similar:

$2.9B \leq 8000$.

TABLE 11-3. **Man-Hour Requirements and Capacities for the Two-Product Company**

Department	Man-Hours per Unit		Department Capacities (man-hours per month)
	A	B	
1	3	0	6000
2	0	2.9	8000
3	2.5	2	7500
4	1.3	1.5	5000

Department three is used by both products. Product A requires 2.5 hours per unit, and B, 2 hours per unit. The monthly capacity is 7500 hours. Therefore, the constraint on the time requirements for the two products is

$2.5A + 2B \leq 7500$.

Similarly, for department four, the capacity constraint is

$1.3A + 1.5B \leq 5000$.

Assuming the nonnegativity constraints on variables, the linear optimization model is shown in the computer input in Figure 11-10 (a).

Interpretation of Computer Solution

The optimal solution shown in Figure 11-10 (b) specifies an output of 2000 units of product A, and 1250 units of product B. The maximum contribution possible is indicated as $143,750 per month. Compare this optimal contribution with the production manager's proposed schedule which has a contribution of

$(50)(615) + (35)(2600) = \$121{,}750$.

The optimal schedule would increase contribution by $22,000, or 18.1 percent.

Now let us beware of jumping to the conclusion that the original schedule is a poor one. The optimal contribution could be obtained only if the units could be sold. Here, we observe internal controversy, for the sales manager says that he could sell 2200 units of A, and only 1500 units of B. He charges that the production manager will create a horrible inventory problem with his proposed schedule by producing 2600 units of B. Furthermore, he claims they will miss a market opportunity for product A.

```
LPENTER
ENTER THE NAME OF THIS PROJECT TWO PRODUCT COMPANY
MAXIMIZE OR MINIMIZE: MAX
OBJECTIVE FUNCTION: Z=50A+35B
ENTER CONSTRAINT EQUATIONS, (STRIKE JUST A CARRIAGE RETURN TO STOP INPUT)
 (1) 3A≤6000
 (2) 2.9B≤8000
 (3) 2.5A+2B≤7500
 (4) 1.3A+1.5B≤5000
 (5)
                                    (a)
      LPRUN
                          TWO PRODUCT COMPANY

      THE OPTIMAL VALUE OF THE OBJECTIVE FUNCTION IS:    143750.000

                   THE VARIABLES IN THE SOLUTION ARE

      VARIABLE    A      AT LEVEL    2.0000E3
                  B                  1.2500E3
                  SLK2               4.3750E3
                  SLK4               5.2500E2

      DO YOU WISH SENSITIVITY ANALYSIS? YES

                         SHADOW        LB          CURRENT       UB
      CONSTRAINT    1   2.0833E0     3.2609E3     6.0000E3     9.0000E3
                    2   0.0000E0     3.6250E3     8.0000E3     7.2370E75
                    3   1.7500E1     5.0000E3     7.500 0E3    8.2000E3
                    4   0.0000E0     4.4750E3     5.0000E3     7.2370E75

      PRICE         A                4.3750E1     5.0000E1     7.2370E75
                    B                0.0000E0     3.500 0E1    4.0000E1
      -> END <-
                                    (b)
```

FIGURE 11-10. **Two-Product Company: (a) computer input and (b) computer solution**

Of course, we note from the optimal solution that neither of the product mixes proposed by the production manager or the sales manager seems entirely appropriate. The production manager's schedule has a relatively low contribution. The sales manager's contribution is larger [(50) (2,200) + (35) (1,500) = $162,500], but is it feasible? No, the sales manager's schedule would require 6600 hours in department one, 8500 hours in department three, and 5110 hours in department four, all exceeding capacities. Only department two's capacity would be capable of handling the sales manager's proposal. You should check these calculations to be sure you understand the implications of the sales manager's proposal.

The optimal solution indicated in Figure 11-10 shows that departments one and three would be fully utilized, and that departments two and four would have slack capacity of 4375 hours and 525 hours respectively. One of the questions to be answered is whether or not the slack capacity can be used by a third product.

Sensivity Analysis

Now let us examine the sensitivity analysis given for the Two-Product Company, also shown in Figure 11–10. The shadow prices for the capacities of departments two, and four are zero. Therefore, with the present line of products, man-hour requirements, and contribution rates, there is no advantage in expanding these departments. However, the shadow price for department one is $2.08 per man-hour of capacity, and this shadow price is valid in the range of 3261 to 9000 man-hours per month. Also, the shadow price for department three is $17.50, valid in the range of 5000 to 8200 man-hours per month.

The bounds on the contributions in the objective function indicate that for product A, the $50 contribution could increase without bounds and the optimum solution would not change. On the other hand, the $35 contribution for product B is valid for the present solution between 0 and $40, but the solution would change if the contribution rate were to increase above $40 per unit. This later contribution is therefore sensitive to increases (which may be unlikely), but not to decreases.

Introduction of a Third Product

After seeing the computer optimal solution and sensitivity analysis for the existing two products, both the production and sales managers wish to evaluate the potential impact of the proposed new product C, *before* it is introduced. They are both excited about the new product, but for different reasons. The sales manager sees the hope of added contributions. The expanded sales may be the basis for a salary increase and/or a promotion for him. The production manager sees the new product as a way of using his slack capacity. Reports on plant utilization have indicated that he has not been very effective in scheduling production, as indicated by low output per man-hour. The optimal solution of Figure 11–10 seems to verify the report results. The production manager fears the loss of his job.

Product C has uniqueness, and market tests indicate that it can command a contribution of $75 per unit. The sales manager raises the question again of whether or not there is sufficient existing capacity. The production manager contends that existing capacities are adequate and that, indeed, a reason that product C is so attractive is that it fits in so well, using slack capacity. The analyst says, "Let's not argue, let's compute."

The man-hour requirements for product C are: 0.15, 2.5, 3.5, and 1.5, respectively for each of the four departments.

Three Products–Interpretation of Computer Solution

With the addition of product C, the linear optimization model becomes the computer input shown in Figure 11–11(a). Note that the objective function and

```
            LPENTER
    ENTER THE NAME OF THIS PROJECT THREE PRODUCT COMPANY
    MAXIMIZE OR MINIMIZE:  MAX
    OBJECTIVE FUNCTION:  Z=50A+35B+75C
    ENTER CONSTRAINT EQUATIONS, (STRIKE JUST A CARRIAGE RETURN TO STOP INPUT)
    (1) 3A+0.15C≤6000
    (2) 2.9B+2.5C≤8000
    (3) 2.5A+2B+3.5C≤7500
    (4) 1.3A+1.5B+1.5C≤5000
    (5)
                                    (A)
            LPRUN
                            THREE PRODUCT COMPANY

        THE OPTIMAL VALUE OF THE OBJECTIVE FUNCTION IS:    160714.286

                        THE VARIABLES IN THE SOLUTION ARE

        VARIABLE    C      AT LEVEL    2.1429E3
                    SLK1               5.6786E3
                    SLK2               2.6429E3
                    SLK4               1.7857E3

        DO YOU WISH SENSITIVITY ANALYSIS? YES

                                SHADOW          LB          CURRENT         UB
        CONSTRAINT     1       0.0000E0       3.2143E2      6.000UE3      7.2370E75
                       2       0.0000E0       5.3571E3      8.000UE3      7.2370E75
                       3       2.1429E1       0.0000E0      7.500UE3      1.1200E4
                       4       0.0000E0       3.2143E3      5.000UE3      7.2370E75

        PRICE          A                     -7.2370E75     5.000UE1      5.3571E1
                       B                     -7.2370E75     3.500UE1      4.2857E1
                       C                      7.0000E1      7.500UE1      7.2370E75
        -> END <-
                                    (B)
```

FIGURE 11-11. **Three-Product Company:**
(a) computer input and
(b) computer solution

all four constraints must be altered to take product C into account. You should check to see that you understand the new linear optimization model.

The solution to the Three-Product Company case is shown in Figure 11-11(b). The results are rather startling, since the optimum solution calls for production of only product C. The results are impressive in that the contribution is actually increased from $143,750 for the two-product case to $160,714 when product C is added to the line. However, it is no longer a product line, since product C dominates completely.

The production manager probably would not have generated this solution. According to his comment, he envisioned using the slack available in departments two and four from the previous solution, or the generous slack capacity available in his initially proposed schedule. Actually, however, slack is now available in three departments. The reason that product C dominates is that it is so profitable compared to the original two products. Perhaps the most important questions that need to be answered are related to the risks involved in dropping products A and B, and concentrating only on the new product C. Also, we need to be concerned about the size of the potential market for product C.

While the analysis provided by linear optimization models does not deal with risks, we can obtain some insight by looking at the bounds on the prices for the three products in the sensitivity analysis shown in Figure 11-11. In Figure 11-11, the lower bound on the attractive contribution for product C is $70, compared to the current contribution of $75. If the estimated contribution for product C decreases by $5 or more, the solution will change. Therefore, it might be worthwhile to examine the effects of a contribution for product C of less than $70 to see what the new solutions would look like and to see what would happen to the optimal value of the objective function.

The solution in Figure 11-11 is also risky because all capacity is turned over to product C. The production and sales managers both realized that their bread and butter had been in products A and B and that the market for the new product as an introduction is probably limited to 50 units. The production manager also accepted the sales manager's estimates for the markets for products A and B of 2200 and 1500 units respectively.

Three Products—Market Constraints

The market constraints are added to the linear optimization model for the three-product case, and the new model is shown as the computer input in Figure 11-12(a). With the market restrictions, we see that the net contribution of adding product C to the product mix is only $672, compared with the two-product case. Nevertheless, the solution calls for the maximum production of product C permitted by the market constraint, reflecting again the attractive contribution rate for product C.

Note that departments two and four still have slack capacity, and that the new solution indicates slack in constraints [5] and [6], the market constraints for A and B respectively. This means that we did not satisfy the sales manager's estimate of the market for these two products. Looking at the shadow prices in Figure 11-12(b), we see that there is still a $2.08 shadow price on the capacity for department one, a $17.50 shadow price on the capacity for department three, and that there is a $13.44 shadow price on the market constraint for product C, indicated by constraint [7]. That means that if the market can realistically be expanded for the new product, we could gain an additional $13.44 for each unit up to 741 units.

The bounds on the contribution rates (prices) are also useful in mapping strategies. Note that the lower bound for product A is only $6.25 below the current value. If the contribution drops below $43.75, the solution will change. The contribution for product B can fall to zero before the solution will change. However, we find that the contribution rate for the new product C is less sensitive than for product A. The estimated contribution rate would have to be in error by more than −$13.44 before the solution would change.

We can see from the analysis of the Two- and Three-Product Company structures that a number of computing runs may be useful to the manager. By posing *what if* questions and scenarios for change, and by examining the sensitivity analysis, the manager can obtain a great deal of information that can help him in the decision-making process. The value of linear optimization models to the manager is not simply in obtaining an optimal solution to a problem, but in interacting with the model and its variations to obtain information and insights.

FEED MIX SELECTION

To illustrate a different type of problem that can be analyzed using a linear optimization model, let us consider the selection of different grains in a feed mix. A feed and grain producer may purchase and mix three different types of grain to produce feed for cattle. The cattle feed must meet minimum standards for four basic nutritional ingredients according to the current federal regulations. The percentage of each of these nutritional ingredients in each unit weight of each grain and the minimum federal regulations are shown in Table 11–4. For example, one pound of wheat contains 0.1 pounds of ingredient 1, 0.2 pounds of ingredient 2, etc.; and one pound of feed must contain 0.1 pounds of ingredient 1, 0.1 pounds of ingredient 2, etc.

The current market forecast is for sales of 10,000 pounds of cattle feed during the next month. Wheat currently costs $0.10 per pound, barley costs $0.12 per pound, and rye costs $0.08 per pound. How many pounds of each grain should be purchased and mixed to meet the sales forecast at minimum cost, while meeting the federal regulations?

TABLE 11–4. **Nutritional Ingredients in Grains**

Nutritional Ingredient	Proportion of Each Nutritional Ingredient in			Minimum Federal Regulation for Feed
	Wheat	Barley	Rye	
1	0.10	0.10	0.15	0.10
2	0.20	0.00	0.15	0.10
3	0.30	0.20	0.10	0.15
4	0.30	0.25	0.20	0.20

```
                    LPENTER
ENTER THE NAME OF THIS PROJECT THREE PRODUCT COMPANY WITH MARKET RESTRICTIONS
MAXIMIZE OR MINIMIZE: MAX
OBJECTIVE FUNCTION: Z=50A+35B+75C
ENTER CONSTRAINT EQUATIONS, (STRIKE JUST A CARRIAGE RETURN TO STOP INPUT)
 (1) 3A+0.15C≤6000
 (2) 2.9B+2.5C≤8000
 (3) 2.5A+2B+3.5C≤7500
 (4) 1.3A+1.5B+1.5C≤5000
 (5) A≤2200
 (6) B≤1500
 (7) C≤50
 (8)
                              (A)
          LPRUN
                      THREE PRODUCT COMPANY WITH MARKET RESTRICTIONS

   THE OPTIMAL VALUE OF THE OBJECTIVE FUNCTION IS:    144421.875

                    THE VARIABLES IN THE SOLUTION ARE

   VARIABLE   A      AT LEVEL      1.9975E3
              B                    1.1656E3
              C                    5.0000E1
              SLK2                 4.4947E3
              SLK4                 5.7981E2
              SLK5                 2.0250E2
              SLK6                 3.3438E2

   DO YOU WISH SENSITIVITY ANALYSIS? YES

                       SHADOW         LB           CURRENT        UB
   CONSTRAINT   1     2.0833E0      5.1975E3      6.0000E3      6.6075E3
                2     0.0000E0      3.5053E3      8.0000E3      7.2370E75
                3     1.7500E1      5.1688E3      7.5000E3      8.1687E3
                4     0.0000E0      4.4202E3      5.0000E3      7.2370E75
                5     0.0000E0      1.9975E3      2.2000E3      7.2370E75
                6     0.0000E0      1.1656E3      1.5000E3      7.2370E75
                7     1.3438E1      0.0000E0      5.0000E1      7.4074E2

   PRICE        A                   4.3750E1      5.0000E1      3.1875E2
                B                   0.0000E0      3.5000E1      4.0000E1
                C                   6.1563E1      7.5000E1      7.2370E75
   -> END <-
                              (B)
```

FIGURE 11-12. **Three-Product Company with market restrictions: (a) computer input and (b) computer solution**

Decision Variables The decision variables are the number of pounds of each grain—wheat (W), barley (B), or rye (R)—to include in the feed.

Objective Function The objective is to minimize the total cost of the grain. The cost of wheat will be $0.1W$, barley $0.12B$, and rye $0.08R$, so we wish to

minimize $Z = 0.1W + 0.12B + 0.08R$.

Constraints The first four constraints simply ensure that the minimum federal requirements for each ingredient are met. From Table 11-4, at least 0.1 of the total sales forecast of 10,000 pounds, or $(0.1)(10,000) = 1000$ pounds, should be nutrient 1. This constraint is imposed by

$$0.1W + 0.1B + 0.15R \geq 1000.$$

Similar constraints can be written for the other three ingredients. We must also meet the sales forecast for the feed, so

$$W + B + R = 10,000$$

is the final constraint.

Figure 11–13 shows the computer input and solution for this problem. The complete formulation is shown as the computer input (a). According to the computer solution (b), we should purchase 2500 pounds of wheat (W) and 7500 pounds of rye (R) to mix for the feed. Since the variable corresponding to barley (B) does not appear in the solution, its optimal value is zero.

Notice that the computer solution gives us some new variables that we did not ask for, $SUR1$, $SUR2$, and $SUR4$. These are surplus variables related to constraints [1], [2], and [4], and are similar to slack values, except that they correspond to the use of greater than or equal to ($\geq$) relationships in constraints rather than the less than or equal to ($\leq$) relationships encountered in the previous problems. Some problem formulations may include both types of constraints, so the solution will involve both slack variables and surplus variables.

For example, if $W = 2500$, $B = 0$, and $R = 7500$, then from constraint [1], there are $(0.1)(2500) + (0.1)(0.0) + (0.15)(7500) = 1375$ pounds of ingredient 1 in the feed. The difference between 1375 and the federal requirement of

```
         LPENTER
         ENTER THE NAME OF THIS PROJECT FEED MIX PROBLEM
         MAXIMIZE OR MINIMIZE: MINIMIZE
         OBJECTIVE FUNCTION:Z=.1W+.12B+.08R
         ENTER CONSTRAINT EQUATIONS, (STRIKE JUST A CARRIAGE RETURN TO STOP INPUT)
          (1) .1W+.1B+.15R≥1000
          (2) .2W+.15R≥1000
          (3) .3W+.2B+.1R≥1500
          (4) .3W+.25B+.2R≥2000
          (5) W+B+R=10000
          (6)
                                   (A)
              LPRUN
                              FEED MIX PROBLEM

         THE OPTIMAL VALUE OF THE OBJECTIVE FUNCTION IS:       850.000

                          THE VARIABLES IN THE SOLUTION ARE

              VARIABLE    W         AT LEVEL    2.5000E3
                          R                     7.5000E3
                          SUR1                  3.7500E2
                          SUR2                  6.2500E2
                          SUR4                  2.5000E2
                                   (B)
```

FIGURE 11–13. **Feed mix problem: (a) computer input and (b) computer solution**

a minimum of 1000 pounds, or 375 pounds, is the value of the surplus variable, *SUR*1. Test your understanding of this important point by interpreting the meaning of *SUR*2 and *SUR*4. The sensitivity analysis for the feed mix problem is considered in exercise 21.

This formulation of the feed mix problem is a simplification of an important class of applications of linear optimization models. Actual applications have been reported by Chappell [1974] and by Lyons and Dodd [1975]. Also, related models that allocate the use of food ingredients to meet nutritional requirements at minimum cost have been used by Balintfy [1975] in food management applications such as might be found in university dormitories, military installations, hospitals, and other large institutions supplying food service.

WHAT SHOULD THE MANAGER KNOW?

Linear optimization models can become very complex, involving an enormous number of variables and constraints, and a manager's initial reaction could easily be one of rejection. However, the manager need not concern himself with the mathematical complexities. The real value for him lies in being aware of the characteristics of problems for which linear optimization models may be useful, so that he can both suggest applications and evaluate proposals for application. In addition, a knowledge of the nature of model formulation, information requirements, and particularly interpretation of results is important for the manager. If he so chooses, he need not know the mathematical methods of the linear programming solution technique. Given the existence of linear programming computer codes similar to the one used in this chapter, the manager can assume that if the problem can be put in standard form for input, the "black box" will perform its function and provide the solution output, complete with sensitivity analysis.

Problem Characteristics

What is the nature of problems for which linear optimization methods are applicable? Linear optimization models are of value in problems that involve the allocation of limited resources to competing demands. The chemical production, product planning, and feed mix examples all had this general characteristic. In the chemical production and product planning examples, the limited resources were the productive capacities and the limited market demands; the objective was to maximize the use of the resources with respect to a criterion—maximum profits. In the feed mix example, the limited productive resources were the raw materials and limited market demands, and the objective was to optimize the use of the different ingredients in order to minimize costs.

Applications of linear optimization models in the analysis of production problems are commonplace today. In addition to the kinds of problems described here, these models have been used to analyze multiple plant location problems and scheduling problems. The problems at the end of this chapter provide examples of the analysis of production problems using linear optimization models. Examples of applications in other areas, including marketing, finance, manpower and personnel management, urban planning, and education, are provided in Chapter 12.

Model Formulation

The manager needs to know and understand something about formulating linear models in order to use the services of staff analysts appropriately and to interpret results. He needs to be able to think in terms of the criterion function and the constraints to his problem. If he can formulate the simpler kinds of problems we used as examples in this chapter, he can work effectively through analysts to help formulate more complex problems, for as we noted, the more complex problems are straightforward extensions of the concepts involved in the simple ones.

Interpretation of Results

The heart of the managerial function is focused in the interpretation of results and in decision making. While the solution output has obvious value for the manager, the power of the results is greatly enhanced by the sensitivity analysis. The manager can put himself in the interactive mode that we discussed in connection with predictive models. He can raise intelligent *what if* questions if he understands the meaning of shadow prices and the upper and lower bounds on solutions. These questions often result in additional computing runs to evaluate alternatives that are not automatically generated within the optimizing model.

Extensions of Linear Optimization Models

An extension of linear optimization models called goal programming has been used in a number of production-oriented applications. For example, Lee and Moore [1973] applied the methodology to distribution problems in which management had a hierarchy of goals such as guaranteed delivery to a specific customer, use of certain routes because of union agreements, fulfillment of a transportation cost budget, and so on. The constraints were the supplies available at origin points, the market demands, and the goals. The solution procedure using linear programming successively seeks the achievement of goals in their order of priority, and higher priority goals are considered as constraints that cannot be violated.

Another important extension of the general concept of a linear optimization model is the integer valued optimization model. Integer valued optimization models are formulated much like linear optimization models, except that some of the variables are required to have integer values in the final solution. Integer values (the numbers 0, 1, 2, 3, 4, etc.) have no fractional parts.

There are two important types of integer variables that appear in optimizing models. The first type, integer decision variables, simply represents the number of units of a product, a machine, or some other resource that should be produced or allocated, much like the ordinary decision variables in linear optimization models. Decision variables required to have integer values often represent expensive resources. For example, a company planning a product distribution system will not consider a solution requiring them to build 3.5 warehouses to be particularly meaningful. Similarly, an oil company may wish to purchase either 4 or 5 supertankers, but not 4.3 supertankers.

In some cases, a linear programming problem can be solved by ignoring the integer restrictions, and the variables that are required to have integer values can be rounded off to the nearest integer solution. Such a solution may or may not be the best integer solution that can actually be obtained. When significant costs or other resources are involved, the additional computational burden generally associated with integer programming models may be justified in order to find the best integer solution.

The second type of integer variable is a *logical* variable that allows the optimizing model to evaluate mutually exclusive alternative decisions and to analyze various combinatorial problems. An example of a combinatorial problem is the selection of three of ten alternative sites for new warehouses. These logical integer variables generally indicate *yes* or *no* decisions rather than the number of units used or produced.

The optimizing models with integer values provide a powerful tool of analysis for managers. The computational burden for these problems, however, has inhibited their widespread use until recently. Extremely large linear optimization models can be solved on the computer by efficiently programmed versions of the simplex algorithm. However, there is no single algorithm that is equally general when applied to integer optimization models. A solution strategy may perform satisfactorily for some problems, but not so well for others.

The choice of a particular integer programming algorithm is an issue for the technical analyst. Nevertheless, it is important that the manager work closely with the analyst so that the formulation of the model with integer variables can be as efficient as possible.

Check Your Understanding

1. Which of the following mathematical expressions are linear? Why?
    a. $x + y = 1$
    b. $x^2 + y^2 = 10$
    c. $1/x + 2x = 10$
    d. $x + xy + y = 1$
    e. $x_1 + x_2 + x_3 + x_4 = 1$

2. Graph each of the following constraints on a separate graph and shade or cross-hatch the areas of the graph that include admissible points.
   a. $x + y \leq 4$
   b. $x + y \geq 10$
   c. $2x + 3y = 15$
   d. $x \leq 10$
3. Outline the model-building process used for developing linear optimization models.
4. How are alternatives generated within the structure of the model-building process?
5. In the break-even analysis example, explain why we were able to simply drop the variable f (fixed cost) from the objective function.
6. In the break-even analysis example, there was a slack capacity of 100 units per month. Suppose that the demand constraint had been $x \leq 400$. How would the concept of slack apply?
7. In the chemical production example, the objective function that we developed was a statement of contribution to profit and overhead. Why maximize this function instead of an expression for profit? Isn't it really profit that we wish to maximize?
8. Suppose that in the chemical production problem, the availability of time on machine A is drastically reduced to only 40 hours because of a breakdown. How does this change the solution space shown in Figure 11-6? Is it likely to change the optimum number of units of each chemical to produce?
9. Explain the concept of shadow prices. How can a manager use his knowledge of shadow prices in decision making?
10. What is the interpretation of the upper and lower bounds on the shadow prices indicated in Figure 11-8? Of what value is this information to a manager?
11. What is the interpretation of the upper and lower bounds on the "prices" given in Figure 11-8? Of what value is this information to the manager?
12. What may be the practical value of knowing that the bounds on one or more prices may be "tight"?
13. Suppose we have a machine that is flexible and can be used to process various sizes of a product by a simple adjustment. The capacity of the machine is greater for small sizes. The capacity of the machine for three sizes is $x_1 = 500$ per month, $x_2 = 1000$ per month, and $x_3 = 2500$ per month. The monthly capacity of the machine for an average mix is stated to be 1500 per month. Write the capacity constraint expression for the machine.

Problems

14. The Elmore Electronics Corporation is a manufacturer of two kinds of electronic test equipment: oscilloscopes (O) and vacuum tube voltmeters (V). The physical facilities are organized into three main departments: the circuit board

TABLE 11-5. **Monthly capacities for the Elmore Electronic Corporation**

	Time Requirements (hours/unit)		Hours Available Next Month
	Oscilloscopes (O)	Voltmeters (V)	
Chassis Department (C)	4.5	2.0	2000
Circuit Board Department (CB)	6.3	1.5	2500
Assembly Department (A)	7.0	3.0	3000

TABLE 11-6. **Costs and Prices for the Elmore Electronics Corporation**

Costs and Prices (per unit)	Oscilloscopes (O)	Voltmeters (V)
Sales prices	$170	$55
Costs		
Variable labor	20	5
Material	50	10
Overhead (at current volume)	40	10

department (CB), the chassis department (C) and final assembly (A). Monthly capacities for each of the two products in the three departments are given in Table 11-5, and financial data are given in Table 11-6.

Current market forecasts for the two products for the coming month are for 400 oscilloscopes and 600 voltmeters.

Formulate a linear optimization model for the manager of Elmore that can be used as a basis for scheduling production for next month.

15. Elmore is contemplating the addition of a third product for the coming month, which it thinks will have a broad appeal to TV repairmen. It is a portable circuit board tester that can quickly check a standard circuit board by setting dials and switches to standard settings. The product has been market tested and estimates of the market and production costs have been made.

The foremen in the chassis and circuit board departments state that they can absorb the small added load with present facilities and labor force. The assembly department foreman, however, states that he must enlarge his labor force to a total of 3500 available hours in order to absorb the new product load.

The new product is dubbed (P) for *portable* and alternate plans must be generated to include the item in next month's production schedule. The manager is delighted with the prospect that the new product may go into production, partly because overhead costs will be spread over a larger product base, making existing products more "profitable." He estimates that the per unit overhead costs will decline to $38 for oscilloscopes and $9 for voltmeters.

The portable circuit board testers (P) will sell for $400 each, and initial cost estimates indicate that variable labor will be $100, materials $125, and allocated overhead $60 per unit. Initial sales estimates are set at 50 for next month. Hours requirements in the three departments for P are estimated to be 9 per unit in the chassis department, 10 per unit in the circuit board department, and 15 per unit in assembly. Reformulate Elmore's problem as a linear optimization model.

16. The Goodwear Shoe Company has three plants, all of which can produce the full line of shoes: dress shoes (D), which yield a net contribution of $10 each; work shoes (W), which yield $8; and sport shoes (S), which yield $4.

    A decline in the market has caused an excess capacity in all three plants amounting to 550, 650, and 300 units per day in plants 1, 2, and 3 respectively (regardless of shoe type). Even though there is excess capacity, there is an in-process inventory capacity limit because of physical layout limitations. These limitations, in turn, limit output rates. The three plants have available 1000, 850, and 400 square feet of storage space respectively. Shoe lines D, W, and S require 1.0, 1.5, and 0.8 equivalent square feet of storage respectively. Sales forecasts are 700, 850, and 750 respectively for shoe lines D, W, and S.

    Formulate a linear optimization model that will provide management with a program of how many of each shoe type to produce in each plant. The model must meet the constraints and maximize contribution.

17. The Appliance Manufacturing Company produces air conditioners (A), refrigerators (R), and electric stoves (S). The manufacturing facility needs for the three product lines are common in certain respects, which accounts for the fact that manufacturing costs are generally low. The facilities are composed of a machine shop, which fabricates a variety of parts needed in all three products; a metal stamping department, which stamps out a variety of sheet metal parts for all three products; a unit department, which produces the refrigeration units used in A and R; and independent assembly lines for each of the three products.

    Because some of the facilities are shared between the product lines, specifying their capacities posed a problem. The manufacturing manager finally resolved the difficulty by computing the limiting capacity of the machine shop if, for example, it were entirely devoted to each of the three products. He summarized these results in Table 11–7.

TABLE 11-7. **Capacities of Shop Facilities for Air Conditioners, Refrigerators, and Stoves**

	Department Capacity for:		
	Air Conditioners	Refrigerators	Stoves
Machine shop	6000	7000	8000
Stamping department	9000	5000	4000
Unit department	7000	6000	---
A Assembly	5000	---	---
R Assembly	---	4000	---
S Assembly	---	---	3000

TABLE 11-8. **Refinery and Market Data**

		Percentage of Optimal Throughput for Each Crude			
Crude	Delivered Price per Gallon (cents)	Regular Gas	High-Test Gas	Diesel Fuel	Fuel Oil
Oklahoma	14	30	10	40	20
West Texas	12	20	10	60	10
Wyoming	10	10	---	30	60
Pennsylvania	18	30	50	20	---
Present market requirement (gallons per hour)	---	20,000	15,000	28,000	33,000

The contribution rates for the three products were $60, $50, and $40 per unit respectively for A, R, and S. Also, the maximums that the marketing department estimated could be sold in the coming planning period were 4000, 3000, and 2000 respectively, for A, R, and S.

Formulate a linear optimization model designed to maximize contribution within the constraints under which the company must operate.

18. A refinery operating in Nebraska uses four crude oils: Oklahoma, West Texas, Wyoming, and Pennsylvania. These crudes have different delivered costs as indicated in Table 11-8. The refinery makes four basic end products: regular

gas, high-test gas, diesel fuel, and fuel oil. The catalytic cracking and reforming characteristics of the refinery dictate a limited and different input mix of the crude oils, as is also indicated in Table 11–8. For example, 30 percent of the Oklahoma crude must be used for regular gas, 10 percent for high-test gas, 40 percent for diesel fuel, and the remaining 20 percent for fuel oil.

The objective is to minimize crude oil costs, but meet market requirements. Let A, B, C, and D represent the number of gallons of crude oil from Oklahoma, West Texas, Wyoming, and Pennsylvania respectively that must be used per hour.

Formulate the refinery problem as a linear optimization model.

19. The Three Mines Company owns three different mines that produce an ore that, after being crushed, is graded into three classes: high, medium, and low grade. There is some demand for each grade of ore. The Three Mines Company has contracted to provide a smelting plant with 12 tons of high-grade, 8 tons of medium-grade, and 24 tons of low-grade ore per week. Operating costs are $180 per day for mine W, $200 per day for mine X, and $160 per day for mine Y.

The three mines have different capacities. Mine W produces 6, 3, and 4 tons per day of high-, medium-, and low-grade ores respectively. Mine X produces 3, 1, and 2 tons per day of the three ores, and Mine Y produces 1, 1, and 6 tons per day of the three ores.

How many days per week should each mine be operated to fill the orders and minimize operating costs? Let W, X, and Y represent the number of days per week each of the mines operates. Formulate the Three Mines Company's problem as a linear optimization model.

20. Mesa Plastics Company is a bulk producer of sheet plastic, which they sell in three sizes (thicknesses). They have two plants located on the same site. Plant B is of later design and was specifically built to produce sizes 1 and 2 economically, since these two sizes had the largest demand. However, plant B is less economical than A for size 3. Time requirements for the three products in the two plants and the variable hourly costs and time availability for plants A and B are shown in Table 11–9. Sales revenue and maximum demand for the three products are shown in Table 11–10. Management is considering how production should be allocated to the two plants for the upcoming period so as to maximize contribution.

A computer input and output for a linear optimization model is given in Figure 11–14. How do you interpret the results?

TABLE 11-9. **Time Requirements, Costs, and Capacities for the Mesa Plastics Company**

	Hours per 100 Pounds	
	Plant A	Plant B
Size 1	0.25	0.20
Size 2	0.40	0.25
Size 3	0.35	0.40
Variable costs per hour	$250	$300
Maximum available hours per week	100	100

TABLE 11-10. **Sales Revenue and Maximum Demand for the Mesa Plastics Company**

Size	Sales Revenue per 100 Pounds	Maximum Demand per Week (100s of pounds)
1	$100	310
2	$120	300
3	$150	125

21. The sensitivity analysis for the feed mix problem is shown in Figure 11–15. Using Figure 11–15 along with the computer input and solution shown in Figure 11–13, answer the following questions:
    a. Suppose that the federal requirement for ingredient 3 were lowered from 0.15 to 0.12. What would be the effect on the optimal solution? Would the cost of the feed increase or decrease? By how much?
    b. Suppose that the federal regulation for ingredient 2 were lowered from 0.1 to 0.05. Would the solution change? How do you know?
    c. Suppose the accountant of the firm rushes in with the news that the price of wheat has increased from $0.10 per pound to $0.12 per pound. Should the optimal mix for the feed be changed? How do you know?

```
                              MESA PLASTICS COMPANY
        MAXIMIZE OR MINIMIZE: MAX
        OBJECTIVE FUNCTION:  Z=37.5A1+40B1+20A2+45B2+62.5A3+30B3
        ENTER CONSTRAINT EQUATIONS,
        (001)  0.25A1+0.4A2+0.35A3≤100
        (002)  0.2B1+0.25B2+0.4B3≤100
        (003)  A1+B1≤310
        (004)  A2+B2≤300
        (005)  A3+B3≤125
        (006)
             LPRUN
                              MESA PLASTICS COMPANY
        THE OPTIMAL VALUE OF THE OBJECTIVE FUNCTION IS:  33250.000
                           THE VARIABLES IN THE SOLUTION ARE

        VARIABLE    A1     AT LEVEL    1.8500E2
                    B1                 1.2500E2
                    B2                 3.0000E2
                    A3                 1.2500E2
                    SLK1               1.0000E1

        DO YOU WISH SENSITIVITY ANALYSIS?   Y
                              SHADOW         LB           CURRENT         UB
        CONSTRAINT    1       0.0000E0       9.0000E1     1.0000E2        7.2370E75
                      2       1.2500E1       9.2000E1     1.0000E2        1.3700E2
                      3       3.7500E1       1.2500E2     3.1000E2        3.5000E2
                      4       4.1875E1       1.5200E2     3.0000E2        3.3200E2
                      5       6.2500E1       0.0000E2     1.2500E2        1.5375E2

        PRICE
                      A1                     2.0000E1     3.7500E1        4.0000E1
                      B1                     3.7500E1     4.0000E1        5.7500E1
                      A2                    -7.2370E75    2.0000E1        4.1875E1
                      B2                     2.3125E1     4.5000E1        7.2370E75
                      A3                     2.5000E1     6.2500E1        7.2370E75
                      B3                    -7.2370E75    3.0000E1        6.7500E1
        ">END<"
```

FIGURE 11-14. **Computer input and output for the Mesa Plastics Company**

```
        DO YOU WISH SENSITIVITY ANALYSIS?  YES
                              SHADOW         LB           CURRENT         UB
        CONSTRAINT    1       0.0000E0      -7.2370E75    1.0000E3        1.3750E3
                      2       0.0000E0      -7.2370E75    1.0000E3        1.6250E3
                      3       1.0000E-1      1.0000E3     1.5000E3        3.0000E3
                      4       0.0000E0      -7.2370E75    2.0000E3        2.2500E3
                      5       7.0000E-2      8.3333E3     1.0000E4        1.5000E4

        PRICE         W                      8.0000E-2    1.0000E-1       1.6000E-1
                      B                      9.0000E-2    1.2000E-1       7.2370E75
                      R                     -7.2370E75    8.0000E-2       1.0000E-1
```

FIGURE 11-15. **Sensitivity analysis for the feed mix problem**

References

1. Balintfy, J. L., "A Mathematical Programming System for Food Management Applications," *Interfaces,* Vol. 6, No. 1, Part 2, November 1975.
2. Buckley, J. W., M. R. Nagarai, D. L. Sharp, and J. W. Schenck, *Management Problem-Solving with APL,* Melville Publishing Co., Los Angeles, 1974.
3. Chappell, A. C., "Linear Programming Cuts Costs in Production of Animal Feeds," *Operational Research Quarterly,* Vol. 25, No. 1, March 1974; reprinted in *Readings in Management Science,* edited by E. Turban and N. P. Loomba, Business Publications, Dallas, Texas, 1976.
4. Charnes, A., and W. W. Cooper, *Management Models and Industrial Applications of Linear Programming,* Vols. 1 and 2, John Wiley & Sons, New York, 1961.
5. Daellenbach, H. G., and E. J. Bell, *User's Guide to Linear Programming,* Prentice-Hall, Englewood Cliffs, N.J., 1970.
6. Dantzig, G. B., *Linear Programming and Extensions,* Princeton University Press, Princeton, N.J., 1963.
7. Hillier, F. S., and G. J. Lieberman, *Introduction to Operations Research,* second edition, Holden-Day, San Francisco, 1974.
8. Lee, S. M., and L. J. Moore, "Optimizing Transportation Problems With Multiple Objectives," *AIIE Transactions,* Vol. 5, No. 4, December 1973, pp. 333–38.
9. Lyons, D. F., and V. A. Dodd, "The Mix-Feed Problem," *Operational Research,* North-Holland Publishing Co., Amsterdam, 1975.
10. Machol, R. E., *Elementary Systems Mathematics: Linear Programming for Business and the Social Sciences,* McGraw-Hill, New York, 1976.
11. Wagner, H. M., *Principles of Operations Research,* second edition, Prentice-Hall, Englewood Cliffs, N.J., 1975.

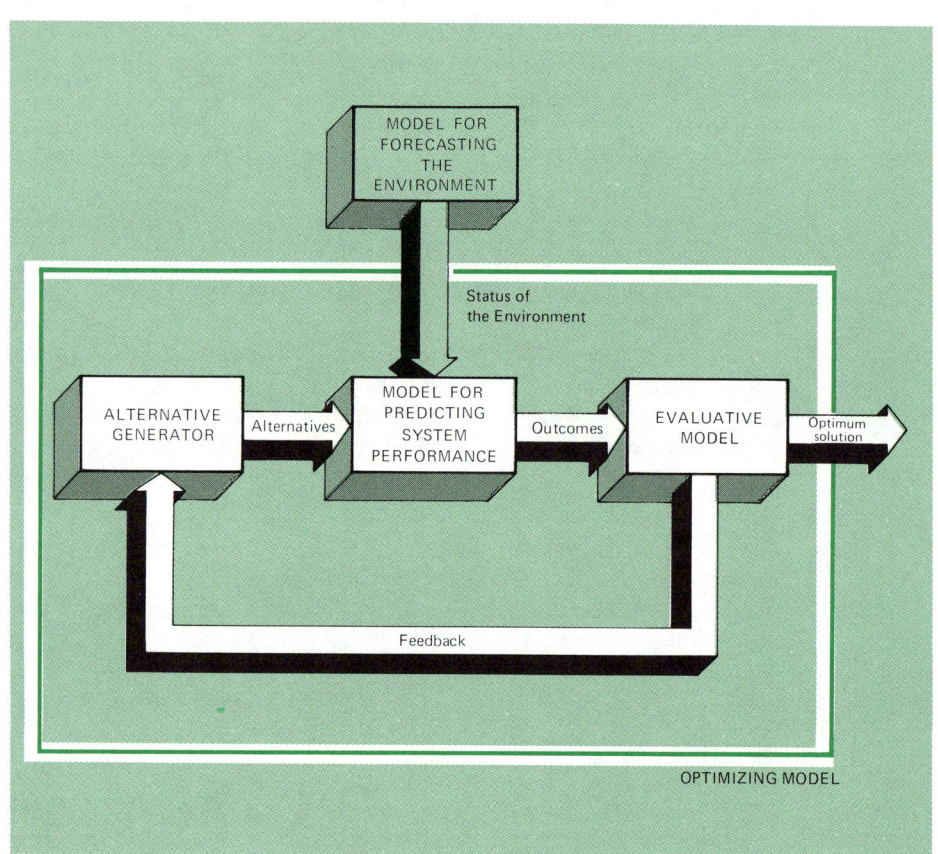

12

APPLICATIONS OF LINEAR OPTIMIZATION MODELS

Chapter 11 provided numerous examples of the use of linear optimization models to analyze production problems. Now let us think more broadly about the format of this model to see the range of problems that can be analyzed through its use. Such problems occur in profit and not-for-profit enterprises and in various organization functions such as finance, marketing, and personnel planning.

In this chapter, we give examples of applications of linear optimization models in a variety of situations. In order to avoid extraneous details, these examples have necessarily been simplified. However, real-world counterparts of each of them are in routine use.

We have categorized these examples into finance, marketing, personnel, and the not-for-profit sector. In studying these examples, you should be looking for the common threads in these applications that make them amenable to analysis by linear optimization models. This awareness will aid you in identifying potential applications of this powerful analytical tool in the real world.

LINEAR OPTIMIZATION MODELS FOR FINANCIAL DECISIONS

There are many financial decisions that can be successfully analyzed using linear optimization models. The general financing mix problem has been approached by linear optimization methods at various levels in organizations. At the overall enterprise level we can raise the question of the most profitable combination of financing sources, such as equity versus debt. Or, for the shorter term use of funds, we may ask what is the most profitable allocation of funds to accounts receivable, planned payments for purchases, cash needs for operation, and cash surplus from operations? Robichek, Teichroew, and Jones [1965] formulated linear optimization models in which the objective was to minimize net interest cost while meeting cash needs. The sources of short-term funds were pledges of accounts receivable at specific interest costs, stretched payments for purchases at a cost of loss of discounts, and short-term loans. There were constraints on the amounts of all sources. Smith [1974] has collected several examples of the use of linear optimization models for the management of working capital.

Through an extension of linear programming, Hughes and Lewellen [1974] have formulated the capital rationing problem in which limited capital funds are allocated to specific capital investment projects. The objective is to select from among the complete set of investment opportunities those projects that will provide the highest possible returns without exceeding the allowed budget.

A number of other applications are reviewed in the survey *Quantitative Analysis of Financial Decisions* by Mao [1969]. The examples presented here demonstrate how financial and production decisions can be integrated, and how portfolio selection and investment decisions can be analyzed.

Financing the Production Decision

In Chapter 11, we studied the linear optimization model for the chemical manufacturing firm that produces two products. This example shows how financial and production considerations for that firm can be integrated into a linear optimization model for production planning. The relevant production and financial data are summarized in Table 12-1. The firm also must pay fixed expenses of $400 in dividends and $500 on plant and equipment each month. The balance sheet for the firm at the end of December is shown in Table 12-2.

The company's two products are sold on terms of one month credit, but the variable costs of labor and materials must be paid immediately. For simplicity, we assume that the firm produces no more of each product than the monthly demand figure, so inventory is zero for both products.

The firm has a policy of maintaining a cash asset position of at least $5000 each month. In addition, the terms of the bond indenture require that the firm maintain a balance of at least $13,500 in short-term assets at all times (short-term assets are the sum of cash, accounts receivable, and inventory, or $14,000 at the end of December). How many units of each chemical product should the firm produce in January in order to maximize profits while observing these financial restrictions?

TABLE 12-1. **Data for the Chemical Manufacturing Company**

	Production			Financial		
	Product				Product	
	x	y			x	y
Machine A (hr)	2	4	Sales price		$350	$450
Machine B (hr)	3	2	Variable costs		290	400
Monthly demand (units)	16	18	Unit contribution to profit and overhead		60	50
Total Available Time (hr per mo)			Fixed cash expenses		$900	
Machine A	80					
Machine B	60					

TABLE 12-2. **Balance Sheet for Chemical Manufacturing Company (end of December)**

Cash assets	$ 7,000	Bank loan	$ 7,000
Accounts receivable	7,000	Long-term bonds	7,000
Inventory	0	Equity	10,000
Plant and equipment	10,000		$24,000
	$24,000		

Decision Variables As before, we let CHEMX be the number of units of chemical x produced in January, and CHEMY is the number of units of chemical y.

Objective Function The objective of the production plan is to maximize the contribution to profit and overhead:

maximize Z = 60 CHEMX + 50 CHEMY.

Constraints First, we have the same constraints on machine time and demand that were described in Chapter 11. For machine A,

2 CHEMX + 4 CHEMY ≤ 80,

and for machine B,

$$3\ CHEMX + 2\ CHEMY \leq 60.$$

The demand constraints are $CHEMX \leq 16$ and $CHEMY \leq 18$.

Now let us consider the additional financial constraints on the production decision. The cash asset position at the end of January must be at least \$5000. The beginning balance is \$7000, and the collection of the accounts receivable will add an additional \$7000, for a total of \$7000 + \$7000 = \$14,000 of available cash. However, the fixed cash expenses of \$900 per month and the variable costs of $290\ CHEMX + 400\ CHEMY$ must be paid in January, so we require

$$14{,}000 - 900 - 290\ CHEMX - 400\ CHEMY \geq 5000,$$

which simplifies to

$$290\ CHEMX + 400\ CHEMY \leq 8100.$$

The constraint on short term assets is developed in a similar manner. In January, the short term asset position of \$14,000 is reduced by the fixed cash expenses, \$900, and by the payment of the variable costs, $290\ CHEMX + 400\ CHEMY$. The asset position is increased, however, by the revenue generated by the sales of the products, or $350\ CHEMX + 450\ CHEMY$. In order to ensure that the short term asset position is at least \$13,500, the constraint

$$14{,}000 - 900 - 290\ CHEMX - 400\ CHEMY + 350\ CHEMX + 450\ CHEMY \geq 13{,}500$$

is needed. This simplifies to

$$60\ CHEMX + 50\ CHEMY \geq 400.$$

The computer input and solution for this formulation are shown in Figure 12-1. The linear optimization model is the input (a) and the solution is shown as (b). Notice that the optimal solution, $CHEMX = 12.58$ and $CHEMY = 11.13$, differs from the solution determined in Chapter 11. This is because of constraint [5] on the cash position of the firm. The interpretation of this result and an examination of the sensitivity analysis are presented in exercise 1.

Formulation of a Portfolio Selection Problem

The selection of an investment portfolio is a common problem. The objective is to maximize expected returns, but this objective is often constrained by policies that require diversification of investments. Suppose we are managing a portfolio and are dealing in four types of securities: the electronics industry, utilities, financial institutions, and the chemical industry. Data on permissible percentages of the portfolio to be invested and current expected yields are shown in Table 12-3.

```
            LPENTER
ENTER THE NAME OF THIS PROJECT  FINANCING THE PRODUCTION DECISION
MAXIMIZE OR MINIMIZE: MAXIMIZE
OBJECTIVE FUNCTION:Z=60CHEMX+50CHEMY
ENTER CONSTRAINT EQUATIONS, (STRIKE JUST A CARRIAGE RETURN TO STOP INPUT)
  (1) 2CHEMX+4CHEMY≤80
  (2) 3CHEMX+2CHEMY≤60
  (3) CHEMX≤16
  (4) CHEMY≤18
  (5) 290CHEMX+400CHEMY≤8100
  (6) 60CHEMX+50CHEMY≥400
  (7)
                                  (A)
      LPRUN
                       FINANCING THE PRODUCTION DECISION

THE OPTIMAL VALUE OF THE OBJECTIVE FUNCTION IS:       1311.290

                        THE VARIABLES IN THE SOLUTION ARE
   VARIABLE  CHEMX  AT LEVEL   1.2581E1
             CHEMY             1.1129E1
             SLK1              1.0323E1
             SLK3              3.4194E0
             SLK4              6.8710E0
             SUR6              9.1129E2
                                  (B)
```

FIGURE 12-1. **Production problem with financial constraints: (a) computer input and (b) computer solution**

In addition, the electronics and financial industries are considered to be relatively high risk investments, so we require that the total percentage of the portfolio invested in both of them should be less than or equal to 40. Further, we wish to ensure that the investment in utilities should be at least 50 percent of the total investment in electronics and financial securities.

Decision Variables The decision variables are the proportions of the portfolio to be invested in each of the four types of securities—E, U, F, and C.

TABLE 12-3. **Permissible Investment Limits and Current Yields**

Type of Security	Limits (%)		Expected Yield (%)
	Minimum	Maximum	
Electronics (E)	10	30	12
Utilities (U)	15	---	8
Financial (F)	5	20	10
Chemicals (C)	20	35	9

Objective Function The objective is to maximize the total yield. Therefore, we wish to maximize the proportion of the fund in electronics, E, times the yield for these securities, 0.12, plus similar terms for each of the other security types. Stated in mathematical terms, we have

$$\text{maximize } Z = 0.12E + 0.08U + 0.10F + 0.09C.$$

Constraints The decision variables represent proportions, so they should sum to 1.0. Thus, our first constraint is

$$E + U + F + C = 1.0.$$

Next, we need constraints to enforce the minimum and maximum restrictions on the investment in each type of security, as shown in Table 12-3. For the electronics industry we can simply write $E \geq 0.1$ and $E \leq 0.3$ to reflect these requirements. Similar constraints can be written for the other three security types.

Also, the total investment in the electronics and financial securities must be less than or equal to 0.4, which is guaranteed by the constraint

$$E + F \leq 0.4.$$

Finally, the investment in utilities must be at least 50 percent of this total. That is, we must have

$$U \geq 0.5 (E + F),$$

which can be written as

$$0.5E + 0.5F - U \leq 0.$$

The complete formulation of this problem is shown in Table 12-4. The computer input, solution, and the sensitivity analysis are presented in exercise 2.

Investment Planning

This example illustrates how linear optimization models can be used to analyze investment decisions over several time periods. The manager of Sophisticated Investments, Inc., has four investment opportunities to consider for the next three years. The investments differ in terms of availability, duration, rate of return, and the maximum allowable investment. The relevant data are summarized in Table 12-5. The firm can invest up to $500,000 in an apartment house (A) at the beginning of the second year, but must then hold it for the remaining two years of the planning horizon. The government bonds (B) are considered a safe investment and can be purchased each year. The municipal bonds (C) will be available at the beginning of the third year and can be held for only one year, but the firm wishes to invest no more than $500,000 in them.

Finally, the mutual funds (D) can be purchased now, but they must be held for exactly two years. The amount of the mutual fund investment is unlimited.

The manager would like to invest $1 million so that the return over the three-year planning horizon will be maximized. The total funds available at the beginning of year 2 will be the amount invested in the government bonds plus its interest payment. The total available at the beginning of year 3 will be the amount invested in government bonds in year 2 plus its interest payment and the amount invested in the mutual fund plus its interest payment.

TABLE 12-4. **Linear Optimization Model for the Portfolio Selection Problem**

maximize $Z = 0.12E + 0.08U + 0.10F + 0.09C$

subject to

proportions	$E + U + F + C = 1.0$
minimum limit on E	$E \geq 0.1$
maximum limit on E	$E \leq 0.3$
minimum limit on U	$U \geq 0.15$
minimum limit on F	$F \geq 0.05$
maximum limit on F	$F \leq 0.2$
minimum limit on C	$C \geq 0.2$
maximum limit on C	$C \leq 0.35$
limit on sum	$E + F \leq 0.4$
limit on U	$0.5E - U + 0.5F \leq 0$
	$E, U, F, C \geq 0$

TABLE 12-5. **Investment Opportunities for Sophisticated Investments, Inc.,**

Investment	Available	Duration	Projected Annual Rate of Return	Investment Limitations
Apartment house (A)	At beginning of second year	Two years	0.15	Maximum of $500,000
Government bonds (B)	Now	Renewable each year	0.09	Unlimited
Municipal bonds (C)	At beginning of third year	One year	0.10	Maximum of $500,000
Mutual fund (D)	Now	Two years	0.12	Unlimited

Decision Variables The decisions are the investments to be made in opportunities A, B, C, and D at the beginnings of years 1, 2, and 3. Therefore, we define A2 as the investment in the apartment house (A) in year 2. Also, B1, B2, and B3 are the investments in the government bonds in each of the three years, C3 is the investment in municipal bonds in year 3, and D1 is the mutual fund investment in year 1.

Objective Function The objective is to maximize the total return from the investments over a three-year period. For example, the annual rate of return from the apartment house investment is 15 percent, or 0.15 A2 in years 2 and 3 (recall from Table 12-5 that this investment must be held for two years). Thus, the total return from the apartment house would be (2)(0.15) A2, or 0.3 A2. (For simplicity we ignore the compounding of interest.) Verify that the appropriate objective function is

    maximize Z = 0.3 A2 + 0.09 B1 + 0.09 B2 + 0.09 B3 + 0.1 C3 + 0.24 D1.

Constraints The only investment opportunities at the beginning of year 1 are the government bond and the mutual fund. Since $1 million are available for investment at this time,

    B1 + D1 = 1,000,000,

and both of these investments are otherwise unlimited in amount.

At the beginning of the second year, the apartment house opportunity is available (A2), along with the government bonds (B2). The money available for the investment is the amount invested in government bonds in year 1, B1, plus interest, 0.09 B1, for a total of 1.09 B1. Thus,

    A2 + B2 = 1.09 B1.

The constraint

    A2 ≤ 500,000

enforces the limitation on the apartment investment.

In year 3, the investment opportunities are government bonds (B3) and municipal bonds (C3). The available cash is from the government bond investment in year 2 plus interest of 9 percent, and from the mutual fund investment in year 1 plus two years of interest accumulation for a total of 24 percent. Thus,

    B3 + C3 = 1.09 B2 + 1.24 D1

The limitation on the investment in municipal bonds is enforced by

    C3 ≤ 500,000.

The complete problem formulation is shown in Table 12-6. The interpretation of the computer solution is the subject of exercise 3.

TABLE 12-6. **Formulation of the Investment Planning Model**

maximize $Z = 0.3\ A2 + 0.09\ B1 + 0.09\ B2 + 0.09\ B3$
$\qquad + 0.1\ C3 + 0.24\ D1$
subject to $\qquad\qquad\qquad B1 + D1 = 1{,}000{,}000$

$\qquad\qquad A2 + B2 - 1.09\ B1 = 0$

$\qquad\qquad\qquad\qquad\qquad A2 \leq 500{,}000$

$\qquad B3 + C3 - 1.09\ B2 - 1.24\ D1 = 0$

$\qquad\qquad\qquad\qquad\qquad C3 \leq 500{,}000$

$\qquad\qquad A2, B1, B2, B3, C3, D1 \geq 0$

LINEAR OPTIMIZATION MODELS FOR MARKETING DECISIONS

A wide range of marketing problems are candidates for analysis with linear optimization models. One classical allocation problem is selecting media for a limited promotion and advertising budget. Although the simple linear optimization model formulation of this problem has some serious limitations, it does provide a basis for bootstrapping into the more complex models that are in use for analyzing these decisions today.

Retailing and sales force management models are also important for managers of the marketing function. For example, models may be used to determine the optimum size of a sales force and to divide geographical regions into equitable sales territories.

Product transportation and distribution networks are now routinely analyzed by linear optimization models and their extensions. Since applications of these distribution models are so commonplace, we devote Chapter 14 to a review of them.

Aaker's survey [1973] of the applications of management science in marketing includes a discussion of several linear optimization models. Kotler [1971] also summarizes many of these studies. The following examples deal with the media selection problem and the determination of sales territories.

Advertising Media Selection

The independent party of Democrats and Republicans has a limited budget of only $600,000 to spend in promoting their candidate. They wish to maximize the exposure of their candidate within the limited budget through the media (magazines, newspapers, radio, and television). They have obtained data on the costs, exposure ratings per unit, and the number of voters reached per unit for each media type, as shown in Table 12-7.

TABLE 12-7. **Costs and Exposure Ratings for Media**

Media	Cost per Advertising Unit	No. of Voters Reached per Unit	Exposure Rating per Unit
Magazines (M)	$20,000	10,000	100
Newspapers (N)	15,000	30,000	400
Radio (R)	5,000	20,000	200
Television			
Prime time (TVP)	40,000	35,000	600
Other (TVO)	10,000	15,000	150

The exposure rating per unit is a subjective measure of the effectiveness of an advertising message in each media. It takes into account the profile of the voters reached by each media (age, income, political party, etc.) and the impact of the message as presented through the media.

After examining the exposure rating data, the campaign manager states: "We obviously should put the entire $600,000 into TV advertising on prime time." Campaign committee members object, however, feeling that this approach is too risky and may not reach some important kinds of voters. The committee then agrees that no more than $250,000 will be spent on any single medium, such as TV. They also feel that no more than $350,000 should be spent on the two printed media, magazines and newspapers. Further, they specify that the budget for the radio advertisement should be at least 25 percent of the total TV budget, and that the nonprime time TV budget (TVO) should be at least 50 percent of the prime time budget (TVP). They also wish to ensure that they reach at least 250,000 voters. The committee agrees that their objective is to maximize the total exposure rating of the messages.

Decision Variables The decision variables are the numbers of advertising units for each of the targeted media — M, N, R, TVP, and TVO.

Objective Function The stated objective is to maximize the sum of the exposure ratings per unit. The aggregate exposure rating for magazine units will be 100M, using the exposure rating per unit data in Table 12-7. The function that the committee wishes to maximize is the sum of the aggregate ratings for each of the media, or,

maximize $Z = 100M + 400N + 200R + 600TVP + 150TVO$.

Constraints The first constraint is on the total budget of $600,000. From Table 12-7 we see that the total amount spent for magazine advertising would be 20M, in thousands of dollars. The total budget constraint is then

$20M + 15N + 5R + 40TVP + 10TVO \leq 600.$

Budget constraints on each of the media must also be formulated to ensure that no more than $250,000 is spent on it. For example, the constraint for magazines is

$20M \leq 250.$

The constraints for the other media are similar, except that we must aggregate the two kinds of TV time; that is, we must have

$40TVP + 10TVO \leq 250.$

The committee wishes to ensure that no more than $350,000 is spent on the printed media, so

$20M + 15N \leq 350.$

Further, they also require that the radio budget be at least 25 percent of the total television budget, so

$5R \geq 0.25(40TVP + 10TVO).$

This constraint simplifies to

$5R - 10TVP - 2.5TVO \geq 0.$

The nonprime time TV budget must be at least 50 percent of the prime time budget, so

$10TVO \geq 0.5(40TVP).$

Finally, they wish to reach 250,000 voters, so from Table 12-7,

$10M + 30N + 20R + 35TVP + 15TVO \geq 250.$

The complete formulation of this problem is shown in Table 12-8. The computer input and output are presented as part of exercise 4. Engle and Warshaw [1964] and Bass and Lonsdale [1966] discuss more sophosticated approaches to modeling the media selection problem for actual applications.

Determination of Sales Territories

A company has two salesmen, Able and Baker, who must serve customers in six different geographic sales zones. A map of the area and the six sales zones is shown in Figure 12-2. The number in parentheses in each sales zone is the number of customers or accounts in the zone. For example, there are 20 customers to be served in zone 1. Salesman Able currently lives in zone 5, and

TABLE 12-8. **Formulation of the Advertising Media Selection Problem**

maximize $Z = 100\,M + 400\,N + 200\,R + 600\,TVP + 150\,TVO$

subject to

$$20\,M + 15\,N + 5\,R + 40\,TVP + 10\,TVO \leq 600$$
$$20\,M \leq 250$$
$$15\,N \leq 250$$
$$5\,R \leq 250$$
$$40\,TVP + 10\,TVO \leq 250$$
$$20\,M + 15\,N \leq 350$$
$$5\,R - 10\,TVP - 2.5\,TVO \geq 0$$
$$10\,TVO - 20\,TVP \geq 0$$
$$10\,M + 30\,N + 20\,R + 35\,TVP + 15\,TVO \geq 250$$
$$M, N, R, TVO, TVP \geq 0$$

salesman Baker lives in zone 3. The company wishes to assign some proportion of the customers in each zone to each salesman. In making this assignment, the company wishes to equalize the numbers of customers assigned to each salesman and to assign a salesman districts that are close to his home in order to minimize his travel time.

Decision Variables We can let $XA1$ be the *proportion* of the customers in zone 1 assigned to Able (A), and $XB1$ be the proportion assigned to Baker (B). Looking ahead to the constraints, we will require that $XA1 + XB1 = 1.0$, so that if $XA1 = 0.4$, then $XB1 = 0.6$. Since there are 20 customers in zone 1, if $XA1 = 0.4$ and $XB1 = 0.6$, then $(0.4)(20) = 8$ would be assigned to Able and $(0.6)(20) = 12$ to Baker.

Two similar decision variables would be required for each of zones 2 through 6, so that a total of twelve decision variables are needed.

Objective Function The objective is to assign these customers so that the travel time is minimized. Since travel time generally depends on distance, we can focus on the distance from each salesman's home to the center of each sales zone. The center of each sales zone is approximated by a dot as shown in Figure 12-2. For simplicity, we assume that Able and Baker live in the center of zones 5 and 3 respectively.

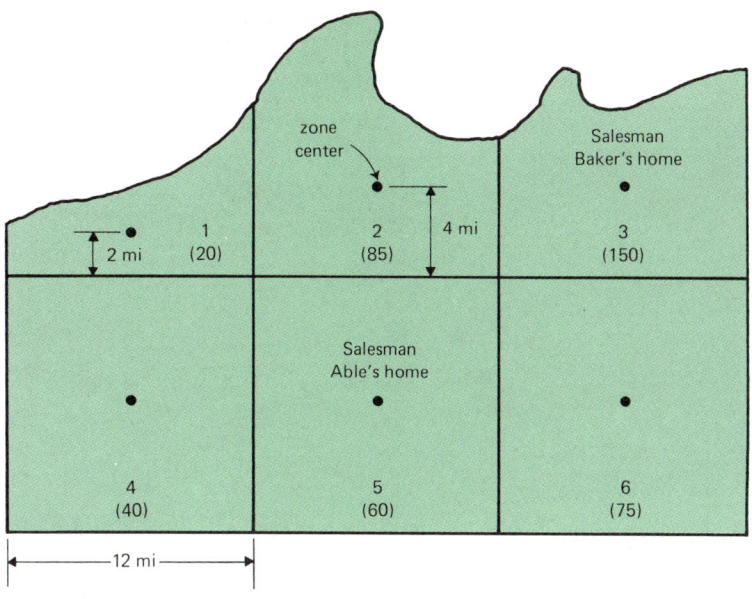

FIGURE 12-2. **Map of Sales area to be Divided between Able and Baker**

Travel between two points is seldom in a straight line, especially in populated areas. We generally move in east-west and north-south directions according to routes determined by rectangular city blocks. Therefore, we will measure the distances in Figure 12-2 according to east-west and north-south distances. For example, to get to the center of zone 1, Able must travel 12 miles west and 8 miles north. Finally, in order to place a severe penalty on long distances, we will square both the east-west distance and the north-south distance, and sum the result as a measure of how far each zone is from each salesman. Thus, the squared rectangular distance from Able's residence to zone 1 is $(12)^2 + (8)^2 = 208$. The squared rectangular distances from Able and Baker to the other zones are shown in Table 12-9.

For the objective function, we will minimize the sum of the squared rectangular distances multiplied by the proportion of the customers in each zone seen by each salesman. That is, we

$$\begin{aligned}
\text{minimize } Z = &\text{ the squared rectangular} & = 208\,XA1 + 100\,XA2 + 244\,XA3 \\
&\text{ distances for Able} & + 144\,XA4 + 0\,XA5 + 144\,XA6 \\
&\text{ plus the squared rectangular} & = 580\,XB1 + 144\,XB2 + 0\,XB3 \\
&\text{ distances for Baker} & + 676\,XB4 + 244\,XB5 + 100\,XB6.
\end{aligned}$$

Notice that minimizing the *squared* rectangular distances does not violate our requirement that the relationships be linear because these squared distances are

CHAPTER 12 APPLICATIONS OF LINEAR OPTIMIZATION MODELS

TABLE 12-9. **Squared Rectangular Distances in Sales Territories**

	From:	
To District	Able	Baker
1	$(12)^2 + (8)^2 = 208$	$(24)^2 + (2)^2 = 580$
2	$(0)^2 + (10)^2 = 100$	$(12)^2 + (0)^2 = 144$
3	$(12)^2 + (10)^2 = 244$	$(0)^2 + (0)^2 = 0$
4	$(12)^2 + (0)^2 = 144$	$(24)^2 + (10)^2 = 676$
5	$(0)^2 + (0)^2 = 0$	$(12)^2 + (10)^2 = 244$
6	$(12)^2 + (0)^2 = 144$	$(0)^2 + (10)^2 = 100$

merely coefficients in a linear expression. None of the decision variables are squared.

Constraints The constraints are very simple. As mentioned previously, since $XA1$ and $XB1$ are the proportions of the customers in zone 1 assigned to Able and Baker respectively, we require that $XA1 + XB1 = 1.0$. We need similar constraints for zones 2 through 6.

Finally, the total number of customers in the six zones is $20 + 85 + 150 + 40 + 60 + 75 = 430$. Dividing these equally, we wish to assign 215 customers to each salesman. Since the decision variables are the proportions of the customers in each zone assigned to each salesman, this constraint is written as

$$20\ XA1 + 85\ XA2 + 150\ XA3 + 40\ XA4 + 60\ XA5 + 75\ XA6 = 215$$

for salesman Able. Since exactly 215 customers are assigned to salesman Able by this constraint, then $430 - 215 = 215$ will also be assigned automatically to Baker. Therefore, we do not require a similar constraint for salesman Baker, even though including it in our formulation would do no harm.

The complete problem formulation is shown in Table 12–10. The computer solution and its interpretation are the subject of exercise 5.

Hess and Samuels [1971] provide additional details regarding the sales districting model and discuss its use by a major pharmaceutical company, CIBA, to determine sales territories, and by IBM to determine service territories for typewriter servicemen. More recently, Standard Oil of Indiana has used a variant of this approach to determine sales territories. It has also been used to define police patrol areas in cities (see Heller, Markland, and Brockelmeyer [1971]). Also of interest is the use of this model to determine legislative districts consistent with the "one man-one vote" Supreme Court decision. This reapportionment

TABLE 12-10. **Linear Optimization Model for Determining Sales Territories**

minimize $Z = 208\, XA1 + 100\, XA2 + 244\, XA3 + 144\, XA4 + 0\, XA5 + 144\, XA6$
$+ 580\, XB1 + 144\, XB2 + 0\, XB3 + 676\, XB4 + 244\, XB5 + 100\, XB6$

subject to

$$XA1 + XB1 = 1$$
$$XA2 + XB2 = 1$$
$$XA3 + XB3 = 1$$
$$XA4 + XB4 = 1$$
$$XA5 + XB5 = 1$$
$$XA6 + XB6 = 1$$
$$20\, XA1 + 85\, XA2 + 150\, XA3 + 40\, XA4 + 60\, XA5 + 75\, XA6 = 215$$
$$XA1, XA2, XA3, XA4, XA5, XA6, XB1, XB2, XB3, XB4, XB5, XB6 \geq 0$$

analysis was originally made for the state of Delaware, and the model has since been used in other states and countries [Hess et al., 1965].

LINEAR OPTIMIZATION MODELS FOR PERSONNEL PLANNING DECISIONS

Linear optimization models can be used to schedule employee work hours on a short-term basis and to determine personnel needs over a longer planning horizon. The latter analysis provides the basis for employee recruitment and training programs. Charnes, Cooper, and Niehaus [1972] report on the extensive use of linear optimization models for personnel planning in the navy. Charnes, Cooper, Lewis, and Niehaus [1975] also describe how these models may be used to assist in meeting equal employment opportunity goals. Models for this same purpose are under development in major corporations. Linear optimization models have also been used to determine equitable executive compensation plans (see Charnes, Cooper, and Ferguson [1955]). Here we present a simple model for scheduling work shifts and a long-term model for planning staffing activities.

Nurse Scheduling

Nurses at the Good Samaritan Hospital come on duty every four hours and work eight-hour shifts. Management has found this idea of six staggered shifts to be more effective in minimizing the disruption and communication problems that occur when a shift is changed.

The hospital has also done an analysis of the work required during each of the six four-hour periods of the day. This varies from period to period as follows:

Time of Day	Period	Minimum Number of Nurses Required per Period
2 A.M.– 6 A.M.	1	25
6 A.M.–10 A.M.	2	60
10 A.M.– 2 P.M.	3	50
2 P.M.– 6 P.M.	4	35
6 P.M.–10 P.M.	5	55
10 P.M.– 2 A.M.	6	40

Each nurse works for eight consecutive hours. Nurses who begin work in periods 2, 3, and 4 are paid $40 per day, and those beginning in periods 1, 5, and 6 are paid $50 per day to compensate for the inconvenient hours. How many nurses should be scheduled to begin work each period in order to minimize the daily payroll costs?

Decision Variables The decision variables are the number of nurses beginning work in each of the six periods, which we define as $N1$, $N2$, $N3$, $N4$, $N5$, and $N6$.

Objective Function We wish to minimize daily payroll costs, so we

minimize $Z = 50\ N1 + 40\ N2 + 40\ N3 + 40\ N4 + 50\ N5 + 50\ N6$.

Constraints The constraints for this problem simply enforce the minimum personnel requirements. The total number of nurses available during period 2 must be at least 60. This total is equal to the number of nurses beginning work in period 1 plus the number that go on duty at 6:00 A.M. in period 2. That is, we require

$N1 + N2 \geq 60$.

The other constraints are similar. For example, the total number of nurses on duty during period 3, $N2 + N3$, must be at least 50, so

$N2 + N3 \geq 50$

is the second constraint. Test your understanding by writing down the other four constraints.

The complete problem formulation is shown in Table 12–11. The computer solution and the sensitivity analysis are discussed in exercise 6.

TABLE 12-11. **Nurse Scheduling for Good Samaritan Hospital**

$$\text{minimize } Z = 50\,N1 + 40\,N2 + 40\,N3 + 40\,N4 + 50\,N5 + 50\,N6$$

subject to
$$N1 + N2 \geq 60$$
$$N2 + N3 \geq 50$$
$$N3 + N4 \geq 35$$
$$N4 + N5 \geq 55$$
$$N5 + N6 \geq 40$$
$$N1 + N6 \geq 25$$
$$N1, N2, N3, N4, N5, N6 \geq 0$$

Personnel Planning and Scheduling

The employees in the manufacturing department of a major company are classified as machinists. A three-month production forecast indicates that 4000 hours of machinist time will be required in January, 4500 in February, and 4200 in March. The department has 30 machinists available on January 1, and each worker averages 150 hours of productive work each month.

Newly hired machinists must be trained for one month before being able to contribute any productive hours. This training is conducted by an experienced machinist and requires 75 worker-hours of time, so that the total productive pool of worker-hours is reduced. Each month there is a turnover rate of 10 percent among the machinists, since some quit and others are transferred to other positions in the company.

If excess worker-hours are available in a month, workers are assigned to maintenance activities rather than being laid off. A machinist makes $1200 per month, and a trainee makes $1000 during the month of training. How many trainees must be hired in January and February in order to meet the three-month personnel forecast and yet minimize the total payroll cost in the department?

Decision Variables The obvious decision variables for this problem are *TRAINJ* and *TRAINF*, the number of trainees hired in January and February respectively. In addition, we need to define decision variables for the number of machinists available for work in February and March, *MACHF* and *MACHM*.

Objective Function The objective is to minimize the payroll costs for the trainees hired in January and for the machinists and trainees in February and March. This objective is accomplished by

minimize $Z = 1000\,TRAINJ + 1200\,MACHF + 1000\,TRAINF + 1200\,MACHM$.

Notice that we do not include in the objective function the cost of ($1200)(30) = $36,000 for the 30 machinists available in January because we have no control over this value. This cost may be ignored as a fixed cost, since it would not affect the solution.

Constraints Each machinist contributes, on the average, 150 productive hours per month and 4000 are required in January. However, each trainee hired in January will demand 75 productive hours in the training program. Since 30 machinists are available on January 1, we must have

$$(30)(150) - 75\ TRAINJ \geq 4000$$

or, after subtracting 4000 from both sides of the inequality and rearranging,

$$75\ TRAINJ \leq 500.$$

The number of machinists available in February, MACHF, is equal to 90 percent of the work force in January, because of the turnover, plus the number of trainees hired in January. Therefore, we write,

$$(30)(0.9) + TRAINJ = MACHF$$

as another constraint. In order to meet the worker-hour requirement in February,

$$150\ MACHF - 75\ TRAINF \geq 4500.$$

Test your understanding by writing down the two constraints needed for March.

TABLE 12–12. **Linear Optimization Model for Personnel Planning**

$$\text{minimize } Z = 1000\ TRAINJ + 1200\ MACHF + 1000\ TRAINF + 1200\ MACHM$$

subject to
$$75\ TRAINJ \leq 500$$
$$MACHF - TRAINJ = 27$$
$$150\ MACHF - 75\ TRAINF \geq 4500$$
$$MACHM - TRAINF - 0.9\ MACHF = 0$$
$$150\ MACHM \geq 4200$$
$$TRAINJ, MACHF, TRAINF, MACHM \geq 0$$

The complete formulation for this problem is shown in Table 12–12. The interpretation of the computer solution is the subject of exercise 7.

LINEAR OPTIMIZATION MODELS IN THE PUBLIC AND NOT-FOR-PROFIT SECTOR

Linear optimization models have been applied to many managerial problems in the public and not-for-profit sectors. For example, in the health care field Revelle, Feldmann, and Lynn [1969] have developed a mathematical model that predicts future states of the disease tuberculosis. Controls in the form of therapy, vaccinations, or prophylaxis may be superimposed on the actual processes, thus altering the future course of the disease. Linear programming is used to select the forms of control that achieve specific reductions at minimum cost. Sensitivity analysis can then be used to determine the marginal cost of an even greater reduction in the future disease level.

Linear programming has also been applied to the problem of integrating public schools, as reported by Franklin and Koenigsberg [1973]. The objective function and constraints in their models can be modified so that the solution of each formulation provides a policy or point of view. The authors emphasize that school authorities, judges, and the public can see the logical implications of each point of view and select school assignment plans on a rational basis. Notice that there is not even a hint that the purpose of the linear programming models is to provide *the answer*. Rather its purpose is to generate the consequences in terms of costs and school assignments of different levels of desegregation and of different approaches. The selection of the best approach is still a matter for the school authorities, the judges, and the public to decide.

Problems of the environment have also been studied by using linear programming. Glassey and Gupta [1974] have developed a linear model of the production, use, and recycling of various paper and related products. The linear programming analysis indicates that if 70 percent of the potentially recoverable paper had been recycled in 1970, the annual virgin pulp consumption could have been reduced from 45 million tons to 28 million tons (or by 38 percent). The reduction in the annual cost of collecting and disposing of solid waste would have been approximately $238 million, which presumably could be used to offset the cost of collecting and processing wastepaper. In a related study, Ignall, Kolesar, and Walker [1972] used a linear optimization model to improve crew assignments for solid waste collection.

Several of our previous examples involved elements of the public and not-for-profit sector. The media selection formulation was placed in the context of "selling" a political candidate rather than a new product. The formulation of the nurse scheduling problem remains unchanged for a public, not-for-profit, or private hospital. To further demonstrate the breadth of the applications of linear optimization models, we present an application in urban planning and a school desegregation model.

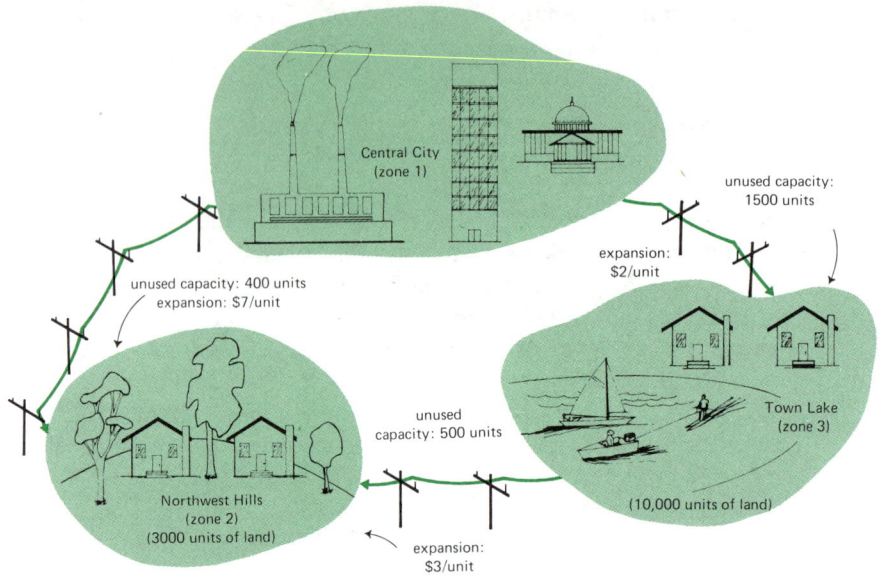

FIGURE 12-3. **Network of existing electrical lines in Capital City**

Land-Use Allocation

Capital City is undergoing a period of rapid urban development. The new growth in the city is restricted to two planning zones, Northwest Hills (zone 2) and Town Lake (zone 3). The central city (zone 1) is overcrowded, and there is no available land for further expansion.

The three zones are linked by networks of electrical lines as illustrated in Figure 12-3. The arrows alongside the lines indicate the direction of flow of the utility. For example, electrical power can flow from the central city to Northwest Hills, but not vice versa. Also shown on Figure 12-3 is the unused capacity available on each of these lines. For example, an additional 400 units of electrical power could be transmitted from the central city (zone 1) to Northwest Hills (zone 2). The capacity in each of these utility lines can be expanded at a unit cost also shown in Figure 12-3. The additional electrical transmission capacity from zone 1 to zone 2 can be increased above 400 units for $7 per unit (all units have been conveniently scaled). Also, as shown in Figure 12-3, there are 3000 units of available land in Northwest Hills and 10,000 units of available land in Town Lake.

The city expects to have 600 new residential developments and 400 new industrial developments over the next ten years. Each new residential development requires 7 units of land, and 2 units of electricity. Each new industrial development requires 9 units of land and 3 units of electricity.

346   PART IV OPTIMIZING MODELS

The city can control the growth by issuing permits for the developments in each zone. How many units of each type (residential and industrial) should the city allow to be developed in each zone (2 and 3) in order to minimize the costs of expanding the existing utility lines?

Decision Variables The decisions are the numbers of developments of each type that should be allowed in each zone over the next ten years. We define $R2$ and $R3$ as the units of residential development (R) in each of zones 2 and 3. Similarly, $I2$ and $I3$ are the units of industrial development (I) in each of the respective zones.

On each of the existing utility lines there is some unused capacity. We can let $UC12$ represent the number of units of electrical power transmitted from zone 1 to zone 2 through the unused (U) capacity (C) of 400 units. In a similar manner, $UC13$ is the electrical transmission on the unused capacity from zone 1 to zone 3, and $UC32$ is the transmission on the unused capacity from zone 3 to zone 2.

We also need to define variables representing any expansions (X) of the capacities (C) of the electrical lines. Suppose we let $XC12$ represent the number of units of expansion (X) required on the electrical line from zone 1 to zone 2. In a similar manner, we define $XC13$ and $XC32$. No new utility lines are to be considered.

Objective Function From the point of view of the city, the objective is to minimize any costs of expanding the existing electrical lines. Using the expansion costs from Figure 12-3, the city wishes to

minimize $Z = 7\ XC12 + 2\ XC13 + 3\ XC32$.

Constraints We assume that the 600 new residential units and the 400 new industrial units will be developed. Therefore, we have

$R2 + R3 = 600$

and

$I2 + I3 = 400$.

Next we must consider the available land in each zone. Since each unit of new residential development requires 7 units of land, and each new industrial development requires 9 units of land, we must have

$7\ R2 + 9\ I2 \leq 3000$

because there are only 3000 units of available land in zone 2. Similarily, we have

$7\ R3 + 9\ I3 \leq 10{,}000$

for zone 3.

Now let us focus on the electrical power lines. In zone 2, any new developments will generate a demand for additional units of electrical power. This power must flow into zone 2 on the line from zone 1 to zone 2, on the line from zone 3 to zone 2, or on both. Thus, we can write a constraint for zone 2 in words as follows:

$$\begin{pmatrix} \text{additional demand} \\ \text{for power in zone 2} \end{pmatrix} = \begin{pmatrix} \text{total additional flow} \\ \text{from zone 1 into zone 2} \end{pmatrix} + \begin{pmatrix} \text{total additional flow} \\ \text{from zone 3 into zone 2} \end{pmatrix}.$$

Since each unit of residential development requires 2 units of electricity, and each unit of industrial development requires 3 units of electricity, the additional demand for power in zone 2 will be $2\,R2 + 3\,I2$. The number of additional units of electrical power that actually flow from zone 1 into zone 2 on the unused capacity of 400 units is $UC12$. However, the capacity on the line from zone 1 to zone 2 can be expanded by $XC12$, so the *total* additional flow on this line is given by $UC12 + XC12$. Similarly, the total additional flow of electrical power on the line from zone 3 to zone 2 is given by $UC32 + XC32$, where the unused capacity $UC32$ must be less than or equal to 500 units. The electrical power constraint for zone 2 becomes

$$2\,R2 + 3\,I2 = UC12 + XC12 + UC32 + XC32,$$

and the limitations on the unused capacity shown in Figure 12-3 are enforced by

$$UC12 \leq 400$$

and

$$UC32 \leq 500.$$

Notice that electrical power may flow from zone 3 into zone 2. Therefore, the additional power flowing into zone 3 from zone 1 must equal the additional demand for power generated by new developments in zone 3 *plus* the additional flow from zone 3 into zone 2. Again, writing this constraint in words, we have

$$\begin{pmatrix} \text{additional demand} \\ \text{for power in zone 3} \end{pmatrix} + \begin{pmatrix} \text{total additional flow} \\ \text{from zone 3 into zone 2} \end{pmatrix} = \begin{pmatrix} \text{total additional flow} \\ \text{from zone 1 into zone 3} \end{pmatrix}.$$

The additional demand for power in zone 3 is given by $2\,R3 + 3\,I3$, and the electrical power transmitted from zone 3 into zone 2 is $UC32 + XC32$. The total additional flow of power from zone 1 into zone 3 is given by $UC13 + XC13$. The constraint is

$$2\,R3 + 3\,I3 + UC32 + XC32 = UC13 + XC13.$$

Since the unused capacity of the electrical line from zone 1 to zone 3 is 1500 units, we require

$$UC13 \leq 1500.$$

TABLE 12-13. **Land-Use Allocation Model for Capital City**

minimize $Z = 7\ XC12 + 2\ XC13 + 3\ XC32$

subject to
$$R2 + R3 = 600$$
$$I2 + I3 = 400$$
$$7\ R2 + 9\ I2 \leq 3000$$
$$7\ R3 + 9\ I3 \leq 10{,}000$$
$$2\ R2 + 3\ I2 - UC12 - XC12 - UC32 - XC32 = 0$$
$$2\ R3 + 3\ I3 + UC32 + XC32 - UC13 - XC13 = 0$$
$$UC12 \leq 400$$
$$UC32 \leq 500$$
$$UC13 \leq 1500$$
$$R2, R3, I2, I3, UC12, XC12, UC13, XC13, UC32, XC32 \geq 0$$

The complete problem formulation is shown in Table 12-13, and the analysis of the computer solution is the subject of exercise 8. This model can be extended to consider simultaneously the expansion of several types of utility lines, including water, sewer, and natural gas. Bagby and Thesen [1976] describe an actual application of an extended version of this model for allocating land-use developments in the military installation of Fort Campbell, Kentucky. The result indicated a distribution of the anticipated land uses so that no additional utility investments were required.

School Desegregation Model

A school district includes two schools, A and B, located as shown on the map in Figure 12-4. The school district is divided into five census tracts. School A is roughly in the center of tract 2, and school B is in the center of tract 5. The students in the district are primarily from two major ethnic groups, X and Y. The numbers of students from each ethnic group in each census tract are also shown in Figure 12-4. For example, in census tract 1 there are 50 students from ethnic group X and 10 students from ethnic group Y. When students were assigned to schools simply on the basis of geographic distance, the proportion of students in ethnic group X enrolled in school A was substantially higher than the proportion enrolled in school B.

The district has decided to reassign the students to the schools so that the total enrollments in the two schools are equal and so that the proportion of students in each ethnic group is identical in each school. In carrying out this reassignment, the district wishes to minimize the total number of student-miles traveled by the students. For example, if 30 students must travel 9 miles from tract 1 to school A, this corresponds to $(30)(9) = 270$ student-miles. We assume that travel distances are rectangular in the east-west and north-south directions. As a rough approximation, these distances are measured from the dot in the center of each census tract as shown in Figure 12-4. Table 12-14 contains the estimates of the distances from each tract to each school. These distances are then multiplied by the number of students in each ethnic group in the respective tract in order to obtain student-miles for each ethnic group. These calculations are also shown in Table 12-14.

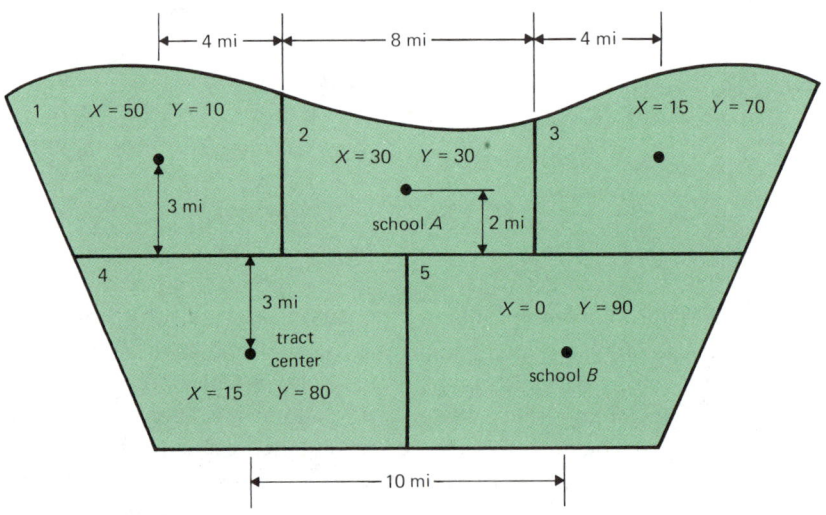

FIGURE 12-4. **Map of census tracts and school locations**

TABLE 12-14. **Calculation of Student Miles for Each Tract and Ethnic Group**

	From Tract:				
	1	2	3	4	5
School A					
Distance to school	8 + 1 = 9	0 + 0 = 0	8 + 1 = 9	5 + 5 = 10	5 + 5 = 10
Student-miles for:					
X	(9)(50) = 450	(0)(30) = 0	(9)(15) = 135	(10)(15) = 150	(10)(0) = 0
Y	(9)(10) = 90	(0)(30) = 0	(9)(70) = 630	(10)(80) = 800	(10)(90) = 900
School B					
Distance to school	13 + 6 = 19	5 + 5 = 10	3 + 6 = 9	10 + 0 = 10	0 + 0 = 0
Student-miles for:					
X	(19)(50) = 950	(10)(30) = 300	(9)(15) = 135	(10)(15) = 150	(0)(0) = 0
Y	(19)(10) = 190	(10)(30) = 300	(9)(70) = 630	(10)(80) = 800	(0)(90) = 0

Decision Variables We let $XA1$ be the *proportion* of students of ethnic group X from tract 1 assigned to school A, and $XB1$ be the proportion of students of group X from tract 1 assigned to school B. In a similar manner, we would define $YA1$ and $YB1$ for ethnic group Y. Thus, there are four decision variables for each of the five census tracts, for a total of twenty decision variables.

Objective Function We can minimize the student-miles traveled by minimizing the proportion of students in an ethnic group that must travel a long distance to a school. For example, if $XA1 = 1.0$, then we add 450 student-miles to the total traveled, using the student-miles figure in Table 12–14. However, if $XA1 = 0.1$, we add only $(0.1)(450) = 45$ student-miles to the total. Therefore, we would like to

minimize Z = the total student-miles
traveled to school A $\quad = 450\, XA1 + 90\, YA1 + 135\, XA3 + 630\, YA3$
$\qquad\qquad + 150\, XA4 + 800\, YA4 + 900\, YA5$

plus the total student-
miles traveled to school B $\quad = 950\, XB1 + 190\, YB1 + 300\, XB2 + 300\, YB2$
$\qquad\qquad + 135\, XB3 + 630\, YB3 + 150\, XB4 + 800\, YB4.$

Constraints Since $XA1$ and $XB1$ are the proportions of students of ethnic group X from tract 1 assigned to schools A and B respectively, we must have $XA1 + XB1 = 1$ to ensure that all of the students are assigned. Similarly, we have $YA1 + YB1 = 1$ for the ethnic group Y. Two similar constraints are needed for each of the other four census tracts.

Next, we wish to ensure that the number of students assigned to each school is equal. There are a total of 390 students in the district. Thus, the enrollment in school A is $390/2 = 195$, so we have

$50\, XA1 + 10\, YA1 + 30\, XA2 + 30\, YA2 + 15\, XA3$
$\quad + 70\, YA3 + 15\, XA4 + 80\, YA4 + 90\, YA5 = 195$

for school A. If exactly 195 students are assigned to school A, $390 - 195 = 195$ will automatically be assigned to school B. Therefore, there is no need to include a similar constraint for school B, even though it would do no harm.

Finally, there is a total of 110 students of ethnic group X in the district. If we assign 55 to school A and 55 to school B, the proportions of the ethnic groups in each school will be identical. Thus we require that

$50\, XA1 + 30\, XA2 + 15\, XA3 + 15\, XA4 = 55.$

If this constraint is satisfied, then again the identical constraint for school B would be automatically satisfied, so it is not explicitly included in the model.

The complete formulation is shown in Table 12–15, and the computer results are analyzed in exercise 9. There have been numerous examples of actual applications of linear optimization models to school desegregation problems. Two examples are described by Belford and Ratliff [1972] and Clarke and Surkis [1967]. A similar model to minimize transportation costs in a school district has been implemented by McKeown and Workman [1976].

TABLE 12-15. **School Desegregation Model**

minimize $Z = 450\ XA1 + 90\ YA1 + 135\ XA3 + 630\ YA3 + 150\ XA4 + 800\ YA4 + 900\ YA5 + 950\ XB1 + 190\ YB1 + 300\ XB2 + 300\ YB2 + 135\ XB3 + 630\ YB3 + 150\ XB4 + 800\ YB4$

subject to

$$XA1 + XB1 = 1$$
$$YA1 + YB1 = 1$$
$$XA2 + XB2 = 1$$
$$YA2 + YB2 = 1$$
$$XA3 + XB3 = 1$$
$$YA3 + YB3 = 1$$
$$XA4 + XB4 = 1$$
$$YA4 + YB4 = 1$$
$$XA5 + XB5 = 1$$
$$YA5 + YB5 = 1$$

$$50\ XA1 + 10\ YA1 + 30\ XA2 + 30\ YA2 + 15\ XA3 + 70\ YA3 + 15\ XA4 + 80\ YA4 + 90\ YA5 = 195$$

$$50\ XA1 + 30\ XA2 + 15\ XA3 + 15\ XA4 = 55$$

$XA1, XB1, YA1, YB1, XA2, XB2, YA2, YB2, XA3, XB3, YA3, YB3,$
$XA4, XB4, YA4, YB4, XA5, XB5, YA5, YB5 \geq 0$

WHAT SHOULD THE MANAGER KNOW?

There have been literally thousands of successful applications of linear optimization models in the analysis of significant managerial problems. These problems have been in virtually every functional area of the firm, and in the public and not-for-profit sectors of the economy as well as in the private sector. Thus, no matter what specialization or functional field appeals to a manager, and no matter what sector of the economy he is working in, he should be familiar with this powerful tool of analysis.

We have presented a breadth of examples of applications in order to emphasize this important point. In addition, a careful study of these different applications should enhance your ability to recognize potential applications in practice and to participate in the development and use of the appropriate linear optimization model.

Check Your Understanding

1. The computer input and solution for the problem of financing the production decision were shown in Figure 12-1. The corresponding sensitivity analysis is shown in Figure 12-5. Using Figures 12-1 and 12-5, answer the following questions:
    a. When the chemical production problem was analyzed in Chapter 11 (see Figures 11-7 and 11-8), an additional unit of capacity on machine A was worth $3.75. According to Figure 12-5, it is worth nothing ($0.00) when the financial constraints are added. Why?

```
DO YOU WISH SENSITIVITY ANALYSIS? YES

                        SHADOW          LB              CURRENT         UB
CONSTRAINT      1       0.0000E0        6.9677E1        8.000UE1        7.2370E75
                2       1.5323E1        4.5310E1        6.000UE1        6.5300E1
                3       0.0000E0        1.2581E1        1.600UE1        7.2370E75
                4       0.0000E0        1.1129E1        1.800UE1        7.2370E75
                5       4.8387E-2       7.0400E3        8.100UE3        8.9000E3
                6       0.0000E0       -7.2370E75       4.000UE2        1.3113E3

PRICE           CHEMX                   3.6250E1        6.000UE1        7.5000E1
                CHEMY                   4.0000E1        5.000UE1        8.2759E1
-> END <-
```

FIGURE 12-5. **Sensitivity analysis for the production problem with financial constraints (exercise 1)**

   b. What is an additional unit of machine B capacity worth to the firm when the financial constraints are considered?
   c. Suppose the company changes its policy and requires a cash asset position of only $4500. Would the contribution to profit be increased? If so, by how much?

2. Figure 12-6 gives the computer input, solution, and sensitivity analysis for the portfolio selection linear optimization model discussed in the text and given in Table 12-4.
    a. What is the appropriate interpretation of the objective function value of 0.097?
    b. Suppose we have $100,000 to invest. How much should be purchased of each security?
    c. What is the meaning of $SUR2 = 0.2$? $SLK6 = 0.1$?
    d. Suppose that the upper bound on the electronics securities increased from 30 to 35 percent. How would the solution change?
    e. Suppose that the yield in electronics increased from 12 to 15 percent. Would the solution change? How do you know?

f. If the yields were known for certain, we would clearly invest our entire portfolio in electronics securities. What is the purpose of the upper and lower limits on the investments? Are these limits firm or subjective? Criticize this model in terms of its practical usefulness.

```
        LPENTER
ENTER THE NAME OF THIS PROJECT PORTFOLIO SELECTION
MAXIMIZE OR MINIMIZE: MAXIMIZE
OBJECTIVE FUNCTION:Z=.12E+.08U+.1F+.09C
ENTER CONSTRAINT EQUATIONS, (STRIKE JUST A CARRIAGE RETURN TO STOP INPUT)
    (1) E+U+F+C=1
    (2) E≤.1
    (3) E≤.3
    (4) U≥.15
    (5) F≥.05
    (6) F≤.2
    (7) C≥.2
    (8) C≤.35
    (9) E+F≤.4
    (10) .5E-U+.5F≤0
    (11)
        LPRUN
                    PORTFOLIO SELECTION

THE OPTIMAL VALUE OF THE OBJECTIVE FUNCTION IS:      0.097

            THE VARIABLES IN THE SOLUTION ARE

VARIABLE  E     AT LEVEL    3.0000E-1
          U                 2.5000E-1
          F                 1.0000E-1
          C                 3.5000E-1
          SUR2              2.0000E-1
          SUR4              1.0000E-1
          SUR5              5.0000E-2
          SLK6              1.0000E-1
          SUR7              1.5000E-1
          SLK10             5.0000E-2

DO YOU WISH SENSITIVITY ANALYSIS? YES

                        SHADOW         LB           CURRENT        UB
CONSTRAINT     1        8.0000E-2      9.5000E-1    1.0000E0       7.2370E75
               2        0.0000E0       -7.2370E75   1.0000E-1      3.0000E-1
               3        2.0000E-2      2.0000E-1    3.0000E-1      3.5000E-1
               4        0.0000E0       -7.2370E75   1.5000E-1      2.5000E-1
               5        0.0000E0       -7.2370E75   5.0000E-2      1.0000E-1
               6        0.0000E0       1.0000E-1    2.0000E-1      7.2370E75
               7        0.0000E0       -7.2370E75   2.0000E-1      3.5000E-1
               8        1.0000E-2      2.0000E-1    3.5000E-1      4.0000E-1
               9        2.0000E-2      3.5000E-1    4.0000E-1      4.3333E-1
              10        0.0000E0       -5.0000E-2   0.0000E0       7.2370E75
PRICE          E                       1.0000E-1    1.200UE-1      7.2370E75
               U                       -7.2370E75   8.000UE-2      9.0000E-2
               F                       8.0000E-2    1.000UE-1      1.2000E-1
               C                       8.0000E-2    9.000UE-2      7.2370E75
```

FIGURE 12-6. **Portfolio selection problem (exercise 2)**

3. The computer input and solution for the investment planning model are shown in Figure 12-7.
   a. What are the total interest payments received from the investments over the three-year time horizon?
   b. Interpret the solution. How much should be invested each year in each opportunity?
   c. The shadow price for the first constraint is 0.3516. How do you interpret this number?
   d. Notice that the shadow price for constraint [5] is 0.01, and yet each dollar invested in opportunity C3 returns 0.1 percent. How do you reconcile this result? (Hint: Consider the other opportunity for investment in year 3.)
   e. What difficulties would you foresee in implementing this model in the real world? How might they be overcome?

```
          LPENTER
    ENTER THE NAME OF THIS PROJECT   INVESTMENT PLANNING MODEL
    MAXIMIZE OR MINIMIZE: MAXIMIZE
    OBJECTIVE FUNCTION:Z=.3A2+.09B1+.09B2+.09B3+.1C3+.24D1
    ENTER CONSTRAINT EQUATIONS, (STRIKE JUST A CARRIAGE RETURN TO STOP INPUT)
    (1) B1+D1=1000000
    (2) A2+B2-1.09B1=0
    (3) A2≤500000
    (4) B3+C3-1.09B2-1.24D1=0
    (5) C3≤500000
          LPRUN
                           INVESTMENT PLANNING MODEL

    THE OPTIMAL VALUE OF THE OBJECTIVE FUNCTION IS:    386600.000

                        THE VARIABLES IN THE SOLUTION ARE

    VARIABLE    A2       AT LEVEL      5.0000E5
                B1                     4.5872E5
                B3                     1.7119E5
                C3                     5.0000E5
                D1                     5.4128E5

    DO YOU WISH SENSITIVITY ANALYSIS? YES

                            SHADOW          LB             CURRENT        UB
    CONSTRAINT    1       3.5160E-1      8.6194E5       1.0000E6       7.2370E75
                  2       2.4000E-1     -1.5048E5       0.0000E0       5.0000E5
                  3       6.0000E-2     -1.1642E-10     5.0000E5       6.5048E5
                  4       9.0000E-2     -1.7119E5       0.0000E0       7.2370E75
                  5       1.0000E-2      0.0000E0       5.0000E5       6.7119E5

    PRICE       A2                       2.4000E-1      3.000E-1       7.2370E75
                B1                       2.4600E-2      9.000E-2       1.4657E-1
                B2                      -7.2370E75      9.000E-2       1.4190E-1
                B3                      -1.0000E0       9.000E-2       1.0000E-1
                C3                       9.0000E-2      1.000E-1       7.2370E75
                D1                       1.8343E-1      2.400E-1       3.6540E-1
    -> END <-
```

FIGURE 12-7. **Investment planning problem (exercise 3)**

4. Figure 12-8 gives the computer input, solution, and sensitivity analysis for the advertising media selection problem discussed in the text.
   a. How many advertising units should be purchased in each media?
   b. What if the exposure rating per unit of newspapers (N) were higher? Would the solution change?

```
          LPENTER
ENTER THE NAME OF THIS PROJECT ADVERTISING MEDIA SELECTION
MAXIMIZE OR MINIMIZE: MAXIMIZE
OBJECTIVE FUNCTION: Z= 100M+400N+200R+600TVP+150TVO
ENTER CONSTRAINT EQUATIONS, (STRIKE JUST A CARRIAGE RETURN TO STOP INPUT)
 (1) 20M+15N+5R+40TVP+10TVOS=600
 (2) 20M≤=250
 (3) 15N≤=250
 (4) 5R≤=250
 (5) 40TVP+10TVOS=250
 (6) 20M+15N≤=350
 (7) 5R-10TVP-2.5TVO≥=0
 (8) 10TVO-20TVP≥=0
 (9) 10M+30N+20R+15TVO+35TVP≥=250
(10)
          LPRUN
                          ADVERTISING MEDIA SELECTION.
THE OPTIMAL VALUE OF THE OBJECTIVE FUNCTION IS:     1⁰166.667
                     THE VARIABLES IN THE SOLUTION ARE

        VARIABLE   N        AT LEVEL     1.6667E1
                   P                     5.0000E1
                   TVP                   1.6667E0
                   TVO                   3.3333E0
                   SLK2                  2.5000E2
                   SLK5                  1.5000E2
                   SLK6                  1.0000E2
                   SUR7                  2.2500E2
                   SUR9                  1.3583E3

DO YOU WISH SENSITIVITY ANALYSIS? YES

                          SHADOW         LB           CURRENT        UB
        CONSTRAINT   1    1.5000E1      5.0000E2      6.0000E2      7.5000E2
                     2    0.0000E0      0.0000E0      2.500UE2      7.2370E75
                     3    1.1667E1      1.0000E2      2.5000E2      3.5000E2
                     4    2.5000E1      1.0000E2      2.5000E2      3.5000E2
                     5    0.0000E0      1.0000E2      2.500UE2      7.2370E75
                     6    0.0000E0      2.5000E2      3.500UE2      7.2370E75
                     7    0.0000E0     -7.2370E75     0.0000E0      2.2500E2
                     8    0.0000E0     -5.0000E1      0.000UE0      1.0000E2
                     9    0.0000E0     -7.2370E75     2.500UE2      1.6083E3

        PRICE       M                  -7.2370E75     1.000UE2      3.0000E2
                    N                   2.2500E2      4.000UE2      7.2370E75
                    R                   7.5000E1      2.000UE2      7.2370E75
                    TVP                 6.0000E2      6.000UE2      1.3000E3
                    TVO                -1.5000E2      1.500UE2      1.5000E2

-> END <-
```

FIGURE 12-8. **Advertising media selection problem (exercise 4)**

c. The budget limitations of $250,000 on each of the media were subjectively set. If you were to consider increasing this budget allocation to one of these media, which one would you choose? Why?

d. This model assumes that the first advertisement in each of the media has just as much impact as the second, which has the same impact as the last advertisement. Is this a reasonable assumption? Criticize this formulation in terms of its use in the real world. Can you think of ways to improve its realism?

5. The computer input and solution for the sales territory determination problem are shown in Figure 12-9. (The sensitivity analysis is omitted.)

  a. Which sales zones should be assigned to Able and which to Baker?
  b. Redraw the map in Figure 12-2 and shade in the area assigned to Able. How would you suggest dividing up zone 6?
  c. Suppose the company is willing to consider an assignment of zones that gives at least 210 customers to Able and at least 210 customers to Baker. Reformulate the problem to allow for this change.
  d. Rather than simply using the number of customers in each area, are there other measures that might be more appropriate for an equitable distribution of sales zones? In other words, evaluate this model. What changes would you suggest before using it in practice?

```
LPENTER
ENTER THE NAME OF THIS PROJECT DETERMINATION OF SALES TERRITORIES
MAXIMIZE OR MINIMIZE: MINIMIZE
OBJECTIVE FUNCTION:Z=208XA1+100XA2+244XA3+144XA4+0XA5+144XA6+580XB1+144XB2
                    +0XB3+676XB4+244XB5+100XB6
ENTER CONSTRAINT EQUATIONS, (STRIKE JUST A CARRIAGE RETURN TO STOP INPUT)
(1) XA1+XB1=1
(2) X.2+XB2=1
(3) XA3+XB3=1
(4) XA4+XB4=1
(5) XA5+XB5=1
(6) XA6+XB6=1
(7) 20XA1+85XA2+150XA3+40XA4+60XA5+75XA6=215
(8)
LPRUN
                              DETERMINATION OF SALES TERRITORIES

THE OPTIMAL VALUE OF THE OBJECTIVE FUNCTION IS:          557.867

                        THE VARIABLES IN THE SOLUTION ARE

       VARIABLE   XA1    AT LEVEL    1.0000E0
                  XA2                1.0000E0
                  XA4                1.0000E0
                  XA5                1.0000E0
                  XA6                1.3333E-1
                  XB3                1.0000E0
                  XB6                8.6667E-1
```

FIGURE 12-9. **Sales territories problem (exercise 5)**

6. The computer input, solution, and sensitivity analysis for the nurse scheduling problem are shown in Figure 12–10.
   a. How many nurses should come on duty each period? Verify that this schedule satisfies the minimum requirements.
   b. The shadow price for constraint [2] is 0.0. How do you interpret this?
   c. Suppose nurses come on duty only at 6:00 A.M., 2:00 P.M., and 10:00 P.M., and work 8 consecutive hours. Those arriving at 6:00 A.M. and 2:00 P.M. are paid $40 per day, and those arriving at 10:00 P.M. are paid $50. Determine by hand the number of nurses needed on each shift, based on the data in the example, and compute the total daily payroll costs. Which system would you recommend?

```
        LPENTER
ENTER THE NAME OF THIS PROJECT NURSE SCHEDULING
MAXIMIZE OR MINIMIZE: MINIMIZE
OBJECTIVE FUNCTION:Z=50N1+40N2+40N3+40N4+50N5+50N6
ENTER CONSTRAINT EQUATIONS, (STRIKE JUST A CARRIAGE RETURN TO STOP INPUT)
  (1)  N1+N2≥60
  (2)  N2+N3≥50
  (3)  N3+N4≥35
  (4)  N4+N5≥55
  (5)  N5+N6≥40
  (6)  N1+N6≥25
  (7)
        LPRUN
                       NURSE SCHEDULING

THE OPTIMAL VALUE OF THE OBJECTIVE FUNCTION IS:    5850.000

              THE VARIABLES IN THE SOLUTION ARE

     VARIABLE   N1     AT LEVEL     5.0000E0
                N2                  5.5000E1
                N4                  3.5000E1
                N5                  2.0000E1
                N6                  2.0000E1
                SUR2                5.0000E0

     DO YOU WISH SENSITIVITY ANALYSIS? YES

                         SHADOW        LB          CURRENT      UB
     CONSTRAINT   1      4.0000E1    5.5000E1     6.000E1    7.2370E75
                  2      0.0000E0   -7.2370E75    5.000E1    5.5000E1
                  3      3.0000E1    3.0000E1     3.500E1    4.0000E1
                  4      1.0000E1    5.0000E1     5.500E1    6.0000E1
                  5      4.0000E1    3.5000E1     4.000E1    4.5000E1
                  6      1.0000E1    2.0000E1     2.500E1    3.0000E1

     PRICE    N1                    4.0000E1    5.000E1     8.0000E1
              N2                    1.0000E1    4.000F1     5.0000E1
              N3                    3.0000E1    4.000E1     7.2370E75
              N4                    1.0000E1    4.000E1     5.0000E1
              N5                    4.0000E1    5.000E1     8.0000E1
              N6                    2.0000E1    5.000E1     6.0000E1
 -> END <-
```

FIGURE 12–10. **Nurse scheduling problem (exercise 6)**

7. The computer input, solution, and sensitivity analysis for the personnel planning problem are shown in Figure 12-11.
   a. How many trainees should be hired in January? In February?
   b. Suppose the machinists are paid $2000 per month. Would this change be likely to alter the solution? Why or why not?
   c. The results are not integer valued. How would you implement this solution in practice? In other words, if you were in charge of recruiting and training, what would you do?

```
         LPENTER
ENTER THE NAME OF THIS PROJECT PERSONNEL PLANNING
MAXIMIZE OR MINIMIZE: MINIMIZE
OBJECTIVE FUNCTION:Z=1000TRAINJ+1200MACHF+1000TRAINF+1200MACHM
ENTER CONSTRAINT EQUATIONS, (STRIKE JUST A CARRIAGE RETURN TO STOP INPUT)
  (1) 75TRAINJ≤500
  (2) MACHF-TRAINJ=27
  (3) 150MACHF-75TRAINF≥4500
  (4) MACHM-TRAINF-.9MACHF=0
  (5) 150MACHM≥4200
  (6)
         LPRUN
                     MANPOWER PLANNING

THE OPTIMAL VALUE OF THE OBJECTIVE FUNCTION IS:    74048.276

                  THE VARIABLES IN THE SOLUTION ARE

   VARIABLE   TRAINJ AT LEVEL     3.3448E0
              MACHF               3.0345E1
              TRAINF              6.8966E-1
              MACHM               2.8000E1
              SLK1                2.4914E2


DO YOU WISH SENSITIVITY ANALYSIS? YES

                         SHADOW         LB           CURRENT        UB
   CONSTRAINT   1        0.0000E0       2.5086E2     5.0000E2       7.2370E75
                2       -1.0000E3       2.3678E1     2.7000E1       3.0345E1
                3        5.9770E0       3.7725E3     4.5000E3       4.6667E3
                4       -1.4483E3      -9.6333E0     0.0000E0       1.0000E0
                5        1.7655E1       4.0500E3     4.2000E3       5.6450E3

   PRICE       TRAINJ                  -3.0000E2     1.0000E3       7.2370E75
               MACHF                   -1.0000E2     1.2000E3       7.2370E75
               TRAINF                  -2.8400E3     1.0000E3       2.4444E3
               MACHM                   -1.4483E3     1.2000E3       7.2370E75
  -> END <-
```

FIGURE 12-11. **Personnel planning problem (exercise 7)**

8. The computer input, solution, and sensitivity analysis for the land-use allocation problem are shown in Figure 12-12.
   a. Which utility lines will require expansion? By how much?
   b. How many residential developments should be given building permits in each zone? How many industrial developments?

c. Suppose an additional 100 residential developments (700 rather than 600) are actually needed. How much extra will it cost the city for the expansion of the utility lines?

d. The city wishes to charge each industrial development a building permit fee equal to the marginal cost of the necessary utility line expansion. What should the fee be?

```
            LPENTER
ENTER THE NAME OF THIS PROJECT LAND USE ALLOCATION
MAXIMIZE OR MINIMIZE: MINIMIZE
OBJECTIVE FUNCTION:Z=7XC12+2XC13+3XC32
ENTER CONSTRAINT EQUATIONS, (STRIKE JUST A CARRIAGE RETURN TO STOP INPUT)
 (1) R2+R3=600
 (2) I2+I3=400
 (3) 7R2+9I2≤3000
 (4) 7R3+9I3≤10000
 (5) 2R2+3I2-UC12-XC12-UC32-XC32=0
 (6) 2R3+3I3+UC32+XC32-UC13-XC13=0
 (7) UC12≤400
 (8) UC32≤500
 (9) UC13≤1500
(10)
            LPRUN
                        LAND USE ALLOCATION

THE OPTIMAL VALUE OF THE OBJECTIVE FUNCTION IS:       4000.000

                   THE VARIABLES IN THE SOLUTION ARE

        VARIABLE   XC13   AT LEVEL      5.0000E2
                   UC12                 4.0000E2
                   UC13                 1.5000E3
                   UC32                 4.5714E2
                   R2                   4.2857E2
                   R3                   1.7143E2
                   I3                   4.0000E2
                   SLK4                 5.2000E3
                   SLK8                 4.2857E1

DO YOU WISH SENSITIVITY ANALYSIS? YES

                              SHADOW        LB          CURRENT        UB
        CONSTRAINT    1       4.0000E0      4.2857E2    6.0000E2      1.3429E3
                      2       6.0000E0      2.3333E2    4.0000E2      9.7778E2
                      3       0.0000E0      1.4000E3    3.0000E3      3.1500E3
                      4       0.0000E0      4.8000E3    1.0000E4      7.2370E75
                      5      -2.0000E0     -4.2857E1    0.0000E0      4.5714E2
                      6      -2.0000E0     -7.2370E75   0.0000E0      5.0000E2
                      7      -2.0000E0      3.5714E2    4.0000E2      8.5714E2
                      8       0.0000E0      4.5714E2    5.0000E2      7.2370E75
                      9      -2.0000E0      0.0000E0    1.500E3       2.0000E3

        PRICE        XC12                   2.0000E0    7.000E0       7.2370E75
                     XC13                   0.0000E0    2.000E0       7.0000E0
                     XC32                   0.0000E0    3.000E0       7.2370E75
                     UC12                  -7.2370E75   0.000E0       2.0000E0
                     UC13                  -7.2370E75   0.000E0       2.0000E0
                     UC32                   0.0000E0    0.000E0       0.0000E0
                     R2                    -7.2370E75   0.000E0       0.0000E0
                     R3                     0.0000E0    0.000E0       7.2370E75
                     I2                     0.0000E0    0.000E0       7.2370E75
                     I3                    -7.2370E75   0.000E0       0.0000E0
-> END <-
```

FIGURE 12-12. **Land-use allocation problem (exercise 8)**

e. How many additional units of electricity will be transmitted on each of the three electrical lines after the expansion?
f. What other considerations might be included in a real-world application of an urban planning model?

9. The computer input and solution for the school desegregation problem are shown in Figure 12–13. (The sensitivity analysis is omitted.)

   a. Verify that 195 students are assigned to school A and that 195 are assigned to school B. Also, verify that 55 students from ethnic group X are assigned to each school.
   b. Notice that $XB1 = 0.5$, so that $(0.5)(50) = 25$ students from ethnic group X in zone 1 are assigned to school B, even though they must travel 19 miles. The 30 students from ethnic group X in zone 2 are assigned to school A, even though they would only have to travel 10 miles to school B. If 25 students from ethnic group X in zone B were assigned to school B, then the 25 in zone 1 assigned to B could be reassigned to school A. Would this be a better solution? If so, what is wrong with the model?

```
          LPENTER
ENTER THE NAME OF THIS PROJECT SCHOOL DESEGREGATION
MAXIMIZE OR MINIMIZE: MINIMIZE
OBJECTIVE FUNCTION:Z=450XA1+90YA1+0XA2+0YA2+135XA3+630YA3+150XA4+800YA4+0XA5
                    +900YA5+950XB1+190YB1+300XB2+300YB2+135XB3+630YB3+150XB4
                    +800YB4+0XB5+0YB5
ENTER CONSTRAINT EQUATIONS, (STRIKE JUST A CARRIAGE RETURN TO STOP INPUT)
  (1) XA1+XB1=1
  (2) YA1+YB1=1
  (3) XA2+XB2=1
  (4) YA2+YB2=1
  (5) XA3+XB3=1
  (6) YA3+YB3=1
  (7) XA4+XB4=1
  (8) YA4+YB4=1
  (9) XA5+XB5=1
 (10) YA5+YB5=1
 (11) 50XA1+10YA1+30XA2+30YA2+15XA3+70YA3+15XA4+80YA4+90YA5=195
 (12) 50XA1+30XA2+15XA3+15XA4=55
 (13)
          LPRUN
                    SCHOOL DESEGREGATION

THE OPTIMAL VALUE OF THE OBJECTIVE FUNCTION IS:       2505.000

                    THE VARIABLES IN THE SOLUTION ARE

VARIABLE    XA1       AT LEVEL     5.0000E-1
            YA1                    1.0000E0
            XA2                    1.0000E0
            YA2                    1.0000E0
            YA3                    1.0000E0
            YA4                    3.7500E-1
            XA5                    1.0000E0
            XB1                    5.0000E-1
            XB3                    1.0000E0
            XB4                    1.0000E0
            YB4                    6.2500E-1
            YB5                    1.0000E0
```

FIGURE 12–13. **School desegregation problem (exercise 9)**

c. Suggest an alternative objective function and reformulate the problem. (Hint: See the sales territory model.)
d. Suppose the district wishes to ensure that there are at least 180 students enrolled in each school and that at least 45 students from ethnic group X are enrolled in each school. Reformulate the problem to impose these constraints.

Problems

10. A Federal Home Loan Bank makes essentially four kinds of loans, which yield the following annual interest rates:

First mortgages	10%
Second mortgages	16%
Home improvement loans	18%
Loans against accounts	5%

    The bank has a maximum lending capability of $2 million and must stay within the following limits and policies:
    a. First mortgages must be at least 45 percent of all mortgages and at least 25 percent of loans outstanding.
    b. Second mortgages cannot exceed 30 percent of loans.
    Formulate the bank's loan problem as a linear optimization model designed to maximize interest income within the stated policy limits.

11. Clyde's, a men's store in a small college town, wishes to place an order for its three major lines of apparel: casual sportswear, suits and sports coats, and sweaters. Clyde's receives a greater profit per unit from suits and sports coats, but the required floor space for displays and sales time is also greater. The per unit profit for sweaters is the lowest, but the required floor space and sales time are also low.

    Clyde's feels obligated to carry a full line of clothing, so the buyer feels that he must order at least 100 units of casual sportswear, 100 units of suits and sports coats, and 200 units of sweaters for the season. Otherwise, he would like to order a mix of apparel that, if sold, would maximize his profits.

    The store has only 3000 square feet of floor space and only 1600 salesman hours available for customer service. The buyer has made rough estimates of the floor space and salesman-hour requirements per 100 units of each line of clothing. The results are shown in Table 12–16. Finally, the buyer feels that he could sell a maximum of 1000 units of the casual sportswear, 2000 units of suits and sports coats, and a virtually unlimited number of units of sweaters. How many units of each line should he order for the season, assuming that he wishes to maximize profits? Formulate the buyer's problem as a linear optimization model.

TABLE 12-16. **Sales Data for Clyde's**

Line of Clothing	Average Profit per Unit	Salesman-Hours per 100 Sold	Floor Space (sq ft per 100 units)
Casual sportswear	$ 7.00	30	50
Suits and sports coats	20.00	100	75
Sweaters	5.00	10	40

12. A local power plant has had a visit from the air pollution control authorities. After considerable technical analysis, the plant has been ordered to reduce solid pollutants by 50,000 lb per year, oxides of sulfur by 40,000 lb per year, and hydrocarbons by 50,000 lb per year.

    The plant currently uses coal as a fuel. Extensive engineering analysis indicates that substantial reductions in pollutants could be achieved by installing and operating precipitators, using fuel oil, or using natural gas. The annual cost of each of these control methods is as follows:

Control Method	Annual Cost
Precipitator (P)	15
Coal to oil (CO)	10
Coal to gas (CG)	18

    Fractional or multiple installations of each of these methods may be used.

    The engineering analysis also indicated estimates of the possible improvement in each of the three types of pollutants for each of the three control methods. These data are shown in Table 12-17. Formulate the pollution control problem as a linear optimization model.

TABLE 12-17. **Potential Improvement in Air Pollutants by Three Control Methods (in 1000s of lb)**

Pollutant	Precipitator	Coal to Oil	Coal to Gas
Solids	30	32	40
Oxides of sulfur	35	20	30
Hydrocarbons	28	10	40

13. Mr. George Overstreet has decided to run for the city council of his home town. He faces stiff opposition in the primary election as well as in the fall. The resources for his campaign are limited in terms of both time from volunteer workers and money.

Mr. Overstreet has divided the town into city blocks as a basic campaign unit. He can take three different actions on each block: door-to-door canvassing, placement of lawn signs, and a district-wide mailing. The estimated average time and cost per city block of each of these actions is shown in Table 12–18. Mr. Overstreet estimates that he can allocate a total of 8 hours of volunteer worker time and a total of $7 to each block over both the primary and the fall campaign.

TABLE 12–18. **Alternative Campaign Actions**

Effort	Time per Block (hr)	Dollars per Block
Door-to-door canvassing	2	$ 0.00
Lawn signs	1	3.50
District-wide mailing	0	10.50

After a preliminary analysis, Overstreet has made estimates of the impacts of each of the three campaign strategies. The results are shown in Table 12–19. For example, if a block is canvassed door-to-door in the primary campaign, Overstreet expects to receive a net additional 1.5 votes. We say "net additional" votes, because the door-to-door canvassing stimulates voter participation in general, with some of the additional votes going to his opponent.

TABLE 12–19. **Net Effects of Campaign Action on Votes**

	Net Additional Votes	
Effort	Primary	Fall Election
Door-to-door canvassing	1.5	4.0
Lawn signs	1.8	0.25
District-wide mailing	10.0	20.0

Suppose Overstreet wishes to obtain a net additional vote of at least 2.0 per block from his campaign efforts in the primary, and then maximize the net additional vote in the fall election. How should he allocate his resources?

Overstreet has formulated his problem using a linear optimization model. He defined CP as the proportion of city blocks that can be canvassed (C) during the primary (P) and CF as the proportion canvassed in the fall (F). For example, if $CP = 0.5$, then half of the blocks should be canvassed in the primary. He also assumed that he may have $CP > 1.0$. For example, he would interpret $CP = 2.5$ to mean that each block should be canvassed 2.5 times prior to the primary.

Likewise, SP and SF are the proportions receiving signs (S) in the primary and fall respectively, and MP and MF are the proportions receiving a direct mailing (M). The complete problem formulation is shown as the computer input in Figure 12-14, along with the solution.

a. How many additional votes in each block does Overstreet expect to receive from his fall campaign efforts?
b. Suppose Overstreet could *hire* additional campaign workers for $1 per hour. Should he spend $1 for an hour of campaign worker time?
c. Suppose that Overstreet would like to generate a net additional vote in each block of 5.0 from the efforts during the primary. How many net additional votes in the fall election would he be giving up?
d. Criticize the assumptions of this model. (Hint: Compare this model to the media selection model.)*

```
        LPENTER
ENTER THE NAME OF THIS PROJECT  CAMPAIGN RESOURCE ALLOCATION
MAXIMIZE OR MINIMIZE: MAXIMIZE
OBJECTIVE FUNCTION:Z=4CF+.25SF+20MF+0CP+0SP+0MP
ENTER CONSTRAINT EQUATIONS, (STRIKE JUST A CARRIAGE RETURN TO STOP INPUT)
(1) 2CP+SP+2CF+SF≤8
(2) 3.5SP+10.5MP+3.5SF+10.5MF≤7
(3) 1.5CP+1.8SP+10MP≤2
(4)
        LPRUN
                        CAMPAIGN RESOURCE ALLOCATION

THE OPTIMAL VALUE OF THE OBJECTIVE FUNCTION IS:      25.333

                    THE VARIABLES IN THE SOLUTION ARE

VARIABLE  CF      AT LEVEL     4.0000E0
          MF                   4.6667E-1
          MP                   2.0000E-1

DO YOU WISH SENSITIVITY ANALYSIS?  YES

                       SHADOW         LB          CURRENT         UB
CONSTRAINT    1       2.0000E0      0.0000E0     8.0000E0      7.2370E75
              2       1.9048E0      2.1000E0     7.0000E0      7.2370E75
              3      -2.0000E0      0.0000E0     2.0000E0      6.6667E0

PRICE     CF                        3.0000E0     4.0000E0      7.2370E75
          SF                       -7.2370E75    2.5000E-1     6.6667E0
          MF                        1.0000E-6    2.0000E1      2.6667E1
          CP                       -7.2370E75    0.0000E0      1.0000E0
          SP                       -7.2370E75    0.0000E0      5.0667E0
          MP                       -6.6667E0     0.0000E0      2.0000E1
-> END <-
```

FIGURE 12-14. **Campaign resource allocation problem (exercise 13)**

---

*This problem is based on an analysis by Southwick and Zionts [1975] of Southwick's campaign for the Town Council of Amhurst, New York. (He won!) For a discussion of the actual use of a linear optimization model in planning a political campaign, see Barken and Bruno [1972].

References

1. Aaker, David A., "Management Science in Marketing: The State of the Art," *Interfaces,* Vol. 3, No. 4, August 1973.
2. Bagby, G., and A. Thesen, "A Network Flow Model for Allocation of Land Uses to Sectors," *Management Science,* Vol. 22, No. 11, July 1976.
3. Barken, J. D., and J. E. Bruno, "Operations Research in Planning Political Campaign Strategies," *Operations Research,* September–October 1972.
4. Bass, F. M., and R. T. Lonsdale, "An Exploration of Linear Programming in Media Selection," *Journal of Marketing Research,* Vol. 3, 1966.
5. Belford, P. C., and D. Ratliff, "A Network-Flow Model for Racially Balancing Schools," *Operations Research,* Vol. 20, No. 3, 1972.
6. Charnes, A., W. W. Cooper, and R. Ferguson, "Optimal Estimation of Executive Compensation by Linear Programming," *Management Science,* Vol. 1, No. 2, January 1955.
7. Charnes, A., W. W. Cooper, K. A. Lewis, and R. J. Niehaus, "A Multi-Objective Model for Planning Equal Employment Opportunities," OCMM Research Report No. 23, Office of Civilian Manpower Management, Washington, D.C., October 1975.
8. Charnes, A., W. W. Cooper, and R. J. Niehaus, *Studies in Manpower Planning,* U.S. Navy Office of Civilian Manpower Management, Washington, D.C., July 1972.
9. Clarke, S., and J. Surkis, "An Operations Research Approach to Racial Desegregation of School Systems," *Socio-Economic Planning Sciences,* Vol. 1, 1967.
10. Engle, J. F., and M. W. Warshaw, "Allocating Advertising Research," *Journal of Advertising Research,* Vol. 4, No. 3, 1964, pp. 42–48.
11. Franklin, A. D., and E. Koenigsberg, "Computed School Assignments in a Large District," *Operations Research,* Vol. 21, No. 2, March–April 1973, pp. 413–26.
12. Glassey, C. R., and V. K. Gupta, "A Linear Programming Analysis of Paper Recycling," *Management Science,* Vol. 21, No. 4, December 1974, pp. 392–408.
13. Gray, P., and C. Cullinan-James, "Applied Optimization—A Survey," *Interfaces,* Vol. 6, No. 3, May 1976.
14. Heller, N. B., R. E. Markland, and J. A. Brockelmeyer, "Partitioning of Police Districts into Optimal Patrol Beats Using a Political Districting Algorithm: Model Design and Validation," School of Business Administration, University of Missouri, Saint Louis, 1971.
15. Hess, W. H., and S. A. Samuels, "Experiences with a Sales Districting Model: Criteria and Implementation," *Management Science,* Vol. 18, No. 4, Part II, December 1971.

16. Hess, W. H., J. Weaver, H. Siegfeldt, J. Whelan, and P. Zitlau, "Nonpartisan Political Redistricting by Computer," *Operations Research,* Vol. 13, No. 6, November–December 1965.
17. Hughes, J. S., and W. G. Lewellen, "Programming Solutions to Capital Rationing Problems," *Journal of Business, Finance and Accounting,* Vol. 1, No. 1, Spring 1974.
18. Ignall, E., P. Kolesar, and W. Walker, "Linear Programming Models of Crew Assignments for Refuse Collection," *IEEE Transactions on Systems, Man and Cybernetics,* November 1972, pp. 661–666.
19. Kotler, P., *Marketing Decision Making: A Model Building Approach,* Holt, Rinehart & Winston, New York, 1971.
20. McKeown, P. and B. Workman, "A Study in Using Linear Programming to Assign Students to Schools," *Interfaces,* Vol. 6, No. 4, August 1976.
21. Mao, J. C. T., *Quantitative Analysis of Financial Decisions,* Collier-MacMillan, London, 1969.
22. Revelle, C., F. Feldmann, and W. Lynn, "An Optimization Model for Tuberculosis Epidemiology," *Management Science,* Vol. 16, No. 4, December 1969, pp. 190–211.
23. Robicheck, A. A., D. Teichroew, and J. M. Jones, "Optimal Short Term Financing Decisions," *Management Science,* Vol. 12, No. 1, September 1965, pp. 1–36.
24. Smith, K. V., editor, *Management of Working Capital,* West Publishing Co., St. Paul, 1974.
25. Southwick, L., and S. Zionts, "Optimal Resource Allocation in a Local Election Campaign," *Interfaces,* Vol. 6, No. 1, November 1975.

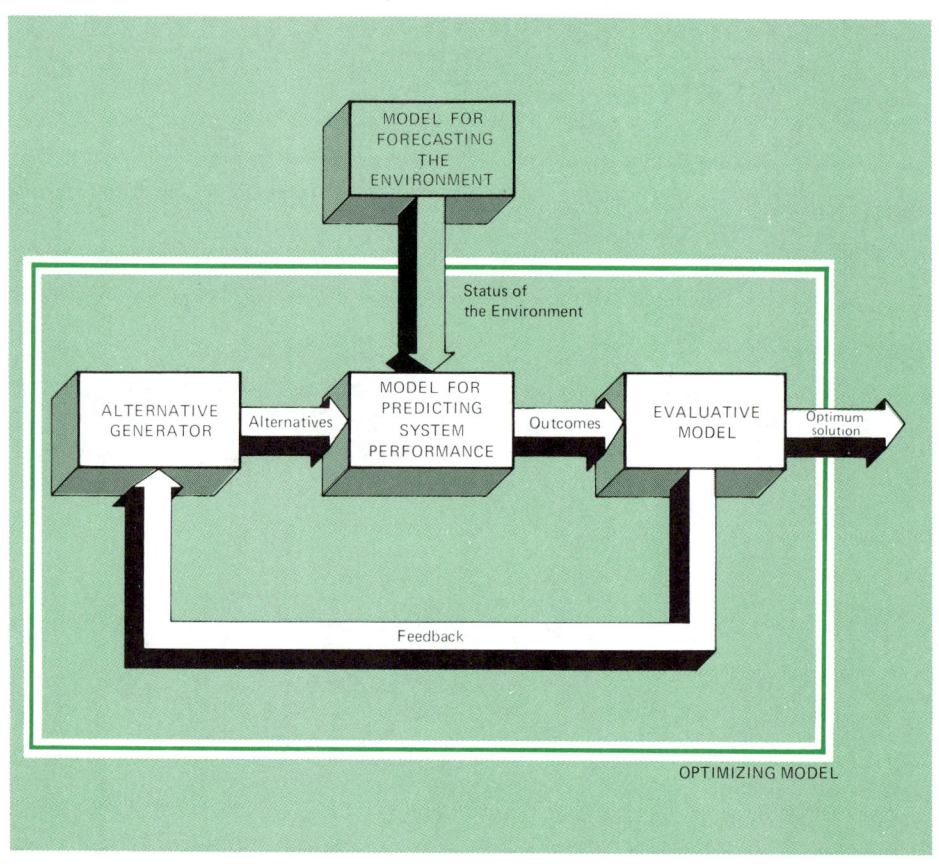

13

THE SIMPLEX METHOD

In the previous two chapters we discussed the formulation and interpretation of linear optimization models, assuming that the solution was provided by a computer program. Now let us look inside the linear programming solution technique, the *simplex method*. An understanding of how the simplex algorithm functions will contribute to a more effective interpretation of results.

We first present an algebraic development of the solution strategy as an aid to understanding the solution process. Next the simplex algorithm is explained as a series of steps that can be formulated for computer solution. In effect, the algorithm is reduced to a series of mechanical steps, based on organizing the data into a tableau.

We shall use the chemical production problem as a vehicle for discussion. Since we can represent that problem in graphic form, and since we already know the answer, we can see readily what is happening at each stage of the solution. We shall simplify the problem slightly by eliminating the demand constraints. Recall that for the stated problem, these constraints were not effective in dictating the optimal solution anyway. Eliminating them provides a simpler, more direct explanation of the procedure.

Formulation

The statement of the problem was one of allocating time on machines A and B to the two products, x and y, in such a way that contribution to profit and overhead would be maximized. The time requirements on the two machines for each product were given and the total available time on the two machines was limited. (Rereading the Chapter 11 formulation may be of value, but all conditions for the problem are the same except that we will assume that we can sell all products produced within the limits of machine capacity.) Therefore, the resulting linear optimization model is

maximize $Z = 60x + 50y$,
subject to
  $2x + 4y \leq 80$ (machine A),
  $3x + 2y \leq 60$ (machine B),
  $x \geq 0$ (minimum production for chemical x),
  $y \geq 0$ (minimum production for chemical y).

Graphic Solution

Figure 13-1 shows the constraints plotted on a graph and identifies the feasible solution space, *abcd*, and the previously determined optimal allocation of machine time at point *c*; that is, produce $x = 10$ units and $y = 15$ units. Recall also that the contribution for the optimal solution was $1350.

We have plotted in Figure 13-1 the linear objective function for two values of total contribution, $Z = \$900$ and $Z = \$1200$. When we set $Z = \$900$, for example,

$60x + 50y = 900$.

Then, when $x = 0$, we must have $y = 18$, since $60(0) + 50(18) = 900$, and when $y = 0$, we have $x = 15$, since $60(15) + 50(0) = 900$. The resulting straight line is very simple to plot on Figure 13-1. The "$900 line" within the constraints defines all of the feasible solutions that would produce a contribution of $Z = \$900$. Since our objective is to maximize contribution, what happens if we increase Z to $1200? Since the slope of the objective function has not changed, the line for $Z = \$1200$ is parallel to the $900 line, and closer to point *c*, as we note in Figure 13-1. It is now rather obvious for the simple problem that if we substituted larger and larger values of Z in the objective function, lines parallel to the $900 and $1200 lines would result, and a line through point *c* would define a combination of *x* and *y* with the maximum possible contribution within the feasible solution space. Figure 13-1 then provides us with a clear picture of the problem and the relationships for various solutions evaluated by the objective function.

ALGEBRAIC SOLUTION

Let us now proceed through the algebraic steps of the simplex solution to the chemical production problem.

Slack Variables

First, let us note the physical meaning of the constraints on available time for machines A and B. For machine A, since *x* requires 2 hours per unit and *y*

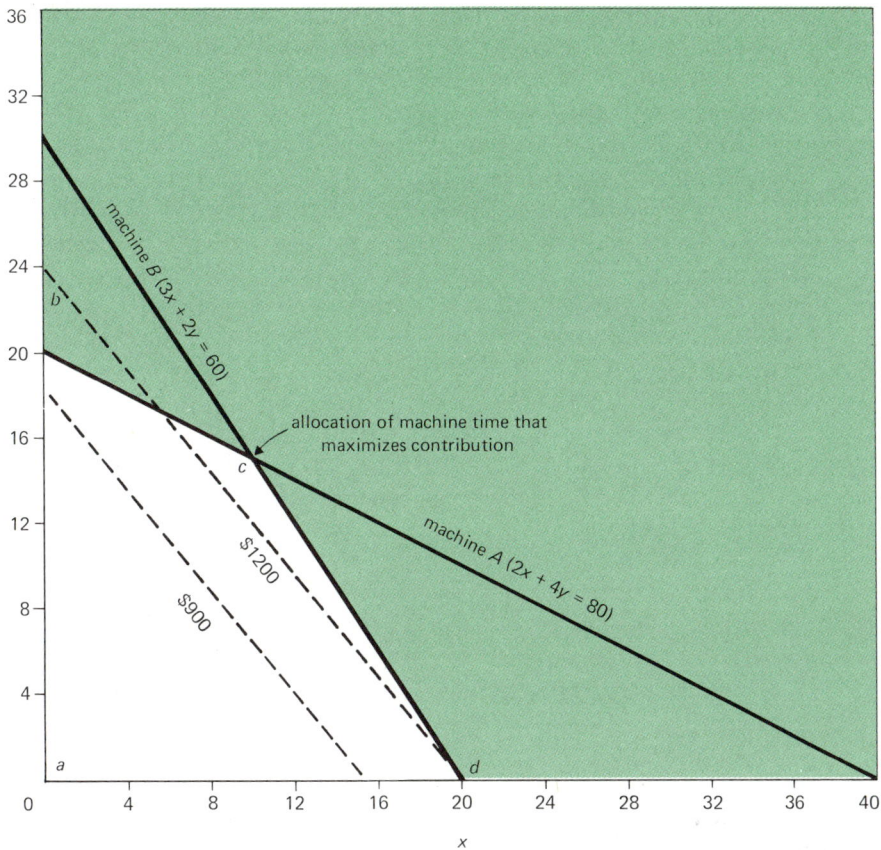

FIGURE 13-1. **Graphic solution of example used for algebraic interpretation of the simplex method**

requires 4 hours per unit, and we are limited to a total of 80 hours, we wrote the inequality constraint

$$2x + 4y \leq 80, \tag{1}$$

and for machine B,

$$3x + 2y \leq 60. \tag{2}$$

The inequalities state that the use of machines A and B is less than or equal to 80 and 60 hours respectively; that is, there *could* be idle machine time. If we take up the slack available, we could convert inequalities (1) and (2) into equations by defining *slack variables* to represent the possible idle time. Therefore,

$$2x + 4y + W_A = 80, \tag{3}$$
$$3x + 2y + W_B = 60, \tag{4}$$

CHAPTER 13 THE SIMPLEX METHOD

where W_A is the idle time for machine A, and W_B the idle time for machine B. We also require W_A and W_B to be nonnegative (W_A, $W_B \geq 0$). The constraints plotted in Figure 13-1 are then lines that indicate the full use of the two machines when $W_A = W_B = 0$. Solutions that involve some idle time are permissible and would fall below one or both of the constraint lines, and would be within the solution space *abcd*.

The effect of solutions involving slack (idle machine time) is easy to see through examples. Assume that the production schedule is 9 units of chemical *x*, and 14 units of chemical *y*. Since 2 hours per unit of *x* and 4 hours per unit of *y* are required of machine A time, and machine A has a total of 80 hours available, we have from equation (3)

$$W_A = 80 - (2)(9) - (4)(14) = 80 - 74 = 6 \text{ hours.}$$

There are 74 productive hours, and the slack in machine A time is taken up as idle time of 6 hours.

Similarly, the idle time on machine B from equation (4) would be

$$W_B = 60 - (3)(9) - (2)(14) = 60 - 55 = 5 \text{ hours.}$$

Now examine Figure 13-1 and note that the point ($x = 9$, $y = 14$) falls inside the feasible solution space, but not on any of the constraint lines. This type of solution is called *nonbasic*.

With the slack variables now in the formulation, the objective function is actually

$$\text{maximize } Z = 60x + 50y + (0)W_A + (0)W_B.$$

The zero coefficients for the slack variables are appropriate, since they make no contribution to profit. The total contribution of the nonbasic solution is

$$Z = (60)(9) + (50)(14) + (0)(6) + (0)(5) = 540 + 700 + 0 + 0 = \$1240.$$

Let us return to our two equations, (3) and (4), with four unknown variables, plus the objective function that we shall use as an evaluative model. Now, recall from simple algebra that we can solve equations simultaneously if there are the same number of unknowns as equations. If we set any two of the four variables to zero, we can solve the two equations simultaneously to find the values of the other two. This is exactly what we will be doing in the following step-by-step procedure.

Solution Procedure

Step 1. *Establish an initial solution.* To start, let us develop a trivial solution whose implications we know and understand—the worst possible solution. We assume no production; that is, $x = y = 0$. We know then that all of the available time on the two machines will be idle, and using the objective function to evaluate the solution, we know that $Z = 0$, since we have produced nothing. Let us solve equations (3) and (4) for W_A and W_B as follows:

$$W_A = 80 - 2x - 4y, \qquad (5)$$
$$W_B = 60 - 3x - 2y, \qquad (6)$$

and our statement of the objective function is

$$Z = 60x + 50y. \qquad (7)$$

If x and y are zero, the values of W_A and W_B are

$$W_A = 80 - 2(0) - 4(0) = 80,$$
$$W_B = 60 - 3(0) - 2(0) = 60.$$

The evaluation of this solution by the objective function is

$$Z = 60(0) + 50(0) = 0,$$

which is the contribution expected when nothing is produced. Note that this is point a in Figure 13-1.

Step 2. *Can the initial solution be improved?* Now, we need a test for optimality in order to know whether to stop or to continue in search of a better solution. We look at the last statement of the objective function, equation (7), and note that both x and y have positive contributions. In other words, we can improve the initial solution by introducing either x or y into the solution with nonzero values.

This is the test: if we examine the last statement of the objective function and find variables in it that improve the objective function, then the solution can be improved. If at some point in the procedure we find only variables that offer no positive contribution to the objective function, then no improvement is possible and we have an optimal solution.

Step 3. *Selecting the incoming variable.* We can improve the solution by making either x or y nonzero. Let us choose the variable that provides the greatest improvement per unit. Since in equation (7), a unit of x earns \$60 and a unit of y only \$50, we select x as the variable to enter the solution with a nonzero value. We shall refer to x as the *incoming variable*. In doing so, we have determined the direction of change in our solution, since x will *increase* from its initial value of zero.

Step 4. *Determine the amount of change in x.* We know that allocating productive time to x will improve the objective function value. For each unit of x produced, we obtain a contribution of \$60. Now, how many units of x should we produce? Since we have found an advantageous direction of change, we wish to press this advantage by producing the maximum possible amount of x, within the constraints of the problem. Suppose we solve equations (3) and (4) for x. From (3) we obtain

$$x = 40 - 2y - \frac{W_A}{2}, \qquad (8)$$

and from (4),

$$x = 20 - \frac{2y}{3} - \frac{W_B}{3}. \tag{9}$$

In the initial solution, $y = 0$. What if W_A were set equal to 0 along with y? From (8), x would equal 40. If W_B were set equal to zero along with y, x would equal 20 in (9).

The smaller of these two numbers, 20, determines how large x can become. From (9), there is no way that x can become larger than 20 without either y or W_B being a negative number, and this is not permitted. This can also be seen in Figure 13–1, since equation (8) refers to the constraint for machine A and equation (9) to the constraint for machine B. Note that $x = 40$ is not in the feasible solution region, but that 20 is the maximum value of x in the feasible region. Therefore, equation (4) determines how large we can make x.

Now let us pause to examine the logic of what we have done in terms of the actual chemical production problem. Machine A has 80 hours available and the time to process chemical x is 2 hours per unit, so if all of the machine A time were allocated to chemical x, as proposed by the solution at this stage, we can produce

$$\frac{80 \text{ hours available}}{2 \text{ hours per unit}} = 40 \text{ units of chemical } x.$$

This is the result obtained from equation (8), if $y = 0$ and $W_A = 0$.

Now let us examine machine B in a similar way. Machine B has 60 hours available, and the time to process chemical x is 3 hours per unit. If all of the machine B time were allocated to the production of chemical x, then the maximum output would be

$$\frac{60 \text{ hours available}}{3 \text{ hours per unit}} = 20 \text{ units of chemical } x.$$

This is the result obtained from equation (9), if $y = 0$ and $W_B = 0$.

Therefore, when machines A and B are considered as a system, the output is limited by machine B to 20 units of chemical x. Also, since the solution at this stage limits x to 20 units, there will be some idle time in machine A because it will produce somewhat less than it could. The values of the slack variables from equations (5) and (6) are

$W_A = 80 - (2)(20) - (4)(0) = 40$ hours,
$W_B = 60 - (3)(20) - (2)(0) = 0$ hours.

In order to increase x to 20, we must reduce W_B to 0, as seen in equation (9). Thus, we will again have a solution with two nonzero values, x and W_A, and with two variables, y and W_B, set equal to zero. To determine the effect of setting

x equal to 20 on W_A, we substitute $20 - 2y/3 - W_B/3$ from (9) into (5), and obtain

$$W_A = 80 - 2\left(20 - \frac{2y}{3} - \frac{W_B}{3}\right) - 4y,$$

which simplifies to

$$W_A = 40 - \frac{8y}{3} + \frac{2W_B}{3}. \tag{10}$$

Thus, with $y = W_B = 0$, we have $W_A = 40$.

Expressions (9) and (10) would be obtained if we simply solved equations (3) and (4) simultaneously for the common values of x and W_A, when y and W_B are assumed to be constants.

We also substitute (9) as the value of x into the last statement of the objective function, equation (7). The objective function then becomes

$$Z = 60\left(20 - \frac{2y}{3} - \frac{W_B}{3}\right) + 50y = 1200 + 10y - 20W_B. \tag{11}$$

With y and W_B set to zero, (11) gives the total contribution of the solution $x = 20$ and $W_A = 40$, which is 1200.

To summarize, by letting y and W_B be zero, we obtain the solution

$x\ \ = 20$, from (9),
$W_A = 40$, from (10),
$y\ \ = 0$,
$W_B = 0$,
$Z\ \ = 1200$, from (11)

This solution is an obvious improvement over the first solution, since the value of the objective function has now increased from zero to $1200. We can see from Figure 13-1 that the second stage of our solution is represented by point d.

Now you may be asking yourself the question: "If we are going to set y and W_B equal to zero anyway, why do we carry them along as excess baggage in equations (9), (10), and (11)?" The answer is that we obtain additional information from having them in (9), (10), and (11). For example, in (11) we now see that an additional unit of y will increase the value of the objective function Z by $10 per unit. Why is the increase only $10 per unit, since the contribution per unit from y as shown in the original formulation is $50 per unit? To increase y from its current value of zero, we will have to decrease x, which has a per unit contribution of $60. However, (11) tells us that the *net effect* of increasing y from the *current solution* will be worth $10 per unit. We can now use the "excess baggage" in (9) and (10) to quickly determine how large to make y.

Let us reflect on these marginal values in the objective function in the context of the actual chemical production problem. From equation (11) the contributions are $10 per unit for chemical y, and $-\$20$ per hour for W_B. Since all of the available time for machine B is allocated to chemical x in the current solution, we cannot process units of chemical y unless we process fewer units of chemical x. Chemical y requires 2 hours per unit on machine B, and chemical x requires 3 hours per unit. If we process one unit of y, we must reduce x by 2/3 units, since y requires 2/3 the time of x on machine B. The result is that while we gain $50 by producing a unit of y, we lose $(2/3)\$60 = \$40$ by processing 2/3 unit less of x. The net gain is, therefore, only $\$50 - \$40 = \$10$, as indicated in equation (11).

Now, how about the $-\$20$ contribution for W_B shown in equation (11)? It says, if we reduce the idle time of $W_B = 60$ hours to only 59 hours, the net cost will be $20. The physical significance of this action is as follows: if we increase the idle time in machine B from $W_B = 0$ to $W_B = 1$, we forego the contribution of 1/3 unit of chemical x (it requires 3 hours per unit of x on machine B), or $(1/3)\$60 = \$20$.

Thus the revised objective function of equation (11) states the marginal values of changing the production plan from the present solution. We could gain $10 per unit by producing chemical y and sacrificing some production of chemical x. We would lose $20 per hour if idle time were introduced into machine B's operations. Obviously, the best next step is to change the production plan by introducing the processing of some of chemical y, even though we sacrifice some output of chemical x. Of course, the question is, how many units of chemical y?

Step 5. *Repeat steps 2, 3, and 4.* Since y has a positive coefficient in (11), we would like to increase it from its current solution value of zero. Notice that W_B has a negative coefficient in (11). The value of the objective function would increase if we could *decrease* W_B. However, W_B is zero in the current solution, and so it cannot be reduced any further. Therefore, we select y as our entering variable.

Using the "excess baggage" in (9) and (10), we solve for y and obtain

$$y = 30 - \frac{3x}{2} - \frac{W_B}{2} \tag{12}$$

from (9) and

$$y = 15 - \frac{3W_A}{8} + \frac{W_B}{4} \tag{13}$$

from (10). W_B is equal to zero in the current solution; setting $x = 0$ gives $y = 30$ from (12), while setting $W_A = 0$ gives $y = 15$ from (13), with the latter being more restrictive. Therefore, we can make $y = 15$ in the revised solution.

Substituting the right hand side of (13) for y in (9) gives

$$x = 20 - \frac{2}{3}\left(15 - \frac{3W_A}{8} + \frac{W_B}{4}\right) - \frac{W_B}{3},$$

which simplifies to

$$x = 10 + \frac{W_A}{4} - \frac{W_B}{2}. \tag{14}$$

Again, we would obtain (13) and (14) by solving (3) and (4) simultaneously for x and y while treating W_A and W_B as constants (check this yourself).

We also substitute the value of y given by equation (13) in the last statement of the objective function (11), and we obtain

$$Z = 1350 - \frac{15W_A}{4} - \frac{35W_B}{2}, \tag{15}$$

or alternately, we can substitute the values of x and y given by equations (13) and (14) in the original statement of the objective function which includes slack variables, $Z = 60x + 50y + (0)W_A + (0)W_B$, and obtain

$$Z = 60 \left(10 + \frac{W_A}{4} - \frac{W_B}{2}\right) + 50 \left(15 - \frac{3W_A}{8} + \frac{W_B}{4}\right) + 0 + 0$$

$$= 600 + \frac{60W_A}{4} - 30W_B + 750 - \frac{150W_A}{8} + \frac{50W_B}{4}$$

$$= 1350 - \frac{15W_A}{4} - \frac{35W_B}{2}.$$

Of course, this is identical with equation (15).

When W_A and W_B are zero, the values of the variables and of the objective function are then as follows:

y = 15, from (13),
x = 10, from (14),
$W_A = 0$,
$W_B = 0$,
Z = 1350, from (15).

We see that this is point c in Figure 13–1, and we know that this is the optimal solution by inspection of Figure 13–1. According to our procedure, however, we know this is true by examining the last statement of the objective function, equation (15). We note that the only possible way that the contribution could be increased is by decreasing either W_A, W_B, or both, since their respective coefficients in (15) are negative. Since the solution at this stage already specifies that W_A and W_B are at their minimum values of zero, and since none of the variables can take on negative values, there is no way to increase contribution, and we have met the requirements for the test of optimality.

Shadow Prices

Recall that the sensitivity analysis provided by the computer program in Figure 11–8 indicated that the value for a marginal unit of capacity for machine A was

$3.75 and for machine B, $17.50. Where do we find these values in the algebraic solution? They are contained in the last statement of the objective function, equation (15). The significance of the coefficients $-15/4$ and $-35/2$ for W_A and W_B respectively is that they are the shadow prices for marginal units of capacity. In other words, for every unit of W_A added in the solution at this point (idle time on machine A), contribution declines by $15/4 = \$3.75$. But conversely, if the original capacity of machine A had been 81 hours instead of 80, net contribution could have been increased by $3.75.

Thus, the coefficients of the slack variables in the objective function are the shadow prices and indeed, had this equivalent meaning at every stage of the solution. In the initial statement of the objective function, equation (7), x and y had marginal contribution rates of 60 and 50 respectively and W_A and W_B had zero rates. In the second stage of solution the objective function was represented by equation (11), and y had a contribution rate of 10 and W_B a rate of -20.

Characteristics of the Simplex Solution

The optimizing model we have developed involved a trial solution of the constraint equations, an evaluation of that solution by the objective function, and a test for optimality. If the optimality test indicated that improvement was possible, we determined the direction of change of the solution (selection of the entering variable) and the amount of change (testing constraints to see how much the entering variable could be increased and selecting the most restrictive equation). This generated a new solution, which was subjected to the same procedure until the test for optimality indicated that no further improvement was possible. The general nature of the algorithmic solution is summarized by Figure 13-2. In Figure 13-2 the predictive model and the objective function are modified to reflect the values of the decision variables for each stage of the solution.

Note that, in fact, we did not consider all possible feasible solutions. Rather, we proceeded to the optimum solution by considering only three alternate solutions, points *a*, *d*, and finally *c* in Figure 13-1. There are an infinite number of combinations of the four variables that we did not bother with as we converged on the optimum solution. For example, proceeding from *a* to *d*, we considered none of the feasible solutions along the line *ad*, which would have yielded progressively larger values of contribution as x increased. Instead, we jumped from *a* to *d*. Similarly, we did not consider any of the feasible solutions along the line *dc*, although each one would have progressively yielded a larger contribution as we converged on the optimum. For example, the point ($x = 16$, $y = 6$) results in $W_A = 24$, $W_B = 0$, and a contribution of $1260.

Also, we did not consider any of the feasible solutions that fell inside the solution space *abcd*. We should note that all of these other solutions that we did not consider, those that lie inside the solution space but not on constraint lines, are feasible solutions that involve more than two of the four variables with

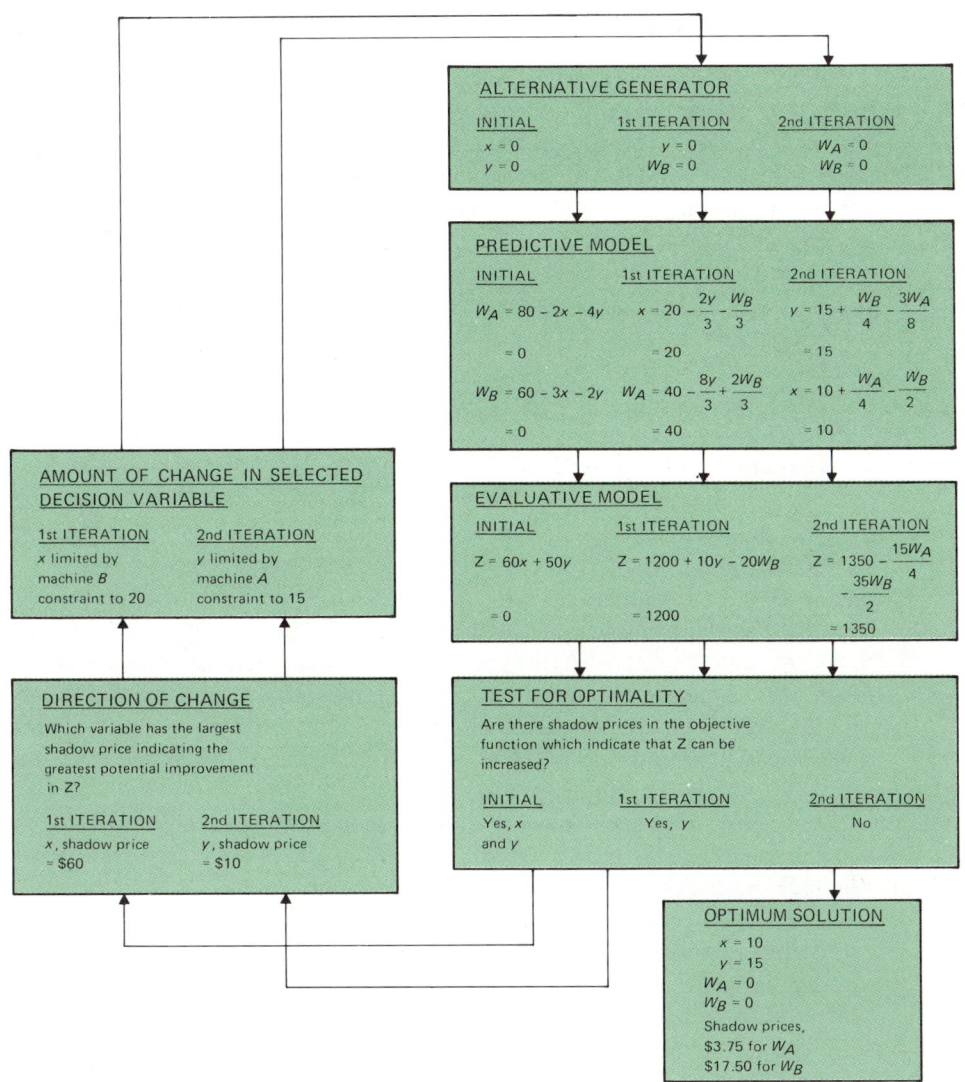

FIGURE 13-2. **Optimizing model indicating initial solution and two iterations for the chemical production problem**

positive values. By requiring that we deal only with solutions where two, and only two, variables could be positive, we jumped from corner to corner, rather than moving more slowly in a larger number of steps along the sides of the solution space or even within its interior. The solutions that involve only two of the four variables are called *basic solutions*. There are only four such basic solutions in our example, at points a, b, c, and d. Feasible solutions that involve more than two of the four variables are nonbasic solutions.

In the larger scale problems, we are doing a similar thing; that is, moving from one basic solution to a better one, jumping over an entire set of other feasible solutions that are in between. These basic solutions are always at the corners of two- and three-dimensional problems, and conceptually at the equivalent of corners of multidimensional problems. This solution strategy is advantageous, since it can be shown that if a linear optimization model actually has an optimal solution, it will lie at a corner point. The proof of this important result is beyond our scope in this discussion, but it provides the rationale for the simplex algorithm.

THE SIMPLEX ALGORITHM

We used simple, even naive problems to explain linear optimization models and the simplex solution technique. The power of linear programming, however, is in the solution of large-scale problems, and the key to their solution has been the simplex algorithm. The simplex algorithm uses the algebraic logic we have just discussed, but reduces this logic to a very efficient set of arithmetic and logical operations so that computing effort is minimized. When the algorithm has been developed in a rigorous way, the computing effort can be further minimized by programming the algorithm for computers. Large-scale problems of resource allocation can then be formulated and solved at reasonable cost. Without the simplex algorithm and without computers, the solution of large-scale problems would be entirely out of reason.

We shall now present a more rigorous description of the simplex method, so that the logic can be programmed on a computer. In reducing the simplex algorithm to a set of rigorous rules, there is a risk that we may begin to think of it as a mechanical procedure, losing contact with what is being accomplished at each stage of solution. We shall try to maintain contact with the meaning of each step by using the chemical production problem as an example again, and relating our manipulations to the process of the preceding algebraic development and to the graphic solution shown in Figure 13–1.

Recall that after the addition of the slack variables to account for idle time, our two restricting equations for machines A and B were respectively

$$2x + 4y + W_A + (0)W_B = 80,$$
$$3x + 2y + (0)W_A + W_B = 60,$$

and the objective function was

$$\text{maximize } 60x + 50y + (0)W_A + (0)W_B = Z.$$

To minimize the recopying of x, y, W_A and W_B, let us rearrange the two restricting equations with the variables at the heads of columns and the coefficients of these variables in rows to represent the equations. The equal signs have also been dropped.

x	y	W_A	W_B	
2	4	1	0	80
3	2	0	1	60

Next we place the coefficients from the objective function above the variables, and to the right we place beside the constants 80 and 60, two columns that identify the variables in the solution and their contribution rates in the objective function, as shown in Table 13-1. This format for a linear optimization model is called the simplex tableau.

Table 13-1 shows the condition of the tableau for the initial solution. Recall that in the algebraic interpretation we started with an initial trivial solution where all of the available machine time was idle. The stub of the tableau identifies the variables in the solution that are nonzero and shows their values. Also shown in the far right column of the stub is the contribution to the objective function made by each of these variables.

TABLE 13-1. **Initial Simplex Tableau**

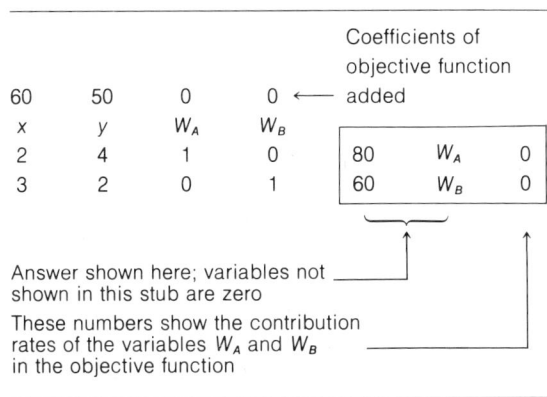

Before proceeding, let us name the various parts of the tableau as shown in Figure 13-3. The objective row contains the coefficients that show the contribution rates for each of the variables in the objective function. For example, the contribution of each unit of x is $60 per unit, y is $50 per unit, W_A is 0, etc. The variable row simply identifies the variable associated with each of the coefficients in the various columns.

The solution stub will always contain three columns. The variable column shows the variables that have positive values (basic variables) at a given stage of solution, *and the variables not shown in the variable column have a value of zero.* The constant column shows the value of each of the variables in the solution. The objective column shows the contribution rates of the variables in

FIGURE 13-3. **Nomenclature of the simplex tableau**

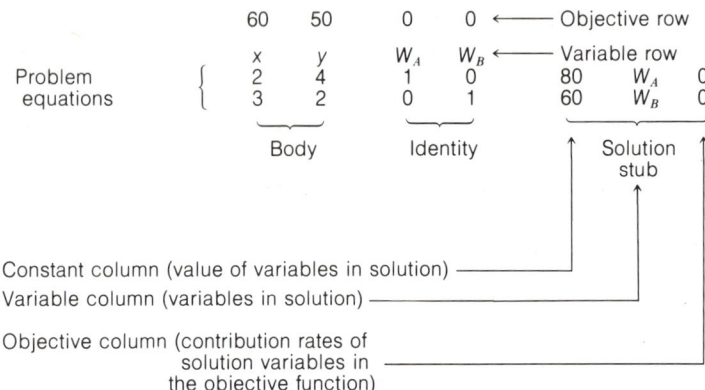

the solution, and these coefficients come from the objective row. For example, in the initial solution, the coefficients above W_A and W_B are zeros.

The body and identity will vary in size, depending on the particular problem. The initial identity will be that portion of the tableau showing the coefficients for slack variables.

We must not lose sight of the fact that the coefficients in the body and the identity are the coefficients of the variables in the variable row, and that the numbers in the constant column are the numerical values of the right-hand side of the constraint equations. They are equations at every stage of solution.

Improving the Initial Solution

To improve the initial solution, we use the test for optimality: "Are there coefficients in the objective function that indicate that Z can be increased?" If there are, we know that we can substitute a variable in the solution that has a higher contribution rate to the objective function than one of the variables now in the solution. In order to establish a systematic index of potential improvement we develop an *index row* of coefficients, that will be placed just below the present initial tableau. The index numbers will appear under the body, the identity, and the constant column, and are calculated from the following formula:

index number = (number in objective row at head of column)
$\quad - \sum$ (numbers in column) × (corresponding   (16)
number in objective column).

Recall that the numbers in the objective column represent the contribution rates of the variables that are in the solution to the two constraint equations in the initial tableau. The numbers in the column, such as the coefficient 2 under column x, are the coefficients of the variables for which the index row is being computed. What we have then is a modification of the objective function to reflect the marginal contribution rates of variables not now in the solution. If the coefficient for any of the variables is positive, they are candidates for changes in allocation.

For our problem, the index row numbers are as follows:

1. index number for first column of body
   $= 60 - (2 \times 0 + 3 \times 0) = 60$
2. index number for second column of body
   $= 50 - (4 \times 0 + 2 \times 0) = 50$
3. index number for first column of identity
   $= 0 - (1 \times 0 + 0 \times 0) = 0$
4. index number for second column of identity
   $= 0 - (0 \times 0 + 1 \times 0) = 0$
5. index number for constant column
   $= 0 - (80 \times 0 + 60 \times 0) = 0$

We now place the index numbers in the initial simplex tableau as indicated in Table 13-2. We see that this was a trivial step in that we have merely copied the objective row coefficients and inserted the value of the objective function, 0, as the left-hand side of the objective function equation. Note, however, that this trivial transformation occurs only when the objective column contains all zeros, that is, when the variables in the solution all have the value of zero.

Before proceeding, let us compare the initial simplex tableau with equations (5), (6), and (7), which represented the initial solution in the algebraic method. Equation (5) takes the following form, if we transpose all of the variables to the left of the equal sign, leaving the constant on the right:

$2x + 4y + W_A = 80.$

The coefficients of this equation are exactly the same as those of the first row under the variable row of Table 13-2, excluding the variable and objective columns.

Next, equation (6) takes the following form when rearranged:

$3x + 2y + W_B = 60.$

The coefficients of this equation are identical with those of the second row under the variable row.

Finally, equation (7) takes the following form when rearranged:

$60x + 50y + (0)W_A + (0)W_B = Z.$

Again, these are the coefficients of the index row, recalling that in the initial solution, $Z = 0$.

TABLE 13-2. **Initial Simplex Tableau with Index Row Included**

	60	50	0	0			
	x	y	W_A	W_B			
	2	4	1	0	80	W_A	0
	3	2	0	1	60	W_B	0
Index row →	60	50	0	0	0		

TABLE 13-3. **Initial Simplex Tableau with Key Column, Row, and Number Identified**

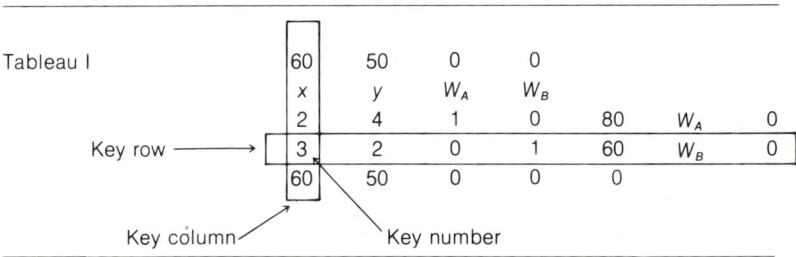

Selecting the Key Column and Key Row We can see from Table 13-2 that the column headed by the variable x has the greatest improvement potential, since it has the largest positive coefficient in the index row (contribution rate is $60), so we select it as the *key column*. This selection means that the variable x will be introduced into the solution in favor of W_A or W_B. The selection of the key column then determines the "direction of change" as indicated in the flow chart for this example in Figure 13-2.

To determine whether x will replace W_A or W_B, we must select a key row. To do this, we *divide each number in the constant column by the corresponding positive nonzero number in the key column*. The resulting quotients are compared, and the key row is selected as the row yielding the smallest nonnegative quotient. For our problem, the quotients are:

first row, $\dfrac{80}{2} = 40$,

second row, $\dfrac{60}{3} = 20$ (key row).

Through the selection of the key row, we are determining which of the two constraint equations will be the more restrictive on the value of x. See equations (8) and (9) to verify that we have performed exactly the same computation as we did at that point in the algebraic development. The essence of this step is related easily to Figure 13-1. If y is 0, we can see from Figure 13-1 that the maximum value for x in the machine A constraint equation is 40. Similarly, the maximum value for x in the machine B constraint equation is 20 when y is set to 0. Note that the latter is point d in Figure 13-1. The second row is selected as the key row, then, because the point d is in the feasible solution set, whereas, the value of $x = 40$ is not feasible.

Since the second row limits the value of x, it is designated the key row, and the number at the intersection of the key row and the key column is designated the *key number*. Table 13-3 shows the initial tableau with the key column, key row, and key number identified.

Developing an Improved Solution

With the key column and key row selected, we can now prepare a new tableau representing an improved solution. The first step in developing the new tableau is to calculate the coefficients for the *main row*. This main row appears in the relative position in the new tableau as the key row in the preceding tableau. It is computed by dividing the coefficients of the key row by the key number. Table 13-4 shows this development. The variable and its objective number from the head of the key column, that is, x and 60, are placed in the stub of the main row replacing W_B and 0 from the previous tableau. The balance of the objective and variable columns in the stub is copied from the previous tableau and the new tableau developed to this point now appears in Table 13-5.

Now all of the remaining coefficients in the new tableau, including the constant column, the body, identity, and index row can be calculated by the following formula:

$$\text{new number} = \text{old number} - \frac{\begin{pmatrix}\text{corresponding}\\ \text{number of}\\ \text{key row}\end{pmatrix} \times \begin{pmatrix}\text{corresponding}\\ \text{number of}\\ \text{key column}\end{pmatrix}}{\text{key number}} \quad (17)$$

1. first row, constant column,
   new number $= 80 - (60 \times 2)/3 = 40$
2. first row, first column of body,
   new number $= 2 - (3 \times 2)/3 = 0$
3. index row, first column of body,
   new number $= 60 - (3 \times 60)/3 = 0$

The remaining coefficients can be calculated in the same way and the completed improved solution is shown in Tableau II in Table 13-6.

Note that the solution at this stage is $x = 20$, $W_A = 40$, $y = 0$, $W_B = 0$, and that the value of the objective function is 1200, as shown in the solution stub. (While the right-hand side of the index row in Table 13-6 is -1200, when transposed and solved for Z, as in equation (11), the value is $Z = 1200 + 10y - 20W_B = 1200$, a positive contribution, since y and W_B are zero in the solution.)

TABLE 13-4. **Simplex Tableau with Main Row of New Table**

Tableau I

	60	50	0	0			
	x	y	W_A	W_B			
	2	4	1	0	80	W_A	0
	3	2	0	1	60	W_B	0
	60	50	0	0	0		

Tableau II

	1	$\tfrac{2}{3}$	0	$\tfrac{1}{3}$	20	Main row

TABLE 13-5. **Simplex Tableau with Variable and Objective Columns Completed**

Tableau I

	60	50	0	0			
	x	y	W_A	W_B			
	2	4	1	0	80	W_A	0
	3	2	0	1	60	W_B	0
	60	50	0	0	0		

Tableau II

						W_A	0
	1	$\tfrac{2}{3}$	0	$\tfrac{1}{3}$	20	x	60

TABLE 13-6. **Simplex Tableau with First Iteration Completed**

Tableau I

	60	50	0	0			
	x	y	W_A	W_B			
	2	4	1	0	80	W_A	0
	3	2	0	1	60	W_B	0
	60	50	0	0	0		

Tableau II

	0	$2\tfrac{2}{3}$	1	$-\tfrac{2}{3}$	40	W_A	0
	1	$\tfrac{2}{3}$	0	$\tfrac{1}{3}$	20	x	60
	0	10	0	−20	−1200		

Now, let us pause again and compare the coefficients in Tableau II of Table 13-6 with those of equations (9), (10), and (11) in the algebraic method. Equations (10), (9), and (11), when rearranged, are as follows:

$$\frac{8y}{3} + W_A - \frac{2W_B}{3} = 40 \tag{10}$$

$$x + \frac{2y}{3} + \frac{1W_B}{3} = 20 \tag{9}$$

$$10y - 20W_B = Z - 1200 \tag{11}$$

The coefficients of these equations check with the coefficients in Tableau II of Table 13-6, exclusive of the variable and objective columns.

Third and Optimal Solution

Next, we examine the index row of Tableau II in Table 13-6, and we see that potential improvement still exists, since the coefficient 10 appears under the variable y. The index row has only one positive number, and y is selected as the key column for the next iteration. The key row is selected in the same way as previously and the two quotients are:

first row, $40/(8/3) = 15$ (key row),

second row, $20/(2/3) = 30$.

The first row has the smallest nonnegative quotient, so it is selected as the key row. A new main row is calculated as before, by dividing the coefficients in the main row by the key number. The new variable y and its objective number are entered in the stub, and the new numbers in the body, identity, and index row are computed as before. The remaining variable and its objective number are copied from the preceding iteration tableau, and Table 13-7 shows the new solution in Tableau III.

The new solution in Table 13-7 is optimal, since no further improvement is indicated in the index row; that is, the shadow prices are either zero or negative. The values of the variables in the solution for maximum contribution are given in the solution stub. The values of the variables for the optimal solution are: $x = 10$, $y = 15$, $W_A = 0$, $W_B = 0$, and the value of the objective function is $1350. Of course, all these values check with our previous algebraic solution and with the graphic solution. Note also that the final index row yields the shadow prices obtained previously for W_A and W_B.

TABLE 13-7. **Simplex Tableau Second and Final Iterations Completed**

Tableau I

	60	50	0	0			
	x	y	W_A	W_B			
	2	4	1	0	80	W_A	0
	3	2	0	1	60	W_B	0
	60	50	0	0	0		

Tableau II

0	$2\frac{2}{3}$	1	$-\frac{2}{3}$	40	W_A	0
1	$\frac{2}{3}$	0	$\frac{1}{3}$	20	x	60
0	10	0	-20	-1200		

Tableau III

0	1	$\frac{3}{8}$	$-\frac{1}{4}$	15	y	50
1	0	$-\frac{1}{4}$	$\frac{1}{2}$	10	x	60
0	0	$-3\frac{3}{4}$	$-17\frac{1}{2}$	-1350		

Again, let us examine Tableau III in Table 13-7 and compare it to the equivalent algebraic step. Equations (13), (14), and (15), when rearranged, are as follows:

$$y + \frac{3W_A}{8} - \frac{1W_B}{4} = 15 \tag{13}$$

$$x - \frac{1W_A}{4} + \frac{1W_B}{2} = 10 \tag{14}$$

$$-\frac{15W_A}{4} - \frac{35W_B}{2} = Z - 1350 \tag{15}$$

The coefficients of these equations check with the coefficients of the first, second, and index rows of Tableau III, in the body, identity, and constant column.

To summarize, we have been making an important point by comparing the coefficients in the tableaus with those of the comparable equations in the algebraic method. The point is that the tableau method of solution actually accomplishes the equivalent steps of the algebraic method, but by an efficient mechanical procedure. There is no recopying of the variables required. By following the procedure carefully, one can solve problems of moderate size by hand much more quickly (and probably accurately) than by the algebraic method. What is really important, however, is that the computations can be computerized so that large-scale problems can be solved.

Summary of the Procedure

The simplex tableau approach can be summarized by the following steps:
1. Formulate the problem and the objective function.
2. Develop the initial simplex tableau, including the initial trivial solution and the index row numbers. The index row numbers in the initial tableau are calculated by the formula:

$$\text{index number} = \begin{pmatrix} \text{number in} \\ \text{objective} \\ \text{row at head} \\ \text{of column} \end{pmatrix} - \sum \begin{pmatrix} \text{numbers} \\ \text{in} \\ \text{column} \end{pmatrix} \times \begin{pmatrix} \text{corresponding} \\ \text{number in} \\ \text{objective} \\ \text{column} \end{pmatrix}.$$

3. *Select the key column*, the column with the largest positive number in the index row of the body or the identity.
4. *Select the key row*, the row with the smallest nonnegative quotient obtained by dividing each number of the constant column by the corresponding positive number in the key column.
5. *The key number* is at the intersection of the key row and key column.
6. *Develop the main row of the new tableau.*

$$\text{Main row} = \frac{\text{numbers in key row of preceding tableau}}{\text{key number}}.$$

The main row appears in the new tableau in the same relative position as the key row of the preceding tableau.

7. *Develop the balance of the new tableau.*
    a. The variable and its objective number at the head of the key column are entered in the stub of the new tableau to the right of the main row. These new numbers replace the variable and objective number from the key row of the preceding tableau.
    b. The remainder of the variable and objective columns are reproduced in the new tableau exactly as they were in the preceding tableau.
    c. The balance of the coefficients for the new tableau are calculated by the formula:

$$\text{new number} = \text{old number} - \frac{\begin{pmatrix} \text{corresponding} \\ \text{number of} \\ \text{key row} \end{pmatrix} \times \begin{pmatrix} \text{corresponding} \\ \text{number of} \\ \text{key column} \end{pmatrix}}{\text{key number}}$$

8. Repeat steps 3 through 7c until all the index numbers (not including the constant column) are negative or zero. An optimal solution then results.
9. The resulting optimum solution is interpreted in the following manner: the solution appears in the stub. The variables shown in the variable column have the values shown in the corresponding rows of the

constant column. The value of the objective function is shown in the constant column, index row. All variables not shown in the stub are zero. The shadow prices that indicate the value of a marginal unit of each variable not in the solution are shown in the index row of the final solution.

The output for the computer solution, including sensitivity analysis for the simplified chemical production problem, is shown in Figure 13-4. Note that the format is the same as the computer output illustrated in Chapter 11, showing the optimal value of the objective function, the optimal value of the decision variables, the shadow prices, and the upper and lower bounds on the right-hand values of the constraints and of the prices in the objective function.

SENSITIVITY ANALYSIS

The manager can use the sensitivity analysis shown in Figure 13-4 in the ways that we indicated in Chapter 11. To an alert manager, the optimum solution not only provides answers—given assumptions about resources, prices, and capacities—but should raise questions about what would happen *if* conditions should change. Some of these changes might be imposed by the environment, such as changes in resource costs and market constraints, or they might occur if resources were curtailed. Some, however, represent questions raised by the manager because they are changes that he can initiate, such as enlarging capacities or adding new activities. Obviously, it is possible to answer some of these questions by new computer runs, but why make the added runs if the information is already available in the present optimal solution? Sensitivity analysis is focused on the objective function and on the values for the right-hand sides of the constraints. Let us now consider how such analyses are developed.

Analysis of the Objective Function

We have already referred to the shadow prices and their significance. What happens if the unit prices (contributions or costs) in the objective function change? Would the optimal solution remain comprised of the same combination of decision variables? (Of course, the *value* of the objective function would change if the prices changed.)

Changes in Nonbasic Variables For our example, let us first consider the prices for the nonbasic variables W_A and W_B, which are not in the optimal solution. If we could sufficiently increase the profitability of idle time, the solution could change. (This is seemingly ridiculous for the chemical production example, but consider other cases, where a value is placed on idle resources, for example, government agricultural subsidies. Of course, another company might be willing to pay rent on available idle capacity.)

```
                              LPRUN
                        CHEMICAL PRODUCTION
      THE OPTIMAL VALUE OF THE OBJECTIVE FUNCTION IS:   1350.000
                    THE VARIABLES IN THE SOLUTION ARE
       VARIABLE  X      AT LEVEL    1.0000E1
                Y                   1.5000E1
       DO YOU WISH SENSITIVITY ANALYSIS? Y
                              SHADOW       LB         CURRENT        UB
       CONSTRAINT     1      3.7500E0    4.0000E1    8.0000E1     1.2000E2
                      2      1.7500E1    4.0000E1    6.0000E1     1.2000E2

       PRICE    X                        2.5000E1    6.0000E1     7.5000E1
                Y                        4.0000E1    5.0000E1     1.2000E2
```

FIGURE 13-4. **Computer solution and sensitivity analysis for the simplified chemical production problem**

Recall that the rows in the simplex tableau actually represent equations at every stage of the solution. If the W_A contribution were increased by Δ, then the initial index row in the tableau becomes

$$60 \quad 50 \quad (0 + \Delta) \quad 0.$$

For convenience in this section, we rewrite this row inserting the variables, and the corresponding equation is

$$60x + 50y + (0 + \Delta)W_A + (0)W_B = Z.$$

If we perform the simplex transformations at each iteration as before, the index row in the final tableau would become

$$(0)x + (0)y + \left(\frac{-15}{4} + \Delta\right)W_A - \frac{35W_B}{2} = Z - 1350.$$

Notice that these are the coefficients of the final index row of Tableau III in table 13-7, except that $+\Delta$ is added to the coefficient of W_A.

For the solution in Table 13-7 to remain optimal, the coefficient of W_A must be negative or zero. This means that

$$\frac{-15}{4} + \Delta \leq 0$$

or $\Delta \leq \frac{15}{4}$. Otherwise, if $\Delta > \frac{15}{4}$, the coefficient of W_A becomes positive, and by the rules of the simplex algorithm, W_A would enter the solution in exchange for x or y. The *absolute values* of the final index row coefficients of the *nonbasic* variables represent the largest positive increments to the original objective function coefficients for those variables that would not alter the current optimal solution.

Basic Variables   Now, what is the effect of changing the contribution of basic variables in the final solution, such as x and y? For example, within what range is the coefficient for x valid for the current solution? If we add an increment Δ_x to the contribution for x in the initial index row, we have

$$(60 + \Delta_x)x + 50y + (0)W_A + (0)W_B = Z.$$

Again, if we perform the simplex arithmetic transformations at each iteration, the final index row is

$$\Delta_x x - \frac{15W_A}{4} - \frac{35W_B}{2} = Z - 1350. \tag{18}$$

However, since x is a basic variable, its coefficient must equal 0 in every row, including the index row, except for the row in which its coefficient is 1 (row 2 in this example). If we alter the index row of Tableau III in Table 13-7, according to equation (18), we have the revised Tableau III shown in Table 13-8.

Note now, that there is a positive contribution of Δ_x, so we must perform another iteration in the usual way. The key column and row are determined and shown in Table 13-8, and the coefficients of Tableau IV are generated according to the rules.

TABLE 13-8. **Final Iteration With the Contribution of Basic Variable x Increased by Δ_x**

Tableau III						
0	1	$\frac{3}{8}$	$-\frac{1}{4}$	15	y	50
1	0	$-\frac{1}{4}$	$\frac{1}{2}$	10	x	60
Δ_x	0	$-\frac{15}{4}$	$-\frac{35}{2}$	-1350		
Tableau IV						
0	1	$\frac{3}{8}$	$-\frac{1}{4}$	15	y	50
1	0	$-\frac{1}{4}$	$\frac{1}{2}$	10	x	60
0	0	$\left(-\frac{15}{4} + \frac{\Delta_x}{4}\right)$	$\left(-\frac{35}{2} - \frac{\Delta_x}{2}\right)$	$(-1350 - 10\Delta_x)$		

Examine the index row of Tableau IV in Table 13–8. For this current solution to remain optimal, the coefficients of W_A and W_B must remain negative or zero. Therefore, we require

$$-\frac{15}{4} + \frac{\Delta_x}{4} \leq 0$$

for W_A. Simplifying, we obtain $\Delta_x \leq 15$. Similarly we have

$$-\frac{35}{2} - \frac{\Delta_x}{2} \leq 0$$

for W_B, so $\Delta_x \geq -35$. Thus, the *change* to the original contribution of x, 60 must be between -35 and 15 units. This means that the same solution will be optimal if the contribution of x is any number as small as $60 - 35 = 25$ or as large as $60 + 15 = 75$, as long as the other data in the problem remain unchanged. A similar analysis for chemical y indicates its range to be 40 to 120. Check these bounds on x and y with the computer sensitivity analysis in Figure 13-4.

Sensitivity of Right-Hand Side Constants

Now if the resources were to change, under what conditions would the solution change? These resources for our problem were the available hours on machines A and B of 80 and 60 hours respectively. First, let us consider the machine A constraint. If we added an increment of hours, Δ_A, to the 80-hour limit, the initial tableau becomes

2	4	1	0	$(80 + 1\Delta_A)$	W_A	0
3	2	0	1	$(60 + 0\Delta_A)$	W_B	0
60	50	0	0	$(\ 0 + 0\Delta_A)$		

Notice that we have added a new variable to this problem on the right-hand side of the equations. The coefficients of this new variable are 1 in row 1, and 0 in row 2 and in the index row. These are the same coefficients as for the variable W_A, the slack variable for row 1. In applying the simplex method, we divide every coefficient in a row by the same constant, or we multiply every coefficient in a row by the same constant. The result is that if the coefficients of two different variables are identical in every row in the initial tableau, they will be identical after every iteration, including the final one. Therefore, it is not necessary to re-solve the initial tableau with Δ_A added to the right-hand side. We know that the solution would be

0	1	$\frac{3}{8}$	$-\frac{1}{4}$	$\left(15 + \frac{3\Delta_A}{8}\right)$	y	50
1	0	$-\frac{1}{4}$	$\frac{1}{2}$	$\left(10 - \frac{\Delta_A}{4}\right)$	x	60
0	0	$\frac{-15}{4}$	$\frac{-35}{2}$	$-1350 - \frac{15\Delta_A}{4}$		

where the coefficients of Δ_A are identical to those of W_A.

For the optimal solution to be feasible, the optimal values of the basic variables must be nonnegative. Therefore, we have the relation

$$15 + \frac{3}{8}\Delta_A \geq 0$$

from row 1, which simplifies to $\Delta_A \geq -40$. From row 2,

$$10 - \frac{1}{4}\Delta_A \geq 0$$

or $\Delta_A \leq 40$. The same basic variables will be "in the solution" as long as $-40 \leq \Delta_A \leq 40$, or as long as the available hours on machine A are between $80 - 40 = 40$ and $80 + 40 = 120$. However, in this case the *values* of these basic variables would change.

Note in the index row the value of the objective function, Z, is $1350 + (15/4)\Delta_A$. This value emphasizes that $15/4$ is the shadow price, or marginal value, of an additional hour on Machine A. This shadow price is valid for any number of machine hours within the range of 40 to 120.

For example, suppose we can obtain 10 additional hours of time on machine A by changing our maintenance techniques. Thus, $\Delta_A = 10$, which is within the range -40 to $+40$. The new values of the basic variables are given by

$$y = 15 + \frac{3\Delta_A}{8}$$
$$x = 10 - \frac{\Delta_A}{4}$$

Substituting $\Delta_A = 10$, we obtain

$$y = 15 + \frac{3(10)}{8} = 18.75,$$
$$x = 10 - \frac{10}{4} = 7.50,$$

and the new value of the objective function is

$$Z = 1350 + \frac{15(10)}{4} = 1387.5.$$

We can apply the same type of analysis for the machine B constraint. Suppose we add an increment of Δ_B to the 60-hour limit on machine B in the initial set of equations. Then the coefficients for Δ_B in the final set of equations will be the same as the coefficients for W_B in the final set of equations. Therefore, the right-hand sides of the final set of equations, and the associated values of Δ_B will be

$$15 - \frac{\Delta_B}{4} \geq 0,$$

which gives $\Delta_B \leq 60$ from row 1, and

$$10 + \frac{\Delta_B}{2} \geq 0,$$

which gives $\Delta_B \geq -20$ from row 2. The range for the right-hand side constant for machine B is then $60 - 20 = 40$, and $60 + 60 = 120$, or 40 to 120. Check these ranges with the computer sensitivity analysis in Figure 13-4. (Note that these ranges are not the same as those given in Figure 11-8 because the constraint set included market limitations in that problem.)

These bounds apply when each right-hand side constant is varied independently. A similar, but more complex analysis is called for when several changes are made simultaneously [see Wagner, 1975].

EXTENSIONS OF THE SIMPLEX ALGORITHM

The simplex algorithm may be extended to deal with alternate optimal solutions and with degenerate solutions, as well as with other forms of the constraints (as described later in this section). These extensions are of definite interest to the manager.

Alternate Optimal Solutions The identification of alternate optimal solutions is important, since they provide flexibility for the manager in his decisions. What if one of the coefficients of a nonbasic variable is 0 in the index row of an iteration, and the other coefficients are all positive? Recall that the coefficients of the nonbasic variables indicate how much the objective function will change with a unit increase in the associated variable. If the coefficient in the index row is 0, then the corresponding variable can enter the solution without changing the value of the objective function. If this occurs when there are no positive coefficients in the index row, the existing solution is optimal, but the solution that would be found by "bringing in" the variable with the 0 coefficient would also be optimal. It would have the same objective function value since the change per unit is 0.

Degeneracy When one or more of the basic variables are actually "in the solution" with a value of 0, the solution is said to be degenerate. This condition was the cause for some alarm in the early days of linear programming, since theoretically the simplex algorithm can fail if degeneracy occurs. However, this failure has never been reported in a practical problem, so the issue now seems of concern only to analysts.

Minimizing an Objective Function The procedure with which we have been dealing is a maximizing one, but it can also be applied to minimize an objective function. Suppose that we had wished to maximize the time that the equipment was in use. Using the chemical production problem as an example, the objective function would have been

$$\text{minimize } Z = W_A + W_B,$$

since W_A and W_B represent the slack or idle time on machines A and B respectively. To convert the minimizing objective function for use in the maximizing algorithm that we developed, we simply multiply the foregoing statement by -1 and obtain

$$\text{maximize } Z = -W_A - W_B.$$

This change does not alter the objective function, but makes it possible to use the maximizing procedure. We may also alter the procedure to minimize an objective function by changing one simple rule in the algorithm. When selecting the entering variable, the one with the most negative number in the index row is selected, rather than the one with the largest positive number. All other steps remain exactly the same.

Requirements The constraints in the example problem were both restrictions that the values of the left-hand sides be less than or equal to the maximum amounts of time available on machines A and B. There may be situations, however, in which we are given a requirement that some combination of the variables must be greater than or equal to a given number. For example, the inequality

$$3x + 2y \geq 12$$

has a requirement of at least 12. To convert this statement to an equation, we must *subtract* a slack variable, and the result is

$$3x + 2y - W_1 = 12.$$

A slack variable that is subtracted in a requirement is sometimes called a *surplus variable* because it indicates an excess supply relative to the right-hand side constant (see the feed mix problem in Chapter 11).

As it stands, this equation cannot be used in the simplex method because the coefficient for W_1 is -1. The simplex method requires that each row must have exactly one variable with a coefficient of $+1$, which appears in the identity. When all of the constraints are restrictions, this requirement is achieved for the initial set of equations by adding the slack variables. We can accomplish the same objective in this case by addition of an *artificial variable U*, so that the equation becomes

$$3x + 2y - W_1 + U = 12.$$

The artificial variable is included simply as a computational device that permits us to stay within the rules of the algorithm. Consequently, an artificial variable is not wanted in the optimum solution. To be sure that the artificial variable will always be zero in the optimum solution, we may assign an arbitrarily large negative contribution to it in the objective function, which we shall call $-M$. The $-M$ is in reality an overwhelming cost in relation to the positive contributions in the objective function, so that as the objective function is maximized through the usual procedure, the artificial variable is driven to zero.

Equations A problem may state that a certain combination of variables must total some exact quantity. To fit into the requirements of the simplex format we must have a variable in the equation with a coefficient of $+1$ that appears in the identity. For example, the equation

$$2x + 3y = 90$$

can be modified to fit into the simplex format by adding an artificial variable U. The equation then becomes

$$2x + 3y + U = 90.$$

As with the approach for requirements, a $-M$ price is assigned to the artificial variable U in the objective function so that the artificial variable is always zero in the optimum solution.

Nonlinear Expressions The simplex algorithm can only be applied to problems that can be transformed into systems of linear equations. If nonlinear relationships exist, in some cases it may be possible to approximate them with linear relationships. If this can be accomplished, the powerful simplex algorithm can still be used. The use of linear approximations to nonlinear relationships is a topic of importance for the analyst, but clearly beyond our scope here. However, the manager should be willing to work with the analyst in evaluating whether or not such approximations can be used. When linear approximations cannot be used and the analyst must work with the nonlinear relationships, the algorithms become much more complex, and problem solution becomes much more costly.

WHAT SHOULD THE MANAGER KNOW?

In Chapter 11 we argued that the manager need not concern himself with the mathematical complexities of the linear programming solution technique. Yet, in this chapter, we have presented that technique in some detail. The relevant question at this point is, "What should the manager know about the simplex algorithm?"

The Simplex Algorithm It is most unlikely that a manager would ever consider solving a practical linear programming problem by hand. The computational effort would not be justified, since standard computer codes are available that can efficiently handle problems involving more than 1000 constraints. Therefore, the rationale for studying the algorithm must be based on other considerations.

A manager should not be intimidated by the techniques of management science. Understanding the basic strategy of the simplex algorithm may be helpful in appreciating what linear programming can and cannot do. After all, when reduced to simplest terms, the nature of the simplex technique is to solve simultaneous equations successively in a sequence controlled by a test for optimality. The logic of the method is straightforward and relatively simple to comprehend. This knowledge may make the manager more comfortable in dealing with technical analysts and more confident in using the results of computerized solutions to linear optimization models.

The manager should be sufficiently familiar with linear programming to be able to exploit certain simple extensions in problem formulation. For example, if the solution indicates that an alternative optimal solution exists, it should be welcomed as providing additional flexibility and a further opportunity to exercise judgment. Flexibility in the form of the objective function and the constraints is also important in increasing the number of real-world problems that can be formulated as linear optimization models.

Check Your Understanding

1. The Elmore Electronics Corporation was presented as exercise 14 in Chapter 11. Continue your study of that problem by creating a graphic means of solution.
    a. Plot the constraints on a graph, using the number of oscilloscopes (O) for the horizontal axes, and the number of voltmeters (V) for the vertical axes.
    b. Plot the objective function on the same graph for the value of Z = $36,000. Which two constraints appear to limit the size of the contribution?
    c. Solve simultaneously for values of O and V the two equations that limit the size of total contribution.
    d. Look at your graph of constraints. Are there any constraints that can be ignored completely since they have no possible effect, that is, they are redundant?
2. What is the function of slack variables in the simplex method of solution?
3. What is the physical meaning of slack variables in the following types of constraints?
    a. constraint on the capacity of a machine
    b. constraint on the size of the market
    c. constraint on the total expenditure on advertising in various media
4. Explain the rationale of step 1, "establish an initial solution," in the algebraic solution. Why start with the worst possible solution?

5. In the algebraic solution procedure, what is the test for determining whether or not an initial or other solution can be improved?
6. Suppose in attempting to improve a solution, we have several variables with positive contributions in the objective function. How do we select the incoming variable?
7. Given that we have selected the incoming variable, which indicates the variable that will increase from its initial value of zero, how do we determine how much to increase the value of that variable? What limits the size of the incoming variable?
8. When we have decided on the limiting size of the incoming variable by testing to determine the maximum value it can have in either of the constraints, how do we modify the objective function in order to determine whether or not we now have an optimum solution?

    In the text example, the original contribution y in the objective function was $50 per unit. Why is the contribution of y only $10 at the end of Tableau II?
9. What is the test for optimality in the algebraic procedure?
10. Following is a linear optimization model for a simplified version of the Elmore Electronics Corporation problem that you solved graphically in exercise 1. Now solve it using the algebraic procedure we have outlined:

    maximize $Z = 100O + 40V$,
    subject to
    $$6.3O + 1.5V \leq 2500,$$
    $$7O + 3V \leq 3000,$$
    $$O, V \geq 0.$$

11. Place the preceding problem solved by the algebraic method into the optimization model framework of Figure 13-2. As is done in Figure 13-2, divide the steps into alternative generator, predictive model, evaluative model, test for optimality, direction of change, amount of change, and optimum solution. For your example problem, indicate each iteration for each block equivalent to Figure 13-2.
12. What is a feasible solution? A basic solution? Identify both kinds of solutions in Figure 13-1. Can a feasible solution be basic? Must a feasible solution be basic?
13. In analyzing the sensitivity of the cost coefficients of *nonbasic* variables in the objective function, suppose that the initial objective function (index row in equation form) were $10x + 5y + (0)A + (0)B = Z$. After all of the simplex transformations, the equation representing the index row of the final simplex tableau is $(0)x + (0)y - 5A/17 - 30B/17 = Z - 2900/17$.

    If the contribution for A were increased from zero to $(0 + \Delta)$, what would the coefficient for A be in the index row of the final tableau? If $\Delta = 1/2$, would the solution change?
14. Now, let us consider sensitivity analysis for the *basic* variables in the objective function indicated in exercise 13. Suppose that an increment, Δ_y, is added to

the contribution for y. The initial objective function (index row in equation form) becomes $10x + (5 + \Delta_y)y + (0)A + (0)B = Z$. After we perform the simplex arithmetic transformations, the final index row in equation form is, $\Delta_y y - (5A/17) - (30B/17) = Z - 2900/17$. The simplex tableau at this stage of solution would then be:

x	y	A	B			
0	1	5/17	−4/17	180/17	x	5
1	0	−2/17	5/17	200/17	y	10
0	Δ_y	−5/17	−30/17	−2900/17		

a. Is the solution still optimal? Why?
b. If the solution is not optimal, perform the necessary simplex iterations to make it optimal.
c. From (b), what is the sensitivity of the basic variable y in the objective function; that is, what is the range in the value of the cost coefficients of y that will maintain the same final simplex solution?

15. In sensitivity analysis of the right-hand side constants of the constraints, why is it not necessary to re-solve the initial tableau if an increment Δ is added to one of the right-hand side constants?

16. Suppose that the initial and final simplex tableaus for a problem were as follows:

Initial							
x	y	A	B				
4	5	1	0	100	A	0
5	2	0	1	80	B	0
10	5	0	0	0		
Final							
0	1	5/17	−4/17	180/17	x	5
1	0	−2/17	5/17	200/17	y	10
0	0	−5/17	−30/17	−2900/17		

a. Note that the right-hand side constant limits resource A to 100 units. If resource A were increased to $100 + \Delta_A$, what is the range in the size of Δ_A that would keep the same basic variables in the solution shown in the final tableau?
b. What is the range in the value of the right-hand side of the resource A constraint?
c. What is the shadow price on resource A that is associated with the right-hand side range?

Problems

17. The Two-Product Company was formulated as a linear optimization model in Chapter 11, with computer input and solution given. With that formulation, solve the problem by the simplex methods of this chapter.

18. A manufacturer has two products, both of which are made in two steps by machines A and B. The process times for the two products on the two machines are as follows:

Product	Machine A (hr)	Machine B (hr)
1	4	5
2	5	2

    For the coming period, machine A has available 100 hours and B has available 80 hours. The contribution for product 1 is \$10 per 100 units and for product 2, \$5 per 100 units. Using the methods of the simplex tableau, formulate and solve the problem for maximum contribution.

19. Consider the following linear optimization model:

    $$\text{maximize } Z = 3x_1 + x_2 + 4x_3,$$
    $$\text{subject to } 6x_1 + 3x_2 + 5x_3 \leq 25,$$
    $$3x_1 + 4x_2 + 5x_3 \leq 20,$$
    $$x_1, x_2, x_3 \geq 0.$$

    After adding slack variables and performing one simplex iteration, we have the following tableau:

3	−1	0	1	−1	5	x_4	0
3/5	4/5	1	0	1/5	4	x_3	4
3/5	−11/5	0	0	−4/5	−16		

    If the above result is not optimal, perform the next iteration. Indicate the resulting values of the variables and the objective function.

20. Consider the following linear optimization model:

    $$\text{maximize } Z = 3x_1 + 6x_2 + 2x_3,$$
    $$\text{subject to } 3x_1 + 4x_2 + x_3 \leq 2, \quad \text{(resource A)}$$
    $$x_1 + 3x_2 + 2x_3 \leq 1, \quad \text{(resource B)}$$
    $$x_1, x_2, x_3 \geq 0.$$

    If you add x_4 and x_5 as slack variables, you have the following tableau at the final iteration of the simplex method:

1	0	−1	3/5	−4/5	2/5	x_1	3
0	1	1	−1/5	3/5	1/5	x_2	6
0	0	−1	−3/5	−6/5	−12/5		

a. State the optimal values for each x_j and the value of the objective function.
b. Suppose the number of units of resource A is increased to 3. What are the optimal values for each x_j and the value of the objective function? (Note: Do not rework the problem. Use the techniques of sensitivity analysis.)
c. Suppose that the company can only guarantee that the price of x_3 is between 1.5 and 2.5. Should additional study be undertaken to determine the exact figure, or will the solution remain unchanged if the price of x_3 falls within this range? Show why.
d. Suppose that the company can purchase additional units of resource A at a cost of $0.75 per unit. Would this be a wise investment? Why or why not?

21. Mesa Plastics Company was formulated as exercise 20 in Chapter 11 with computer input and solution given. Using the simplex methods of this chapter, we obtained the simplex tableau shown in Table 13-9.
    a. Identify the optimal solution.
    b. What are the shadow prices?

TABLE 13-9. **Final Simplex Tableau for Mesa Plastics**

37.5	40	20	45	62.5	30	0	0	0	0	0			
X_{1A}	X_{1B}	X_{2A}	X_{2B}	X_{3A}	X_{3B}	W_A	W_B	W_1	W_2	W_3			
0	0	0.0875	0	0	0.15	1	1.25	−0.25	−0.3125	−0.35	10	W_A	0
0	1	−1.25	0	0	2	0	5	0	−1.25	0	125	X_{1B}	40
1	0	1.25	0	0	−2	0	−5	1	1.25	0	185	X_{1A}	37.5
0	0	1	1	0	0	0	0	0	1	0	300	X_{2B}	45
0	0	0	0	1	1	0	0	0	0	1	125	X_{3A}	62.5
0	0	−21.875	0	0	−37.5	0	−12.5	−37.5	−41.875	−62.5	−33,250		

References

1. Charnes, A., and W. W. Cooper, *Management Models and Industrial Applications of Linear Programming*, Vols. 1 and 2, John Wiley & Sons, New York, 1961.
2. Daellenbach, H. G., and E. J. Bell, *User's Guide to Linear Programming*, Prentice-Hall, Englewood Cliffs, N.J., 1970.

3. Dantzig, G. B., *Linear Programming and Extensions,* Princeton University Press, Princeton, N.J., 1963.
4. Hillier, F. S., and G. J. Lieberman, *Introduction to Operations Research,* second edition, Holden-Day, San Francisco, 1974.
5. Machol, R. E., *Elementary Systems Mathematics: Linear Programming for Business and the Social Sciences,* McGraw-Hill, New York, 1976.
6. Wagner, H. M., *Principles of Operations Research,* second edition, Prentice-Hall, Englewood Cliffs, N.J., 1975.

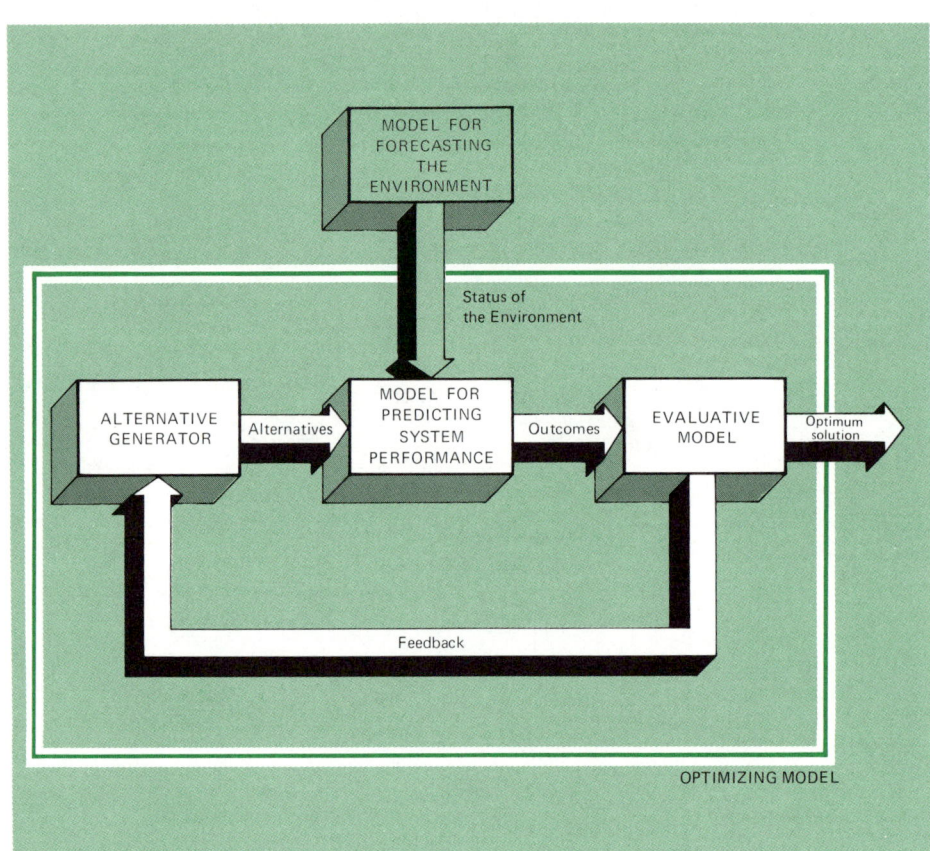

14

NETWORK MODELS— TRANSPORTATION AND TRANSSHIPMENT

Network models are an important special case of linear optimization models for three reasons. First, many real-world problems can be modeled by using networks. Problems related to the determination of transportation and distribution systems are routinely solved in many organizations by this method. A special form of a network, known as the *transportation model*, takes its name from this use. A generalization of the transportation model is the *transshipment model*, which allows greater flexibility in the nature of the distribution system being analyzed. These models can also be used as aids in assigning workers to jobs. Other network models can be used to determine the longest or shortest path through a network. These models can be used to schedule activities in large-scale projects. The latter models include the network scheduling techniques PERT and CPM. This chapter presents the transportation and transshipment network models. The network scheduling models are discussed in Chapter 15.

A second important feature of network models is that there is a visual interpretation in addition to the mathematical formulation. The ability to visualize a network, much like a decision tree, significantly reduces problems of communication between managers and technical analysts and among managers. Since one of the most important factors limiting the use of management science models by managers is their confidence in the model, this feature cannot be overemphasized.

Finally, the third advantage of the network is that the corresponding mathematical formulation has a special structure that allows extremely large problems to be solved very quickly by using specialized versions of the simplex algorithm for solving linear programming problems. The resulting low cost encourages the user to run the model many times to gain full advantage of it. An additional bonus is that integer-valued optimal solutions are obtained automatically. When a problem cannot be formulated as a network problem and an integer-valued solution is required, the additional computational effort can become quite burdensome.

These three advantages of network models—the large number of potential real-world applications, the visual interpretation, and an efficient solution strategy—are so important that the modern manager should be familiar with problems that can be analyzed with networks. Therefore, we shall present several examples of these models and concentrate on how they are formulated.

THE TRANSPORTATION MODEL

The transportation model is a special form of network optimization models that is routinely applied to problems of allocating the production from several factories to different warehouses or other distribution centers. The purpose of the model is to aid in selecting the most economical transportation routes for the required shipments. Such decisions must be made regularly in many large organizations. This same model can also be used to analyze other problems with a similar mathematical structure that do not involve the selection of transportation routes.

An Example Problem

Suppose we have the product distribution problem illustrated in Figure 14–1. We have three factories located in Chicago, Detroit, and Atlanta, which produce the same product. There are five major product distribution centers in Milwaukee, Cincinnati, Des Moines, Buffalo, and New York City. The weekly capacity in terms of units produced varies among the factories as follows:

Factory	Supply (units/week)
Detroit (A)	19
Chicago (B)	28
Atlanta (C)	25
	72

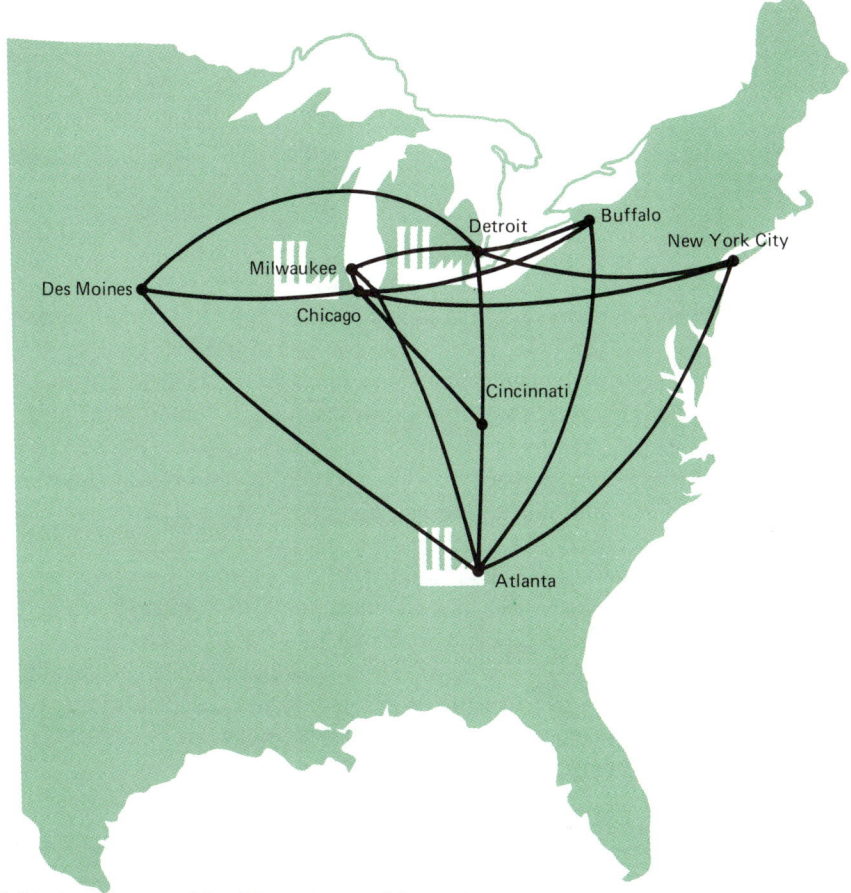

FIGURE 14-1. **Geographical locations of factories and distribution points**

The average weekly shipment required in each product distribution center is given below:

Distribution Center	Demand (units/week)
Milwaukee (V)	11
Cincinnati (W)	13
Des Moines (X)	7
Buffalo (Y)	17
New York City (Z)	<u>24</u>
	72

Notice that the total weekly supply of the product of 72 units is equal to the total weekly demand.

The costs of shipping depend on which factory ships to which distribution center because the shipping distances vary. These costs are as follows:

	Distribution Center				
Factory	Milwaukee (V)	Cincinnati (W)	Des Moines (X)	Buffalo (Y)	New York City (Z)
Detroit (A)	12	12	14	10	14
Chicago (B)	4	12	10	16	18
Atlanta (C)	16	14	12	18	16

These costs are expressed in dollars per unit shipped. For example, the Detroit factory can ship one unit of our product to Milwaukee for $12. Our problem is to determine how much should be shipped where by whom. This solution must consider the factory capacities and the distribution center demands, as well as the costs of the shipments.

Let us first consider whether this problem might be formulated as a linear optimization model. It is a *resource allocation problem*, since we are trying to allocate shipments of the product among 15 different alternative routes, so we will define a decision variable for each route. Further, there are constraints on our decisions. We assume that we must meet the demand at each of the 5 distribution centers, and we cannot ship more than the available supply from each of the 3 factories. The appropriate evaluative model will simply involve a single criterion under certainty, cost. The detailed formulation of this linear optimization model will be left for an exercise, but it will be a relatively complex model with 15 decision variables and 8 constraints.

The Network Now let us see how this problem can be modeled as a network. Suppose we take the map in Figure 14–1 and rearrange it by placing all of the factories on the left and all of the distribution centers on the right. Rather than using pictures of the factories and warehouses, we will use circles to represent them both. These circles are labeled with a letter to identify the factory or the distribution center; for example, the circle labeled A corresponds to the Detroit factory, while the circle labeled Y corresponds to the Buffalo distribution center. The routes between the factories and the warehouses at the distribution centers are represented by arrows. This configuration is illustrated in Figure 14–2.

Now we can write the number of units available at each factory with a plus sign in front of it and the number of units required at each warehouse with a minus sign in front of it. The plus sign indicates that units are placed into the system at the corresponding circle, while the minus sign indicates that units are removed. Finally, we write the cost per unit of shipping on each of the corresponding arrows. For example, the cost of shipping from factory A to distribution center X is $14 per unit, which is written on the arrow from the factory circle A to the distribution center circle X (see Figure 14–2).

Unless you are an extremely sophisticated mathematician, Figure 14–2 probably conveys more information in an easily understood manner than the

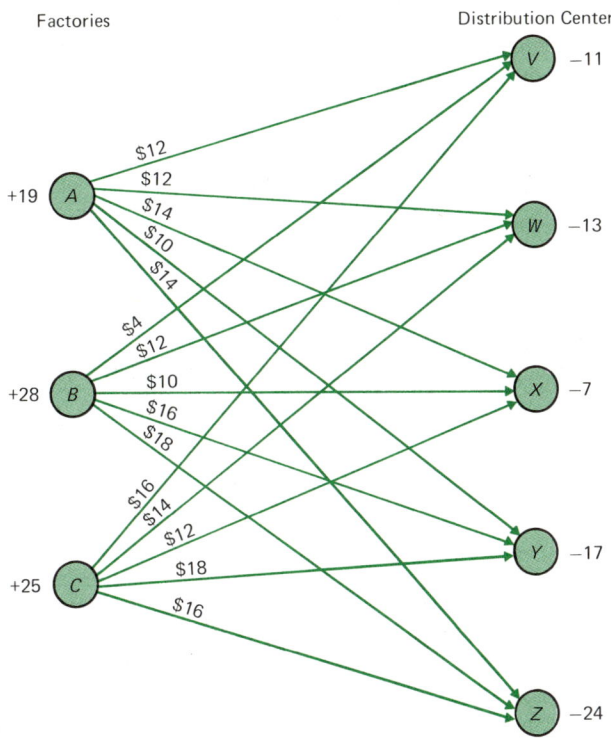

FIGURE 14-2. **Network formulation of the transportation problem**

mathematical relationships in a linear optimization model formulation of this same problem. This ability to portray the logic of the model graphically is one of the important advantages of network models. Thus, the problem of communication between a manager and an analyst is greatly simplified when network models are used.

More formally, the circles in Figure 14-2 are called *nodes*, and the arrows are called *arcs*. We shall use these terms in the following discussion.

The Transportation Table The information in Figure 14-2 can also be entered in a table especially suited for analyzing transportation problems, as shown in Table 14-1. There is one row for each factory and one column for each distribution center. The number of units available from the factory are written to the right of each row, and the number of units required at each center are written at the bottom of each column. Further, the costs are written in the small boxes; for example, the cost of shipping one unit from factory B to center V is $4. Also notice that each large square is labeled with letters that correspond to

CHAPTER 14 NETWORK MODELS: TRANSPORTATION AND TRANSSHIPMENT

its row and column. For example, the large box labeled BX is in row B and column X. These large boxes correspond to the shipping routes between the factories and the distribution centers.

TABLE 14-1. **The Transportation Table**

To Dist. Centers / From Factories	V (Milwaukee)	W (Cincinnati)	X (Des Moines)	Y (Buffalo)	Z (New York City)	Available at Factories
A (Detroit)	AV 12*	AW 12	AX 14	AY 10	AZ 14	19
B (Chicago)	BV 4	BW 12	BX 10	BY 16	BZ 18	28
C (Atlanta)	CV 16	CW 14	CX 12	CY 18	CZ 16	25
Required at Distribution Centers	11	13	7	17	24	72

*Per-unit cost ($) of shipping from factory to distribution center.

THE STEPPING-STONE ALGORITHM

We shall now present one algorithm for solving transportation problems by hand. The required calculations can be performed using the transportation table shown in Table 14-1. This algorithm is presented to emphasize that the special structure of the transportation problem makes its solution much easier than ordinary linear programming problems. While other, more efficient algorithms for solving transportation problems by hand are available, they are more complex conceptually. Since the chances that you will ever have to solve a real-world transportation problem by hand are remote, we have selected this particular algorithm because of its intuitive appeal. For reasons that will become apparent as you study the algorithm, it is called the *stepping-stone method* for solving transportation problems. Details regarding alternative solution strategies are provided in Dantzig [1963] and Wagner [1975].

An algorithm must provide the following:
1. an initial solution
2. a test for improvement
3. a means of improving the solution

We shall now consider each of these requirements.

An Initial Solution The simplest approach to obtaining an initial solution is to ignore the distribution costs. The rules for obtaining this initial solution are as follows:

Step 1. Start allocating supply to demand in the upper left-hand corner (the northwest corner) of the transportation table.

Step 2. Allocate as many units as possible while observing the restrictions on total supply for the row and on total demand for the column.

Step 3. If the demand in the column is met, move to the right to the box in the next column. Go to step 2.

Step 4. If the supply for the row is exhausted, move down to the box in the next row. Go to step 2.

Let us illustrate these rules by applying them to Table 14–2. We begin with box AV in the first row and the first column (step 1). We see that factory A has 19 units available, and distribution center V requires only 11. We assign the 11 from factory A to center V, as indicated by the 11 circled in box AV of Table 14–2 (step 2). We have met the demand at V, so we move to the right under column W (step 3), and assign the balance of the supply from A, 8 units, to W (step 2). Now that the supply has been exhausted, we drop down to row B (step 4) and assign the balance of W's requirement, 5 units, from the capacity of factory B (step 2). We continue in this fashion, stair-stepping down the table until all of the assignments have been made, as shown in Table 14–2. The total cost associated with this solution, $1016, is also calculated in Table 14–2 by multiplying the number of units shipped to each warehouse from each factory by the appropriate shipping cost per unit. (The circled number representing the number of units assigned to a box is multiplied by the number in the upper right hand corner of the box, and the results are summed.)

Notice that the application of this northwest corner rule determines a solution that satisfies the restrictions on supply and demand at each factory and at each warehouse. The solution can easily be checked by summing the entries in each row and in each column. Thus, the solution is feasible. Also, there are three rows and five columns in Table 14–2. The number of cells in the table with assignments is $3 + 5 - 1 = 7$. In general, if n is the number of rows in a transportation table, and m is the number of columns, we want $n + m - 1$ assignments in the table. Otherwise, we call the solution *degenerate,* and special procedures are required for dealing with degenerate solutions, as we shall see.

TABLE 14-2. **Initial Solution by the Northwest Corner Rule**

To Dist. Centers \\ From Factories	V (Milwaukee)	W (Cincinnati)	X (Des Moines)	Y (Buffalo)	Z (New York City)	Available at Factories
A (Detroit)	AV 12 (11)	AW 12 (8)	AX 14	AY 10	AZ 14	19
B (Chicago)	BV 4	BW 12 (5)	BX 10 (7)	BY 16 (16)	BZ 18	28
C (Atlanta)	CV 16	CW 14	CX 12	CY 18 (1)	CZ 16 (24)	25
Required at Distribution Centers	11	13	7	17	24	72

Total distribution cost:

AV: 11 × 12 = 132
AW: 8 × 12 = 96
BW: 5 × 12 = 60
BX: 7 × 10 = 70
BY: 16 × 16 = 256
CY: 1 × 18 = 18
CZ: 24 × 16 = 384
             $1,016

A Test for Improvement Is the initial northwest corner solution in Table 14-2 the best possible solution? We can answer this question by examining each of the empty boxes in the transportation table to determine whether it would be better to move some of the units into it. In doing so, we want to be sure that any new solution satisfies the supply and demand restrictions shown in the right column and in the bottom row in the transportation table.

For example, we can begin with the first empty box in the first column, box BV, which corresponds to shipping from factory B (in Chicago) to warehouse V (in Milwaukee). Just for the moment, suppose we ship only one unit along this route. To indicate this shipment we place a small +1 in the upper right-hand corner of box BV, as shown in Table 14-3. What does this additional unit do to our supply and demand constraints?

The supply at factory B is only 28 units, but this additional unit plus the 5 shipped from B to W, the 7 shipped from B to X, and the 16 shipped from B to

TABLE 14-3. **Evaluation of Box *BV***
For shifting one unit to *BV*, the change in cost is
$$+4 - 12 + 12 - 12 = -8.$$
This change is a net improvement in cost.

To Dist. Centers From Factories	V (Milwaukee)	W (Cincinnati)	X (Des Moines)	Y (Buffalo)	Z (New York City)	Available at Factories
A (Detroit)	AV 12 (−1) ⑪	AW 12 (+1) ⑧	AX 14	AY 10	AZ 14	19
B (Chicago)	BV 4 (+1)	BW 12 (−1) ⑤	BX 10 ⑦	BY 16 ⑯	BZ 18	28
C (Atlanta)	CV 16	CW 14	CX 12	CY 18 ①	CZ 16 ㉔	25
Required at Distribution Centers	11	13	7	17	24	72

Y sum to 29. In order to observe the supply restriction of 28 units, let us reduce the number of units shipped from factory *B* to distribution center *W* by one unit. We denote this change by placing a −1 in the corresponding box of the transportation table, as illustrated in Table 14-3.

However, when we remove one unit from the demand at distribution center *W*, we need to compensate. Notice that if we add one unit in box *AW* of the transportation table and subtract one unit from box *AV*, all of our original constraints on supplies and demands will be met. We have subtracted exactly one unit from each row and from each column that has one unit added to it, and *vice versa*. Thus, we again have a feasible solution, as shown in Table 14-3.

Now, in the boxes with the +1's, we will incur additional costs of 4 + 12 = 16. However, the boxes with −1's indicate savings, since one unit fewer will be shipped in each. The savings from this trial solution are 12 + 12 = 24. Thus, we would incur an additional cost of 16 but a savings of 24, resulting in a *net* savings of 8 for each additional unit we ship from factory *B* to distribution center *V*. These savings suggest that a desirable *direction of change* in the initial solution would be increasing the number of units shipped from factory *B* to outlet *V* from its initial value of 0 units.

Now we know that this initial solution can be improved by shifting units into the empty box BV. But what about the other empty boxes? We would reduce the total cost by $8 for each unit we shift into box BV, but what if we could obtain an even greater cost reduction per unit by shifts into other empty boxes?

We can evaluate the other empty boxes using the same strategy as in the evaluation of box BV. This strategy can be summarized by the following steps:

Step 1. Determine a closed path, starting at the empty box being evaluated, and "stepping" from boxes with assignments back to the original box. Right angle turns in this path are permitted only at boxes with assignments and at the original empty box. Since only the boxes at the turning points are considered to be on the closed path, both empty and assigned boxes may be skipped over. The boxes at the turning points are often called the "stepping stones" on the path.

Step 2. Beginning at the box being evaluated, we assign a +, and then alternate minus and plus signs at the assigned boxes on the corner points of the path.

Step 3. Sum the unit costs in the boxes with plus signs, and subtract the unit costs in the boxes with minus signs. If we are minimizing costs (maximizing profits), the result is the *net change* in the cost (profit) per unit from the changes made in the assignments.

Step 4. Repeat this procedure for each empty box in the transportation table.

Steps 1 and 2 correspond to the intuitively appealing strategy of assigning a single unit to the empty box, then adjusting the shipments in the boxes with assignments until all of the row supply and column demand constraints are satisfied. Step 3 simply calculates the cost (or contribution to profit) that would result from such a modification in the assignments.

If the net changes are all greater than or equal to 0, and if we are minimizing costs, or if they are all less than or equal to 0, and we are maximizing profits, we have found an optimal solution. Otherwise, we could shift units into an empty box and reduce the cost (or increase the profit).

The application of these steps to the empty box BV is shown by the heavy black arrows in Table 14-3. Notice that the closed path forms a simple rectangle. However, the evaluation of all empty boxes is not so easy. For example, the closed path for evaluating box AZ is shown in Table 14-4. The path is $+AZ - CZ + CY - BY + BW - AW$, and the net change is $+14 - 16 + 18 - 16 + 12 - 12 = 0$. Thus, switching units into box AZ would neither increase nor decrease the distribution costs associated with the initial solution.

The net change in cost associated with each of the empty boxes is written in the bottom left-hand corner of the empty boxes in Table 14-4. For example, the net change of -8 is in box BV, and the net change of 0 is in box AZ. The computations of these net changes are shown in Table 14-5.

TABLE 14-4. **Evaluation of Empty Boxes**
For shifting one unit to AZ, the change in cost is
$+14 - 16 + 18 - 16 + 12 - 12 = 0$.
Notice that box BX is not on this path.

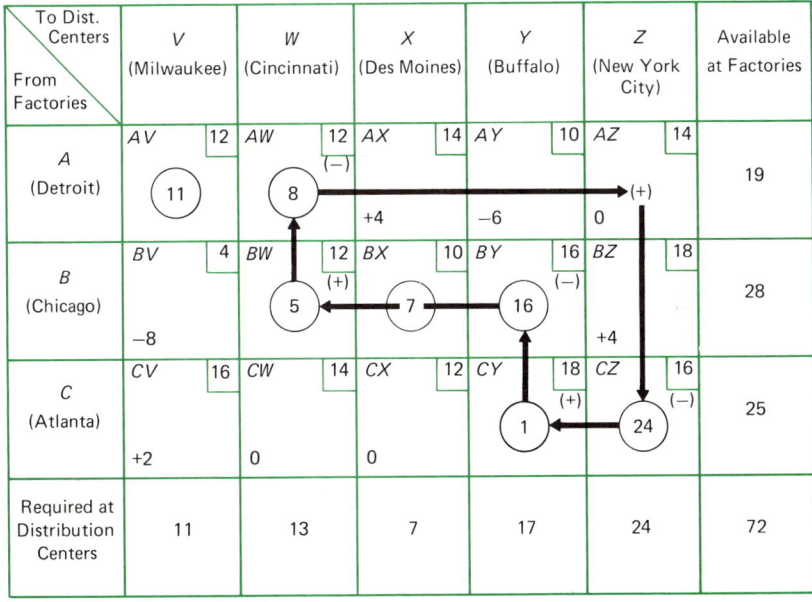

TABLE 14-5. **Summary of Calculations of Net Changes in Cost**

Empty Box	Closed Path	Calculation of Net Change from Moving One Unit into Each Empty Box	
AX	$+AX - BX + BW - AW$	$+14 - 10 + 12 - 12$	$= +4$
AY	$+AY - BY + BW - AW$	$+10 - 16 + 12 - 12$	$= -6$
AZ	$+AZ - CZ + CY - BY + BW - AW$	$+14 - 16 + 18 - 16 + 12 - 12 =$	0
BV	$+BV - BW + AW - AV$	$+4 - 12 + 12 - 12$	$= -8$
BZ	$+BZ - CZ + CY - BY$	$+18 - 16 + 18 - 16$	$= +4$
CV	$+CV - CY + BY - BW + AW - AV$	$+16 - 18 + 16 - 12 + 12 - 12 = +2$	
CW	$+CW - CY + BY - BW$	$+14 - 18 + 16 - 12$	$= 0$
CX	$+CX - CY + BY - BX$	$+12 - 18 + 16 - 10$	$= 0$

The calculation of these net changes corresponds to the "test for optimality" in the simplex method of solving linear optimization models.

Improving the Solution Each negative net change indicates the amount by which the total solution would be reduced if one unit were shipped in the corresponding box, and each positive net change indicates the amount by which it would be increased.

Notice that in Table 14–4, two empty boxes, *AY* and *BV*, have negative net changes. Which one shall we choose in determining the new solution? One reasonable rule for small problems and hand solutions is to always select the one with the most negative net change (if minimizing costs) or the most positive (if maximizing profits). Thus, we would like to shift units into box *BV*, since the net change per unit for *BV* of -8 is more negative than the net change per unit of -6 for *AY*.

We save $8 for each unit we can shift into *BV*, so we would like to shift as many units as possible. To determine how many units to shift, we need to consider the evaluation path for box *BV* shown in Table 14–3. In the boxes in Table 14–3 with the minus signs (*AV* and *BW*), we are removing units. Clearly we cannot remove more than 11 units from *AV* or more than 5 units from *BW*. The smaller of these numbers is 5, so the most we can shift around is 5 units. This 5 units is the appropriate *amount of change* in the desirable direction. The results of the shift of 5 units are shown in Table 14–6. Notice that we have added 5 units to the boxes on the evaluation path of *BV* with a plus sign (*AW* and *BV*), and subtracted 5 units from the boxes on the evaluation path of *BV* with a minus sign (*AV* and *BW*). The net savings for this change is $8 per unit times the 5 units that were shifted, or $8 × 5 = $40 saved. Also add the total number of units in each row and in each column to confirm that the factory capacity constraints and the distribution center demands are still met.

Summarizing, to improve the solution we first identify the open box with the most negative net change (if minimizing costs) or the most positive (if maximizing profits). We then determine the closed path used to evaluate that box and carry out the following steps:

Step 1. Determine the minimum number of units assigned to a box on the path that was marked with a minus sign.

Step 2. Add this number to the empty box and to all other boxes on the path marked with a plus sign. Subtract this number from boxes on the path marked with a minus sign.

From Table 14–5, the empty box with the most negative net change is *BV*, and its closed path is $+BV - BW + AW - AV$. The minimum number of units assigned to *BW* or *AV* is 5 (step 1). Carrying out step 2 results in the revised solution shown in Table 14–6. These calculations are summarized in Table 14–7.

TABLE 14-6. **A Revised Solution**

To Dist. Centers \ From Factories	V (Milwaukee)	W (Cincinnati)	X (Des Moines)	Y (Buffalo)	Z (New York City)	Available at Factories
A (Detroit)	AV 12 ⓖ	AW 12 ⑬	AX 14	AY 10	AZ 14	19
B (Chicago)	BV 4 ⑤	BW 12	BX 10 ⑦	BY 16 ⑯	BZ 18	28
C (Atlanta)	CV 16	CW 14	CX 12	CY 18 ①	CZ 16 ㉔	25
Required at Distribution Centers	11	13	7	17	24	72

TABLE 14-7. **Summary of Calculations in Revision of the Initial Solution**

Boxes on Closed Path of BV	Current Assignment in Box	Sign of Box	Smallest Number in Box with a Minus Sign	Revised Assignment in Box
BV	0	+	5	5
BW	5	−	5	0
AW	8	+	5	13
AV	11	−	5	6

Further Revisions Now we repeat the entire process in order to determine if this new solution is optimal, or if it can be revised in order to reduce costs even further. The *net changes* for each empty box in the new solution are shown in the lower left-hand corner of the empty boxes in Table 14-8. Also illustrated in Table 14-8 is the closed path for evaluating box *CW*. Since there are negative *net change* numbers in boxes *AX*, *AY*, and *AZ*, the solution can be improved still further.

The box with the most negative net change of -14 is AY. The closed path for AY is $+AY - BY + BV - AV$ (verify this). The smallest number of units assigned to the boxes with a negative sign, BY and AV, is 6 units in AV. Therefore, we would add 6 units into boxes AY and BV, and subtract 6 units from boxes BY and AV as shown in Table 14-9. The revised solution is shown in Table 14-10.

We would continue to repeat the entire process until none of the *net change* values are negative.

TABLE 14-8. **Net Changes for the Empty Boxes and the Closed Path for Box CW**

To Dist. Centers From Factories	V (Milwaukee)	W (Cincinnati)	X (Des Moines)	Y (Buffalo)	Z (New York City)	Available at Factories
A (Detroit)	AV 12 (+) 6	AW 12 (−) 13	AX 14 −4	AY 10 −14	AZ 14 −8	19
B (Chicago)	BV 4 (−) 5	BW 8	BX 12 7	BY 10 16	BZ 16 (+) 4	28
C (Atlanta)	CV 16 10	CW 14 (+) 8	CX 12 0	CY 18 1	CZ 16 (−) 24	25
Required at Distribution Centers	11	13	7	17	24	72

TABLE 14-9. **Summary of Calculations in the Revision of the Solution Shown in Table 14-8**

Boxes on Closed Path of AY	Current Assignment in Box	Sign of Box	Smallest Number in Box with a Minus Sign	Revised Assignment in Box
AY	0	+	6	6
BY	16	−	6	10
BV	5	+	6	11
AV	6	−	6	0

TABLE 14-10. **The Second Revision of the Solution**

To Dist. Centers From Factories	V (Milwaukee)	W (Cincinnati)	X (Des Moines)	Y (Buffalo)	Z (New York City)	Available at Factories
A (Detroit)	AV 12	AW 12 ⓘ13	AX 14	AY 10 ⓘ6	AZ 14	19
B (Chicago)	BV 4 ⓘ11	BW 12	BX 10 ⓘ7	BY 16 ⓘ10	BZ 18	28
C (Atlanta)	CV 16	CW 14	CX 12	CY 18 ⓘ1	CZ 16 ⓘ24	25
Required at Distribution Centers	11	13	7	17	24	72

An Optimal Solution After two more revisions of the solution, we obtain the results shown in Table 14-11. The evaluation of the empty boxes in Table 14-11 reveals that there are no negative net changes, so there are no shifts of units that will lead to a further reduction in the costs. Therefore, this is an *optimal solution*.

The total cost of shipping according to this solution is $826 as computed in Table 14-11. Thus, through a simple (but tedious) analysis, we have reduced the cost of the initial solution by $1016 − $826 = $190, which is an 18.7 percent reduction.

In a problem more realistic in terms of size, determining a good solution by hand would be much more difficult; however, the potential cost savings are even greater than in this example. These much larger problems can be solved efficiently using a modified version of the simplex method for linear programming.

Alternate Optimal Solutions The fact that empty boxes AZ and CX have zero net change evaluations in Table 14-11 is important and gives us flexibility in determining the final plan of action. These zero net changes allow us to generate other solutions that have the same total distribution cost as the optimal solution shown in Table 14-11. For example, since empty box CX has a zero evaluation, we may make the shifts in assignments as indicated by its closed path and generate the alternate optimal solution shown in Table 14–12. The managerial implication of this result is that the single unit shipped from Atlanta to Cincinnati could also be shipped to Des Moines and the total cost would be unchanged. As long as the costs are equal, the manager might have a slight preference for the solution in Table 14–12, since no more than two factories ship to any one distribution center, whereas all three factories must ship to Cincinnati in the Table 14–11 solution.

Another alternate optimal solution could be determined by shifting the solution in Table 14–11 along the closed path of empty box AZ. A manager might want to generate many alternate optimal solutions, if they exist, before making a final decision.

Degeneracy If n is the number of rows, and m is the number of columns in a transportation table, we want $n + m - 1$ assignments in the table. A solution with fewer than $n + m - 1$ assignments is called a *degenerate solution*. Such a

TABLE 14–11. **An Optimal Solution**

To Dist. Centers / From Factories	V (Milwaukee)	W (Cincinnati)	X (Des Moines)	Y (Buffalo)	Z (New York City)	Available at Factories
A (Detroit)	AV 12 / 8	AW 12 / 2	AX 14 / 4	AY 10 / 17	AZ 14 / 0	19
B (Chicago)	BV 4 / 11	BW 12 / 10	BX 10 / 7	BY 16 / 6	BZ 18 / 4	28
C (Atlanta)	CV 16 / 10	CW 14 / 1	CX 12 / 0	CY 18 / 6	CZ 16 / 24	25
Required at Distribution Centers	11	13	7	17	24	72

Total distribution cost:

AW: 2 × 12 = 24
AY: 17 × 10 = 170
BV: 11 × 4 = 44
BW: 10 × 12 = 120
BX: 7 × 10 = 70
CW: 1 × 14 = 14
CZ: 24 × 16 = 384
                $826

TABLE 14-12. **An Alternate Optimal Solution**

To Dist. Centers From Factories	V (Milwaukee)	W (Cincinnati)	X (Des Moines)	Y (Buffalo)	Z (New York City)	Available at Factories
A (Detroit)	AV 12	AW 12 ②	AX 14	AY 10 ⑰	AZ 14	19
B (Chicago)	BV 4 ⑪	BW 12 ⑪	BX 10 ⑥	BY 16	BZ 18	28
C (Atlanta)	CV 16	CW 14	CX 12 ①	CY 18	CZ 16 ㉔	25
Required at Distribution Centers	11	13	7	17	24	72

solution may arise when the rules for improving the solution are applied, or even in determining an initial solution by the northwest corner rule.

An example in Table 14-13 shows that a degenerate solution will arise if the rule for improving the solution is followed by shifting the minimum number of units in a box marked with a minus sign. This minimum number, 6, occurs in two boxes, AV and BX.

Note that the problem in Table 14-13 is only a slight modification of the problem we have been using. The demand requirements in columns V and X have been changed by one unit each. Otherwise, the northwest corner rule was applied to determine the initial solution, the empty boxes were evaluated as before, and changes in assignments were made when they indicated potential improvement.

When the shift of 6 units occurs, the assignments in boxes AV and BX both go to 0, as shown in Table 14-14. We have only 6 assignments in Table 14-14 rather than the $3 + 5 - 1 = 7$ assignments we obtain in a nondegenerate solution. The practical effect is that several of the empty boxes in Table 14-14 cannot be evaluated in the usual way, since a closed path cannot be established for them. For example, try to devise a closed path for evaluating box AV or box CX.

The degeneracy can be resolved, however, by regarding one of the two boxes where assignments have disappeared as an assigned box with an extremely small allocation, which we shall call an ϵ allocation. This allocation is illustrated in Table 14-15, which also shows the closed path for box CX.

Conceptually, we shall regard the ϵ allocation as being infinitesimally small, so that it does not affect the supply and demand totals. The allocation, however, does make it possible to meet the $n + m - 1$ restriction on the number of assignments so that evaluation paths may be established for all empty boxes. The ϵ allocation is then manipulated as though it were the same as any other allocation. If in subsequent manipulations, the ϵ cell is the one that limits shifts and assignments, the ϵ is simply shifted to the cell being evaluated, and the usual procedure is then continued.

Unequal Supply and Demand Suppose that the capacities at the three factories in this example had been 20, 30, and 30 respectively. Then the total potential supply of $20 + 30 + 30 = 80$ units is 8 more than the total demand of $11 + 13 + 7 + 17 + 24 = 72$ units. How do we adjust for the unequal supply and demand totals? Simply by defining a "dummy" distribution center with a

TABLE 14-13. **Transportation Table in which Degeneracy Will Occur**

To Dist. Centers From Factories	V (Milwaukee)	W (Cincinnati)	X (Des Moines)	Y (Buffalo)	Z (New York City)	Available at Factories
A (Detroit)	AV 12 (−) 6	AW 12 13	AX 14 (+)	AY 10	AZ 14	19
B (Chicago)	BV 4 (+) 6	BW 12	BX 10 (−) 6	BY 16 16	BZ 18	28
C (Atlanta)	CV 16	CW 14	CX 12	CY 18 1	CZ 16 24	25
Required at Distribution Centers	12	13	6	17	24	72

Boxes on Closed Path of AX	Current Assignment in Box	Sign of Box	Smallest Number in Box with a Minus Sign	Revised Assignment in Box
AX	0	+	6	6
BX	6	−	6	0
BV	6	+	6	12
AV	6	−	6	0

TABLE 14-14. A Degenerate Solution

To Dist. Centers \ From Factories	V (Milwaukee)	W (Cincinnati)	X (Des Moines)	Y (Buffalo)	Z (New York City)	Available at Factories
A (Detroit)	AV 12	AW 12 ⓘ13	AX 14 ⓘ6	AY 10	AZ 14	19
B (Chicago)	BV 4 ⓘ12	BW 12	BX 10	BY 16 ⓘ16	BZ 18	28
C (Atlanta)	CV 16	CW 14	CX 12	CY 18 ⓘ1	CZ 16 ⓘ24	25
Required at Distribution Centers	12	13	6	17	24	72

TABLE 14-15. The ϵ Allocation and the Closed Path for Box CX

To Dist. Centers \ From Factories	V (Milwaukee)	W (Cincinnati)	X (Des Moines)	Y (Buffalo)	Z (New York City)	Available at Factories
A (Detroit)	AV 12 ⓘϵ	AW 12 ⓘ13	AX 14 ⓘ6	AY 10	AZ 14	19
B (Chicago)	BV 4 ⓘ12	BW 12	BX 10	BY 16 ⓘ16	BZ 18	28
C (Atlanta)	CV 16	CW 14	CX 12 (+)	CY 18 ⓘ1	CZ 16 ⓘ24	25
Required at Distribution Centers	12	13	6	17	24	72

CHAPTER 14 NETWORK MODELS: TRANSPORTATION AND TRANSSHIPMENT

demand equal to the difference between the total supply and the total demand; that is, with a demand of $80 - 72 = 8$ units. The cost of shipping from each factory to this dummy center will be zero. Naturally, any units assigned by our solution strategy to this nonexistent center would not actually be produced and shipped, which justifies the use of the zero costs. This strategy will help us in determining the appropriate production schedule in each factory. If the demand in a problem exceeds the supply, a similar strategy could be adopted by adding a dummy row with zero costs of shipping. These dummy shipping routes correspond to slack variables in the equivalent linear programming formulation of the problem. The initial table with the dummy distribution center to absorb the excess demand is shown in Table 14–16.

TABLE 14–16. **A Transportation Table with a Dummy Distribution Center to Adjust for Unequal Total Supplies and Demands**

To Dist. Centers From Factories	V (Milwaukee)		W (Cincinnati)		X (Des Moines)		Y (Buffalo)		Z (New York City)		D (Dummy)		Available at Factories
A (Detroit)	AV	12	AW	12	AX	14	AY	10	AZ	14	AD	0	20
B (Chicago)	BV	4	BW	12	BX	10	BY	16	BZ	18	BD	0	30
C (Atlanta)	CV	16	CW	14	CX	12	CY	18	CZ	16	CD	0	30
Required at Distribution Centers	11		13		7		17		24		8		80

Summary of the Stepping-Stone Method

The application of the stepping-stone method to the transportation model is equivalent to the use of the simplex method for solving linear optimization models. However, the special structure of the transportation model provides certain computational advantages that are exploited in the stepping-stone algorithm. For example, in a transportation problem, it is very easy to find an initial starting solution involving only decision variables, rather than the starting solution with all slack variables or with some artificial variables in the general simplex algorithm.

The evaluation of the empty boxes in the transportation table is equivalent to the calculation of shadow prices for the corresponding variables in the linear programming formulation. Again, the special structure of the transportation model simplifies the calculations so much that they can be easily accomplished by hand. Similarly, the shift of units to improve a solution is equivalent to the computations required to produce a new tableau in the simplex algorithm.

While it is most unlikely that you will ever be involved in solving a practical transportation problem by hand, learning to solve these simple problems emphasizes how the special structure of the network simplifies the computations of linear programming. This awareness should make you even more sensitive to possible applications of network models.

The Practical Use of the Transportation Model

The transportation model is routinely used in determining transportation and distribution policies for many large organizations. When production capacity exceeds the demand for a product, this same model can also be used to determine the production schedule at each of the factories. Excellent discussions of the analysis of large distribution systems are provided by Geoffrion [1976] and by Zierer, Mitchell, and White [1976]. In actual practice, organizations may use such models on an annual or semiannual basis to revise their transportation and distribution policies.

One obvious limitation of the transportation model is that it assumes the units to be shipped from each source to each destination are identical and interchangeable. However, many organizations have multiple products with different demands in the different market areas. It may not be appropriate to solve the distribution problem for each product independently of the others because it is cheaper per unit when large quantities are shipped on the same routes. The transportation problem with multiple products (the multicommodity problem) can be formulated mathematically, and algorithms for its solution have been proposed. However, the multicommodity problems cannot be represented by a network. Consequently, they are much harder to solve computationally and require much more computer time. For these reasons their practical usefulness is limited.

An alternative is to define a *standard commodity bundle* for the organization, that represents a combination of the multiple products proportional to their respective market demands. This strategy works well when the relative market demands for the products do not differ significantly in each market area. For example, suppose a firm manufactures two products. The total demand for product 1 is 1500 units, while the total demand for product 2 is 500 units. Thus, product 1 outsells product 2 at a ratio of 3 to 1. Further, this sales proportion is relatively constant in each of the different market areas. Then the organization can solve its transportation and distribution problems by assuming a standard commodity bundle with a total demand of $1500 + 500 = 2000$ units. Suppose the cost of shipping product 1 from a particular factory to a specific outlet is $2 per unit, while the cost of shipping product 2 from the same factory to the same outlet is $1 per unit. Then, the cost of shipping each unit of the standard commodity bundle from this factory to this outlet would be $(\$2)(0.75) + (\$1)(0.25) = \$1.75$. The transportation model could then be applied to analyze this problem.

It is also possible to add lower and upper bounds on the number of units to be shipped along each route (or arc). For example, we might require that the number of units shipped from factory 1 to distribution center 2 be at least 30 but no more than 40. We could write these lower and upper bounds as the pair (30, 40), and place them next to the appropriate arc in the network. Mathematically, this corresponds to adding very simple constraints to the linear programming formulation of the problem. The simple form of these constraints means that they can be satisfied with little additional computational burden. When lower and upper bounds are placed on the routes, the resulting model is often called a *capacitated* transportation problem.

It is also important to recognize that an optimizing model, such as the transportation model, may be used to answer *what if* questions and to provide data for a more extensive analysis of a broader problem. For example, suppose a firm is currently producing a product at three different factories, each of which is operating at near capacity. Further, a market analysis shows that the demand for the product is expected to grow even higher over the next ten years before leveling off. The company may be trying to decide 1) whether or not to build a new factory, and 2) if so, in which of several alternative locations.

In order to analyze this problem, the company could estimate the total production and distribution costs associated with manufacturing the product in the three existing factories over the expected market life of the product. This estimate could be made by solving the transportation problem with the new market forecasts for each year in the estimated market life of the product and discounting the results to determine the equivalent present values of the costs. Next, the assumption could be made that a factory was built at one of the locations under consideration and the transportation problem could be re-solved for each of the years in the market life of the product, given this new factory. The estimated costs of producing and distributing with this new factory, plus the cost of constructing it, could then be compared with the cost of operating the existing factories, perhaps using overtime.

By repeating the analysis for the alternative sites under consideration, the costs implications of the various choices could be estimated. These results would play an important role in the determination of the new plant site, if a plant is to be built. Naturally, we recognize that the president of the company may still choose to construct a new plant in Columbus, Ohio, because he or she has relatives there, but at least the opportunity costs of such a decision would be clear.

THE TRANSSHIPMENT MODEL

Another limitation of the transportation model is the assumption that direct routes exist from each factory (or supply point) to each distribution center (or demand point). Again, in the real world, things are not always so simple. Major transportation routes actually pass through major distribution centers before going to smaller market areas.

Suppose we wish to redistribute goods among eight cities (the circled letters) as shown in Figure 14–3. The arrows, or arcs, indicate possible shipping routes. The arcs point in a specific direction indicating that goods can only be shipped along the route in that direction. In some cases, as for example between cities d and e, there are arcs pointing in two different directions indicating that goods can be shipped from e to d, or from d to e. The number associated with each city is the supply (plus) or demand (minus) at that location. For example, city a has a supply of 10, city c has a demand of -3, and city e has neither a supply nor a demand. Notice that some cities may have goods shipped *through* them. These cities, b, d, e, f, and g, have arrows pointing into and out of them, and are called transshipment points.

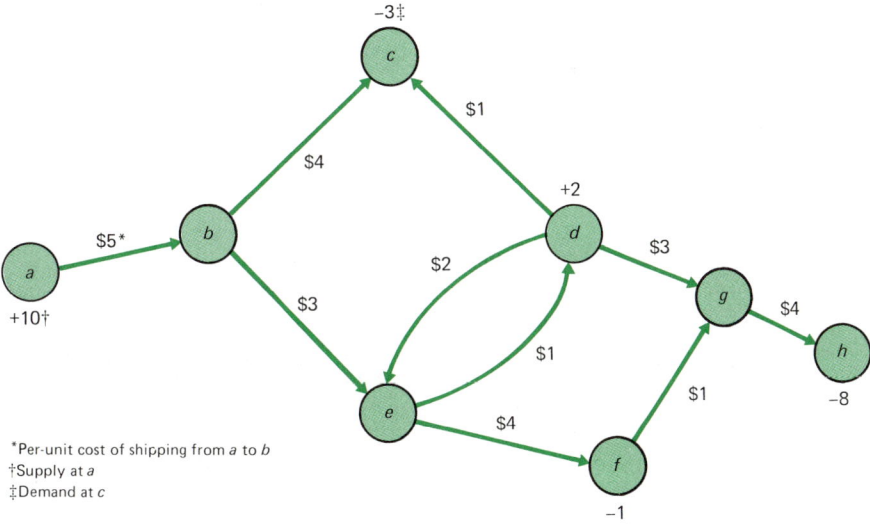

*Per-unit cost of shipping from a to b
†Supply at a
‡Demand at c

FIGURE 14–3. **Example of a Transshipment Problem**

A network such as this one that includes transshipment points is called a *transshipment problem*. As in the case of the transportation problem, the fact that the model can be represented as a network means that extremely efficient computer codes exist for its solution. Furthermore, there is a strong relationship between the mathematical structures of the transshipment and the transportation models. This relationship makes it possible to treat the transshipment problem as a transportation problem, and to develop a transportation table for it. The simple rules that allow this transformation of a transshipment problem into a transportation problem are omitted here, but they may be found in Wagner [1975].

AN EXAMPLE OF THE USE OF A NETWORK MODEL

We shall now present an example of the actual use of a network model to aid in solving a real-world problem. This example illustrates the following points:
1. A network model may be used for problems other than those related to transportation and distribution issues.
2. Optimizing management science models can be successfully applied to problems in the public and not-for-profit sectors.
3. The visual interpretation of a network model is an important advantage in communicating its logic to individuals who have not been formally exposed to management science techniques.
4. The computational advantage of a particular model formulation can significantly enhance its practical usefulness.
5. An optimizing model does not always "solve" the problem, but it can be a helpful aid to the decision maker.

The problem is the assignment of faculty members to courses during the three quarters of an academic year. The particular implementation we describe took place in the Graduate School of Management (GSM) at UCLA (for further details, see Dyer and Mulvey [1976]).

The faculty/course scheduling problem is complicated by the lack of a clearly defined objective to serve as the evaluative model that guides a solution process. The preferences of the faculty members must be balanced against the needs and desires of the students, while administrative policies and resource constraints must also be considered. Even these constraints are "loose," and some may be recognized only as the solution evolves.

How can one go about formulating an optimizing model for aiding a decision maker in analyzing a problem such as this one? First, the model builder may look for analogies with more familiar models. For example, he might note that each faculty member teaches a specific number of courses per academic year (usually five quarter courses per year at GSM). Thus, he might view a typical faculty member as "supplying" five course section equivalents, one unit of which is defined as the time and effort equal to the actual teaching of one course section. Further, each course "demands" one course section equivalent for each section that is to be offered. Thus, if three sections of course MGT 240 are to be offered during the year, the annual demand is three course section equivalents. This analogy suggests that the problem might be modeled as a transportation problem, with each faculty member being represented as a supply point that supplies course section equivalents into the system, and with each course viewed as a demand point that takes course section equivalents out of the system. An arc from a particular faculty member to a particular course would indicate that he could teach that course. Otherwise, the arc would be omitted.

In addition, the courses are taught over three quarters, and the schedule must be determined by quarters. Thus, the analogy went further. The quarters could be viewed as transshipment points, with the course section equivalents of the faculty "shipped" through particular quarters to corresponding quarter transshipment points for the courses. The network model that resulted from this analogy is shown in Figure 14-4 for a department with two faculty and three courses.

The flow on the arcs of the network is in course section equivalents. The nodes in the network are either faculty or course related. For each faculty member, there are up to four nodes corresponding to the annual, fall, winter, and spring schedules respectively. However, if a faculty member is not teaching during a particular quarter, the corresponding node is deleted. There are similar sets of nodes for the courses. Figure 14-5 portrays several examples of how

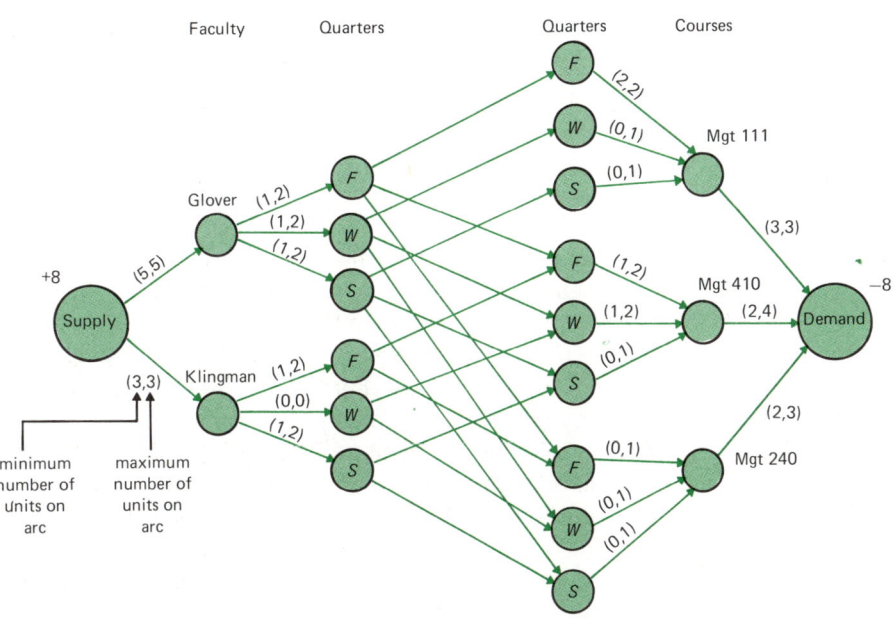

FIGURE 14-4. **Network representation of the faculty/course scheduling problem**

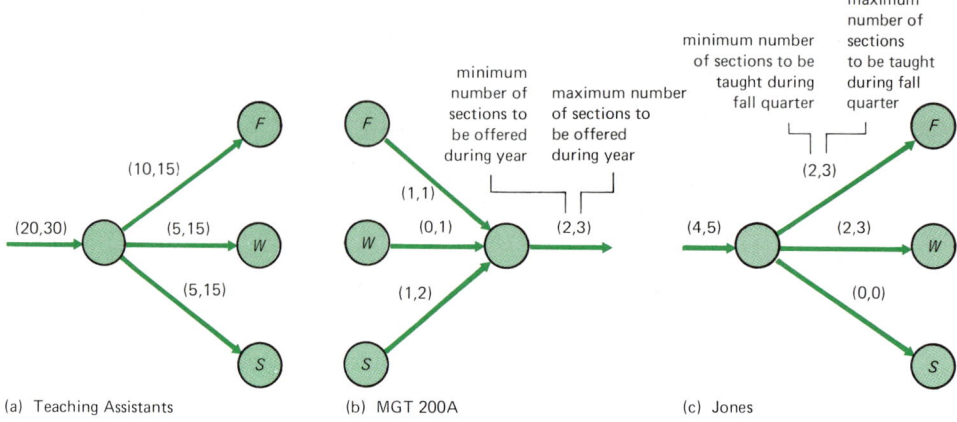

FIGURE 14-5. **Individual faculty/course nodes and associated arcs (examples)**

lower and upper bounds of the flows on the arcs can be useful in achieving various objectives. As illustrated in Figure 14-5(a), the total number of course sections to be offered by teaching assistants during the year is restricted to between 20 and 30. However, any one quarter cannot have more than 15 course sections offered by teaching assistants because of the capacity restrictions of the other arcs.

Similar restrictions determine the number of offerings of the courses. For example, MGT 200A will be offered either two or three times during the academic year as shown in Figure 14-5(b). One section will be offered during the fall as indicated by the corresponding minimum and maximum flow restrictions of one. At least one section will be offered during the spring quarter, and a third section *may* be offered during either the winter or the spring. The determination of whether this third section will actually be offered, and during which of the two quarters, will be made by the model, based on the availability of faculty resources. Thus, the user is able to incorporate many options within the context of a simple network model. Further, this visual interpretation makes it easy to convey the logic of the model to actual users.

The desires of the faculty members receive consideration in the model in two ways. Subject to administrative policies, a faculty member may determine the number of courses he will teach each quarter by manipulating the lower and upper bounds of the flow restrictions as illustrated in Figure 14-5(c). Jones will be assigned all five of his courses in the fall and winter and be free from formal teaching duties in the spring. In addition, the optimization in the model is carried out with respect to the "preference weights" of the faculty members for teaching the various courses. These preference weights range from -2 to $+2$, and are assigned by the faculty members.

Thus, it would appear that the evaluative model for this formulation is "maximize faculty happiness." However, it was assumed that the objective of maximizing faculty "happiness" and student "satisfaction" are complementary. Faculty members generally prefer teaching courses that are consistent with their professional abilities and teaching styles. Similarly, students generally prefer instructors who are enthusiastic about a course and its contents. While there may be some exceptional cases, it was not felt that these occurrences justify the burden of collecting additional information beyond simple expressions of faculty preference. In addition, information concerning the needs and desires of the students can be used to determine the lower and upper bounds on the number of sections of each course offered per academic year, and by quarter.

This network formulation is extremely attractive from a computational standpoint. The current costs of solving this model for GSM (with approximately 1000 nodes and 4500 arcs*) is in the range of $0.50 to $1 for the optimization, and $4 to $7 for a complete run, including input and output charges. Prior to recent developments in the field of network optimization, the cost of solving the same model would have been approximately $50 per run, which would have greatly inhibited its usefulness. The advantage of this low cost encourages the scheduler to make use of the model much more freely.

Although a number of considerations relevant to the faculty/course scheduling problem can be incorporated into this network model, and it has an obvious computational advantage, this formulation is only a crude approximation to the "ideal" model that would actually solve the scheduling problem in a single run. Therefore, the actual solution strategy for the problem is iterative, with the model providing a "first cut," and approximate solution that must be modified by the decision maker to include more subtle issues not considered in the model.

We emphasize again that a model need not be sufficiently detailed to "solve" a problem in a single computer run in order to be useful. Rather, the manager should view it as a decision-making aid that efficiently does much of the required computational work for him, but that must be used intelligently in order to actually provide some benefit.

WHAT SHOULD THE MANAGER KNOW?

Network models are among the most practical and useful management science models because they have many advantageous characteristics.
1. Many real-world problems can be formulated with network models.
2. The visual interpretation of the network reduces the problem of communication between the manager and the analyst.

---

*Note that each arc in a network corresponds to a variable in the equivalent linear programming formulation.

3. Efficient computer codes are available to analyze the networks, and integer valued solutions are obtained automatically.

These advantages enhance the practical usefulness of the transportation and transshipment models.

Problem Characteristics

The transportation and transshipment models may be applied to problems that require the allocation of units from sources of supply to sources of demand. The most obvious examples of such problems are the product distribution problems of large organizations. Certainly these models have been used to advantage for analyzing such problems in many instances. In addition, by solving transportation or transshipment problems several times for new facilities located on alternative sites, the problem of locating new facilities can also be analyzed.

It is also possible to use this model to assign workers to tasks, as illustrated in the description of the actual application of this methodology to the problem of faculty/course scheduling. This methodology is the basis for assigning military manpower to different jobs, as described by Charnes, Cooper, Niehaus and Sholtz [1970], and assigning workers to shifts as described by Segal [1974].

Thus, if the manager is studying any problem and recognizes that the task is to allocate units of a resource from sources of supply to sources of demand, he should consider formulating the problem with a transportation or transshipment model.

Formulation and Information Requirements

The formulation of large-scale transportation and transshipment problems will probably be the responsibility of an analyst with specialized skills in management science. However, the visual interpretation of these models makes it easy for the manager to get involved in this task and to satisfy himself that the logic of the model is correct. This involvement on the part of the manager significantly reduces the problem of validating the model.

The information requirements are the shipping costs per unit on each route, the supply capacities at the supply points, and the demands. The latter may be market demands, which are based on market surveys or other marketing estimates. Sensitivity analysis can be used to determine if the solution is particularly sensitive to changes in any one of these estimates. Then, when changes occur in the estimates, the sensitivity analysis can be used to determine whether or not a new solution needs to be calculated, or what the potential costs of *not* changing an existing distribution policy actually are.

Computational Considerations

The computational advantage of the network formulation is significant. Table 14–17 shows the time required to solve several transshipment problems on a CDC 6600 computer and gives an estimate of the costs of solving these problems based on computer charges of $0.04 per second [Mulvey, 1975]. A transportation problem with 8000 nodes would require a transportation table with a total of 8000 rows and columns. Yet it is possible to solve such a problem in approximately 80.5 seconds on a large computer at an estimated cost of $3.22. This result is not only of interest to technical analysts. The important practical implication is that the manager can use such a model freely once it has been formulated. Making 50 different runs to explore *what if* questions under various scenarios would cost only $161. The potential savings from such analyses can run into millions of dollars (for examples see Geoffrion [1976]).

One of the problems in Table 14–17 includes 35,000 arcs. Recall that an arc corresponds to a variable in a linear programming formulation. Can you imagine keypunching in the data for this problem! Naturally, special computer programs have been written to develop the input data for problems of this size.

In order to emphasize again the power of these solution methods, we suggest that when you are solving a transportation problem by hand with a total of 8 or 10 rows *and* columns and perhaps 16 variables, you should take a second look at the solution times and costs in Table 14–17.

TABLE 14–17. **Solution Times and Costs for Large Transshipment Problems**

Problem	No. of Nodes	No. of Arcs	Solution Time* (seconds)	Solution Cost†
1	8000	15,000	80.5	$3.22
2	5000	23,000	80	3.20
3	3000	35,000	63	2.52
4	5000	15,000	51	2.04
5	3000	23,000	37.5	1.50

*On a CDC 6600.
†Assuming $0.04 per second.

Advantages and Disadvantages of the Model

The advantages of the transportation and transshipment models have been discussed. The only disadvantage is that they are somewhat restricted in the amount of problem detail that can be incorporated. Some important logic in a problem may not be amenable to formulation in the network format. This situation occurred in the faculty/course scheduling problem, but the computational advantage of the network formulation suggested that a man-machine solution strategy would be successful. The network model could be used to provide an approximate solution, that could then be adjusted by hand to determine the final solution. This same strategy might be of value in other practical situations.

Check Your Understanding

1. Explain the significance of the visual interpretation of a network.
2. Comment on the following statement: "A manager does not need to worry about how efficient a computer program is for solving a problem. The machine can run all night so long as it finally gets *the* answer."
3. What is the significance of the notion of a "standard commodity bundle"? When can it be used?
4. Modify steps 1 through 4 of the northwest corner rule for finding an initial solution so that it becomes the "northeast" corner rule. That is, modify the steps so that you begin in the upper right-hand corner (the northeast corner) of the transportation table. Apply this new northeast corner rule to the introductory example shown in Table 14–1.
5. Apply the *northwest* corner rule to the transportation table shown in Table 14–18. What happens? The supply in row 1 and the demand in column 1 are met simultaneously by an allocation of 50 units. If no entry appears in row 1, column 2 or in row 2, column 1, the solution will be *degenerate*. Place an ϵ in row 1, column 2 (the shipment from factory 1 to outlet 2), and continue to allocate the remainder of the units to the boxes using the northwest corner rule.
   a. Evaluate the empty box in row 1, column 3.
   b. How many units can be shifted into the box in row 1, column 3 (hint: not zero, but a "very small" number)?
   c. Make this shift, and continue to apply the stepping-stone algorithm until the optimal solution is obtained.
6. Begin with the solution shown in Table 14–10. Apply the stepping-stone algorithm until an optimal solution is obtained. Have you found the optimal solution shown in Table 14–11? If not, have you found an alternate optimal solution? (Compute the total cost of the solution and compare it with the result in Table 14–11.)

TABLE 14-18. **Example Problem**

Factory \ Retail Outlet	1 (Kansas City)	2 (Atlanta)	3 (Detroit)	Available at Factories
1 (Chicago)	3	2	3	50
2 (New York)	10	5	8	70
3 (Dallas)	1	3	10	20
Required at Outlets	50	60	30	140

7. Begin with the optimal solution shown in Table 14–11. Generate the alternate optimal solution that could be determined by shifting units into empty box *AZ*. What is the managerial implication of this result?

Problems

8. Suppose we use the following shipments as an initial solution in the example problem shown in Table 14–18:
    Ship 20 units from factory 1 to outlet 2.
    Ship 30 units from factory 1 to outlet 3.
    Ship 30 units from factory 2 to outlet 1.
    Ship 40 units from factory 2 to outlet 2.
    Ship 20 units from factory 3 to outlet 1.
   a. Check to see that this initial solution satisfies the supply constraints at the factories and the demand constraints at the retail outlets.
   b. Compute the total shipping costs for this initial solution.
   c. Suppose we ship one unit from factory 1 to outlet 1. Compute the *net savings* that result. Have you found a desirable *direction of change*?
   d. How many units can be shifted around to the route from factory 1 to outlet 1. In other words, what is the appropriate *amount of change* in the desirable direction?

e. Revise the solution by shifting the necessary units. Check to see that the supply and demand restrictions are satisfied.

f. Now compute the *net savings* from shipping one unit from factory 2 to outlet 3 while observing the supply and demand restrictions. If this is a desirable direction of change, compute the appropriate amount of change and shift the necessary units.

g. Evaluate each empty box in the revised solution. Have you found an optimal solution?

9. Formulate the example network problem of Figure 14–2 as a linear optimization model. The decision variables will be the amount shipped from each factory to each distribution center. It is helpful to number the factories from 1 to 3, and to number the distribution centers from 1 to 5. Then the decision variables can be defined as x_{24}, for example, where x_{24} is the amount shipped from factory 2 to center 4. Since there are 3 factories and 5 distribution centers, you will have $(3)(5) = 15$ decision variables. When you finish with your formulation, look back at Figure 14–2. Which formulation is easier to understand?

10. Factories 1 and 2 distribute an identical product through two regional warehouses. Normal production costs are $2 per unit at factory 1, and $4 per unit at factory 2. Normal capacity is 100 units at each plant. Shipping costs are as follows:

Factory	Warehouse 1	Warehouse 2
1	$2	$4
2	3	1

The demand at warehouse 1 is 75 units, and demand at warehouse 2 is 125 units.

a. Set up the transportation table that you would use to determine the optimal production-shipping schedule. Do *not* work the problem.

b. Now assume that the demand at warehouse 2 has increased to 150 units. Suppose that additional overtime capacity of 20 units is available at each plant. Overtime production costs are $3 per unit at plant 1 and $5 per unit at plant 2. Set up the new transportation table that you would use to determine the optimal production-shipping schedule utilizing both regular and overtime capacity. Do *not* work the problem (Hint: Overtime capacity can be treated like a new factory with its own supply and costs).

c. Use the northwest corner rule to obtain an initial solution and solve for the optimal production-shipping schedules for (a) and (b) above.

11. Temple-Stark, Inc., produces a cleaning fluid at its plants in Albuquerque and Boston. Cleaning fluid sells for $0.50 a can in the Midwest and Southwest (serviced by warehouses located in Omaha and Houston respectively) and for $0.55 a can in the Rocky Mountains, which are served by a warehouse in Salt Lake City. Transportation costs per can are as follows:

Transportation Cost to:

From	Salt Lake City	Omaha	Houston
Albuquerque	$0.07	$0.08	$0.05
Boston	0.10	0.05	0.09

Production information is as follows:

Plant	Monthly Capacity	Unit Production Cost
Albuquerque	1700	$0.35
Boston	1800	0.29

a. Suppose the monthly demand is for 1300 cans in Salt Lake City, 1200 cans in Omaha, and 1000 cans in Houston. Set up a transportation table that could be used to determine the optimum production-shipping schedule. Do *not* work the problem.

b. Suppose the monthly demand is for 1200 cans in Salt Lake City, 1000 cans in Omaha, and 1000 cans in Houston. Set up a transportation table that could be used to determine the optimum production-shipping schedule. Do *not* work the problem.

c. Use the northwest corner rule to obtain an initial solution and solve for the optimal production-shipping schedules for cleaning fluid for (a) and (b) above.

12. Factories A, B, and C distribute an identical product through three regional warehouses, X, Y, and Z. Monthly factory capacities are 160, 190, and 150 units respectively. Monthly warehouse requirements average 150, 160, and 90 units respectively. The unit distribution costs differ as follows:

From	To: X	Y	Z
A	$ 3	$5	$ 8
B	5	6	15
C	12	7	4

The current shipping schedule is as follows:

From	To	No. of Units
A	X	150
A	Y	10
B	Y	150
B	Z	40
C	Z	50

a. Set up a transportation table that could be used to determine the optimum shipping plan.
b. Use the current shipping schedule as the initial solution. Evaluate the net savings (cost) associated with shipping one additional unit on each of the following routes while observing the supply and demand restrictions:

From	To
A	Z
A	dummy warehouse
B	X
B	dummy warehouse
C	X
C	Y

c. If one or more of the evaluations in (b) reveals a net savings, shift the units in the transportation table. Interpret the results.
d. Evaluate the net savings (cost) associated with shipping one additional unit on each of the unused routes in the revised table. Is the solution optimal? How do you know?

13. Four workers are available, each of whom may be assigned to only one of four jobs. The number of minutes required to perform each job by each worker is shown in the table below:

Worker	Job 1	Job 2	Job 3	Job 4
1	2	4	5	---
2	7	3	2	3
3	9	---	8	6
4	---	6	2	3

The empty *cells* indicate that the worker does not have the necessary skills to do the particular job.

a. Set up a transportation problem that can be used to assign one worker to each job so that the *sum* of the minutes required for the jobs is minimized. What is the appropriate interpretation of the supply and the demand in this case?

b. Draw the network corresponding to this problem.

c. Use an initial solution of 1s in row 1, column 1; row 2, column 2; row 3, column 3; and row 4, column 4. This solution is degenerate. Place ϵ's in row 1, column 2; row 2, column 3; and row 3, column 4. Solve by the stepping-stone method.

d. If, after a little practice, worker number four can perform job two in 2 minutes instead of 6, should the solution be changed? If so, what should it become?

14. Texas Electronics, Inc., has just received a large government contract to deliver radar units to three different locations over a three-year period. The radar units are currently manufactured in plants in Atlanta (A) and Boston (B). Each plant has a normal capacity of 100 units per year. However, an extra shift could be added in either or in both plants that could boost the annual capacity by an additional 75 units in each plant. Any units produced on an extra shift would cost an additional $2 per unit (these costs are "scaled" so they are simple numbers).

The units must be shipped to Rhode Island (R), South Dakota (S), and Tennessee (T). The annual demands vary over the three-year period of the contract as shown in the following table:

Demand in Year:	Location		
	R	S	T
1	50	60	100
2	75	70	120
3	100	80	150

The per-unit costs of shipping also vary as follows:

From	To:		
	R	S	T
A	$3	$1	$5
B	8	2	4

On the basis of these data, a management science analyst has determined the optimum production-shipping schedule for each of the three years by using the transportation model and a special-purpose computer program. The results are shown in Table 14–19.

TABLE 14-19. **Production-Shipping Schedule for Texas Electronics**

	To:		
From	R	S	T
Year 1			
A (normal)	50	50	0
A (extra shift)	0	10	0
B (normal)	0	0	100
B (extra shift)	0	0	0
Year 2			
A (normal)	75	25	0
A (extra shift)	0	45	0
B (normal)	0	0	100
B (extra shift)	0	0	20
Year 3			
A (normal)	100	0	0
A (extra shift)	0	75	0
B (normal)	0	0	100
B (extra shift)	0	5	50

As an alternative, Texas Electronics, Inc., can purchase a new plant in Chicago (C), operate it for three years, and sell it at an estimated total net loss of $1000. This new plant has a normal capacity of 130 units per year, and an extra shift could produce an additional 100 units per year, although there would be an estimated incremental cost of $2 per unit manufactured on the second shift. It costs $2 per unit to ship from Chicago to Rhode Island, $6 to ship to South Dakota, and $3 to ship to Tennessee.

The management science analyst has also performed a *what if* analysis of the optimum production-shipping schedule, based on the assumption that the plant in Chicago has been purchased. His results are shown in Table 14-20. Should Texas Electronics, Inc., purchase this new plant? Based on the monetary criterion alone, what is the appropriate decision? What other factors might alter this decision?

15. The Stellar Steel Company makes automotive parts that are used in the assembly of automobiles. At present, the company has three plants, one in

TABLE 14-20. **Production-Shipping Schedule for Texas Electronics with Chicago Plant**

	To:		
From	R	S	T
Year 1			
A (normal)	0	60	0
A (extra shift)	0	0	0
B (normal)	0	0	20
B (extra shift)	0	0	0
C (normal)	50	0	80
C (extra shift)	0	0	0
Year 2			
A (normal)	0	70	0
A (extra shift)	0	0	0
B (normal)	0	0	65
B (extra shift)	0	0	0
C (normal)	75	0	55
C (extra shift)	0	0	0
Year 3			
A (normal)	20	80	0
A (extra shift)	0	0	0
B (normal)	0	0	100
B (extra shift)	0	0	0
C (normal)	80	0	50
C (extra shift)	0	0	0

Cleveland, one in Denver, and one in Philadelphia. These plants supply four automobile assembly plants in Oakland, Gary, Houston, and Newark. Of late, the output from the company's plants has not been able to keep pace with its orders. As a result, the company has decided to build a new plant to expand its productive capacity. It is considering San Francisco and Atlanta as possible sites; both appear to be excellent choices in terms of subjective, noncost factors.

TABLE 14-21. **Production-Distribution Data for the Stellar Steel Company**

Demand		Production	
Assembly Plant Requirements (units per month)		Normal Production Load (units per month)	Production Costs (per unit)
Oakland	9,000	Denver	6,000	$0.48
Gary	10,000	Philadelphia	14,000	0.50
Houston	12,000	Cleveland	15,000	0.52
Newark	15,000	Atlanta (estimate)	---	0.49
	46,000			
		San Francisco (estimate)	---	0.53
			35,000	

Transportation Costs ($ per unit)

From	To: Gary	Houston	Newark	Oakland
Cleveland	$0.25	$0.55	$0.40	$0.60
Denver	0.35	0.30	0.50	0.40
Philadelphia	0.36	0.45	0.26	0.66
Atlanta	0.35	0.30	0.41	0.50
San Francisco	0.60	0.38	0.65	0.27

The production and output requirements for each of the existing plants, together with the estimated production costs of the two locations are shown in Table 14-21. Transportation costs from all these plants to the assembly plants are also given. Which of the two new locations should be selected on the basis of the cost criterion?

16. A firm is attempting to manage its cash balance so that it obtains the maximum return on its assets.* It has forecasted the cash payments it can expect from its accounts receivables, and the accounts payable from its own commitments in each of the next three months as shown:

---

*Based on V. Srinivasan, "A Transshipment Model for Cash Decisions," *Management Science*, Vol. 20, No.10, June 1974.

Month	Forecasted Cash Inflow (in $ thousands)	Forecasted Accounts Payable (in $ thousands)
1 (Jan.)	10	40
2 (Feb.)	20	60
3 (Mar.)	40	50
	70	150

The firm can delay payment of an account by one month and pay a penalty of 2 percent. However, it cannot delay payment by more than one month.

The firm also has two marketable securities. Security A matures on March 1 with a face value of $50,000, while security B matures on February 1 with a face value of $20,000. These securities could be sold early, if necessary, to provide cash for the accounts receivable. The penalties are as follows:

Number of Months Before Maturity	Penalty (percent)
1	0.5
2	1.5

In addition, the firm has a line of credit with a bank. The interest charges for borrowing are as follows:

Borrow in Month	Interest Charge (percent)
1 (Jan.)	4.0
2 (Feb.)	3.0

This credit can be used to cover the excess cash demands over the total cash availabilities during this three-month period.

Finally, any excess cash available during one month may be invested in short-term securities which mature in 30 days or 60 days. The returns from these securities are as follows:

Maturity (days)	Return (percent)
30	0.75
60	1.60

Formulate the cash management problem as a transshipment problem. Assume that all of the accounts payable, including those for March, must be paid before April 1. (Hint: Define nodes representing "cash" in each month that are the transshipment nodes. The other nodes will be either "sources" or "sinks.")

References

1. Charnes, A., W. Cooper, R. Niehaus, and D. Sholtz, "A Model for Civilian Manpower Management in the U.S. Navy," in *Models of Manpower Systems,* edited by A. Smith, English Universities Press, 1970.
2. Dantzig, G., *Linear Programming and Extensions,* Princeton University Press, Princeton, 1963.
3. Dyer, J., and J. Mulvey, "An Integrated Optimization/Information System for Academic Planning," *Management Science,* Vol. 22, No. 12, August 1976.
4. Geoffrion, A., "Better Distribution Planning with Computer Models," *Harvard Business Review,* Vol. 54, No. 4, July–August 1976.
5. Klingman, A., A. Napier, and J. Stutz, "Netgen: A Program for Generating Large Scale Capacitated Assignment, Transportation, and Minimum Cost Flow Network Problems," *Management Science,* Vol. 20, No. 5, January 1974.
6. Mulvey, J., "Special Structures in Network Models and Associated Applications," Ph.D. dissertation, The Graduate School of Management, The University of California, Los Angeles, 1975.
7. Segal, M., "The Operator Scheduling Problem: A Network Flow Approach," *Operations Research,* Vol. 22, No. 4, July–August 1974, pp. 808–823.
8. Srinivasan, V., "A Transshipment Model for Cash Decisions," *Management Science,* Vol. 20, No. 10, June 1974.
9. Wagner, H., *Principals of Management Science,* Prentice-Hall, Englewood Cliffs, N.J., 1975.
10. Zierer, T.K., W. A. Mitchell, and T. R. White, "Practical Applications of Linear Programming to Shell's Distribution Problems," *Interfaces,* Vol. 6, No. 4, August 1976.

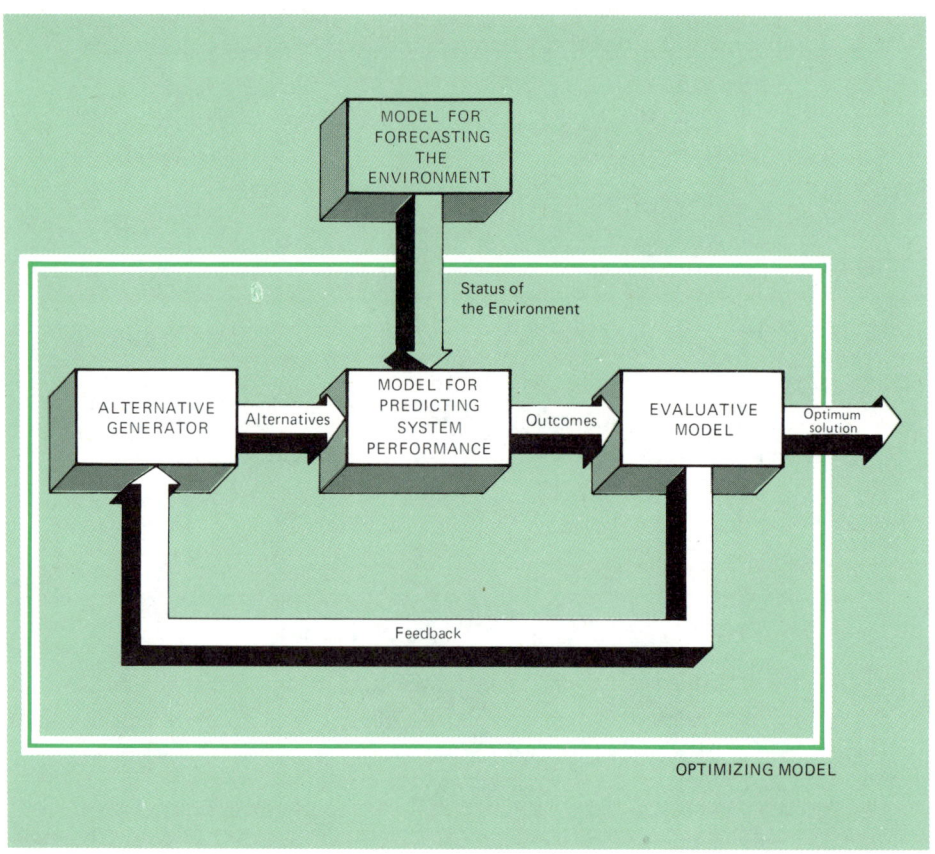

NETWORK SCHEDULING MODELS: PERT AND CPM

Another important class of network models involves the determination of the longest or the shortest path through a network. In most real-world applications, the length of the path is not actually a measure of distance, but rather a measure of money or of time. If the measure is time, the longest path through the network may be of interest as an estimate of the duration of a large-scale project. This latter concept is the basis for the well-known network scheduling techniques PERT and CPM.

These network models also share the following important characteristics:
1. Many real-world problems can be formulated with network scheduling models.
2. The visual interpretation of the network reduces the problems of communication.
3. Efficient computer codes are available to analyze the networks.

Therefore, a manager should be able to recognize opportunities for using these models.

NETWORK SCHEDULING MODELS

Network scheduling models are used to plan, schedule, control, and evaluate complex projects and tasks. The basic idea is to analyze a complex project—for example, the development of a new weapons system, the construction of a large building, or the production of a motion picture—by identifying the specific tasks that must be accomplished to complete the project and interrelating them in a network.

The network planning techniques known as the critical path method (CPM) and the Program Evaluation and Review Technique (PERT) were originally developed in the 1950s. PERT was first used to help manage the successful Polaris project, and since that time, some form of network scheduling model has been required for every government defense contract.

The nodes in the network scheduling models represent "events" in the project.[*] An event generally corresponds to the beginning or end of a specific task, or "activity," that must be performed as part of the project. The activities are represented by the arcs in the network.

The rules of logic in the network are relatively simple. Suppose an activity D can be started only after activities A, B, and C have been completed. This situation would be diagramed as shown in Figure 15-1. Thus, all activities represented by arcs into an event node must be completed before an activity represented by an arc out of an event node can begin.

In addition, because of restrictions imposed by most computer routines that analyze network schedules, two activities cannot have the same beginning and ending event nodes. Thus, if activities B and C can begin after activity A, and activity D can begin after activities B and C have been completed, we might be tempted to diagram this relationship as shown in Figure 15-2(a). However, since computer codes identify activities by their beginning and ending nodes, they could not distinguish between activity B and activity C, which both begin with event 2 and end with event 3. Therefore, a "dummy" activity is used as shown in Figure 15-2(b). The dummy activity has a time duration of zero and is used for logical purposes in the network.

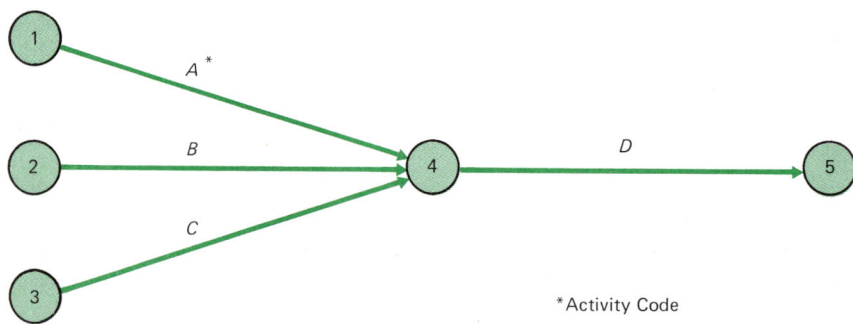

FIGURE 15-1. **Activity D can begin only after activities A, B, and C have been completed.**

*Activity Code

---

[*]We are presenting the "activities on the arcs" approach to network scheduling, although it is also possible to develop "activities on the nodes" models.

PART IV OPTIMIZING MODELS

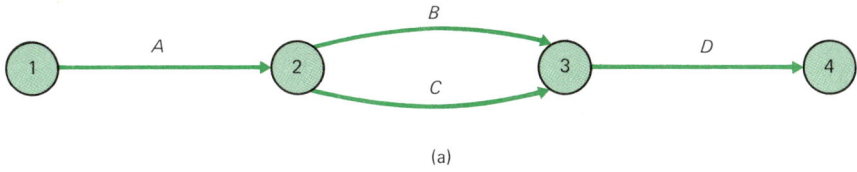

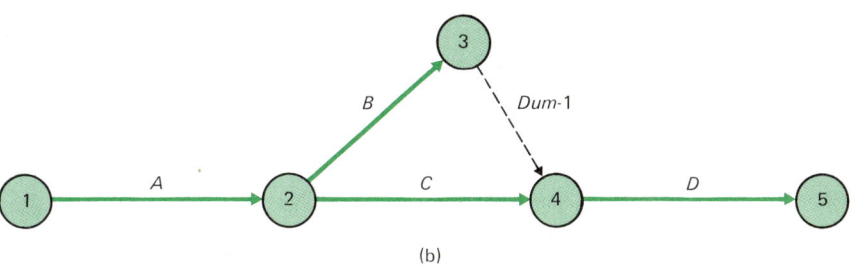

FIGURE 15-2. **Network diagraming rules**

Drawing the Network

Now, consider a simple example of a project that might be analyzed by using network scheduling. Suppose we wish to conduct a market survey. Our first activity, A, will be to study the purpose of the survey. After completing this task, we can hire data collection personnel (B) and design the questionnaire (C). After both B and C are completed, we can train the personnel (D). However, after completing only the design of the questionnaire (C), we can begin selecting households for our survey (E), even before the personnel have been hired (B). Finally, after completing tasks (D) and (E) we can take the survey (F). These tasks and the precedence relationships are shown in Table 15-1. Try to construct your own network for analyzing this problem before looking at the solution in Figure 15-3. Notice that one dummy activity was required to indicate that activity D cannot start until *both* activities B and C have been completed, but activity E depends only on activity C.

Just the construction of such a network could be a significant managerial aid in dealing with a complex problem. In preparing Table 15-1, it was necessary to do an *activity analysis*; that is, the activities required to complete the project had to be identified and the technical precedence relationships among the activities had to be determined. These precedence relationships are the statements of which activities must immediately precede an activity.

The value from the network can be enhanced if the activity analysis also uses estimates of the time required to complete each activity, and these are included in the network. In order to determine these time estimates, decisions must be made regarding the methods and tools to be used in completing each activity. Again, this forces the manager to break down the project into its individual tasks, and to plan each of these in detail before beginning the project. Suppose that the time estimates for the activities in the market survey are 2 weeks for A, 4 weeks for B, 2 weeks for C, 1 week for D, 2 weeks for E, and 3 weeks for F. These time estimates are shown in parentheses on the network in Figure 15-4.

TABLE 15-1. **Activities Required and Immediate Predecessors for the Market Survey**

Activity Code	Description	Immediate Predecessors
A	Study purpose	---
B	Hire personnel	A
C	Design questionnaire	A
D	Train personnel	B, C
E	Select households	C
F	Survey	D, E

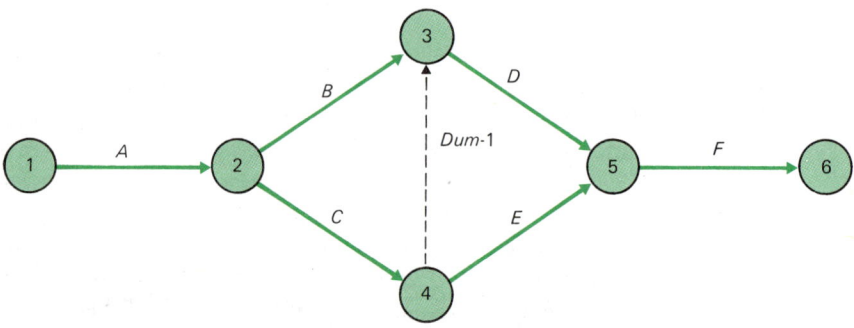

FIGURE 15-3. **Network diagram for the market survey**

Network Analysis

Given these time estimates, the network may be analyzed to provide additional information of importance to managers. The most obvious information of interest is the total length of time required for the project. Since we are interested in completing each of the activities, the total time for the project will be equal to the *longest path* through the network. Thus, we apply a simple algorithm to obtain this estimate.

This algorithm computes the "earliest" and "latest" start and finish times for each of the activities. The early start and finish times are simply the earliest that each activity can be started and finished respectively, given the technical precedence relationships in the network. The latest start and finish times are the latest that an activity can be started and finished respectively, *without delaying the total time to complete the project.* The difference between the early and late start (finish) time is the "slack" associated with an activity. This slack is the amount of time that a particular activity could be delayed without delaying the completion of the project. This information can be very useful to managers in scheduling work and the use of equipment. The activities with zero slack cannot be delayed without delaying the entire project. These activities are on the longest path through the network, which is called the *critical path.*

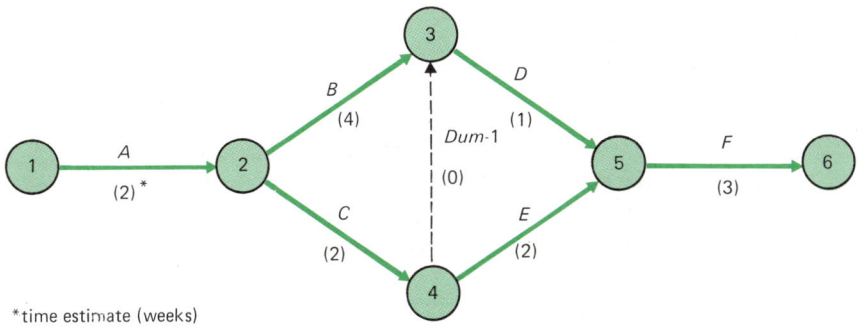

*time estimate (weeks)

FIGURE 15-4. **Time estimates for the activities in the network diagram**

Earliest Start and Finish Times We can begin with zero as the starting time for the project, which becomes the earliest start time (*ES*) for the first activity. Given *ES* for an activity, the earliest finish time (*EF*) is simply *ES* + activity time. The procedure for computing *ES* and *EF* is as follows:

Step 1. Place the value of the project start time to the left of the beginning activity in the position shown for the early start time in Figure 15-5. In Figure 15-5 we see a zero for the *ES* of activity A. The early finish time is then *ES* + activity time, or 2 weeks for activity A. This *labels* activity A.

Step 2. Consider any activity not yet labeled, all of whose predecessors have been labeled with their *ES*'s and *EF*'s. The *ES* for this activity is the *largest number* in the *EF* position of its immediate predecessors. That is to say, the earliest an activity can begin is the earliest that *all* of its predecessor activities are finished. The *ES* for activity B in Figure 15-5 is 2 weeks.

Step 3. The *EF* for this activity is *ES* + activity time. For activity B, *EF* = 2 + 4 = 6 weeks.

Step 4. Repeat steps 2 and 3 until the last activity is labeled. This label is the *length* of the critical (longest) path in the network, and the total duration for the project.

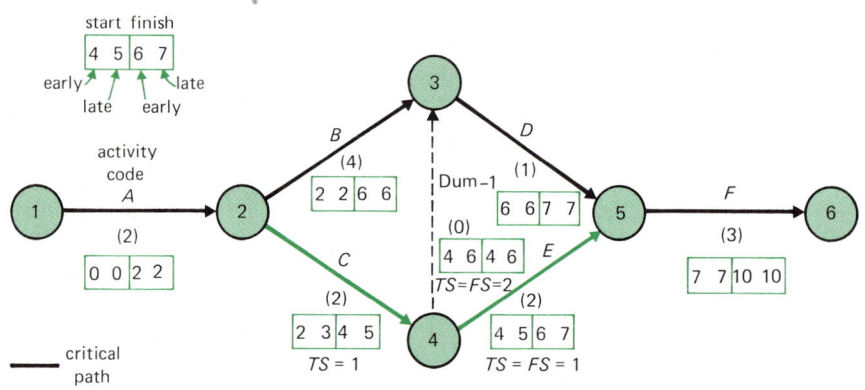

FIGURE 15-5. **Network diagram for the market survey showing early and late start and finish times, and critical path. *TS* = total slack; *FS* = free slack**

In our simple example, the length of the critical path is 10 weeks, which is the minimum amount of time required to complete the market survey.

Latest Start and Finish Times If we assume that the target for completing the market survey is the *EF* time of 10 weeks, then we have defined the latest finish time (*LF*) of 10 weeks, allowing no slack in the project as a whole. Therefore, the latest start time (*LS*) for the final activity is *LF* − activity time. The procedure for computing *LS* and *LF* for the remaining activities is as follows:

Step 1. Label the *LF* and *LS* values for the terminal activities as shown in Figure 15-5. For the market survey, *LF* = 10, and *LS* = 7 for activity F.

Step 2. Consider any activity not yet labeled, all of whose successors have been labeled with their *LS*'s and *LF*'s. The *LF* for this activity is the *smallest number* in the *LS* position of its immediate successors. That is to say, the latest that an activity can be finished is the latest that *any* of its successors can start. The *LF* for activity E in Figure 15-5 is 7 weeks.

Step 3. The *LS* for this activity is *LF* − activity time. For activity E, *LS* = 7 − 2 = 5 weeks.

Step 4. Repeat steps 2 and 3 until the initial activity is labeled.

Slack and Critical Path Total slack (*TS*) for an activity is the maximum time that the activity can be delayed beyond its *ES* without delaying the project completion time. The critical activities are those that are in the sequence of the longest time path through the network, and therefore the activities on this path all have minimum possible *TS*. Since for our example the target date and the *EF* for activity *F* (the final activity) are the same, all critical activities will have zero *TS*. The project target date may of course be later than the *EF* of the final activity, in which case all activities on the critical path would have the same *TS* equal to the difference between the project target date and the final *EF*. Then all noncritical activities will have greater *TS* than critical activities.

Free slack (*FS*) is the amount of time that an activity can be delayed without delaying the *ES* of any other activity. Free slack for an activity never exceeds its *TS*. Free slack is computed as the difference between the *EF* for that activity and the earliest of the *ES* times of all of its immediate successors. For example, activity *E* has $FS = 1$, since the *ES* of its successor is 7 and its own *EF* is 6.

An Example Network scheduling techniques are often applied to large-scale projects, such as the development of the Polaris missile or the construction of the Mexico City subway. However, they can also be used to analyze relatively simple operations, such as rebuilding a device known as a tool cutter-grinder. This latter example is realistic, yet simple enough to present in its entirety.

The first step is the activity analysis, which generates the activities required, the activity time requirements in days, and the technical precedence requirements to build a tool cutter-grinder, as shown in Table 15-2. The network corresponding to this activity analysis is then generated, and the critical path analysis is performed, as illustrated in Figure 15-6. For practical problems, these computations are actually performed by computer codes. The output from a computer code that has analyzed the tool cutter-grinder network is shown in Figure 15-7.

Extensions and Managerial Uses of Network Scheduling Techniques

There are numerous extensions of the network scheduling techniques that enhance their practical usefulness to managers. One important extension is the use of probabilistic time estimates. The time estimate for completing a particular activity may be uncertain, especially in research and development activities where there is no previous experience to use as a guide. Therefore, instead of a single time estimate for an activity, *three* time estimates are obtained. The three different time estimates are:

    1. The *optimistic time, a,* is the shortest possible time in which the activity may be accomplished if all goes well. The estimate is based on the assumption that the activity would have no more than one chance in 100 of being completed in less than this time.

TABLE 15-2. **Rebuilding a Tool Cutter-Grinder**

Activity Code	Description	Days Required	Immediate Predecessors
A	Disconnect and move	0.2	---
B	Connect power and pretest	0.2	A
C	Remove electrical units	0.2	B
D	Clean machine	0.3	C
E	Remove and disassemble mechanical units	0.2	C
F	Clean machine parts	0.4	D
G	List mechanical parts	0.5	F
H	Order machine parts	0.5	G
I	Receive machine parts	1.0	H
J	Paint cross slides	25.0	I
K	Machine parts	1.5	G
L	Inspect and list electrical parts	1.0	K
M	Paint motor	1.0	L
N	Assemble motor	0.8	P, Q, R
O	Machine saddle	2.5	H
P	Machine slides	2.0	V
Q	Machine table	2.0	L
R	Paint machine	2.0	M
S	Scrape slides	1.0	N
T	Scrape table	1.0	G
U	Scrape saddles	0.5	E
V	Machine gibs	2.0	K
W	Install spindle	1.0	J, O, T
X	Assemble parts	1.0	J, O, S, T
Y	Scrape gibs	0.5	U
Z	Assemble head	1.0	J, O, T
AA	Install motor and electrical parts	0.3	Y
BB	Assemble cross slides	0.4	J, O, T
CC	Connect power and test	0.5	AA, BB, Z, W, X
DD	Touch up, move, reinstall	0.3	CC

Source: Data from R. D. Archibald and R. L. Villoria, *Network-Based Management Systems,* John Wiley & Sons, New York, 1967; used by permission.

2. The *pessimistic time, b,* is the longest time that an activity could take under adverse conditions, barring acts of nature. This time estimate is based on the assumption that the activity would have no more than one chance in 100 of being completed in a time larger than b.
3. The *most likely time, m.*

These three time estimates are reduced to a single time estimate t_e, the mean of the implied probability distribution for the activity time. In addition, the *variance* of this distribution, σ^2, can also be estimated. The formulas are:

$$t_e = \frac{1}{6}(a + 4m + b), \tag{1}$$

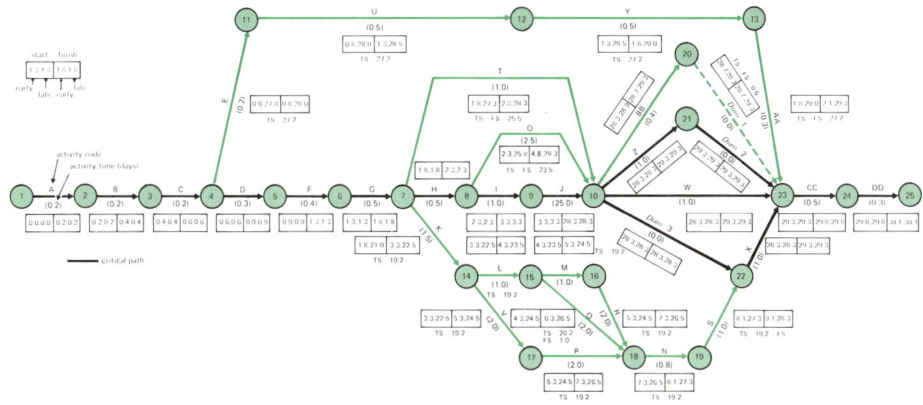

FIGURE 15-6. **Arrow diagram for rebuilding Cincinnati No. 2 cutter-grinder showing early and late start and finish times, and critical path.** *TS* = total slack; *FS* = free slack
Adapted from R. D. Archibald and R. L. Villoria, Network Based Management Systems, John Wiley & Sons, New York, 1967.

$$\sigma^2 = \left[\frac{1}{6}(b-a)\right]^2. \tag{2}$$

The t_e estimates are then used in the computation of the critical path for a project exactly as before. However, the total time for the critical path is now interpreted as the *mean* estimate.

When we add several random variables, the sum is also a random variable with a normal probability distribution, even if the random variables that are added are not normally distributed. The mean of this normal distribution is equal to the sum of the means of the individual random variables, and the variance is equal to the sum of the variances of the random variables. Therefore, the length of the critical path is the mean of a normal probability distribution whose variance is equal to the sum of the variances of the individual activities on the critical path.

Management can then compute the *probability* of completing the project in any specified length of time. For example, since the length of the critical path is only the mean of a normal probability distribution for the total project time, there is only a 50 percent chance that the project will actually be completed by this time. Management can plan, reschedule, or even renegotiate contracts on the basis of the expected outcomes and risk levels. Obviously, however, the output

CRITICAL PATH SCHEDULE Job No. 50787, Date issued 7-17-62, Page 1

Operation Code	i	j	Days Req'd.	Earliest Start	Earliest Finish	Latest Start	Latest Finish	Days Slack	Free Slack
A	1	2	.2	.0	.2	.0	.2	.0	**
B	2	3	.2	.2	.4	.2	.4	.0	**
C	3	4	.2	.4	.6	.4	.6	.0	**
D	4	5	.3	.6	.9	.6	.9	.0	**
E	4	11	.2	.6	.8	27.8	28.0	27.2	.0
F	5	6	.4	.9	1.3	.9	1.3	.0	**
G	6	7	.5	1.3	1.8	1.3	1.8	.0	**
H	7	8	.5	1.8	2.3	1.8	2.3	.0	**
I	8	9	1.0	2.3	3.3	2.3	3.3	.0	**
J	9	10	25.0	3.3	28.3	3.3	28.3	.0	**
K	7	14	1.5	1.8	3.3	21.0	22.5	19.2	.0
L	14	15	1.0	3.3	4.3	22.5	23.5	19.2	.0
M	15	16	1.0	4.3	5.3	23.5	24.5	19.2	.0
N	18	19	.8	7.3	8.1	26.5	27.3	19.2	.0
O	8	10	2.5	2.3	4.8	25.8	28.3	23.5	23.5
P	17	18	2.0	5.3	7.3	24.5	26.5	19.2	.0
Q	15	18	2.0	4.3	6.3	24.5	26.5	20.2	1.0
R	16	18	2.0	5.3	7.3	24.5	26.5	19.2	.0
S	19	22	1.0	8.1	9.1	27.3	28.3	19.2	19.2
T	7	10	1.0	1.8	2.8	27.3	28.3	25.5	25.5
U	11	12	.5	.8	1.3	28.0	28.5	27.2	.0
V	14	17	2.0	3.3	5.3	22.5	24.5	19.2	.0
W	10	23	1.0	28.3	29.3	28.3	29.3	.0	**
X	22	23	1.0	28.3	29.3	28.3	29.3	.0	**
Y	12	13	.5	1.3	1.8	28.5	29.0	27.2	.0
Z	10	21	1.0	28.3	29.3	28.3	29.3	.0	**
AA	13	23	.3	1.8	2.1	29.0	29.3	27.2	27.2
BB	10	20	.4	28.3	28.7	28.9	29.3	.6	.0
CC	23	24	.5	29.3	29.8	29.3	29.8	.0	**
DD	24	25	.3	29.8	30.1	29.8	30.1	.0	**
Dum-1	20	23	.0	28.7	28.7	29.3	29.3	.6	.6
Dum-2	21	23	.0	29.3	29.3	29.3	29.3	.0	**
Dum-3	10	22	.0	28.3	28.3	28.3	28.3	.0	**

**Critical Operations

FIGURE 15-7. **Sample output of network analysis program for the tool cutter-grinder**

is no better than the input data, and there is a danger that the very existence of such precise probability statements will give an aura of accuracy that may not be justified.

The network schedule can also be used to study questions from time/cost trade-offs. In order to estimate the time required to complete an activity, assumptions regarding the level of manpower and the resources to be used must be made. In some cases, it may be advantageous to develop multiple time estimates for multiple levels of resource input. The critical path analysis could be performed with each activity by using a maximum of its resources. Then, for activities with slack, resources could be reduced, extending the time for the activity but not increasing the time for the network, as long as the time extension does not exceed the slack on the activity's path.

In some cases, even activities on the critical path may be extended when the cost savings exceed the costs of delaying the project completion. Computer algorithms are also available to perform such analyses. Managers may also wish to use the early start-late start information for activities not on the critical path to schedule their start in such a way as to smooth the manpower requirements over the total life of the project, or to make the most efficient use of other limited resources, such as special-purpose machinery.

Finally, the network schedule can be used for project control. Cost estimates can be developed for the activities and these data can be entered into computer programs along with the time estimates. As work on a project progresses, the actual cost and time figures can be compared with the estimates. Areas in which significant cost or time overruns are occurring can be indentified easily, and managerial actions can be considered to overcome them. For example, if a time overrun is occurring on a network path that has a relatively large slack value, the manager may choose to do nothing. However, if the time overrun is on the critical path or on one with little slack, he may wish to take immediate action. These topics are treated in further detail at a managerial level in Weist and Levy [1977], while more technical issues are examined in Moder and Phillips [1970] and in Archibald and Villoria [1967].

WHAT SHOULD THE MANAGER KNOW?

Network scheduling techniques are widely used in many organizations. It is likely that the modern manager will be involved at some point in his career with projects for which network scheduling is used. Therefore, you should have an understanding of the benefits that can be obtained from this important tool.

Problem Characteristics

Network scheduling methods are advantageously applied to complex, large-scale projects. Generally, these are one-of-a-kind projects, so that previous plans and experience for completing this type of effort are not available. Among the successful applications that have been reported are the following cases:
1. construction of new homes, shopping centers, subways, etc. [Glasser and Young, 1961; O'Brian, 1965]
2. introduction of new products [Wong, 1964]
3. major maintenance efforts [Reeves, 1960]

4. pilot production runs [Odom and Blystone, 1964]
5. development of new weapon systems [Fazar, 1961]

Thus, any time the manager confronts a problem that is complex in that it requires the completion of several interrelated activities, is relatively large in terms of the resource requirements, and is nonroutine (no one in the organization has had significant experience in dealing with this type of problem previously), a network scheduling technique should be considered as a managerial aid.

Formulation

The manager and all persons who will be responsible for some of the activities to be performed should be involved in formulating the initial network. Some experts claim that 90 percent of the benefits of the technique are obtained from this exercise. The activities must be identified and the interrelationships must be clarified. Responsibility for accomplishing each activity must be assigned to individuals, and the person responsible should be involved in determining how to conduct the activity and in estimating the time required for its completion. This involvement provides the participants with an overview of the entire project and an understanding of how their activities relate to others.

Computational Considerations

Once the initial network has been formulated, it can be entered into the computer for analysis. Rather than providing the answer, the result of this analysis should be the basis for another round of planning with the managers involved in the project. Issues of trading off costs versus time and of manpower smoothing can be raised. Alternative solutions can be generated by moving activities from their early start to their late start times. Several computer runs would doubtless be required before the final plan is determined.

When the project is under way, the actual time and cost performances can be entered into the computer to compare against the initial estimates. Potentially, areas of cost or time overruns can be identified early, and managerial action can be taken.

Interpretation

The manager must be careful not to put too much reliance on the network. Just because the network terminates before the project due date does not mean that the actual project will. Thus, the manager must ensure that the data used in the analysis are an accurate portrayal of what is actually occurring in the project.

Disadvantages of the Network Scheduling Models

Network scheduling, especially for the control of a project, can be relatively costly. The costs of obtaining information and updating the network may not justify the benefits of the method in relatively small projects. As a rough rule of thumb, O'Brian [1965] suggests that computer network scheduling techniques are probably not justified on projects involving costs of $100,000 or less and should be questioned on projects even up to $500,000 in costs. However, the hand calculations for these networks are so straightforward that smaller projects can be organized with a simple analysis and "back of the envelope" calculations.

Even if computer network scheduling and control techniques are not used, the manager should always consider an initial planning session devoted to the construction of a network. Again, much of the value of a management science model is not in the solution it provides, but in the knowledge gained in the process of its formulation.

Check Your Understanding

1. What is an *event* in a project? How does it relate to an *activity*?
2. What is the function of a *dummy* activity?
3. What is the managerial significance of information regarding the *slack* associated with an activity? How might this information be used?
4. What is the *critical path*? What is its managerial significance?
5. What is the difference between *free slack* and *total slack* for an activity? What is its managerial significance?
6. Suppose that the target for completing the market survey shown in Figure 15–5 is twelve weeks, so that the late finish time (*LF*) for the terminal activity *F* is 12. Compute the revised late start and late finish times for the activities. Also compute the revised total slack and free slack for each activity.
7. The following comment was heard in industry: "Every time the PERT chart is revised, the management sends a bunch of supervisors to check on the activities on the critical path. When they ask us for time estimates for our activity, we always revise our actual estimates to ensure that our activity won't be on the critical path. We don't want a bunch of supervisors hanging around!" What are the implications of this comment for the proper use of network scheduling techniques in real-world situations?
8. Suppose the critical path of a project was determined by using probabilistic time estimates. The mean length of the critical path is 12 days, and the variance (determined by summing the variance of each activity on the critical path) is 4 days. Thus, the standard deviation associated with the critical path is $\sqrt{4} = 2$ days. Using the area under the standarized normal curve in Table C–1 of

Appendix C, compute the probability that the project will actually be completed in 10 days, 12 days, 14 days, 16 days.

9. Describe how the network schedule may be used to accomplish each of the following:
   a. a time/cost trade-off analysis
   b. a resource scheduling and allocation analysis
   c. cost control

Problems

10. A small maintenance project consists of ten jobs, whose precedence relationships are identified by their node numbers as shown in Table 15–3.
    a. Draw an arrow diagram representing the project.
    b. Calculate early and late start and finish times for each job.
    c. How much total slack does job *d* have? Job *f*? Job *j*?
    d. Which jobs are critical?
    e. If job *b* were to take 6 days instead of 3, how would the project finish date be affected?

TABLE 15–3. **Jobs for a Small Maintenance Project**

Job	Network Description (initial node, final node)	Estimated Duration (days)
a	(1, 2)	2
b	(2, 3)	3
c	(2, 4)	5
d	(3, 5)	4
e	(3, 6)	1
f	(4, 6)	6
g	(4, 7)	2
h	(5, 8)	8
i	(6, 8)	7
j	(7, 8)	4

11. An architect has been awarded a contract to prepare plans and specifications for an urban renewal project. The job consists of the following activities and their estimated times.

Activity	Description	Immediate Predecessors	Time (days)
a	Preliminary sketches	---	2
b	Outline of specifications	---	1
c	Prepare drawings	a	3
d	Write specifications	a, b	2
e	Run off prints	c, d	1
f	Have specifications printed	c, d	3
g	Assemble bid packages	e, f	1

a. Draw an arrow diagram for this job, indicate the critical path and calculate the total slack and free slack for each activity.
b. During the first day of work it is learned that activity c (prepare drawings) will take 4 days instead of 3. What effect does this delay have on the project completion date and project management?

12. The following tasks are required for the production of a play:

Activity	Description	Immediate Predecessors	Time (weeks)
a	Play selection	--	3
b	Casting	a	4
c	Costume design	a	3
d	Set design	a	2
e	Set construction	d	4
f	Rehearsals	b	3
g	Dress rehearsals	c, e, f	2
h	Printing tickets and programs	b	6

a. Draw the arrow diagram for this play.
b. Calculate the early and late start and finish times for each activity, and the total slack and free slack for each activity.
c. Indicate the critical path.

13. Consider the project network shown in Figure 15-8.
    a. Supply the information indicated in the following table:

Activity	Network Description (initial node, terminal node)	Time (weeks)	ES	EF	LS	LF	TS	FS
a	(1, 2)	2						
b	(1, 3)	3						
c	(2, 4)	4						
d	(3, 4)	1						
e	(4, 5)	3						
f	(4, 6)	2						
g	(5, 6)	0						
h	(5, 7)	3						
i	(6, 7)	1						
j	(7, 8)	2						

b. If activities e and f both require the use of a special piece of equipment (i.e., cannot be performed at the same time), what adjustment would you make? In particular, how would the project duration be affected?

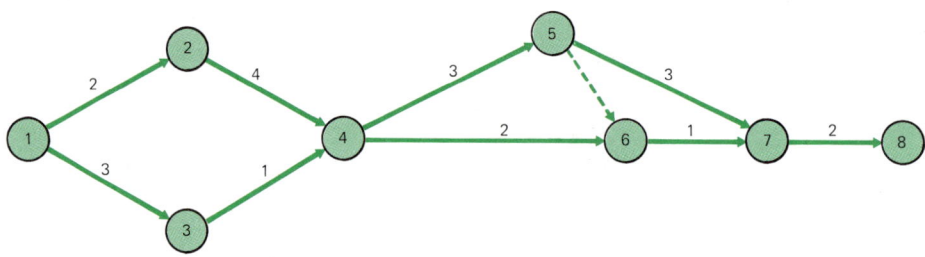

FIGURE 15–8. **Project network (exercise 13)**

14. An established company has decided to add a new product to its line. It will buy the product from a manufacturing concern, package it, and sell it to a number of distributors selected on a geographical basis. Market research has indicated the volume expected and size of sales force required. The steps shown in Table 15–4 are to be planned. The precedence relationships among these activities are shown in Figure 15–9. As the figure shows, the company can begin to organize the sales office, design the package, and order the stock immediately. Also, the stock must be ordered and the packaging facility must be set up before the initial stocks are packaged.
   a. Draw the arrow diagram for this project.
   b. Calculate the early and late, start and finish times for each activity, and the total and free slack for each activity.
   c. Indicate the critical path.
15. Probabilistic time estimates have been obtained for the activities in the simple project network shown in Figure 15–10.
   a. For example, the estimate of the "optimistic time," a, for job a is 1; the

TABLE 15-4. **Planning Activities for New Product Introduction (exercise 14)**

Activity	Description	Time (weeks)
a	Organize sales office	6
b	Hire salesmen	4
c	Train salesmen	7
d	Select advertising agency	2
e	Plan advertising campaign	4
f	Conduct advertising campaign	10
g	Design package	2
h	Set up packaging facilities	10
i	Package initial stocks	6
j	Order stock from manufacturer	13
k	Select distributors	9
l	Sell to distributor	3
m	Ship stock	5

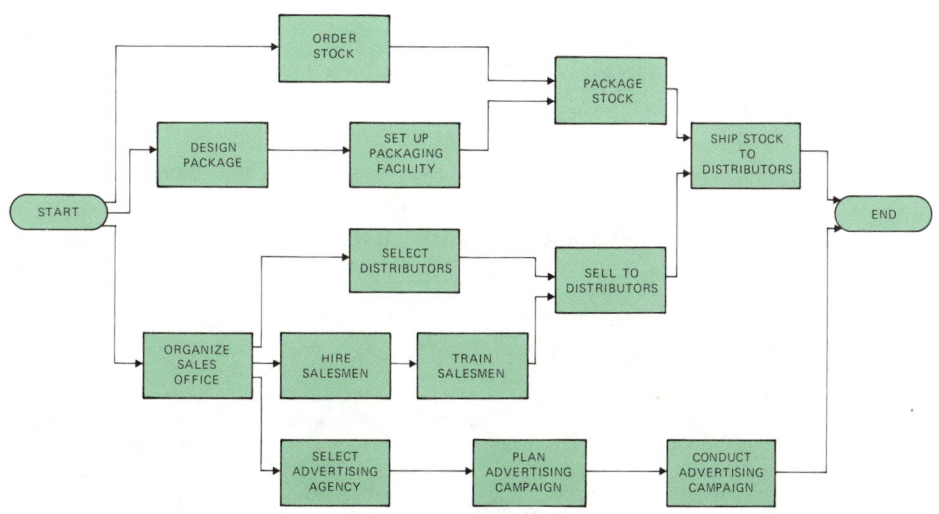

FIGURE 15-9. **New product introduction— precedence diagram (exercise 14)**

CHAPTER 15 NETWORK SCHEDULING MODELS: PERT AND CPM

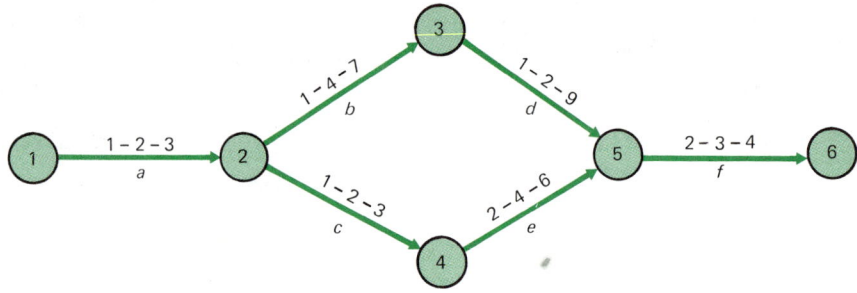

FIGURE 15-10. **Project network (exercise 15)**

estimate of the "most likely time," *m,* for job *a* is 2; and the estimate of the "pessimistic time," *b,* for job *a* is 3. Using the formulas (1) and (2) from the chapter discussion, calculate the mean and variance for each activity time.
b. Using the mean values, determine the critical path and its mean duration.
c. Sum the variances of the times of the activities on the critical path to obtain the variance associated with the mean duration of the project.
d. Using the area under the standardized normal curve in Table C-1 of Appendix C, compute the probability that the project will actually be completed in 10 days, 12 days, 14 days, 16 days.
e. A penalty cost of $50,000 must be paid if the project is not completed in 12 days. For an additional cost of $20,000, the management can guarantee that activity *d* can be completed in exactly 1 day. Should they pay the $20,000 for sure, or accept the risk regarding the penalty cost? Use the expected monetary value evaluative model as a guide to your recommendation.

16. For the network shown in Figure 15-11, determine the critical path and the probability of finishing the project in less than 32 time periods. The optimistic, most likely, and pessimistic time estimates are shown above each activity.

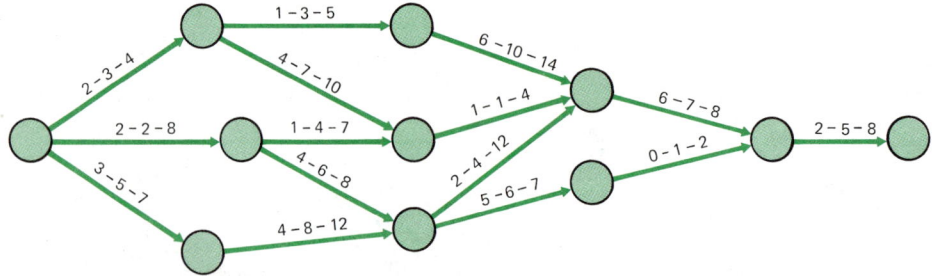

FIGURE 15-11. **Project network (exercise 16)**

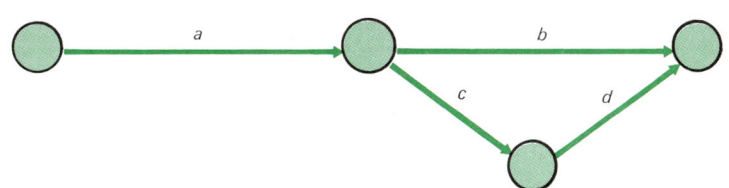

FIGURE 15-12. **Project network (exercise 17)**

17. Miller Manufacturing Company is engaged in the small project shown in Figure 15-12. The times required to accomplish each activity depend on the level of resources allocated to it. For example, activity a can be accomplished in 3 days with a normal allocation of resources. However, for an additional $400 worth of resources, the time can be reduced to 2 days, and for another allocation of $400 worth of resources, it can be cut to 1 day. No further reductions are possible. Similar reductions in time are possible for the other activities. The data for each activity are as follows:

Activity	Minimum Time (days)	Normal Time (days)	Cost to Reduce Time by 1 Day
a	1	3	$400
b	3	7	100
c	2	4	400
d	2	5	200

   a. What is the normal project duration and the minimum project duration?
   b. Overhead costs of $450 per day are incurred for every day the project is not completed. What is the optimum duration of the project considering both overhead costs and the costs to reduce the time on each activity?

18. A small maintenance project consists of the jobs in the following table. With each job is listed its normal time and a minimum time (in days). The cost in dollars per day of reducing the time for each job is also given.

Job	Network Description (initial node, terminal node)	Minimum Time (days)	Normal Time (days)	Cost to Reduce Time by 1 Day
a	(1, 2)	6	9	$20
b	(1, 3)	5	8	25
c	(1, 4)	10	15	30
d	(2, 4)	3	5	10
e	(3, 4)	6	9	15
f	(4, 5)	1	2	40

a. What is the normal project duration and the minimum project duration?
b. Overhead costs are $50 per day. What is the optimum length schedule in terms of both time reduction and overhead costs? List the scheduled durations for each job for your solution.

References

1. Archibald, R., and R. Villoria, *Network-Based Management Systems,* John Wiley & Sons, New York, 1967.
2. Fazar, W., "Navy's PERT System," *Federal Accountant,* Vol. 11, December 1961.
3. Glasser, L., and R. Young, "Critical Path Planning and Scheduling: Application to Engineering and Construction," *Chemical Engineering Progress,* Vol. 57, November 1961.
4. Levy, F., G. Thompson, and J. Wiest, "The ABC's of the Critical Path Method," *Harvard Business Review,* Vol. 41, No. 5, October 1963.
5. Moder, J., and C. Phillips, *Project Management with CPM and PERT,* second edition, Reinhold Corporation, New York, 1970.
6. O'Brian, J., *CPM in Construction Management,* McGraw-Hill, New York, 1965.
7. Odom, R., and E. Blystone, "A Case Study of CPM in a Manufacturing Situation," *Journal of Industrial Engineering,* Vol. 15, No. 6, November–December 1964.
8. Paige, H. W., "How PERT-Cost Helps the General Manager," *Harvard Business Review,* Vol. 40, No. 2, March–April 1962.
9. Reeves, E., "Critical Path Speeds Refinery Revamp," *Canadian Chemical Processing,* Vol. 44, October 1960.
10. Wiest, J., and F. Levy, *A Management Guide to PERT/CPM: with GERT/PDM/DCPM,* second edition, Prentice-Hall, Englewood Cliffs, N.J., 1977.
11. Wong, Y., "Critical Path Analysis for New Product Planning," *Journal of Marketing,* Vol. 28, No. 4, October 1964.

PART V

SYNTHESIS

SYNTHESIS

In Chapter 1, we argued that a model simplifies a problem solver's view of a problem by leaving out much information and by creating categories. In a similar manner, an introductory textbook simplifies a complex body of knowledge by leaving out much information (recall our numerous comments that such details were primarily of interest to analysts) and by creating categories (called chapters). A useful model contains not only the important categories, but also the essential interrelationships among these categories. Continuing the analogy, the material in a textbook will be of significant value only if the reader understands the interrelationships among the materials within different chapters, as well as the more specific details in each chapter.

As you have read each chapter, the title and the introduction have identified the nature of the problems and of the associated mathematical models and solution techniques to be discussed. In the real world there are no titles or introductory statements to tell you that a particular problem can best be modeled and analyzed using linear programming or any other technique of management science. An ability to recognize key problem characteristics that aid in identifying the appropriate form of the model must be developed. This ability can be of significant value in enhancing the problem-solving skills of a manager, even if a formal, mathematical analysis is not performed.

The later statement raises another important question: When should a formal, mathematical analysis of a problem be performed? There are no firm rules for selecting a particular model or for deciding whether to perform an analysis, but we shall attempt to provide some guidance in Chapter 16.

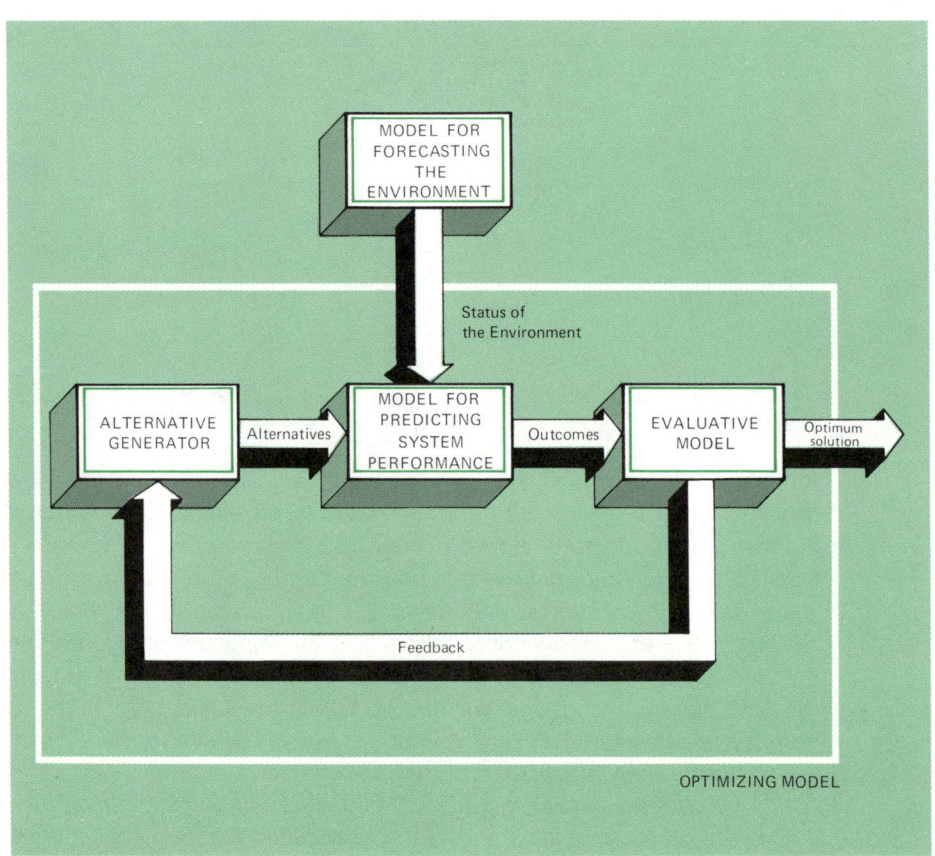

16

WHAT SHOULD THE MANAGER KNOW?

What should the manager know about the tools, techniques, and concepts of management science/operations research? At the end of each chapter, we have addressed this important question in terms of the specific materials included within the chapter. Now it is time to address this question by looking across the chapters in order to gain an appreciation for the total body of knowledge associated with the hybrid term "management science/operations research." In doing so, we shall first consider whether a formal, mathematical analysis should be used to deal with a particular, real-world problem. Next, we shall provide some summary guidelines for matching problems with models and solution techniques. These guidelines also serve as a means of summarizing and synthesizing the topics we have covered.

WHEN SHOULD MANAGEMENT SCIENCE/OPERATIONS RESEARCH BE USED?

We have presented numerous examples of "successful" applications of the models and tools of management science/operations research to real-world problems, but it is clear that not every real-world problem should be dealt with by formally applying these models and tools. How can an intelligent decision be made with regard to the use of these approaches? Perhaps some insights can be gained by considering what is meant by the term "successful application."

Benefits Versus Cost

The use of a formal, mathematical model in the analysis of a problem is "successful" if the benefits exceed the costs. The costs include the time for model formulation, the time and cost of data collection, the time and cost of the development of necessary computer programs, and the cost of any computer runs required for the formal analysis.

These costs can be substantial and can easily exceed subjective estimates of the benefits that might result from an analysis. However, the continuing research and development in the fields of computer hardware design and information systems, and the development of efficient computer programs for performing the analyses guarantee that these costs will continue to decrease, so that in the future the potential benefits of applying formal mathematical models will exceed the costs in a growing number of problem areas.

This relationship between the benefits and costs of analysis can be illustrated diagrammatically as shown in Figure 16-1. The gross benefits of applying formal mathematical models to problems within an organization increase rapidly as the problems with the highest payoff are analyzed first, and continue to increase, but at a decreasing rate. The costs of applying the models are initially small, but increase at an increasing rate. However, the costs associated with 1965 technology, in terms of computers, information systems, and computer programs, increase much faster than the costs associated with 1975 technology. Therefore, the number of problems to which the formal analysis should be applied in order to maximize *net benefits* has increased from point A in 1965 to point B in 1975 (see Figure 16-1). It is likely that this increase will continue, making it even more important for the modern manager to have model-building skills in the future.

In any particular situation, a rough estimate of the potential benefits and costs will have to be made. For example, the expenses from the product transportation and distribution system of a large organization may run into the millions of dollars annually. A large-scale formal analysis of the system could easily be justified, even if the costs of the analysis were several hundred thousand dollars.

In other situations, computer programs may be available that can analyze a problem by using readily accessible data. The costs of the analysis may be only a few hundred dollars, and these costs can easily be justified, even in small organizations dealing with relatively small problems.

Conceptual Value

Suppose that you estimate that a formal mathematical model-building effort is not justified in a particular situation — perhaps because adequate data or the appropriate computer programs are not available, and the cost or time required to develop them is prohibitive. Are the concepts of model building still of use in the problem-solving effort?

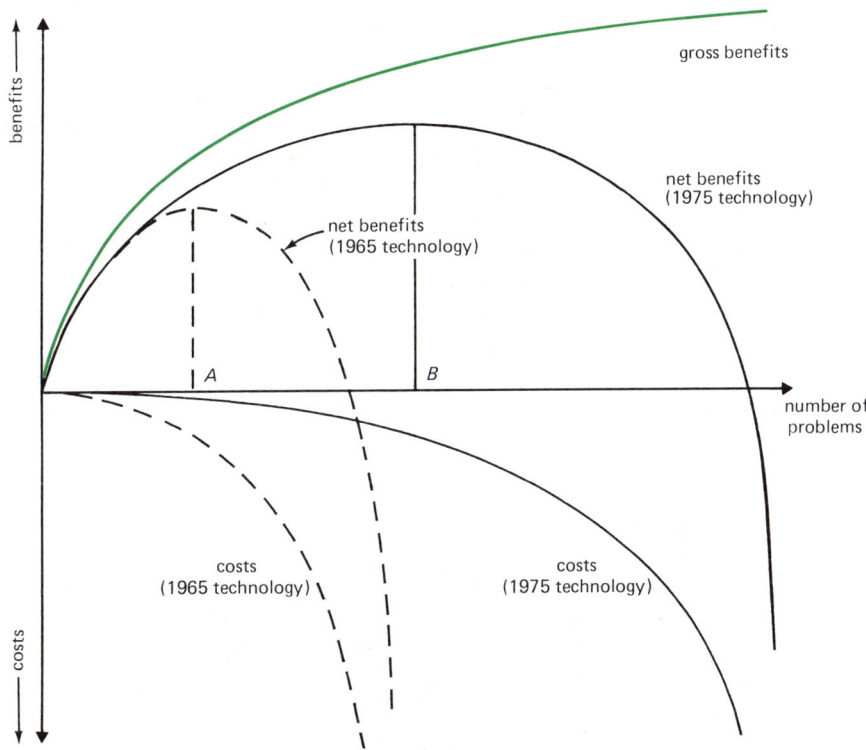

FIGURE 16-1. **Benefits and costs of analysis**

What you have learned may seem at first to be some detailed knowledge about linear optimization models, corporate planning models, network models, waiting-line models, decision trees, and so on. But it should have been more than that. Formal models should also teach us something about the basic structure of certain kinds of important problems.

For example, in studying linear optimization models we learn not only the structure and application of this important model but also something fundamental about allocation problems in general. We learn to handle the effects of interacting and competing demands for limited resources and, perhaps more important, we learn the general nature of optimum solutions. Understanding these general concepts is important, because they should carry over into situations for which the formal model is not applicable. In the practical operating situation, allocations of limited resources must often be made on an intuitive basis, either because there is not time for formal analysis or because the most important variables are not quantifiable. We believe that a manager can exercise intuitive judgment most effectively if he understands the basic nature of a formal problem and the probable nature of good solutions.

Another excellent example is the general waiting-line model. The individual who understands formal waiting-line models should be able to make a good snap judgment about the level of service to provide in a practical situation because he realizes the great value of idle time of the server. The value of idle time, of course, is a concept that runs contrary to our fundamental training to conserve time, yet in the design of many systems, provision of apparent overcapacity is the key to success.

Thus, one benefit of an understanding of formal mathematical model building is that it provides alternative ways of thinking about a problem—as a linear optimization model, a network model, or a waiting-line model. In each case, thinking about a model in these terms can also help determine the information that should be collected and the probable nature of the best solution. These benefits should accrue to a manager with model-building skills even if no formal analysis is undertaken.

CHOOSING A MODEL

Which model should be used in analyzing a specific problem, either formally or simply as a way of thinking about the problem? Perhaps this issue is not critical, since there is often no *one correct way* of modeling a problem. Additional insights may be obtained by trying to conceptualize a problem in terms of different mathematical forms—as a linear optimization model or a network model, for example. However, some models do "match" better with a particular problem than others, and thus offer greater insights into the problem. Therefore, it is important to be able to recognize key characteristics of a problem that have implications for model selection.

One strategy is to look for the problem characteristics that can be related to the categories of models shown in the now familiar Figure 16–2. In thinking about a problem, we may ask ourselves about the nature of the problem environment. Can it be *forecast* with relative certainty, or is risk a major factor to be considered in the decision? Some of the models we have studied are appropriate for problems in which important elements can only be described in terms of probability statements. Examples are the waiting line models and the Monte Carlo simulation models. Other models assume that the environment is relatively certain. These include the important optimizing models described in Part IV and the computer-based corporate simulation models discussed in Chapter 6.

A second question relates to the nature of the relationships among the important elements in the problem. In effect, we are trying to identify the nature of the mathematical expressions that may exist in the *predictive* model. The corporate simulation models and the elementary inventory models use simple, algebraic relationships. The relationships are required to be linear expressions in order to use the linear optimization models. If the relationships can be described with a network of arrows and circles, then one of the models in Chapter 14 or 15

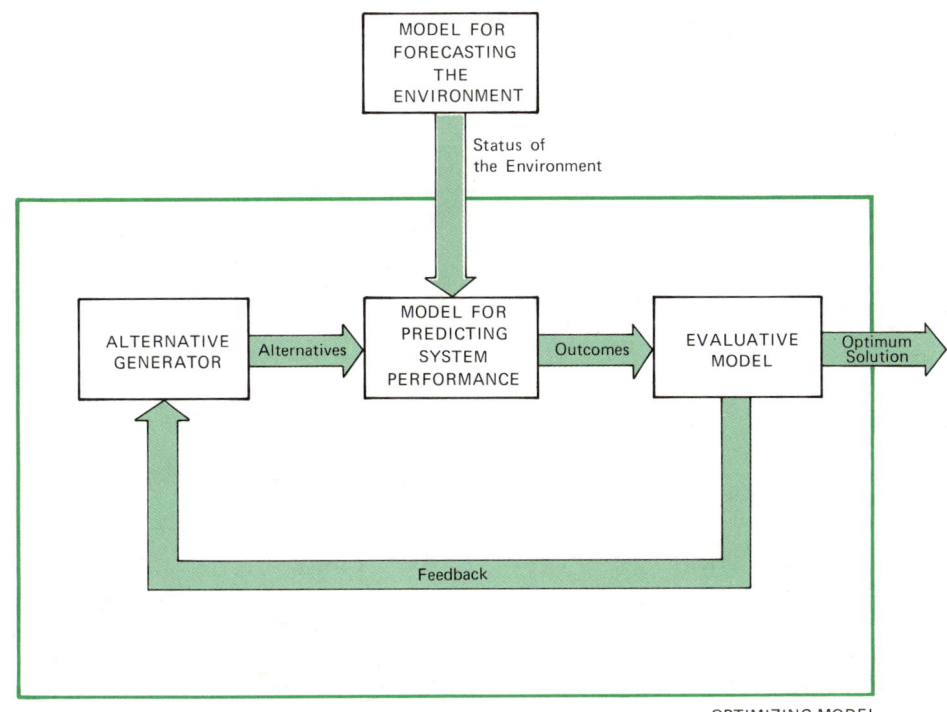

FIGURE 16-2. **Models of management science**

might be appropriate. An important issue in a problem might be how the relationships among the problem elements change over time. If so, the Markov chain models might be helpful in analyzing the transition of problem elements from one state to another.

Finally, a third question relates to the purpose of the analysis. If we are seeking the *best* solution to a problem according to some clearly defined, quantifiable function of the decision variables (*evaluative model*), then we should look to the optimizing models of Part IV. If we only wish to predict the outcomes of selecting an alternative, or the impact of changing one element of the problem on the other elements, then one of the predictive models of Part III would be appropriate.

Table 16-1 provides a summary of the topics we have covered and a description of the assumptions regarding the nature of the environment, the predictive model, and the evaluative model for each topic. Like any other model, Table 16-1 omits some information in simplifying and summarizing these assumptions. As you gain experience with the techniques and tools of management science, you may recognize exceptions or quibble with some of the categories in Table 16-1. However, we hope that this summary will be helpful to the beginner in relating the materials.

TABLE 16–1. **Assumptions Regarding the Nature of the Environment, the Predictive Model, and the Evaluative Model**

Chapter	Title	Environment	Relationships Among Elements	Objective
2	Probability and Expected Value	Risky	Outcomes from predictive models, optimizing models, or subjective estimates	Maximize expected value
3	Decision Trees	Risky	Outcomes from predictive models, optimizing models, or subjective estimates	Maximize expected value
4	Evaluative Models Based on Utility Functions	Certain or risky	Outcomes from predictive models, optimizing models, or subjective estimates	Maximize (expected) utility
5	Forecasting the Environment	Risky	Statistical	Minimize forecast error
6	Building Mathematical Models to Predict System Performance	Certain	Simple, algebraic	Complex and/or not defined quantitatively
7	Predicting the Effects of Risk: Markov Chains	Risky	Probability of transition from state to state over time	Complex and/or not defined quantitatively
8	Predicting the Effects of Risk: Waiting Line Theory	Risky	Waiting lines and service facilities	Complex and/or not defined quantitatively
9	Predicting the Effects of Risk: Monte Carlo Simulation	Risky	May involve several waiting lines and service facilities	Complex and/or not defined quantitatively
10	Elementary Optimizing Models for Inventory Management	Certain or risky	Simple, algebraic and statistical	Minimize costs
11	Linear Optimization Models	Certain	Linear expressions	Maximize (minimize) a quantifiable function of the decision variables
12	Application of Linear Optimization Models	Certain	Linear expressions	Maximize (minimize) a quantifiable function of the decision variables
13	The Simplex Method	Certain	Linear expressions	Maximize (minimize) a quantifiable function of the decision variables
14	Network Models: Transportation and Transshipment	Certain	Network	Maximize (minimize) a quantifiable function of the decision variables
15	Network Models: PERT and CPM	Certain	Network	Maximize (minimize) a quantifiable function of the decision variables

Matching Problem Characteristics and Models

Let us now illustrate how the summary in Table 16-1 might be used. Suppose we ask questions about the environment, the nature of the relationships among elements, and the purpose of the analysis of a specific problem. We identify the following problem characteristics:

1. a relatively certain environment
2. simple algebraic relationships among the elements of the problem
3. no clearly defined quantifiable objective

Then from Table 16-1 the predictive models described in Chapter 6 seem most likely to provide a useful analysis.

As a second example suppose we ask similar questions about a second problem and obtain the following conclusions:

1. a relatively risky environment
2. the logical relationships and/or the parameters change as a function of time
3. no clearly defined, quantifiable objective

Again from Table 16-1 the Markov chain models provide the appropriate "match."

Finally, this questioning procedure might lead to the following set of problem characteristics in another study:

1. a relatively certain environment
2. linear relationships among the elements of the problem
3. a clearly defined, quantifiable function of the decision variables to be maximized (minimized)

This time, a linear optimization model would be selected from Table 16-1.

Turn back through the book to any problem description, either in the text or in the problem section. Read it carefully, and then ask the following questions:

1. What is the nature of the environment (certain or risky)?
2. What is the nature of the relationships among the problem elements?
3. Is there a clearly defined, quantifiable function of the decision variables to be maximized (minimized)?

See if your answers to these questions for a problem in a particular chapter are consistent with the summary for that chapter shown in Table 16-1. If not, try to reconcile the differences.

Example: The Cash Management Problem The cash balance of a firm normally fluctuates because of a lack of synchronization between cash inflows from accounts receivable, cash sales, and so forth, and cash outflows from payments on accounts and notes payable. The cash management problem is concerned with optimally financing these outflows with cash-on-hand, lines of credit, or sales of marketable securities, while investing net inflows in the appropriate marketable securities.

Suppose you were presented with the cash management problem of a large organization. How would you make your analysis? Are any of the models of management science appropriate for aiding this analysis? What questions should you ask, and what additional information would you require?

First of all, let us take stock of what we know from this brief problem description. What is the nature of the environment? Can a firm accurately forecast its inflows and outflows of cash over a time horizon of several months? The answer depends on the nature of the organization and the stability of its market. It may also depend on the degree of detail that is required in the analysis. Very few firms can forecast cash inflows and outflows with *complete* certainty, but the assumption that they can may be a reasonable abstraction from reality for the purposes of analysis.

We shall consider the following three different conditions of the environment:

1. The outflow of cash is relatively constant over time.
2. The inflows and outflows of cash can be described only by probability statements.
3. Cash inflows and outflows vary, but these variations can be forecast with certainty.

Each of these conditions has implications for the choice of the appropriate model.

Skipping to the last question in our list of three, is there a clearly defined function of the decision variables to be maximized (minimized)? At first glance, the objective seems clear: maximize the returns (minimize the costs) from the cash management decisions. The returns are from the interest paid on marketable securities and from discounts commonly offered by creditors for early payments. The costs are from interest charges from the lines of credit, from losses on the sales of marketable securities that must be sold before maturity, and from the costs of the transactions.

But is the problem really this simple? Excess cash deposits improve a firm's credit rating and the banker's goodwill at the cost of earnings foregone from investments in securities. The determination of an appropriate "minimum" cash balance will require the consideration of issues other than short-term profits. However, it may still be appropriate to adopt the assumption of a single quantifiable objective function for the purpose of analysis, realizing that we are abstracting from and simplifying reality in order to gain the advantage of alternative ways of viewing this problem.

Now let us couple our assumption of a quantifiable objective function with each of the three different conditions of the environment. It is generally necessary to know the nature of the environment before we can identify the relationships among the problem elements. Suppose the outflow of cash is relatively constant over time. Given this condition in the environment, would it be possible to express the relationships among the problem elements in terms of simple, algebraic statements? Perhaps so. We might view the cash management problem in the following manner. All cash outflows are to be made from a cash account. There is a cost associated with *holding* cash in this account, since it could be earning interest in marketable securities. There is also a cost of adding cash to this account, since marketable securities must be sold or lines of credit must be used. These latter *transaction* costs are similar to *reordering* costs in inventory management models. Thus, we have an analogy. We have a constant demand for cash, a holding cost, and a reordering (transaction) cost. The relationships among these elements can be expressed as simple, algebraic statements. The simple economic order quantity model of Chapter 10 could be employed to determine the maximum size of the cash account and frequency with which it should be replenished. Such an approach to cash management was suggested by Baumol [1952] in one of the first formal analyses of this problem.

Suppose the outflows of cash are not constant and can be described only by probability statements. It would be natural to adopt one of the inventory models described in Chapter 10 that account for risk. An example of such an extension is provided by Miller and Orr [1966].

The simple inventory models have been criticized on the grounds that they do not take into account all of the information that is actually available regarding cash inflows and outflows. The argument is that our third condition, that variations in cash inflows and outflows can be forecast with certainty, is actually correct. With these detailed forecasts, more complex models involving more detailed decision variables can be formulated.

Many firms *can* provide reasonable sales forecasts, from forecasting models such as those described in Chapter 5, and historical data can be used to relate sales to payments on accounts receivable. This information provides a reasonably certain forecast of cash inflows from sales. In addition, the firm may hold securities that can be sold before maturity to generate additional cash inflows if necessary, but these inflows result from controllable decisions by the cash manager.

Similarly, production (or service activity) level forecasts can be used as the basis for estimating cash outflow requirements, and it may be possible to obtain reasonably certain estimates of these. Cash outflows for the purchase of securities also result from controllable decisions.

Given these certain forecasts, it is a straightforward task to formulate a linear programming model of the cash management problem. The relationships among the problem elements can be written as linear expressions involving the following decision variables:

1. payment schedules for the predicted purchases in periods 1, 2, . . .
2. transactions to be made on the securities held by the firm at the beginning of the planning period
3. the new investments to be made in securities in periods 1, 2, . . .
4. the use of the available lines of credit in periods 1, 2, . . .

An example of such a formulation is presented by Orgler [1969, 1970]. This model provides a detailed guide to cash management decisions. The only criticism of Orgler's model is that the level of detail may actually be too high. The complexity of the model may hinder its acceptance and use by managers.

Srinivasan [1974] took advantage of another analogy in constructing a different model of the cash management problem. Cash inflows and marketable securities are *sources* of funds, while accounts payable and the purchases of securities are *uses*. "Sources and uses" sounds like "supplies and demands." Recall the transportation and transshipment models of Chaper 14. Given the certain forecasts of cash inflows and outflows, Srinivasan realized that it would be possible to develop a *network model* of the cash management problem (see exercise 16 in Chapter 14).

The resulting transshipment formulation is shown in Figure 16-3. Suppose there are only three time periods. The three nodes labeled C1, C2, and C3 denote cash availabilities in periods 1, 2, and 3 respectively. Notice that it is possible to "ship" excess cash from period 1 to periods 2 and 3, and from period 2 to period 3. Since this could be accomplished by investing in short-term securities that mature in periods 2 and 3, there would be a negative cost (a contribution) on each of these arcs. The positive number by each cash node represents the forecast of the cash inflow in that period from payments on accounts receivable.

The nodes labeled A1, A2, and A3 represent the accounts payable by the firm in periods 1, 2, and 3 respectively. The forecasts of the amounts are shown as negative numbers written by the nodes. Cash available in period 1 may be used to pay accounts in period 1, as indicated by the arc from node C1 to node A1. Cash available in period 2 may be used to pay accounts in period 1 with an interest penalty (a cost on the arc from node C2 to node A1) or to pay accounts in period 2 (A2) at no charge. All accounts must be paid after a delay of no more than one period, so there is no arc from node C3 to node A1.

Nodes SA and SB represent marketable securities held by the firm. SA matures in period 3 at a face value of 50, so there is no cost on the arc from node SA to node C3. However, SA could be sold at a penalty to provide cash in periods 1 or 2. These penalty costs would be on the arcs from SA to C1 and to C2. Similarly, security SB matures in period 2, so there is no arc from SB to C3.

Node CR represents the line of credit of the firm, which could be used in any of the three periods to obtain additional cash. The costs on the arcs from CR would represent interest payments.

The advantages of this model are that it has the visual interpretation of Figure 16-3, and the relevant information can be summarized in a transportation table in a convenient, easy to understand format. Srinivasan [1974] estimates that the computer run time would be about 3 percent of that required for a linear programming model of the same cash management problem in a

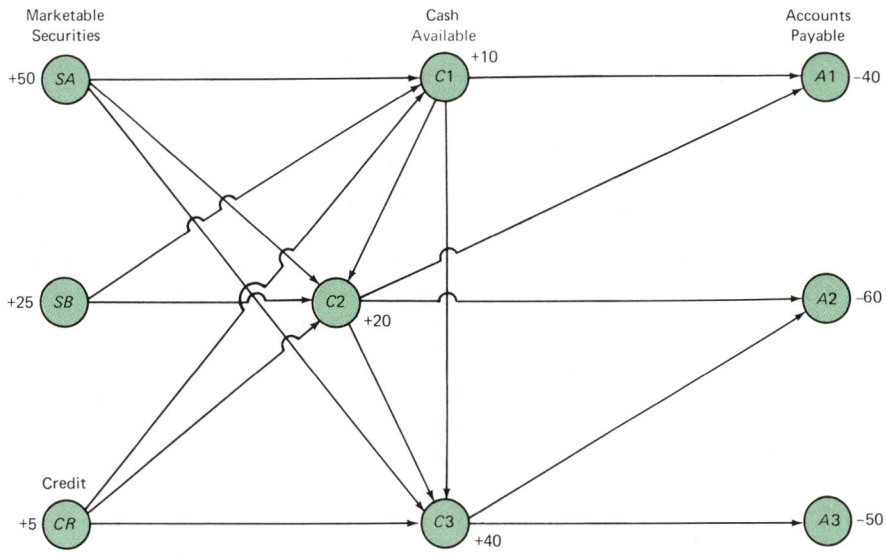

FIGURE 16-3. **A transshipment model formulation of the cash management problem**

large organization. Since it is proposed that this model should be run each day, such considerations can become important.

The transshipment formulation does have some disadvantages, since some details included in Orgler's linear optimization model must be omitted. (Srinivasan [1974] presents a more complete discussion.)

In summary, this example illustrates several important points. First, there is no one model that is "best" for analyzing a particular problem. We have seen that the cash management problem may be analyzed using a simple inventory model, and inventory model that allows probabilistic demand statements, a linear optimization model, or a network model. The choice of the appropriate model is dependent on the nature of the environment, the desired level of detail in the model, and the costs of computation. Such decisions should not be left entirely to a staff analyst, but should involve the individual who will actually be using the model.

Second, the appropriate model can be identified by determining the nature of the environment, the nature of the relationships among the problem elements, and the objective of the analysis. This process is not automatic and requires judgment, but the manager can play an important and valuable role in it.

Adding Complexity

Unfortunately, real-world problems are not always categorized as neatly as those we have presented here. It may actually be necessary to combine ideas from several types of models in order to analyze a complex problem. Moses [1975] describes the implementation of a corporate simulation model with an embedded linear optimization model that simply provides additional information to the simulation model.

Another example in which substantially different kinds of models have been coupled together is reported by Buffa [1972, pp.690-704] concerning the firm of Van Den Berghs & Jurgens, a subsidiary of Unilever. In general, a number of planning models of the type discussed in Chapter 6 are coupled together in a complex planning system. There are a raw material model, a distribution model, a packaging model, marketing models, brand models, a fixed expenses model, a cash flow model, an expense extraction model, a cost type model, and a divisional model. The company is a major producer of margarine and other fat products, and crude oil costs are of significance. Therefore, the formulation for each of the product groups is chosen on the basis of refined oil costs. The formulations themselves are generated by an off-line linear programming model, and entered into the system as necessary by way of the formulations model. Thus, we have an optimizing model coupled with a set of predictive models.

Finally, an excellent example of the coupling of different kinds of models was developed by Hax and Meal [1975] and applied as a planning system in a process manufacturing firm described as being analogous to a chemical plant or steel mill. The example firm is a multiplant, multiproduct operation with three distinct seasonal patterns. There is a strong incentive to maintain a nearly level manufacturing rate for the following reasons:

1. The capital cost of equipment is very high compared with the cost of shift premium for labor, and the plants normally operate three shifts five days a week with occasional weekend work.
2. The labor union is very strong and exerts pressure to maintain constant production levels throughout the year for employment stabilization.

System Structure In structuring the system, levels of aggregation for the various items produced were developed first. The extent to which sets of decisions regarding production were interdependent was examined. If two sets of decisions were found to be independent, they were totally separated in the hierarchy of decisions. Beginning at the most detailed level, items sharing a major "set up" cost were grouped into "families." Thus, scheduling decisions for items in a family were very dependent, while the opposite was true for items in different families. It was also found that decisions for a family in one time period were strongly tied to decisions for the same family in other time periods. This time dependence resulted from the need to accumulate seasonal inventories in both product families. Product families were aggregated into "types" if they shared a common seasonal pattern and production rate. This process facilitated seasonal planning, since only the aggregate for all families in the type needed to be considered in developing the plan.

The next step in the process was the development of a hierarchy of decisions based on the relationships developed in the aggregation process. The following steps were developed:

1. assignment of families to plants
2. seasonal planning
3. scheduling of families
4. scheduling of items

In addition to the preceding steps, basic inventory models were used to establish minimum production run lengths and overstock limits. The complete decision sequence is shown in Figure 16-4. A brief description of the several submodels and the nature of their interaction follows.

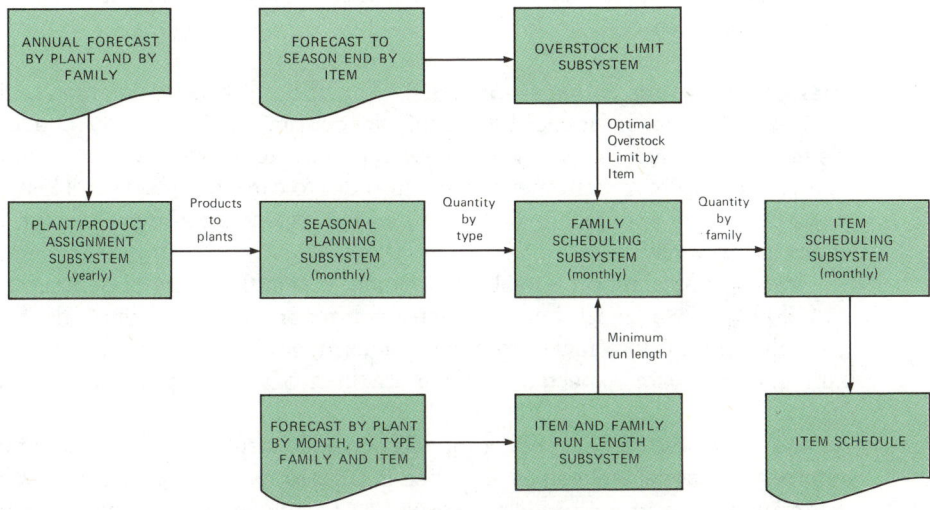

Figure 4. Decision sequence in planning and scheduling

FIGURE 16-4. **Decision sequence in planning and scheduling**

From A. C. Hax and H. C. Meal, "Hierarchical Integration of Production Planning and Scheduling," in Studies in the Management Science. Vol. 1, "Logistics," edited by M. A. Geisler, North Holland—American Elsevier, 1975, used by permission.

Plant Product Assignment Subsystem (PAS) The PAS system determines the plant locations at which each family should be manufactured. The model balances the cost of interterritory transportation against the incremental capital investment cost required to manufacture the product family in question. The model is run annually to take account of new products and changes in variable manufacturing cost and demand patterns.

Seasonal Planning Subsystem (SPS) SPS, the aggregate planning subsystem, determines the production requirements and seasonal stock accumulations by product type for each plant. The objective is to minimize total regular and overtime production costs plus inventory holding costs, subject to constraints on available regular and overtime labor. Demand and safety stock requirements must also be met. Linear programming was used as the solution technique.

Family Scheduling Subsystem (FSS) The FSS subsystem is used to schedule enough production for the families in a product type to use the time allocated to the type by the SPS. This production includes the accumulation of the necessary seasonal stock.

Item Scheduling Subsystem (ISS) The ISS subsystem determines the production quantities for each item within the constraints of the family schedules determined by the FSS. As in FSS, overstock limits are observed and an attempt is made to maximize customer service. In order to carry out this task, Hax and Meal developed approaches that equalized the expected run out times for the items in the family.

Hax and Meal report a total development cost in the range of $150,000 to $200,000. While exact benefits were not reported, cost reductions from smoother production, fewer emergency interruptions, and reduced inventory carrying cost were expected to be more than $200,000 per year in each plant.

Most of these more complex models generally result from a bootstrapping approach to model building as described in Chapter 6. A manager who has the basic knowledge of the models and solution techniques that we have studied should have no difficulty in participating in the development of more complex models such as these and in using their results.

WHAT SHOULD THE MANAGER KNOW?

We have come full circle. In the introduction, we argued that the modern manager should have the following skills:

1. The ability to recognize situations in which management science might be used effectively.

2. The ability to conduct two-way communication with a technical specialist; that is, he must be able to
   a. explain the nature of his problem to a specialist in a meaningful way
   b. understand the specialist's product sufficiently well to verify its appropriateness and potential usefulness.
3. The ability to understand the results of management science studies so that he can obtain full value from the information available to him.
4. The ability to conceptualize a problem in terms of a particular model of management science, even if no formal analysis is performed.
5. The ability to formulate models appropriate for analyzing small, straightforward problems, utilize standard computer programs written by others to obtain the solutions, and interpret the results.

If you have mastered these skills, you have added an important dimension to your managerial growth and abilities.

References

1. Baumol, W. J., "The Transactions Demand for Cash: An Inventory Theoretic Approach," *Quarterly Journal of Economics*, Vol. 66, 1952, pp. 454–56.
2. Buffa, E. S., *Operations Management: Problems and Models*, third edition, John Wiley & Sons, New York, 1972.
3. Eppen, G. D., and E. F. Fama, "Cash Balance and Simple Dynamic Portfolio Problems with Proportional Costs," *International Economic Review*, Vol. 10, 1969, pp. 119–33.
4. Hax, A. C., and H. C. Meal, "Hierarchical Integration of Production Planning and Scheduling," in *Studies in the Management Science, Vol. 1, Logistics*, edited by M. A. Geisler, North Holland-American Elsevier, 1975.
5. Miller, M. H., and D. J. Orr, "A Model of the Demand for Money by Firms," *Quarterly Journal of Economics*, Vol. 80, 1966, pp. 413–35.
6. Moses, M. A., "Implementation of Analytical Planning Systems," *Management Science*, Vol. 21, 1975, pp. 1133–43.
7. Neave, E. H., "The Stochastic Cash Balance Problem with Fixed Costs for Increases and Decreases," *Management Science*, Vol. 16, 1970, pp. 472–90.
8. Orgler, Y., "An Unequal-Period Model for Cash Management Decisions," *Management Science*, Vol. 16, 1969, pp. B77–B92.
9. ———, *Cash Management: Methods and Models*, Wadsworth Publishing Company, Belmont, Calif., 1970.
10. Srinivasan, V., "A Transshipment Model for Cash Management Decisions," *Management Science*, Vol. 20, June, 1974, pp. 1350–63.
11. White, D. J., and J. M. Norman, "Control of Cash Reserves," *Operational Research Quarterly*, Vol. 16, 1965, pp. 309–28.

APPENDIXES

APPENDIX A

REVIEW OF SOME MATHEMATICAL CONCEPTS

The following review of mathematical concepts is intended as a "prompter" or reminder to those who have been exposed to comparable materials elsewhere. As with the other review materials in these appendixes, it is not intended as a substitute for rigorous mathematics courses.

SETS

Set theory is part of the language of modern mathematics and is often used in the analysis of managerial problems, particularly those associated with probability analysis.

Definitions

Set A set is a *well-defined collection of objects*. All of the letters in the alphabet define a set. The last five letters in the alphabet define a set. The letters in the word *number* define a set. The English language is full of words often used as synonyms for the term *set*, such as a *swarm* of bees, a *team* of horses, a *clutch* of eggs, a *bed* of oysters, a *tyranny* of deans, a *covey* of quail, and a *group* of students.

If the definition is vague, we do not have a set. For example, it would be difficult to think in terms of lovers, hippies, or analysts as sets because the definitions of these terms may not be crystal clear to everyone.

Elements Each object of a set is called an *element*. For example, the set of all of the odd integer numbers between 1 and 99 contains the number 25 as an element.

Notation

It is common to denote a set by a capital letter and to define it by enclosing the elements with braces, for example,

$A = \{a, b, c\}$,
$B = \{$the six odd numbers between 6 and 18$\}$,
$C = \{$colors of the American flag$\}$,
$D = \{$the months of the year$\}$.

Empty Set A set with no elements in it is called an empty set, usually denoted by the symbol ϕ or by $\{\ \}$.

Element in a Set If c is an element in the set A, then in notational form $c \in A$. On the other hand, if c is *not* an element of the set A, then $c \notin A$.

Equal Set Two sets are identical or *equal* if an only if each and every element of set A is also an element of set B, and if each and every element of set B is also an element of set A. For example, $A = B$ if

$A = \{a, b, c\}$,
$B = \{c, b, a\}$.

The order in which the elements are listed is irrelevant. If $C = \{1,2\}$, and $D = \{1, 2, 3\}$, then the two sets are not equal and the standard notation is $C \neq D$.

Subset If each element of set C is also an element of set D, then set C is a subset of D. To denote this relationship, we use the inclusion sign ($\subset$), for example, $C \subset D$ when $C = \{1, 2\}$ and $D = \{1, 2, 3\}$.

Universal Set The set that includes all of the elements is called the *universal set*, commonly denoted by $\mathcal{U}$.

Venn Diagram

Graphic representations of sets in the form of Venn diagrams are often useful. The universal set $\mathcal{U}$ is usually denoted graphically as a rectangle. A circle within the rectangle then denotes a set, as shown in Figure A-1. Therefore, Figure A-1 shows that the set A is a subset of the universal set $\mathcal{U}$, or symbolically, $A \subset \mathcal{U}$.

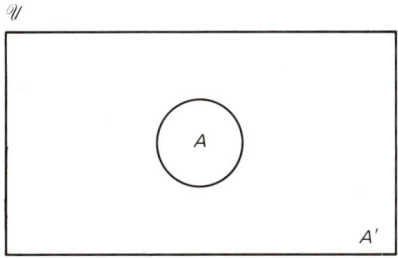

FIGURE A-1. **Venn diagram showing the set A as a subset of the universal set $\mathcal{U}$. The complement of set A contains all elements not in A, that is, A'.**

Complement Note in Figure A-1 that all of the elements of the universal set $\mathcal{U}$ which are *not* in set A are denoted by the *complement* set A', read A prime.

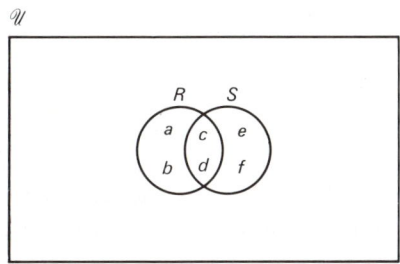

FIGURE A-2. **Venn diagram showing the intersection of sets R and S, since both sets contain c and d. The new set is denoted $R \cap S$.**

Intersections When there are common elements in two sets, we describe them as having an intersection as shown in Figure A-2. In Figure A-2, the universal set is all of the letters of the alphabet, and $R = \{a, b, c, d\}$, and $S = \{c, d, e, f\}$. Thus, we have a new set defined by the intersection of R and S comprised of the elements c and d, and this new set is denoted as $R \cap S$, where $\cap$ is read as the "intersection" of R and S.

Union The union of two sets is defined as a new set consisting of those elements belonging to either or both. For example, in Figure A-2, $R = \{a, b, c, d\}$ and $S = \{c, d, e, f\}$. However, the *union* of R and S is a set that is denoted symbolically as $R \cup S = \{a, b, c, d, e, f\}$.

APPENDIX A REVIEW OF SOME MATHEMATICAL CONCEPTS

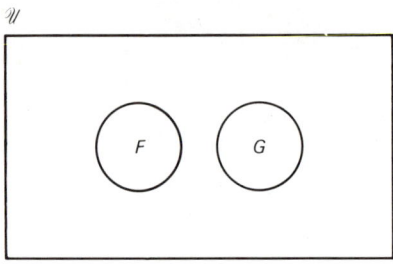

FIGURE A-3. **Venn diagram of disjoint or mutually exclusive sets F and G**

Disjoint or Mutually Exclusive Sets If two sets have no common elements, they are said to be *disjoint* or *mutually exclusive*. They can, nevertheless, be a part of the same universal set, as shown in Figure A-3. For example, the universal set might be composed of all of the college football teams. The set $F =$ {all of the teams in the Pacific Eight Conference} and $G =$ {all of the teams in the Big Ten Conference}. There are no teams common to the two defined sets; they are mutually exclusive, or disjoint.

Functions

A function is a particular kind of relationship where for each element x of set S, a single value y can be determined in set Y. For example, suppose that the number of items held in inventory is the set $X = \{1, 2, 3\}$, and the corresponding cost of holding items in inventory is the set $Y = \{30, 40, 50\}$.

Domain The set X of the number of items held in inventory is defined as the domain.

Range The set Y is defined as the range.

Thus, when we have one set defining a domain and a corresponding set defining a range for the domain, the association between the two sets is called a function. When a functional relationship exists we can express the relationship in terms of an equation. For our example, we note that each additional unit of inventory adds $10 to the cost, so there must be a fixed cost of $20. The equation is then

$$y = 20 + 10x. \tag{1}$$

Independent and Dependent Variables The inventory cost y is dependent on the number of units in inventory x. Therefore, the number of units x defines the domain and is designated the *independent* variable, and since y *depends* on x, we designate y as the dependent variable.

The Graph of a Function

The graphic representation of a function is another way of showing that for a given element x of set X, one and only one value of y is determined in the set Y. Standard graphic representation of a function designates the horizontal axis for the independent variable x and the vertical axis for the dependent variable y, as shown in Figure A–4. Then to plot equation (1) we determine points on the graph by paired values (x, y), by substituting values of x in equation (1) and computing corresponding values of y. For example, three paired values from equation (1) are (1, 30), (2, 40), and (3, 50). These values are plotted in Figure A–4 and connected by a line that defines the relationship within the stated domain and range.

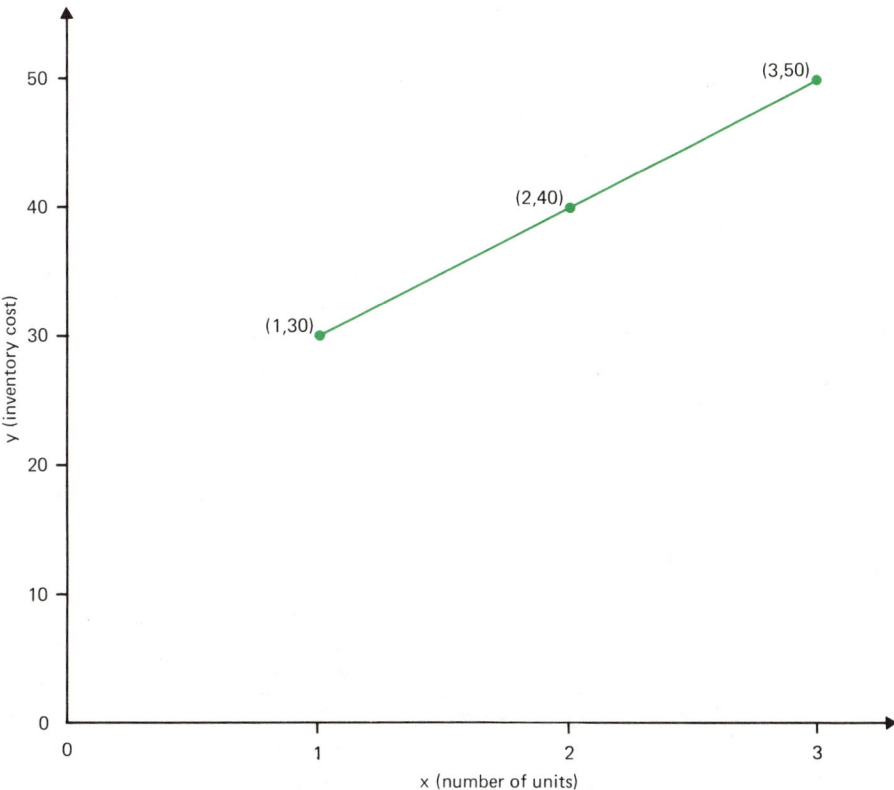

FIGURE A–4. **Graph of the equation $y = 20 + 10x$ for the domain $X = \{1, 2, 3\}$ and the range $Y = \{30, 40, 50\}$**

Functional Notation

It is common to state the dependent side of an equation y in terms of its functional dependency by substituting $f(x)$ for y so that equation (1) would read

$$f(x) = 20 + 10x. \tag{2}$$

The functional notation $f(x)$ is read, "the value of the function at x," or usually condensed to read simply "f of x."

The dependent variable might be a function of several independent variables and the functional notation is shorthand for stating this fact. For example, overall production cost y might be dependent on several variables, such as the number of units produced x_1, wage rates x_2, overtime used x_3, materials used x_4, and inventory costs x_5. In functional notation we could state the dependency relationship as

$$y = f(x_1, x_2, x_3, x_4, x_5). \tag{3}$$

Linear Functions

In the previous section we used a relationship between the number of items held in inventory to inventory cost as an example to discuss the nature of a function. The result was equation (1), $y = 20 + 10x$, which is a linear function because there are no squared or higher powers of variables, nor were there cross product terms of variables, such as xy. Graphically, linear functions plot as straight lines.

The Slope-Intercept Form A linear equation with one independent variable can be placed in the slope-intercept form by solving for the dependent variable y, as follows:

$$y = a + bx,$$

where a is the constant or y intercept term (the value of y when $x = 0$), and b is the slope of the line, as shown in Figure A–5. The slope b is simply the amount y increases for a *unit* increase in the independent variable x. The slope can be either negative, or positive as it is in Figure A–5. Since only two points need be established to plot the equation for a straight line, one point is established by the y intercept, and one additional point can be established by substituting a value of x in the equation and computing the corresponding value of y.

The Standard Form The standard form for a linear equation is

$$Ax + By = C, \tag{4}$$

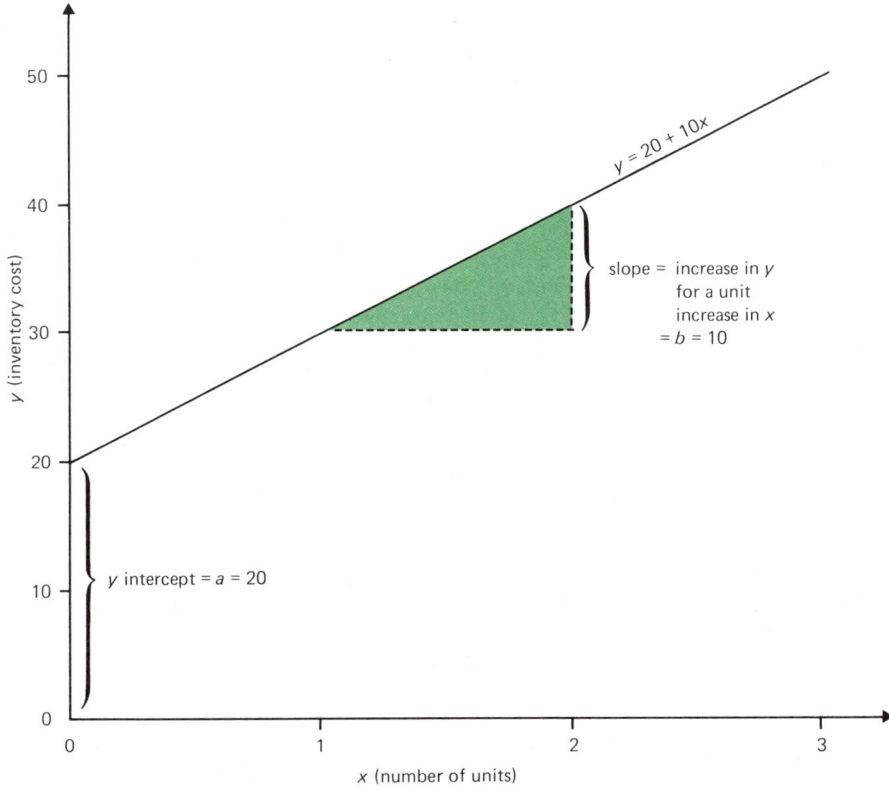

FIGURE A-5. **Graphic relationships for a linear equation of the form $y = a + bx$**

where A, B, and C are constants. To convert to the slope-intercept form, we simply solve for y and obtain

$$y = \frac{C}{B} - \frac{Ax}{B}.$$

Equation (1) can be placed in standard form by rearranging as follows:

$$-10x + y = 20,$$

and the coefficients of the standard form for equation (1) are $A = -10$, $B = 1$, and the constant $C = 20$.

Solving Simultaneous Linear Equations

Suppose we own two machines, both of which can perform the same operation; however, the fixed and variable costs of using the two processes are different. The costs are a function of the number of units produced and are therefore

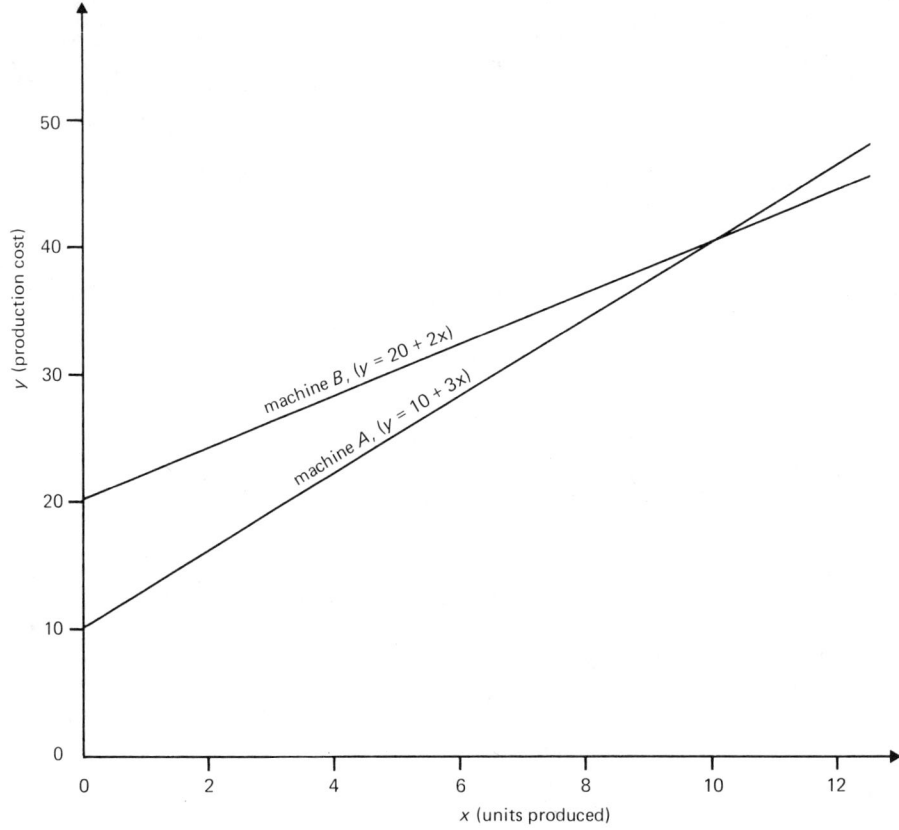

FIGURE A-6. **Simultaneous solution of equations A and B occurs where the graphs of the two equations intersect — the point at which the two equations have common values of x and y.**

expressed in general terms as $f(x) = a + bx$, where a represents the fixed costs and b the variable costs.

For machine A, the fixed costs are $10 to set up the machine, and the variable costs are $3 per unit produced. The cost equation is then, $y = 10 + 3x$.

For machine B, the fixed costs are $20 to set up the machine, and the variable costs are only $2 per unit produced. The machine B cost equation is then, $y = 20 + 2x$.

The two cost equations are plotted in Figure A-6. We wish to determine the volume at which the costs are equal for the two machines. This volume can be seen to be the value of x common to the two equations, that is, where the two lines cross in Figure A-6, yielding the same cost and number of units produced.

Analytically, we determine this point by solving the two equations simultaneously. Recall from basic algebra that if we have two independent equations and two unknowns, we can solve simultaneously to determine the values of the two unknowns, in our case x (number of units) and y (cost for x units). More generally, if we have n independent equations and n variables, we can solve simultaneously to determine the values of the n variables.

We can take two approaches to solution, substitution and Gaussian elimination.

Substitution For our simple example, the easiest procedure is to solve for one variable, using one of the equations, and insert that expression in the other equation. This process produces an equation that has eliminated one of the variables, and we can then determine a numerical value for the remaining variable. Then we substitute this numerical value back into the first equation and solve for the value of the second variable.

Using our example, the value of y for machine A is, $y = 10 + 3x$. Substituting this value of y in the machine B equation, we have

$10 + 3x = 20 + 2x,$
$x = 10 \text{ units}.$

Now, inserting $x = 10$ in the machine A equation we have, $y = 10 + 3(10) = \$40$. Therefore, the volume is $x = 10$ units, and the cost is $y = \$40$ for either machine. Below 10 units machine A is more economical, and above 10 units machine B is more economical. Compare this result with the point where the graphs of the two equations cross in Figure A-6.

Gaussian Elimination Though it is not necessary to do so, let us rearrange the equations for machines A and B in standard form,

$A, -3x + y = 10,$
$B, -2x + y = 20.$

Suppose we wish to eliminate the variable x from one of the two equations by Gaussian elimination. First, we divide equation A by its x coefficient (-3) to obtain

$A, \quad x - \dfrac{1y}{3} = \dfrac{-10}{3},$
$B, -2x + y = 20.$

Then, we multiply A by the negative of the x coefficient in equation B, $-(-2) =$

2, and add the resulting equation A to equation B. This process results in the revised equations

$$A, \quad x - \frac{1y}{3} = \frac{-10}{3},$$
$$B, \quad \frac{1y}{3} = \frac{40}{3}.$$

To see how B was obtained, the calculations are shown below:

$$2x - \frac{2y}{3} = \frac{-20}{3} \quad \text{(from multiplying A by 2)}$$
$$\underline{-2x + y = 20} \quad \text{(from B)}$$
$$\frac{1y}{3} = \frac{40}{3} \quad \text{(adding equals)}$$

Next, divide B by the y coefficient ($\frac{1}{3}$), which gives

$$A, \quad x - \frac{1y}{3} = \frac{-10}{3},$$
$$B, \quad y = 40.$$

The solution for y, 40, is the same as the one obtained previously by substitution. Finally, multiply B by the negative of the y coefficient in equation A, $-(-\frac{1}{3}) = \frac{1}{3}$, and add the resulting equation B to equation A:

$$A, \quad x = 10,$$
$$B, \quad y = 40,$$

which gives the solution of 10 units for x. Again, the calculations for this step are shown below:

$$x - \frac{1y}{3} = \frac{-10}{3} \quad \text{(from A)}$$
$$\underline{\frac{1y}{3} = \frac{40}{3}} \quad \text{(from multiplying B by 1/3)}$$
$$x = \frac{30}{3} \quad \text{(adding equals)}$$

APPENDIX B

REVIEW OF SOME CONCEPTS OF STATISTICS

The following review of statistical concepts is intended as a "prompter" or reminder to those who have been exposed to comparable materials elsewhere. As with the other review materials in these appendixes, it is not intended as a substitute for a rigorous course in statistics.

UNIVERSE AND SAMPLE

A sample is drawn from a *universe* or *population* and is therefore a subset of a universe or population.

A *finite universe* might be a lot of 1000 parts produced on a lathe. Any of the dimensions produced might in themselves be considered a finite universe.

An *infinite universe* might be represented by the time required for a worker to perform the lathe operation.

If we selected 100 parts from the 1000 and measured their diameters, we would have a sample distribution of diameters. If we let the selection of the sample of 100 parts be based strictly on chance, we would have a *random sample*.

It is often true that the entire universe data are difficult and expensive to obtain, or impossible in the case of an infinite universe. Therefore, one of the important objectives of statistics is to infer from a sample distribution the characteristics of the universe distribution.

Parameters are designated as the characteristics of the universe, such as the mean, variance, and range (these terms will be defined later).

Statistics are designated as characteristics of a sample drawn from a universe and are intended to infer the characteristics of the universe.

Notation

It is of some importance to retain the distinction between *parameters* and *statistics,* and we shall attempt to do this through a system of notation. In general, when we are referring to the parameters of a universe, we shall use one set of symbols, and when we are referring to the statistics of a sample, we shall use another set. In most instances, we shall be dealing with statistics rather than parameters. The notation is as follows:

μ = the population mean (parameter),
$\bar{x}$ = the mean of a sample drawn from the population (statistic),
σ^2 = the population variance (parameter),
s^2 = the variance of a sample drawn from the population (statistic).

DESCRIPTIVE STATISTICS

One major area of the study of statistics has to do with the precise and efficient ways of describing what otherwise would be a mass of data that would communicate very little worthwhile information. Table B–1 illustrates this point. It lists measurements of the diameters of a sample of 50 shafts from a production lot of 10,000. By scanning the table we can pick out the maximum reading, 1.0043 inches, and the minimum reading, 0.9954 inches, but any generalization about the diameters of the 50 shafts is difficult. Similarly, inferences about the entire lot of 10,000 shafts are difficult.

Frequency Distributions

The situation is improved by grouping the data into a frequency distribution. This process involves tabulating the number of shaft measurements that fall into certain class intervals, as in Table B–2. Immediately we observe some characteristics of the data that were difficult to see before. For example, we see that the high and low readings represent a small minority of the cases, and that a large percentage of the shafts measured somewhere between 0.9982 inch and 1.0018 inch, with the largest number occurring around 1.0000 inch. When the data are plotted in a histogram (see Figure B–1) the general relationships show up clearly. We see that we have a fairly symmetrical bell-shaped distribution of the measurements, centering on 1.0000 inch.

TABLE B-1. **Diameters of 50 Shafts**

1.0039	0.9956	1.0026	1.0004	1.0005
1.0014	0.9996	0.9994	0.9977	1.0023
0.9980	1.0025	1.0043	1.0004	0.9989
1.0000	1.0028	0.9954	0.9974	0.9992
0.9973	0.9994	1.0009	1.0033	1.0005
0.9996	0.9998	1.0026	1.0031	1.0034
0.9996	0.9998	1.0026	1.0031	1.0034
1.0010	0.9995	0.9976	1.0009	0.9991
0.9999	0.9979	0.9983	0.9972	0.9998
1.0003	0.9968	1.0013	1.0007	1.0041
1.0037	1.0012	0.9985	1.0018	0.9987

TABLE B-2. **Frequency Distribution of the Data in Table B-1**

Class limits (in.)	Frequency (no. of shafts)
0.9946–0.9955	1
0.9956–0.9965	1
0.9966–0.9975	4
0.9976–0.9985	6
0.9986–0.9995	7
0.9996–1.0005	11
1.0006–1.0015	7
1.0016–1.0025	3
1.0026–1.0035	6
1.0036–1.0045	4
	50

The Normal Distribution The smooth bell-shaped curve that has been superimposed on the histogram of Figure B-1 is called the normal or Gaussian distribution. We see that the distribution of diameter measurements fairly well approximates the normal distribution. The term *normal distribution* does not

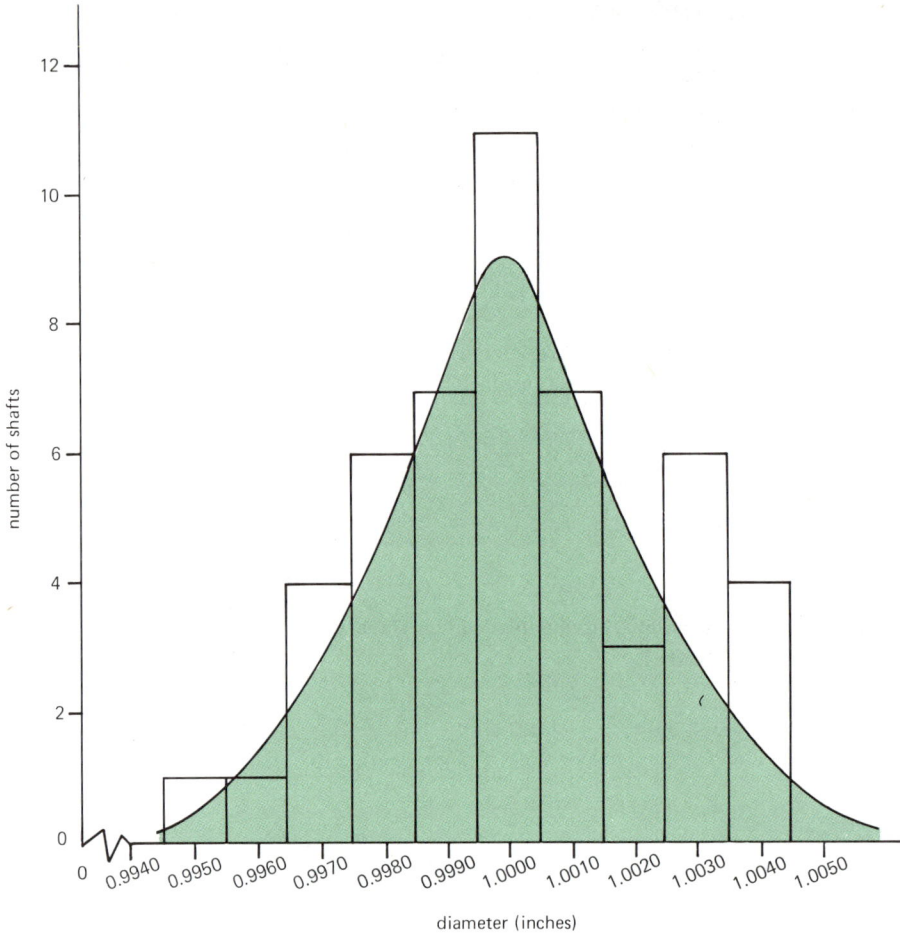

FIGURE B-1. **Histogram of 50 shaft diameter measurements**

imply that distributions which do not approximate it are abnormal. The curve for the normal distribution has a specific mathematical function, so that for a distribution to approximate normality, the occurrence frequencies must follow closely the general pattern indicated in Figure B-1. There are statistical tests that can be used to determine how closely a distribution approximates normality. If there is anything "normal" about the normal distribution, it may be that a great number of actual distributions in industry, science, and nature can be closely approximated by it. Thus a large part of statistical method is based on the normal distribution. Table C-1 in Appendix C gives areas under a standardized normal curve.

Other Distributions There are a number of other important distributions that are useful in management science. For example, the Poisson and the negative exponential distributions are used in waiting line theory and are useful in determining buffer inventory levels.

Techniques parallel to those discussed here for the normal distribution have been developed for these other distributions as well as for situations in which no specific distribution is implied. We will review general statistical methods for the normal distribution and will not attempt to review the details of analysis for the other distributions.

Measures of a Distribution

Several characteristics of distributions can be used to describe or specify them. In Figure B-1 we note that, first, the measurements tend to group around some central value; second, there is variability, that is, no one value represents the whole; third, the distribution is symmetric; and fourth, there is one peak or mode. To describe a distribution we need measures of central value, variability, and symmetry and an observation of the number of modes. Note that if a distribution can be assumed to be normal, only the first two measures will specify it, since a normal distribution is unimodal and symmetric. Therefore, we shall discuss measures of central value and of variability.

Measures of Central Value A measure of central value in the population is often made from a random sample drawn from the population. Suppose that the values for n individual items in a random sample are represented by x_1, x_2, x_3, ..., x_i, ..., x_n. Then the arithemetic mean $\bar{x}$ of the sample can be computed by

$$\bar{x} = \frac{\sum_{i=1}^{n} x_i}{n} = \frac{x_1 + x_2 + x_3 + \cdots + x_{n-1} + x_n}{n}.$$

The Greek letter Σ means "sum of," and the x_i are the individual observations, which are numbered from 1 to n, where n is the total number of observations.*
Therefore, for our shaft diameter example, we calculate $\bar{x}$ from Table B-1 as follows:

$$\bar{x} = \frac{1.0039 + 1.0014 + 0.9980 + \cdots + 0.9987}{50} = 1.0002.$$

The result, $\bar{x}$, is the estimate of the population mean of the parent distribution. There are two other measures of the center of a distribution, the

---

*There is a short-cut method for calculating the mean based on the grouped data of Table B-2.

median and the mode. The *median* is that point on the horizontal scale which divides the area under the histogram into two equal parts.

The *mode* is the most frequently occurring value. On a histogram it is the midpoint of the class interval that has the largest frequency of occurrence. For the data of Table B–2, represented by the histogram of Figure B–1, the mode is 1.0000. Note then, that for a symmetrical distribution, the mean, the median, and the mode will all be equal.

Measures of Variability or Dispersion The *range*, which is the simplest and most easily determined measure of variability, is the difference between the highest and lowest values in the distribution. For the data of Table B–1, the range is $1.0043 - 0.9954 = 0.0089$ inch. It is not as stable a measure as the variance, since it is based on only two values instead of the entire set of data.

The *variance* is the most commonly used measure of variability in statistics because of its stability as a measure and because of other valuable properties that we shall discuss. The sample variance is defined by

$$s^2 = \frac{\sum_{i=1}^{n}(x_i - \bar{x})^2}{n - 1}.$$

It is simply the sum of the squares of the differences between the individual observations and the mean of a distribution, divided by $n - 1$. For the data of Table B–1, where we have already computed $\bar{x} = 1.0002$, the variance 0.00000494 is calculated as follows:

$$s^2 = \frac{(1.0039 - 1.0002)^2 + (1.0014 - 1.0002)^2 + (0.9980 - 1.0002)^2 + \cdots + (0.9987 - 1.0002)^2}{49}$$

$$= 0.00000494;$$

It is the estimate of the actual population variance of the parent distribution.

The *standard deviation* is the square root of the variance and is commonly denoted by s. For the data of Table B–1,

$$s = \sqrt{s^2} = \sqrt{0.00000494} = 0.00222.$$

The standard deviation has special properties that are useful to us. If we consider a normal distribution with mean, μ, and standard deviation, σ, it is true that 68.27 percent of the area under the curve (equivalent to the frequency of occurrence in the histogram) is included within the limits of $\mu \pm \sigma$; 95.45 percent is included within the limits $\mu \pm 2\sigma$; and 99.73 percent is included within the limits $\mu \pm 3\sigma$ (see Figure B–2).

The significance of Figure B–2 is that we can now make a probability statement about values that we presume come from the universe or population

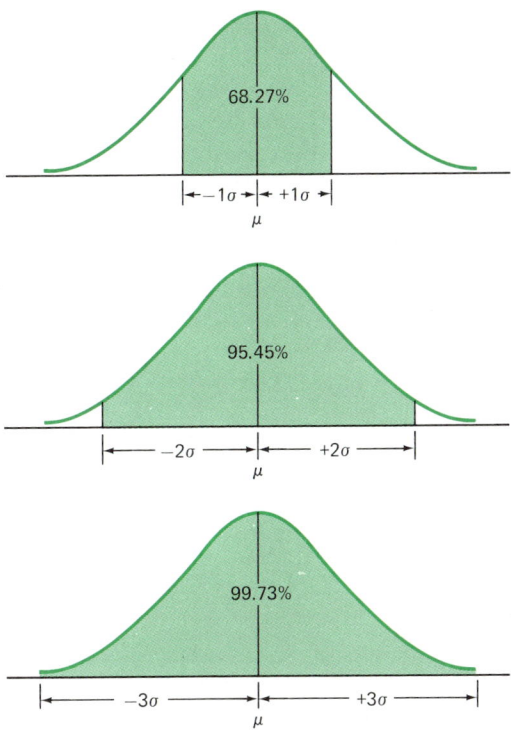

FIGURE B-2. **Areas under the normal curve for different σ limits**

from which the sample distribution is drawn. Using the shaft diameter example, which had an $\bar{x} = 1.0002$ inch and $s = 0.00222$ inch, we can say that there is a 0.9545 probability that shafts coming from the lot or universe from which the sample was drawn will have outside diameters measuring between 0.99576 and 1.00464 inches, and that there is only a 0.0455 probability that shafts will measure outside these limits. Similarly, virtually all shafts will measure between 0.99354 and 1.00686 inches, and there is only a 0.0027 probability that any shafts will measure outside these limits.

REGRESSION AND CORRELATION

The statistical methods known as regression and correlation can help answer such questions as the following: What is the relationship between product demand and gross national product? How good is the relationship? Is it good enough to help predict product demand?

The regression line that best represents a set of points, $(x_1, y_1), (x_2, y_2), \ldots,$ $(x_i, y_i), \ldots, (x_n, y_n)$, is often needed as a basis for an estimating function. Take the data represented by the scatter diagram of Figure B–3. An estimate of job difficulty has been developed by a system of points that varies with the degree that jobs require certain factors of skill, education, experience, physical fitness, etc. In Figure B–3, estimates of job difficulty have been plotted versus existing wages for the job. The line that best fits the points is commonly the linear regression line, that is, the line that minimizes the squares of the wage deviations from it, as well as setting the simple deviations to zero. This least squares line is the linear function

$$y = a + bx,$$

$$\text{where } b = \frac{\sum_{i=1}^{n} x_i y_i - \bar{x} \sum_{i=1}^{n} y_i}{\sum_{i=1}^{n} x_i^2 - \bar{x} \sum_{i=1}^{n} x_i},$$

$$a = \bar{y} - b\bar{x},$$

y_i's = wages,
x_i's = point ratings.

The line can be computed easily with the aid of a calculator and plotted on the scatter diagram as the line of best fit for the given points. Table B–3 shows this computation for the data of Figure B–3. Since the resulting equation, $y = a + bx$, is a straight line, the value computed for a is the point where the line intersects the vertical axis, and the computed value for b is the slope of the line. For the data of Figure B–3, the equation of the line is $y = 1.903 + 0.0141\ x$. The line intersects the wages axis at \$1.903, and for each point of job difficulty we add \$0.0141. The regression line is superimposed on the scatter diagram in Figure B–3.

Let us note further the assumed structure with which we are dealing in the regression equation. For each level of job difficulty there is a distribution of wages. The reasons for variation might be related to the people on the jobs, their skills, seniority, etc., and to errors made in appraising both jobs and people. The distributions are assumed to be normal. They each have a mean that falls on the regression line and they have equal variances. These assumptions are diagramed in Figure B–4.

The regression equation is often used to estimate y within certain probability limits, given a value of x, since the value of x specifies a normal distribution with a mean and a variance. The probability that y will be beyond certain values is specified by the standard deviation limits.

There are other regression techniques that are appropriate when a straight line does not represent the data. Also, there are appropriate techniques for multiple regression, where there are more than two variables to be related.

Correlation is a measure of the degree of relationship between two variables. Although many times we suspect that a relationship exists because of

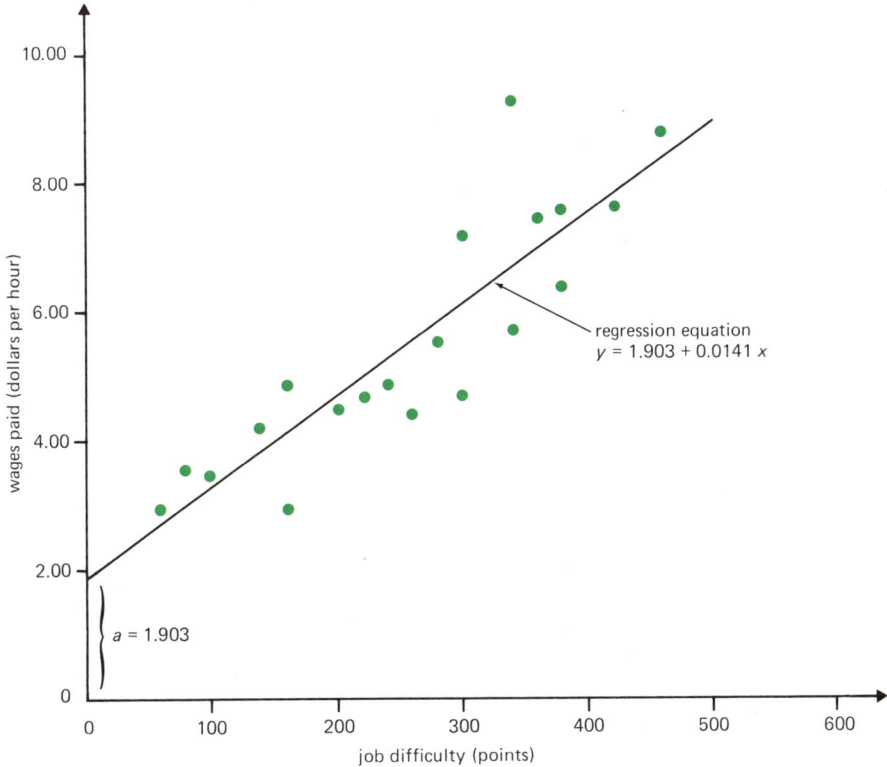

FIGURE B-3. **Scatter diagram showing difficulty points versus wages paid, with regression line**

the appearance of a scatter diagram, a correlation coefficient tells us how close that relationship is.

Correlation coefficients vary from -1.00 to $+1.00$. Figure B-5 illustrates this general picture. Thus a correlation coefficient, r, of 0.85 indicates a higher degree of relationship than 0.50, and similarly an r of -0.85 indicates a higher degree of relationship than -0.50. It is important to note, however, that $r = 0.90$ does not imply twice as close a relationship as $r = 0.45$, since our ability to forecast y, given x, is better indicated by r^2, the square of the correlation coefficient. Loosely speaking, $r = 0.90$ ($r^2 = 0.81$) is about twice as good as $r = 0.636$ ($r^2 = 0.405$).

TABLE B-3. **Computation of Regression Line Coefficients *a* and *b* for the Data from Figure B-3**

x (points)	y (wages)	xy	x^2
60	3.00	180	3600
80	3.60	288	6400
100	3.50	350	10,000
140	4.20	588	19,600
160	2.96	---	---
160	4.90	---	---
200	4.50	---	---
220	4.70	---	---
240	4.90	---	---
260	4.40	---	---
280	5.60	---	---
300	4.70	---	---
300	7.20	---	---
340	5.70	---	---
340	9.30	---	---
360	7.50	---	---
380	6.40	---	---
380	7.60	---	---
420	7.65	---	---
460	8.80	---	---

$\Sigma x = 5180.0 \quad \Sigma y = 111.11 \quad \Sigma xy = 32{,}436.6 \quad \Sigma x^2 = 1{,}600{,}400.0$

Computation of regression coefficients:

$N = 20, \quad \bar{x} = \dfrac{\Sigma x}{N} = \dfrac{5180}{20} = 259.0, \quad \bar{y} = \dfrac{\Sigma y}{N} = \dfrac{111.11}{20} = 5.555,$

$b = \dfrac{\Sigma xy - \bar{x}\Sigma y}{\Sigma x^2 - \bar{x}\Sigma x} = \dfrac{32{,}436.6 - 259 \times 111.11}{1{,}600{,}400 - 259 \times 5180} = 0.0141,$

$a = \bar{y} - b\bar{x} = 5.555 - 0.0141 \times 259 = 1.903,$

$\Sigma y^2 = 685.5341.$

Equation of regression line, $y = 1.903 + 0.0141\, x$.

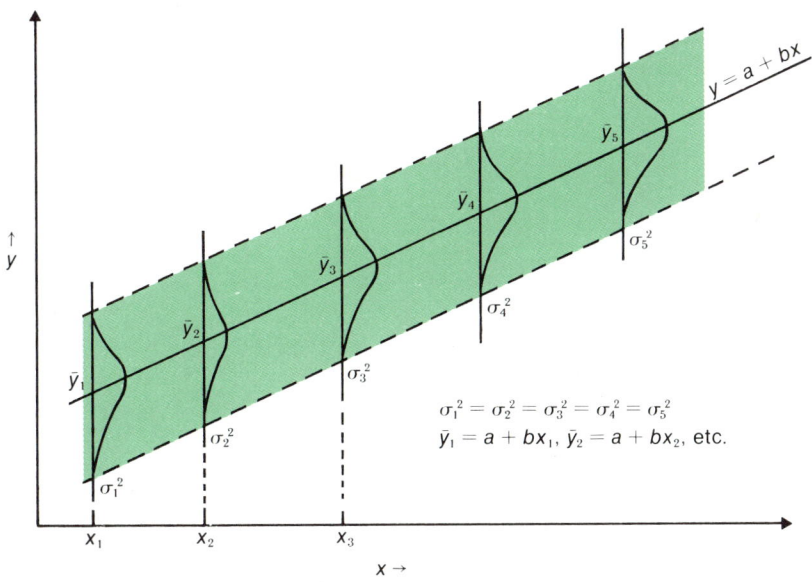

FIGURE B-4. **Diagram of assumptions in regression analysis**

Calculation of Correlation Coefficients The correlation coefficient may be calculated by the following formula:

$$r = \frac{\sum_{i=1}^{n}(x_i - \bar{x})(y_i - \bar{y})}{ns_x s_y}$$

The deviations from the means from each pair of observations are multiplied. There are as many such multiplications as there are observations. The entire set is summed and divided by $ns_x s_y$. It is actually simpler computationally to use

$$r = \frac{n\sum_{i=1}^{n} x_i y_i - \sum_{i=1}^{n} x_i \sum_{i=1}^{n} y_i}{\sqrt{\left[n\sum_{i=1}^{n} x_i^2 - \left(\sum_{i=1}^{n} x_i\right)^2\right]\left[n\sum_{i=1}^{n} y_i^2 - \left(\sum_{i=1}^{n} y_i\right)^2\right]}}.$$

All of the necessary components to compute r from the preceding formula are included at the bottom of Table B-3, and the result is $r = 0.87$.

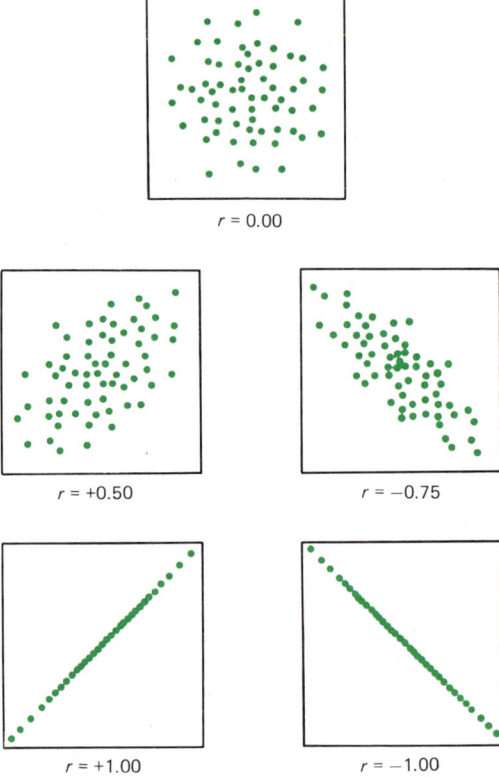

FIGURE B-5. **Scatter diagrams for different correlation coefficients**

Reliability of Correlation Coefficients Too often correlation coefficients are quoted without any indication of how much confidence we are justified in placing in them. There are statistical tests that allow us to make a probability statement about observed r's. By adopting a significance level we may be able to say, for example, that we are 95 percent sure that an $r = 0.80$ observed for a sample will not be less than 0.75 for the parent population.

One easy check is to compare the observed value of r with the values given in Table B-4. This table gives the critical values of r that must be exceeded for various numbers of observations n, to be confident that r is not really zero for the parent population. The critical values are given for both the 95 and 99 percent confidence levels. This test assumes that both of the variables, x and y, are normally distributed.

TABLE B-4. **Critical Values of *r* for 95 Percent and 99 Percent Confidence**

n	95%	99%	n	95%	99%	n	95%	99%
10	.632	.765	30	.361	.463	50	.279	.361
12	.576	.708	32	.349	.449	60	.254	.330
14	.532	.661	34	.339	.436	70	.235	.306
16	.497	.623	36	.329	.424	80	.220	.287
18	.468	.590	38	.320	.413	100	.197	.256
20	.444	.561	40	.312	.403	150	.161	.210
22	.423	.537	42	.304	.393	200	.139	.182
24	.404	.515	44	.297	.384	400	.098	.128
26	.388	.496	46	.291	.376	1000	.062	.081
28	.374	.479	48	.284	.368			

Note: These values must be exceeded for a given sample size *n* to be sure that the value of *r* is not really zero for the parent population.

Source: W. J. Dixon and F. J. Massey, *Introduction to Statistical Analysis*, second edition, © 1957 by the McGraw-Hill Book Company; used by permission.

APPENDIX C

TABLES

TABLE C-1. Areas Under the Normal Curve

Areas under the normal curve to the left of x for decimal units of σ' from the mean, $\bar{x}'$

x	Area	x	Area	x	Area	x	Area
$\bar{x}' - 3.0\sigma'$	0.0013	$\bar{x}' - 1.5\sigma'$	0.0668	$\bar{x}' + 0.1\sigma'$	0.5398	$\bar{x}' + 1.6\sigma'$	0.9452
$\bar{x}' - 2.9\sigma'$	0.0019	$\bar{x}' - 1.4\sigma'$	0.0808	$\bar{x}' + 0.2\sigma'$	0.5793	$\bar{x}' + 1.7\sigma'$	0.9554
$\bar{x}' - 2.8\sigma'$	0.0026	$\bar{x}' - 1.3\sigma'$	0.0968	$\bar{x}' + 0.3\sigma'$	0.6179	$\bar{x}' + 1.8\sigma'$	0.9641
$\bar{x}' - 2.7\sigma'$	0.0035	$\bar{x}' - 1.2\sigma'$	0.1151	$\bar{x}' + 0.4\sigma'$	0.6554	$\bar{x}' + 1.9\sigma'$	0.9713
$\bar{x}' - 2.6\sigma'$	0.0047	$\bar{x}' - 1.1\sigma'$	0.1357	$\bar{x}' + 0.5\sigma'$	0.6915	$\bar{x}' + 2.0\sigma'$	0.9772
$\bar{x}' - 2.5\sigma'$	0.0062	$\bar{x}' - 1.0\sigma'$	0.1587	$\bar{x}' + 0.6\sigma'$	0.7257	$\bar{x}' + 2.1\sigma'$	0.9821
$\bar{x}' - 2.4\sigma'$	0.0082	$\bar{x}' - 0.9\sigma'$	0.1841	$\bar{x}' + 0.7\sigma'$	0.7580	$\bar{x}' + 2.2\sigma'$	0.9861
$\bar{x}' - 2.3\sigma'$	0.0107	$\bar{x}' - 0.8\sigma'$	0.2119	$\bar{x}' + 0.8\sigma'$	0.7881	$\bar{x}' + 2.3\sigma'$	0.9893
$\bar{x}' - 2.2\sigma'$	0.0139	$\bar{x}' - 0.7\sigma'$	0.2420	$\bar{x}' + 0.9\sigma'$	0.8159	$\bar{x}' + 2.4\sigma'$	0.9918
$\bar{x}' - 2.1\sigma'$	0.0179	$\bar{x}' - 0.6\sigma'$	0.2741	$\bar{x}' + 1.0\sigma'$	0.8413	$\bar{x}' + 2.5\sigma'$	0.9938
$\bar{x}' - 2.0\sigma'$	0.0228	$\bar{x}' - 0.5\sigma'$	0.3085	$\bar{x}' + 1.1\sigma'$	0.8643	$\bar{x}' + 2.6\sigma'$	0.9953
$\bar{x}' - 1.9\sigma'$	0.0287	$\bar{x}' - 0.4\sigma'$	0.3446	$\bar{x}' + 1.2\sigma'$	0.8849	$\bar{x}' + 2.7\sigma'$	0.9965
$\bar{x}' - 1.8\sigma'$	0.0359	$\bar{x}' - 0.3\sigma'$	0.3821	$\bar{x}' + 1.3\sigma'$	0.9032	$\bar{x}' + 2.8\sigma'$	0.9974
$\bar{x}' - 1.7\sigma'$	0.0446	$\bar{x}' - 0.2\sigma'$	0.4207	$\bar{x}' + 1.4\sigma'$	0.9192	$\bar{x}' + 2.9\sigma'$	0.9981
$\bar{x}' - 1.6\sigma'$	0.0548	$\bar{x}' - 0.1\sigma'$	0.4602	$\bar{x}' + 1.5\sigma'$	0.9332	$\bar{x}' + 3.0\sigma'$	0.9987
		$\bar{x}'$	0.5000				

σ' units from the mean, $\bar{x}'$, associated with given values of the area under the normal curve to the left of x

x	Area	x	Area
$\bar{x}' - 3.090\sigma'$	0.001	$\bar{x}' + 3.090\sigma'$	0.999
$\bar{x}' - 2.576\sigma'$	0.005	$\bar{x}' + 2.576\sigma'$	0.995
$\bar{x}' - 2.326\sigma'$	0.010	$\bar{x}' + 2.326\sigma'$	0.990
$\bar{x}' - 1.960\sigma'$	0.025	$\bar{x}' + 1.960\sigma'$	0.975
$\bar{x}' - 1.645\sigma'$	0.050	$\bar{x}' + 1.645\sigma'$	0.950
$\bar{x}' - 1.282\sigma'$	0.100	$\bar{x}' + 1.282\sigma'$	0.900
$\bar{x}' - 1.036\sigma'$	0.150	$\bar{x}' + 1.036\sigma'$	0.850
$\bar{x}' - 0.842\sigma'$	0.200	$\bar{x}' + 0.842\sigma'$	0.800
$\bar{x}' - 0.674\sigma'$	0.250	$\bar{x}' + 0.674\sigma'$	0.750
$\bar{x}' - 0.524\sigma'$	0.300	$\bar{x}' + 0.524\sigma'$	0.700
$\bar{x}' - 0.385\sigma'$	0.350	$\bar{x}' + 0.385\sigma'$	0.650
$\bar{x}' - 0.253\sigma'$	0.400	$\bar{x}' + 0.253\sigma'$	0.600
$\bar{x}' - 0.126\sigma'$	0.450	$\bar{x}' + 0.126\sigma'$	0.550
$\bar{x}'$	0.500		

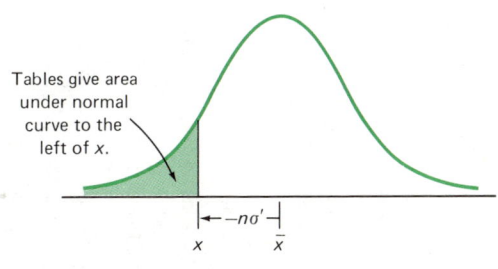

Tables give area under normal curve to the left of x.

TABLE C-2. Values of L_q for $M = 1 - 15$, and Various Values of $r = \lambda/\mu$. Poisson Arrivals, Negative Exponential Service Times

r	1	2	3	4	5	6	7	8	9
0.10	0.0111								
0.15	0.0264	0.0008							
0.20	0.0500	0.0020							
0.25	0.0833	0.0039							
0.30	0.1285	0.0069							
0.35	0.1884	0.0110							
0.40	0.2666	0.0166							
0.45	0.3681	0.0239	0.0019						
0.50	0.5000	0.0333	0.0030						
0.55	0.6722	0.0449	0.0043						
0.60	0.9000	0.0593	0.0061						
0.65	1.2071	0.0767	0.0084						
0.70	1.6333	0.0976	0.0112						
0.75	2.2500	0.1227	0.0147						
0.80	3.2000	0.1523	0.0189						
0.85	4.8166	0.1873	0.0239	0.0031					
0.90	8.1000	0.2285	0.0300	0.0041					
0.95	18.0500	0.2767	0.0371	0.0053					
1.0		0.3333	0.0454	0.0067					
1.2		0.6748	0.0904	0.0158					
1.4		1.3449	0.1778	0.0324	0.0059				
1.6		2.8444	0.3128	0.0604	0.0121				
1.8		7.6734	0.5320	0.1051	0.0227	0.0047			
2.0			0.8888	0.1739	0.0398	0.0090			
2.2			1.4907	0.2770	0.0659	0.0158			
2.4			2.1261	0.4305	0.1047	0.0266	0.0065		
2.6			4.9322	0.6581	0.1609	0.0426	0.0110		
2.8			12.2724	1.0000	0.2411	0.0659	0.0180		
3.0				1.5282	0.3541	0.0991	0.0282	0.0077	
3.2				2.3856	0.5128	0.1452	0.0427	0.0122	
3.4				3.9060	0.7365	0.2085	0.0631	0.0189	
3.6				7.0893	1.0550	0.2947	0.0912	0.0283	0.0084
3.8				16.9366	1.5184	0.4114	0.1292	0.0412	0.0127

r	1	2	3	4	5	6	7	8	9	10	11	12	13	14	15
4.0					2.2164	0.5694	0.1801	0.0590	0.0189						
4.2					3.3269	0.7837	0.2475	0.0827	0.0273						
4.4					5.2675	1.0777	0.3364	0.1142	0.0389	0.0128					
4.6					9.2885	1.4867	0.4532	0.1555	0.0541	0.0184					
4.8					21.6384	2.0708	0.6071	0.2092	0.0742	0.0260					
5.0						2.9375	0.8102	0.2786	0.1006	0.0361	0.0125				
5.2						4.3004	1.0804	0.3680	0.1345	0.0492	0.0175				
5.4						6.6609	1.4441	0.5871	0.1779	0.0663	0.0243	0.0085			
5.6						11.5178	1.9436	0.6313	0.2330	0.0883	0.0330	0.0119			
5.8						26.3726	2.6481	0.8225	0.3032	0.1164	0.0443	0.0164			
6.0							3.6828	1.0707	0.3918	0.1518	0.0590	0.0224			
6.2							5.2979	1.3967	0.5037	0.1964	0.0775	0.0300	0.0113		
6.4							8.0768	1.8040	0.6454	0.2524	0.1008	0.0398	0.0153		
6.6							13.7692	2.4198	0.8247	0.3222	0.1302	0.0523	0.0205		
6.8							31.1270	3.2441	1.0533	0.4090	0.1666	0.0679	0.0271	0.0105	
7.0								4.4471	1.3471	0.5172	0.2119	0.0876	0.0357	0.0141	
7.2								6.3135	1.7288	0.6521	0.2677	0.1119	0.0463	0.0187	
7.4								9.5102	2.2324	0.8202	0.3364	0.1420	0.0595	0.0245	0.0097
7.6								16.0379	2.9113	1.0310	0.4211	0.1789	0.0761	0.0318	0.0129
7.8								35.8956	3.8558	1.2972	0.5250	0.2243	0.0966	0.0410	0.0168
8.0									5.2264	1.6364	0.6530	0.2796	0.1214	0.0522	0.0220
8.2									7.3441	2.0736	0.8109	0.3469	0.1520	0.0663	0.0283
8.4									10.9592	2.6470	1.0060	0.4288	0.1891	0.0834	0.0361
8.6									18.3223	3.4160	1.2484	0.5286	0.2341	0.1043	0.0459
8.8									40.6824	4.4806	1.5524	0.6501	0.2885	0.1298	0.0577
9.0										6.0183	1.9368	0.7980	0.3543	0.1603	0.0723
9.2										8.3869	2.4298	0.9788	0.4333	0.1974	0.0899
9.4										12.4189	3.0732	1.2010	0.5287	0.2419	0.1111
9.6										20.6160	3.9318	1.4752	0.6437	0.2952	0.1367
9.8										45.4769	5.1156	1.8165	0.7827	0.3588	0.1673
10.0											6.8210	2.2465	0.9506	0.4352	0.2040

APPENDIX C TABLES

TABLE C-3. Table of Random Digits

03689	33090	43465	96789	56688	32389	77206	06534	10558	14478
43367	46409	44751	73410	35138	24910	70748	57336	56043	68550
45357	52080	62670	73877	20604	40408	98060	96733	65094	80335
62683	03171	77109	92515	78041	27590	42651	00254	73179	10159
04841	40918	69047	68986	08150	87984	08887	76083	37702	28523
85963	06992	65321	43521	46393	40491	06028	43865	58190	28142
03720	78942	61990	90812	98452	74098	69738	83272	39212	42817
10159	85560	35619	58248	65498	77977	02896	45198	10655	13973
80162	35686	57877	19552	63931	44171	40879	94532	17828	31848
74388	92906	65829	24572	79417	38460	96294	79201	47755	90980
12660	09571	29743	45447	64063	46295	44191	53957	62393	42229
81852	60620	87757	72165	23875	87844	84038	04994	93466	27418
03068	61317	65305	64944	27319	55263	84514	38374	11657	67723
29623	58530	17274	16908	39253	37595	57497	74780	88624	93333
30520	50588	51231	83816	01075	33098	81308	59036	49152	86262
93694	02984	91350	33929	41724	32403	42566	14232	55085	65628
86736	40641	37958	25415	19922	65966	98044	39583	26828	50919
28141	15630	37675	52545	24813	22075	05142	15374	84533	12933
79804	05165	21620	98400	55290	71877	60052	46320	79055	45913
63763	49985	88853	70681	52762	17670	62337	12199	44123	37993
49618	47068	63331	62675	51788	58283	04295	72904	05378	98085
26502	68980	26545	14204	34304	50284	47730	57299	73966	02566
13549	86048	27912	56733	14987	09850	72817	85168	09538	92347
89221	78076	40306	34045	52557	52383	67796	41382	50490	30117
97809	34056	76778	60417	05153	83827	67369	08602	56163	28793
65668	44694	34151	51741	11484	13226	49516	17391	39956	34839
53653	59804	59051	95074	38307	99546	32962	26962	86252	50704
34922	95041	17398	32789	26860	55536	82415	82911	42208	62725
74880	65198	61357	90209	71543	71114	94868	05645	44154	72254
66036	48794	30021	92601	21615	16952	18433	44903	51322	90379
39044	99503	11442	81344	57068	74662	90382	59433	48440	38146
87756	71151	68543	08358	10183	06432	97482	90301	76114	83778
47117	45575	29524	02522	08041	70698	80260	73588	86415	72523
71572	02109	96722	21684	64331	71644	18933	32801	11644	12364
35609	58072	63209	48429	53108	59173	55337	22445	85940	43707
73703	70069	74981	12197	48426	77365	26769	65078	27849	41311
42979	88161	56531	46443	47148	42773	18601	38532	22594	12395
12279	42308	00380	17181	38757	09071	89804	15232	99007	39495

INDEX

Aaker, D. A., 335, 366
Ackoff, R. L., 170
Activity analysis, 448, 449
Ahl, D. H., 133, 138
Algorithm, 270
   simplex, 380-390
   stepping stone, 410-422
   transportation, 410-422
Alternative generator, 261
Archibald, R., 454, 457, 466
Artificial variables, 396, 397
Averages. See Moving averages
Averill, B., 205

Bagby, G., 349, 366
Balintfy, J. L., 244, 315, 325
Barkdoll, G., 170
Barken, J. D., 366
Baron, R., 205
Base case runs, 150
Basic variables, 379, 381
Bass, F. M., 133, 138, 337, 366
Baumol, W. J., 481, 487
Bell, E. J., 325, 403
Belford, P. C., 352, 356
Benton, W. K., 128, 138
Bierman, H., 49
Blystone, E., 458, 466
Bonini, C. P., 49
Boodman, D. M., 282
Bootstrapping, 146, 266
Boulden, J. B., 153, 170
Bounding problem, 143

Bounds, in sensitivity analysis, 301
Box, G. E. P., 130, 139
Brand switching, 177-184
Brigham, F., 206
Brockelmeyer, J. A., 366
Brown, R. G., 122, 139, 282
Brown, R. V., 76, 100
Bruno, J. E., 366
Buchan, J., 282
Buckley, J. W., 297, 325
Buffa, E. S., 122, 139, 147, 153-158, 170, 171, 218, 282, 484, 487
Buffer stocks, 272-277
Burdick, D. S., 244

Capital costs, 260
Cash management problem, 479-483
Causal forecasting methods, 124-129
   econometric, 129
   multiple regression, 128
   regression, 125-128
   reliability, 126
Chambers, J. C., 129, 135, 139
Chappell, A. C., 315, 325
Charnes, A., 185, 195, 325, 341, 366, 403, 432, 444
Choosing a model, 476-483
Chu, K., 244
Church, J. G., 122, 139
Churchman, C. W., 170

Clarke, S., 352, 366
Claycamp, H. J., 133, 139
Coefficient of determination, 127
Conditional outcome, 21-23
Conditional probability, 29
Constraints, 289-291, 294, 295, 304, 306, 311, 312
Controllable variables, 142
Cooper, W. W., 188, 195, 325, 341, 366, 403, 432, 444
Correlation, 509-515
   coefficients, 512, 513
   reliability of, 513
Costs, inventory models, 258
   capital, 260
   handling and storage, 259
   production, 259
   shortages, 260
Cox, D. R., 218
CPM (Critical Path Method), 448
Critical path, 453
Cullinan-James, C., 366

Daellenbach, H. G., 325, 403
Dantzig, G. B., 325, 403, 444
Decision Tree, 53-76
   rolling back, 55-57
   value of perfect information, 57-59, 63-66
Decision variables, 142, 289, 293, 303, 312

Decoupling, 256
Degeneracy (degenerate solution), 395, 420
Delphi method, 132
Demand, components of, 114-116
  maximum, 273-276
Dependent variables, 494
Dewey, J., 3, 15
Dietz, R. V., 170
Distribution, 504-509
  measures of, 507-509
  normal (bell shaped), 505
Dixon, W. J., 515
Dodd, V. A., 315, 325
Dummy activities, 448
Dyer, J., 100, 195, 428, 444

Econometric forecasting methods, 129, 130
Elmaghraby, S. E., 170
Emshoff, J. R., 243
Engle, J. F., 337, 366
Entering variables, 373
Environment, forecasting of, 111-139
EOQ (Economic Order Quantity), 264-272
Eppen, G. D., 487
ϵ (epsilon) allocation, 421
Equilibrium in Markov Chains, 182
Erlang, A. K., 198
Evaluative models, 12, 19-100
  decision trees, 53-76
  expected value, 35-42
  multiple criteria, 89-93
    additive model, 91, 92
  single criterion under certainty, 22
  single criterion under risk, 34-42
  subjective probabilities, 26
  utility theory, 243
Evans, G. W., 243
"Excess baggage," 375, 376
Expected value, 35-42
Exponentially weighted moving average, 118-123
  modifications for shortest term, 123

  seasonal adjustments, 121, 122
  trend effects, 121, 122

Fama, E. F., 487
Fazar, W., 458, 466
Feinberg, A., 100
Feldmann, F., 345, 367
Ferguson, R., 341, 366
Financial decisions, linear optimization models, 327-335
Fishburn, P. C., 84, 100
Fitzsimmons, J. A., 234-238, 243, 244
Flamholtz, E., 188, 195
Forecasting, 111-139
  causal methods, 124-129
  components of demand, 114-116
  econometric, 129, 130
  exponential, 118-124
  historical analogy, 135
  life cycle analysis, 135
  long term, 132-135
  moving averages, 117, 118
  multiple regression, 128
  regression analysis, 125-128
  S-curve analysis, 135
  selection of model, 130
  time series methods, 116-124
  use of, 111-114
Franklin, A. D., 345, 366
Frequency, relative, 84. See also distribution
FSS (Family Scheduling Subsystem), 486
Function,
  domain of, 494
  graph of, 495
  slope intercept form, 496
  standard form, 496
  linear, 496, 497
  range of, 494

Geoffrion, A., 100, 170, 171, 433, 444
Gershefski, G. W., 171
Gerstenfeld, A., 139
Glasser, L., 457, 466
Glassey, C. R., 345, 366
Gnugnuoli, G., 242, 244

Goal programming, 316
Gray, P., 366
Grayson, C., 100
Gupta, V. K., 345, 366

Hamilton, W. F., 159, 171
Hammond, J. S., 100
Harris, F. W., 255
Hausman, W. H., 49
Hax, A. C., 484, 487
Heller, N. B., 366
Hess, W. H., 366, 367
Hierarchy of planning process, 485
Hillier, F. S., 325, 403
Hodges, J. L., 50
Hodgsdon, R. A., 130, 131, 139
Howard, R. A., 68, 76, 100
Huang, D. S., 128, 139
Hughes, J. S., 328, 367

IBM Corporation, 244
Idle time, 476
Ignall, E., 345, 367
Incident generator, 234
Incoming variable, 373
Independent variables, 494
Index row, 382-384
Information, value of, 40-42
  perfect, 57-59, 63-66
Inland Steel Company, 159, 161-163
  scenarios, 162
Input-transportation-output module, 107
Intersection, 493
Inventory:
  buffer, 257
  costs of, 258
  cycle, 256
  functions of, 255
  pipeline, 256
  seasonal, 258
ISS (Item Scheduling Subsystem), 486

Jackson, J. R., 3-5, 15, 100
Jelmert, A., 188, 195
Jenkins, G. M., 130, 139
Joint probability, 28, 32
Jones, J. M., 49, 76, 328, 367

Keeney, R., 84, 92, 100
Kemeny, J., 195
Key number, 385
King, C. W., 133, 138
Kirkpatrick, C. A., 50
Kiviat, P. J., 243
Klingman, A., 444
Koenigsberg, E., 282, 345, 366
Kolesar, P., 345, 367
Kotler, P., 335, 367

Leach, A. G., 139
Lead time, 273
Lee, S. M., 325
Lee, W. B., 159, 171
Lehmann, E. L., 50
Levin, R. I., 50
Levy, F. K., 457, 466
Lewellen, W. G., 328, 367
Lewis, K. A., 341, 366
Liddy, L. E., 133, 138
Lieberman, G. J., 325, 403
Liebman, L. H., 195
Limiting row, 384
Linear function, 288, 496-500
Linear optimization models, 285-367
   applications of, 327-367
   breakeven model, 288-293
   computer solutions, 297-303
   feed mix example, 312
   model building process, 287
   nature of, 286
   ratio constraints, 303-305
   sensitivity analysis, 300
   two product example, 293
Linear programming, 369-403
   interactive code, 297-302
   See also Simplex method
Little, J. D. C., 147, 171
Logical relationships, 142
Long term forecasting methods:
   Delphi, 132
   historical analogy, 135
   life cycle analysis, 135
   market surveys, 133
Lonsdale, R. T., 337, 366
Lynn, W. R., 345, 367
Lyons, D. F., 315, 325

Mabert, V. A., 130, 139

Machol, R. E., 325, 403
MAD (Mean Absolute Deviation), 123
Magee, J. F., 74, 76, 282
Maisel, H., 242, 244
Makridakis, S. A., 128-131, 139, 171
Management science/ operations research, 3-15, 473-487
   adding complexity, 484
   benefits versus cost, 474
   choosing a model, 476-483
   conceptual value, 474
   introduction to, 3-15
   manager and, 10, 11
   matching problem characteristics and models, 479
   maturation period, 5
   models, 7-10
   problem solving, 3-7
   when to use, 477
Mao, J. C. T., 328, 367
Marginal (unconditional) probabilities, 32
Market surveys, 133
Marketing decisions, linear optimization models, 335-341
Markland, R. E., 366
Markov chains, 173-195
   analysis, 185
   brand switching, 177
   equilibrium, 182
   geriatric ward, 185
   transition probabilities, 174
   use of, 184
Markowitz, H. M., 244
Martin, E. W., 14, 15
Mason, R. D., 14, 15, 50
Massey, F. J., 515
Matheson, J. E., 68
Matrix:
   transition, 176
   of transition probabilities, 176, 178
McKewon, P., 352, 367
McLaughlin, C. P., 159, 171
Meal, H. C., 484, 487
Measure:
   of central value, 507
   of variability (or dispersion), 508

Meier, R. W., 242-244
Meredith, J., 185-187, 195
Miller, D. W., 282
Miller, M. H., 481, 487
Mitchell, W. A., 444
Mode, 508
Model:
   choosing, 476-483
   components of, 141-143
   computer based predictive, 151-163
   creating, 143-148
   evaluative, 19-100
   integer programming, 316
   inventory, 255-282
   logical relationships, 142
   managerial use of, 159-163
   network, 405-466
      scheduling, 445-466
      transportation, 405-445
   optimizing, 249-252
   parameters, 142
   plywood example, 152-159
   predictive, 105-244, 261
   problem solving, 3-7
   purchase order quantity, 260-272
   queuing, 197-218
   simulation, 221-244
      validation of, 234
   transportation, 405-445
   transshipment, 427
   waiting line, 197-218
Model building, 141-162
   analysis, 149
   appropriate detail, 147
   bootstrapping, 146
   bounding problem, 143
   interpretation, 150
   logical relationships, 142
   validation, 148
Moder, J., 457, 466
Monte Carlo, 222-231
Moore, L. J., 325
Morris, W. T., 147, 171
Morse, P. M., 218
Moses, M.A., 159, 171, 484, 487
Moving averages, 117-123
   exponentially weighted, 118-123
MRCA (Market Research Corp. of America), 189

Mullick, S. K., 129, 135, 139
Multiple criteria in evaluative models, 89-93
  additive model, 91-93
  identifying criteria, 91
Mulvey, J., 428, 433, 444
Murphy, R. C., 171

Nagarai, M. R., 325
Napier, A., 171, 244
Neave, E. H., 487
Negative exponential distribution, 204
Nelson, C. R., 130, 139
Nelson, R. T., 218
Network:
  models, 405-466
  scheduling, 445-466
  transportation, 405-445
Newell, T., 242-244
Niehaus, R., 188, 195, 341, 366, 432, 444
Nonbasic variables, 381, 390
Normal distribution, 505
Norman, J. M., 487
North, D. W., 68
North, H. Q., 133, 139
Notation:
  functional, 496
  set theory, 492
  statistical, 504

Objective function, 289, 294, 304, 312
Objective probabilities, 26
O'Brian, J., 457, 459, 466
Odom, R., 458, 466
Ogden, J., 171
Oil shales. See POCO
Operations research. See Management science/operations research
Optimality, 249-252
  test for, 251, 264, 265, 373, 416
Optimization models:
  integer variables, 316
  goal programming, 316
  inventory, 255-282
  linear, 285-367
  linear programming, 369-403
  network, 405-466

Orgler, Y. E., 482, 483, 487
Orr, D. J., 481, 487

Paige, H. W., 466
Parameter, 142
  sensitivity, 158
Parker, G. C., 127, 128, 139
PAS (Plant Product Assignment Subsystem), 486
Pazer, H. L. 242-244
Pegels, C., 188, 195
Personnel planning decisions, linear optimization models, 341-345
PERT (Program Evaluation and Review Technique), 448
Pessemier, E. A., 133, 138
Phillips, C., 457, 466
POCO (Pacific Oil Company), 30-33, 37-40, 59-66, 88-90
Poisson distribution function, 200-202
Posterior probability, 34
Predictive models, 12. See also Forecasting
Price sensitivity, 302
Probabilities:
  conditional, 29
  joint, 28, 32
  marginal, 32
  posterior, 34
  revised prior, 34
  transition, 174, 176
  unconditional (marginal), 32
Problem solving, 3-7
Programming:
  linear, 369-403
  interactive code, 297-302
Public and not-for-profit, linear optimization models, 345-352
Pyke, D. L., 133, 139

Quantity discounts, 268
Queue length, 207, 208
Queuing theory. See waiting line theory

Raiffa, H., 67, 76, 84, 92, 100
RAND Corp., 132

Random Sample, 503
Range, 508
Ratliff, D., 352, 366
Reeves, E., 457, 466
Regression analysis, 125-128, 509-512
  multiple, 128
Reisman, A., 149, 171
Reitman, J., 243, 244
Reorder point, 261, 262, 273
Revelle, C., 345, 367
Revised prior probability, 34
Rising, E. J., 205
Risk, 173-244
  averse, 80, 84
  neutral, 84
Rivett, P., 171
Robichek, A. A., 328, 367
Rolling back decision tree, 55-57
Rosenthal, B., 171
Ruhl, G. J., 171
RUNNER, 130, 131

Saaty, T. L., 218
Samuels, S. A., 366
Scavullo, R. V., 170
Scenario, Inland Steel, 161
Schauland, H., 171
Schenck, J. W., 325
Schlaifer, R., 50, 76
Schriber, T. J., 244
Schreiber, A. N., 171
S-curve analysis, 135
Seaberg, C., 159, 171
Seaberg, R. A., 159, 171
Segal, M., 432, 444
Segura, E. L., 127, 128, 139
Sensitivity analysis, 150, 158, 300-302, 390-395
Service levels, 272
Service systems, 197-215
  multiple-channel, single-phase, 207-211
  single-channel, single-phase, 202-207
  time distributions, 202-207
  waiting line models, 200-215
    finite, 198
    infinite, 200-215
Sets, 491-494
  complement, 493

disjoint (mutually exclusive), 494
empty, 492
equal, 492
subset, 492
universal, 492
Set theory, 491-494
Shadow prices, 301, 377, 390
Sharp, D. L., 325
Sholtz, D., 432, 444
Shortages, 267
SIBYL, 130
Siegfeldt, H., 367
Simplex method, 369-403
  algebraic solution, 370-380
  algorithm, 380-390
  alternate optimal solutions, 395
  degeneracy, 395
  formulation, 369
  graphic solution, 370
  minimizing an objective function, 395
  sensitivity analysis, 390-395
Simulation:
  CALL, 238
  computer, 231
  discrete event, 223
  discrete time updating, 223
  of emergency medical system, 233-238
  languages, 239
  Monte Carlo, 223-231
Simulator, 234
Single criterion under certainty, 22
Single criterion under risk, 34-51
  conditional and joint probabilities, 29
  decision trees, 53-75
    value of information, 40-42
  expected value model, 35-40
  value of perfect information, 57, 58, 63-66
Sisson, R. L., 243
Slack variables, 370
Smith, D. D., 129, 135, 139
Smith, W. L., 218
Snell, J., 195

Southwick, L., 367
Spetzler, C. S., 27, 50, 100
SPS (Seasonal Planning Subsystem), 486
Srinivasan, V., 442, 444, 482, 487
Stael von Holstein, C. S., 27, 50
Standard deviation, 508
Standard error of estimate, 128
Starr, M. K., 282
Statistics, 503-515
  descriptive, 504-509
Stephenson, G. G., 159, 171
Stutz, J., 444
Strauch, R. E., 171
Subjective expressions of worth, 79-81
Substitution, 99
Surkis, J., 352, 366
Surplus variables, 314
Sutherland, G. L., 243

Taubert, W. H., 122, 139, 282
Teichroew, D., 328, 367
Thesen, A., 349, 366
Thompson, G., 466
Time series forecasting methods, 116-124
  exponentially weighted averages, 118-124
  modifications, for shortest term, 123
  seasonal, 121
  trend, 121
  moving averages, 117, 118
Transitions matrix, 176
  probabilities of, 174, 176
Transshipment, 427
Trigg, D. W., 139
Trinkl, F., 188, 195
TRW Company, 133

Unconditional (marginal), probabilities, 30-32
Union, in sets, 493
Universe, of data, 503
  finite, 503
  infinite, 503
Urban, G. L., 147, 171
Utility functions, 79-100
  additive, 91

construction of, 81
as an evaluative model, 84
single criterion, 80-89
weights of in multiple criteria, 92

Value:
  of information, 40
  of perfect information, 63
Van den Burgh & Jurgens, 159, 484
Variables, 141
  artificial, 396
  basic, 379
  controllable, 142
  decision, 289
  dependent, 494
  entering, 373
  incoming, 373
  independent, 494
  integer, 316
  nonbasic, 381, 390
  slack, 299, 370
  surplus, 314
Variance, 508
Venn diagram, 493
Villanueva, R., 244
Villoria, R., 454, 457, 466

Wagner, H. M., 218, 325, 403, 444
Waiting line theory, 197-215
  costs and capacity, 211-213
  infinite models, 200
  model structures, 198
  Poisson arrivals, 200-202
  service distributions,
    constant, 206
    negative exponential, 205
    unspecified, 202
Walker, W., 345, 367
Wallace, G. F., 243
Warshaw, M. W., 337, 366
Weaver, J., 367
Weights, assessing, 92
Weist, J., 457, 466
"What if" questions, 150, 165
What should the manager know?
  See Management science/operations research

Wheelwright, S. C., 75, 76, 99, 100, 128-131, 139, 171
Whelan, J., 367
White, D. J., 487
White, T. R., 444

Whybark, D. C., 139
Wong, Y., 457, 466
Workman, B., 352, 367
Wyman, F. P., 244

Young, R., 457, 466

Zierer, T. K., 444
Zeleny, M., 171
Zionts, S., 367
Zitlau, P., 367